P9-CTP-020

J

ADOLESCENT DEVELOPMENT

McGRAW-HILL SERIES IN PSYCHOLOGY
Consulting Editors
Norman Garmezy
Richard L. Solomon
Lyle V. Jones
Harold W. Stevenson

Adams Human Memory
Beach, Hebb, Morgan, and Nissen The Neuropsychology of Lashley
Berkowitz Aggression: A Social Psychological Analysis
Berlyne Conflict, Arousal, and Curiosity
Blum Psychoanalytic Theories of Personality
Brown The Motivation of Behavior
Brown and Ghiselli Scientific Method in Psychology
Butcher MMPI: Research Developments and Clinical Applications
Campbell, Dunnette, Lawler, and Weick Managerial Behavior, Performance, and
   Effectiveness
Cofer Verbal Learning and Verbal Behavior
Crafts, Schneirla, Robinson, and Gilbert Recent Experiments in Psychology
Crites Vocational Psychology
D'Amato Experimental Psychology: Methodology, Psychophysics, and Learning
Davitz The Communication of Emotional Meaning
Deese and Hulse The Psychology of Learning
Dollard and Miller Personality and Psychotherapy
Edgington Statistical Inference: The Distribution-free Approach
Ellis Handbook of Mental Deficiency
Ferguson Statistical Analysis in Psychology and Education
Forgus Perception: The Basic Process in Cognitive Development
Franks Behavior Therapy: Appraisal and Status
Ghiselli Theory of Psychological Measurement
Ghiselli and Brown Personnel and Industrial Psychology
Gilmer Industrial and Organizational Psychology
Gray Psychology Applied to Human Affairs
Guilford The Nature of Human Intelligence
Guilford Psychometric Methods
Guilford and Fruchter Fundamental Statistics in Psychology and Education
Guilford and Hoepfner The Analysis of Intelligence
Guion Personnel Testing
Haire Psychology in Management
Hirsch Behavior-genetic Analysis
Hirsch The Measurement of Hearing
Hurlock Adolescent Development
Hurlock Child Development
Hurlock Developmental Psychology
Jackson and Messick Problems in Human Assessment
Krech, Crutchfield, and Ballachey Individual in Society
Lakin Interpersonal Encounter: Theory and Practice in Sensitivity Training

ADOLESCENT DEVELOPMENT

Fourth Edition

Elizabeth B. Hurlock

McGraw-Hill Book Company

New York   St. Louis   San Francisco   Düsseldorf   Johannesburg   Kuala Lumpur
London   Mexico   Montreal   New Delhi   Panama   Rio de Janeiro   Singapore
Sydney   Toronto

Adolescent Development

This book was set in Optima by Black Dot, Inc.
The editors were John Hendry and James R. Belser;
the designer was J. E. O'Connor;
and the production supervisor was Ted Agrillo.
The drawings were done by Vantage Art, Inc.
The printer and binder was Kingsport Press, Inc.
Cover photograph: Farrell/Greene. Omikron.

Library of Congress Cataloging in Publication Data
Hurlock, Elizabeth Bergner, 1898-
Adolescent development.
Bibliography: p
1. Adolescent psychology. I. Title.
[DNLM: 1. Adolescence. 2. Adolescent psychology.
WS 460 H965a   1973]
BF724.H8 1973   155.5   72-8695
ISBN 0-07-031457-8

To my husband, Irland McKnight Beckman

Contents

Preface

In revising a textbook, an author faces two major problems. The first is what new material to include and what old material to exclude. I have, of course, made extensive use of the newer studies in all areas of adolescent development. I also decided that, because of the popular interest in adolescent activism and the extensive research being done in this area, a new chapter, "Adolescent Nonconformists," should be added. On the other hand, I have not included a new chapter on cognitive development during adolescence, even though many other textbooks in this area of development include such a chapter. There were two reasons for this decision. First, most students are familiar with the important aspects of intelligence—meaning of intelligence, growth of intelligence, constancy of the IQ, and measurement of intelligence—from a basic course in general or educational psychology. Second, because many of the studies of cognitive development are based on younger or decidely older subjects, and because no attempt has been made in this book to cover development during childhood, adulthood, or old age, there seemed to be too little material from studies of cognitive development during adolescence to make a meaningful chapter. Instead, studies relating to cognitive development, especially in the areas of moral development and family relationships, have been included in the chapters specifically related to those areas of development.

The second major decision an author of a textbook faces is how to make the revision more useful as a learning experience for students and more valuable as a teaching aid for the instructor. To achieve these goals, several radical changes have been made in this, the fourth, edition.

Boxes are used to highlight important points. The material for them has been taken from many research studies, the most important of which are indicated by references.

To avoid breaking the reader's train of thought, relatively few citations are given throughout the text. They appear only when there is a reference to a specific study, when an author is directly quoted, or when some debatable point is made. However, all the sources from which the material for the chapters has been drawn are given in the bibliography for that chapter at the end of the book.

When a large amount of material is presented in a chapter, it is sometimes difficult to know what are the most important points. To aid the reader, a brief section of chapter "highlights" has been added at the end of each chapter. This is not strictly a summary of the chapter; only the most important points are repeated, but this device should prove helpful in reviewing the chapter. The reader may want to read the "highlights" before as well as after studying the chapter.

Two topics, moral and sexual development during adolescence, were given two chapters each in the previous edition. Here both are covered in a single chapter. This was done partly to shorten the book and partly to counteract the false impression that these two topics are the most important areas of development during the adolescent years. No major topics have been omitted by combining chapters. Instead, topics usually covered in other courses in psychology have been treated more briefly in this edition.

Most of the chapter bibliographies have been shortened and made more selective. This has been done mainly by eliminating many of the studies made before 1955. This, I felt, would help those who want to pursue a topic further to select important recent studies while being able to locate, in the bibliographies of these recent studies themselves, references to older studies in the same areas.

I owe thanks to three groups in particular. First, to the many researchers whose studies I have used in the preparation of this book and whose names appear in the chapter bibliographies; second, to my professional colleagues in the area of developmental psychology who gave me invaluable suggestions as I was revising this book; and third, to the students who have written to tell me what parts of the third edition they found to be confusing, contradictory, or in need of further explanation. Seeing the book through student eyes has been a tremendous help in planning and writing this revision.

Elizabeth B. Hurlock

Chapter 1

Adolescence: Age of Transition

The word "adolescence" comes from the Latin verb *adolescere,* which means "to grow" or "to grow to maturity." Adolescence is a period of transition when the individual changes physically and psychologically from a child to an adult. As Sorenson (167) has characterized it:

Adolescence is much more than one rung up the ladder from childhood. It is a built-in, necessary transition period for ego development. It is a leave-taking of the dependencies of childhood and a precocious reach for adulthood. An adolescent is a traveler who has left one place and has not reached the next. . . . It is an intermission between earlier freedoms . . . and subsequent responsibilities and commitments . . . a last hesitation before . . . serious commitments concerning work and love.

AGE OF ADOLESCENCE

Broadly speaking, adolescense begins when the individual attains sexual maturity and ends when independence from adult authority is legally assured. In the United States the individual is legally mature at the age of 18 years. Marking off the beginning of adolescence is difficult because the age of sexual maturing varies greatly. On the average, adolescence extends from 13 to 18 years for girls and from 14 to 18 for boys.

Since the behavior patterns of the young and of the older adolescent differ, adolescence may be divided into two periods, *early* and *late,* the dividing line at age 17. Box 1-1 describes the subdivisions and the names commonly applied to them.

The dividing line between early and late adolescence is not determined by physiological changes but by differences in behavior patterns. The average adolescent becomes a senior in high school sometime during his seventeenth year. The status of a senior is usually quite different from that of underclassmen; it is more prestigious and it has rights, privileges, and responsibilities not given to underclassmen. From the point of view of the students, the seniors are the big wheels who run everything.

When an adolescent becomes a senior in high school, his status in the home likewise becomes more clearly defined and more prestigious. Parents suddenly realize that in a year's time their adolescent son or daughter will be away at college, in a vocational training school, in the armed services, married, or earning a living. Aware of the changes that will soon be taking place, parents grant the adolescent new privileges and responsibilities. Even younger siblings treat a senior in high school differently from a sophomore or junior. This changed status in the home and school provides the adolescent with the necessary motivation to live up to social expectations.

BOX 1-1   SUBDIVISIONS OF ADOLESCENCE

Early Adolescence
Girls: From about 13 to 17 years, depending on when the girl matures sexually. Boys: From about 14 to 17 years, depending on the age of sexual maturity. The early adolescent years are called the "teen years," and the young adolescent, a "teen-ager."

Late Adolescence
From 17 to 18 years. The late adolescent years are sometimes referred to as "youth." The older adolescent is called a "young man" or "young woman," which implies that the characteristic behavior of this period approximates that of an adult.

Long versus short adolescence

A late-maturing child will have a shorter-than-average early adolescence while an early maturer will have a longer-than-average one. As girls mature earlier than boys, the average girl has 4 years of early adolescence—from 13 to 17—while the average boy has only 3 years—from 14 to 17. An adolescent who is academically accelerated will reach senior status at the age of 16 or earlier. Hence, his late adolescence will begin earlier than that of the average student. One who is academically retarded will be treated according to the standards for his academic level. Consequently, neither in school nor at home will he have acquired the status at which he is encouraged to behave like an older adolescent.

There are both advantages and disadvantages to a longer-than-average or shorter-than-average adolescence. A child who matures early is subjected to the indefinite status associated with early adolescence longer than his age-mates; this affects him unfavorably. On the other hand, a shorter-than-average early adolescence may be a handicap because it deprives the adolescent of the time needed to learn the social skills his age-mates have been learning over a longer period (32).

Adolescence versus puberty

Puberty, when sexual maturing occurs, is a part of adolescence but is not synonymous with it because adolescence includes *all* phases of maturing, not sexual maturing alone. Puberty is an overlapping period; approximately one-half of it overlaps the end of childhood, and one-half, the early part of adolescence. On the average, puberty covers 4 years. About 2 years are spent in preparing the body for reproduction and about 2 are spent in completing the process.

The first 2 years of puberty are known as "preadolescence." The individual is called a "preadolescent" or a "pubescent child." He is not an adolescent because he is not sexually mature. Nor is he characteristically a child because many of his physical features and behavior patterns have begun their transformation to those of an adult.

TRADITIONAL BELIEFS VERSUS SCIENTIFIC EVIDENCE

Tradition holds that radical changes take place in the individual as he emerges from childhood. He is supposed to shed, automatically, the undesirable traits acquired during childhood and to develop, in some mysterious way and with little or no effort, desirable traits that will serve him well when he reaches maturity. The selfish child, for example, is expected to turn into a considerate, kindly adult; and the careless, to develop habits of neatness and orderliness.

This point of view was popularized early in the twentieth century by G. Stanley Hall, usually called the "Father of Child Study in America." According to Hall, the changes in adolescence marked a "new birth" of the individual's personality. Hall believed that the changes resulted from sexual maturing and were, thus, biologically generated. Because the changes are so rapid and pronounced, Hall described adolescence as a period of "storm and stress," a time when the individual is erratic, emotional, unstable, and unpredictable (69, 71).

Interest in the problems of adolescence, aroused by the work of Hall and his followers, has led many psychologists, sociologists, and anthropologists to study large groups of adolescents from different social classes, cultures, and economic levels. One of the pioneer studies, made by Hollingworth shortly after the First World War, refuted the idea that all children are changelings who, at puberty, develop into new and different personalities (83). Gradually, scienfific research has brought together evidence to disprove the traditional point of view. No longer is it possible to claim that a metamorphosis will take place in the adolescent years. Rather, it is now believed that the traits present in childhood will probably become more deep-rooted with the passage of time (95).

If storm and stress were biologically generated, then they would be found in all adolescents and in all civilizations. Such is not the case. Furthermore, studies of the relationship of sexual maturing to emotional tensions have shown that emotional tensions persist long after sexual maturing has been completed. They have also revealed that social and economic conditions and pressures are largely responsible for the difficulties the individual has in passing from childhood into adulthood (123, 153).

Modern scientific research has thus disproved many traditional beliefs which were widely accepted and responsible for much misunderstanding (134, 179, 188). Garn (63) expressed the change in point of view thus:

Traditionally, in our culture, adolescence is a period of stress and strain but there is no physiological reason for it. Twenty milligrams of testosterone is not unsettling except to a few dozen sebaceous glands. "Adolescent rebellion" occurs in the hypogonadal lad as well as in the normal boy. Growth, itself, does not result in awkwardness. Despite a raft of elementary textbooks, an overnight increase of two-hundredths of an inch hardly unsettles the balance of Joe, or Pete, or Tom, or Dick. We cannot blame undesirable adolescent behavior on growth,

Figure 1-1 How many parents react to typical adolescent behavior. (Adapted from George Clark: "The Neighbors." © 1972 New York News, Inc. World Rights Reserved. Used by permission.)

"The discouraging part is that she knows exactly what she's doing."

genes, or glands, but only on a culture that has no meaningful place for the adolescent. This, however, does not lessen the vicissitudes of adolescent growth and its effect on the adult-to-be. The fat adolescent is unhappy in a lean milieu. . . . In the sports-oriented school the lean or nonmuscular boy may gravitate into an intellectual corner, or into a mischievous group. Lacking muscular outlets the muscular lad is more likely to find prestige in an antisocial gang. Differences in growth rate, physique, and fat-patterning may have tremendous repercussions on the adolescents themselves.

SOCIAL ATTITUDES TOWARD
ADOLESCENCE

The transition from childhood to adulthood is normally a difficult period for the social group as well as for the individual (52, 67, 103). Adolescence has been called the "terrible teens," and the label "teen-ager" has, as Lane pointed out, become the "journalistic equal of hoodlum, gangster, junior public enemy" (109). The unfavorable stereotype of the adolescent has had a damaging effect on adults' attitudes and relationships with adolescents as well as on adolescents' attitudes toward themselves and their relationships with adults. This has served to widen the "generation gap" that always exists between adults and young people in every culture (52). See Figure 1-1.

Parents and other adults who accept the unfavorable stereotype of the adolescent are concerned about how successfully adolescents will make the transition into adulthood. While their concerns vary, three are almost universal in America. These are explained in Box 1-2.

Many adolescents view adulthood with a mixed feeling of anticipation and fear. They wonder if they are capable of assuming the responsibilities that go with freedom. Certainly parental anxiety and concern about the adolescent's ability to cope with his problems and to achieve a satisfactory adult status do not build up the adolescent's self-confidence. Instead, they increase his anxiety and lead to even stronger negative feelings about himself and his abilities (99).

Knowing how adults feel about adolescence

makes adolescents resentful toward adults. They feel they are being prejudged or judged unfairly because a handful of their age-mates have attracted nationwide publicity for their antisocial behavior.

TRANSITION MEANS CHANGE

Whether he likes it or not, a child cannot remain a child forever. The onset of puberty brings rapid changes in body size and structure. When physical development reaches a certain point, the child is expected to grow up psychologically and put away childish things. Accompanying the physical changes there are changes in interests. No longer, for example, do childhood playmates or play activities satisfy the adolescent. He finds himself taking a new interest in the other sex, in social activities, and in books, movies, and television programs that he formerly scorned.

Furthermore, more new problems arise than the adolescent has ever had to solve in so short a time before. He realizes that because he looks like an adult he is expected to behave as an adult. But he does not know how to do so. As he moves away from the home into the peer group, he no longer has models of de-

sirable behavior so readily available nor does he have a stable environment to facilitate identification. In addition, he must learn to stand on his own feet and face the world without his parents and teachers to act as buffers, as they did when he was a child.

Making the change from childhood to adulthood is too big a task for a short time. Therefore, the child must have time to make the change. That is the function of adolescence. Stone and Church have called adolescence a "way station" in development (171). The Hechingers (80) have also emphasized the transitional nature of adolescence and have pointed out the role adults should play in helping children to make the transition:

The task now is to make it clearly understood that adolescence is a stage of human development, not an empire or even a colony. The mission of the adult world is to help teen-agers become adults by raising their standards and values to maturity rather than by lowering adulthood to their insecure maturity. The task for the adult world is to make adolescence a step toward growing up, not a privilege to be exploited.

As in the childhood years, development in adolescence follows an orderly sequence or

---

BOX 1-2 COMMON ADULT CONCERNS ABOUT ADOLESCENTS

Appearance and Manners
The adolescent is stereotyped as homely because his body does not conform to adult proportions, his skin is often pimply, and his hair is sometimes stringy or greasy. In dress, he may be extremely fastidious or sloppy. He is unsure of himself and this makes him say and do things in a gauche manner.

Defiance of Adult Authority
Many adolescents go out of their way to do the opposite of what they have been told to do, thus engaging in acts which are physically or psychologically damaging. They often refuse to listen to adult reason and claim that adults do not "understand" or are "old-fashioned."

Future Plans
When adolescents go downhill academically, idle away their days, or devote "too much time" to protests, adults fear that they are not sufficiently serious about preparing themselves for the competitive world in which they will soon find themselves.

pattern. The behavioral changes that take place in preadolescence and early adolescence are great and they accompany the rapid physical changes that occur at that time. As physical development slows down in late adolescence, changes in behavior are also slower.

SOCIAL EXPECTATIONS FOR CHANGES

Since the pattern of development is similar for all, with slight individual differences, every cultural group expects individuals of a given age to do the things they are capable of doing. These expectations are expressed in the form of "developmental tasks"—behavior patterns a person must learn if he is to be reasonably successful and happy (10, 64, 75). The important developmental tasks the social group expects American boys and girls to master during the transition from childhood to adult-

---

BOX 1-3 DEVELOPMENTAL TASKS OF ADOLESCENCE

*Achieving new and more mature relations with age-mates of both sexes

*Achieving a masculine or feminine social role

*Accepting one's physique and using the body effectively

*Achieving emotional independence of parents and other adults

*Achieving assurance of economic independence

*Selecting and preparing for an occupation

*Preparing for marriage and family life

*Developing intellectual skills and concepts necessary for civic competence

*Desiring and achieving socially responsible behavior

*Acquiring a set of values and an ethical system as a guide to behavior

---

hood have been listed by Havighurst (75). These are given in Box 1-3.

Adolescence is a long period, and many young adolescents have little motivation to master the developmental tasks for their age. By the senior year in high school, however, they realize that adulthood is rapidly approaching; this provides them with the necessary motivation to prepare themselves for their new status As a result, they make greater strides toward the goal of maturity than they did in early adolescence. Whether the developmental tasks will be fully mastered by the time they reach legal maturity will depend upon how strong their motivation is, upon their opportunities for learning, and upon the kind of foundations they have when they reach adolescence (189).

Successful achievement of the developmental tasks for one period in life leads to success with later tasks, while failure leads not only to personal unhappiness and disappointment but also to difficulties with later tasks. Good achievement on a particular developmental task at one age is followed by good achievement on a similar task at later ages. Also, good achievement on one developmental task is generally associated with good achievement on other tasks at the same age. Good peer relationships, for example, link with success in other developmental tasks for that age level.

Regardless of whether the adolescent has successfully mastered the developmental tasks of adolescence, he is, in most "advanced" cultures, automatically given the status of adult when he reaches the age of legal maturity. This is in direct contrast to more simple cultures where young people must demonstrate to their elders, in "puberty rites," that they are prepared to assume the rights, privileges, and responsibilities of the adult status.

DIFFICULTIES IN MAKING TRANSITION TO ADULTHOOD

Just knowing social expectations as spelled out in developmental tasks is not enough to enable the child to make the transition to adulthood successfully. Under any circumstances and at any time in life, adjusting to change is difficult; the more radical the change, the more difficult it is. Keniston (100) has stressed the universality of this problem:

Growing up is always a problem, whether in Samoa, Nigeria, or Yonkers. It entails abandoning those special prerogatives, world views, insights and pleasures that are defined by the culture as specifically "childish" and substituting for them the rights, responsibilities, outlooks, and satisfactions that are suitable for the culturally defined "adult." Although the concepts of "childish" and "adult" differ from one culture to another, every culture requires some change in the child's habitual ways of thinking, feeling, and acting—a change which involves psychic dislocation and therefore constitutes a "problem" for the individual and the culture. . . . In societies where the transition to adulthood is unusually painful, young people often form their own "youth culture" with a special set of antiadult values and institutions in which they can at least temporarily negate the feared life of the adult. But somehow children must be induced to accept their roles as adults if the society is to continue.

Studies of adolescents who find the transition into adulthood especially difficult have revealed that they fall into four major categories:

First, adolescents who must enter the world of work at 16 or 17 years of age are forced to learn to be adults almost overnight. They are deprived of the time in late adolescence when their contemporaries who remain in college or professional training schools can make the transition more slowly and with less trauma.

Second, the student who must depend on others for economic support into the early years of adulthood is, as Blos has pointed out, "living in the twilight of an arrested transition which renders the adolescent self-conscious and ashamed" (31). If he can earn some money and be at least partially independent while he pursues his studies he will escape some of the difficulties that dependency brings (46, 74).

Third, girls are more handicapped than boys in making the transition to adulthood because parents tend to encourage their daughters to be dependent. Though boys from the middle and upper socioeconomic groups may remain economically dependent while pursuing their education, they are permitted greater psychological independence than girls (22, 48, 131, 183).

Fourth, children who have not mastered the developmental tasks of childhood are ill-prepared at adolescence to make the changes necessary for a smooth transition into adulthood. Eisenberg (53) has written:

Optimal development in adolescence depends on successful accomplishment of the developmental tasks in infancy and childhood. Thus, clinical experience has indicated that adolescence is likely to be particularly stormy, prolonged, and sometimes poorly resolved if it follows a childhood marked by severe deficit.

Factors contributing to difficulties in transition

How easy it will be for the adolescent to make the transition into adulthood will depend partly upon the individual, partly on environmental aids or obstructions, and partly on adult expectations. Of the many factors that influence the ease or difficulty of the transition, the following eight are the most important.

Speed of transition   At no other period does the individual undergo such a sudden and drastic change in so short a time and at no other age is he less prepared to cope with the problems this change brings. The change is especially difficult if the adolescent goes to work immediately after finishing high school.

Length of transition   Rapid maturers, those who seem to grow up overnight, find adjustment especially difficult. They are expected to behave like adults simply because they look like adults.

On the other hand, a prolonged adolescence also brings problems. The adolescent gets into the habit of being dependent, and this, like all habits, is difficult to overcome later.

Discontinuities in training Much of the stress and strain of adolescence is due to discontinuities in training. For example, the assumption of responsibility during adolescence is difficult because the child has been trained to be dependent and submissive. Schonfeld (158) has commented on the consequences:

Too many of today's affluent adolescents tend to follow the philosophy of "let John do it." John may be parents, teachers or Uncle Sam. . . . [Such adolescents] ask a girl to go steady and drop her if they find someone else who strikes their fancy. They come late for part-time jobs and drop them without notice, and they rush into marriage with no thought of how they are going to support the marriage. This irresponsibility has often been cultivated in the individual since early childhood. Yet parents and teachers are surprised when it does not miraculously disappear with adolescence.

Degree of dependency How dependent the young adolescent will be is determined mainly by the kind of training he received in childhood, how much encouragement he has to be independent, and how successfully he handles the independence he is granted. Parents often foster dependency because they feel that adolescents are not ready to assume responsibility for their own behavior. As a result, many adolescents find it difficult to make the transition to adulthood.

Ambiguous status In tradition-bound societies, the child is expected to follow in the footsteps of his parents; this gives him a pattern of behavior to imitate. In a democratic society, by contrast, it is assumed that every individual should be free to choose his own pattern of self-development. As a result, he is deprived of the guidance and help given in tradition-bound societies where the behavior of youth is regulated by a defined code (99, 152).

Conflicting demands The adolescent is confronted with conflicting demands from parents, teachers, contemporaries, and the community. He is confused and exasperated by being told, "You are old enough to know better," and then, in almost the next breath, "You are not old enough to do this or that." He is told to take responsibilities, to show some judgment, and to make decisions. Then he is treated as a child and is expected to obey his parents and teachers.

Degree of realism When the adolescent begins to look like an adult, he is permitted an added degree of freedom. Far too often this encourages him to set unrealistic goals for himself, to believe that the obstacles in his way are removed, and that he can now be and do what he chooses. If he discovers that he is not ready, either physically or psychologically, to play the adult role, he becomes dissatisfied with himself and this weakens his motivation to try to achieve an adult status (56, 152).

Motivation The adolescent goes through a period of wondering how he will meet the new problems life presents. He would like to grow up but he is unsure of his ability to cope with adulthood. So long as this feeling of insecurity exists, there will be little motivation to make the transition into adulthood. As the barriers to growing up are lowered or removed by parents, teachers, and society, the adolescent can see the possibility of reaching the goal of adulthood, and motivation to make the transition is normally increased.

EFFECTS OF TRANSITION TO ADULTHOOD

Few adolescents make the transition from childhood to adulthood without any "emotional scars." Sometimes the scars are minor; sometimes they are so damaging that the adolescents give up the struggle and remain immature for the rest of their lives. Certain effects of the transition are more common and more damaging than others. These are instability, preoccupation with problems, problem behavior, and unhappiness.

Instability

Instability comes from feelings of insecurity, and insecurity, in turn, comes when the individual must abandon habitual patterns and substitute new ones. The adolescent can no longer behave like a child, but he is unsure of his ability to do what society now expects of him.

Feelings of insecurity are always accompanied by emotional tension; the individual is worried and concerned or he is angry and frustrated. Rarely is he happy when insecure because he realizes that his behavior reflects his lack of self-confidence. Emotional tension may express itself outwardly or inwardly; the adolescent may be aggressive, self-conscious, or withdrawn.

Instability is also shown in behavior patterns that are not related to emotionality. Some adolescents overwork in school, others throw themselves feverishly into sports, while some devote most of their time to social activities. Others show their instability by shifts in likes, in interests, in vocational aspirations, and in friendship choices.

As adolescence progresses, the individual gradually becomes more stable. How early and how successfully he will achieve stability depends partly on his motivation to speed up the transition to maturity and partly on the opportunity he has to do so. When he discovers that people regard his instability unfavorably, this may motivate him to become more stable and dependable.

With increasing stability, the adolescent makes better personal and social adjustments. He is happier and freer from emotional tensions. Long-continued and pronounced instability indicates that the individual is having difficulties—either through his own fault or the fault of his environment—in breaking off childish habits and establishing more mature ones. As a result, he will make poorer adjustments than one could anticipate for his age level.

Preoccupation with problems

Adjustment to new situations always brings problems. For several reasons, at adolescence the problems seem worse than they actually are or than they would seem at other ages. *First,* the problems of adolescence cover a wider scope and affect more people than the problems of childhood. *Second,* the transition to adulthood is rapid at first and so many problems are likely to pile up at once that the adolescent has no time to adjust to one before he is deluged by others. *Third,* the adolescent has had little experience in handling his problems *alone.* In childhood, he sought help from parents. Now he must learn to stand on his own feet.

Common problems of adolescence The problems that occupy the time and attention

---

BOX 1-4   TYPICAL PROBLEMS OF ADOLESCENTS

Personal Problems
The adolescent is preoccupied with problems relating to his home (relationships with family members, discipline), school (grades, relationships with teachers, extracurricular activities), physical condition (health, exercise), appearance (weight, attractiveness of features, sex appropriateness), emotions (temper outbursts, moodiness), social adjustment (acceptance by peers, leadership roles), vocation (choice, training), and values (morals, drugs, sex).

Problems Characteristic of Adolescence
The ambiguous status of the adolescent gives rise to such concerns as achieving greater independence, being misunderstood or judged by unfavorable stereotypes, and having more rights and privileges and fewer responsibilities imposed by parents. Such problems as achieving economic independence, assuming the approved sex role, and preparing for family life present special difficulties. Adolescent problems are intensified if the developmental tasks of childhood have not been thoroughly mastered.

of adolescents are myriad. Roughly, they can be divided into two major categories: personal problems and problems characteristic of adolescence. Box 1-4 lists some typical problems of each category (2, 3, 12, 55, 61, 65, 132, 149, 165).

Many of the problems that face the young adolescent also face the older one. This indicates that he did not solve the problems to his satisfaction during the early period. The older adolescent, for example, is still concerned about his appearance. If he remains in the academic world after high school, he is still concerned about grades and success in extracurricular activities. Likewise, he still finds relationships with members of the opposite sex a problem, though often less so than when he was a teen-ager.

Solution of problems Solving a problem is never easy. It is especially difficult for adolescents who, as children, have become overly dependent on parents and teachers. Adolescents face numerous problems that their parents and many of their teachers did not face as adolescents and thus feel incapable of helping young persons solve (8).

Furthermore, while many adolescents would like to go to their parents, they feel that they will not get a sympathetic hearing or will create the impression that they are incapable of exercising the independence they have been able to achieve. Others regard their parents as symbols of the childhood they want to leave behind.

After breaking away from their parents, many adolescents feel themselves adrift and in need of new sources of help. Some turn to teachers, ministers, older siblings, adult relatives, and family friends. Others regard all adults as authority figures and want to avoid putting themselves in a position of submission to them. They then turn to members of the peer group for help. Or lacking confidence in the help they get from their peers, they may turn to unseen advisers, getting their help by mail, through advice columns in newspapers, magazines, or over radio and television.

Even when they turn to parents for help, adolescents tend to be cautious about which parent they will go to and what problems they will discuss. Both boys and girls tend to feel that their mothers are more tolerant and understanding. How frequently the adolescent will turn to his parents for help depends not so much upon the relationship he has with them as upon the nature of the problem. The more serious the problem the more resistant he is to seeking parental help. Problems relating to sex, to boy-girl relationships, or to religious doubts are least likely to be discussed with parents (49).

In Figure 1-2, some of the problems discussed by boys and mothers and by girls and fathers are ranked according to the difficulty of the discussion.

Problem behavior

The third common effect of the transition from childhood to adulthood is that it usually gives rise to "problem behavior" of minor or major severity. At any age, a person's behavior is regarded as problem behavior if it causes inconvenience and trouble for others. Certainly at no time in the growing-up process is one's behavior likely to be as troublesome to others as during adolescence, especially in the early period.

The main reason adolescence is called a "problem age" is that the adolescent is too often judged by adult standards rather than by standards suitable for his age. For example, the typical adolescent is egocentric. As Elkind has pointed out, "While the adolescent is self-critical, he is frequently self-admiring too. Much of the boorishness, faddish dress and loudness is to attract attention to himself (55). His egocentrism also makes him uncooperative, selfish, inconsiderate of others and prone to talk about himself and his problems. Such behavior is suggestive of immaturity and leads to unfavorable judgments.

The young adolescent is more of a problem to himself than to others. He is not adjusted to his new role in life, and as a result, he is confused, uncertain, and anxious. Instead of being expected to behave in a way that is consistent with his level of development, he is sometimes treated like a child and expected to behave like an adult. Consequently, in ad-

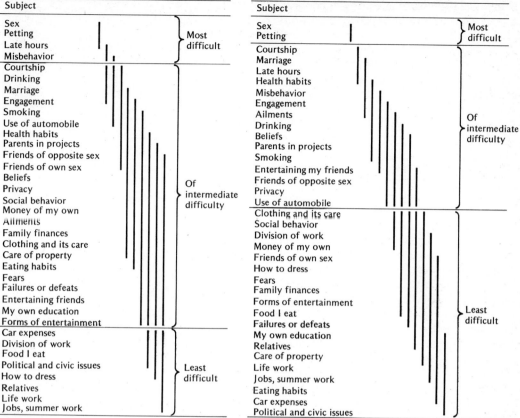

Figure 1-2 Some of the problems young adolescents find difficult to discuss with their parents. (Adapted from M. C. Dubbé: What parents are not told may hurt. *Family Life Coordinator*, 1965, **14,** 51–118. Used by permission.)

dition to his own problems he finds, as Horrocks has said, that "adults and their unreasonable ways and points of view are really the problems" he must cope with (85). While he remains in this state of confusion and uncertainty, he is tense and nervous. This leads to aggressive, attention-seeking, disruptive behavior or to moodiness, irritability, and general unhappiness. Regardless of what form his behavior takes, he is usually regarded by adults as a person who is immature and unpleasant to live or work with (148). To make the situation worse, so many studies by psychologists and psychiatrists have emphasized the behavior of the poorly adjusted adolescent that there is widespread impression that *all* adolescents are problem cases.

As adolescence progresses, problem behavior gradually diminishes if the adolescent is making the transition into adulthood successfully. The adolescent becomes less of a problem to himself and to the social group. If the adolescent is not making a good transition, problem behavior will continue and he will seem even more immature and troublesome than earlier when he looked less like an adult.

Unhappiness

The fourth and by far the most damaging effect of the transition into adulthood is the unhappiness that is so prevalent among adolescents. Studies reveal that adolescence stands close to the top of the list of unhappy ages (84,

127). For most people, happiness depends mainly on a feeling of adequacy to do what society expects; it means freedom from worry and nagging responsibility, combined with the achievement of one's hopes and ambitions. Because of the problems the adolescent must face and the conflicts that arise when he is prevented from achieving the status he feels entitled to, it is understandable that adolescence is seldom a truly happy period in our society (177, 180, 181).

Causes of unhappiness That unhappiness in adolescence is either directly or indirectly environmental in origin is shown by three lines of evidence. *First,* the fact that unhappiness is far from universal suggests that conditions in the life pattern of adolescents rather than in their hereditary endowment are responsible. In most simple societies, for example, adolescence is one of the happiest periods of life (24, 123). Furthermore, in many industrialized societies, it is a far happier period than in the United States (6, 137, 154).

Second, there are sex differences in happiness which are based on the differential ways boys and girls are treated and on what parents and the social group expect of them. While boys are given greater freedom than girls, more demands are placed on boys to achieve and to live up to unrealistic expectations. By contrast, many girls, especially those from middle- and upper-class families, regard adolescence as a happy age because they are protected, are subjected to fewer pressures, and are encouraged to use this time as a stepping-stone to meeting the "right people"

and making a successful marriage (85, 127, 181).

Third, adolescents from unfavorable home environments which have low socioeconomic status or frictional family relationships have fewer happy experiences and fewer happy memories of their childhood than adolescents from more favorable environments (58, 84, 180). Normally, happiness as shown in an optimistic outlook on life increases as adolescence progresses. As Tuddenham has pointed out, "Increased optimism is a usual concomitant of passage from stormy adolescence to serene maturity" (181).

Unhappiness in adolescence has many causes. The most common are summarized in Figure 1-3.

Effects of unhappiness on behavior The unhappiness of adolescence manifests itself in different patterns of behavior for different individuals and also for the same individual at different times, depending on the satisfaction derived from the behavior. The manifestations of unhappiness explained in Box 1-5 are widely observed (14, 18, 50, 112, 146, 159, 175, 179). A careful study of Box 1-5 will show how damaging unhappiness is during adolescence—perhaps more so than at any other period in the life span. For three major reasons, unhappiness should be controlled.

First, unhappiness leads to behavior that perpetuates unhappiness. The adolescent who shows his unhappiness by moodiness or antisocial behavior discovers that social reactions to him are so unfavorable that he is neglected or rejected. This accentuates his unhappiness and leads to other forms of behavior that increase social neglect or rejection.

Second, unhappiness often becomes habitual. It leaves its mark on the person's facial expression and on his characteristic methods of adjusting to people and life situations. A study of loneliness, which showed how unhappiness stemming from loneliness becomes persistent, concluded that "how happily a person gets along as an adult in his job, in his family and social life, depends a great deal on how he

Figure 1-3 Unhappiness has many causes.

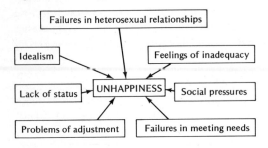

got along with other children when he was young" (136).

Third, unhappiness leads to poor personal and social adjustments which may in time lead to personality disorders. Whether they will or not depends largely on the form of expression unhappiness takes. For example, the adolescent who eases the pangs of unhappiness by retreat into the daydream world is more likely to develop a personality disorder than the one who expresses his unhappiness by being quarrelsome.

SUCCESS IN MAKING THE TRANSITION TO ADULTHOOD

Some adolescents are successful in mastering the developmental tasks of adolescence before they reach the age of legal maturity, some lag behind the norm for their age level, and some never make the grade. The majority of American adolescents, especially those from middle- or upper-class homes, reach legal maturity with some "unfinished business" of adolescence which they eventually finish during the early years of adulthood. Jersild (89) has written:

The adolescent not only continues many tasks of life that he began in earlier years; he also leaves unfinished many tasks that are the business of adolescence but are carried over into adult life. There is something of the uncompleted work of adolescence in every adult. The big issues with which the adolescent strives—issues relating to his attitudes toward himself and others, issues pertaining to his relationship to authority, sex, responsibilities he should seek to carry or to shirk—are not completely settled just because he officially has finished the adolescent years. There are issues he must face as long as he lives. Even some of the issues that seem to have been settled—such as the choice of a vocation and even the choice of a mate—are not as completely settled as they seem to be.

For most adolescents, unfinished business is limited to those developmental tasks which have been particularly difficult or have been played down by parents as of little value. Because of the high value Americans place on popularity, for example, most middle-class adolescents are encouraged to master the developmental task of learning how to get along with age-mates of both sexes. With the trend toward vocational specialization and the long period of training this requires, adolescents are encouraged at home or in school to select and prepare for an occupation. By contrast, they are given little training either in the home or the school in preparing for marriage and family life. Nor are they encouraged, in many homes, to achieve emotional independence of parents and other adults. Because preparing for a chosen life career often requires financial dependency, adolescents of both sexes are handicapped in achieving a socially approved masculine or feminine role in society.

Simple versus "advanced" cultures

Unfinished business would not be permitted among adolescents in simpler cultures. The disgrace to the adolescent and his family would be so great that the adolescent could never hope to be a respected member of the cultural group nor could his parents ever again hope to have the social esteem they formerly enjoyed. The puberty rites—ceremonials in which the boy or girl is tested by the elders of the group—ensure that the adolescent has mastered the group's demands before he is granted the status of adulthood. The developmental tasks vary from one culural group to another and depend on what each group has found to be essential for success in adult living in that group. In a warlike tribe, for example, success in fighting is more highly valued than success in hunting or fishing—tasks which are more highly valued in less warlike tribes (123).

Parents from simpler cultures know what will be expected of their children and they begin to train them in the developmental tasks of their group as soon as the children are capable of learning. Furthermore, knowing that they will be tested when they reach puberty, children have a strong motivation to master the tasks. Under such conditions, neither the child nor his parents can afford to let any unfinished business exist.

Few "advanced" cultures test the readiness of the adolescent for adult status. When he reaches the legal age set for adulthood, whether it be 16 or 18 or 21, he is automatically an adult. The motivation to master the developmental tasks is often weak and many adolescents carry unfinished business into adulthood.

Dangers of unfinished business

Even though the adolescent in our culture is not submitted to a testing procedure and denied the status of an adult if he fails the test, the unfinished business of adolescence can be damaging.

First, the individual who is immature at adulthood has, more likely than not, been immature throughout adolescence. If he has been a late maturer and has not had the environmental encouragement or the motivation to learn what his age-mates have learned, he has doubtless developed a feeling of personal inadequacy. Such inadequacy is usually expressed either in aggressive attempts to achieve the status of his age-mates or in withdrawal and working below capacity.

A *second* consequence of unfinished business at adulthood is that the habit of behaving immaturely becomes a way of life and is rarely overcome. Studies of adults at middle and old age have revealed that their pattern of adjustment is similar to that of their adolescent years. Those who made poor adjustments in adolescence, for example, usually continued to do so as adults (170, 181).

At adolescence, the individual is at the "crossroads of life." Before he reaches adulthood, he must decide which road he will take. If he does not take the right road—the road that will lead to behavior the social group expects of him—he is likely to develop feelings of inadequacy which will color the pattern of his future adjustments. If he takes the right road, he will be more acceptant of himself because the social group will be more acceptant of him.

AIDS IN MAKING THE TRANSITION TO ADULTHOOD

Left to his own devices, the adolescent is likely to employ a trial-and-error approach to mastering the developmental tasks essential to transition to adulthood. While he may learn from his mistakes, he wastes valuable time that might be spent in more constructive activities and he weakens his self-confidence and motivation to carry through with tasks that have proved to be difficult. In time, this may lead to a shunning of the difficult tasks and a concentration on the easier ones; thus he reaches adulthood with unfinished business in certain important areas.

As in all learning, guidance is valuable in learning the developmental tasks. A clue to the value of guidance comes from studies of adolescents in cultures where parents do not expect their children to make the transition into adulthood unaided. They know the demands of the social group, and to avoid the possibility of failure, they help their children prepare for the tests they must pass in the puberty ceremonials. Instead of placing obstacles in the way of learning, they guide and encourage and thus build up their children's

confidence. As a result, the unhappiness so characteristic of American adolescents is almost unheard of.

The more complex the culture, the more guidance the individual needs in meeting new demands. Guidance is essential if the transition is to be made successfully and with minimum psychological damage. According to Anderson, "Our task with adolescents is to facilitate the movement from the security of childhood to the responsibility of adult life" (9).

Guidance is not limited to parents, but must be assumed by all who live or work with adolescents. The responsibility of the school is especially great. Frank has described the kind of guidance that the school should provide for adolescents (60):

The schools should not try to prepare them for future living by specific instruction and training for tasks they will meet later, but help them to meet their present adolescent problems. . . . Here, as in all other ages, the best preparation for tomorrow is to live adequately today, to deal with today's requirements so as to be able to go forward without too much "unfinished business."

Each adolescent has his own individual problems and therefore guidance must be personalized. A system of aid meant for all adolescents of a cultural group without regard for individual differences, as Horrocks has warned, "always runs the danger of subverting them in one direction and causing them to develop along too narrow lines" (85).

Chapman has suggested four principles for facilitating the transition of the American adolescent into adulthood. These are given in Box 1-6. In addition, Chapman has suggested "three basic L's" for making this transition easier and happier: love, limitations, and letting them grow up (39). This means that the transition will be facilitated if the adolescent knows that he is loved by people who are significant in his life, if he has the security that comes from knowing what the limitations on his behavior are so that he has guidelines for conforming to social expectations, and if he is given an opportunity to grow up and be independent instead of being overprotected and treated like a child.

HIGHLIGHTS OF CHAPTER 1

1. Adolescence (from the Latin word meaning "to grow to maturity") is a transitional period extending from the time the individual becomes sexually mature until he reaches legal maturity.

2. Adolescence is divided into two periods: early and late adolescence. The dividing line is at 17 years—when the average American adolescent becomes a senior in high school and is recognized by the social group as a near adult.

3. Children who become sexually mature later than the average (13 years is average for girls and 14 to 15 for boys) have a shorter-than-average early adolescence and this may delay their mastery of the developmental tasks. Children who mature earlier than the average are often frustrated by the long, indefinite status associated with early adolescence.

4. Puberty, the time when sexual maturing occurs, overlaps late childhood and early adolescence. It differs from adolescence because it refers only to physical maturing while adolescence refers to *all* phases of maturing.

5. The traditional beliefs that the adolescent will automatically shed undesirable and childish traits and replace them with desirable traits and that adolescence is inevitably a period of storm and stress have not been substantiated by scientific evidence.

6. Social attitudes, based largely on unfavorable cultural stereotypes, have intensified adult concern about the adolescent's appearance and manners, his defiance of adult authority, and his lack of conscientiousness about preparing for adult life.

7. Since the pattern of transitional changes in adolescence is predictable and is followed in much the same way by all adolescents in a given culture, the social group sets up expectations of behavioral patterns in the form of developmental tasks which the adolescent must master if he is to be reasonably successful and happy.

8. Transition into adulthood is difficult for adolescents for four reasons: (1) They are expected to assume new roles when they complete their education; (2) they must depend on others for economic support, sometimes even into early adulthood; (3) they are often forced into a dependency status by parents; and (4) they are often not given an opportunity to master the developmental tasks of childhood which are a necessary foundation for their new roles.

9. Transition into adulthood is influenced by such factors as the speed and length of the transition; discontinuities in training; degree of dependence on parents; ambiguous status in the group; conflicting demands from parents, teachers, and peers; the adolescent's unrealistic aspirations; and his motivation to make the transition.

10. The most common damaging effects of the transition are instability, preoccupation with problems (both personal and those characteristic of the adolescent period), problem behavior, and unhappiness.

11. Unhappiness in adolescence, which is far from universal and more typical of boys than girls, leads to behavior which perpetuates unhappiness. Such behavior often becomes habitual, predisposing the adolescent to make poor personal and social adjustments and often leading to personality disorders.

12. Success in making the transition into adulthood is facilitated by love and understanding from parents and other significant people in the adolescent's life, by limitations on his activities as guidelines for socially approved behavior, and by encouragement to learn to be both mature and autonomous.

Chapter 2

The Changed Body

Photograph by Farrell/Greene
Omikron

The first recorded reports of puberty changes go back to the days of Aristotle. In his *Historia animalium* Aristotle states that when boys are "twice seven years old," they begin to "engender seed." At this time hair begins to appear on the pubes and the voice alters, getting harsher, more uneven, and somewhat shrill. Girls at the same age experience the first menstrual flow. When this occurs, Aristotle said, the breasts have swelled to the height of two fingers' breadth, and the girl's voice has become deeper. Aristotle noted also that behavioral changes accompany these changed physiological states. He mentioned among other behavioral changes the tendencies to be ardent, irritable, passionate, and sanguine. Girls at this age, according to Aristotle, are in need of constant surveillance because of their developing sex impulses (5).

The effects of body changes on attitudes and behavior have been proved by scientific studies. When changes are rapid, the individual cannot make adequate adjustments to them. Bühler, who has labeled this period of adolescence the "negative phase," has helped to focus scientific attention on the marked behavioral changes that come with sexual maturing. Most of the changes, Bühler noted, are unfavorable and are expressed in confusion, feelings of insecurity, and "anti" attitudes toward life (18). Generally, however, the worst of the negative-phase behavior is over by the time girls become sexually mature at the "menarche," or first menstruation. The same holds true for boys when their sex organs reach a level of functional maturity.

Tanner (155) has been equally emphatic about how important this period is in the life span:

For the majority of young persons, the years from twelve to sixteen are the most eventful ones of their lives so far as their growth and development is concerned. Admittedly during fetal life and the first year or two after birth developments occurred still faster, and a sympathetic environment was probably even more crucial, but the subject himself was not the fascinated, charmed, or horrified spectator that watches the developments, or lack of developments, of adolescence.

MEANING OF PUBERTY

Physical changes take place throughout the adolescent years, but the majority come in late childhood and early adolescence. This is known as the "puberty phase." The word "puberty" comes from the Latin *pubertas,* which means "age of manhood." It refers to the time when the reproductive organs mature and begin to function. The word "phase" suggests that the transition from childhood to adulthood is relatively rapid.

Accompanying the changes in the reproductive organs are changes in the rest of the body; these, in turn, lead to changes in interests, attitudes, and behavior. Physical development continues after sexual maturity has been attained, but at a progressively slower rate, and the psychological and behavioral changes become less and less pronounced (41). The more complex the culture, the longer the time needed to learn to think, act, and feel like an adult. Consequently, the transitional period for *psychological* maturity is longer today than it was in the time of our great grandparents, extending several years beyond the end of puberty.

Even though puberty is a relatively short period in the total life span and only a part of adolescence, it is divided into three stages: the prepubescent, the pubescent, and the postpubescent. These three stages and an explanation of what changes occur in each are given in Box 2-1.

AGE OF PUBERTY

Puberty begins with the beginning of the transformation of the child's body into an adult's and ends when the transformation is completed. The individual is considered a "child" until he is sexually mature; he is then called an "adolescent." Figure 2-1 shows how puberty overlaps both childhood and adolescence.

Criteria of sexual maturity

To be able to determine the age of puberty, one must have reasonably accurate criteria to indicate when the transformation of the body begins and when the child becomes sexually mature. Among girls, the menarche, or first menstruation, has been used for centuries as the best single criterion of sexual maturity. Scientific studies have shown that the menarche comes at neither the beginning nor the end of the period of physical changes taking place at puberty. Instead, the menarche may be regarded as the midpoint of puberty. This is justified by evidence that a period of "adolescent sterility," lasting 1 month or longer, follows the menarche. During adolescent sterility, "ovulation," or the ripening and release of a ripe ovum from a follicle in the ovary, does not occur, and the time between menstrual periods ranges from 2 to 6 months. This is evidence that sexual maturing has not been completed (113, 126).

Among boys, the first "nocturnal emission," or "wet dream," has been popularly used as a criterion of sexual maturity. During sleep, the penis sometimes becomes erect and "semen," or fluid containing sperm cells, spurts out. This is the normal way for the male reproductive organ to rid itself of excessive amounts of semen. However, nocturnal emissions have been found to occur after some pubertal development has taken place and therefore cannot be used as a criterion of the onset of puberty. Furthermore, not all boys experience this phenomenon, or not all recognize it as such.

The most dependable single criterion of sexual maturity in boys and girls is the assessment of the state of their *bone development* by means of x-rays (50, 153). Studies reveal that genital growth always occurs at a certain point in the bone development of the individual. X-rays of the long bones of the hands and knees, taken at different times during the preadolescent growth spurt, make it possible to determine just when puberty begins and at what rate it is progressing. The maturity determiners in the bones are successive changes in the outline of the shaft ends and in the contour of epiphysical ossification centers (63, 143)

Reported ages of sexual maturing

Extensive studies of youngsters of different cultural and racial backgrounds, and of different socioeconomic levels within these groups, report that both boys and girls follow

Figure 2-1 Puberty overlaps the end of childhood and the beginning of adolescence.

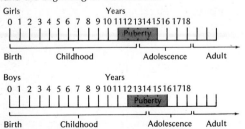

reasonably predictable patterns in sexual maturing. For example, American girls reach maturity or are pubescent between the ages of 12.5 and 14.5 years, with an average (about 50 percent) of 13 years for girls of the middle and upper socioeconomic groups and 13.5 for girls of the lower groups. Boys mature approximately a year later than girls. Thus, the age for sexual maturing in boys falls between 14 and 15.5 years, with an average (about 50 percent) of 14.5 years. The other 50 percent of boys and girls are about equally distributed between ages below and above the averages (10, 126, 151, 153, 164). Those who mature earlier than the average are known as "early maturers"; those who mature later than the average are called "late maturers."

Differences between the sexes are espe-cially marked between the ages of 12 and 14 years, when there are many more mature girls than boys. This difference shows itself not only in the larger and more mature bodies of girls but also in their more mature, more aggressive, and more sex-conscious behavior. Age differences in sexual maturing *within a sex group* cause many social problems during the junior and early senior high school period. These problems often lead to poor schoolwork and undisciplined behavior.

Although sexual maturing follows a fairly predictable pattern, there are variations. Johnston has said, "The time clock that governs the developmental process in children is an individual one" (70). Variations in the age of sexual maturing are due to variations in the functioning of the endocrine glands which

---

BOX 2-2 FACTORS INFLUENCING AGE OF SEXUAL MATURING

*Heredity
Age of maturing "runs in the family." For example, girls have their first men-struation at approximately the same age as their mothers and sisters.

*Intelligence
Children of superior intelligence mature sexually slightly earlier than those of average or below average intelligence.

*Health
Good health, due to good prenatal and postnatal care, results in earlier ma-turing.

*Nutrition
A predominantly carbohydrate diet during childhood generally results in late maturing, while a predominantly protein diet leads to early maturing.

*Family Socioeconomic Status
The better the socioeconomic environment, the greater the chances of early maturing. Because of substandard medical care and nutrition, children from poor socioeconomic backgrounds often mature later, as do those from rural environments.

*Body Size
Children who are taller and fatter than their age-mates reach sexual maturity earlier.

*Body Build
Children with feminine-type bodies (broad hips and shorts legs) tend to be early maturers, while those with masculine-type bodies (broad shoulders and long legs) tend to be late maturers.

are responsible for the transformation of the child's body into an adult body. Box 2-2 lists a number of the most important factors that influence the age of sexual maturing (15, 34, 118, 126, 151, 153, 164, 172).

Effect of age of sexual maturing on body development

The pattern of body development differs according to whether the child matures earlier or later than the average age for his sex group or at approximately the average age. In the late maturer, growth is usually irregular and asymmetrical, with growth of the body dimensions and of the internal organs lagging behind growth in stature. This is in direct contrast to the early maturer, whose growth is more regular and who shows less organic imbalance. Though late maturers may be abnormally small in late childhood, they do not necessarily end up as small adults.

Age of maturing affects the pattern of development of different body tissues as well as the pattern of development of body dimensions. Early-maturing girls, for example, are larger than late-maturing girls in total breadth of calf and in the breadths of fat, muscle, and bone within the calf. This difference is also seen in boys who mature early, though to a lesser degree.

TIME NEEDED FOR MATURING

There are such marked individual variations in the time needed for sexual maturing that it is impossible to give a really precise estimate of how long it will take. Approximately 1 to 2 years are needed for the preliminary changes from an asexual to a sexual state. During this time changes in preparation for sexual maturity are taking place throughout the body. After the sex organs have reached a point in their development where they begin to function, another year or two are required to complete their development and the other changes throughout the body which accompany maturity of the sex organs. This means that the average child requires from 2 to 4 years to make the transition. Children who require

less than the average time are known as "rapid maturers"; those who require more are called "slow maturers" (10, 73, 172).

Effect of rate of maturing on development

The pattern of development at puberty is greatly influenced by the speed of development. Rapid maturers have more spurts of rapid growth; their periods of acceleration and slowing down come abruptly; and they attain adult proportions very quickly. Their sex organs and secondary sex characteristics develop early, and the osseous development is accelerated.

Slow maturers, by contrast, have less intense periods of acceleration; their growth is more even and gradual; and it continues for a longer time. The sex organs and secondary sex characteristics develop at a slower rate than the average, thus reaching their mature level later. The osseous development is also later. At maturity, slow maturers are usually larger than rapid maturers (10, 106, 154).

CAUSES OF PUBERTY CHANGES

For centuries the exact cause of sexual maturation was completely unknown. Aristotle seemed to believe that in boys the physical changes of puberty were dependent upon some activity of the testes because, when boys were castrated, their voices remained high-pitched and pubertal hair did not appear. People knew, of course, that the bodies of little boys and girls began to change, but they did not know what lay behind the changes and why they occurred in such a regular, predictable manner.

A partial answer to the mystery of sexual maturation has come from the work of endocrinologists who have discovered a close relationship between the pituitary gland, located at the base of the brain, and the gonads, or sex glands.

Role of the pituitary

The anterior lobe of the pituitary gland produces two hormones that are closely related to puberty development. These are the *growth* hormone, which is influential in determining the size of the individual, especially the limbs, and the gonad-stimulating, or *gonadotropic,* hormone, which, when acting on the gonads, stimulates them to increased activity.

Just before puberty there is a gradual increase in the gonadotropic hormone. At the same time the gonads become more sensitive to this hormone. The combination of these two conditions initiates puberty. What is responsible for the increased supply of the gonadotropic hormone or the increased sensitivity of the gonads to the hormone, at the more or less predictable age at which puberty changes occur, has not yet been fully explained. Some hereditary factor is unquestionably at work.

Role of the gonads

The gonads, the second of the endocrine glands to play an active role in bringing about puberty changes, are the sex glands. The female gonads are called the "ovaries," and the male, the "testes." Just before puberty the gonadotropic hormone from the pituitary gland is produced in sufficient quantity to cause the immature gonads to grow and develop into mature testes and ovaries. With their development comes the production of germ cells, as well as hormones that bring about sex changes in the growth and development of the *genital organs* and *secondary sex characteristics.*

As the ovaries develop, their primary function is to produce germ cells, called "ova," for the perpetuation of the race. Likewise, changes occur in the other reproductive organs, such as the development of the uterus, the Fallopian tubes, and the vagina. Accompanying these changes comes cyclic menstrual bleeding or menstruation. In addition, there is the development of the secondary sex characteristics of the female body.

The male gonads, or testes, like the female ovaries, are stimulated to development at puberty by the gonadotropic hormone. The testes have a dual function. They produce "spermatozoa," or sex cells, which are needed for reproduction, and they produce one or more hormones that control the physical and psychological adjustments necessary in the carrying out of the reproductive function. The physical adjustment includes the development of secondary sex characteristics, as well as further development of the testes themselves, the prostate gland, the seminal vesicles, and the penis.

Interaction of gonads and pituitary

After the gonadal sex hormones are stimulated by hormones from the pituitary gland, they in turn act on the pituitary and cause a gradual reduction in the amount or the effectiveness of the growth hormone. The gonadal sex hormones eventually stop the action of the growth hormone completely. If there has not been enough of the growth hormone in late childhood and early puberty, the individual's growth will be arrested and he will be below average in height. If, on the other hand, production of the gonadal hormones in adequate quantity is delayed, the individual's growth continues too long, and his body, especially his limbs, becomes too large. It is thus obvious that the pituitary gland and the gonads must function in a reciprocal manner, with properly timed action on the part of both, if growth is to be normal (102, 126, 137, 175).

Abnormal glandular functioning

An inadequate supply of gonadal hormones *delays puberty* and prevents normal development of the sex organs and of the secondary sex characteristics. In delayed puberty, the secondary sex characteristics in girls are normal but the uterus is small and undeveloped. Boys are somewhat effeminate in appearance, while girls tend to be somewhat masculine in their looks and ways. They usually have a childish appearance and often seem immature (69, 137).

Accelerated puberty, known as "puberty precox," comes from an excessive supply of the gonadotropic hormone during the early years of childhood. This affects the gonads, and the individual matures too soon, even to the production of spermatozoa and ova. While there is no evidence of what causes the excessive supply of gonadotropic hormone at an early age, there is evidence that it is not caused by inheritance (69, 130, 137).

PHYSICAL TRANSFORMATION AT PUBERTY

In a relatively short time, the child's body is transformed into that of an adult. The exterior changes are often so radical that the adolescent may not be recognized at first glance by those who have not seen him in 2 or 3 years. The changes that take place within the body—in the size, shape, and functioning of the different organs and glands—are not visible, but are equally as great.

A convenient classification of the changes includes four major categories: growth in body size, changes in body proportions, development of the primary sex characteristics, and development of the secondary sex characteristics. In spite of individual differences in the rate of the changes, the pattern of the changes is similar for all children and, hence, predictable.

Growth in body size

The first major physical change that takes place at puberty is growth in body size. There is a growth spurt during which the body reaches its adult size. While there may be an addition of weight with advancing age, the *normal* weight for body height and build is achieved at this time. The puberty growth spurt begins a year or two before the sex organs become functionally mature and lasts for 6 months to a year afterward. This entire period is commonly called the "adolescent growth spurt." Since the most rapid growth occurs in the preadolescent period, it more correctly should be called the "preadolescent growth spurt."

The growth spurt for girls begins between the ages of 8.5 and 11.5 years, with a peak of rapidity in growth occurring, on the average, at 12.5 years. After this, the rate declines until

it gradually comes to a standstill between 15 and 16 years. Boys have a similar pattern of rapid growth, but they start later and grow for a longer time than girls. In the average pattern, the spurt begins between 10.5 and 14.5 years, with a peak of rapidity around 14.5 years, and then a gradual decline until 17 or 20, when growth is completed (51, 102, 151, 153).

Body size is measured in terms of height and weight. Since the puberty growth spurt affects the two differently, however, they will be discussed separately.

Height Height is regulated by the growth hormone from the anterior lobe of the pituitary gland. In adequate amounts it enables healthy well-nourished children to attain their maximum normal size. In the absence of an adequate amount of the growth hormone, dwarfism occurs in more or less pronounced forms, depending upon the degree of deficiency of the hormone. Too much of the growth hormone has the opposite effect and produces giantism. The most important fact about the growth hormone is that *it must be produced at the right time* if the child is to grow normally (102, 115).

Growth in height follows a fairly regular pattern and usually, though not always, precedes that in weight. The pattern of height growth differs somewhat for boys and girls, as may be seen in Figure 2-2.

How tall or short the individual will be when his growth is completed depends upon many factors. Children tend, on the whole, to resemble their parents in height (10, 67, 94). Adolescents with ectomorphic (tall and slender) builds are taller, as adults, than adolescents who were mesomorphic (short, stocky, and muscular). This difference in build is noticeable throughout the growth years but becomes more pronounced after the puberty changes have been completed (142, 153).

Of the environmental influences on adult height, nutrition is the most important single factor. Children from the higher economic groups, on the average, become taller adults than those from the lower groups because they have better nutrition and care during the growth years (55, 127, 151).

Age of maturing likewise influences the ultimate height of both boys and girls. By the age of 15 years, differences between early and late maturers begin to disappear. After that, late maturers not only catch up with their early-maturing contemporaries but usually outstrip them. The result is that late maturers are taller as adults than their childhood measures would have indicated, while early maturers have shorter-than-expected adult stature. Children who mature at a slow rate are generally taller as adults than those who mature at a more rapid rate (62, 73).

Weight Increase in weight during adolescence is due largely to growth in the bones and muscles. The *bones* grow larger as well as heavier. They change in shape, proportions, and internal structure. By the time the girl is 17 years old, her bones are mature or nearly mature in size and ossification; boys' bones complete their development approximately 2 years later. At maturity, about 16 percent of the body weight is provided by the bones.

In childhood, the *muscles* contribute about 25 percent of the total body weight and, by maturity, approximately 45 to 50 percent. Muscles contribute more to body weight in boys than in girls; in girls fat is a heavier contributor than in boys. The most pronounced increase in muscle tissue comes between 12 and 15 years for girls and between 15 and 17 years for boys (66, 102).

Girls make their greatest gain in weight just before and just after puberty. On the average, 10 pounds are gained 2 years before puberty. The largest increase, an average gain of 14 pounds, occurs in the year immediately preceding puberty, and an additional gain of 10 pounds comes in the year following puberty. This means that in 3 years the average increase in weight for girls is 34 pounds.

For boys, the weight spurt comes a year or two later than for girls. Their pattern of weight increase varies more than that for height. The mean gain during the pubertal period is 39.92 pounds, with a range from 17.2 to 64.81 pounds. The maximum growth in

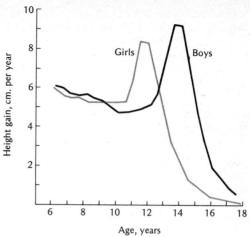

Figure 2-2 Puberty spurt in height growth for boys and girls (1 cm = 0.39 in.). (Adapted from J. M. Tanner: *Growth at adolescence,* 2d ed. Oxford: Blackwell Scientific Publications, 1962. Used by permission.)

weight comes with or after the maximum growth in height (38, 52, 55).

Age of maturing affects the pattern of weight increase during puberty. Early-maturing girls are, for example, 33.6 percent heavier than late-maturing girls at the point of greatest contrast, which falls between the ages of 11.5 and 12.5 years. Among boys, those who mature before their fourteenth birthday are heavier than those who mature later, and those who mature between their fourteenth and fifteenth birthdays are heavier at all ages than those who mature after their fifteenth birthday (66, 73).

Adolescents often experience a "fat period" early in sexual maturing. This is due in part to the hormonal dislocation that accompanies sexual maturing and in part to the increased appetite that accompanies rapid physical growth. The fat look normally disappears as height increases and as hormonal balance is restored.

In boys, the fat period comes at or near the onset of the period of rapid growth for height and the onset of the spurt in penis growth. At this time, boys tend to have marked accumulations of fat around the nipples and over the abdomen, hips, and thighs. The facial appearance is altered by increase of fat about the cheeks, neck, and jaw. This fat period lasts for approximately 2 years, after which the body regains its normal proportions.

The fat period among girls comes with the onset of puberty. At this time, appetite increases, and the girl often overeats. Like the boy, the girl develops fat in areas of the body where fat is considered inappropriate, especially over the abdomen and hips. As puberty development continues, the fat appearance of the girl generally disappears although her weight may not change. This occurs when her legs lengthen and her whole body becomes taller (66, 95, 162).

Relatively few adolescents remain fat. In fact, at the very time when weight increases most, when sexual maturity is achieved, adolescents begin to look scrawny. Their muscles and bones are growing rapidly, so that their shoulders, legs, and arms make their bodies bigger and heavier, but more slender. Only when the body is covered with fat tissue does it look fat.

BOX 2-3 CHANGES IN PROPORTIONS IN BODY EXTERIOR

*Head
During puberty, the head grows slowly compared with the rest of the body. At maturity, it is one-sixth of total body length as compared with one-fourth at birth.

*Face
The forehead becomes higher and wider and the nose grows rapidly early in puberty; both reach their adult size by pubescence. The mouth widens, the flat lips of childhood become fuller, and the jaw becomes more pronounced though the changes are not completed until maximum height has been attained.

*Trunk
Toward the end of puberty, a waistline develops; it appears to be high because the trunk has grown less than the legs. By the time the trunk reaches its mature size, early in adolescence, the waistline drops below the middle of the trunk and the shoulders (greater in boys) and hips (greater in girls) broaden.

*Legs
Just before puberty, the legs become relatively longer than the trunk and are four times as long as they were at birth. At maturity, they are five times as long. As they lengthen, legs become noticeably shaped, owing to fat in girls and muscles and fat in boys.

*Arms
Just before and immediately after puberty, the arms begin to lengthen. This makes the arms seem proportionally too long until the trunk reaches its mature length. The arms take on shape at puberty, owing to fat in girls and muscles and fat in boys.

*Hands and Feet
Hands and feet reach their mature size and shape before the arms and legs. Their growth is completed 4 to 5 years before maximum stature is attained; hence they seem proportionally too large and conspicuous.

Changes in body proportions

The second major physical transformation that takes place at puberty consists of changes in body proportions, both exterior and interior. Growth is asynchronous. That is, the peak rate of growth in different parts of the body does not necessarily occur at the same time. Not only do the different parts grow at different rates but they reach maximum development at different times. However, while each part of the body has its own peculiar pattern of development, all parts conform in a general way to the patterns for growth in height and weight. Consequently, changes in body proportions are predictable.

Changes in body exterior As different areas of the body exterior reach their mature size and shape, there are changes in appearance. Until all parts have fully developed, it is impossible to predict what the mature appearance of the adolescent will be.

According to tradition, the child improves in appearance as he takes on the body and facial features of an adult. Within limits, this is true. The lanky body, the shapeless arms and legs, and the face whose parts are out of proportion, especially the adult-sized teeth in a childish mouth, improve as they reach adult shapes and proportions. Some adults, however, are less attractive than they were as young children, before they reached the lanky age of late childhood, though many improve their looks by careful selection of clothes, cosmetics, and even plastic surgery. Consequently, they may only *appear* to be more attractive than they were as children.

Box 2-3 lists the changes in proportions that take place in the body exterior during puberty and the pattern of the changes (10, 44, 102, 106, 107, 109). These are shown graphically in Figure 2-3.

The body build of the individual, after the puberty changes have been completed, varies somewhat according to the age at which the maturing process occurred. Late-maturing boys, for example, are characteristically of slender build, long-legged at all ages, and relatively weak at the ages when they are

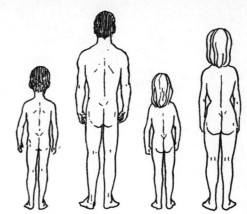

Figure 2-3 Changes in body proportions as children mature.

lagging behind their contemporaries in size. Early-maturing boys are usually large, strong, and broad-hipped. Late-maturing girls have slightly broader hips than those who mature early. Late maturers of both sexes tend to have slightly broader shoulders than those who mature early (10, 102, 106).

Changes in body interior Internal growth is not so readily apparent as external growth but it is just as pronounced. It is closely correlated with growth in height and weight and, like external growth, is asynchronous, with different organs reaching their peak growth at different ages. Because of the asynchronous growth of the different internal organs, adolescence is characterized by a temporarily increased physiological instability.

During puberty the organs of the *digestive system* attain almost their mature size and shape. The stomach becomes longer and less tubular; thus its capacity increases. The intestines grow in length and circumference, and the smooth muscles in the stomach and intestinal walls become thicker and stronger; this results in stronger peristaltic movements. The esophagus increases in length, and the liver in weight.

In the *circulatory system*, there is an increase in the size of the heart and in the length and thickness of the walls of the blood vessels.

The heart grows so rapidly that, in the 17- or 18-year-old, it is twelve times as heavy as at birth. The increase in the size of the veins and arteries during this time, by contrast, is only 15 percent. By the end of adolescence, the ratio of the size of the heart to the arteries is 290 to 61, as compared with a ratio of 25 to 20 at birth.

As a result of growth in the lungs, there are marked changes in *respiration* during adolescence. Breathing is slower than in childhood, though the volume of inhaled and exhaled air is greater. The greater oxygen consumption of boys after puberty is due to their having more muscle than fat tissue, as compared with girls, not merely because they have larger bodies.

The glands of the *endocrine system* grow at different rates and reach maturity at different ages. The adrenal glands, attached to the kidneys, lose weight during the first year of life and do not regain their birth weight until the middle of adolescence. The thyroid glands, located in the throat, enlarge in girls at the time of the menarche; this produces irregularities in the basal metabolic rate. The gonads of both boys and girls grow rapidly at puberty and reach adult size late in adolescence or early in adulthood (45, 66, 102, 115, 127).

Development of primary sex characteristics

The third important physiological transformation that occurs during puberty is the development of the primary sex characteristics. The primary sex characteristics are the sex organs proper; their function is to produce offspring. During childhood the sex organs are small and inconspicuous and do not produce cells for reproduction. With the onset of puberty all this is changed. The period at which functional maturity occurs, the "pubescent stage," is the true dividing line between the sexually immature and the sexually mature individual.

Since the primary sex characteristics of boys and girls differ in both structure and function, and since the patterns of their development also differ, they will be discussed separately.

Male sex organs The male sex organs consist of both external and internal genitalia. Those on the outside of the body are the penis and the scrotum, or sac containing the testes, while those on the inside are the vas deferens and its associated parts, the prostate gland and the urethra. Growth of the primary sex characteristics follows a pattern and is similar for all boys even though the timing of the different stages varies according to the rate of maturing. This pattern, as shown in Box 2-4, has five stages (16, 93, 102, 105).

When the male reproductive organs are functionally mature, *nocturnal emissions* generally occur. The first nocturnal emission occurs most frequently between the ages of 12 and 16 years. It may be caused by a dream of sex excitement, or it may be set off by other stimulating circumstances, such as being too warmly covered, sleeping on the back, wearing tight pajamas, having a full bladder, or having constipated bowels. The boy may not

---

BOX 2-4 DEVELOPMENT OF MALE PRIMARY SEX CHARACTERISTICS

Stage I
Penis, testes, and scrotum are essentially the same as in early childhood.

Stage II
Testes and penis have noticeably enlarged; highly pigmented hair has appeared.

Stage III
The penis has appreciably lengthened; hair has become coarser.

Stage IV
Larger testes and penis of increased diameter are apparent. Pubic hair looks adult but its area is smaller.

Stage V
Genitalia are adult in size and shape; pubic hair is adult.

---

be conscious of what is taking place until he sees the telltale spot on his bedclothes or pajamas.

Female sex organs The most important part of the female reproductive apparatus consists of two ovaries, the organs producing the ova or eggs. They begin a spurt of rapid growth between the ages of 12 and 18 years, which continues for some time. When the girl reaches puberty, the eggs begin to ripen, one approximately every 28 days, or every menstrual cycle. It enters the Fallopian tube, or passageway from the ovary to the uterus, and then passes into the uterus, or womb. It later passes through the vagina, or passage leading from the uterus to the outside genital opening.

The ovaries and the uterus grow rapidly during puberty. The ovaries do not reach their mature weight and size until the girl is 20 or 21 years old, even though they start to function in approximately the middle of the puberty period (66, 126, 137).

The first definite indication a young girl has of her sexual maturity is the menarche. A period of adolescent sterility follows the menarche. At this time the endocrine glands do not pour their hormones into the bloodstream with proper intensity to make ovulation and reproduction possible. The duration of this period in the human female is extremely variable, from 1 month to 7 years. Even after several menstrual periods, it is questionable whether a girl's sexual mechanism is mature enough to make it possible for her to conceive (126, 137, 152).

The menarche is the beginning of a series of periodic discharges that will occur fairly regularly every 28 days until the woman reaches the menopause, in her forties or fifties. These periodic discharges are know as "menstruation," from the Latin word *menses* meaning "month." It refers to the lunar month of 28 days.

In the young adolescent, the interval between each menstrual period varies greatly. The time between periods is usually longer during the summer months, for example, than during the winter. The variability decreases with age. There are likewise marked variations in the length of the period of the flow. In the first few menstrual periods, it is not at all uncommon for the flow to last only a day or even less. Later, it may last from 1 to 14 days. The average is 3 to 5 days.

It is not unusual for menstruation during the first few years following puberty to be accompanied by physical discomfort or pain. The most common disturbances are headaches, backaches, cramps, or severe abdominal pains. There may be vomiting, fatigue, bladder irritability, soreness of the genital organs, pain in the legs, swelling of the ankles, and skin irritations. As the menses become more regular, the disturbances become less and less severe. Circulatory congestion, which is relieved by the menstrual flow, is partially responsible for these disturbances (66, 102, 126, 137).

Development of secondary sex characteristics

The fourth and, unquestionably, the most dramatic physical transformation that occurs during puberty is the development of the secondary sex characteristics—the physical features that make girls "feminine" and boys "masculine" in appearance. They play an important indirect role in mating by making members of one sex appealing to members of the other sex, but they are not directly related to reproduction. In Box 2-5 are shown the important male and female secondary sex characteristics (62, 66, 69, 100, 126, 153).

The development of the secondary sex characteristics is due to the increased supply of hormones from the gonads during puberty. These hormones not only stimulate the growth of the sex organs—the primary sex characteristics—but are also responsible for the development of the secondary sex characteristics.

Again, growth is asynchronous. The secondary sex characteristics develop at different times and reach maturity at different ages. Early or late maturers follow much the same pattern as those who mature at the average age for their sex group, though the different characteristics appear earlier or later.

Each of the important secondary sex characteristics develops according to a predictable pattern. A few examples will show how predictable the pattern is and explain why, if pubescent boys and girls are unaware of the pattern, they are disturbed by the length of time it takes for them to be transformed into sex-appropriate adults.

The change in the boy's *voice*, which is one of the most obvious indications of pubertal maturing, is due to the rapid growth of the larynx (Adam's apple) and the lengthening of the vocal cords that stretch across it. In time, the vocal cords nearly double their length. This results in the drop of an octave in pitch. There is also an increase in volume, and the tonal quality is pleasanter than that of the high-pitched childish voice. It is rather unusual for the beginning of the change to occur before some pubic hair is present. Huskiness precedes actual change in pitch, while vocal instability and loss of control of the voice do not come until the change in tone is one octave in extent. On the average, the voice does not begin to acquire the deeper tone characteristic of a mature male until the boy is 15, but roughness of tone and unexpected changes in pitch continue until he is 16 or 18 years old.

Several important changes take place in the *skin* at puberty and during the remaining years of adolescence. The soft, delicate, transparent skin of the child gradually becomes thicker and coarser as the individual matures sexually. At the beginning of puberty, there is a definite increase in the thickness of subcutaneous tissue. The soft coloring of the transparent skin of the child becomes deeper. Pores enlarge, and facial hair not only grows heavier but is supplemented by coarse and more pigmented hair in regions of the body where no hair grew in childhood.

Shortly before puberty the "apocrine" *sweat glands* begin to enlarge, but they do not attain full development until puberty is well advanced. The functioning of these glands, especially in the axillae, or armpits, begins even before the axillary hair makes its appearance. The characteristic odor of axillary perspiration may be detected first at puberty. It becomes more pronounced in the early years of adolescence, particularly during emotional tension. Among girls, increased secretion from these glands occurs during the premenstrual and menstrual portions of the menstrual cycle.

The "sebaceous," or *oil-producing, glands,* become especially large and active at puberty. They are for a time associated with disproportionately small ducts. This causes a temporary maladjustment in their functioning, which continues until the maturation process is completed. The result is a skin disturbance known as "acne." When the matter from the sebaceous glands cannot drain properly because of the disproportionately small ducts leading from the temporarily too large glands, it forms into hard plugs in the pores at the openings of the gland ducts. These are known as "comedones" or "blackheads." They are most often found on the nose, the chin, and the center of the forehead. When the plugged pores are overfilled, they easily become inflamed, and pimples appear on the surface of the skin.

SIGNIFICANCE OF BODY TRANSFORMATION

The radical body changes described above have psychological as well as physical repercussions. The physical changes determine not only what the young adolescent can do but also what he wants to do. And what he wants to do is largely determined by the *physical* repercussions of the changes.

Bodily changes are usually accompanied by fatigue, listlessness, and other symptoms of poor health. These are exaggerated when bodily changes occur rapidly or when the pubescent is expected to assume more responsibilities at home and at school than when he was a child.

Furthermore, owing to changes in the digestive system, the pubescent often suffers from digestive disturbances. These are frequently accompanied by anemia, which further increases the pubescent's general state of fatigue and listlessness. In addition, digestive disturbances are often responsible for headaches and general feelings of wretchedness which dampen the motivation of the pubescent to do what he is capable of doing and what members of the social group expect him to do. Since he is not actually sick, adults and even peers have an unsympathetic attitude toward him, and this encourages him to develop feelings of martyrdom. Pubescent girls, for example, often find that family members, teachers, and peers are critical of their absence from school when they suffer from cramps during their menstrual periods and intimate that they are being truants (133).

The *psychological* repercussions that follow the physical transformation at puberty come mainly from social expectations of mature attitudes and behavior. When the pubescent begins to look more like an adult than a child, social expectations, as defined by the developmental tasks described in Chapter 1, place a heavy psychological burden on the adolescent.

One of the most difficult developmental tasks for the young adolescent is acceptance of his changed body and physique. He must not only adjust to the normal changes that accompany puberty but he must also accept his new size and shape as the physique he will have for the remainder of his life. Sooner or later, most adolescents do this.

Most children look forward to the day when they will be grown-up, but changes in their bodies frequently cause more distress than pleasure. Many adolescents report that they would like to change their physical characteristics and that they know specific ways in which they would like to be different (4, 33).

Dissatisfaction with appearance is generally at its height shortly after sexual maturity has been achieved, during the high school age. After that, adolescents who are well adjusted show an increasingly more acceptant attitude toward themselves and their appearance. Boys tend to have an unfavorable opinion of their abilities while girls tend to be critical of their appearance (3).

"Body cathexis," or degree of feeling of satisfaction with the body or its various parts, is more important to girls than to boys because society places more value on appearance in girls. Unless the adolescent girl is satisfied with her body after the transformation of puberty, she will develop feelings of anxiety and insecurity. This is true of boys also, but to a lesser extent because of the lower value boys place on physical attractiveness (25, 134).

While all adolescents are affected by the physical changes of puberty, the extent of effects will depend upon a number of factors, the most important of which are given in Box 2-6.

The effects of body changes may be divided into two categories: those which are sources

BOX 2-6 FACTORS INFLUENCING EFFECTS OF BODY CHANGES

Rapidity of Change
Rapid growth and physical change so alter the body that the pubescent who cannot readily accept his new physique and revise his physical self-image may become overly self-conscious.

Lack of Preparation
How much knowledge and forewarning the adolescent has of the changes taking place in his body will markedly influence his attitude toward the changes.

Childhood Ideal
Any feature that greatly deviates from the adolescent's childhood ideal of himself as a grown-up will be a source of concern.

Social Expectancy
The adolescent's attitude toward his body and facial features is influenced by what he *believes* the significant people in his life, especially parents and members of the peer group, think of them.

Stereotypes
Body builds or facial features associated with unfavorable stereotypes of the adolescent lead to unfavorable self-concepts and unsocial behavior.

Social Insecurity
The adolescent knows that physical appearance affects social acceptance. A physical feature that is unfavorably judged will make the adolescent socially insecure.

---

of concern and those which affect attitudes and behavior. The former are responsible, either directly or indirectly, for the latter. Sources of concern and effects on behavior are discussed in detail below.

CONCERNS ABOUT TRANSFORMED BODY

All adolescents have a lively interest in their developing bodies. They constantly compare themselves with their contemporaries and are distressed when their own development falls short. As Havighurst has pointed out, "It is a rare youngster who is never worried during this period with the question: Am I normal?" (65) Physical conditions are a source of concern because they represent real or fancied social handicaps. From the point of view of

adjustment, it matters little whether the handicaps are real or imagined.

Girls, as a group, are more concerned about their developing bodies than boys because, to them, their bodies are more closely related to their roles in life, especially in courtship and marriage (48, 87, 166). Furthermore, girls know that they can use cosmetics and select clothes to enhance their good features and camouflage the bad, and this heightens their interest in their bodies and intensifies their concern about them (11, 134).

Studies of sources of concern have revealed that they center around three questions: Am I normal? Am I sex appropriate? and What can I do to make my body come up to my childhood ideal? Concern about normality often arises because the pubescent does not know that different parts of the body develop at different rates and reach maturity at different ages. He is also ignorant of the fact that nature's timetable differs for different individuals and, therefore, he worries when his body differs in any respect from the bodies of his age-mates.

Long before puberty, boys and girls learn what constitutes sex appropriateness of appearance and what role a sex-appropriate appearance plays in successful social adjustments. Consequently, they are concerned about any aspect of their bodies that suggests sex inappropriateness (139). Knowing, for example, that boys like slender girls with long legs and well developed breasts, girls are naturally concerned when their bodies do not match this image (30, 170, 171).

It is an unusual pubescent who, as a child, did not have an ideal image of what he wanted to look like as a grown-up. Childhood body ideals are fostered by mass media and by family, peer, and general cultural attitudes (139). When the pubescent compares his body with his ideal, he usually has adequate reason to be concerned.

Studies of sources of concern reveal that the adolescent is generally disturbed by *one physical characteristic* which he feels is homely or disproportionate, which is sex inappropriate, or which does not come up to social standards. He may also be concerned because of a personal dislike for a trait that does not come up to his childhood ideal (91, 139).

In Box 2-7 are given the most common concerns pubescents have about their developing bodies (21, 35, 42, 48, 126, 131, 136, 138, 167). Individual concern may become focused on one specific aspect to the exclusion of others. A boy with a bad case of acne may not realize that he also has perspiration odor, for example.

Intense and persistent concern about the changing body is apparent when adolescents take steps to bring their bodies closer to their ideals and to the cultural stereotype of what is sex appropriate. They know, as Brislin and Lewis have pointed out, that "it is very re-warding to be with someone who is physically attractive" and that a body that conforms to cultural standards will enhance their chances of social acceptance (13). To achieve this end, they seek plastic surgery to improve a facial feature, such as a "big" nose (97, 110), they submit to orthodontic treatment in the hope of improving the shape and appearance of the mouth (8, 14, 90), they get contact lenses or glasses with modish frames (59, 60, 98), they go on rigorous diets if they think they are too fat (17, 165), and they seek dermatological aid for acne and other skin disorders (83).

EFFECTS OF BODY TRANSFORMATION ON BEHAVIOR

Most of the changes in attitude and behavior during the prepubescent stage are, unfortunately, unpleasant. The child seems to go in reverse in that many socially desirable traits built up during late childhood disappear. As was noted earlier in the chapter, Charlotte Bühler has called this period the negative phase (18). Behavior is markedly affected for only a relatively short time, however—for about 6 to 12 months. This period immediately precedes the pubescent stage—when sexual maturity is established. The few months before the menarche in girls and before nocturnal emissions, pubic hair, and other signs of sexual maturing in boys are unquestionably among the most difficult of the whole growth pattern. While the prepubescent does nothing terribly wrong, he is troublesome and irritating, and friction between parent and child generally reaches its peak in both frequency and intensity (35, 41).

When sexual maturity has been achieved, the pattern of behavior changes. As Macfarlane et al. have said, "This tension [which] may be due to the physiological changes, to social aspects of maturing, or more probably to both of these factors" decreases (96). But the change does not occur suddenly. Josselyn writes: "Practically every child is somewhat overwhelmed for a short period by the effects of the physiological maturing process. His

BOX 2-7 COMMON CONCERNS ABOUT THE CHANGING BODY

Sex Differences in Development
Boys are smaller, shorter, and less developed than girls for 2 to 5 years. Girls are bigger and more developed than boys and have an interest in boys which is not reciprocated.

Body Build
Boys are sometimes short and stocky, deviating from the sex-appropriate triangular shape. Girls may be tall or stocky, deviating from the sex-appropriate hourglass shape.

Secondary Sex Characteristics
Scanty or abundant facial and bodily hair, voice cracks, and undeveloped muscles concern boys. Undeveloped breasts and hips and hair on the face and limbs and in the armpits disturb girls.

Skin Disturbances
Acne and pimples are unattractive to boys and are incorrectly but traditionally attributed to masturbation or one of the "social diseases." Skin disturbances mar attractiveness and are often believed to be a sign that a girl is menstruating.

Axillary Perspiration
Boys worry about perspiration odor and stain and fear perspiration will be interpreted as a sign of embarrassment. Girls dislike perspiration odor and stain on their clothing and fear that perspiration will be interpreted as a sign that they are menstruating.

Physical Defects
Physical defects often prevent boys from engaging in sports and other masculine activities. Girls feel that physical defects mar their attractiveness.

---

defenses are inadequate to deal with the strain to which he is exposed" (77).

Gradually, however, the young adolescent, now a sexually mature person, adjusts to these physical and psychological upheavals. He becomes more energetic and shows a desire for strenuous activity and competitive sports; he shows an interest in social activities, in members of the opposite sex, and in clothes and appearance; he shows better emotional control, less restlessness, less boredom, a less critical attitude toward family and friends, and a stronger motivation to do things. In each successive month of the postpubescent period, there are evidences of improved behavior and shifts from negative to positive social attitudes.

During the transition from prepubescent negative phase behavior to the more mature behavior of late adolescence, certain patterns are common, though not necessarily universal. Those which have the greatest effect on the pubescent's self-concept and personal and social adjustment fall into four major divisions: changes in accustomed behavior patterns, changes in interests, behavior affecting social adjustment, and behavior affecting personal adjustment.

Changes in accustomed behavior patterns

With the rapid and uneven growth characteristic of the prepubescent period, boys and girls who formerly had good control over their bodies and whose skills closely approximated those of adults become clumsy, awkward, and uncoordinated. How *awkward* the pubescent is will depend largely upon how rapid the growth spurt has been and how much his patterns of behavior have been dislocated (145, 149).

Boys in particular go through a period of conspicuous awkwardness, primarily because their growth spurt is more rapid than that of girls. Furthermore, boys tend to be emotionally disturbed by their awkwardness and are more likely than girls to withdraw from situations where their awkwardness will make them conspicuous. Girls, by contrast, try to overcome their awkwardness. They take dancing lessons, for example, not so much for the fun of it, but to learn to move their bodies more gracefully (57, 68).

Tension in the arteries, resulting from disproportions between the size of the heart and of the arteries, causes the pubescent to be *restless* and *incessantly active,* with a desire to consume his newly released energy. But because he is frequently embarrassed by his awkwardness, he restrains this desire. As a result, he twitches and squirms like a preschooler, finding it difficult to stand or sit in one position for any length of time.

Some of the restlessness of the pubescent comes from inner tensions resulting from *heightened emotionality.* Unlike the child who is able to release pent-up emotional energy in active play, the pubescent who withdraws from sports and games lacks this form of emotional catharsis. He becomes moody and sulky, only to burst out in temper tantrums or fits of uncontrolled crying at the slightest provocation. How heightened emotionality affects the behavior of the pubescent and adolescent will be discussed in detail in Chapter 3.

The pubescent characteristically shows a *disinclination to work.* He does as little as possible at home and at school, often letting his home duties remain undone and his schoolwork go unprepared. Even though parents and teachers accuse the pubescent of willful "laziness," his laziness has a physiological basis. It is a direct result of the rapid physical growth of puberty which saps his energy and makes him so tired that he has

neither the zest nor the motivation to do more than is absolutely necessary. When he is blamed or punished for not doing what is expected of him, he builds up resentments which further reduce his motivation (57, 123).

In no area are changes in behavior patterns more marked than in *eating.* Normally, the active schoolchild has a healthy appetite, and if he is well adjusted, he eats what is placed before him, though like people of all ages he has his favorite foods. By contrast, the pubescent not only has a finicky appetite but also turns away from his old favorites and develops new ones.

The finicky appetite of the pubescent is shown in rapid shifts from overeating to undereating, varying with his emotional ups and downs. In spite of rapid growth, which requires increased food intake, the pubescent picks at his food when he is emotionally disturbed and eats ravenously when the emotional disturbances are cleared up. The change from old favorites to new ones comes partly from the pubescent's revolt against foods associated with the dependency of childhood in favor of foods regarded as grown-up. The shift in food preferences also comes from physiological changes. These may be glandular, but more often they are related to the sense organs for smell. As taste is largely dependent on smell, the growth of the hairy network in the pubescent's nostrils—part of the secondary sex characteristic of body hair—makes food which in childhood seemed tasty now seem so bland as to be unappetizing. The pubescent therefore prefers food that is more "tasty" (61, 66, 127, 148). A study of food cravings has revealed that whenever a person is depressed he has a desire to eat compulsively, especially sweets. Among girls, the tension and depression of the premenstrual and menstrual periods are commonly accompanied by a craving for sweets (147).

Changes in interests

The child shows a keen interest in play and social activities with the peer group as well as in reading and television watching, but the pubescent often loses interest in these activities. He becomes "bored," withdraws from social contact with his peers, and spends much of his time in solitude, lolling around or daydreaming. This change is due in part to the general state of fatigue that accompanies rapid growth and glandular changes.

One very common interest at puberty is expressed in a *preoccupation with sex*. While children have an interest in different aspects of sexuality, this interest is far less intense and less constant than at puberty. As his body changes, the pubescent's attention becomes focused on sex and his new sexual sensations. Knowing that his parents and contemporaries are aware of his changing body serves to heighten his interest. One of the first ways in which the pubescent manifests this interest ordinarily is in exploring the body and engaging in masturbation (14).

Even before the body transformation is completed, interest in sex is turned outward and revealed in the increased attention the adolescent gives to members of the opposite sex, in impressing them with his newly changed body and sex-appropriate appearance, and in showing them that he is no longer a child but a near adult. Girls often try to attract the attention of boys with coyness and affected mannerisms and by calling attention to their feminine physical characteristics, especially their breasts. Boys put more emphasis on displaying their strength. The reserve that accompanied the early changes in the body gives way to sexual showing off as puberty draws to a close. Much of the conversation and most of the daydreams of the young adolescent likewise center on sex.

Behavior affecting social adjustment

At puberty, the child who behaved in a cocky show-off manner often develops a *shyness* that is reminiscent of babyhood. When he is shooting up in height, the pubescent may, for a year or two, be very self-conscious about his size. This makes him shy in the presence of others and gives rise to a desire to withdraw from all social situations or to make himself inconspicuous when he must be with others. Figure 2-4 shows the characteristic pattern of shyness for boys and girls from 7 to 14 years of age.

Once adolescents become accustomed to their larger bodies, they show a marked decrease in shyness and an increase in self-importance. No longer must they look up when they speak to adults. Now they can meet them on an equal footing physically; for that reason, they soon come to expect the rights and privileges that adults enjoy.

Unlike the child who craves the companionship of others and is unhappy when he is away from members of the peer group, the pubescent often shows a *desire for isolation*. This is due, in part, to the fatigue from rapid growth that makes him want to shun strenuous play and, in part, to the shyness and self-consciousness that his changed body has fostered. Not only does the pubescent withdraw from peer companionship but he also withdraws from family activities, shutting himself up in his room where he will not be disturbed.

The child spends considerable time and effort learning to get along with people so that he will be accepted by them, but the pubescent usually develops an *antagonistic attitude toward others*—family members, teachers, and peers. He tends to be critical and derogatory of everything they say or do. Many of his childhood friendships are strained to the breaking point (146).

The special targets for the pubescent's

Figure 2-4 Characteristic patterns of shyness in boys and girls. (Adapted from J. Macfarlane, L. Allen, and M. P. Honzik: *A developmental study of the behavior problems of normal children between twenty-one months and fourteen years.* Berkeley, Calif.: University of California Press, 1954. Used by permission.)

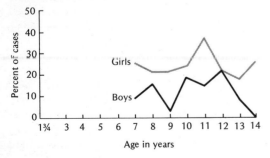

antagonism are members of the opposite sex. While *sex antagonism* is pronounced during the gang age of late childhood, it usually reaches a peak of intensity during puberty. Boys resent the larger size and greater sophistication of girls their own age, and girls resent the fact that boys are not subjected to the periodic discomforts of menstruation that they experience. Instead of withdrawing from members of the opposite sex, as happens in childhood, pubescents express their hostility in criticism, derogatory comments, and belittling remarks about the achievements of members of the opposite sex.

So long as children are smaller than adults, they may resent adult authority but they usually do not resist it except by breaking rules on the sly or pretending that they forgot a rule. With the changes in body size and build, however, the pubescent feels that he is now on a par with adults and this makes him bolder in his resistance to adult authority. Except when discipline is strictly authoritarian, the pubescent tends to argue with parents and teachers about rules and often openly defies them.

Many of the *misdemeanors* of puberty are a direct outgrowth of the pubescent's resentful attitude toward rules and those in authority. While children break rules more because they forget them or do not understand them, pubescents often do so to declare their independence. This is especially true of girls, who in childhood conform more submissively than boys. In the premenstrual and menstrual periods, girls have been reported to be especially "naughty" (26, 74, 169).

Behavior affecting personal adjustment

The fourth common behavioral effect of body changes in puberty relates to behavior influencing personal adjustment. Unfortunately, this behavior often leads to poor personal adjustment. The pubescent is concerned about body changes that do not conform to those of his age-mates or to his concept of what he wanted to look like when he was grown-up; he is apt to be *excessively modest,* trying to keep his body covered so that others will not see the changes that disturb him. This is

markedly different from the child, who not only lacks modesty but often delights in displaying his body and comparing different features, especially the sex organs, with those of peers.

Children who are most confident and boastful of their achievements are likely to be hardest hit by *lack of self-confidence* during puberty. Awkwardness, for example, and social rejection following antisocial behavior play havoc with self-confidence and lead to feelings of inadequacy and inferiority (3).

Since lack of self-confidence is ego-deflating, many pubescents retreat from the real world into the world of daydreams. *Daydreaming* may serve to bolster self-confidence if the daydreams center on themselves as "conquering heroes." But many daydreams of the puberty period are of the "suffering hero" or martyr variety in which the pubescent sees himself as misunderstood, misjudged, and mistreated. These may further intensify his lack of self-confidence and increase his feelings of worthlessness (78).

While children may, in a temper outburst, *threaten to commit suicide* if they are frustrated in what they want to do, they rarely attempt to carry out the threat. This is not true of pubescents. They have a prevailing belief that they are "worthless," and only a slight frustration may convince them that they are such total failures that the only way out is to take their own lives. Few suicide attempts at puberty are fatal, but they are danger signals of poor personal adjustment. This matter will be discussed in detail in Chapter 15 in connection with personality development in adolescence. While boys and men at most ages threaten or carry out suicide more than girls and women, there is evidence that, during the premenstrual and menstrual periods, girls are often so depressed physically that their poor self-concepts make them highly vulnerable to attempted suicide (159).

Long-term effects of behavior changes at puberty

Sooner or later, most adolescents adjust to the physical changes that take place during puberty. As a result, they show less of the unsocial behavior that leads to poor social and personal adjustments. The adolescent adjusts partly because he becomes better satisfied with his body than he was earlier, partly because he learns how to bring out his good features and camouflage the bad ones, and partly because he feels better physically as the rapid growth that sapped his strength slows down (142).

When the body transformation is completed, the adolescent then reverts to the adjustive patterns of behavior acquired in childhood. If he enjoyed contacts with peers and needed social acceptance to be happy, he usually has a strong motivation to replace the unsocial behavior of puberty with behavior that conforms to socially approved standards. As a result, the puberty changes have only a temporary effect on his behavior.

Adolescents who made poor personal and social adjustments during childhood are likely to be more seriously damaged psychologically by puberty. Consequently, though puberty per se is not responsible for the psychological damage, it tends to exaggerate and prolong it. Excessive eating, for example, is usually only temporary in pubescents who, as children, were well adjusted. Children whose poor adjustment encouraged them to overeat as compensation for lack of peer acceptance, however, are likely to continue to overeat and remain fat in adolescence (17, 95). Well-adjusted adolescents learn to curb their appetites and avoid obesity, which they know is a handicap to social acceptance.

EFFECTS OF DEVIANT SEXUAL MATURING

Nothing gives a young adolescent a greater feeling of security and self-confidence than being so much like the members of the peer group that nothing about him attracts personal attention. On the other hand, nothing is so disturbing as being different especially when the difference is ever present and readily apparent, as in physical appearance. The child who looks like a young adult while his classmates still look like children, for example, is so embarrassed that he would rather receive failing grades than get up to recite in class so that his near-adult body will be in full view. As Eisenberg puts it (46):

The sensitivity of the adolescent to the good opinion of his peers and the dependence of his sense of identity upon the attainment of competence in an adult role renders him psychologically vulnerable to variations in physiological development, such as precocious or delayed growth, facial acne, obesity, enlarged mammary glands in the male, or inadequate or overabundent breast development in the female. These deviations from the expected pattern of maturation . . . may lead to major psychological trauma if not offset by sensitive guidance.

Children and adolescents invariably regard being different as being inferior; so long as they are like their age-mates, they regard themselves as normal. A slight temporary difference causes no real concern; a conspicuous difference leads the adolescent to wonder what is the matter. While problems often arise from being out of step with one's age-mates, lagging behind them is often interpreted as being less bright and, hence, inferior. This anxiety is often exaggerated by parental concern.

The transformation of the body at puberty affects *all* boys and girls to some extent, but the deviant maturers are affected most—whether deviant in the length of time needed for sexual maturing (slow and rapid maturers) or deviant in the age of maturing (early and late maturers).

Effects of deviations in rate of sexual maturing

Some children seem to turn into adults overnight while others proceed at a snail's pace. If deviations in the rate of maturing are slight, either a year more or less than peers of the same sex, the effects are not great. If the rate varies by more than a year in either direction, however, the effects are likely to be damaging or even traumatic.

In addition to wondering if they are normal, slow and rapid maturers are confronted with complex adjustment problems. Studies of normal, early, and late maturers *suggest* certain effects that deviant rates of maturing may have but more specific information awaits further research.

The more rapid the transformation, the more upsetting it is to the child both physically and psychologically. Not only is the rapid maturer bigger and better developed than his agemates, but he is out of step with them in his interests. He has the interests of a young adolescent while they continue to be interested in childish things.

Similarly, the awkwardness which normally accompanies the body transformation is often so accentuated in the rapid maturer that frequently he withdraws from social contacts to avoid embarrassment. The grumpiness, social withdrawal, and other patterns of antisocial behavior characteristic of the negative phase of puberty are more pronounced in the rapid maturer (46, 73, 149).

The slow maturer is spared most of these problems because he has more time to adjust to body changes. He may, however, become overconcerned about his slow development and wonder whether something is wrong with him and whether he will ever turn into an adult (43, 168).

Effects of deviations in time of sexual maturing

The psychological significance of deviant sexual maturing differs for early and late maturers. Early maturers have a shorter childhood and, therefore, less time to enjoy the relative freedom that comes with childhood. On the other hand, they have a longer adolescence, which means more time to make the social and emotional adjustments needed for successful adulthood. Deviant development is difficult, however, for both early and late maturers. Adults tend to treat children in accordance with their physical age rather than their chronological age. They expect too much of early maturers, and too little of late maturers.

While early and late maturing affect individuals differently, they also affect members of the two sexes in a slightly different way. On the whole, early maturing is more advantageous to boys, and late maturing to girls. Under no circumstances, however, can one say that there is a greater advantage to being a deviant maturer than to being an average

---

BOX 2-8 COMMON EFFECTS OF DEVIANT TIMING OF SEXUAL MATURING

Early Maturing

Boys
*Favorable reputation based on superior athletic skills
*Often chosen for leadership roles
*Popular with girls because of social interests, skills, and sophistication
*Self-confidence and favorable self-concept because of favorable social treatment

Girls
*Unfavorable reputation of being "stupid" or "fast" based on large size and precocious social interests.
*Envied by other girls for grown-up looks and clothes
*Often aggressive with boys because of earlier interest in dating
*Social expectations may be too high because of mature appearance

Late Maturing

Boys
*Rarely chosen for leadership roles
*Embarrassed, self-conscious, and shy because of small undeveloped body
*Rejected by girls in social activities because of lack of sophistication
*Self-rejectant because of unfavorable social attitudes

Girls
*Popular with peers and often selected as leader
*Resentful of being treated as a child
*Reputation of being "nice" based on lack of social and sexual aggressiveness
*In step with boys of own age and hence not subjected to excessive criticism and ridicule
*Often plagued by doubts about normalcy.

maturer; it is a matter of which causes less psychological damage. In Box 2-8 are given the common effects of early and late sexual maturing on boys and girls (22, 43, 73, 106, 114, 168).

Long-term effects

Little scientific attention has been devoted to the effects of deviation in rates of sexual maturing, and so it is impossible to say whether the effects of rapid and slow maturing will be temporary or long lasting. From scientific knowledge of the effects of reinforcement on learning, however, it is possible to *speculate* that *rapid maturers* can be psychologically damaged by awkwardness, by self-consciousness and concern about normalcy, and by social attitudes that they are "stupid" because they act young but are so much larger and better developed than their classmates. If social attitudes become favorable, as they do when a rapid-maturing boy develops into a superior athlete or a rapid-maturing girl into an attractive, socially sophisticated teenager, the psychological scars will quickly fade. Similarly, if the young adolescent learns to control his awkwardness, the self-consciousness he felt will be replaced with pride in achievement.

In *slow maturers,* the psychological damage is more likely to be persistent because they have a longer-than-usual time to develop and reinforce maladjustive behavior patterns. The habit of being critical and derogatory, for example, can readily become entrenched unless the adolescent makes special effort to develop more socially desirable patterns of speech. Daydreaming, likewise, can become so habitual that the adolescent will derive more enjoyment from his daydream world than from the real world and, hence, make little effort to confront his very real problems.

Several genetic studies of early and late maturers have been made. These studies cover the lives of enough boys and girls, from childhood into the early forties, to indicate how persistent the effects of the deviations are (4, 73). There is little or no evidence of the waning of either the psychological damage or the psychological well-being caused by early and late sexual maturing. The concept of self is highly influenced by the way significant people—mainly parents, siblings, and members of the peer group—treat the adolescent. And how they treat him will depend on his physiological age—how old he looks—rather than his chronological age. Whether the adolescent develops a healthy or an unhealthy self-concept, it is likely to persist and to affect the quality of his behavior long after the circumstances that led to the self-concept have disappeared.

Studies of the long-term effects of early or late maturing on a group of men up to the age of about 35 found that those who had been *early maturers* were socially more active and more often held leadership roles in their communities than did the late maturers. As Ames stressed, "Early maturers tend to either become or remain socially active in adulthood, whereas late maturers tend to either remain or become less socially active as a group" (4).

Men who were early maturers are reported to be more dominant, to make better impressions on others, to be more self-controlled and more willing and able to carry social responsibilities than are those who were late maturers. As a result, they are more successful vocationally than the late maturers. The pattern of behavior of men who were *late maturers* is based on unfavorable self-concepts developed during adolescence. Compared with early maturers, they tend to be rebellious, touchy, impulsive, self-indulgent, and lacking in self-insight—characteristics of immaturity which are reflected in poor personal, social, and vocational adjustment (4, 71).

To date, there have been few reports of the long-term effects of deviant sexual maturing among girls (142). Consequently, speculation about its effects are based on information about the long-term effect on boys and the short-term effect on girls. If an early maturing girl develops feelings of embarrassment and shame because she suspects others regard her as older and more stupid than her average-maturing classmates, it is doubtful that her feelings of personal inadequacy will disappear when her contemporaries finally catch up to her. In fact, such feelings do not disappear during the high school years and there is little evidence that they disappear later (72, 114).

Furthermore, reputations, once established, tend to persist. Should the early-maturing girl acquire the reputation of being "fast" or "not nice" because her behavior is different from that of her age-mates—even though it is in accordance with her physiological development—it will not be easy for her to live down this reputation.

Markedly delayed sexual maturing cannot fail to leave psychological scars which are difficult if not impossible to erase. After a period of being different and of being treated as inferior, boys develop an unfavorable self-concept which is so firmly reinforced that it affects all their adult personal, social, and vocational adjustments. It is quite unlikely that girls would be any less seriously damaged.

Deviant maturing *need not* do temporary or permanent damage to the individual. What impact the age of maturing will have depends partly on childhood foundations and partly on the treatment the individual receives from the significant people in his life during puberty and throughout the adolescent years.

It should also be stressed that deviant age of sexual maturity per se is not responsible for the temporary or permanent psychological scars or advantages early or late maturers may experience. The early-maturing boy, for example, is not made more outgoing, self-confident, poised, and mature in his behavior just because he matured several years before his age-mates or even because this gave him a headstart in acquiring mature social skills. This development was due, in part, to social expectations of more mature behavior and to better opportunities to learn to behave in a more mature way. As Jones and Bayley have said, there is "clear evidence of the effect of physical maturing on behavior. Perhaps of greater importance, however, is the repeated demonstration of the multiplicity of factors, psychological and cultural as well as physical, which contribute to the formation of basic personality patterns" (74). This point of view was also expressed by Jones and Mussen: "Each individual's personality structure is determined by a complex of interacting variables, including rate of maturation" (75).

HIGHLIGHTS OF CHAPTER 2

1. The puberty phase is divided into three stages: (1) the prepubescent stage when bodily changes and secondary sex characteristics are beginning to develop but the reproductive function is not yet developed, (2) the pubescent stage when sex cells are produced in the sex organs but the bodily changes are not yet complete, and (3) the postpubescent stage when the sex organs function in a mature way and the body has attained its mature size and shape.

2. Puberty changes require approximately 4 years to be completed.

3. Variations in the age of puberty are influenced by such factors as heredity, health, intelligence, nutrition, home environment and family socioeconomic status, body size, and body build.

4. Puberty changes are brought about by increased supplies of the growth and gonadotropic hormones from the anterior lobe of the pituitary gland. The growth hormone is responsible for the puberty growth spurt and the gonadotropic for the maturing of the sex organs and the development of the secondary sex characteristics.

5. The physical transformation occurring at puberty includes four categories of change: (1) growth in body size, (2) changes in body proportions, both exterior and interior, (3) the development of the primary sex characteristics, or the sex organs, and (4) the development of the secondary sex characteristics, or the physical features which distinguish the male from the female body.

6. The physical transformation of puberty has psychological as well as physical repercussions, with the psychological coming mainly from social expectations for mature attitudes and behavior when the adolescent's body has achieved adult size and shape.

7. The conditions influencing the effects of puberty changes include rapidity of the changes, degree of preparation for the changes, how closely

the changes conform to a childhood ideal, and the degree of social security the pubescent experiences.

8.   Common concerns about the changing body include sex differences in age of maturing, sex appropriateness of body build and secondary sex characteristics, skin disturbances, axillary perspiration, and physical defects.

9.   The physical changes of puberty affect the pubescent's behavior in a number of ways, the most common of which are changes in accustomed behavior patterns and changes in interests and behavior which affect personal and social adjustments.

10.   While most adolescents adjust successfully to the physical changes of puberty, those who have made poor personal and social adjustments in childhood are likely to be psychologically damaged by them to some degree.

11.   Deviant sexual maturing may be in the rate of maturing (rapid or slow) or in the time when maturing begins and is completed (early or late).

12.   As is true of anything that makes the adolescent different from his peers, deviant sexual maturing may have either temporary or permanent effects. Those effects which evince unfavorable attitudes toward the pubescent and unfavorable treatment of him are most likely to be permanent.

Chapter 3

Transition in Emotionality

One of the most common dreads of adolescence is its alleged stormy nature. Adults dread adolescence because the storminess of the adolescent makes him hard to live and work with. Adolescents dread it because storminess is embarrassing to them. Just when they are trying to convince themselves and others that they are growing up, they find themselves giving way to emotional outbursts and behaving like temperamental children.

Dread of adolescence has been intensified by the traditional belief that it is characterized by *Sturm und Drang,* a label which received the scientific stamp of approval from G. Stanley Hall when he called adolescence a "period of storm and stress" (51). The word "storm" suggests that anger, with its accompanying temper outbursts, is a prominent, if not the dominant, emotion at this age. "Stress" suggests the existence of factors, emotional and physical, which disrupt normal functioning. It implies a generally upset condition which leads to deterioration of both physical and psychological functioning.

The traditional explanation of the storm and stress of adolescence was that it was due to the physical changes that accompany the transformation of the body at this time. Before there was knowledge of the functioning of the endocrine glands, the explanation was given in terms of the predominance of one of the body humors. Intense and irrational fears, or "phobias," for example, were attributed to a predominance of black bile (12, 39).

Later, as medical research discovered the role of the endocrine glands in emotionality, they were blamed for adolescent storm and stress. Furthermore, as it was found that glandular changes are responsible for the body transformation at puberty, it was accepted that the body changes and the storm and stress were inevitably linked, because both were caused by the glands. This led to a resigned dread of adolescence—a belief that there was nothing anyone could do to prevent the adolescent's emotional upsets.

Acceptance of these beliefs reinforced an equally common traditional belief that the unpleasant emotionality resulting from the body transformation would necessarily make the adolescent an unhappy person. That adolescence could be a happy period was thus almost inconceivable.

Since the days of G. Stanley Hall, at the turn of the present century, scientific interest in adolescent emotionality has given rise to a great deal of research on the subject. As a result, "storm and stress," as used by Hall, has been replaced by the term "heightened emotionality" (108). Scientific studies have also challenged the traditional beliefs about adolescent emotionality by providing information on the causes and forms of expression of those emotions which seem to become heightened in the typical adolescent.

MEANING
OF HEIGHTENED EMOTIONALITY

"Heightened emotionality" is a relative term. It means more-than-normal emotionality for a *given person.* The criterion of heightened emotionality must therefore include a comparison of how the person reacts at a particular time with how he normally or usually reacts. When a normally serene or restrained person experiences heightened emotionality, he may appear, in comparison with others, to be quite calm. In comparison with his usual behavior, however, he is emotionally upset (21).

To the psychologist, heightened emotionality extending over a period of time is what fever is to a doctor—a danger signal. And, like fever, its effects may be far-reaching. For example, the adolescent who is experiencing an unhappy ending to a romance is nervous and tense not only in situations related to the romance but in his home, school, and social relationships. His schoolwork suffers, he quarrels with his friends and family, and in a general way he makes himself thoroughly obnoxious to everyone.

Most investigators of adolescent emotions agree that adolescence is a period of heightened emotionality. Josselyn writes, "The normal adolescent is inevitably a mixed-up person, but not at all in the sense of being a psychologically sick person" (71). *Any emo-*

Escape mechanisms

Moodiness

Nervous habits

HEIGHTENED
EMOTIONALITY

Emotional outbursts

Finicky appetites

Quarrelsomeness

Figure 3-1 Common expressions of heightened emotionality in adolescence.

tion can be heightened in the sense that the person experiences it, whether it be a form of anger, jealousy, fear, or happiness, in a stronger and more persistent manner than is usual for him. An adolescent may experience deep depression in a moment of self-criticism or experience great self-admiration when he excels in some task that is important to him and the peer group (38).

Heightened emotionality is never hidden. Though it may not always be readily recognized, it is expressed in some kind of behavior. As Hornick has said of anxiety, "One of the commonest paths of anxiety in adolescence is acting out, acting up, or just plain action" (62). Figure 3-1 illustrates some of the ways in which heightened emotionality is expressed in adolescence.

EVIDENCE CONTRADICTING TRADITIONAL BELIEFS ABOUT HEIGHTENED EMOTIONALITY

Scientific studies of heightened emotionality during adolescence have provided evidence that contradicts most of the traditional beliefs referred to above. This evidence is important because it shows that there is far less need to dread the adolescent years as a time of storm and stress than was once believed. It also shows that the adolescent does not have to go through a period that is embarrassing to him and annoying to his parents and teachers. This becomes apparent when one examines the evidence regarding the conditions responsible for heightened emotionality, the traditional beliefs about the universality and persistence of heightened emotionality during the adolescent years, and the relationship between heightened emotionality and unhappiness.

Evidence regarding causes of heightened emotionality

While there is ample evidence that the glandular changes which are responsible for the physical changes at puberty do upset body homeostasis temporarily, other physical conditions unrelated to glandular changes are also responsible for heightened emotionality (57). And, for the most part, these are controllable.

It has been found, for example, that emotional tension, in the form of anxiety or frustration, causes nutritional disturbances and these, in turn, intensify and prolong emotional tension. Improper nutrition predisposes the individual to emotional tension. Unquestionably, poor nutrition is, as Peckos has said, "at the basis of some of the stresses and strains of adolescence" (115).

Anemia from iron deficiency causes apathy, accompanied by increased anxiety and irritability. A deficiency in calcium, common during periods of rapid growth, leads to irritability and emotional instability. Prolonged malnutrition, from insufficient diet or from poor choice of foods, invariably leads to emotional disturbances. Fatigue predisposes the individual to moodiness and gloominess, often accompanied by irritability and the tendency to fly off the handle in an emotional outburst (58, 114, 139).

On the other hand, studies show that heightened emotionality is most often environmental and social in origin. It results from the necessity of breaking off old habits of thought and action and establishing new ones. While the adjustment is taking place, the adolescent is emotionally upset. After the adjustment has been made, he settles down, and excessive emotionality usually disappears.

During the period of adjustment, the adolescent may have strong feelings of insecurity and uncertainty, which predispose him to heightened emotionality. Since these feelings are mainly a product of environmental and social factors, one can safely conclude that heightened emotionality during adolescence is more often attributable to social factors than to glandular changes, as was formerly believed. Box 3-1 describes the most common conditions that predispose the adolescent to heightened emotionality (21, 27, 37, 42, 127).

Evidence regarding the universality and persistence of heightened emotionality

Contrary to traditional belief, there is evidence that heightened emotionality is not characteristic of the entire period of adolescence, but only of the last year or two of childhood and the first year or two of adolescence when developmental change is greatest. The more sudden and pronounced the physical changes, the greater the disturbance to body homeostasis and the greater the likelihood of heightened emotionality (37, 108, 114).

As development slows down, heightened emotionality becomes less of an everyday occurrence. Heightened emotionality generally reaches its peak between the ages of 11 and 12 years. Thirteen- to fourteen-year olds, Gesell et al. have reported, are often irritable. They get excited easily and are more likely to explode than to control their feelings. A year later, the young adolescent tries to cover up his feelings; this leads to moodiness. By the time the adolescent is 16, he "doesn't believe in worrying," with the result that he takes a calmer approach to his problems (44).

Heightened emotionality may again become common in late adolescence, depending largely on environmental circumstances in the adolescent's life. If he spends the closing years of adolescence in an educational institution, for example, he will be facing the unknown world of work and other problems he has never before encountered. Doubts about his adequacy to get and hold a job may readily lead to heightened emotionality.

BOX 3-1 PREDISPOSING CAUSES
OF HEIGHTENED EMOTIONALITY

Adjustment to New Environments
As the adolescent leaves the world of childhood, radical changes may take place in his pattern of life. Since he is often unprepared for his new roles, he experiences strong and unusual feelings of inadequacy.

Social Expectations of More Mature Behavior
When the adolescent begins to look like an adult, he is expected to act accordingly. Constant pressure to live up to social expectations often causes a generalized state of anxiety.

Unrealistic Aspirations
Childhood aspirations are often unrealistic, and when the adolescent fails to attain them, he develops feelings of inadequacy. If he projects the blame for his failure on others, he adds feelings of martyrdom to his feelings of inadequacy.

Social Adjustments to the Other Sex
Learning what to talk about, how to behave correctly in social situations, and how to be popular with members of the other sex is perplexing to an adolescent. While learning, he often experiences intense nervous tension and general emotional excitement.

School Problems
When the adolescent begins to recognize the importance of education to vocational success, emotional tension often replaces the "why worry" attitude of childhood.

Vocational Problems
What to do after leaving school, worry over the prospects of getting and holding a job, and dread of the demanding life of the work world build up tension and worry.

Obstacles to Doing What He Wants to Do
Financial limitations or family restrictions which prevent the adolescent from doing what his friends do often lead to emotional upsets.

Unfavorable Family Relationships
Too strict parental discipline, too little independence for the adolescent's level of development, and lack of parental understanding of adolescent interests lead to family friction and contribute to emotional tension.

Gesell and his associates, Ilg and Ames, have labeled periods of heightened emotionality as times of "disequilibrium"—when insecurities, tensions, and indecisions are readily recognized. They are times when the individual is "out of focus," when his behavior causes more problems for others than is normal, and when he is less happy and well adjusted than usual. However, no two individuals express their disequilibrium in exactly the same way: instead, each has his own characteristic method of expression (5, 44).

Studies of adolescents reveal that not all, by any means, experience sufficient storm and stress to disturb either themselves or the adults in their lives. While all experience emotional instability from time to time, this is characteristic of *all* people of *all* ages (22, 42, 55, 108).

Evidence regarding heightened emotionality and unhappiness

As noted earlier, any emotion may be experienced in a heightened and intense form in adolescence, and undoubtedly most young people have moments of great happiness when they are satisfied and content with themselves. Adults as well as adolescents, however, expect adolescence to be a time of emotional disturbance and upheaval. There is little evidence that this expectation is realistic (108). Hornick has remarked that emotionally disturbed adolescents are just more visible than those who make the transition into adulthood with greater composure (62). Since it is traditionally believed that the heightened emotionality of adolescence is expressed primarily in rebelliousness and antisocial behavior, it is taken for granted that every adolescent will inevitably be unhappy.

Those adolescents who deviate markedly from the norm in the time and rate of sexual maturing are the ones most likely to experience damaging and prolonged heightened emotionality. Deviant sexual maturing brings many personal and social problems, as explained in Chapter 2. Boys often experience more pronounced heightened emotionality than girls, because they are expected to solve their problems with less guidance from parents and teachers (55). Adolescents who, as children, experienced many emotional disturbances due to unfavorable conditions in their lives, especially poor parent-child relationships, develop the habit of overreacting emotionally to things which children brought up under more favorable conditions learn to react to more calmly. Consequently, as adolescents, the former tend to experience more heightened emotionality than the latter (21).

As was pointed out in Chapter 1, adolescents in simpler cultures who have successfully completed their puberty rites, as well as in many advanced cultures, find adolescence one of the happiest periods of life. Studies of American adolescents find no evidence that adolescence is always a period of storm and stress, though many experience more unhappiness in adolescence than in childhood. But this is usually only transitory.

In summary, most of the causes of heightened emotionality are social and environmental. There is no evidence that heightened emotionality is constant or that unhappiness is either universal or persistent (25, 38, 104, 152).

COMMON EMOTIONAL PATTERNS IN ADOLESCENCE

In adolescence, there are marked changes in the stimuli that give rise to emotions, just as there are changes in the form of emotional response. However, there is a similarity between childhood and adolescent emotions in that at both ages the dominant emotions tend to be unpleasant—mainly fear and anger in their various forms, grief, jealousy, and envy. The pleasant emotions—joy, affection, happiness, or curiosity—occur less frequently and with less intensity, especially during the *early* years of adolescence.

Social factors are largely responsible for the dominance of the unpleasant emotions, for the form of expression each emotion takes, and for the kind of stimulus that gives rise to the emotion. Similarly, social factors are important in determining what the adolescent will respond to emotionally. If it is the "thing to do" to laugh at jokes about members of other ethnic groups, the adolescent will respond to such jokes with laughter. Furthermore, as different social classes have different values and expectations, social-class differences in emotional responses are greater in adolescence than in childhood when the individual was less aware of and less influenced by social pressures.

Only a limited amount of research has been done on emotional stimuli and responses in adolescence. Furthermore, the techniques used in the study of childhood emotions are superior to those used in the study of adolescent emotions. In spite of these constraints, an attempt will be made to give a reasonably complete picture of the emotions commonly found among American adolescents.

Fear

By the time the child reaches adolescence, he has learned that many of the things he used to fear are neither dangerous nor harmful. This does not mean that fear vanishes, but that children's fears are replaced by more mature ones. The adolescent, for example, is far more likely to be afraid of social situations than of animals. Furthermore, the adolescent is more likely to "borrow trouble," to imagine things that might happen to frighten him, than

the child. The fears of adolescents may be divided into four types. In Box 3-2 these typical fears and examples of each are spelled out (43, 63,105, 124, 127, 151).

Adolescent fear is different from childhood fear for two reasons. The first is a *change in values*. The more important a thing is to a person, the more likely he is to be afraid if he feels that he is going to lose it or be unable to attain it. Speaking or acting in front of a group of teachers, parents, and peers is far less frightening to a child than to an adolescent because the adolescent is more anxious to create a good impression. As a result, audience sensitivity or stage fright is more common among adolescents.

The second reason for the age difference in fears is that the adolescent has many *more new experiences* to cope with than the child. Anything new and difficult is likely to give rise to fear, but the child is usually protected, while the adolescent is constantly confronted with the new and different as his social horizons broaden.

Fears differ from one adolescent to another because fears are closely related to what is

---

BOX 3-2   TYPICAL FEARS OF ADOLESCENTS

Natural Phenomena and Material Objects
In this category are such fear-inducing stimuli as bugs, snakes, dogs, storms, high places, fire, and airplanes.

Social Relationships
Fears of people and social situtations are expressed in two ways: shyness and embarrassment. Both come from feelings of social inadequacy. *Shyness* makes the adolescent ill at ease in the presence of a person on whom he wants to make a good impression. *Embarrassment* arises when the adolescent does something that he fears will lead to unfavorable social judgments.

The Self
In this category are fears of serious illness, of incapacitation, of personal inadequacy in social or vocational situations, and of failure in school.

The unknown
Adolescents fear having to stay in the house alone, being in a strange place with strange people, undergoing surgical operations, and being unable to cope in many other situations.

important to the particular individual. There are, however, certain predictable variations. Girls' fears, on the whole, are different from those of boys of the same age. These *sex* differences are determined largely by sex differences in values. Girls put higher value on personal safety than boys, for example, and so they have more fears of animals and strangers than boys. Girls also talk more about their fears than boys (43).

Social-class differences in fears are likewise common. Adolescents of the lower social classes tend to show more fear of parental threat, while those of the middle classes are more afraid of strangers and of social attitudes (6).

Fear *responses* in adolescence follow a fairly stereotyped pattern. The pattern has two elements: rigidity of the body and avoidance of the fear situation. When the adolescent is frightened, his body becomes rigid; he trembles and perspires. If the fear is relatively mild, as in embarrassment, he blushes. If it is more intense, his face turns pale.

The adolescent learns to avoid situations by "running" *before* such situations arise. He thus avoids the embarrassment or humiliation of having others see that he is frightened. If he is afraid of a social situation, for example, he will plan some other activity for that time and will then rationalize the avoidance to himself and to others by stressing the pressure of more important duties and responsibilities.

Worry

As the number and intensity of fears decrease, worry is substituted for fear. Worry is a variety of fear that comes mainly from imaginary causes. In all worry, there is an element of reality, but it is exaggerated out of all proportion. Thus, worry may be considered an emotional reaction to "borrowed trouble"; the trouble may come but it has not up to the present.

Like fear, worry is *specific* in that it is related to a person, thing, or situation. An adolescent worries about an examination, about his adequacy to make a speech before a group, or about whether he will get a job. Because it is the "thing to do" to worry during adolescence, social pressures tend to increase the frequency and intensity of worry. Many adolescents worry because their friends worry more than they do. Worries parallel fears in the sense that they are closely related to what is important to the individual. If it is important to the adolescent to create a good impression when he speaks before a group or participates in an athletic contest, for example, he will worry about whether he will do so, even before he begins the activity.

Since worries are influenced by values, and values change with *age*, the worries of young adolescents are different from those of older adolescents. As adolescents grow older, their outlook on life is more like that of an adult. Thus, the severity as well as the source of worries is more closely related to reality as the adolescents mature. Changes in worries as boys and girls progress through adolescence are illustrated in Figure 3-2. If the adolescent remains in school or college throughout the adolescent years, many of the worries confronting him will be the same as those which concerned him when he was younger. If he goes to work, his worries will be more likely to center on getting and holding a job.

Since boys and girls have different interests and values, there are *sex* differences in worries. Boys worry more about their abilities and vocations. They also worry more about where and how to get the money they need for their social lives. As appearance and social acceptance are more important to girls, their worries focus on these problems. Girls also verbalize their worries more than boys (43, 44, 68).

While there is relatively little difference in the amount of worrying adolescents of different *socioeconomic groups* do, what they worry about usually is different. One of the most pronounced socioeconomic differences in worries relates to school. Being admitted by a college of their choice, preparing for their future vocations, and meeting the "right" people in school and college are more highly

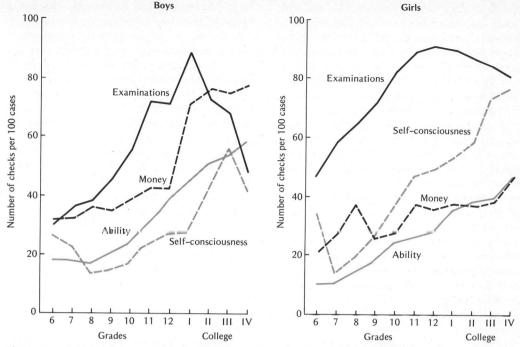

Figure 3-2 Age trends in some worries during adolescence. The trends after grade 12 would be different for adolescents who go to work at that time. (Adapted from S. L. Pressey and R. G. Kuhlen: *Psychological development through the life span.* New York: Harper & Row, 1957. Used by permission.)

valued by boys and girls of the middle and upper groups than by those of the lower socioeconomic groups. Lower-class adolescents' school worries tend to center on their adequacy to recite in class if called on by the teacher and their relationships with a teacher whom they regard as hostile to them because of their lower-class status (6).

The adolescent who is worried about something generally talks about his worries to his friends or teachers, or he may write to a newspaper or magazine columnist. The major reason for verbalizing his worry is to gain sympathy, understanding, and help. That the adolescent shows little desire to avoid the things that worry him, as he does the things that frighten him, and that he is willing to let others know of his emotional state suggest that worry is more socially acceptable in adolescence than fear.

Another common response to worry is a harassed look—a look of preoccupation with something not present and of disregard of what is present. The adolescent who fails to respond to what is happening around him and appears to be looking off into space is sooner or later asked what is the matter. This gives him the opportunity to verbalize his worries.

Anxiety

Anxiety, like worry, is a form of fear. It is, as Jersild (68) has said, a

. . . persisting distressful psychological state arising from an inner conflict. The distress may be experienced as a feeling of vague uneasiness or foreboding, a feeling of being on edge, or as any of a variety of other feelings, such as fear, anger, restlessness, irritability, depression, or other diffuse and nameless feelings.

As in worry, the threat that gives rise to

anxiety is more often imaginary than real. The adolescent anticipates trouble more than being actually faced with it. Anxiety differs from worry and fear in one major aspect: It is a *generalized emotional state* rather than a specific one. In other words, the individual is not anxious about a specific thing; he is stirred up generally or in a state of jitters.

Anxiety often develops from repeated and varied worries. The more often the adolescent worries and the more different worries he has, the more likely it is that his worries will develop into a generalized state of anxiety. What he is anxious about, like what he worries about, is culturally determined. For example, when the cultural group places high value on appearance, on popularity, on academic achievement, or on being like others of the same age group, anxiety is likely to develop if the adolescent feels that he has not measured up to cultural expectations.

The characteristic *behavior patterns* of an anxious person are those of unhappiness, restlessness, unaccountable moodiness, mood swings, irritability, and dissatisfaction with self and others. Furthermore, as Jersild has said, there is reason to believe that the adolescent is suffering from anxiety if he seems sullen and "ornery"; if he "overreacts," by being greatly upset by little things or bitterly angry at something that seems trivial to others; if he "underreacts" by being apathetic and unmoved in situations where normally a person would experience some emotion; if he is driven by compulsions to the point where he is in a constant "fever of activity"; if he acts distinctly "out of character" by behaving contrary to his normal patterns; if he is rigid, self-righteous, and dogmatic in his attitudes; or if he imposes impossible standards on himself (68).

In general, the expressions of anxiety fall into three major categories: behavior patterns, effects on achievement, and susceptibility to group influences. Box 3-3 describes the characteristics of these categories (31, 41, 56, 62, 118, 149).

Anger

The most intense anger stimuli in adolescence are social, that is, related to people. Objects and situations are much less important anger stimuli, both in number and intensity. The most common causes of anger among junior and senior high school students are being

---

BOX 3-3 COMMON EXPRESSIONS OF ANXIETY IN ADOLESCENCE

Behavior Patterns
To cover up self-dissatisfaction, the anxious adolescent may withdraw into a daydream world, use defense mechanisms, project the blame for his self-dissatisfaction on others, use mass media as forms of escape, or engage in antisocial behavior.

Effects on Achievement
Anxiety may increase the speed of performance in an activity but not necessarily the accuracy of performance. It is especially detrimental in situations in which preparation is impossible, where reasoning is involved, or in which failure has been experienced previously.

Susceptibility to Group Influences
Any anxiety, but especially socially oriented anxiety, makes the adolescent so suggestible that he reacts as the group expects him to in the hope of improving his social acceptance.

---

teased, being unfairly treated, having a sibling take their property or impose on them, being lied to, being bossed, having sarcastic remarks made to them, or having things not go right. Among college students, social causes of anger include thwarted self-assertion, such as unjust accusations, insulting or sarcastic comments, unwelcome advice, contradictions, being teased and bossed, and not being invited to a party.

In addition to social causes, interruption of habitual activities, such as study and sleep, failure in activities undertaken, and frustrated plans give rise to anger. Thwarting of some course of action involving self-assertion invariably leads to anger (57, 68, 85). Boys are more often angered than girls by things that do not work as they want them to work and by their own ineptitude. Girls are more often angered by people and social situations. This difference is due in part at least to the fact that girls are given less freedom than boys and are more often thwarted in what they want to do by people (43, 71).

Throughout adolescence, the number and severity of anger experiences depend not so much upon the age and sex of the individual as upon the environment in which he lives and works. The more environmental thwarting there is, the greater and the more frequent will be the anger experiences (57, 71, 85).

Temper tantrums not unlike those of young children are fairly common during early adolescence. In his anger, the young adolescent will kick and throw things, stamp his feet, leave the room and slam the door, refuse to speak, and lock himself in his room until his anger subsides. Many girls, at puberty or during the early part of adolescence, burst into tears when they become angry. Most adolescents know, as Zander has pointed out, that expressions of hostile feelings are usually "kept out of sight by well-mannered people," and so they are embarrassed and ashamed after a temper outburst (157). As a result, fighting and other aggressive forms of behavior are gradually replaced by more mature patterns.

The older adolescent usually substitutes

verbal attacks for the physical attacks he used earlier. He name-calls, swears, and lashes back with bitter sarcasm. He tries to get revenge by belittling and ridiculing. Whenever possible, and in whatever way possible, he humiliates his adversary. The emotional energy that might be used for attacks on others is often spent in pacing the floor, in restlessness, or in strenuous exercise. Instead of immediately releasing emotional tension, the angry adolescent learns to hold back his overt responses until they will be most effective.

How long anger lasts in the adolescent depends on his age and on how he handles his anger. The older adolescent tends to be angry longer, not because his anger is more severe but because he has learned to suppress its expression. As a result, it smolders in the form of an angry mood. This is especially true in girls, who have learned to suppress the expression of anger to win social approval, and in both boys and girls who have been trained by strict authoritarian methods or subjected to the religious belief that one must turn the other cheek (10, 157).

Annoyances

Annoyances are irritations or unpleasant feelings, not so intense as anger, which have been built up as a result of conditioning; they come from exasperating experiences with people, things, or even one's own acts. Annoyances are more common and more important in adolescence than anger. They differ from anger in two major respects; *first,* the individual derives pleasure from talking about the things that annoy him, and *second,* annoyances are invigorating, while anger, tends to have a depressing effect (68).

Most annoyances are social in origin. Adolescents are more annoyed by people, especially by their speech, behavior, and mannerisms, than by any other single cause. They are also annoyed by things that do not work out as hoped, such as a party being canceled at the last minute or a "drop" quiz, and by their own ineptitude, as when they try to fix something that is broken only to find that it does not work after all the time and effort spent on it (24, 81).

Since social relationships provide the source of most annoyances, and since social relationships are so important for adolescents, as will be seen in Chapter 4, annoyances not only persist but become more intense with age. Poorly adjusted adolescents, particularly, are annoyance-prone. Adolescents who are popular with classmates and teachers and have reasonably good relationships with their families experience fewer annoyances than those who are unpopular or have frictional family relationships (81).

The *response* to annoying situations is very different from the response to anger-provoking situations. Instead of aggressively attacking the source of annoyance, adolescents try to block it out or avoid it. Studies of social acceptance reveal that adolescents shun a classmate who annoys them. They treat him as if he were not present and exclude him from their activities. This will be discussed in more detail in Chapter 5.

Similarly, the adolescent shuns places or things which annoy him. Instead of making aggressive attacks on situations in an attempt to improve them, he usually withdraws and selects situations more to his liking. In addition, in his own behavior, the adolescent tries to avoid the mannerisms of others that annoy him.

Frustrations

Frustrations are a response to interference with the satisfaction of some need. They may result from deprivation arising out of the environment or from the individual's inability to reach a goal because of personal inadequacy. Frustrations are accompanied by feelings of helplessness; this gives rise to anger which may be either mild or excessive. While both annoyances and frustrations are forms of anger, they differ in one major respect: Annoyances arise mainly from social situations whereas many frustrations arise from the individual's own ineptitude (32, 85, 90).

Among the most common frustrations are sex-inappropriate or unattractive physique, poor health which limits participation in peer group activities, insufficient money to take part in peer group interests, personality traits that interfere with social acceptance, and lack of ability to reach self-established goals. Most of these obstacles to achievement originate within the adolescents themselves. Conflicts with parents, lack of social techniques, and conflicts with family standards—all environmental in origin—are less frequent sources of frustration (32, 68, 95).

While most frustrations are accompanied by some degree of anger, other reactions, such as those given in Box 3-4, are common (19, 32, 90, 95, 159).

How the adolescent *perceives a situation* will influence his reaction to it. If he has found people in authority, whether parents or teachers, to be a source of frustration, for example, he will perceive *anyone* in authority, even a peer who has been selected for a leadership role, as a possible threat. Consequently, he will react more aggressively than if his past experiences had colored his present perceptions more favorably. On the whole, the well-adjusted adolescent tends to perceive situations realistically and accurately and thus does not feel as apprehensive about new situations as the poorly adjusted (68, 151).

Jealousy

Jealousy occurs when a person feels insecure or afraid that his status in the group or in the affections of a significant person is threatened. The stimulus to jealousy is always social in origin. It can be aroused by any situation involving people for whom the individual has a deep feeling of affection or whose attention and acceptance he craves. Thus, in jealousy, two emotional elements are strong: fear and anger. Whether fear of loss of status is stronger than anger will depend on the situation.

Jealousy stimuli in adolescence are quite individualized. They depend largely on what makes a person feel insecure. And the degree of insecurity depends on the value the person places on relationships with certain people. As the adolescent grows older, more threats to security come in relationships outside the home than within it. Thus in late adolescence sibling jealousy is less common than peer jealousy.

Sibling jealousy during adolescence comes mainly when younger siblings are given privileges at an age earlier than the adolescent himself was given them or when parents seem to favor a sibling. If the independence that comes with privileges did not mean so much to him, he would have less reason to be jealous.

The high value placed on social acceptance is at the basis of much of the jealousy the adolescent experiences outside the home. He becomes jealous of classmates who are more popular than he. The less secure he feels in his social relationships with the peer group, the more likely he is to be jealous of those whose social acceptance seems assured.

The curve of jealous reactions normally has two peaks, the first occurring during the preschool years, and the second in adolescence. Among girls, jealousy tends to be stronger during the preschool years, and among boys, in adolescence (97). Adolescent jealousy generally reaches a peak during the years when dating becomes important. Dating is a new experience and the adolescent feels unsure of his ability to deal with the problems it gives rise to. In addition, the high social value placed on popularity with members of the opposite sex makes the adolescent jealous of peers who achieve greater success in this area than he. For example, a girl is likely to be extremely jealous of an age-mate who dates boys regarded as the big wheels of the class or who starts to go steady sooner than she. Boys show less jealousy in dating situations than girls. But the prestige value of achievement in sports and in making the "right" college is greater for boys. Consequently, when boys are jealous of their peers, it is generally in strictly "masculine" areas of behavior.

Typically, the jealous *reaction* of the adolescent is verbal. Instead of a bodily attack on the individual who made him jealous, the adolescent will usually fight back with words. This substitute reaction takes many forms, the most common of which are sarcasm, ridicule, and talking about the individual in a derogatory manner when he is not present to defend himself. A more subtle form of verbal attack is to make derogatory comments about the qualities, whether they be athletic ability, looks, or intelligence, which have made another a threat to the adolescent. Through these comments, he hopes to reduce the threat to his own status in the group. Regression to earlier forms of behavior is far less common among adolescents than among children. However, emotionally immature adolescent girls may whine or cry when their jealousy is aroused, while immature boys may physically attack their rivals (44, 68, 120).

Envy

Envy is similar to jealousy in that it is an emotion directed toward an individual. It differs from jealousy in one major respect, however. It is not the individual per se who stimulates envy, but the *material possessions* of that individual. An adolescent girl, for example, may be envious of a classmate whose clothes and home are superior to hers. And because she envies this girl, she reacts to her in much the same way as if she were angry or jealous. Envy is, in reality, covetousness.

Each year, as the child grows older, he is increasingly aware of how important material possessions are to social acceptance. To a young adolescent, they are status symbols—an indication of his status in the social group. The adolescent realizes that material possessions not only give him prestige in the eyes of others but that they are essential to social acceptance. The better the material possessions, the greater will be his prestige and the greater his chances of acceptance (3, 4, 111).

While envy may be expressed in different patterns of behavior, the typical adolescent *reaction* is verbal. The adolescent who is envious will tell those whose possessions he envies how "lucky" they are and will often hint or openly suggest that they share their possessions with him, claiming that his parents are too poor or "too tight" to give him the possessions he craves. Often the envious adolescent will try to minimize the value of the possessions of others or even ridicule them, thus compensating for his lack of them. This sour-grapes attitude helps the adolescent to overcome the anger he feels when he realizes that others have more than he.

An adolescent may react to envy by trying to convince himself that he is satisfied with what he has. This "Pollyanna" attitude is usually a product of childhood training. It is closely related to home situations where the adolescent realizes that his parents have made personal sacrifices to give him things they can ill afford to give. Most adolescents, however, feel resentful of parents who have not been able to give them the things their friends have.

Envy sometimes leads to *action,* either stealing or working. Studies of juvenile delinquency show that stealing is one of the most common misdemeanors among girls and that it ranks high among the misdemeanors of boys. Typically, girls steal clothing, cosmetics, and costume jewelry while boys are more likely to steal cars. This will be discussed in Chapter 12 in connection with juvenile delinquency. The envious adolescent may turn his energies into more socially acceptable behavior and work to earn the money to buy status symbols. He may take an out-of-school job, or he may study hard to get into a prestige college and prepare for a high-paying occupation in the future.

Curiosity

For most adolescents the chief source of new interests is their own and their friends' sexual maturation. Few reach adolescence with so complete a knowledge of the physiology and psycholgoy of sex that there is nothing new to stimulate their curiosity. Aside from interest in sex, the adolescent is also curious about scientific phenomena, world affairs, religion, and moral issues. These, however, are far less universal in their appeal than sex (101).

The adolescent generally talks about the things that arouse his curiosity and asks questions about them. For example, he talks about sex to his friends or to any adults who are willing to discuss the matter with him. Books containing factual information about sex or a romantic treatment of sex in daily life are eagerly read by both boys and girls in the hope of supplementing their knowledge. In addition, the adolescent gets firsthand information about the meaning of sex through stimulation of the sex organs and from contacts with members of the other sex. This subject will be discussed in detail in Chapter 13. Curiosity about other matters is also satisfied by talking, asking questions, and reading.

Affection

Affection is a pleasant emotional state of relatively mild intensity; it is a *tender attachment* for a person, an animal, or an object. While commonly used interchangeably with "love," it differs from love in that, *first,* love is a stronger emotional state; *second,* love is normally directed toward a member of the opposite sex; and *third,* love has components of sexual desire. Affection may be directed toward members of the opposite sex, but it does not have elements of sexual desire nor does it have the intensity of love.

Affections are built up through pleasant associations; they are not innate. People tend to like those who like them and are friendly toward them. It is unlikely that a pleasant emotion would become associated with persons who were indifferent, unfriendly, or rejecting. Since a tender attachment for another comes from pleasant experiences, a reciprocal liking is developed; this leads to increasingly pleasant associations. As a result, affection grows with time; the more pleasant associations a person has with another, the more he likes him and shows it in his behavior (82).

The stimuli that arouse affection in adoles-

cence differ from those in childhood in a number of ways. *First,* in childhood, affection is aroused by people, objects (such as toys), and pets. In adolescence, it is aroused primarily by people, rarely by inanimate objects, and only occasionally by animals, mainly family pets.

Second, the stimuli that arouse affection in adolescence have a more intense effect. That is, the affection that the adolescent has for others is characteristically much more intense than that of the child.

Third, the stimuli that arouse affection in children are found primarily within the family; the mother, especially, is a source of affective stimuli. In adolescence, peers or adults outside the home are the most common stimuli for affectionate responses. If the adolescent has few close friends, he is likely to center his affection on some hero, either real or fictional.

Typically, the adolescent *shows* his affection by wanting to be with the person he is fond of, by doing little favors in the hope of making him happy, and by watching and listening with rapt attention to everything he does or says. In addition, he is tolerant of and loyal to the person for whom he has affection. For example, he will defend a close friend for an act which he would condemn in a person for whom he had no affection.

Unlike the child, the adolescent refrains from public physical contact with the person he has affection for. This restraint is due to fear of social disapproval or ridicule. Even a conventional kiss in greeting causes the adolescent great embarrassment if he knows that others are observing him. In addition to fear of social disapproval is fear of rebuff; the adolescent "plays it safe" and avoids any behavior that might interfere with the friendly relationship he has already established.

Grief

Grief, and in its milder forms, sorrow, sadness, and distress, is one of the most unpleasant emotions and is likely to have the greatest physically and psychologically damaging effects. It comes from the loss of something that is highly valued and for which the individual has developed an emotional attachment because it fills an important need in his life (8).

For many adolescents, grief in its various degrees of intensity is a frequent emotional experience, especially during early adolescence. It is one of the major causes of unhappiness at this time. Grief is a relatively new emotion for the adolescent and he must learn to cope with it. He was largely insulated from grief-provoking experiences in childhood by protective parents and by his limited social contacts.

Even more important, with his higher intellectual capacities and insight and his broader social horizons, the adolescent has a more realistic understanding of situations that give rise to grief. When he was a child, for example, he did not comprehend the finality of the loss of a family member or pet through death. Now he does.

Most grief in adolescence is social in origin. It may come from loss due to death, divorce, absence of a person for whom the adolescent has a strong emotional attachment, or breakup of a friendship that has been a source of emotional security, or from the death or running away of a pet that the adolescent has come to regard as a family member.

In its milder form of sadness, grief may occur when the adolescent fails to achieve something which is important to him, such as making an athletic team, being invited to a party, or being accepted by the college of his choice. Since young adolescents tend to be particularly unrealistic in their aspirations—as will be discussed in Chapter 9—they are subject to more sadness from this source than older adolescents (91).

Unlike children, few adolescents show their grief by crying in the presence of others (1, 7). They have learned that crying is considered immature or even a sign of cowardice or weakness. In inhibiting this *overt expression* of their grief, adolescents often induce a general state of apathy which is shown in a variety of ways: they lose interest in people and things around them; become self-bound,

avoiding opportunities for socialization; grow listless and lose their appetite; are unable to sleep soundly; and are unable to concentrate in school. All of these militate against achievement in whatever is undertaken (8).

Some adolescents may have intense feelings of guilt about being partially responsible for the loss they have experienced and some may develop feelings of martyrdom, believing that the loss is a punishment for a wrong they have done. If feelings of guilt and martyrdom are intense, they may lead to psychosomatic illness or to attempts at suicide (91).

Happiness

Unlike most of the emotions already discussed, happiness is generalized rather than specific. It is a state of well-being, of pleasurable satisfaction—the opposite of anger, fear, jealousy, or envy, all of which lead to dissatisfaction. In its milder form, happiness results in a state of "euphoria," a sense of well-being or of buoyancy; in its stronger form, it is known as "joy," a state in which the individual is "walking on clouds."

Happiness is influenced to a large extent by the general physical condition of the individual, though good health alone is not enough to make the adolescent happy nor does it play as important a role in his happiness as it does in the child's. As shown in Box 3-5, the many causes of happiness in its different degrees of intensity may be grouped under four major headings (28, 68, 85, 110, 137, 144).

The *response* in happiness varies little from one individual to another. The body is relaxed, and so is the face. The corners of the mouth turn up in a smile. When the emotion is strong, smiling gives way to laughter. The sounds of laughter vary according to the strength of the emotion. The characteristic laugh of boys is louder and lower in pitch than that of girls (44, 92, 144). Sometimes the sounds can be heard all over the house, though the adolescent soon discovers that uproarious laughter is usually not considered mature. If he laughs or even smiles just because he is happy, for no obvious reason, people are likely to regard him as "crazy." If he smiles or laughs in triumph over others, he is considered a poor sport. If he laughs when others are serious, he gets glances of disapproval from other members of the group.

EFFECTS OF THE EMOTIONS ON ADOLESCENT ADJUSTMENT

Any vivid experience that is accompanied by intense emotion is likely to have a profound effect on one's attitudes, values, and future behavior. The effect may be favorable or unfavorable, depending on the emotion aroused, its intensity, previous experience with the emotion, and the preparation one has had for it. In general, the more pleasant the emotion, the more favorable the effect. The unfavorable effects of unpleasant emotions can be so devastating that control of the emotions is necessary if the individual is to make good personal and social adjustments. Box 3-6 presents both the favorable and unfavorable effects of the emotions on adjustment (22, 37, 42, 64, 85, 148).

Continuous emotional strain, stemming from personal inadequacies or poor environmental conditions, keeps the adolescent stirred up, ready to overrespond to *any* situation. He becomes high strung, uncomfortable, and ineffectual. In time, emotional strain can bring on ill health, both physical and mental.

EMOTIONAL CONTROL

Since the unfavorable effects of the emotions far outweigh the favorable, emotions can have a pervasive and destructive impact if left uncontrolled. Fortunately, emotional habits are still quite unstable during adolescence and are more amenable to change than in later life.

"Emotional control" does not mean repression or elimination. It means learning to approach a situation with a rational attitude, to respond to it with the mind as well as the emotions, and to avoid reading meanings into situations that could give rise to emotional overreactions. This is control of the *mental* aspects of an emotional state. In addition, emotional control means harnassing the *overt motor or verbal expression* of the emotions. Achieving emotional control is one indication of emotional maturity (27, 31).

Effects of emotional control

Just keeping the overt expression of the emotions under control is not an indication of emotional maturity. They must be kept under control in a way that wins social approval and, at the same time, does the least possible physical or psychological damage to the person himself. *Wholesome* emotional control, Jourard has explained, necessitates behavior "which will produce certain valued consequences. These consequences include the riddance of undesired tensions, or the attainment of desired ones, and the maintenance and enhancement of other values. These other

---

BOX 3-6   EFFECTS OF EMOTIONS ON ADJUSTMENT

Favorable Effects

Excitement and Relaxation
Emotions add excitement to daily life. Even if an emotion is unpleasant, the aftermath is a state of relaxation which is always pleasurable.

Body Strength and Endurance
Under emotional stress, a person can often perform feats that would otherwise be impossible. Even when the activity is completed, the person is not tired or physically exhausted.

Motivation
In their milder forms, all emotions serve as a drive to action related to the emotions that have been aroused. In their stronger forms, emotions tend to paralyze related action.

Unfavorable Effects

Physical Debility
Emotional tension upsets body homeostasis and leads to digestive disturbances, loss of appetite, and headaches. Prolonged emotional tension leads to loss of weight, loss of energy, and a generally run-down condition.

Efficiency Loss
Emotional stress results in flightiness, instability, and inconsistency of performance. It leads to errors in motor skills, speech disturbances, and accidents. Poor concentration impedes memorizing, reasoning, and recall.

Personality Maladjustments
Unpleasant emotions make a person irritable and moody. Irritability leads to impatience and an uncooperative attitude, while moodiness results in either withdrawn or aggressive behavior.

Emotional Habits
With repetition, unpleasant emotional responses tend to become habitual. The result is a worried, anxious, or angry adolescent, whose responses— even to happiness—are tinged with displeasure.

---

values include . . . self-respect, one's job, friendships, etc." By contrast, *unwholesome* emotional control occurs when a person does not "respond emotionally as he is supposed or expected to, and when his emotionally-provoked behavior endangers his health, safety, his position, or anything else which he or society deems important" (72).

Two criteria determine whether the control is socially approved: *first,* social reactions to the individual's behavior, and *second,* the aftereffects of the emotional control on his physical and psychological well-being. If social reactions to his emotional control are satisfactory, the first criterion is fulfilled. But this alone is not enough. If the control is such that it makes the individual nervous, edgy, and irritable, it will damage his physical and psychological well-being and, in time, affect his social relationships. While the person may be judged more favorably by the social group when he controls the overt expressions of his anger than when he "blows his top," he is likely to experience fatigue, shame, and guilt or to feel martyred because he has been picked on but not allowed to retaliate.

While some people who suffer from anxiety and depression can control these unfavorable emotional states by the use of alcohol or tranquilizers, these are only stopgap measures and thus cannot be considered desirable means of emotional control. When their effects end, the emotional states return. Furthermore, with continued use, the amount of the psychological pain-killer must be increased to achieve the desired results and this, in time, leads to a habitual reliance which is characteristic of the addict (58, 59).

Influence of social expectations on emotional control

The social group does not require the adolescent to control his emotions at all times or in all places. Instead, it expects him to learn when he may express them and when he must control them. It also expects him to learn socially acceptable patterns of emotional expression. Too little control creates the impression that the adolescent is immature for his age. Too much control, in addition to damaging his physical and psychological well-being, creates the impression, as Jourard has pointed out, that he is "less than human" (72).

Emotional control is expected to increase with *age.* Early maturers, unfortunately, are subjected to more rigid social expectations than their age-mates who continue to resemble children (37, 70). *Boys,* at all ages, are more or less expected and permitted to express their emotions more overtly than girls *except fear,* which brands boys as cowards. Boys who express their emotions openly are likely to be envied and admired by the peer group. While some expression of anger in the form of tears may be tolerated in girls, many genuinely intense emotional expressions must be stifled if social approval is sought (43, 93).

Each *social class* has its own approved ways for boys and girls to express and control their emotions. In general, the lower-class boy knows that aggressive attacks in anger are regarded as manly, while the lower-class girl knows that such behavior will only win her social disapproval. In general, the middle-class boy or girl knows that verbal attacks carefully camouflaged as wit will be tolerated when he is angry or that laughing will be condoned in some situations and not in others (110, 111, 157).

Even when the adolescent learns to control his emotions to conform to social expectations, the harmful effects of emotional arousal are by no means eliminated. When an emotion is aroused but direct expression of it is suppressed, it does not die out at once. Like a dammed-up stream, the emotional energy will find some new outlet. This substitute form of expression is often physically or psychologically damaging. Of the many indirect expressions of controlled emotions, those given in Box 3-7 are the most common (27, 68, 72, 110, 157, 159).

ACHIEVING SOCIALLY APPROVED EMOTIONAL CONTROL

The adolescent needs guidance in learning how to avoid some of the damage that comes from bottling up emotional energy. Jourard has suggested two rules that can help if *both* are followed. The first rule is to admit that one has the emotion he has tried to control, and the second is to subject the cognitive or mental aspects of the emotional response to reality testing (72).

If the adolescent is jealous, for example, he must admit his jealousy to himself even though he has hidden it so well that others do not suspect it. Then he must submit his jealousy to reality testing. That is, he must look at it objectively and without bias to see if it is justified—if he has any reason to be jealous and if he can achieve the attention and affection he craves by some means other than by attacking, directly or indirectly, the person who has aroused the jealousy.

Wholesome control of the emotions is possible only when the adolescent has "ego strength"—the ability to refrain from emotional outbursts if he decides that is what he wishes to do or to let loose his feelings if that is what he wants. In discussing the factors that promote ego strength, Jourard (72) writes:

One such factor is autonomy, the possession of a high degree of skill and competence in many areas, so that the person is not obligated to be overly dependent on others. . . . Security is another factor, whether it is the by-product of diverse skill, or an assured source of income. Insecure persons are very prone to anxiety, and they may dread expressing their feelings because they believe that if they do so, they may lose status, their job, or friendships. Reality-contact can also promote healthy emotional behavior; the person can determine realistically what values are at stake in an emotional situation and what dangers are associated with suppression and expression of feelings. Autonomy, security, and reality-contact appear to make it possible for a person to choose how he will react under emotion, rather than reacting in a stereotyped manner with "explosions," with repression, or suppression.

Role of catharsis in emotional control

The safest and surest way to minimize the damaging effects of emotional control is "emotional catharsis," purging the mind and body of pent-up emotional energy. Catharsis has two aspects—mental and physical—both of which must be carried out if homeostasis is to be regained. Mental catharsis alone achieves better results than physical catharsis alone. Once the mind is cleared of the emotion, further physical disturbances will not build up. But mental catharsis alone is inadequate because it does not eliminate the bodily preparation for action that has already taken place (16, 42, 79).

The adolescent is anxious to control his emotions in order to create the impression that he is grown up, but the more control he exerts, the more damaging the effects. Furthermore, since the most common and most intense emotions of the adolescent are the most damaging ones—fear, anxiety, frustration, grief, jealousy, and envy—he needs the purging effects of catharsis. This is especially true during the heightened emotionality of early adolescence (37, 42).

Physical aspect of emotional catharsis The physical aspect of emotional catharsis consists of the elimination of pent-up physical preparation for action. When one controls the expression of an emotion, emotional energy remains dammed-up, ready for use, until it is drained off. The adolescent purges the body of the physical harm of this dammed-up energy by giggling, laughing, crying, strenuous physical exertion in work or play, and in the case of older adolescents, sexual behavior—petting, necking, or intercourse (15, 98, 128).

The kind of purge used will depend largely on what the adolescent has discovered from

past experience will give him the greatest satisfaction and, at the same time, conform to socially approved patterns of behavior. An adolescent may, for example, get greater relief of the physical tensions of emotions through sexual activity than through other means. But unless the social group sanctions his use of this outlet, he will be forced to make a decision: Would he rather risk the disapproval of the group or use a more acceptable outlet, such as sports, which gives him less personal satisfaction?

Although all the common forms of physical catharsis purge the body of pent-up emotional energy, not all are possible or practicable for every adolescent. For example, strenuous activity in *sports* is an excellent emotional cathartic. But to be able to engage in sports, the adolescent must have enough skill to get on a team or enough social acceptance to be included in the sports of the peer group.

Because of the social approval of *work* which leads to a constructive end, an emotionally mature person learns to use some form of work as physical catharsis as soon after he has controlled his emotions as possible. He thus is able to avoid much physical and psychological damage.

The least satisfactory way to purge the body of pent-up emotional energy is *crying*. Many adolescent girls who giggle uncontrollably alternate their giggling with crying and frequently end the giggling with uncontrollable crying. They quickly discover that such a performance is considered babyish. Boys who learned early in childhood that crying is regarded as a sign of being a sissy rarely indulge in this form of catharsis. Crying is also a poor catharsis because it often leaves the adolescent exhausted and moody. The longer and harder the crying, the more energy used. In addition, crying tends to arouse unhappy feelings about oneself and about life in general.

Mental aspect of emotional catharsis The mental aspect of emotional catharsis consists of ridding the mind of the attitudes that gave rise to the emotional state the individual is trying to control. To purge his mind of these attitudes, the adolescent must understand them. In this way, he can minimize their influence and replace them with more wholesome attitudes. Unwholesome attitudes will not automatically disappear just because the adolescent controls their overt expression. Rather, they must be replaced by wholesome attitudes.

Four things are essential to purge the mind of unwholesome attitudes: *First,* a recognition of the feelings that persist even after the overt expression of an emotion has been controlled; *second,* the ability to communicate one's feelings to others to get a more objective perspective; *third,* a willingness to communicate with others and understand one's feelings; and *fourth,* access to people with whom one is able and willing to communicate. Only

by bringing one's feelings out in the open and seeing them through the eyes of another person who is not personally involved can one hope to get a perspective that will lead to wholesome feelings. As Worchel has pointed out, there is a therapeutic effect to mental catharsis "due to insight or new learning as the individual verbalizes his previous experiences" (156).

If new insight and new learning do not result from the catharsis, much of its therapeutic value is lost. Just blowing off emotional steam or talking about one's irritations or worries will have little value; the experience must lead to a changed point of view, new attitudes, and a new perspective if it is to have a drive-reducing effect when a similar situation develops in the future. Merely expressing anxiety feelings concerning an anticipated failure, for

---

BOX 3-8 COMMON DIFFICULTIES IN MENTAL CATHARSIS

Difficulty in Expressing Feelings
Because of authoritarian childhood training which emphasized covering up one's feelings, the adolescent may find it just as hard to express his pleasures as his gripes.

Willingness to Communicate
Years of family conflict, criticism, punishment, and lack of overt expression of parental affection will make the adolescent unwilling to disclose his troubles to his parents even though he is in desperate need of help. An insecure status in the peer group will make the adolescent hesitant to discuss his problems with peers for fear of losing what status he has. If teachers or other adults are regarded as unsympathetic, the adolescent will not try to get help from them.

Lack of Confidants
Many adolescents are so on the fringe of social life that they have no real friends with whom they can explore their personal feelings.

Lack of Guidance in Developing a Perspective
Parents and peers often lack the ability to help the adolescent subject his unwholesome attitudes to reality testing, and teachers and counselors often have to concentrate on the most intractable students. Even if excellent facilities for guidance are available, many adolescents resist the "uncovering process" which is necessary to discover the cause of their unwholesome attitudes because it seems to threaten their security and self-esteem.

example, will not eliminate the underlying threat. In fact, the more one thinks and talks about a threat, the more anxious he is likely to become (16, 98, 129).

Adolescents are faced with a number of difficulties in attempting to free themselves of mental attitudes that predispose them to emotional hang-ups. Box 3-8 explains the most common difficulties (15, 26, 33, 36, 78, 117, 136).

Some adolescents, more by trial and error than by guidance, discover ways of dealing with their negative attitudes. The three most common ways are wit, literary expression, and daydreams. The adolescent who through *wit*—a joke or cartoon—can show his pent-up hostility toward a person or group may reduce his hostility, at least temporarily. Social disapproval of his witty attacks, however, may outweigh the value he receives from this catharsis (16, 110).

Literary expression is less likely to arouse social disapproval and thus may be a more satisfactory catharsis than wit. Adolescents who find it difficult to express themselves verbally in face-to-face situations sometimes are able to do so in letters, diaries and journals, or

Figure 3-3 The ages at which boys and girls keep diaries. (Adapted from R. G. Kuhlen: *The psychology of adolescent development,* 2d ed. New York: Harper & Row, 1963. Used by permission.)

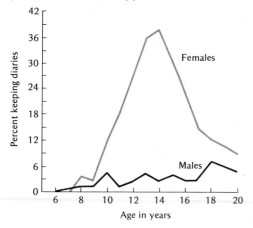

school or college newspaper columns. Just writing down their feelings freely, however, usually has only a temporary cathartic effect. They must also get new perspectives on their problems if the effect is to be long-lasting (85, 94, 125).

The diary is the most personal form of literary expression and is thus the best substitute for mental catharsis. As Baruch has pointed out, "Keeping a diary . . . might almost have been invented to meet adolescent needs" (9). Many adolescents do not keep diaries merely because they do not take the time to do so, but most are afraid that other family members will get hold of the diaries and ridicule or criticize what they have written. Girls more than boys use the diary as a confidant, recording in it their personal problems, aspirations, and emotional reactions (85). Sex and age differences in diary keeping are shown in Figure 3-3.

Adolescents, especially during the junior and senior high school years, often use the social columns of the school paper to let off emotional steam about classmates they dislike. This may give the writer temporary emotional relief, but it is not a satisfactory pattern of catharsis. First, it is not an outlet that he can continue to use after he leaves school, and second, it does not lead to the learning experiences that will change his perspective (69).

The most unsatisfactory substitute for mental catharsis is *daydreaming*. Since the adolescent has no check on reality in his daydream, he is likely to allow himself to wallow in distorted images of himself as a martyr until he persuades himself that he actually is a martyr. Then when he leaves the daydream world and is confronted with emotion-arousing situations, he reacts to them with the distorted attitudes developed in his daydreams rather than subjecting them to reality testing (18, 40, 87).

Success of catharsis in emotional control

The success of catharsis in emotional control may be judged from two frames of reference—

the *immediate* and the *long term*. If the adolescent's physical and mental states are restored to normal, the catharsis has been a
success, at least for the time being. But temporary success is not enough. Permanent
relief can be achieved only when the cause
of the unhealthy and damaging condition is
diagnosed and treated so that it will not
recur.

Three widely accepted criteria of assessing
emotional maturity are given in Box 3-9. When
an adolescent can ask, "Why should I worry
and get ulcers?" about an examination or can
philosophically face a frustration or defeat,
there is positive evidence that he is well along
on the road to emotional maturity.

HIGHLIGHTS OF CHAPTER 3

1. Heightened emotionality, which means
more-than-normal emotionality for a given person,
can occur with any emotion.

2. Scientific evidence contradicts the traditional beliefs that heightened emotionality is
caused by the glandular changes of puberty and
that it is inevitable and characteristic of *all* adolescents throughout the adolescent period.

3. The emotions of adolescents are different
from those of children in two ways: The stimuli that

give rise to emotions differ and the form of the emotional response is different. They are similar in that
the dominant emotions in both groups tend to be
unpleasant.

4. The common emotional patterns of adolescence include fear, worry, anxiety, anger, annoyances, frustrations, jealousy, envy, curiosity, affection, grief, and happiness in the forms of euphoria
and joy.

5. Emotions have both favorable and unfavorable effects on the adolescent's personal and social
adjustments.

6. On the favorable side, emotions provide
sources of enjoyment, motivation, and bodily
strength and energy; on the unfavorable side, emotions disturb body homeostasis, efficiency, and
personality.

7. With repetition, emotions develop into
habits. Thus, if the pleasant emotions become habitual, they can be aids to adjustment; if the unpleasant ones become habitual, as is more likely,
they become liabilities to adjustment.

8. Emotional control has two aspects: control
over the way one interprets an emotional stimulus
and control over the overt expression of the emotion that has been aroused.

9. The social group expects the adolescent to
achieve greater emotional control as he grows older,
and the judgments made of him are greatly in-

fluenced by how closely he conforms to group expectations.

10.   Emotional control is aided by physical and mental catharsis. The former serves to eliminate pent-up physical energy, and the latter, to change attitudes.

11.   Four essentials to satisfactory mental catharsis are: recognition of persistent feelings, ability to communicate feelings to others as an aid to getting a more wholesome perspective of them, willingness to communicate with others, and access to people with whom one can and will communicate.

12.   The adolescent who learns when and how to control his emotions, aided by emotional catharsis, is regarded by the social group as an emotionally mature person.

Chapter 4

Transition in Socialization

Photograph by Farrell/Greene
Omikron

The foundations of socialization are laid during the childhood years, and the adolescent is expected to build on these foundations the attitudes and behavior patterns that will fit him to take his place in the adult world. The social group expects him to master four developmental tasks: He must establish new and more mature relationships with age-mates of both sexes, desire and achieve socially responsible behavior, develop intellectual skills and concepts necessary for civic competence, and achieve a more autonomous state through achieving emotional independence of parents and other adults.

Transition to adult socialization is difficult for adolescents because the patterns of social behavior learned in childhood are no more suited to mature social relationships than is the clothing worn by a child suited to the adult body. Nor are the patterns of social behavior many adolescents learn as a part of the youth culture of their high school and college days suited to the adult world. As adolescents finish their formal schooling and go out into the world of work, they must revise many of their attitudes, values, and patterns of behavior if they are to make satisfactory adjustments to their new roles.

Most adolescents are aware of the transition they must make in this area of development. They know, for example, that childish behavior and immature attitudes alienate friends. The awareness of the need for change is especially strong when they emerge from puberty into adolescence and discover that they have lost more friends, affection, and respect than they have gained.

Adolescent girls, even more than boys, are concerned about how to improve their social adjustments. This is not because boys make better social adjustments than girls. Rather, the difference may be traced to two causes. *First,* girls, age for age, are more mature in their attitudes than boys, and, as a result, view problems from an adult perspective earlier than boys. *Second,* the social life of girls is more dependent on the kind of social adjustments they make.

MEANING OF SOCIALIZATION

"Socialization" is the process of learning to conform to group standards, mores, and customs. It is the ability to behave in accordance with social expectations. As Child (27) has explained:

Socialization . . . is a broad term for the whole process by which an individual, born with behavioral potentialities of enormously wide range, is led to develop actual behavior which is confined within a much narrower range—the range of what is customary and acceptable for him according to the standards of his group.

Socialization is generally judged in terms of *social activity.* It is assumed that the better the socialization of the individual, the more active he will be socially. This, however, is not necessarily so. How active the individual is socially will depend upon many factors other than degree of socialization. An adolescent from a large family, for example, may conform well to group standards, but have so many home duties and so little money that it is impossible for him to participate in group activities as he would like.

Whether an adolescent is social, unsocial, or antisocial must be judged both objectively and subjectively. *Objectively,* he is judged in terms of his behavior; *subjectively,* he is judged in terms of his feelings and attitudes. Both kinds of criteria are necessary because adolescents have learned to conceal many of their unsocial feelings behind "fronts" which help them to avoid social disapproval. For example, the adolescent may appear to be interested in what someone is saying while, in reality, he is bored.

Four criteria may be used in judging a *social* adolescent: (1) behavior which conforms to the approved standards of the group, (2) proper playing of the social role prescribed by the group, (3) social attitudes that lead to approved behavior, and (4) personal satisfaction from social behavior.

An *unsocial* adolescent is one who fails to conform to one or more of the criteria of a social person, owing to ignorance of social expectations. By contrast, an *antisocial* person is aware of what the group expectations are, but does not conform because, for one reason or another, he does not wish to (24, 161, 168).

Role of social expectations in socialization

Guidelines to direct the adolescent's mastery of social expectations are expressed in terms of developmental tasks. Each cultural as well as each subcultural group sets up its own standards with its own guidelines to help the adolescent make the transition from childish social attitudes and behavior to those considered adult-appropriate.

The social group has many reasons for expecting the adolescent to replace his childish attitudes and behavior with those more suited to his new developmental status. It realizes that no adolescent or adult can be happy if he is friendless and that his needs for social contacts cannot be met outside the group context. Furthermore, in a culture which places high prestige on popularity, the adolescent who lacks friends thinks of himself as a social failure. This soon becomes a generalized belief. He then regards himself as a failure in all respects (28, 78). This, added to his loneliness, is likely to make him so emotionally unstable that he has difficulty fitting into any social group. Wagner (161) has written:

Recently our society has seen chaos brought about by the rejected loner. Each day we read of brutal acts committed by lonely people who have never been accepted by society. A President was slain by one and several women in a beauty salon in Arizona were wantonly murdered by another. The testimony of the offenders revealed that as teenagers they never felt they were part of the group. Lacking attention, they committed acts such as those mentioned above to get the spotlight focused on them. They wanted someone to know that they existed. Rejected by their peers and unable to better themselves, they became loners.

From the long-term view, the value of so-cialization is not limited to happiness and favorable self-concepts; it influences the degree of success the person achieves in life. With the growing complexity of business and social life, the adolescent must be prepared to meet a wider variety of people and adjust to a wider variety of social situations than adolescents of past generations.

Unquestionably the most important reason for fostering socialization in the adolescent is that the pattern of social adjustment established in adolescence is likely to determine his level of socialization throughout the remainder of his life. A study of middle-aged people revealed that those who had not made good social adjustments in adolescence regarded themselves as social failures or near failures as adults. Those who had made good social adjustments in adolescence were more satisfied with their social lives in adulthood, just as they had been in their school days (67). Follow-up studies of shy, retiring children have shown that, as adolescents, they made poor social adjustments. This pattern persisted into adulthood. By contrast, socially well-adjusted children are likely to become well-adjusted adolescents and adults (13, 70, 111).

Difficulty of making social transition

While the child has to revise his pattern of social behavior when he enters school, he has a great deal of help from parents and teachers. By the time he has been in school for 6 or more years, adults usually assume that he is equipped to handle the problems of adolescent transition alone.

Adolescents themselves are aware of the magnitude of the task that confronts them and often feel inadequate to cope with it. Feeling that parents do not understand their problems and that teachers do not have time to help with problems unrelated to academic work, they generally turn to their peers for advice and help. Sometimes they read books that have a "how to win friends" theme or write to newspaper columnists for advice.

Educators, who recognized the unique social and academic problems of the young adolescent, established the junior high schools as "shock absorbers" to ease the transition from childish learning to mature studenthood (69). Still, however, the adolescent experiences many worries, anxieties, and frustrations. Unless offered a helping hand, he may revert to the patterns he found satisfactory when he was younger or he may withdraw almost completely from social contacts.

Many factors contribute to the adolescent's difficulties in replacing childish social attitudes and behavior with more adult-appropriate forms. Box 4-1 describes the most notable obstacles (3, 5, 12, 24, 78, 167).

Time needed to make the transition in socialization

Changes in social behavior tend to occur slowly as long as the adolescent is in school and living at home. If parents and teachers treat him like a child, he has little motivation to behave like an adult. Transition in socialization is normally speeded up, however, in late adolescence. Whether the older adoles-

---

BOX 4-1   DIFFICULTIES IN SOCIAL TRANSITION

Poor Foundations
Poor training and identification with poorly adjusted people in the formative years provide poor foundations on which to build adult-appropriate patterns of social behavior in adolescence.

Lack of Guidance
Parents and teachers often believe that the adolescent will automatically become better socialized. Adolescents who "don't like being bossed" often reject adult advice.

Lack of Suitable Models to Imitate
Models from the mass media are often unsuitable because their patterns of behavior do not always conform to approved group standards. Imitating a popular peer usually means learning patterns of behavior suited to youth standards, not adult standards.

Lack of Opportunities for Social Contacts
The adolescent who lacks social acceptance and time or money for peer activities will be deprived of opportunities to learn to be social.

Lack of Motivation
The adolescent who derived little satisfaction from social contacts as a child will have little motivation to engage in social activities.

Different Social Expectations
Since different social groups have different standards of approved behavior, the adolescent often feels that he must be a chameleon, changing his colors when he faces different people and situations.

New Kinds of Social Groups
As the childhood gang is replaced by cliques and other social groupings, the adolescent must learn to adjust to members of the other sex as well as to peers with different backgrounds, values, and interests.

cent goes to college or a professional training school, enters the armed services or the world of work, or marries and has a home of his own, social expectations will be quite different from what they were in early adolescence. Furthermore, his environment will provide both more opportunities to learn adult-appropriate social patterns and a greater variety of models to imitate (34, 62). If the adolescent goes away to college, for example, many of the developmental tasks he faces can be resolved more easily and more satisfactorily than if he remains under the parental roof. He will learn to choose his own friends and get along with people from many different backgrounds. And he will have an opportunity to explore his interests and abilities to determine what line of work he wants to undertake, relieved of the proddings and personal aspirations of parents (29).

One reason it takes so long for the adolescent to transform his childish social patterns into adult-appropriate ones is that, if he is to live up to social expectations and achieve acceptance, he must change the whole social structure of his life. Often the transformation is not complete by the time he reaches legal maturity. Changes must be made in five major areas: social groupings, friends, treatment of friends, leaders, and social attitudes and behavior. Each of these major areas of change will be discussed below.

CHANGES IN SOCIAL GROUPINGS

As the gangs of late childhood break up, the preadolescent withdraws from the peer group and passes through a period when he prefers isolation. Both boys and girls lose interest in their former friends and often become antagonistic toward them. For a time, their behavior might justifiably be classed as "antisocial."

As they emerge from the physical transformation that accompanies puberty, young adolescents once again feel the need for a social life. They then attempt to create a society for themselves that will meet their more mature interests and needs. This they do by associating with different kinds of social groupings. Box

4-2 describes the most common social groupings of this age (28, 41, 43, 73, 90, 154).

These groups are more characteristic of early than of late adolescence. However, the older adolescent who goes to college or a professional training school has opportunities to continue this kind of socialization. One who goes to work after completing high school has more contact with older people and the social groups in which he participates are similar to those of the adult (155).

In making the transition from the small play group of the child to the varied groupings of his new world, the adolescent must adjust to larger and more heterogeneous groups than ever before, he must learn to get along with members of both sexes, and he must adjust to a new teacher for every school subject as he enters the departmentalized junior or senior high school. Thus, as his social world enlarges, he must make constant adjustments to new people in new situations as well as to old people in new situations.

How satisfactory the society of the new peer groups will be to the adolescent will depend largely upon the social distance involved in group relationships—the degree of intimacy that exists between two people in a group. Social distance depends partly upon the frequency of contact of group members, but mainly on the degree of emotional warmth built up between two people because of shared interests and values. For example, social distance is greater in cliques than in chum relationships; it is greater in formally organized groups than in crowds (41, 45, 73). Similarly, since the adolescent typically spends more time with peers as he grows older, social distance in peer groups is reduced by the frequency of these contacts.

Evaluation of different peer groups

Peer groups dominate the adolescent's social world and are the strongest social force in his life. However, each kind of group affects his socialization differently. The socializing influence of the various groups must, therefore, be examined.

Chums   A chum plays the role of an ideal sibling, with few of the rivalries and threats to status that a real sibling presents. Chums usually mirror each other in taste, in clothes, in choice of heterosexual partners, and in feelings about parents, siblings, and people different from themselves. Of all adolescent friendships, chum relationships are the most lasting. While chums do quarrel, sometimes very bitterly, a strong bond of mutual affection and common interests usually holds them together.

The adolescent who does not have a chum is likely to be handicapped in learning to make good social adjustments. Being deprived of a close social relationship with someone outside his family is especially hard on an adolescent whose relationship with family members is so strained that he no longer wants to confide in them. Perhaps the most damaging effect of not having a chum is that it deprives the adolescent of a chance of belonging to a clique, since cliques are usually formed from chum groups.

Cliques   A "we" feeling leads the members of a clique to think and act alike. The emotional

Early adolescence

Stage 1: Precrowd stage. Isolated unisexual cliques.

Stage 2: The beginning of the crowd. Unisexual cliques in group–to–group interaction.

Stage 3: The crowd in structural transition. Unisexual cliques with upper status members forming a heterosexual clique.

Stage 4: The fully developed crowd. Heterosexual cliques in close association.

Stage 5: Beginning of crowd disintegration. Loosely associated groups of couples.

Late adolescence

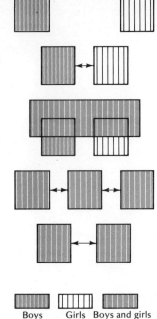

Boys   Girls   Boys and girls

Figure 4-1 Stages in the development of cliques and crowds during the adolescent years. (Adapted from D. C. Dunphy: The social structure of the urban adolescent peer groups. *Sociometry,* 1963, **26,** 230–246. Used by permission.)

attachment of clique members is expressed in two ways: Between members, it arouses strong feelings of friendship and responsibility to render assistance in time of need, and in regard to other groups and outside demands, it results in clique exclusiveness and preference for clique values, even over those of the families of its members.

The clique has a powerful influence on the attitudes, thoughts, and behavior of each member. Phelps and Horrocks have written: "The informal group plays a much more important part in the life of the adolescent than do formally organized groups and may be thought of as a focal area of experience in the process of coming of age" (123). Box 4-3 lists some of the advantages and disadvantages of the clique as far as socialization is concerned (28, 41, 73, 95, 161, 168).

Crowds The advantages of belonging to a crowd are so numerous that every adolescent

at some time should be a crowd member. Crowds have some disadvantages, however, in that they may make the transition into adult socialization more difficult. Box 4-4 shows the most important ways in which crowds influence socialization (28, 41, 72, 131, 161).

Formally organized groups Many educators and church and community leaders recognize the importance of youth groups as a means of keeping young people out of mischief, providing facilities for social activities for those who have few opportunities to socialize, and encouraging a more democratic intermingling of adolescents who otherwise would form small closed cliques. Roughly, formally organized youth groups can be divided into three categories: *special-interest groups,* which pursue a single activity, such as basketball, dramatics, swimming, or handicrafts; *clubs,* which have programs that include many kinds of activities; and *purpose groups,* which are devoted to some idealistic or altruistic purpose, such as the Hi-Y Club.

Formally organized groups offer many of the same opportunities for social participation offered by the more exclusive groupings. They are more democratic, however, and hence have fewer disadvantages than the other groups. Box 4-5 lists the advantages and the most serious disadvantages of formally organized groups (28, 41, 61, 105, 112, 121).

Gangs Adolescents who lack social acceptance among their peers find companionship and a feeling of security and belonging in the gang. Like their better-accepted peers, they learn that they must conform to the standards of behavior set by the gang if they are to retain their status, even when these standards include antisocial or delinquent behavior.

According to Klem (90):

Gang members are held together more by their own shared incapacities than by their mutual goals. . . . They are "drawn" toward the group, dissatisfied, deprived, and making the best of an essentially unhappy situation. . . . The gang member is thrown into his group. He is frustrated, insecure, and trapped in his environment. He is not having much fun, although he makes much of the enjoyment he finds.

Under such conditions, some of the essentials of socialization are fulfilled, such as playing the role the particular social group approves and receiving some satisfaction from social belonging and social behavior with gang-mates. However, the gang member does not fulfill two essential criteria of becoming a social person: acquiring social attitudes that lead to approved behavior in the larger social group and learning proper performance behavior. Consequently, on the whole, the gang leads to the development of antisocial rather than social adolescents (31, 95, 140, 154).

Influence of peer-group belonging on socialization

The peer group is an important socializing influence during adolescence. Since many adolescents are alienated from their families, especially during early adolescence, the peer group is not only a source of emotional security but is also a teacher of socialized attitudes and behavior. It teaches the adolescent how to get along with others—members of his own as well as members of the other sex— how to be considerate of the feelings of others, and how to listen to and be tolerant of the

---

BOX 4-3 INFLUENCE OF CLIQUES ON SOCIALIZATION

Advantages
*A feeling of security and personal importance comes from being a clique member and from having prestige in the eyes of others.

*In the clique, the adolescent can let off pent-up emotional steam, freely expressing his antagonisms, fears, worries, and annoyances.

*The clique provides opportunities to develop social skills that will help the adolescent make good social adjustments.

*The clique sets patterns and standards of behavior which motivate the adolescent to behave in a socially mature way.

*The feeling of security that comes from peer acceptance motivates the adolescent to achieve independence from parents and teachers.

*The clique helps the adolescent adjust in his transition from junior to senior high school and, later, to college.

Disadvantages
*The clique encourages snobbishness and discrimination against nonclique members.

*By encouraging member conformity, the clique stifles individuality.

*The clique stimulates envy on the part of members whose families cannot, or will not, give them what the others have.

*Loyalty to the clique and its values frequently increases the tension between the adolescent and his parents.

*The clique is often a disrupting influence on school or college unity, thus lowering the morale of nonmembers.

*Cliques are tightly knit units that newcomers find hard to penetrate.

*Because of their limited membership and homogeneous makeup, cliques deprive the adolescent of opportunities to learn to adjust to persons of different backgrounds.

BOX 4-4 INFLUENCE OF CROWDS ON SOCIALIZATION

Advantages
*Crowd life offers the adolescent a feeling of security, especially when home relationships are unsatisfactory.

*Crowds provide experience in getting along with different kinds of people and with members of both sexes.

*Crowd life helps the adolescent to understand persons with different backgrounds and different home training experiences.

*Crowds provide an opportunity to acquire social skills and experience in courtship behavior.

*Crowd life offers opportunities to learn to size up others quickly and accurately.

*Crowd values encourage the development of loyalty.

Disadvantages
*Crowd life is so satisfying that it encourages one to neglect home and school responsibilities.

*Crowd exclusiveness encourages snobbishness.

*Noncrowd members are made to feel lonely and rejected.

*The crowd encourages its members to feel self-important and even cocky.

*Crowd values encourage friction with parents about spending money, rules, and privileges.

---

views of others. Wagner has written: ''Perhaps the greatest gift of the peer group is that of empathy. Since all of the members are in the same boat, they can understand each others' problems and offer sympathy and advice that would not be appreciated from parents and teachers'' (161).

In addition, the peer group sets up standards of socially approved behavior and expects its members to conform to them. It demands that members be loyal and committed to the goals of the group if they are to retain their status in it. By providing opportunities for social participation, the group gives the adolescent a chance to develop social perception, which is essential to acceptance. It provides motivation for achievement, even if achievement does not come up to adult expectations at all times. As Wagner has said, ''The peer group makes leaders as well as hoodlums'' (161).

Horrocks and Benimoff (72) have summarized the ways in which the peer group serves as a socializing force in the adolescent's life:

The peer group is the adolescent's real world, providing him a stage upon which to try out himself and others. It is in the peer group that he continues to formulate and revise his concept of self, it is here that he is evaluated by others who are presumably his equals and who are unable to impose upon him the adult world sanctions from which he is typically struggling to free himself. The peer group offers the adolescent a world in which he may socialize in a climate where the values that count are those that are set, not by adults, but by others his own age. Thus, it is in the society of his peers that the adolescent finds support for his efforts at emancipation and it is there that he can find a world that enables him to assume leadership, if his work as a person is such that he can assert leadership. In addition, of course, the peer group is the major recreational outlet of the teenager. For all of these reasons, it would seem of vital importance to the adolescent that his peer group contain a certain number of friends who can accept him and upon whom he can depend.

CHANGES IN FRIENDS

The second major change the adolescent must make in his transition from childish to adult-appropriate socialization is in the kinds of friends he chooses. Childhood friends are, in reality, playmates, not selected primarily for congeniality of interests and values. Only if they have qualities that fit into the more mature social needs of the adolescent will they be adequate for friends during adolescence.

Friends play a crucial role in socialization. Joseph has said that friends may be the most important "area of the adolescent's world" (79). Thus, the kinds of friends the adolescent has will determine, to a large extent, whether he will develop into a social, an unsocial, or an antisocial person.

In the transition from childhood to adolescent friendships, attitudes toward friends change remarkably. The adolescent's attitudes are reflected in his desire to choose his own friends, in the number of friends wanted, in the qualities wanted in his friends, and in the desire to have friends of both sexes. A brief survey will illustrate how radical are the changes that occur in this area of socialization.

Autonomy in Choosing Friends

The adolescent insists upon choosing his own friends. When parents try to persuade him to make friends with persons they consider "right" for him, whether of the same or the opposite sex, the adolescent resists, not because he finds his parents' choices uncongenial but because he resents parental interference.

In selecting his friends, the adolescent often makes choices that prove to be unsatisfactory to him. He is especially likely to become dissatisfied with friends of the opposite sex. As time goes by, he becomes more critical. He discovers, for example, that judging an individual by looks alone is rarely a satisfactory basis for friendship. He also learns that two individuals with different interests and abilities are not likely to have enough in common to form a lasting friendship.

Number of friends

The young adolescent looks upon a large number of friends as a sign of popularity. But by the middle of adolescence, the number of friends is not nearly so important as friends of the right kind. What is meant by "right" will depend upon the cultural pattern of the community. If wealth and social prestige are regarded as primary criteria, the right friends will come from wealthy and socially prominent families. Several right friends are preferred to a large number who are not regarded as right by peer standards (28, 91, 132).

As the adolescent's number of friends decreases, his circle of acquaintances widens. The adolescent will talk about classmates whom he knows only casually if he thinks this will impress others with his popularity with the right people. Like the adult, he learns the art of name-dropping and uses it to gain prestige. To be able to use it successfully, he must know enough about the peers he talks about to create the impression that they are his friends.

Qualities desired in friends

The young adolescent finds that the qualities he thought unimportant in childhood playmates are now essential in the people he wants as friends. A friend must be someone you can trust and depend on, someone you can talk to, and someone whose interests are similar to yours. In addition, friends must make a good appearance, be "nice" to people, and live close enough to be seen frequently (74, 79, 88). Figure 4-2 shows some of the important age changes in girls' values regarding friends. Changes in the desired qualities of friends begin around the junior high school age. Boys' values change in terms of emphasis on certain traits, while girls' values change in terms of totally new traits (28, 128).

Two factors account for the adolescent's revised criteria for selecting friends. The first is a *change in social needs*. In early adolescence, feelings of insecurity in social situations cause adolescents to select as friends those whose interests, values, and backgrounds are similar to theirs; such friends provide an aura of "at-homeness" which fosters feelings of security. In late adolescence, heterosexual interests cause the adolescent to seek friends who can help him make satisfactory adjustments to members of the other sex.

The second major reason for changes in values in the adolescent's selection of friends is a *desire to conform to social expectations*. The adolescent who wants to be well accepted by his peers knows that he must conform to the expectations of the group with which he wishes to be identified. Thus, he shuns those whose lack of social acceptance stems from their lack of conformity to social expectations (6, 88, 136).

Adolescents who are personally and socially insecure are more choosy in the selection of friends than those who are more secure. The insecure are afraid of group opinion. Furthermore, they want to have as friends members of their own sex who are popular enough to flatter their own egos and increase their acceptance with the peer group. But because popular adolescents generally find greater congeniality among other popular adolescents, the boy or girl who is socially insecure is usually thwarted in his attempts to form friendships with popular members of the group.

Friends of the other sex

In adolescence, there is a gradual shift toward a preference for friends of the opposite sex. The shift begins around the middle of the high school period—at about 15 or 16 years of age for girls and a year later for boys. By late adolescence it is usual and normal for an adolescent to have more friends of the opposite sex than of his own sex and to spend an increasingly large percentage of his time with them. At all ages, however, the adolescent wants friends of *both* sexes.

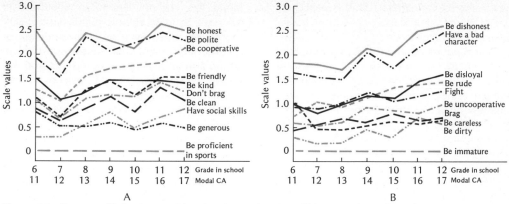

Figure 4-2 Patterns of behavior considered praiseworthy (A) and blameworthy (B) by girls of different ages in early adolescence. (Adapted from S. L. Pressey and R. G. Kuhlen: *Psychological development through the life span.* New York: Harper & Row, 1957. Used by permission.)

As boys and girls become interested in members of the opposite sex and associate with them in cliques and crowds, they form definite opinions about the qualities they expect their friends to possess. Friends of the opposite sex, because their role is that of playmate rather than chum or confidant, are selected by different criteria than are friends of the same sex.

Having no values based on personal experience of what they want in friends of the opposiste sex, but many negative attitudes of what they do not want, both boys and girls in early adolescence tend to build up values based on characters in the mass media and on adults for whom they have had romantic crushes. Most of these concepts are highly unrealistic and influenced by stereotypes of the "ideal" person. What the adolescent's ideal will be will depend on the cultural group. Typically, in America, the ideal boy is an athletic hero, and the ideal girl is one who is popular with boys (9, 28).

Girls like boys who are good-looking, masculine in build, and clean. They want boys to be honest, friendly, considerate, cooperative, good sports and good conversationalists. In fact, they like boys with the characteristics they admire in screen or fictional heroes.

Boys have definite likes and dislikes about girls they select as friends. Above all, they want them to be good-looking, feminine in appearance, and smartly dressed. They want their girl friends to have good manners and to be natural, not show-offs and gigglers. They like girls who have social skills, such as the ability to talk and dance well, who are able to plan something to do when they are out on a date, and who understand that their wallets are not necessarily bulging with wealth. They regard a studious girl as a child—one who still conforms to parental demands. They do not like girls who are too forward and aggressive or who are hypercritical of the boys' appearance, behavior, and manners. And above all else, they want girls to act their age, to be good sports when things do not go as they expected, and not to cry or make a scene in public. Thus, it is apparent that they too are thinking in terms of the ideal girl they have built up from mass media, not the typical girl (32, 106).

CHANGES IN TREATMENT OF FRIENDS

In few areas is the need for transition in social behavior greater than in the way the adolescent treats his friends. This, then, is the third major change the adolescent must make in his socialization patterns. Most adolescents treat their friends in a manner that would, at any other age, cause them to lose the friends they want so very much. This is especially true of young adolescents; it is more characteristic of girls than boys.

What accounts for the shabby way the adolescent treats his friends? *First,* adolescent friendships are very intense and emotionally charged. Since the young adolescent concentrates on a few friends, he tends to put all his "emotional eggs" in one basket and, in a bumbling way, he is trying to make sure that nothing happens to that basket.

Second, adolescents tend to idealize their friends. They put a halo on friends and expect them to behave in a manner that is often beyond their capacities.

Third, the adolescent wants his friends to make a favorable impression on others, thus enhancing his own popularity.

Fourth, the treatment of friends is greatly influenced by habits carried over from childhood when it was all right to fight, physically and verbally, to criticize, to name-call, to make derogatory comments, and to tell jokes at someone else's expense. Once such habits are developed, the responses become automatic when similar situations come up in the future. For example, adolescents are extremely critical of their friends of both sexes. While some take criticism in a good-natured manner, most resent it. Many adolescent quarrels result directly or indirectly from such "friendly" criticism.

Fifth, the degree of loyalty the adolescent feels toward his friends influences his treatment of them. Girls, for example, divulge secrets told them in confidence and may even use the information to further their own interests. They will leave a girl friend in the lurch if, at the last minute, they are asked to go on a date. Boys, by contrast, feel they can count on the loyalty of their friends, and they are sure their friends will support them if their support is needed. In general, they are less ready to entrust their personal secrets to their friends than girls are (52, 79, 87).

Stability of friendships

In childhood, stability among playmates is not of great importance because their emo-tional ties are not strong. In adolescence, however, stability among friends is necessary to provide the individual with a feeling of security and emotional satisfaction which, temporarily at least, he does not get from his family. The adolescent wants friends he can count on, who will be loyal and faithful regardless of what happens. Deprived of such friends, he usually experiences great distress.

Friendship stability varies for members of the two sexes and for all at certain times during the adolescent years. Girls' friendships are more stable than boys' friendships throughout adolescence (79, 84). Friendship fluctuations increase with the onset of pubescence—at about 13 years of age for girls and about 16 for boys. After this, fluctuations tend to decrease until the age of 18, and then begin to increase again as young people graduate from high school, go into college, jobs, or the armed services, or build up new friendships with other "young marrieds" (144, 166).

Broken friendships come from many causes. Some are due to parental pressures or to environmental factors, such as shifts of families from one neighborhood to another. Others come from the formation of cliques where one friend is accepted while the other is not. With new values, especially those relating to looks, ethnic or religious discrimination, socioeconomic status, and popularity with members of the opposite sex, former friends may be replaced by new ones. Because of the high value adolescents place on maturity of behavior, a boy or a girl who does not "act his age" is likely to find old friends dropping away (84, 122). Changes in interests are likewise responsible for broken friendships. A girl who marries and has children soon after graduation from high school will have home-oriented interests while her friend who goes into the business world will have other interests. They will drift apart and establish new friendships with persons sharing their new interests.

Friendships with members of one's own sex stabilize slightly earlier than do friendships with members of the opposite sex. This is to be expected, since friendships with members of the opposite sex are formed for the first time during the adolescent years and the adolescent has had less time to establish values for the selection of friends of the opposite sex.

CHANGES IN LEADERS

The fourth major change the adolescent must make in the socialization patterns established during the childhood years is in the choice of leaders. As the childhood gang is replaced by more mature social groups, a new kind of leader is needed. The individual who fills the social needs of a group will vary according to the adolescents who make up the group, but among both boys and girls certain characteristics of the adolescent leader are fairly universal in our culture. This subject will be discussed in detail in the next chapter.

In childhood, social contacts are mainly for play. In adolescence, the social group meets for many different kinds of activities and therefore needs many different kinds of leaders. There is no such thing as a general leadership quality (40, 54). A very bright adolescent may be chosen as leader in a group of other very bright individuals, but if placed in a group of those duller than he, he is a misfit and unlikely to be the leader. Only when the activity of the group requires the use of his superior intelligence will he be chosen as leader.

To the adolescent, the leader is his representative. Consequently, he wants a leader who will represent him well and add prestige to the group as a whole. A person who makes a good appearance, who has social know-how, and who impresses others with his abilities and self-confidence can be counted on to make a good impression on others. Just as adolescents want to select their own friends and resent adult interference, so do they want to select their own leaders. Even if they make mistakes, as they do in the choice of their friends, they demand the right to make the choice and bitterly resent having a leader selected by others imposed on them (98, 145).

In childhood, the leader is always of the same sex as the members of the gang. In adolescence, when the group is composed of members of both sexes, boys are the leaders.

Only minor leadership roles, such as secretary of the class or chairman of one of the minor committees, are usually entrusted to girls.

CHANGES IN SOCIAL ATTITUDES AND BEHAVIOR

The fifth major change in the transition to adult socialization is in the area of attitudes and behavior. The age of sexual maturing largely determines *when* changes in social attitudes and behavior will occur. Adolescents who mature earlier or later than the average also begin to show changes in attitudes and behavior earlier or later. An early-maturing girl, for example, is interested in boys sooner than her age-mates (32, 78).

Social pressures largely determine the *form* of changed attitudes and behavior. These pressures come mainly from the peer group. To guarantee acceptance by peer-group members, the adolescent tries to change his attitudes and behavior so that they will conform to the standards accepted by the group with which he wants to be identified. If the group is interested in heterosexual social activities, for example, he will develop an interest in members of the other sex and participate in activities with them. Clinging to the old childhood antagonisms, he soon discovers, will lead to social rejection (159).

As a direct result of the changed interests and attitudes that accompany sexual maturing, social behavior during the adolescent years takes on a quite different pattern. Some aspects of the pattern appear in a rudimentary form in late childhood. The adolescent social behavior pattern is marked by heterosexual activities, conformity to the group, self-assertiveness, resistance to adult authority, the desire to help others, prejudice, and social competency.

Heterosexual activities

The most marked change in social behavior is in the area of heterosexual relationships. The adolescent forgets the childhood antagonism between the sexes and develops a lively interest in members of the other sex. For

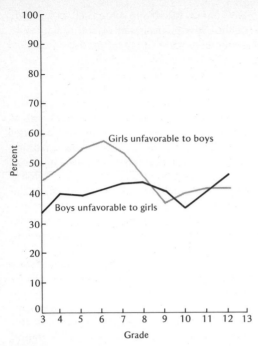

Figure 4-3 Attitude changes toward members of the opposite sex during the early adolescent years. (Adapted from D. B. Harris and S. C. Tseng: Children's attitudes toward peers and parents as revealed by sentence completions. *Child Develpm.,* 1957, **28,** 401–411. Used by permission.)

girls, this comes early in adolescence. For boys, it appears a year or so later, owing to the later sexual maturing of boys (82, 159). See Figure 4-3. Heterosexual relationships and behavior will be discussed at length in Chapter 13.

Conformity to the group

Conformity takes two forms: acquiescence and conventionality. *Acquiescence* means agreement with expressed group opinions in situations involving pressure; the individual shifts to group opinion when his own is different. *Conventionality* means concurrence with the mores and social practices of the individual's culture or subculture. Acquiescence and conventionality generally go hand in hand (116, 170).

Conformity does not begin in adolescence; children are highly sensitive to group opinions and try to conform to the beliefs and behavior of the peer group. But conformity becomes stronger in adolescence. At that time, the opinions of others, especially of one's own age group, are of immense importance (52, 65).

The adolescent does not conform to *all* members of the peer group. He conforms to those who have power in the group and are looked upon as group leaders. Conformity is greatest in early adolescence. The older adolescent shows greater stability and security and the need for group approval is lessened (17, 92, 107). In adolescents whose sexual maturing deviates from that of the group, the pattern may be different. The slow maturer, for example, is not as strongly motivated to conform as his more mature age-mates. As a result, he may be considered different or "queer" (52, 77).

Conformity to the group is more often expressed in behavioral changes than in opinion changes. In manner of dress and in fads, the adolescent follows the crowd. The group ideals, standards, principles, and sometimes even moral concepts become, at least ostensibly, those of each member of the group. Loyalty to the group is shown in the use of language approved by the group, whether it be normal speech, slang, or swearing, and in show-off behavior used by other members of the group (60, 96).

Because of the apparent willingness of adolescents to conform to group values and standards, many adults regard adolescent conformity with alarm; they fear that the adolescent will follow the group wherever it leads and get into trouble. However, as Josselyn has stressed, "What should be of concern is the type of peer group to which he is conforming" because this affects his solution to his social problems (80).

While conformity, within reasonable limits and in degrees appropriate for the adolescent's age and level of development, is an asset to socialization, over- or underconformity is a handicap. In Box 4-6 are given the important influences of different degrees of conformity on socialization during the adolescent years (17, 22, 60, 92, 154).

Self-assertiveness

As the adolescent develops greater self-confidence toward the middle of adolescence, he wants *both* approval and attention. In his desire to become an individual in his own right while, at the same time, achieving status in the group, he discovers that he must call the attention of the group to himself.

To achieve this end the adolescent wears clothing of extreme styles or conspicuous colors, tells off-color jokes, speaks in an authoritative fashion about any and every subject, uses erudite words, and imitates the tone of voice and pronunciation of, say, his favorite TV character (9, 12, 171). Early attempts at self-assertiveness are frequently crude and clownish. Gradually the adolescent learns what is acceptable and what is not. In time crude showing off gives way to more subtle forms of behavior.

Resistance to adult authority

One of the most common ways adolescents assert themselves is through resistance to adult authority. This is not new in adolescence, but is more pronounced than during childhood. While adolescents have an increasing tendency, with age, to challenge authority figures, this tendency generally reaches a peak between the tenth and twelfth grades. After that, it begins to wane, because adults' attitudes and restrictions become less stringent. When parents and teachers realize, as was pointed out in Chapter 1, that the adolescent is approaching adulthood, they usually treat him more like an adult than they did earlier. Consequently, he has less need to challenge authority.

Not only do adolescents challenge home and school authority but they also challenge legal authority—laws and law-enforcement officers. This is more true of boys than of girls (171). The trends in challenging home, school, and legal authority are shown in Figure 4-4.

In the home and school the adolescent girl is surrounded by more restrictions than the boy. Although girls rebel less than boys, they do not placidly accept adult authority. They

---

**BOX 4-6   EFFECTS OF DIFFERENT DEGREES OF CONFORMITY
ON SOCIALIZATION**

Developmentally Appropriate Conformity
Conformity appropriate for the adolescent's age and level of development provides him with a feeling of security and belonging. It aids his acceptance by peers of both sexes and gives him a source of stability. Conformity in appearance and behavior is almost a prerequisite for group acceptance. Conformity in opinions, unless they are verbalized, is not so strictly enforced.

Lack of Conformity
Lack of conformity leads to social neglect or rejection, depending on its visibility. Adolescents can disagree with group values—provided they do not express their opinions—without risking their status, but those who are not reasonably conventional in appearance and behavior are unlikely to gain acceptance. Lack of conformity is less damaging to leaders' acceptance than to followers'.

Overconformity
The adolescent who overconforms loses his identity as a person and, with it, the respect of the peer group. He is in a constant state of anxiety for fear that he will do or say the wrong thing. As a result, he depends on someone else to tell him what his opinions and behavior should be. He often develops a punitive attitude toward those who show individuality, and this lowers his chances of acceptance.

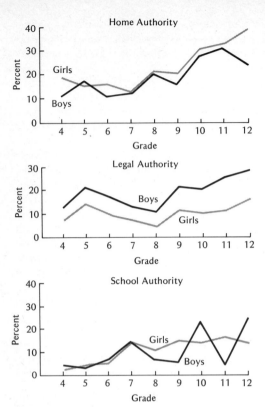

Home Authority

Legal Authority

School Authority

Figure 4-4 Trends in challenging adult authority by boys and girls during early adolescence. (Adapted from S. L. Witryol and J. E. Calkins: Marginal social values of rural school children. *J. genet. Psychol.*, 1958, **92**, 81–93. Used by permission.)

make a contribution to the group themselves. In addition, they learn in school that society expects them to make a contribution, such as doing their share of classroom chores, helping to raise money for a cause by participating in bazaars or collecting "Dollars for Scholars," or doing good in the community through the Scouts. In their classes, especially social studies, emphasis is placed on service to others. By adolescence, most have become other-oriented.

As a result of this shift in attitude, the young adolescent is actively, not passively, interested in the affairs of others. He wants to help them to solve their problems. Emotional outlets and feelings of superiority and security are the chief sources of satisfaction in helping others. Typically, these feelings are weak in adolescents. Therefore, to compensate, they direct their efforts to aiding others. In this way they bolster their self-confidence and gain the feeling of self-importance they crave. As adolescence progresses and feelings of security and self-confidence become stronger, the desire to help others is likely to decrease or to be expressed in critical or derisive remarks.

Prejudice and discrimination

Social discrimination, snobbishness, or "prejudice," as it is generally called, is a social attitude organized and structured in a definable and consistent way; it is an attitude which causes, supports, or justifies discrimination. This attitude is composed of three elements. *First,* there are beliefs, often based on stereotypes, that anyone who does not belong to one's own group or who is different in any way is inferior, while the members of one's group are more important and, thus, superior. *Second,* there is an emotional accompaniment that ranges from indifference to bitter and violent hostility. And *third,* there are beliefs about the appropriate treatment of those regarded as "inferior" (2, 4, 30, 76).

What is regarded as "appropriate threatment" varies. The most common form is withdrawing from members of the group against which there is prejudice, using unfavorable

merely express their resentment against the restrictions in a less aggressive manner (1, 93).

Since resistance to adult authority is so widespread, its forms of expression, together with an explanation of its causes and the reason it has become a major youth problem, will be discussed in detail in Chapter 6.

Helping others

For the most part, young children are self-bound; they expect others to do things for them and to gratify their every wish. Their experience in gang life in late childhood, however, teaches them that, if they want to be accepted members of the gang, they must terms to characterize them, or excluding them from groups and organizations made up of individuals against whom there is no prejudice.

Prejudice is directed against groups that hold a minority position in a given culture. A "minority group" is a subgroup in a larger society that is subjected to discrimination at the hands of another subgroup, the "majority." The terms minority and majority do not have numerical connotations, but are differentiated by control of the economic, political, and ideological mechanisms of the social stratification, stemming from special cultural or physical features, such as race, religion, sex, age, socioeconomic status, occupation, or degree of education. The majority group, even though it may be numerically smaller than the minority, has the power to keep the minority group from achieving comparable social, political and economic status (19, 117, 164).

Origins of prejudice Most prejudice in adolescence is a carry-over from the early years of childhood. The early attitudes of prejudice are strengthened, however, between the ages of 12 and 16. It has been estimated that only about 25 percent of all prejudice develops for the first time after the person reaches 16. At that age, prejudice developed earlier may start to wane but it often becomes stronger (2, 4, 103).

Prejudice is a product of learning. This learning may be in the form of conditioning; the adolescent develops a dislike for a member of a specific group because of some unpleasant experience with him. In time, his conditioned dislike for that individual may spread to all members of his group. Or, prejudice may come from imitation; the adolescent imitates the attitudes and behavior of a person or a group he admires.

Psychological studies of prejudice show that the roots of prejudice go back to early home experiences; the foundations of prejudice are thus homegrown. While most parents *do not intentionally* build up prejudices against people of other groups, it is not un-

common for them to use hostile descriptions and stereotypes in explaining racial, religious, and other differences to their children (30, 169).

Even without direct teaching, the individual will imitate the attitudes and behavior patterns of those whom he admires. The young child admires his parents, and so he will imitate them. Later, he will imitate members of the peer group, and still later, members of the larger social group with which he is identified. If it is "correct" to view and to treat those who do not belong to his group as inferior, he will learn to conform to social expectations and be prejudiced in his attitudes and behavior. *Social contagion* thus intensifies the prejudices established in the home.

No one factor is responsible for the direction of the intensity of prejudice in adolescence. In Box 4-7 are given some of the factors that are responsible (10, 21, 42, 51, 118, 165).

Effects of prejudice The psychological scars of prejudice are intensified in adolescence as prejudice becomes stronger. Prejudice makes the adolescent sensitive to physical and psychological characteristics and names that are part of the stereotype of the group against which he is prejudiced. In his mind, he often magnifies the pejorative aspects of the stereotype.

The scars of prejudice are not limited to adolescents against whom prejudice is directed. They are found also in the personality patterns of adolescents who are prejudiced; but here they are different. *Adolescents who are prejudiced* show it in rude and ruthless denunciations of those whom they consider their "inferiors." They are *intentionally* rude because it gives them personal satisfaction and a feeling of superiority. Even though they may feel guilty about the way they treat members of minority groups, they rationalize and use other defense mechanisms to avoid recognizing the injustice of their behavior. This interferes with the development of healthy attitudes toward self and others and, in time, may result in personality maladjustments.

BOX 4-7   FACTORS INFLUENCING PREJUDICE

*Parents
How great an influence parents have on adolescent prejudice depends—among other things—on the emotional warmth between the adolescent and his parents and on the prestige the parents have, owing to their education, occupation, and community status.

*Sex
Girls, as a group, are less prejudiced than boys and they show their prejudices in a less aggressive way, mainly by ignoring those against whom they are prejudiced.

*Social Proximity
Social proximity may lessen or increase prejudice, depending on the quality of the associations. In general, it is lessened when there is a similarity of interests, values, and education.

*Religion
Adolescents with strong religious interests tend to be less tolerant toward members of minority groups than those whose religious interests are weak or nonexistent.

*Personality
The typical personality syndrome of the prejudiced adolescent, characterized by poor self-acceptance due to feelings of inadequacy and antisocial attitudes, predisposes him to prejudice by making him more willing to accept cultural stereotypes and attitudes that lead to prejudice.

*Cultural Influences
Much prejudice comes from social contagion—acceptance of the prevalent attitude because of a belief that this will win group approval.

*Stereotyping
Since stereotypes are usually unfavorable, they intensify prejudice which originated in other sources, rather than giving rise to it directly.

The effect of prejudice on the *adolescent against whom there is prejudice* is equally damaging. Having been the object of discrimination since early childhood, the person has many unfavorable attitudes toward himself and toward members of the majority group when he reaches adolescence. Allport (2) describes how the foundations of such unfavorable attitudes are established:

A child who finds himself rejected and attacked on all sides is not likely to develop dignity and poise as his outstanding traits. On the contrary, he develops defenses. Like a dwarf in a world of menacing giants, he cannot fight on equal terms. He is forced to listen to their derision and laughter and submit to their abuse. There are a great many things such a dwarf-child may do, all of them serving his ego defenses.

The adolescent develops ways of expressing his resentment toward those who discriminate against him. He shows little interest in establishing friendly relationships with others, even when they try to make him feel that he is wanted; he may even be suspicious of their motives. When he is large enough to feel that he has an even chance to win in a fight, he may express his resentment by aggressive attacks on those who have discriminated against him or on others of their group.

His rebellion, whether expressed or controlled, is usually accompanied by derogation of the group that has discriminated against him and of his own group as well. He feels ashamed of belonging to his group and may try to deny his membership by changing his name, his religion, or any feature, such as shape of nose or texture of hair, that identifies him with that group. Rejection of his group membership usually leads to self-rejection; he comes to dislike himself just as he dislikes the group with which he is identified.

Combating prejudice Many attempts have been made to combat prejudice. Some have been successful but most, unfortunately, have met with failure or only partial success. It has been found, for example, that prejudiced attitudes can be changed more successfully through discussion than through mere exposure to persuasive forms of communication. From discussions with teachers and peers, the adolescent gets a new perspective on the group toward which he was prejudiced (108).

Even more effective in changing attitudes are *interpersonal relationships*. When, for example, black and white students work together in classes in high school or college, there is less prejudice than when they work separately (127). When prejudiced adolescents visit the homes of adolescents against whom there is prejudice, more favorable attitudes on both sides have been reported (11, 157).

Some attitudes are resistant to change, and some change for the worse, especially when contact is *involuntary*. Just being thrown together in the same classroom or on the same athletic team does not necessarily change anyone's attitudes. Whether there will be a decrease in prejudice and an increase in pleasant social interaction will depend partly on the strength of the original attitudes and partly on how pleasurable the interaction between various group members proves to be.

Attitudes tend to become more stable as the adolescent grows older. This suggests that if prejudice is to be combated successfully, the effort must be begun early, even before elementary school life begins. It must be continued during the high school years and during college or the after-school work career (21, 169).

Since the roots of prejudice are in the home, Glad has facetiously suggested that we "abolish the home" (53). Even though adolescents rebel against their parents' attitudes and values, they are still influenced by them. Similarly, even though the adolescent becomes less subject to peer influences as he grows older, there is no time when he is not influenced by them to some degree. When it is the thing to do to discriminate against members of a minority group, therefore, the adolescent will follow the pattern set by the peer group. If prejudice is to be combated successfully, it must be made "unpopular" rather than "fashionable."

How can prejudice be made unpopular? There are no conclusive answers. However, attempts are presently being made to overturn the prevailing stereotypes of different minority groups, such as women, old people, and members of various religious and racial groups, by depicting them in a more favorable light in the mass media, especially in comics, in textbooks, and on the moving-picture and television screens. It is also hoped that adolescents who spend their summer vacations traveling around this country and foreign countries will develop a "world-mindedness" that will encourage them to recognize that differences do not mean inferiorities. This would go a long way toward breaking down some of the prevailing prejudices.

The toughest problem of all in combating prejudice is how to change the prejudiced attitudes of adolescents when these attitudes are closely interrelated with their personality patterns. The first line of attack must center on helping the adolescent gain greater *self-insight,* rather than merely an objective or intellectual insight into the nature of the problem (although that, too, is necessary). In addition, since perception of self precedes perception of others, this means that, if the attitudes of prejudice are to be changed, the adolescent must *accept himself.* Self-acceptance is largely dependent on social acceptance. It is hard for an adolescent to be self-acceptant if he knows that he is not accepted by others. Unfortunately, not all adolescents enjoy the social security that comes from acceptance. Combating prejudice, then, is closely associated with the problem of improving social acceptance. If the adolescent's social acceptance can be improved, his prejudices can be weakened and perhaps uprooted.

Social competency

"Social competency" means a facility in dealing with people and social situations. To be socially competent, the adolescent must know the approved patterns of behavior in different social situations and how to carry them out. As social horizons broaden, new demands are made on the individual. In situations involving peers of both sexes, for example, the adolescent discovers that social acceptance depends partly upon the possession of social skills and interests appropriate for his age and sex group. Adolescents who are superior to their age-mates in such social skills as dancing, conversing, playing cards, or playing a musical instrument have a much better chance of acceptance than those who lack these skills (14).

Boys, as early as the fourth grade, feel more inadequate in social situations than girls. Boys typically rebel against learning *any* social skill for fear of being labeled sissies (52). By adolescence, the gap between the sexes in social competency is wider than it was in childhood.

Most young adolescents are aware of their lack of social skills and are ill at ease in social gatherings. Temporarily, they may withdraw from social situations in fear of the embarrassment that will come from doing the wrong thing. As Strang has observed, "Part of the unnecessary adolescent 'storm and stress' is doubtless due to a lack of the knowledge of the approved behavior in certain social situations" (150).

How social skills are learned Social skills are learned gradually from experience in all kinds of social situations and from practice over a long period. To develop social competency, the adolescent needs, *first,* guidance in the home and school, and *second,* opportunities to use what he has learned. Individuals from the higher socioeconomic groups usually have guidance in their homes to learn what is accepted by the cultural group as correct, while those from the lower socioeconomic groups generally grow up in homes where such guidance is meager (59).

Even when the motivation to learn social skills is strong, the adolescent may run into difficulties when he discovers that there is no universally accepted pattern of such skills. While certain social skills are universally approved, such as the ability to carry on a conversation with people of different ages and interests, others vary from one community or subgroup to another. Ice skating may be an important social skill in one community while folk dancing may be more important in another (120).

Just knowing what to do is not enough. The adolescent must have *opportunities* to put what he knows into practice. Most schools today have extracurricular organizations that offer students opportunities to develop social skills. Unfortunately, many adolescents who lack social skills do not join these organizations. As a result they cut themselves off from the opportunities the organizations offer. This is especially true of adolescents from the lower socioeconomic groups, many of whom, as was pointed out earlier, feel unwanted and rejected in the extracurricular activities of the school or in the social activities of community organizations.

Even more complicated are the problems

stemming from variations in age of sexual maturity. One of the advantages of early maturing is that the individual learns, ahead of his age-mates, the adult-approved social skills. Consequently, he seems more sophisticated, more poised, and more at ease than they (28, 77).

Role of social competency in socialization
Social competency plays so important a role in the kind of social adjustment the adolescent makes that it often compensates for unsocial or even antisocial behavior. A boy with charming manners, for example, will be popular with girls even if he is uncooperative and egocentric. Similarly, a girl who is socially sophisticated will find ready acceptance among boys who, age for age, are less competent in social skills because they know they can count on her to do the right thing at the right time and to keep the conversation rolling. Popularity with members of the opposite sex leads to prestige with members of one's own sex; thus, social competency affects the kind of social relationships the adolescent has with members of both sexes.

Social competency gives the adolescent poise and self-confidence—traits that are of great value in any social situation. These traits, added to the good impression he makes because of his social skills, will go far toward assuring his social approval irrespective of any undesirable traits he may have.

It is apparent, then, that social competency is important enough in the socialization of an adolescent to devote more time and effort to its development than is usually done. Many adolescents recognize this and try to improve themselves by reading books on etiquette, watching and listening to peers who have the reputation of being popular and sophisticated, and studying socially approved patterns of behavior as they are depicted on the screen.

From a practical angle, knowledge of the role played by social competency leads to two positive suggestions: *first,* the earlier the child learns social skills and practices them until they become habitual, the more poised and self-confident he will be when he reaches

adolescence; and *second,* if bad manners can be made unfashionable in childhood, especially among boys, one of the serious obstacles to social acceptance can be removed. While social competency alone will not guarantee acceptance, it goes a long way toward doing so.

HIGHLIGHTS OF CHAPTER 4

1. Socialization, which means learning to behave in accordance with social expectations, is judged objectively in terms of the individual's behavior and subjectively in terms of his feelings and attitudes.

2. An unsocial person fails to conform to social expectations, owing to ignorance of these expectations, while an antisocial person's lack of conformity is due to his lack of desire to conform.

3. Every cultural and subcultural group sets up its own standards and guidelines to help the adolescent make the transition to adult-appropriate social attitudes and behavior.

4. A number of conditions make the transition to adult-appropriate behavior difficult for the adolescent. The most common are poor foundations; lack of guidance, suitable models to imitate, opportunities for social contacts, and motivation; different social expectations; and the necessity of adjusting to new social groups.

5. The time needed to make the transition to adult-appropriate behavior is long owing to the fact that the adolescent must change the whole social structure of his life. This involves changes in social groups with which he is identified, in kinds of friends, in treatment of friends, in the kinds of leaders he selects, and in his social attitudes and behavior.

6. The social groupings of adolescence include chums, cliques, crowds, formally organized groups, and gangs, each of which serves certain needs in the adolescent's life and contributes to his socialization process.

7. Marked changes in the adolescent's attitudes toward his friends are reflected in his desire to choose his own friends, in the number of friends wanted, in the qualities wanted in friends, and in the desire to have friends of the other sex as well as of his own.

8. The way young adolescents treat their friends

contributes to the breakup of many adolescent friendships. This is especially true of friends of the other sex. Improvement in the treatment of friends occurs as adolescence progresses.

9. Stability of friendships is important to adolescents because it provides them with feelings of security and sources of emotional satisfaction.

10. Since adolescent leaders represent their groups in the eyes of others, adolescents want leaders who will add to the prestige of the group.

11. The age at which the adolescent matures sexually is important in determining when changes in social attitudes and behavior will occur.

12. As a result of changed interests and attitudes that accompany sexual maturing, certain kinds of social behavior develop in adolescence, most of which appeared in childhood in less developed forms. The most common of these patterns of behavior include interest in heterosexual activities; marked conformity to peer-group ideals, standards, principles, and behavior patterns; a strong desire for social approval and attention; resistance to adult authority; a desire to help others; prejudice and discrimination; and social competency, or a facility in dealing with people and social situations.

Chapter 5

Social Status

Few experiences are more ego-deflating to an adolescent than being neglected or rejected by his peers and few are more ego-inflating than being accepted or chosen as their leader. Social status—the position one holds in the group—is determined by the degree of one's acceptance by the group members. This is the yardstick by which the adolescent measures himself. Here is how Friedenberg (55) explains the adolescents' reliance on group approval:

Adolescents lack reserves of self-esteem to sustain them under humiliating conditions. . . . [They] are dreadfully concerned about society's appraisal of them and of their worth. . . . They cannot easily assimilate an attack on their dignity or worth, for it produces not merely resentment but intense anxiety. The self is threatened while still ill-defined and in its early stages of construction.

Other people, likewise, evaluate the adolescent by his social status. Their yardstick is the number of friends he has, the status of his friends, and his position as leader or follower in the group. These measures provide evidence of the kind of social adjustment he has made. If he can claim a large number of friends, if he is identified with the "right" crowd, and if he is often chosen as a leader, he is regarded as a "socially well-adjusted person."

As was stressed in Chapter 4, however, an evaluation of adjustment must also take into account the personal satisfaction the adolescent receives from his status. An adolescent may be popular and have a wide circle of friends and acquaintances, but he might prefer to belong to a clique composed of the "big wheels" of the school. He may hold a minor leadership role but prefer a more prestigious role. So long as he is not satisfied, he cannot be considered well adjusted.

In general, there is a close relationship between social status and social adjustment. In fact, there is a close relationship between social acceptance, social status, *and* social activities. The adolescent who is socially well adjusted has high social status and this leads to more than average social activity. The poorly adjusted adolescent has low social status, gains little satisfaction from social activities, and withdraws from them.

The status the adolescent has in the peer group can be measured by two criteria: *first,* the degree of his acceptance by the group and, *second,* the role he plays in that group, whether leader or follower. These two criteria will be discussed in detail in the folowing pages.

MEANING OF SOCIAL ACCEPTANCE

"Social acceptance" means the extent to which a person's company is regarded as rewarding to others in intimate face-to-face relationships. Since the person gives pleasure to others, they accept him, but only to the extent that his companionship is rewarding and positively reinforcing to them.

By contrast, "popularity," in its strictest sense, emphasizes respect and admiration by others. It does not necessarily imply intimate relationships. Naegele highlights the difference between popularity and social acceptance: The respected are "chosen for office, rather than invited to parties" (117). Qualities associated with popularity are not necessarily associated with social acceptance. Studiousness, which usually leads to high marks, may be admired and respected but it does not necessarily make a person a pleasant, rewarding companion.

Since great prestige is associated with a high level of social acceptance in our culture, the American adolescent judges himself and others judge him by the quality and quantity of his friends. In many other cultures, social acceptance is not so important a measure of prestige and adolescents are not greatly disturbed by a low level of acceptance (10, 152). In such cultures, prestige may be closely associated with other factors, such as level of education or family status.

Social expectations and social acceptance

Social acceptance can be achieved only when the adolescent conforms to the expectations of the group with which he wants to be identified. These expectations are based on what the group has found makes people easiest and pleasantest to be with. Since the traits the adolescent likes best in himself are those which conform most closely to the ideals of his group, he most readily accepts as a friend another adolescent who possesses these traits. The traits he dislikes most in himself are generally those the group disapproves. Consequently, he is most likely to reject as a friend anyone who possesses those traits.

If all groups within a culture held the same values, it would not be too difficult for an individual to learn to conform to those values and thus guarantee his acceptance. However, different groups within culture have different values and expectations (13, 124, 139) A girl, for example, may realize that her chances of acceptance in a particular group would be greatly increased if her family background were different. She may try to "reform" her parents, her home, and her siblings. But she is not likely to gain acceptance if the group considers her background "inferior." On the other hand, in a group where most of the members have backgrounds similar to hers, she might win wide acceptance and have a large circle of friends.

The values of various groups in a school are markedly influenced by the kind of school it is. When the goals of the school are highly social, as in a small "finishing school," all groups are likely to place high value on personality, social skills, and socioeconomic status; when the goals are less social, as in an academically oriented school, all groups are likely to place more emphasis on what each adolescent can contribute to the school's activities (31).

Degrees of social acceptance

The continuum of social acceptance ranges from those who are accepted by most of their peers to those who are accepted by very few. Almost none are unanimously accepted or completely isolated. Evidence suggesting that more adolescents fall below average in social acceptance will be discussed later in the chapter. Box 5-1 defines various levels of social acceptance (30, 71, 76, 101, 117).

Most adolescents are able to judge the degree of social acceptance they and others have achieved. This "sociempathic ability" improves with age (6). It comes partly from psychological maturation and partly from learning in a given culture. The greatest gain in ability to perceive the status of others comes between the seventh and eleventh grades. The greatest gain in ability to perceive one's own status comes between the eleventh and twelfth grades (7, 8). Not all adolescents, however, are aware of the degree of acceptance they enjoy. The stars and the isolates are, on the whole, the least aware of how others feel about them. Both groups have so few close friends that they have no way of really knowing how their peers feel. Reasonably well-accepted adolescents have more frequent peer contacts and can better estimate the opinions of others than those who are only marginally accepted (39, 45, 66).

Both boys and girls, but boys especially, tend to overestimate their acceptance. Boys are more accurate, however, in estimating their acceptance by members of the other sex, while girls are more accurate in estimating their acceptance by members of their own sex (8, 17).

Very bright adolescents tend to underestimate their acceptance, and the dull tend to overestimate (100). The more satisfaction the adolescent derives from social contacts, the more accurately he can judge how others feel about him. Awareness of degree of acceptance is better among well-adjusted than among poorly adjusted adolescents (42, 103).

How the adolescent knows what others think of him is not a matter of chance or intuition. Instead, there are many indications from the behavior and speech of others to tell him how he rates with them. Box 5-2 lists the most important of these indicators (84, 102, 114, 153).

FACTORS INFLUENCING SOCIAL ACCEPTANCE

No one trait can ensure the adolescent's social acceptance. Rather, a constellation of traits contributes to behavior patterns that make the adolescent fun to be with and cause peers to judge him as loyal and cooperative.

The relative importance of the different traits that make up the social-acceptance constellation varies from group to group. To be acceptable in one group, a girl must be interested in dating and attractive enough to be popular with boys. In another group, being an outstanding athlete or a good student is more important.

In addition, some factors play a more dominant role in social acceptance among boys than among girls. To be accepted by the leading crowd in high school, Coleman has reported, boys must, above everything else, be good athletes. They must also be socially active, play a leadership role in some activities, and make good grades. For girls, having nice clothes and coming from the "right" family top the list. Being an athlete or making good grades is far less important (30). Lack-

ing such qualities, the adolescent will gain some acceptance, but in crowds that are less prestigious. If he is to make the leading crowd, he must conform—at least outwardly—to its values. Coleman (30) outlines what these values are:

The leading crowd seems to be defined primarily in terms of social success; their personality, clothes, desirability as dates, and—in communities where social success is tied closely to family background—their money and family.

A survey of some of the most important traits in the social-acceptance constellation will show what role each plays among American adolescents.

First impressions

The status of the individual depends partly upon his actual behavior and partly on the mental picture others have of him. It depends to a large extent upon first impressions. If an adolescent is shy, he will create quite a different image from one who is socially at ease. The first will be considered cold and aloof, and the second warm, sympathetic, or friendly (49).

When older adolescents go away to college or professional training schools, to work, or into the armed services, they are often associated with complete strangers for the first time since they started school. First impressions play an important role in determining how they will be accepted. Knowing how members of the new group react also influences their later behavior.

Attractiveness of appearance

Since a person is judged by the impression he makes on others, an attractive appearance aids social acceptance. Appearance affects the person himself as well as others. An adolescent who is dissatisfied with his appearance worries about the effect it will have on social interactions. He becomes self-bound—preoccupied with self—and in time this leads to feelings of inadequacy and unsocial behavior (133, 157).

For boys as well as girls, being attractive is not enough; they must also be sex appropriate in appearance. A masculine-looking boy, for example, has a better chance of acceptance by members of both sexes than an effeminate-looking boy who is a better student and better groomed. Similarly, a girl who creates the impression of being "masculine" will not be so acceptable to members of either sex as a "feminine" girl (133, 157). An attractive appearance is especially important to girls' social acceptance. Popular girls spend more time on their clothes and grooming than do less well-accepted girls (156, 157).

Even before they reach adolescence, most boys and girls discover that clothing is a highly visible insignia of social belonging. If they dress like their peers, it suggests that they belong to the peer group. By adolescence, they discover the camouflage and enhancement values of clothes and recognize their usefulness in covering up or accentuating certain features.

Reputation

The reputation an adolescent acquires is due partly to his behavior and partly to the image he creates in the minds of others. In time, a person's reputation becomes a "halo": Once it has been established, it sticks. An adolescent who acquires an unfavorable reputation finds it difficult if not impossible to live it down. A favorable reputation, by contrast, enables an adolescent to do many things which would be severely criticized in one who was viewed less favorably (117, 125).

Some adolescent boys try to improve their reputations by doing daring things or defying the law—acts which in childhood earned them prestige. But they quickly discover that peer values have changed. Instead of winning favor, such behavior is more likely to lead to

---

BOX 5-2   CUES TO RECOGNITION OF SOCIAL ACCEPTANCE

Treatment by Others
The accepted adolescent is in demand for social activities and can count on the loyalty of his friends. The poorly accepted is made to feel unwanted and unappreciated.

Names and Nicknames
Adolescents called by their formal baptismal names usually enjoy less acceptance than those called by friendly, nondisparaging nicknames.

Designations of Levels of Acceptance
Such labels as "pig," "drag," or "big wheel" tell the adolescent how well accepted he is.

Comments by Peers
Face-to-face confrontations and gossip columns in school and college newspapers give the adolescent a good idea of whether he is well accepted or not.

the reputation of being "bad," "wild," or "delinquent" (61, 84). Doing things that conform to peer values will result in a favorable reputation and, in turn, greater social acceptance.

Behavior that contributes to a favorable reputation differs for members of the two sexes and for adolescents of different socioeconomic backgrounds. Girls, for example, cannot be "too free" with boys if they want to be accepted. But boys who "make conquests" gain prestige in the eyes of their peers. The upper-class boy who has the reputation of being a "gentleman" because of his social skills gains greater acceptance than a boy who has the reputation of being a "slob." A boy from the lower socioeconomic group, by contrast, would be rejected as a sissy if he had exceptionally good manners while one who scorned social skills would be regarded as "masculine" (46, 124).

Social participation

Other factors being equal, the more socially active the adolescent, the better he is known to members of the peer group and the better his chances of acceptance. At both the high school and college levels, accepted adolescents play a much more active role in extracurricular activities of all sorts than do those whose acceptance is lower.

Poorly accepted adolescents do not play regularly on teams, they go to few school parties, and they participate in few extracurricular activities of the school. Their outside activities are often limited to reading for pleasure, listening to the radio, watching television, or going to the movies, usually alone. They rarely serve on school or college committees, and they are never elected to school or college offices (44, 117).

Social participation and acceptance are closely interrelated because the involved adolescent not only makes himself known by his activities but also develops poise and confidence. Thus, he feels free to contribute what he can to the group rather than withdrawing into himself, as characteristically

happens when an adolescent feels the "slap of rejection" (48, 84).

Conversational ability

The quality as well as the quantity of an adolescent's conversation affects his social acceptance. The well-accepted adolescent is almost universally described by his peers as "talkative" or as having a "sense of humor." In any social situation, he seems poised and at ease, never at a loss to know what to say or how to say it. Making a contribution to the group and helping to keep the conversation lively adds to his acceptance. Recognizing this, he feels secure enough in his status to talk without inhibitions. The well-accepted adolescent likes to laugh and joke, thus adding to the enjoyment of others and incidentally increasing his acceptance.

The poorly accepted adolescent, by contrast, adds little to the conversation or the enjoyment of the group. Since he does not joke, he is said to have no sense of humor. Often he is too insecure to enter into the situation and laugh with the group (36, 52).

The quality of the adolescent's conversation is also related to his social acceptance. The adolescent who criticizes his peers and makes derogatory remarks, who complains about trivialities, or who boasts or tells jokes that embarrass others can quickly undermine any favorable impression that his appearance or his participation in group activities might have created (91, 93).

Wit is a two-edged sword. It can win acceptance or rejection. Humorous stories and jokes, especially when focused on the teller —the subjective comic—increase the adolescent's chances of acceptance. Stories and jokes that ridicule others—the objective comic —that are told in a sarcastic or vindictive way or are salacious in content tend to antagonize the hearers (36, 65).

Health

Most popular adolescents appear to be in good health. They are peppy, enthusiastic, and willing to do their share in cooperative activities. The adolescent who is in poor health, especially during the puberty phase, either shuns social activities completely or plays a passive role. Should poor health continue beyond puberty, he will feel like participating in so few peer activities that he will achieve only marginal status in the group; more likely, he will be neglected or rejected (61, 159).

A physical handicap that makes social participation difficult or impossible, such as blindness or lameness, militates against social acceptance. Even though members of the peer group may sympathize with their handicapped classmate, they seldom go out of their way to include in their activities one who cannot carry his share of the load. Furthermore, most handicapped adolescents develop unfavorable self-concepts. These are reflected in attitudes of self-pity or martyrdom and are expressed in behavior which leads to neglect or rejection (35).

Proximity to group

During childhood, children usually select their friends from their immediate neighborhoods because of the transportation problem. By adolescence, transportation presents less of an obstacle, and adolescents select their friends on bases other than proximity. Still, those who live close to the group will be able to participate in more activities than those who are physically isolated.

With the growth of the suburbs, consolidated schools have largely replaced neighborhood schools. Most students in suburban areas must, then, be transported to school by bus or car. Recognizing this as a problem to socialization, schools try to schedule extracurricular activities at times when transported students can take part in them. Being transported, per se, does not therefore have much influence on a student's opportunity to participate in school activities. Consequently, it is safe to say that acceptance depends mostly on the characteristics of the adolescent himself, not on where he lives (40, 47).

This point of view was stressed by Newcomb when he said that "propinquity is a facilitator but not a sufficient condition to develop a positive interaction" (120).

Length of acquaintance

How long an adolescent has known his contemporaries may be advantageous to acceptance or not. It depends on what sort of person he is. When the adolescent enters a group, he establishes his status in the group in a relatively short time. This status then tends to remain constant unless unusual circumstances occur to change it.

Increased length of acquaintance is not likely to improve the acceptance of two kinds of adolescents: those who create unfavorable first impressions and those whose behavior is out of line with group standards. By contrast, social isolates have a good chance of improving their acceptance as the group becomes better acquainted with them. Similarly, newcomers have a chance of improving their acceptance with time, especially if they accept the interests, values, and behavior patterns approved by the group (50, 163).

Kind of group

Acceptance depends in part on the *size* and *nature* of the group. When the group is small, the criteria used to judge the potential acceptance of a new member are mainly personal; he is judged by what he is, has, and can do. When the group is large, he is judged more by what he can contribute to the group, though personal qualities are never overlooked.

When the group is tightly knit, as is true of most small groups, it is difficult for *anyone* to pierce the barriers. It is especially difficult for minority-group adolescents and for newcomers. In a less tightly knit group, members are likely to be more tolerant in accepting new members (162).

If the group is primarily social in nature, acceptance can be gained only when the adolescent demonstrates his social skills and socioeconomic background to the satisfaction of the members. Should the group be less socially oriented, the adolescent's interests and contributions to the group are primary factors in determining his acceptance. A boy who shows marked athletic skills, for example, can gain acceptance in a group where the primary interests are sports because of the contribution he can make to the group's prestige.

Successful groups are usually self-sufficient and self-contained. They do not want to accept new members because newcomers might be a disruptive influence or a threat to some of the older members. An unsuccessful group is more receptive to new members. If they have something to offer the group, their degree of acceptance will depend on the dissatisfaction the members have with the group as it is (158, 161).

Socioeconomic status

High socioeconomic status in relation to the norm for the group usually guarantees that the adolescent will be the center of attention and sometimes the envy of his group. He is judged not only by what he *has* but also by what he and the members of his family *are* in the community. People tend to attribute favorable qualities to those of high income and less favorable qualities to those of low income. Socioeconomic status is, as Luft has explained, a "significant variable in determining how one perceives persons" (104).

Adolescents who have poor social acceptance are often from a lower socioeconomic status than the majority of their classmates. However, adolescents of low socioeconomic status sometimes enjoy high peer acceptance. Such individuals are known as "climbers" if they are operating easily among their peers; they are know as "fringers" if they are only tentatively accepted. Box 5-3 lists some of the reasons why adolescents of low socioeconomic status are handicapped in gaining peer acceptance (19, 33, 104, 124, 138, 141).

Coleman (30) has explained the acceptance value of socioeconomic status among girls:

Money, fancy clothes, good house, new cars, etc.— the "best." They express the fact that being born into the right family is a great help to a girl in getting into the leading crowd. They are not something a girl can change. . . . Her position in the system is ascribed according to her parents' social position and there is nothing she can do about it.

A boy, unlike a girl, can to some extent "escape" his socioeconomic background during adolescence. Most of the boy's social life is spent away from home. Furthermore, a boy has more opportunities to earn money than a girl and the low socioeconomic status of his family is not so great a handicap in getting clothes and money for extracurricular activities.

Possession of skills

Skills will not guarantee social acceptance, though lack of skills may lead to rejection. The adolescent who can participate in group activities and who has enough self-confidence to use his skills has an asset that contributes

---

BOX 5-3   HOW LOW SOCIOECONOMIC STATUS HINDERS SOCIAL ACCEPTANCE

*Lack of money to participate in extracurricular activities or having to work after classes prevents adolescents from becoming active in the peer group.

*Adolescents from low socioeconomic families may feel out of place and, as a result, withdraw from social activities.

*The interests and values of adolescents from lower socioeconomic families are often different from those of active group participants.

*Those from the lower socioeconomic groups are often anxious and ill at ease among peers of higher socioeconomic status and thus are unable to create a favorable impression.

to his acceptance (28, 145). One of the reasons early-maturing boys gain greater peer acceptance than average or late maturers is that their superior physical strength makes superior athletic achievement possible (85, 96). As Coleman has pointed out, "Athletic success seems the clearest and most direct path to membership in the leading crowd" (30). This is not true for girls. A girl who is an outstanding athlete is likely to win the reputation of being "masculine"—which will not enhance her chances of social acceptance (30, 84).

Social skills, accompanied by social know-how, contribute to popularity in adolescence. Knowing the correct thing to do and doing it aids social acceptance. Adolescents who feel incompetent to deal successfully with social situations belong to few school clubs and participate in few extracurricular activities where they would have an opportunity to improve their skills and, as a result, their social acceptance (18, 84, 124).

One of the social skills adolescents must have if they want to be accepted is social insight—the ability to size up social situations quickly and accurately. Adolescents who can tell, from facial expressions, speech, and general behavioral reactions, how others feel about different matters have a good chance of becoming the most popular members of the group. Those who lack normal social insight are regarded as tactless. They unknowingly hurt people's feelings and arouse antagonisms. This militates against future acceptance even though they may improve their social insight. Boys are generally less sensitive to the reactions of others than girls (6, 93, 148).

Intelligence

High intelligence contributes to peer acceptance because it enables the adolescent to take the initiative in crowd activities, plan for the successful carrying out of the activities, and suggest substitute activities when group interest begins to lag. Even more important, it helps the adolescent size up the group's interests and moods quickly and adjust to them (59, 86, 158). An adolescent who is much more intelligent than all other members of the group is apt to be out of step with his contemporaries. He may have different interests, or he may be considered a "brain." (48, 68, 100).

Adolescents who are markedly less intelligent than their peers gain little social acceptance. While they are generally not rejected, they are neglected. They become social isolates even though they would like to participate in group activities. They have little to contribute to the group and its activities and their slowness holds back the other members. Recognizing their lack of acceptance, most dull adolescents become self-conscious and withdrawn, making little effort to participate in group activities (48, 59, 134).

Academic achievement

Being a good student contributes to social acceptance, but if an adolescent is *too good* a student, he is likely to get the reputation of being a brain or a curve raiser. Furthermore, an adolescent who has such good relations with his teachers that his peers consider him a pet or an apple-polisher will find this a handicap to acceptance (81, 116). In a study of high school boys, it was found that the most accepted boys had school marks in the top 25 percent of their classes. The rejected boys had grades in the third 25 percent. In addition, the rejected boys disliked many of their teachers (48).

Adolescents who are well accepted have a better attitude toward school than those who are poorly accepted. Very poor students generally dislike school and are disliked by both their classmates and teachers. They are "pests" in the classroom and tend to argue with their teachers about their grades. They take special delight in disturbing the good students and making it difficult for them to study (48, 116).

Apparently, academic achievement is much less important to social acceptance than some other traits. Adolescents claim they would like to be remembered, as the years pass, as the best athlete or the most popular, not as the best student. Coleman has pointed out that, for the "impressionable" freshman or even sophomore in high school, athletes stand out, not scholars. By the junior or senior year, being a good student contributes more to social acceptance than it did earlier. However, brilliance has little effect in increasing acceptability; studiousness reduces it (30, 31).

For a *boy,* being both a scholar *and* an athlete leads to greater acceptance than being either alone. But of the two, being an athlete is far more important (31, 90). *Girls* with high marks may be respected by members of their own sex and be influential in scholastic affairs. But respect does not necessarily lead to acceptance, especially when the respect is not for social achievements. In most schools, girls with high marks are rated as less popular than girls with lower marks. Only if a girl can be a successful student *and* popular with boys will she win social acceptance among girls. If a girl has *both* beauty and brains, her social acceptance is likely to be high. Of the two, however, beauty will play the larger role (30, 91).

Acceptance of group interests and values

Adolescents feel more comfortable with those whose interests and values are similar to theirs. The most acceptable adolescent, therefore, is the one who conforms most closely to the interests and values of his particular group (124, 127, 150).

Because many of the values of minority groups—whether religious, racial, or socioeconomic—are different from those of the majority, it is difficult for adolescents of minority groups to win acceptance from members of the majority. Rural students, for example, have a minority-group status in many consolidated schools. Even when their economic status is similar to that of town students, their different values in life style, dress, speech, etc., are an obstacle to social acceptance by the town students who regard them as "hicks" (122).

Even when adolescents know the interests and values of the members of the group with which they want to be identified, they must be able or willing to *accept* them. Girls who show little interest in dates, parties, and clothes have little chance of being accepted in a group where these interests dominate. Similarly, boys who do not have the use of a car or whose time is limited by the necessity of working after school will not find acceptance among peers who place a high value on having fun (116, 128, 129).

Family relationships

The home may foster attitudes and behavior patterns that contribute to social acceptance or to peer neglect and rejection. The adolescent who has been overprotected, for example, is likely to be poorly accepted by his peers because of the selfishness and smugness he has learned at home. One who has had more home responsibilities will be more cooperative in the peer group and be better accepted (16, 44).

Parents who encourage their sons and daughters to visit in the homes of their peers, who permit their children to entertain at home and are hospitable to their children's guests, and who are satisfied with the popularity their children enjoy contribute greatly to the social acceptability of adolescents. Adolescents who get along well with their peers, as reflected in their being chosen as friends, generally get along reasonably well with their siblings. In addition, such adolescents are more satisfying to parents (16, 44). See Figure 5-1 for a graphic illustration of this.

The adolescent who is well accepted generally has a favorable attitude toward his family and feels that his home life is both satisfactory and happy. Warnath has stated: "The home thus appears indeed to be a seat of learning for the development of social skills and perhaps of the desire to participate in activities with other individuals" (155). Adolescents who are least satisfied with their homes and have unfriendly feelings toward their parents and siblings are found mostly in the low acceptance groups (44).

Adolescents who enjoy peer acceptance more often come from small families than from large. Those from large families may have so many home responsibilities or such limited amounts of money that they cannot actively participate in a clique or crowd. Only children, if they are pampered at home, are more often poorly accepted than children with one or more siblings. The latter are not usually overprotected and spoiled, but are expected to be cooperative members of the family team—training that prepares them for social acceptance (15).

Studies of the relationship between birth order and social acceptance reveal that first-borns tend to be better accepted than later-borns. Firstborns have a greater affiliation need, and this motivates them to try to win the acceptance of their peers. Further, they are expected to assume more responsibilities at home and are given more opportunities to learn to be mature than their younger siblings; thus they develop qualities that contribute to peer acceptance (4, 136, 140).

Personality pattern

The personality pattern of the adolescent is more important than any other single factor in determining his social acceptance. Constellations of personality traits—or "syndromes" —lead to acceptance, rejection, or neglect. The syndromes contain traits that are liked and admired as well as some that are disliked and disapproved. This means that a well-accepted adolescent is not a paragon of perfection so far as his personality traits are concerned. But the desirable traits outweigh the undesirable. Similarly, a poorly accepted adolescent has some traits which are a social asset, but they are outweighed by those which are a social liability.

In Box 5-4 are given the syndromes that lead to different degrees of social acceptance (44, 48, 71, 91, 154). Note that in both of the acceptance syndromes adolescents are socially oriented. They are friendly and outgoing. In general, they have a good opinion of themselves and their abilities and are free from anxiety. This enables them to turn out-

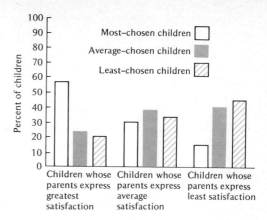

Figure 5-1 Relationship between satisfaction of parents with their children and the degree of social acceptance their adolescent sons and daughters enjoy, as expressed in how often they are chosen as friends. (Adapted from D. Elkins: Some factors related to the choice-status of ninety eighth-grade children in a school society. *Genet. Psychol. Monogr.,* 1958, **58,** 207–272. Used by permission.)

ward, becoming group-oriented rather than self-bound (2, 52, 84, 93). Three kinds of alienation syndromes are described in the box. In each, the adolescent has an unfavorable self-concept, generally resulting from social neglect or rejection, which was caused by his own behavior (5, 102, 106, 146).

EFFECT OF SOCIAL ACCEPTANCE ON ATTITUDES AND BEHAVIOR

The effect of different degrees of social acceptance on the attitudes and behavior of the adolescent will depend on how important social acceptance is to him. When an adolescent's nongroup-oriented interests are limited, when belonging to a given group represents the greatest possible prestige, or when his home and family fail to give him emotional satisfaction, he will have a greater need to be accepted than if these conditions were different.

Success in the "things that count" leads to self-satisfaction and happiness while failure leads to self-dissatisfaction and unhappiness. Since the adolescent sees himself, to a large extent, as members of the peer group see him, his self-concept becomes a mirror image of their concept of him.

Of all adolescents, stars and isolates are most affected by the group. This is not only because their status is most obvious to all but also because it is a more extreme status. Knowing that everyone likes him and wants him as a friend cannot fail to bring ego satisfaction to the star. Realizing that no one wants him as a friend cannot fail to make the isolate question his own worth.

As different degrees of social acceptance have different effects on adolescent attitudes and behavior, they will be discussed under four headings: the influence of social acceptance, of lack of acceptance, of marginal status, and of social neglect.

Influence of social acceptance Attitudes toward and interest in social activities are greatly influenced by how satisfying social participation is. This, in turn, is largely determined by how well accepted one is. Well-accepted adolescents, feeling wanted in different activities, become active participants in them. This provides them with opportunities to learn social skills, to develop greater social insight, and to internalize the values of the group.

The more completely the adolescent is accepted, the more active he is in group affairs and the more prestigious the role he plays. However, being a star has disadvantages as well as advantages. It sets the individual off from the group, with the result that he may have few close, warm friends. Furthermore, he does not reciprocate the affection and respect given him either because he is indifferent or because he does not want to show favoritism and thus alienate any of his friends. As a result, he is less happy and often finds less satisfaction in his social life than the adolescent who is popular but not a star (9, 47, 131).

Influence of lack of social acceptance The adolescent who is not accepted by his peers is unhappy and unsure of himself; he frequently develops a pessimistic attitude toward life and a defeatist attitude toward himself. When this happens, it leads to timidity and resentfulness. Being unaccepted cuts the adolescent off from social contacts, thus depriving him of the fun his contemporaries enjoy and of opportunities to develop social skills, to engage in popular adolescent recreations, and to learn the values of the peer group. Without these opportunities, he is unable to develop sufficient social insight to understand the feelings and attitudes of his contemporaries. This makes him seem tactless and gauche, adding still further to his lack of acceptance.

Box 5-5 shows how lack of social acceptance is likely to influence adolescent behavior (30, 73, 86, 106, 128, 154).

Influence of marginal status The effects of being on the fringe are much the same as those of being unaccepted. The adolescent tends to be insecure and unhappy, living in constant fear of losing what status he has gained. This militates against the development of self-confidence and makes the adolescent hypersensitive. It also affects the way he treats others. To solidify his status, he is likely to try to undercut his competitors, either by actions or by derogatory remarks. This leads to a "peck order" which is resented by those whose status is more secure. In addition, the fringer will be easily influenced by anyone who will accept him (2, 114, 129).

Influence of social neglect Being overlooked and neglected is ego-deflating at any age, but expecially in adolescence when there is a strong desire to be accepted by the peer group. Consequently, the neglectee experiences psychological difficulties and becomes defensive and self-protective. In time, he may become self-bound and develop feelings of martyrdom, which often lead to a martyr complex (1).

PREPONDERANCE OF SOCIALLY ISOLATED

Even in childhood, the curve of acceptance is skewed toward the minus side, indicating that more children are below average in social acceptance than above average. This skew becomes even greater in adolescence. It has been estimated that about 15 to 25 percent of all American adolescents have an acceptance status below the minimum needed for wholesome personality development. However, there is evidence that many more enjoy less acceptance than they want or are striving to achieve (103, 109, 115).

Adolescents' dissatisfaction with their "acceptance quotient" is due, in part, to the greater difficulty of achieving social acceptance in adolescence than in childhood. As was pointed out in the preceding chapter, adoles-

---

BOX 5-5   COMMON EFFECTS OF LACK OF SOCIAL ACCEPTANCE

*Lack of acceptance may motivate attempts to win prestige in unusual lines of endeavor.

*The unaccepted adolescent may become overaggressive, going out of his way to spoil the fun of others.

*The adolescent may develop substitute satisfactions, such as daydreaming and other solitary amusements.

*Nonacceptance may produce anxiety and insecurity which lead to excessive conformity.

*The unaccepted adolescent may try to escape from an environment in which he is an isolate by shunning social activities or withdrawing from school.

---

cents are choosier about their friends than children; they expect their friends to come up to an ideal standard they have set. When friends fall below this ideal, they often criticize them and try to reform them. Furthermore, adolescent social groups are more tightly knit than children's gangs; gaining acceptance to them is difficult, and retaining status, once accepted, is precarious.

The requirements for social acceptance in adolescence are stricter than in childhood. Some of the requirements, such as looks, family socioeconomic status, social skills, and social insight, are of little concern in childhood. And yet many of these are beyond the adolescent's control.

Girls, as a group, enjoy better acceptance by members of both sexes than boys. Since girls mature earlier, they acquire mature social interests and skills earlier. Boys find security in being with girls who appear to be more socially sophisticated than they, while girls regard the less mature boys in their classes as "kids."

In social relationships with members of their own sex, girls enjoy greater social acceptance than boys largely because they try harder to win acceptance. They try harder because social acceptance is usually more important to girls (30, 103, 114).

Improving social acceptability

Since the social-acceptance quotient of most adolescents is far lower than they would like and since unacceptability leads to unhappiness and poor social adjustments, one of the major problems of American adolescents is trying to improve their level of acceptance. As Feinberg et al. have pointed out, "Unpopularity cannot be lightly dismissed as a 'passing phase.'" Instead, it should be dealt with when the individual is plastic and has a strong motivation to change (48).

Unfortunately, lack of social acceptance is often not recognized early enough by those whose responsibility it is to guide the child. Or if it is recognized, those in charge—parents and teachers—tend to believe that the child will "outgrow" his bad habits by the time he reaches puberty. As a result, many children reach adolescence with well-established antisocial habits, with unfavorable reputations, and with poor self-concepts.

Some adolescents initiate their own programs of self-improvement. Even so, most need help in the form of counseling. Studies of attempts to improve the social acceptability of adolescents have brought out three fundamental principles.

First, an adolescent is rejected or neglected for a reason. Therefore, before any headway can be made in improving his acceptance, the cause must be discovered and steps must be taken to correct it. For example, if he does not participate in extracurricular activities, he must become more active. Even more important, he must participate in activities that have prestige in the eyes of his peers, and the quality of his performance must be such that it conforms to group standards. An adolescent who is clumsy and awkward will not improve his acceptance by participating in team sports. Instead, he is likely to increase his rejection.

Second, emphasis should be placed on the development of strong, positive assets rather than merely the correction of negative qualities. As was pointed out earlier, no one has *only* good qualities; rather, positive qualities compensate for negative ones. The adolescent who has a sense of humor and is fun to be with, who develops enough social and self-insight to be tactful, and who is cooperative can compensate for low socioeconomic status or a homely appearance.

Third, since boys are acceptable to their peers for different reasons than girls, emphasis must be placed on the development of strong positive social assets that are important to members of one's own sex, not necessarily of the other sex. Among boys, for example, athletic skills are more important than social skills, while among girls, the reverse is true. Similarly, nonconformity in appearance and behavior is a less serious handicap to social acceptance for boys than for girls—as will be discussed in Chapter 6. If girls want to improve their acceptance, then they must conform more closely to peer standards than boys.

Even with guidance, aid, and strong motivation the adolescent will not find it easy to improve his social acceptance. Pastore has remarked that it is more difficult to change a disliked into a liked person than vice versa (125). Elkins claims that it is easier to adjust the academic requirements to fit the needs of a youngster than to adjust the social environment (44).

A more hopeful note was sounded by Brown: "A person is not born with the traits which make him most desired as a friend, but he can develop them if he so wills and if he has help from mature persons who are sensitive to the adolescent's need for social acceptance" (20).

The first "if" in Brown's statement offers no real problem because almost every adolescent wants to have friends. The second "if," on the other hand, presents a major stumbling block for two reasons.

First, the adolescent may not be fortunate enough to have help from a mature person who is sensitive to his need. Many parents, for example, regard social activities as a waste of time—time that might better be spent on studies or some other "productive" activity. Such parents are often unsympathetic to the adolescent's desire for social acceptance.

Second, even though parents may be both mature and sympathetic, the adolescent may not view them as such. Especially during early adolescence, he may regard any parental advice as interference or bossing, or he may consider it old-fashioned and say it "won't work today because things are different." He may then turn to a peer for advice; but the peer is not a mature person, though he may be sensitive to the adolescent's need.

PERSISTENCE OF LEVEL OF SOCIAL ACCEPTABILITY

The level of social acceptability can be improved, but studies show that the relative statuses of adolescents in a group remain more or less static. The stars remain stars, the isolates tend to remain isolates, and the neglectees tend to remain neglectees. This is true for both boys and girls (19, 47, 125).

Studies also reveal that the most stable statuses are found among those who are best liked. It is most unusual for the popular to fall from grace. By contrast, the least stable statuses are found among those who are least liked. Unpopular adolescents may improve their status or they may become less liked with further acquaintance. Rejectees, especially, are likely to be more disliked with time. Isolates, on the whole, tend to improve their status with further acquaintance (39, 93, 129).

Marked stability in sociometric status begins in the last 3 years of high school. Persistence in status continues into late adolescence and early adulthood. Popular college students were, in general, well accepted throughout their high school days. Those who are poorly accepted in college were poorly accepted in high school (36, 103, 153). Among young adults, those who have large circles of friends were, for the most part, well liked throughout their adolescent years (34, 74, 108). As Jones has explained, the "pattern of social interaction represented by participating in extracurricular high-school activities provided many adolescents with social roles they found intrinsically congenial and likewise useful as a step toward other kinds of satisfying interpersonal relationships" (84).

It is thus apparent that poor social acceptance at one age *does not necessarily guarantee poor acceptance at another age.* Box 5-6 lists reasons for shifts as well as for persistence in social-acceptance level (23, 44, 47, 84, 109, 146). Only when a given adolescent's life pattern conforms to a majority of those reasons responsible for persistence can one predict that his level of social acceptance will remain unchanged as time passes.

STATUS OF LEADER

Every social group, no matter how small, has a leader. When interactions among members of a group become stabilized, a pattern or

BOX 5-6 CONDITIONS AFFECTING STABILITY OF SOCIAL ACCEPTANCE LEVEL

Conditions Favoring Persistence

Personality Traits
Once personality traits become set, whether leading to acceptance or to rejection or neglect, they tend to persist.

Socioeconomic Status
The socioeconomic status of the adolescent's family may favor or impede acceptance, but changes in socioeconomic status are not likely to alter one's acceptance quotient after it has been established.

Interests and Values
The extent of one's knowledge of the interests and values of the group and one's willingness to conform are likely to become more and more stable as time passes.

Reputation
The adolescent's reputation, based on the impression made on group members, tends to be persistent and to encourage the stability of his status in the group, whether it is high or low.

Conditions Favoring Change

Group Values
Shifts in group values by which the adolescent is judged by his peers may result in shifts in his level of social acceptance.

Changes in Groups
Change from one group to another with different interests and values may lead to shifts in acceptance status.

Behavioral Changes
Changes in the adolescent's behavior may enhance or detract from his acceptance, depending on how closely the changes conform to group standards.

---

hierarchy of individual statuses and roles develops, each associated with specific expectations, responsibilities, and loyalties. While statuses and roles are generally consistent within a group, members may have different statuses and roles in other groups. Thus, a leader in one group may become a follower in another group (42, 107).

As was noted earlier, it is often assumed that leaders are better adjusted than followers. That this is not necessarily universally true will become apparent in the discussion below.

Meaning of leader

A "leader" is a person who has the ability to get others to act in a certain way, not because they have to, but because they want to. The leader can influence group opinion and bring it into line with his own personal views.

The group crystallizes around the leader because he can satisfy the needs of the group members. The leader is able to achieve his leadership status for two reasons: *First*, he has demonstrated his mastery of social relationships and has contributed more than other members of the group to the satisfaction of their wants and needs, and *second,* he can arouse emotional reactions in the group members, thus swaying them by loyalty rather than by authority alone (29, 38, 149).

The individual who is selected as a leader is different from the one chosen as a social companion. He is more distant, socially, and exercises a more impersonal influence. (This is especially true of girl leaders.) He has such strong motivation to be a leader that he is willing to expend time and energy and sacrifice personal desires in order to satisfy the needs of the group (29, 79, 89).

Fundamentally, the function of the leader is to maximize the amount of satisfaction that group members derive from their social activities. The more satisfaction the leader provides, the longer the members of the group will want him to remain as leader. The leader provides satisfaction by, *first,* holding the group together as a cohesive unit; *second,* maintaining the group in a state of moving equilibrium; *third,* achieving the purpose for which the group was formed; and, *fourth,* successfully representing the group in nongroup settings (89, 143).

Contrary to popular opinion, leadership is not a specific attribute. As DeHaan (38) has pointed out:

Leadership is not a unitary trait or ability but, rather, it is made up of personal abilities and traits (which in some way make a person prominent and, thereby, eligible for the position as head of a group) plus consistent performance as a socioemotional specialist and a task specialist.

The "socioemotional specialist" is one who is most sensitive to the needs and feelings of others. He can give and receive affection, release tension, achieve agreement in a group, and facilitate a feeling of group solidarity. The "task specialist" is one who is outstanding in the task engaged in by the group (38).

There is little evidence of general leadership ability or of great men who inevitably emerge as leaders. Instead leadership depends on the situation. Thus, the distinctiveness of leaders does not depend on their attributes alone but rather on the relationship of their attributes to those of the other group members and to situational factors. That is why an adolescent may be a leader in one group in which his attributes surpass those of the other group members and a follower in a different group where his attributes are surpassed by those of another adolescent (29).

Kinds of leaders

Adolescents make a distinction between those who lead as a group and those who lead individually. Those who *lead as a group* are known as the "big wheels"—the top crowd or those who run things. They are the members of the leading crowd of any school or college class, and as a group, they set the patterns for the rest of the crowd to follow. This they can do because of their generalized prestige or prominence.

Those who *lead individually* are the "headmen"—the ones who play the role of a true leader by virtue of their activities in relation to the other members of the group. They may lead a small group—a clique or crowd— or they may lead a large group, composed of the different cliques and crowds of a school or college class. The headmen are the real leaders, even in the leading cliques composed of the big wheels.

Adolescent leaders may be subdivided according to the criteria used in making the classification. When subdivided on the basis of *method by which they attain their leadership positions,* they are known as "appointed," "formal," or "informal." The appointed leader is selected for the role by an adult—a teacher or camp counselor—with or without the knowledge and consent of the peer group. The formal and informal leaders, by contrast, achieve their status through the wishes of their peers without adult interference. Formal leadership status comes from an election in which the individual receives more votes than his opponents; the informal leader is not voted on but is so regarded by a majority of the group members. When leaders are subdivided on the basis of their *attitudes* toward their role, they are "voluntary" or "involuntary." The former wants to be a leader; the latter is elected, appointed, or designated as such though he might prefer to be a follower.

Subdivided according to the *method used to lead,* leaders are "authoritarian" or "democratic." The authoritarian leader is bossy, demanding, and inconsiderate of others; he ignores their wishes if they do not coincide with his own. The democratic leader is sensitive to the wishes of the group and willing to comply with group wishes even when they do not agree with his. He is less likely to give direct orders than to make suggestions, he asks for opinions, and he shows concern for the feelings of others. Since the democratic leader's method of control is more rewarding to the followers, their loyalty and affection are usually greater for him than for the authoritarian leader. The larger the group, the more authoritarian the leadership method tends to be.

Some leaders are "group-oriented" and some "self-oriented." The group-oriented leader uses a participatory style of leadership, trying to size up the wants and needs of the group members. He then plans activities that will fit their needs. Furthermore, he is willing to sacrifice personal wishes if they conflict with those of the group. The self-oriented leader is more interested in his own welfare than in that of the group. His followers sense this and withhold their loyalty. He is less likely than the group-oriented leader to retain his status as leader, especially if he is aggressive. Such a leader is a "power seeker" in the sense that he is determined to control others lest others control him. Barclay (11) describes the technique used by a power seeker:

Even at the nursery school stage he may have learned to do this with charm rather than temper tantrums. ("Jeff, you make pretend you're the captain this time and we'll let you be head of the scouting party in the next game.") As he grows older, if his circle holds values that require it, he may in addition take up a noble cause as justification for his efforts to control. If his principal purpose is to dominate, manage or maneuver others, however, he

is still a power-seeker—"a prince with a hero's halo."

When subdivided according to the *activity engaged in,* there are athletic leaders, social leaders, intellectual leaders, and religious leaders. To satisfy the needs of the group, each leader must be a task specialist. He must have some characteristic that enables him to meet the group's needs better than the other group members. The athletic leader, for example, is superior in athletic ability; the intellectual leader has higher scores on mental tests, better academic standing, and interests of a more intellectual nature; the social leader is superior in appearance, dress, manner, and social skills; and the religious leader has greater interest in religious activities than his followers.

Finally, leaders may be subdivided on the basis of *sex:* There are typical girl leaders and typical boy leaders. The girl leader in adolescence is superior in appearance and social skills but somewhat cool and detached in her attitudes toward the group members; this makes her distant and a bit unattainable, the "cool" big wheel. Boy leaders, by contrast, are "good guys," warm, friendly, and liked by everyone. The girl leader is followed because she has flair, is a style setter, and has general prestige in the school, though she is less wanted as a best friend than the boy leader. Because boys have more friendly attitudes and because being led by a girl is not considered sex appropriate for boys, groups composed of members of both sexes are usually led by boys. The one exception to this is social activities where it would be considered sex inappropriate for a boy to be a leader (24, 29, 30, 42, 143).

How leaders are made

Contrary to popular opinion, leaders are made, not born. There is no evidence that a person can automatically step into a leadership role without the training and practice such a role demands.

Case histories of leaders show that leadership is a status achieved over a relatively long period. Whether the individual will be a leader or a follower depends to a large extent on the role he has played earlier, especially during childhood (38, 107).

Early childhood experiences lay the groundwork for leadership ability. Experiences in the home, especially parent-child and sibling relationships, are the most important influence. As the child grows older, relationships with peers and his role in gang life take on greater importance. Still later, specific training and opportunities to play leadership roles in school are significant. These influences are shown in Figure 5-2.

Home influences The adolescent's attitudes toward himself and his ability to be a leader are greatly affected by his parents' and siblings' attitudes toward him, his role in the home, the kind of training he had in childhood, and the characteristic pattern of his home life. Box 5-7 lists some of the experiences in the home that encourage the development of leadership ability (34, 38, 64, 142, 149).

Peer group experiences How the peer group treats a child will have a marked influence on whether he will be a leader or follower in adolescence. Even before the child finishes

Figure 5-2 How leaders are made.

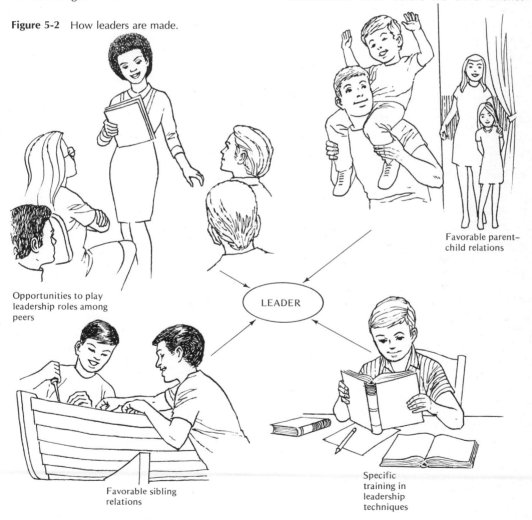

Opportunities to play leadership roles among peers

Favorable parent–child relations

LEADER

Favorable sibling relations

Specific training in leadership techniques

elementary school, it is possible to predict the role he will play in adolescent groups. If he gains a reputation for good leadership in childhood, this will provide a halo which will practically assure adolescent leadership roles (11, 25, 42).

Specific training in leadership Attempts to train adolescents to play the role of leader have reported considerable success in the development of leadership ability and social insight. Training included lessons in diplomacy, with emphasis on the fact that one can get more by requesting than by demanding; reinforcement of the leader's strong points; better understanding and acceptance of self through group counseling; and development of leadership values and abilities, especially personal integrity, consideration of others, and decision making (11, 25, 107).

Many adolescents train themselves by observing and imitating the techniques used by successful leaders or by reading books that suggest ways to develop leadership qualities and techniques.

Distinguishing characteristics of leaders

In our culture, there is a stereotype of what a leader is supposed to be like. The adolescent who most closely resembles the stereotype has the best chance of becoming a leader. He possesses attributes which the members of the group particularly admire (58).

Studies of leadership traits show that the following are of some importance.

BOX 5-7   HOME INFLUENCES ON LEADERSHIP ABILITY

Child Training Methods
Authoritarian training encourages submission to authority and, thus, followership; democratic training encourages initiative, resourcefulness, and other leadership qualities.

Ordinal Position
Firstborns are given more responsibilities and more opportunities to participate in family decision making than later-borns and are thus more likely to assume a leadership role.

Work Assignments
Adolescents who have work assignments in the home and who take outside jobs in their free time develop a maturity of attitude and behavior which leads to peer respect.

Parental Attitudes toward Friends
Parents who guide their children in planning pleasurable at-home activities for their friends give them training for a leadership role.

Sharing in Family Planning
The adolescent who participates in planning family expenditures and activities learns a leadership technique which can be applied to peer group activities.

Range of Interests
If the home encourages a wide range of interests, the adolescent becomes a potential leader in many peer activities.

Social acceptance A well-accepted adolescent may not be a leader, though leaders are usually well accepted. An adolescent may be liked because he is fun to be with, but he may lack other qualities essential to leadership. Being accepted brings him prestige, adds to his self-confidence, and enables him to use his abilities, whatever they may be, for the benefit of the group. Leadership and social acceptance are, thus, interrelated, but the relationship is not absolutely direct (29, 60, 119, 149).

Prestige Social acceptance brings prestige, and prestige is enhanced when the adolescent is selected as a leader. If he is successful in his leadership role, this further enhances his acceptance, his prestige, and the respect others have for him. As a result, the members of the group attribute to him the qualities they admire and shut their eyes to qualities they dislike. Furthermore, because of the favorable reputation he has acquired, he will be chosen for leadership roles in activities for which he is not qualified. As Marak has stated, "A leader's authority extends to many areas not justified by his abilities, after the group members develop conceptions of him as a rewarding person" (107). Should the leader fall short of group expectations, his halo will be tarnished and his prestige will decrease.

Socioeconomic status Studies of the socioeconomic status of leaders show that leaders ordinarily come from higher-income families than nonleaders (3, 89, 118). Coleman has written that adolescents "look upward" for their leaders—to those whose backgrounds are superior to theirs (30). Consequently, upper-class adolescents usually dominate school activities except for athletics.

Skills Adolescence demands many new social skills. However, skills in one situation may give the adolescent enough prestige to facilitate his becoming a leader in situations where his particular skills are not needed. One of the most important skills for leadership during adolescence is skill in conversation.

Among older adolescents, especially, verbal facility and forcefulness of expression are essential to leadership (2, 18).

Social participation In both high school and college, leaders are often found among those who participate in more than the average number of extracurricular activities. Not only do leaders participate in more activities but they spend more of their time in these activities. Furthermore, they are willing to assume responsibilities instead of merely enjoying themselves. They generally hold more than one position of responsibility, and they serve on committees as well as holding offices in many different groups. Transported high school students and off-campus college students are sometimes unable to participate in extracurricular activities and thus have fewer chances of being elected to leadership roles or of serving if they are elected (126, 142).

Social insight To be a leader, the adolescent must have social insight. He must be able to evaluate situations and to know what kind of action to take. He must be perceptive of group needs and be able to satisfy the most important ones. The longer the individual has been a member of a group, the more likely he will be to evaluate group opinion accurately. And the better he understands people, the better he can get along with them (34, 63).

Intelligence In the adolescent leader, social insight is usually accompanied by above-average intelligence, a high level of mental energy, and a liberal point of view. The leader must be intelligent if he is to take the initiative in suggesting new activities, in directing associates, and in making decisions. How much above the average of the group he should be depends upon the activities of the group. A football captain, for example, does not need so high a level of intelligence as the captain of a debating team (112, 160).

Academic achievement Leaders are, on the whole, superior in academic achievement, though some are not. For girls, academic achievement is less of an asset than for boys. A girl who stands too high academically has little chance of being popular enough to be in line for a leadership role (38, 107).

Values The leader must share the values most desired by the group as a whole *at that time*. Even more important, he must conform to these values and let them guide his behavior.

The leader conforms in interpersonal relationships but shows his individuality in his interests. If he is to retain the loyalty of the group, he must neither over- nor underconform. There are no "social rebels" among leaders except in adolescent groups made up of social rebels (80, 112). In discussing the amount of nonconformity necessary to leadership, Barclay (11) has said:

The rule-breaker and value-creator—either child or adult—is a truly "superior person." He is self-respecting and self-directing. He is not swayed by

Figure 5-3 The personality patterns of leaders and nonleaders. (Adapted from R. T. Johnson and A. N. Frandsen: The California Psychological Inventory profile of student leaders. *Personnel Guid. J.*, 1962, **41**, 343–345. Used by permission.)

Standard scores on personality test

desire or need for popular approval and sympathy and can survive personal hurt. He is proud but not vain. His really distinguishing feature, however, is his sensitivity in spheres where others are indifferent, his bravery, his willingness to sacrifice for uncommon ends and his self-sufficiency. Although such persons—when devoid of social sense—can act as powers for ill, the great movers and makers of our culture have had this "masterly" quality.

Appearance Leaders are usually attractive though not necessarily beautiful or handsome. The attractive adolescent can feel confident that he is making a good impression, and he knows that this is an aid to acceptance by peers of both sexes. Because of the high value placed on sex appropriateness of looks as well as of behavior, the adolescent who conforms to the cultural stereotype for his sex group is more likely to be selected as a leader than the one whose appearance falls short of the stereotype (29, 38).

Adolescent leaders must make a good impression if they are to represent the members of the peer group successfully. To make a good impression, the leader must be nice looking, wear becoming, stylish clothes, and be well groomed. A good appearance is especially important for leaders of social activities (30, 133, 137).

Personality Just as there is no one personality trait or combination of traits that assures social acceptability, so there is no one trait or combination that assures one's selection as leader. Certain characteristics, however, are almost inevitably found in leaders. Leaders are *sociable* and *extroverted;* they are *unselfish and outer-bound.* Both male and female leaders tend to be more *masculine* than feminine in their personality patterns. They have more traits that are highly valued in males than in females.

Leaders—except for authoritarian leaders— are *flexible;* they are willing to make changes in the organizational structure of the group if that is to the advantage of the group. They must also be *liberal* and free from biases and prejudices which color their reactions to group members. Leaders must work for the best interest of the group. Thus, *dependability* is one of the outstanding personality traits of all leaders (82, 89, 92). Figure 5-3 shows the typical personality patterns of leaders and nonleaders.

Persistence of leadership

The popular belief that "once a leader, always a leader" is not universally true. Among children, leaders come and go. In adolescence, leadership status is becoming fairly stable, and in adulthood, it is rather stable and fixed. Traits that make for leadership do not develop early and opportunities to engage in activities that develop leadership qualities are not found to any extent in the elementary school. Leadership is developed in junior high school, however, and junior high school leaders are likely to be senior high and college leaders (85, 118, 130).

Studies of the relationship between leadership in school and college and in later life show that the leadership status tends to persist. Women who hold executive positions on boards of charitable institutions, for example, had leadership experience in adolescence. Male business leaders, likewise, were usually leaders in school and college (74, 108, 142).

Some adolescents who held leadership posts no longer do so while others who rarely served as leaders in school become leaders in college or adult life. To understand why this is so, look at Box 5-8, which lists the factors that favor and militate against the persistence of leadership (12, 30, 85, 130, 142, 151).

STATUS OF FOLLOWER

A "follower" is an accepted member of a social group; his interests, opinions, and activities as a group member are initiated, stimulated, and sometimes controlled by the group's leader.

Followers often do as much or even more for the group *quantitatively* than the leader. But, *qualitatively,* their contributions fall short of those of the leader. Many followers, for example, are willing workers on committees.

BOX 5-8   FACTORS INFLUENCING
PERSISTENCE OF LEADERSHIP

Favoring Persistence

*Elected by peers

*Strong motivation to lead

*Group-oriented attitude

*Competence in prestigious activities

*Confidence in ability to lead

*Knowledge of leadership techniques

*Halo effect of good leadership

Militating against Persistence

*Appointed by adult or elected to fill a gap when former leader withdrew

*Weak motivation to lead

*Self-oriented attitude

*Competence in nonprestigious activities

*Lack of confidence in ability to lead

*Poor leadership techniques

*Reputation of being poor leader

Occasionally, they are "middle leaders" who serve as heads of small committees delegated to carry out part of a larger project but their leadership roles have little prestige.

An adolescent may be a follower because the group members perceive him to be less able to meet the needs of the group than the one who is selected as leader. Either he does not have the qualities the members want their leader to have or he has never demonstrated his ability to lead. In addition, as discussed below, he may not want to assume responsibilities or he may never have had an opportunity to do so.

Kinds of followers

Just as there are different kinds of leaders, so there are different kinds of followers. When followers are subdivided according to their *attitudes* toward their role, they may be classed as "voluntary" or "involuntary." The voluntary follower is one who wants to be a follower; he is satisfied with the role he plays and is not anxious to change that role. Either he does not want to put in the time and effort needed to be a leader or he has learned, from past experience, that he derives greater satisfaction from being a follower.

The involuntary follower, by contrast, is not satisfied with his role; he wants to be a leader but has not been given the opportunity. He becomes angry and resentful toward members of the group who are "discriminating against him" and he does not cooperate in group activities. In time, he may be ejected from the group or he may withdraw and try to become the leader in another group.

Subdivided on the basis of their *contributions* to the group, followers may be "constructive" or "destructive." Voluntary followers are usually constructive, and the involuntary, destructive. Constructive followers want to contribute to the school's social life and participate in its extracurricular activities. Because of their contribution, they are well liked and their status is reasonably secure. Any change in their status is generally in the direction of greater acceptance.

Destructive followers not only make few contributions to the group but do much to impede its efforts. They are often called "tear-downers." They either refuse to serve on committees or they do little except criticize other committee members. They go out of their way to criticize the leader and any suggestions he may make. As a result of their critical, uncooperative attitudes, destructive followers are disliked and rejected, or if they are less aggressive, they are neglected.

EFFECT OF GROUP STATUS
ON ATTITUDES AND BEHAVIOR

The effect of status in the group on behavior, attitudes, and personality depends not upon whether the person is a leader or a follower but on how satisfied he is with his status. The leader who is satisfied with his role will be an active participant in group affairs and will adapt his interests to those of the group. Though he may miss close friendships with his peers, he is willing to accept this as one of the prices he must pay for successful leadership.

Similarly, contented followers will contribute what they can to the satisfaction of the group, often doing more than their share. Recognizing that they do not have the ability or the motivation to be leaders, and being unwilling to sacrifice the energy, time, and close personal friendships that the leadership role demands, they are satisfied with their social lives as they are. Like the satisfied leader, they are *socially well-adjusted* people. They not only conform to social expectations but they derive personal satisfaction from the status they have in the group.

By contrast, dissatisfied leaders and followers are *poorly adjusted socially*. The adolescent who is appointed or elected to a leadership status against his will feels uncomfortable and unhappy in the role because he feels inadequate for it. While he may want to be a leader because of the prestige associated with the role, he is afraid. His anxiety is shown by hypersensitivity to the criticism of disgruntled followers; by timidity in introducing new group activities; by mood swings from aggressive to affable—depending on group reactions to his suggestions; and by becoming emotionally involved in the personal affairs of group members and thus creating the impression that he is playing favorites. Sensing that he is not playing his role satisfactorily, he becomes more and more anxious and unsure.

The most dissatisfied group member is the one who wants to be a leader, who feels that he has the capacity to play the role better than the person who is a leader, and who resents having to be a follower. If he convinces himself that he is a martyr whose talents are belittled by jealous rivals, he will become vindictive against any group member who criticizes him.

From this brief survey, it is apparent that

the popular belief that the higher the adolescent's status in the peer group the better his social adjustment is not always true. A leader who is satisfied with his role does conform more closely to the criteria of good social adjustment than a satisfied follower. But a dissatisfied leader is certainly not as well adjusted socially as a satisfied follower. The most poorly adjusted of all is the dissatisfied follower. Only when the attitude of the adolescent toward the status he has in the group is taken into consideration can his social adjustment be assessed fairly and accurately.

HIGHLIGHTS OF CHAPTER 5

1. The status of the adolescent in the peer group is determined by the degree of acceptance he achieves from group members.

2. The social acceptance of the individual is determined by how rewarding his companionship is to the group members; popularity is determined by the respect and admiration he receives from the group.

3. Degree of social acceptance ranges from that of the star who is accepted by most of his peers to that of the isolate, fringer, or neglectee who is accepted by few of his peers. Adolescents who find little satisfaction from the companionship of their peers withdraw and become voluntary isolates; others become neglectees because they have little to offer the group; climbers try to improve their status through identification with a more prestigious group; and fringers are only tentatively accepted by the group.

4. Most adolescents become aware of the degree of acceptance they have achieved by such cues as the way their peers treat them, the names and nicknames by which their peers call them, and the comments made to or about them by their peers.

5. Factors influencing the degree of acceptance the adolescent achieves include first impressions, attractiveness of appearance, reputation, social participation, conversational ability, health, proximity to the group, length of acquaintance, kind of group, family socioeconomic status, intelligence, academic achievement, acceptance of group interests and values, family relationships, and personality patterns.

6. Attitudes and behavior are markedly influenced by the degree of acceptance the adolescent achieves and by how important acceptance is to him.

7. Most adolescents achieve less acceptance than they want or strive for. Improving social acceptance, which is difficult and sometimes impossible, becomes a major problem for adolescents as well as for their parents and teachers.

8. The adolescent's level of acceptance tends to be persistent because many of the factors responsible for it such as his personality, reputation, interests, and values are unlikely to change.

9. Leaders in adolescence may be chosen by their peers or appointed by adults, they may be authoritarian or democratic in their leadership techniques, they may be group- or self-oriented, and they may be general leaders or task specialists who are suited to lead only in specific activities, such as sports or dramatics.

10. Leaders must learn how to play the leadership role. They learn at home, in peer group experiences, and from specific training in leadership techniques.

11. Qualities that distinguish leaders from followers include degree of social acceptance, prestige, skills, socioeconomic status, social participation, social insight, level of intelligence and academic achievement, values, appearance, and personality.

12. Followers, who differ qualitatively more than quantitatively from leaders, may be voluntary, in that they prefer the status of follower, or involuntary, in that they want to be leaders but are not chosen for the role. Voluntary followers make greater contributions to the group and are better accepted by the group than involuntary followers.

Chapter 6

Adolescent Nonconformists

Adolescent nonconformists are not a new breed, as many believe. References to rebellious youth and their attempts to reform society were made by the ancient Greek writers. For the past decade or so, however, student activism has been increasing on American high school, college, and university campuses. It has received worldwide attention in the mass media and has aroused considerable popular concern. The violence that has accompanied many student protests has led to the question, What is to blame for the turmoil? A scapegoat has been sought, and the finger of blame has been pointed at "Spockism" and his "philosophy of permissiveness" and to college and university administrators who "lack backbone" and allow the students to "run the campus." Public and political pressure has forced some college and university presidents to resign and has led to cutbacks in appropriations to state-supported institutions. Reduced alumni contributions have caused fund-raising crises in many private colleges and universities. As a nation, we have been blamed for allowing our youth to set a bad example for the youth of other nations who have likewise been staging protests in their universities.

Whenever emotions are aroused, objectivity flies out the window. Consequently, it is easy to condemn *all* rebellion against established values and patterns of behavior and to fail to see any advantage that might result from raising questions about them. Similarly, it is easy to accuse not only rebellious adolescents of being social misfits and troublemakers but also all the others.

Popular interest in student activism has motivated social scientists—anthropologists, sociologists, and psychologists—to turn their attention to this current educational and social issue. Scientists are concerned with a number of questions, What is at the root of youth's discontent? What kind of adolescent is most likely to become an activist? What advantages or disadvantages will the adolescent and the social group derive from his nonconforming behavior? This chapter will summarize the results of scientific studies.

WHAT IS A NONCONFORMIST?

It is customary among laymen to divide people into two general categories: conformists and nonconformists. *Conformists* accept the values and behavior patterns of their social group and never rebel—at least not overtly—even against unfair demands. Adolescents who fall into this category have been labeled by Block et al. as "apathetic youth" (19). *Nonconformists* reject some or all of the values of the social group and refuse to adhere to the accepted patterns of behavior. Derogatory labels commonly applied to nonconformists include "radicals," "wreckers," "rebels," "activists," "militants," and "hippies." The label used depends largely on the appearance of the nonconformist. If he conforms in speech and appearance but is unconventional in his ideas, values, and behavior, he is likely to be labeled rebel, radical, militant, or wrecker—terms which suggest that his rebellion is more psychological than physical. If he deviates in appearance as well as in values, ideas, and behavior, he is likely to be called a hippie (96, 134).

These labels do not take into consideration some of the fundamental differences among the various kinds of nonconformity. Studies indicate that the motivations for nonconformity differ greatly and that each motivation affects behavior differently. Nonconformists can be categorized on the basis of their motivation. Box 6-1 summarizes the four categories of nonconformists and the characteristics of persons who fall into these categories (56, 67, 79, 82, 88, 161).

Of the four categories, only two can be regarded as "reformers"—the reformers and the activists. The other two categories are *not* reformers because neither takes constructive steps to bring about changes or to improve existing conditions. Equally important, while all activists are reformers, not all reformers are activists; that is, activists, unlike reformers, use aggressive or unsocial means to bring about change.

There have always been nonconformists of all categories. In the past, however, they were less publicized and less vocal than today. In the authoritarian home and school, criticizing and attempting to reform one's elders were not permitted. Furthermore, most adolescents entered the adult world of work and family life where they soon discovered that conformity to existing values and patterns of behavior was essential to survival. As Block et al. have pointed out, until the mid to late 1960s, adolescents were mainly apathetic, conforming, and success-oriented (19). Even today, only a minority are reformers and activists. While many others doubtless watch their bolder peers with interest and envy, they are either too preoccupied with their own problems to become social activists or they are held back by fear of losing the social acceptance they crave and have worked hard to achieve.

This fear is engendered partly by unfavorable social attitudes toward *all* nonconformists, especially those who are disruptive, and partly by the punitive attitudes of parents and teachers. Frustrated would-be nonconformists often develop a resentment of social standards and of the social group that enforces these standards. Such a resentment leads to poor personal and social adjustments.

Adolescents who defy social standards do not make good social adjustments because they are aware of the unfavorable attitudes they arouse. This awareness, in turn, affects their personal adjustments. In whatever category of nonconformity they fall, they are far more likely to be poorly adjusted than those who conform.

CONDITIONS CONTRIBUTING TO NONCONFORMITY

To parents and teachers, reformers and activists are the most troublesome of the different kinds of nonconformists, and so a good deal of research attention has been given to them. With the growing belief that the drug problem is associated with conditions that cause adolescents to become rebels and socially alienated, these categories have also been studied.

The trend among the lay public has been to single out one cause—permissive child training or the generation gap or the ultraliberal doctrines taught in the colleges and universities—and to blame it for the increase in nonconformity. But there is no scientific evidence that one cause alone is responsible. Instead, there is ample evidence that many conditions predispose young people to question the established cultural mores.

Physical maturing

What effect does physical maturing have on different patterns of nonconformity? Physical maturing per se has no direct effect. It does, however, have indirect effects. When the adolescent reaches adult size and appearance, he wants to be autonomous and independent. He rebels against childhood restrictions on his behavior. Erikson has referred to his rebellion as the "revolt of the dependent" (45). The longer the adolescent remains dependent —because of overprotective parents, the need for extended vocational training, or other reasons—the more restless, frustrated, and rebellious he becomes (42).

The pattern of the adolescent's nonconformity will be influenced by his environment —how closely it comes up to his ideals and meets his needs. For example, if the adolescent enters college expecting to meet intellectual challenges and prepare himself to become the kind of adult he has dreamed of becoming, he will understandably be frustrated if his expectations are not met. If he feels that he has no individual identity on a large impersonal campus, that the courses he is required to take are dull and irrelevant, and that the teaching is below the level he was accustomed to in high school, he will not only be rebellious but he will set out to reform the "system." Should his reform efforts

fail, he may turn to activism or become alienated, depending on many factors both in his own experience and in the environment (42, 137).

The generation gap

Adolescent revolt against adult authority is often attributed to a "generation gap" between adolescents and their parents. Those who accept this explanation claim that the generation gap makes it impossible for adolescents and their parents to view life from the same frame of reference and that a clash between them is inevitable. However, the chronological age difference between adolescents and parents today is not appreciably greater than in the past. Why then is adolescent revolt more widespread than in past generations? The answer is to be found not in the generation gap but in the *cultural* generation gap. The cultural generation gap is a result of rapid change in the entire pattern of life in recent years with its new values and new interests.

Perhaps the most significant change in life pattern has come from the greater educational and cultural advantages today's adolescents have. These advantages include the expanded opportunities for higher education, the availability of scholarships and other financial aid to help adolescents take advantage of higher education, the almost universal use of mass media, especially television, the spread of American affluence to families in all social classes (permitting adolescents to remain dependent many years longer than their parents were), and the low cost of world travel (permitting young people to enjoy experiences which their parents dreamed of enjoying after retirement). These differences make it difficult for parents and adolescents to understand each other's interests and values.

While the effects of the cultural gap can be found in all families, they are most severe in socially mobile families and in those having foreign-born parents. Many foreign-born parents came to America in the hope of "bettering themselves." Money, material possessions, and success are important to them, and they cannot understand why such things are not equally important to their children (30, 122). Much the same values are held by socially mobile parents. Prugh (129) draws the following contrast:

Whereas our generation has spent most of its time trying to compete and gain position in a technological world, the new generation is primarily concerned with how they can relate to our society. . . . In refusing to accept the status quo, they have rejected the bestiality and violence of war, and they have been unwilling to overlook or accept fascism and poverty in our own society. They are posing essentially moral questions in their idealism and their social consciousness and concern.

The clash between generational values is probably greatest in three areas: concern with education, choice of vocation, and attitude toward war and sex. To the older generation, higher education meant an opportunity to prepare for a vocation which would provide prestige and the earning capacity to climb the social ladder. Many parents look back with nostalgia to their "happy college years" and are amazed when their children regard college as a "boring" experience and a "necessary evil." To many of today's college students, the value of college is that it provides them an opportunity to understand themselves and the world in which they live (73). Many members of the younger generation plan to use their professional skills in law and medicine, for example, to help the disadvantaged in their communities. Their parents, who may have sacrificed a great deal to support their long and costly training, often find it incomprehensible that their children do not want to use their skills to advance themselves. Draft evasion, burning draft cards, destroying ROTC buildings and demonstrating against war activities in the late 1960s were regarded by many parents as a shameful lack of patriotism. Sexual promiscuity, especially by girls, is also incomprehensible to parents and a source of embarrassment and shame. Many are outraged by the "ultrapermissiveness" of college administrators who permit coed dormitories.

The cultural generation gap could be reduced if parents and adolescents could understand each other's point of view. As will be explained in more detail in Chapter 14, however, communication between parents and children breaks down during the adolescent years. Adolescents accuse parents of being old-fashioned, rigid, and lacking in understanding, while parents accuse their sons and daughters of having wild ideas, of being impractical dreamers, and of not appreciating the opportunities their parents have given them. The consequence is that many parents try to reform the "radical" views of their sons and daughters, and the sons and daughters, in turn, try to convert parents to their values.

If this give and take in the home meets with success, even limited success, adolescents acquire a pattern of meeting clashes in values which they often carry outside the home. If parents and adolescents are unable to communicate, the adolescents withdraw from the home environment, where they have already begun to feel like outsiders. They develop a defeatist attitude which predisposes them to become socially alienated and to seek an environment in which their values are appreciated or at least accepted. They are not revolting against their parents per se but rather against the generational values that their parents represent (168).

When the adolescent is convinced that his parents and teachers will not listen to him and when they label his ideas "impractical," "radical," or "communistic," he is likely to become so enraged that he will turn his energies to violent activities. Just as the child who is unable to communicate his wants and needs to his parents will fly into a temper tantrum, so the adolescent who is rebuffed in his attempts to make others listen to his point of view will become angry and may commit acts of violence (39, 105).

Colleges and universities

Since youth activism on college campuses and in college and university communities has received so much publicity, the public has been quick to blame the institutions of higher education for all the unrest and to accuse faculty members who condone or participate in student demonstrations of encouraging and inciting riots. A close parallel is found among those concerned with adolescent religious doubt and religious inactivity. Many parents and even some members of the clergy accuse the "radical" colleges and universities of turning adolescents into atheists and undermining the religious beliefs learned in the home. This matter will be discussed in more detail in Chapter 11.

Unquestionably, the colleges and universities do contribute—more indirectly than directly—to adolescent nonconformity, especially during late adolescence when reforming and activism normally reach their peak and social alienation is strongest. This indirect contribution comes from three sources.

First, some adolescents are able for the first time in their lives to verbalize their opinions and beliefs free from the fear of parental disapproval. So long as the adolescent is under the parental roof, he feels that he must conform to his parents' views if he wants to retain their affection. Away from home, the restraints are lifted and the adolescent can speak, worship, and dress as he wishes.

Second, contact with students and faculty members of widely different backgrounds and registration in courses of study which increase his knowledge bring about many changes in the adolescents' attitudes and values. For example, as was pointed out in Chapter 4, a decrease in prejudice is a common outgrowth of the adolescent's college experience.

Third, and perhaps most important, in his academic work the adolescent is rewarded for independent thinking. While his capacity for reasoning may not improve, he is encouraged to think independently. That is why many college students begin to question the religious beliefs and social values which they accepted less critically in the more limited environment of the home. This questioning broadens the cultural generation gap and increases the adolescent's desire to change the old-fashioned and "immoral" values of the older generation (22, 52, 69, 106).

Not all colleges encourage independent thinking to this extent. Some of the smaller denominational colleges are less likely to encourage independent thinking than the large universities. Furthermore, some colleges and universities in various subtle or not so subtle ways discourage student activism. Those which permit the expression of adolescent discontent produce the greatest number of adolescent reformers and activists (80, 128).

Home influences

Parents, even more often than college professors, have been blamed for the increase in disruptive adolescent activism and for nonconformity in behavior and appearance. As mentioned earlier, the finger of blame has been pointed at "Spockism" or permissiveness in home discipline. Duvall (40) writes:

Modern parents have taught their young people to be critical and to raise questions about life and its institutions, the country, and "the system." When they demonstrate or engage in a family hassle, youth are doing what they have been taught. This is a generation of young people who have been reared more permissively than previous generations.

While it is true that child-training methods have become more permissive, *not all* of today's adolescents were "Spock babies," and *not all* "Spock babies" are social activists. Other conditions in the home, as shown in Box 6-2, also encourage nonconformity (11, 12, 26, 47, 153, 167).

An interesting finding of some studies of nonconformity is that adolescents brought up by democratic child-training methods were far less likely to be rebellious or to become activists than those whose training was either authoritarian or permissive.

Adolescents subjected to authoritarian training usually conform to parental demands of behavior and dress as long as they live at home because they know they will be punished if they do not do so. Their rebellion outside the home is a way of expressing pent-up frustrations. Those whose desires to rebel or to reform conditions in the home have met parental disapproval and led to no change in conditions often withdraw from the home situation. They become the socially alienated; many are estranged from their parents and other family members.

Permissive discipline does not foster rebellion *in the home* because the adolescent has nothing to rebel against. He is permitted to do much as he pleases because the home is child-oriented. The adolescent himself decides what food he will eat, what hours he will keep, and whether he will take part in family gatherings. *Outside the home,* however, he cannot impose his wishes on others. This makes him rebellious and he attempts to

reform things that are not to his liking. If he makes little or no headway in his reform attempts, he usually tries to force his wishes on others, thus becoming an activist.

The adolescent least likely to become an activist or a socially alienated person is the one brought up by democratic child-training methods (44, 46, 79, 81). He is accustomed to being told why rules and regulations are necessary and is given an opportunity to explain why he may not wish to conform to them. The habit of parent-child communication, established early in childhood, persists into adolescence. This often encourages the adolescent to become a reformer but rarely an activist or socially alienated. Outside the home, he may become an activist if communication between the generations is so restricted that those in authority refuse to listen to him. He may become so infuriated at their authoritarian approach that he will join any group which is determined to be heard and to be given an explanation of why its requests for change and improvement cannot be met. In Chapter 12, Transition in Morality, child training and its effects on adolescent behavior will be discussed in more detail.

Family socioeconomic status and minority-majority group membership are likewise important conditions in influencing adolescent expression of nonconformity. Adolescents whose families are affluent and secure are far more likely to be reformers and activists than are those from economically inferior and insecure homes. The latter are more likely to become socially alienated, feeling that they have no chance of bringing about change in the larger social group. Adolescents from minority racial or religious groups, subjected from early childhood to discrimination and prejudice, suffer from resentments and frustrations that make them easy prey for radical leaders organizing protests against "the hostile establishment."

School influences

Junior and senior high schools both indirectly and directly encourage adolescents to engage in nonconforming behavior. *Indirectly,* the encouragement comes from adolescent frustrations due to lack of autonomy in choosing courses of study and in establishing rules for behavior in the classroom and in extracurricular activities. The students' nonconformity is also indirectly encouraged by boredom due to poor teaching or irrelevant subject matter; by feeling that teachers play favorites and grade unfairly, by heeding the school's emphasis on the need to be interested in social and political questions, and by dislike of school restrictions on hair length, clothing, and extracurricular activities (52, 65, 158, 167).

Directly, schools and teachers encourage student nonconformity when they strike and organize protests for higher wages, shorter working hours, smaller classes, and greater fringe benefits. If school is disrupted and teachers are picketing or holding mass meetings to discuss their demands, students come to believe that they too can get what they want if they strike or protest.

School influences may lead to attempts at reform and to activism or to generally rebellious behavior and social alienation. Students who receive high grades are more likely to demand reforms in a curriculum which they find irrelevant and boring than are poor students (79). Those who are well accepted by their peers know that if they strike or submit demands for reform they will win the favor of their classmates, and they are more likely to take a more aggressive approach than students who are poorly accepted. Since adolescents from middle-class and majority-group families tend to be better accepted than those from lower-class or minority-group families, reforming is the characteristic pattern of nonconformity of the former, and alienation, as shown in truancy and dropouts, is more characteristic of the latter. This subject will be discussed in greater detail in Chapter 10.

As is true of homes, schools that are run by permissive disciplinary methods encourage reforming and activism; those controlled by authoritarian methods encourage rebellion and alienation. Democratic control encourages many attempts at reform, but these are unlikely to be accompanied by protests and strikes because students feel that they can communicate their grievances, receive sympathetic attention, and, at times, achieve change (42, 74, 126).

Peer influences

Adolescents as a group are peer-oriented. They conform to peer standards of dress and behavior even when the standards are contrary to their parents' values. How greatly adolescents will be influenced by the peer group, however, depends to some extent on their level of peer acceptance. When it is the thing to do to grumble and to criticize, whether in school or at home, they will imitate the model set by their peers. Whether they will express their discontent by open rebellion, by attempts at reform, by active protests, or by joining a group of alienated peers will depend largely on the degree of social acceptance they have achieved.

Stars, those who are liked and admired by almost all of their peers, realize that they must watch their step or they might lose their following. Consequently, they tend to be conformists, rarely stirring up trouble by rebellion or protests. This is also true of those who are well liked, though not stars.

By contrast, those who are marginal—the fringers and the climbers—are willing to do almost anything to improve their status in the group. As a result, they become easy prey to the proddings of activist leaders and often join in protest movements. They may even become the leaders in reform and activism, hoping to gain a following and improve their status.

Neglectees, who are overlooked but not actually disliked, and rejectees are less subject to peer pressure and are not likely to become reformers or activists. They often become alienated and are almost always rebels, but they usually do not express their rebellion overtly, as reformers and activists do. Instead, they withdraw.

Regardless of the sociometric status of the adolescent, peer influences on appearance are almost universal. To avoid being regarded as different—which suggests being "inferior" —even the alienated try to look like their peers. Consequently, to a casual observer, all adolescents appear to be "nonconformist," a label which plays an important role in the stereotype of the adolescent and leads to the assumption that, because they look alike, they automatically share similar values and behave in the same manner (85).

Mass media

The mass media, especially the newspapers and television, contribute heavily to adolescent nonconformity in three ways. *First,* they stereotype all adolescents whose grooming and clothing do not reflect approved adult standards as nonconformists and attribute the behavior characteristic of nonconformity to them. As Bandura has pointed out, "The view that adolescence is a period of rebellion is often supported by references to superficial signs of nonconformity, particularly adolescent fad behavior" (10). He goes on to explain how this affects adolescent behavior and contributes to nonconformity.

If a society labels its adolescents as "teen-agers" and expects them to be rebellious, unpredictable, sloppy, and wild in their behavior, and if the picture is repeatedly reinforced by the mass media, such cultural expectations may very well force adolescents into the role of rebel.

The *second* way in which the mass media contribute to adolescent nonconformity is by making real life appear unsatisfying and dull. The "beautiful people," the glamorous, and the rich are presented as the ideal. The adolescent is thus encouraged to protest against a government that spends tax money to send people to the moon or to fight a war rather than to make life pleasanter for its people. As the adolescent develops a more mature outlook on life, some of his dissatisfaction wanes and, with it, some of his desire to find fault and to bring about change.

Presenting vivid pictures of protests among workers and students is the *third* way in which the mass media contribute to adolescent nonconformity. Not only do young people learn the patterns of nonconforming behavior in this way but, even more important, they learn of the rewards. Viewing pickets walking before a factory or school on the television screen and being informed a day or so later that they succeeded in getting what they demanded tells adolescents that the surest way of achieving change is to become an activist.

All adolescents are subjected to the influence of the mass media, but not all become activists or reformers even though they are discontented. Many have learned that attempts at reform are rebuffed or punished. Authoritarian child training, for example, will not make the adolescent satisfied with life, but it may make him afraid to protest overtly and and may alienate him from a life pattern which he finds unsatisfactory.

Idealism

Adolescence is the age of idealism. Typically, the adolescent dreams of a utopia with all the evils of everyday life replaced by qualities that lead to happiness and well-being for all—for self, others, and society at large.

Normally, idealism is at its peak during the early part of adolescence and then is replaced by realism as the adolescent's social horizons broaden and his experiences become more varied. Adolescents who remain in college during later adolescence do not lose their idealism as early as those who assume an adult status in their work or family life immediately after high school.

Idealism increases the adolescent's dissatisfaction with his own life as well as with society and motivates a desire to improve things. In his zest to change things, the adolescent often develops an evangelistic approach, trying to recruit others who are similarly idealistic and dissatisfied to help him (15, 104).

The effect of idealism on adolescent behavior is fairly predictable. At first, the adolescent shows indignation at social injustices; he crusades, often with the help of others, to better things for society at large. He tries to reform his friends to bring them closer to his ideal and he tries to reform himself.

The cost of social reform—in terms of both money and effort—may leave the adolescent so disillusioned that he decides to withdraw from society and seek a life whose pattern he can control. He may break off old friendships and try to find new friends who conform to his ideal. If this is impossible, he may become a "loner." Even more damaging, he may discover that he does not conform to his ideal himself; this may make him so self-dissatisfied that he contemplates or attempts suicide. This matter will be discussed in detail in Chapter 15.

NONCONFORMIST SYNDROMES

In the popular concept, the nonconformist is a maladjusted person. Furthermore, all nonconformists are believed to be alike, rebellious against the mores of the group with which they are identified and unwilling to try to conform. This popular concept is strengthened by the sometimes unusual dress and grooming habits by which nonconformists proclaim to others that they are unlike the larger social group (96).

Just as differences in home environment and family experiences determine what form nonconformist behavior will take, so these differences determine what kind of personality pattern the nonconformist will develop (76, 131, 143). Studies of the personality syndromes of the rebellious and the alienated nonconformists reveal that they are similar in some respects but markedly different in others. Both usually show a high level of intellectual ability, but the rebellious tend to be more creative in their thinking and more motivated toward academic achievement while the alienated tend to be underachievers, truants, and dropouts.

Both the rebellious and the alienated nonconformists are unconcerned about conventionalities and social expectations and both tend to question accepted social values. As Flacks (46) has stated:

They find it difficult to accommodate to institutional expectations requiring submission to adult authority, respect for established status distinctions, a high degree of competitiveness, and firm regulations of sexual and expressive impulses. They are likely to be particularly sensitized to acts of arbitrary authority, to unexamined expressions of allegiance to conventional values, to instances of institutionalized practices which conflict with professed ideals.

Both the rebellious and the alienated show hostility toward all in authority, though they differ in their overt expressions of this hostility. The rebellious protest against authority and the alienated withdraw from situations in which authority is exercised. Both are liberal and tolerant in their social attitudes, though the rebellious tend to be anxious to help those who are discriminated against while the alienated are usually so egocentric that the affairs of others are of little concern to them. While both show signs of poor personal and social adjustments, the rebellious tend to make better adjustments than the alienated (82, 88, 94, 165).

In spite of the similarities in personality syndromes, there are enough differences to justify identifying a "protest-prone" syndrome, as Keniston has labeled it, as distinct from the alienated syndrome (79). Therefore, a general picture of the personality syndromes commonly found among the protest-prone and the alienated nonconformists requires that each be discussed separately.

Protest-prone syndrome

Protest-prone adolescents are often overtly rebellious. They want to reform people and situations that do not measure up to their ideals, even if they must take a determined stand as activists. Studies of protest-prone adolescents report them to be critical, curious, idealistic, individualistic, aggressive, self-confident, emotionally independent, liberal, tolerant, and flexible. They are said to be lacking in self-control, orderliness, and endurance. Many are moody and some are severely depressed by their inability to change things to conform to their ideals (46, 94, 133, 156). In describing the personality of the most aggressive protest-prone adolescent—the activist—Sheehan (140) has said:

A student activist is a young adult with a strong need for identification with an ideology who actively participates in political and social organizations. He is moved by emotional rebellion in which there usually is present a disillusionment and rejection of the values and authority of the elder generation which he wants to replace with values and authority of his own. He has some degree of conflict between awareness of what he is and what he would like to be. He feels alienated from society, somewhat self-punitive, is independent and autonomous and has a need for self-actualization.

Alienated syndrome

The personality syndrome of the alienated nonconformist is characterized by egocentrism. The alienated adolescent is selfish, self-centered, and anxious and insecure about himself and what he wants to do. In general, he is self-dissatisfied, which makes him defensive. He tends to be immature, as shown by shiftlessness, carelessness, lack of self-discipline and persistence, irresponsibility, and impulsiveness. Since he is unrealistic, he tends to be reckless and fatalistic. He is usually a spendthrift, showing little concern for money and material possessions. His attitudes toward others are colored by resentment and hostility, though these are not usually overtly expressed. Alienated adolescents, as a group, are more unhappy than the protest-prone, and this contributes to their poorer personal and social adjustments (75, 85, 164).

SOURCES OF NONCONFORMITY

Just as nonconforming adolescents are psychologically different, so they have different motives for not conforming. While nonconformity is attributed to the physical stress of the puberty changes, Middleton and Putney (111) have pointed out other far more likely sources of motivation:

Clearly adolescent rebellion cannot be attributed solely to the biological maturation process, for adolescence is not a period of storm and stress in every society. Rather, there appear to be structural features in American society conducive to youthful rebellion.

Unquestionably, one motivation of adolescent rebellion is lack of individual identity; another is lack of societal recognition of the adolescent's near-adult status. Adolescents rebel, for example, at being restricted in what they can see on the movie screen without being accompanied by an adult and yet they are given the right to vote and are expected to serve in the armed services, if drafted (150).

As Bealer et al. have explained: "The adolescent seeking his identity in adult society may disagree with his parents regarding when recognition of his maturity should occur. He may wish to engage in activities which symbolize his adulthood while his parents feel that he is still too young. . . . Once the youth is accepted as a member of the adult society, this type of conflict ceases" (13).

Gaining a near-adult status in the home does not mean that the adolescent has no further reason to rebel and no further desire to change things that do not come up to his ideals and expectations. Box 6-3 describes six of the many sources of motivation for activist behavior (19, 75, 96, 133, 164).

While motivations of reform activity listed in the box are especially strong among reformers and activists, they also affect those who become alienated. Having been rebuffed or ignored in their attempts to right what they regard as wrongs, the alienated have become discouraged and disillusioned. They give up their attempts at reform as their disillusion increases. Adolescents who have been accustomed to being listened to when they communicate their grievances become enraged when lines of communication break down; this strengthens their attempts to achieve reform, even if it means taking drastic measures. Unlike the alienated, they are not likely to give up when they are rebuffed. For some, then, activism, rather than alienation, is a more common reaction to rebuffs and disregards. According to Aldridge (4), activism is also a compensation for other things:

BOX 6-3 SOURCES OF ADOLESCENT REFORM

Desire to Help Others
The adolescent sincerely believes that he can improve the lot of others. Targets of altruistic reforms are those for whom the adolescent has the greatest regard and affection.

Desire for Retaliation
The adolescent who is constantly criticized and told how to do things frequently turns around and gives parents and teachers a taste of their own medicine.

Self-assertiveness
The adolescent gets great ego satisfaction from showing others where they are at fault and what they can do to improve themselves.

Showing off
Sometimes the adolescent makes radical suggestions for reform because of the attention this brings.

Conformity to Peer Patterns
The adolescent often follows nonconformist leaders in their critical attacks on society and in clothing and grooming in order to improve his status in the peer group.

Self-defense
Sitting in judgment on others and telling them how they can correct their faults helps the insecure adolescent overcome some of his feelings of inadequacy.

The present college population is so constituted that many of its members are bound to be drawn to activism simply because they are suited to no other role. . . . Hence, their natural impulse is to try to compensate for their failure of ability or interest by involving themselves in some extracurricular activity which happens today to be political activism.

PATTERN OF NONCONFORMIST BEHAVIOR

Nonconformist behavior does not normally begin in adolescence or even at the period of heightened emotionality in early puberty. Instead, it begins in childhood, often during the preschool years. See Figure 6-1. Young children who see adults staging protest marches on TV come to think that protesting is *the* way to get what one wants. If parents and teachers demand certain patterns of behavior from children and threaten punishment if their demands are not met, the youngsters' ideas about getting what they want are reinforced. If parents and teachers criticize children's appearance and behavior and try

to get them to change, the children are exposed to a model which they can imitate if they do not like what someone says or if they do not approve the way things are done at home, at school, or in the community.

As their contacts with people outside the home increase and as their interests in the mass media shift from fairy tales to stories about real people, children build up idealized concepts of what people and life situations *should* be. As they compare their homes and families, schools and teachers, with their idealized concepts, they find faults which they quickly criticize and try to improve. This tendency to be critical and to try to reform becomes stronger with each passing year, reaching a peak during early adolescence and then normally subsiding to some extent as the older adolescent becomes more realistic and tolerant or as he discovers that criticism and attempts at reform antagonize others. Lazar and Klein (91) state that the adolescent's critical attitudes toward his parents stem from a revision of childhood concepts:

By criticizing his parents, the teen-ager is trying to bring them down to life size and helping himself to feel as competent as they are. He is trying to convince himself that "They're not so perfect after all." . . . This effort to accept that his parents are less than perfect is behind much of the teen-ager's arrogance and hostility. Few parents, of course, have ever claimed to be perfect and it is often difficult for them to understand that their child finds it necessary to prove that they are not. But it is useful to keep in mind that, when the teen-ager lashes out, he is not angry because his mother or father tried to fool him with a false picture of perfection: he is simply rebelling against his own childish fantasy of their perfection.

OVERT EXPRESSIONS OF NONCONFORMIST BEHAVIOR

Physical maturity—adult-size and shape—often gives boys and girls the courage to criticize openly those whom they formerly criticized behind their backs. During junior high school, outspoken criticism of family members, teachers, and other adults, as well as

Figure 6-1 The pattern for nonconformist behavior is often laid early in childhood. (Adapted from George Clark: "The Neighbors." © 1972 New York News, Inc. World Rights Reserved. Used by permission.

"I can't wait until I learn to write, so I can draw up a list of demands."

peers, is common and it continues to be so as the adolescent grows older.

Whether criticism is direct or is mere grumbling will depend partly on what the adolescent feels will be to his advantage and partly on how his criticism has been received in the past. If open criticism has been punished in the past, he may have learned to express his hostility covertly, using peers and other tolerant people as sounding boards for his grievances. It is not unusual for adolescents to send anonymous complaints to the school or college newspaper in order to avoid possible repercussions from those in authority.

As early as the gang age of late childhood, both boys and girls often accompany their criticisms with suggestions for improvement, such as "Why don't you do it this way instead of the way you are doing it now?" The older child will try to show the person how to make the change he thinks is needed. An adolescent girl, for example, will not just criticize the length of her mother's skirt but will tell her how long it should be and then pin it at the "fashionable" length. Older children may send a group of student representatives to the faculty committees or administrators with their complaints and suggestions for reform. Should this method fail, they may engage in mass walkouts, demonstrations, and picketing, modeled along the pattern set by labor unions. If this also fails, they may engage in more active protests, seizing buildings, holding administrators as hostages, or destroying school or college property.

Effects of overt expressions

Whether the adolescent expresses his dissatisfaction by grumbling, refusing to conform to expectations, criticizing, or attempting to bring about reforms, his behavior is damaging to the emotional climate of his environment. Criticizing things at home or complaining to parents about things at school arouses unpleasant emotions in those who hear the criticisms as well as in those at whom the criticisms are aimed.

The attitudes of others toward the grumbler, the critic, the rebel, or the reformer are inevitably unfavorable, not only because he is unpleasant to be with but also because he is regarded as poorly adjusted, or as a troublemaker. These attitudes are apparent to the adolescent and they merely add to his already-existing unfavorable self-concept. If others disapprove of him, it is hard for him to like himself. Because of his negative self-concept, he makes poor personal and social adjustments.

One of the ways in which poor personal adjustment expresses itself is in underachievement. In school, the dissatisfied student is almost always an underachiever; he often becomes a truant and dropout. In the home, he may shirk his responsibilities and work below his capacities. Dissatisfaction with his home may cause him to run away or to marry early in the hope of finding a happier home climate. These matters will be discussed in more detail in later chapters.

The effect of nonconforming behavior is as disastrous to friendships with peers as it is to relationships with one's own family. As was pointed out earlier, many adolescent friendships are broken, often permanently, by the critical attitude of one or more members of the peer group. Even more damaging to friendship is an attempt to reform a friend's appearance, behavior, values, or opinions. In heterosexual friendships, reform attempts are more common than in friendships with members of the same sex. Figure 6-2 shows the ages at which frictional relationships with parents and with friends of the opposite sex are most likely. While frictional relationships may stem from many causes, one common cause is criticism accompanied by attempts at reform (33, 74, 127).

When rebellion against authority, criticism of those in authority, or attempts at reform are rebuffed and punished, alienation almost always follows. Not only does the adolescent learn that it is to his personal disadvantage to pursue these tactics but he also realizes that he can make no headway, regardless of how willing he is to accept rebuffs and punishments. Consequently, he feels defeated and withdraws, thus becoming alienated from the

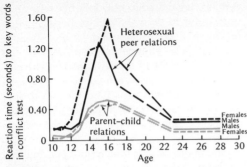

Figure 6-2 Frictional relationships, often caused by criticizing and trying to reform parents and peers of the opposite sex, reach their peak early in adolescence. (Adapted from S. L. Pressey and R. G. Kuhlen: *Psychological development through the life span.* New York: Harper & Row, 1957. Used by permission.)

group that has rebuffed his attempts to improve it.

The adolescent reacts to the peer group, the family, or the school group in much the same way. If members of the peer group rebuff his criticisms and suggestions for reform or punish him by disapproval and lack of acceptance, he is forced to decide which is more important to him—conformity to their standards or attempts to find new friends who are closer to his ideal. Since the desire for peer acceptance is so strong during early adolescence—when criticism and reform are usually at their peak—most adolescents choose the former alternative. They not only try to conform to peer standards but they also curb criticisms and attempts at reform which bring group antagonism and rejection.

TARGETS OF CRITICISM AND REFORM

Just as there is a predictable pattern for nonconformist behavior, so there are predictable targets of adolescent criticism and attempts at reform and predictable times when the targets will be attacked. Variations in the pattern are slight; they depend mainly on sex differences and on the kind of environment in which the adolescent finds himself.

Early criticisms, beginning during the preschool years and growing in frequency during the gang age of late childhood, are concentrated mainly on family members and the home. It is logical, therefore, that during adolescence the *family* and *home* should be major targets for criticism and reform. In Box 6-4 are given the typical home targets during the adolescent years (23, 34, 54, 68, 74).

Another major target of adolescent reform activity is the *school* or *college.* Formal organized protests occur on almost every campus, and informal criticisms of food, dormitories, teaching, and administration are as common and often more outspoken than criticisms of the home. Since the pattern of activity differs in high schools and colleges, the targets of criticism and reform at the two levels differ. Box 6-5 shows how different they are (8, 51, 68, 106, 137, 148).

As the adolescent's social horizon broadens, so does his interest in *community affairs.* Common targets for adolescent criticism and attempts at reform include the inefficiency of the public transportation system, poor radio and television programs, lack of community recreational facilities, dirtiness of the streets, dullness of the church services, age restrictions on movie attendance, and "corruption" of the local government (68, 85, 150).

School and college courses encourage adolescents to develop an interest in *national affairs,* and the mass media reinforce this interest and provide information which leads to criticism of many aspects of national life and national and international policies. Discrimination in hiring, promotion, and housing; pollution; inadequate care for the elderly and sick; and many other social ills become targets for adolescent criticism and reform (68, 79, 125).

Sex differences in criticism and reform

There are predictable sex differences both in the targets for reform and in the tactics used to bring about reform. For girls, the major *targets* are members of the family and the home, while for boys, more interest and zeal are concentrated on educational institutions and community and national life.

To an adolescent girl, her home is her background. She wants it to provide a glamorous setting when she entertains her crowd, especially members of the opposite sex. As Bossard and Boll (23) have pointed out, the home is a status-defining agency:

This explains that oft-noted critical attitude which adolescents, particularly adolescent girls, manifest toward their parents . . . their efforts to "bring up father," to make over the family and the home. The essential tragedy is that their families are a social handicap, or are believed to be so, during these years when the children's chief interest is their social acceptance outside the home.

Even the adolescent boy wants his friends to be impressed by his home. He does not want to be embarrassed when he introduces his parents to his teachers, his friends, or his friends' parents. To avoid being embarrassed he often criticizes his parents and tries to get them to comply with his concept of what "acceptable" parents should be.

Since girls tend to be more conforming than boys, attempts to reform school rules and regulations are more common among boys. Even though girls may have the same complaints as boys, they tend to express their criticism by grumbling and complaining to friends and family members rather than by going directly to their teachers or school administrators. Furthermore, as grades are, on the whole, more important to girls, they curb overt expressions of dissatisfaction, hoping to avoid the possibility of being given poor grades as a penalty.

The *tactics* used by male and female adolescent nonconformists differ considerably. For the most part, girls grumble and criticize, while boys act more aggressively and openly. During the stormy days of campus activism in

---

BOX 6-4   HOME TARGETS FOR CRITICISM AND REFORM

*Parents
The adolescent concentrates on his parents' "imperfections," their appearance, speech, table manners, treatment of each other, failure to participate in community affairs, and their restrictions on his activities. He tries to reform his parents if they differ markedly from his friends' parents or from standards set in the mass media. See Figure 6-3.

*Siblings
The appearance, grooming, speech, table manners, and friends of younger siblings, in particular, are targets of adolescent criticism.

*Relatives
Grandparents, especially grandmothers, are criticized for their grooming, clothes, speech, old-fashioned ideas and values, table manners, religiosity, and "stinginess."

*Home Management
Common criticisms concern menus, food preparation, hours of meals, "laziness" of the cleaning woman, "inefficiency" of the mother, requirements that children carry their load, religious observances, and parental use of liquor.

*Appearance of Home
Girls especially want to remodel the old house or get a new one; they want to rearrange the furniture and purchase new furnishings and laborsaving appliances.

BOX 6-5 TARGETS FOR CRITICISM AND REFORM AMONG STUDENTS

High School

*Teachers: Too old, too many women, favoritism, lack of interest in students and teaching

*Courses: Too few electives and too many required courses

*Grading: Penalty for originality, classroom behavior, or dislike of student; use of grades to select leaders and participants in sports

*Teaching: Too little discussion and use of educational films and too much memory work

*School lunches: Poor food, little choice, and too much supervision in lunchroom

*Extracurricular activities: Too much teacher supervision and banning of students with poor grades

*Rule making: Too little student participation

*School management: Too little student participation in curriculum decisions and choice of teachers

College and University

*Teachers: Impersonal, disinterested attitude toward students and teaching and too much interest in research

*Courses: Overlapping of subject matter, out-of-date facts, irrelevance of subject matter, and omission of information about minority groups

*Grading: Overuse of curve of normal distribution and letter grades

*Teaching: Large classes, too much emphasis on lectures and too little on discussion, dull and irrelevant teaching, too many required courses taught by graduate students

*Food: Dormitory and cafeteria food ill prepared, monotonous, and poorly balanced

*Extracurricular activities: Too much money spent on athletics in order to please alumni, too much emphasis on team sports, too few relevant lectures, and too little student entertainment

*Rule making: Parietal rules and little response to demands for autonomy in dormitory life and extracurricular activities

*College management: Too little student participation and representation in management and faculty and administrative committees

the late 1960s, the ringleaders as well as the majority of participants were boys (51, 52, 98).

This sex difference is explained by two facts: Aggressiveness is considered less sex appropriate for girls than for boys, and girls are trained from early childhood to be more conforming than boys. The difference in response does not mean that girls are more acceptant of the status quo, but rather that they show their nonacceptance in a negative way—by grumbling, complaining, and criticizing—while boys show theirs in a more positive way—by rebelling and attempting to bring about reforms, even by radical measures if necessary.

EVALUATION OF NONCONFORMIST BEHAVIOR

It is commonly assumed that nonconformity in behavior and appearance is a sign of poor adjustment and should be curbed lest the child develop into such a poorly adjusted adult that he will forever be a misfit in society. Before *all* nonconforming behavior is condemned, however, different kinds of nonconformity should be critically analyzed to determine if they are actually as detrimental to personal and social adjustments as often assumed. The following sections attempt to evaluate the effects of rebellion, reforming, activism, and alienation.

Rebellion

In rebelling, the adolescent fails to communicate his reason for nonconformity, except to label the social expectation "unfair" or to state that "I won't do it." A temper tantrum or a sullen refusal to conform to rules and regulations is negative in that it does nothing to remedy the situation which the individual finds unacceptable or intolerable. Others find little reward in trying to explore the cause of his refusal to conform. Then, if he willfully does just the opposite of what the rule or regulation requires, he arouses antagonism and threats of—or actual—punishment. The rebel readily interprets the threat or punishment as personal rejection.

Under such conditions, rebellion can only lead to poor personal and social adjustments. No one who antagonizes others and refuses to comply to standards regarded as appropriate for the group can expect to be judged favorably and accepted by the group. His grumpiness, faultfinding, and criticism are bad for group morale. Other group members may begin to wonder, either consciously or unconsciously, whether their own conformity is justified or whether the rebel is not right.

Those who disagree with the rebel are also affected by his critical remarks. Even if he leaves the group or ceases his attacks, the climate remains emotionally charged.

If the rebel is rejected by the group or senses its disapproval, he can hardly have a favorable opinion of himself. A poor self-concept inevitably leads to poor personal adjustment. If, in addition, the rebel convinces himself that he is right in refusing to comply with social expectations, he is likely to regard himself as a misunderstood and mistreated martyr, which will intensify his poor personal adjustment, lead to further antagonistic behavior, and increase his chances of social rejection.

Reforming

Reformers often play a positive role in their nonconforming behavior. Instead of being tear-downers, as rebels are, they try to be build-uppers. While finding fault with socially accepted patterns of behavior, they also offer suggestions for improvement. Even when their suggestions are impractical, they alert others to existing weaknesses and to the realization that changes might be made to overcome the weaknesses and bring about improvements.

Figure 6-3 Parents are a common target of adolescent reforms. (Adapted from George Clark: "The Neighbors." © 1972 New York News, Inc. World Rights Reserved. Used by permission.)

"You really should get a sports car, Dad. You don't want to fall into that middle-aged family man stereotype."

Social attitudes toward reformers are often unfavorable and reformers are usually regarded as "maladjusted," but these beliefs come not so much from the criticisms and suggested reforms themselves as from the manner in which they are made. More often than not suggestions for reform are made in a rude and derogatory manner, suggesting that the adolescent reformer is sitting in judgment on his parents, teachers, or other adults instead of working with them to improve conditions. It is this holier-than-thou demeanor that antagonizes adults and leads to unfavorable social attitudes toward the reformer (9).

Few adolescent reformers realize that *not all* adults are accustomed to explaining to children or even to adolescents their reasons for setting behavioral standards. Rightly or wrongly, many adults *assume* that young people will recognize that the standards are set to help them make better adjustments to the social group. If adolescents present their reasons for nonconformity in a nonbelligerent and mature manner, the barriers to communication and understanding will sooner or later be lowered, if not totally removed. Unfortunately, too many reformers believe that they are right and that everyone else is wrong. They, therefore, set up barriers to communication and rationalize their behavior by claiming that adults "don't understand" or can't understand because of the "generation gap."

Just as authoritarian social attitudes can discourage creative ideas, so they can discourage behavior arising from creative ideas. Thus, in an authoritarian atmosphere, the potential social value of the reformer can be lost. In discussing young reformers, Prugh (129) has written:

Their energy is boundless, their idealism and candor refreshing—though sometimes somewhat embarrassing to us—and their wealth of new ideas exhilirating, even if at times so many suggestions for change can be anxiety-provoking to members of our generation.

If the adolescent reformer is to make a contribution to the group and, through it, to his own personal and social adjustments, he must learn to channel his creativity and reforming activities into socially approved patterns. As Hurlock warned, "To be positive in its value, reforming must be controlled so that it will assume a socially approved form. Criticizing others and trying to reform them just to put oneself in the limelight or to inflate a deflated ego jeopardizes its usefulness to the individual and to the social group. Furthermore, it antagonizes others and militates against the social acceptance the adolescent craves" (69).

Activism

The value of activism to the adolescent depends upon a number of factors. If activism is approved by the peer group, becoming an activist will strengthen his social acceptance. If activism is a sure way of getting what he wants, then activist behavior will free him of the resentment that comes with constant frustration. Or if activism is a means of ego inflation, he will get temporary satisfaction from participating in activist protests.

The personal satisfaction derived from activism is likely to be greatly overshadowed by the unfavorable social attitudes it gives rise to. The activist may, if backed up by his peers, achieve some of his aims, but not attain the more important and more persistent goals of favorable social attitudes and social acceptance. He may acquire the reputation of being a "radical" and a "troublemaker"; the social group will then shun him as a disturber of the emotional climate or as a danger to the morale of the other group members. Most employers, for example, think twice before hiring a known activist for fear he will be a disruptive influence on the other workers.

On the positive side, activism may have a beneficial shock effect on a group or institution which, through habit or inertia, is not meeting the needs of the group or does not realize that conditions should be improved. Sampson (133) writes:

Student protesters . . . serve the positive function of rocking the boat, conceivably at a time and in a world in which some boats have slow leaks and require frequent rocking just to bail out enough water to keep them afloat.

As Sampson emphasized, however, too much rocking of the boat, especially by those who are inexperienced, serves only to disrupt and tear down instead of creating and building up anew. As a result, much of the potential value of activism is lost unless it is controlled and channeled into realistic reforms.

The shock effect of activism is especially valuable when authoritarian control has reduced communication between those in authority and the rest of the group to a minimum. Under such conditions, activism may be the only means of making those in control listen. The situation is analogous to that of the child who has a temper tantrum because the only answer he ever gets when he makes a request is that "Mother knows best."

Another positive aspect of activism is that it tends to focus on social ills; the goal is usually social improvement rather than personal gain for the activist. Every society needs citizens who will try to help those who cannot help themselves. People who are self-bound, concerned mainly with their own problems and personal welfare, do little to bring about progress for the group as a whole. Without activists who are willing to risk social acceptance for causes they believe strongly in, social ills will never be overcome.

Unfortunately, worthy social goals are often dismissed by the group because of its outrage at the tactics sometimes used by activists. The tactics may seem so antisocial and immature to "straight" members of the social group that they have no desire to cooperate in bringing about admittedly needed changes. As was pointed out above, it is the tactics used by reformers that antagonize others rather than the reforms themselves, and this is equally true of activists.

Sometimes the activist is so enthusiastic about the reform he is attempting to bring about and so convinced that it is essential to the welfare of others that he becomes incensed when members of the social group do not share his enthusiasm. If he regards this as a rebuff—and he often does—it may affect him in one of three ways: *first,* by increasing his belligerency and aggressiveness, *second,* by encouraging him to turn his back on society

and join the socially alienated, or *third,* by encouraging him to become more realistic and to recognize that reforms can best be achieved by "working within the system" rather than by attacking it.

Alienation

Nothing can be said in favor of alienation and much can be said against it. The person who alienates himself from the social group becomes egocentric, concentrating on his own desires and disregarding the interests of others. He makes no contribution to the group but expects the group to sympathize with him. He thinks rules, regulations, and laws were made for others to obey and feels justified in ignoring them himself.

The social group cannot accept the alienated person because of his unsocial attitudes and behavior. He resents his nonacceptance and becomes more hostile, nonconforming, and alienated. In time, he develops a sour-grapes attitude that further disturbs his personal and social adjustments.

Most alienated adolescents are socially rebuffed and, as a result, develop feelings of personal inadequacy. If no one will follow their suggestions for change and improvement, they may lose hope and become apathetic. Even worse, they may come to feel that they have nothing of value to offer—a feeling that may soon become a generalized feeling of inadequacy which stifles attempts to improve anything, including themselves.

As alienated adolescents turn their backs on the social group and try to find meaning in personal experiences, their bitterness and resentment often encourage them to try to deaden the psychological pain of rejection and personal inadequacy by the use of alcohol and narcotics.

LONG-TERM EFFECTS OF NONCONFORMITY

Contrary to popular belief, youthful nonconformity is rarely a passing phase which the adolescent will automatically outgrow. Actually, nonconformity rarely begins in adolescence; its origin may be traced to childhood adjustive patterns. If the foundations for nonconformity are laid in childhood, its symptoms normally become more conspicuous during adolescence.

Furthermore, since nonconformity is not caused by the physical and glandular changes of puberty, even though it may be intensified by them, there is no justification for believing that nonconforming patterns of behavior will disappear when the physical and glandular changes have been completed. It is far more likely that nonconformity will persist into later life.

The long-term effects of nonconformity may be favorable if nonconformity serves as a learning experience, helping the adolescent discover how and within what limits he can contribute to the welfare of the social group

and, through it, to his own personal and social adjustments. Such favorable effects come largely from the development of social insight, which is essential to good adjustments. Emphasizing the value of adolescent social insight, Kirkpatrick (84) writes:

The adolescent has an uncanny capacity for seeing his elders for what they are and classifying by his figures of speech their pomposities, rigidities, and numerous other foibles. . . . The worst thing that could happen to our society would be for our adolescent children to give up the struggle without a good fight and effect a truce or a compromise with life.

Lipset has concluded that once the activists of this generation of students leave the campus and become assimilated into the adult world of work and marriage, they will become

---

BOX 6-6 LONG-TERM EFFECTS OF DIFFERENT KINDS OF NONCONFORMITY

Rebellion
The habitual rebel is uncooperative, refusing to follow rules and carry his share of the social load. His behavior lowers group morale, and he is resented and often rejected by the social group. The rebel is often criticized by those in authority.

Reforming
Attempts to reform others arouse resentments. When rebuffed, the reformer may so doubt his ability to make a contribution that he will alienate himself from the social group.

Activism
Habitual protest deprives the adolescent of an opportunity to learn to make changes in a mature and socially approved manner. The activist may come to think that he is always right and others always wrong.

Alienation
The adolescent who alienates himself from the social group learns to think of himself as inferior because he is different and to feel martyred because others ignore him. Behind a facade of indifference, he suffers acute psychological pain from being denied social acceptance. He may try to ease the pain by excessive use of alcohol, narcotics, and sex. In time, these affect his physcial and mental efficiency, thus further curtailing his chances of becoming a useful and accepted member of the social group. Figure 6-4 shows the percentage of college students who reported their habitual use of different kinds of narcotics when they encounter personal or social problems.

somewhat more conservative but will retain a tendency to fight for what they believe in. They will continue to be a force for social change, which is essential to progress in a democratic society (98).

In spite of the social advantages of nonconformity, there may be long-term personal disadvantage. These are shown in Box 6-6 (67, 75, 86, 114, 133, 143). Since different kinds of nonconformity affect the adolescent differently, their long-term effects will likewise vary.

Rebellion, reforming, activism, and alienation have four common characteristics which affect long-term personal and social adjustments.

First, nonconformity is likely to become habitual. It may, in time, become the person's "normal" or usual way of adjusting to any situation that is not to his liking.

Second, since the person develops a habitual pattern of adjustment, he may acquire a reputation of being a grumbler or a militant. The likelihood of acquiring such a reputation is greater if the person dresses like other nonconformists.

Third, while nonconforming behavior may be modified to some extent as the adolescent gains better social insight and realizes that nonconformity often defeats its own purpose by arousing social antagonism, the modification is usually quantitative rather than qualitative. This means that adolescent grumblers or reformers are likely to be adult grumblers or reformers.

Fourth, and perhaps most damaging, all kinds of nonconformity elicit unfavorable social attitudes and thus make the individual doubt his own worth. This may, in time, lead to feelings of inadequacy and inferiority. As one adult remarked, "I was out to reform the world but didn't succeed in one instance. No one seemed to think my suggestions were worthwhile so I began to think I had nothing to offer. Even now, I blame this as the cause of the inferiority complex I have suffered from ever since I was a teen-ager" (69).

A person who doubts his own worth and feels that he cannot meet the demands of life as successfully as his peers becomes embittered, depressed, and unhappy. The persistence of such a frame of reference has been suggested by Tennyson (152):

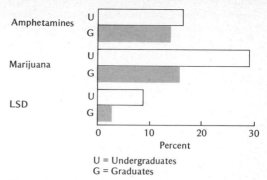

Figure 6-4 The habit of using drugs as psychological pain-killers often begins in college when students encounter personal or social problems they find difficult to cope with. Data based on large sample from nine colleges and universities. (Adapted from G. L. Mizner, J. T. Barter, and P. H. Werme: Patterns of drug use among college students: A preliminary report. *Amer. J. Psychiat.,* 1970, **127,** 15–24. Used by permission.)

Ah, what shall I be at fifty,
Should nature keep me alive,
If I find the world so bitter
When I am but twenty-five?

HIGHLIGHTS OF CHAPTER 6

1. Nonconformists, those who reject the values of the social group and refuse to adhere to its approved patterns of behavior, can be divided into four major categories: rebels, reformers, activists, and alienated.

2. Social attitudes toward nonconformists are unfavorable, especially if their appearance and behavior differ markedly from group-approved patterns.

3. Many conditions contribute to nonconformity. The most common are physical maturing, whose effect is mainly indirect by creating a desire and demand for autonomy, the so-called generation gap, and the influence of schools, colleges, universities, the home, peers, mass media, and adolescent idealism.

4. The personality syndromes of rebels, re-

formers, activists, and the alienated differ, owing mainly to different environmental influences.

5. Two major kinds of personality syndromes have been identified in nonconformists: (1) the protest-prone syndrome, characteristic of rebels, reformers, and activists, and (2) the alienated syndrome, characteristic of the alienated.

6. Adolescents have different motives for nonconformity. The most common are desire to help others or to retaliate, self-assertiveness, showing off, conformity to peer patterns, and self-defense.

7. Nonconformity follows a predictable developmental pattern, often beginning in the preschool years and reaching a peak during adolescence.

8. The common overt expressions of nonconformity include criticism of others and attempts to reform them, grumbling, and rebelling against rules and regulations.

9. Overt expressions of nonconformity lead to unfavorable social attitudes toward the adolescent, which are damaging to his personal and social adjustments.

10. Common targets of criticism and reform include parents, siblings, relatives, the appearance and management of the home, peers, school, college, community, and national affairs.

11. Evaluations of nonconformist behavior reveal that rebellion and alienation are more damaging to the personal and social adjustments of the adolescent than are reforming and activism.

12. Because adolescent nonconformity is rarely a passing phase, its long-term effects are more often damaging to personal and social adjustments than beneficial.

Chapter 7

Recreational Interests and Activities

Social changes bring about important changes in recreation. The urbanization of America over the past fifty years or so has increased the tensions and stresses of everyday life as well as the amount of leisure time the average person has at his disposal. The growth of large cities has made informal home entertaining difficult and has popularized commercial recreations, such as movies, bowling, and professional sports. The prolonged economic dependency of young people due to changes in educational opportunities means that adolescents have much more free time, but perhaps not as much money for recreation as they would like.

Improved transportation has enabled adolescents to engage in recreations away from home and school, free from the supervision of parents and teachers. Social emancipation of women has permitted adolescent girls to engage in recreations formerly limited to boys. And the decline in cultural and religious opposition to many recreations has opened up a whole array of recreational opportunities that were not readily available to adolescents of past generations.

One of the most recent social changes to affect adolescent recreations is the increased heterogeneity of the student bodies of our schools and colleges. This change, together with our recognition of the importance of social acceptance to the social and personal adjustments of children, has presented a major challenge to many educational institutions. When the makeup of the institutions was more homogeneous, discrimination and social acceptance in recreational activities were based primarily on personality or athletic ability. Similarly, when community recreational facilities were centered in the churches, the problem of discrimination was to a large extent eliminated. Today, as was stressed in Chapter 4, this problem is of major importance in many community organizations that offer recreational facilities for adolescents.

Social attitudes toward recreation

Most societies place a high cultural value on work. It was formerly believed that play belonged to early childhood and that the adolescent should devote his time to the serious job of preparing for adulthood. Leisure activities were regarded as loafing and a waste of time.

With automation and the shortening of the work week, more leisure time became available to adults and societal attitudes toward it changed. It is now recognized that people need recreations as they grow older just as children need time to play (45, 100).

Gradually, a new need has been recognized: that of teaching people how to use their recreational time to the greatest advantage. Young people need guidance in selecting recreational activities that will meet their interests and provide healthful relaxation. Holton writes: "To play is no longer a sin but a necessary part of healthy living in a world of many stresses and much uneasiness" (61).

Values of recreation

With the cultural and social change in attitudes toward recreation has come the question, How much recreation does the adolescent need? It is recognized that all play and no work will not make Jack a happy, well-adjusted boy. But a really precise answer to the question is not yet available. Scientific attention has been focused on the values and benefits of recreation. Box 7-1 contains a list of the main benefits the adolescent derives from recreation (3, 29, 41, 83).

Which recreations will best provide these benefits is a highly individual matter. Adolescents differ greatly in their patterns of life and in their needs. An activity may be a recreation for one person and a source of tension and anxiety for another. For example, one person may get pleasure and relaxation from reading the classics while another may get similar benefits only from comics, tabloids, or scandal sheets. One may improve his social status most by learning to play the guitar, whereas another must learn to ice-skate.

One point, however, is almost unanimously agreed upon by those who have studied the recreational interests and activities of adolescents: Adolescent recreational needs are quite different from childhood play needs. The activities which best meet adolescent recreational needs closely approximate those which best meet adult needs.

CHANGES IN RECREATIONAL PATTERNS

With the onset of puberty, changes in recreational activities are essential and, ordinarily, the changes begin to appear naturally. At no time, however, do recreational interests change suddenly. The pace at which they change appears to be determined by the pace of physical changes. When body changes occur at a fairly rapid rate, as at puberty, changes in recreational interests are speeded up. After puberty, when body changes occur at a slower rate, there is a slow and gradual change in recreational interests (29, 92). A number of changes in the recreational activities of adolescents are described below and shown graphically in Figure 7-1.

Changes in time spent in recreation When boys and girls reach adolescence, more of their time must be devoted to home and school responsibilities. With limited leisure, they learn to be more selective in choosing recreational activities.

Changes in number of recreational activities With puberty, many childish play activities are given up as the physical energy needed for games and sports is spent in work of different kinds at home, in school, or on the job. Environmental or economic conditions further limit what the adolescent can do during his leisure time, and so the number and variety of his activities diminish.

Changes in companions By mid-adolescence, interest in members of the opposite sex brings about a marked change in preferred companions. Boys now spend more of their leisure time with girls, and girls spend more time with boys. There is also less difference in the recreational activities of the two sexes than at any time since early childhood when boys and girls played together with the same toys.

BOX 7-1   BENEFITS OF RECREATION

Physical Health
Recreations supply the exercise necessary for good health and reduce the emotional stress that disturbs body homeostasis.

Mental Health
First, recreations provide socially approved outlets for aggressiveness; second, they offer opportunities for self-expression in creative activities; and third, they provide relaxation and thus ease the tensions of everyday life.

Improvement of Social Status
Recreations provide opportunities to get to know members of the peer group, to improve social and athletic skills, and to gain social insight.

Self-evaluation
Peer-group recreations give the adolescent an opportunity to compare his own interests and skills with those of his peers.

Foundations for Adult Recreations
In adolescent recreations the person develops a wide repertoire of interests and discovers which will best meet his adult recreational needs.

Changes in energy expenditure in recreation By the age of 15 or 16 years, adolescents begin to show a preference for sitting around and talking, attending athletic contests as spectators, going to the movies, reading, playing card games, listening to the radio and hi-fi, watching television, and riding in automobiles. Effortless amusements gradually take the place of strenuous play.

Change from informal to formal activities With the onset of adolescence, there is a trend toward more formality. Adolescents make appointments to meet in a specified place and at a definite time. They must be suitably dressed for the activity planned, and the equipment needed for the activity must be correct to the last detail. This formality eliminates much of the spontaneity characteristic of

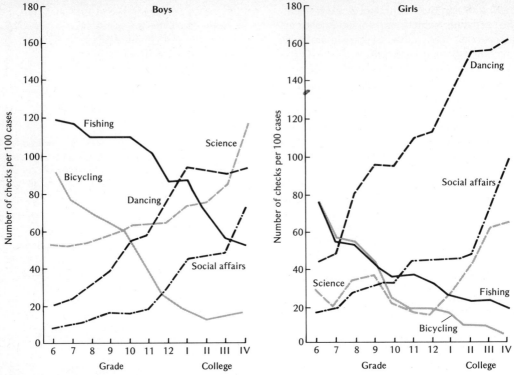

Figure 7-1. Changes in some recreational interests throughout the adolescent years, as found in one study. (Adapted from S. L. Pressey and R. G. Kuhlen: *Psychological development through the life span.* New York: Harper & Row, 1957. Used by permission.)

children's play activities. It is also a handicap for adolescents whose environment and family income make it impossible for them to buy the clothing and equipment needed to keep up with their peers.

Changes in attitudes toward repetition Most children feel happy and secure doing the same thing over and over again; they enjoy rereading stories and comics, seeing the same movies, or hearing the same music. By contrast, adolescents prefer varied, thrilling, and novel experiences.

FACTORS INFLUENCING
ADOLESCENT RECREATIONS

Adolescents not only differ in their recreational needs and preferences, but the needs of any particular adolescent change from time to time. In this section, the factors that influence

recreational interests and activities most are discussed in some detail.

Personal interests By adolescence, most people have discovered which recreations interest them and which bore them, and concentrate on those they find interesting. Many adolescents, for example, prefer recreations that can be engaged in alone or with a few intimate friends. As Strang has pointed out, "Many adolescents are not naturally 'group happy'; it is a strain for them to keep up with the more extrovert teen-agers" (114). Adolescents who are group happy select recreations which involve members of the peer group.

Opportunities to engage in preferred activities Some adolescents have few opportunities to take part in their preferred recreations. Those most likely to be deprived are young people from rural areas, from large families, and from low-income families; members of minority groups; older adolescents; and girls (25, 88). Of these, girls are the largest group of "recreationally underprivileged youth" (29). Two factors account for the girls' deprivation. *First,* schools and communities offer more free activities for boys, and *second,* boys are better able to earn money for commercial recreations. Strang quoted a report of a 17-year-old girl who described her problem in this way (114):

My one big problem is having no place to go at night so I can dance, meet boys, and also eat. Children here at Central don't come from people who have money. So they cannot be always giving partys. . . . I have a boy I wented with most all the time and he came over about three times a week. We either wented for a walk or to the movies—where else could we go? He went to school like me and couldn't pay to be going to dances all the time.

Physical development Adolescents with small physiques show less interest in sports than those whose body builds make success in sports possible. In boys, the quality of muscular tissue is important in determining not only the kind of activity engaged in but also the extent of participation. Recreational interests are more influenced by physiological age than by chronological age. With sexual maturity comes a shift from childish activities to more mature recreations. Sexually mature boys and girls, for example, shift from neighborhood games to social activities with members of the opposite sex (48, 66).

Intelligence Bright adolescents participate in a greater number and variety of recreations than the less bright. In addition, the bright ones spend more time in solitary activities and are more capable of finding satisfaction from their own resources. Typically, the reading interests and preferred radio and TV programs of bright individuals are similar to those of persons several years older than they (76).

Sex Sex differences in recreation begin around the age of 6 years, reach a peak in early adolescence, and then begin to decline as the two sexes spend more of their recrea-

tional time together. These differences are largely due to cultural influences rather than innate differences. For example, a boy might prefer such recreations as drawing and painting but since these are regarded as "feminine," he spends his time on activities considered appropriate for boys, such as sports or reading about sports and science (47, 115).

Environment The environment in which the adolescent lives influences his recreational interests in two ways. *First,* it determines what it is possible for him to be interested in. The number and age of the people present, the climatic conditions, the facilities offered— all play a role in determining what interests the adolescent can develop. *Second,* cultural pressures affect recreational interests. In some communities, it is conventional and correct to be interested in music, art, and the theater. In others, an individual is considered peculiar if he is not interested in fishing, swimming, or sailing.

Family socioeconomic status Recreational interests based on differences in socioeconomic status are less marked in early adolescence than later. They become obvious when some students enter the academic program in high school, preparing for college, and others enter the vocational training program, preparing for jobs. College-oriented adolescents, for example, have less time for recreations and they prefer those with higher prestige value, such as sports, reading, clubs, and social activities with their peers, while the work-oriented spend more time in movie attendance, dancing, and loafing (11, 29).

Peer interests Even though a boy may have little interest in sports, he must feign an interest if he wants to be accepted by boys to whom sports are important. Similarly, girls must feign an interest in boys and dating if they want to belong to a clique or crowd of daters. Because interests developed to serve the purpose of social acceptance often do not fill a real need in the adolescent's life, they are not likely to be permanent (3).

Prestige of recreations The prestige value of different recreations varies from one socioeconomic group to another. The adolescent whose family belongs to a given group will engage in the recreations approved by that group if he wishes to gain acceptance. Bowling, for example, has high prestige value among adolescents of the lower socioeconomic groups, whereas country club membership and social activities have prestige among adolescents of the upper classes. One of the problems of the socially mobile adolescent is the need to acquire an interest and a proficiency in the recreations that have high prestige value in the social group with which he aspires to be associated (83, 86).

Degree of social acceptance The status of the adolescent in the peer group determines to a large extent what his recreational activities will be. If he is well accepted, he will have many more opportunities for recreations involving people than will the less accepted adolescent. This is well illustrated in the case of television watching. While every adolescent enjoys the mass media, Coleman contends that the amount of time an adolescent "stays glued to a TV set" is an indication of his lack of popularity. He adds (29):

Those who are in especially favored positions will not need to escape from the world in which they find themselves, and will turn to the world of mass media less often. Conversely, those in a particularly disadvantaged position will often use this way out of their unfavorable environment. . . . [When he is in a] system that fails to give him status and allow him a positive self-evaluation, the adolescent often escapes to a world where he need not have such a negative self-evaluation: the world of mass media.

A leader who is secure in his status can usually persuade his followers to engage in recreations he enjoys. The less secure leader, by contrast, lets his followers decide what recreations the group will engage in; he hesitates to try to impose his own wishes for fear of jeopardizing his status. Fringers and climbers will spend their recreational time in activities everyone enjoys, regardless of their personal interests. Only the voluntary isolate can engage in the recreations he prefers without worrying about how this will affect his status.

COMMON RECREATIONS OF ADOLESCENCE

In this section, some typical recreations of the American adolescent are described. All these recreations meet some needs in the adolescent's life, though the needs vary from one person to another and, in the same adolescent, from one time to another. An attempt is also made to evaluate the recreations in terms of how well they fill immediate needs and how much they contribute to personal and social adjustments.

Conversations

In adolescence, playing games and engaging in sports that require vigorous physical exertion give way to sitting around and talking to friends. In fact, this is one of the most popular ways for adolescents to spend their leisure time (82, 92). Many boys and girls who were relatively inarticulate as children become very verbal during adolescence. Conversations help the insecure individual establish himself through identification with another person.

The importance of talking to others is evidenced by the tendency of the adolescent to monopolize the family telephone. No sooner has he left his friends than he must call them up. And unlike most adults, adolescents will talk endlessly unless parental restraints are imposed. Boys, as a group, do less telephoning than girls. This is not because boys are more secure and have less need to keep in contact with their friends. It is because they have fewer restrictions on their activities and thus more time for face-to-face talking.

Whether adolescent conversations are face to face or by telephone, certain topics are fairly universal. There are, however, variations in favorite topics in early and in late adolescence.

Difficult as it is to make accurate studies of what *young adolescents* talk about when they are with their peers, their favorite topics appear to be members of the other sex, dates, and matters relating to sex. They also talk about their families, clothes, current happenings in the school and community, and their future vocations. By the senior year in high school, the favorite topics of conversation for boys are ball games, jokes, dates, movies, and politics, and for girls, parties, dates, jokes, books, the movies, movie stars, ball games, and teachers. They like to discuss the personal lives of their heroes—sports figures for boys and movie and TV performers for girls (49, 54).

Characteristically, the young adolescent is either boastful or critical. He talks about personal matters in a *boastful* manner, trying to impress his listeners and increase his prestige. He discusses impersonal matters in a *critical* way, finding fault with everything. He occasionally makes suggestions for reform, but these are most often impractical (48, 114).

Obtaining accurate information about what *older adolescents* talk to their peers about is equally difficult. Their conversational topics are more varied than those of younger adolescents because many have entered the adult world and their lives and interests have taken on a different pattern.

Among college men, dates, fraternities, sports, dancing, clothes, and drugs and drinking rank first in popularity. Among college women, dates, clothes, sororities, food, drugs, and dancing are favorite topics. Sex is one of the most frequent topics of conversation of both boys and girls (24, 39, 49).

The older adolescent boasts less than the younger adolescent because he has discovered that, unless very subtle, boasting wins group disapproval. Older adolescents are critical in their comments, however, and they often offer practical suggestions for change and improvement. This was discussed in Chapter 6.

Nontalkers Some boys and girls talk very little in group situations because they are afraid they will say something that will lead to group disapproval or rejection. This is especially true of fringers and climbers. Group disap-

proval can quickly build up such strong feelings of personal inadequacy that the shy adolescent will shun social situations. He may compensate by carrying on long, imaginary conversations. Another form of compensation is writing. The adolescent may express his thoughts and feelings in voluminous writings, having little fear that anyone else will see them. Or he may dominate the conversation at home. The adolescent who tries to do all the talking during the family dinner is likely to be compensating for not talking when he was with his friends.

To some extent, talking on the telephone is a form of compensation. The adolescent who hesitates to say what he thinks in a face-to-face social situation may find the courage to say it when he cannot see or be seen by another. There is some reason to believe that the use of the telephone as a means of communication is closely associated with a feeling of personal inadequacy.

Evaluation Many adults consider adolescent conversations a waste of time. Though they recognize conversations as recreational, they regard them as damaging in many respects: They believe that too much boasting about possessions and family status leads to distorted attitudes and values and may encourage a hypercritical attitude toward parents, teachers, and all in authority.

Relatively few adults realize that adolescent conversations are a major force in *socialization* because they help adolescents understand themselves and their contemporaries. Even more important, young people have an opportunity in their conversations to discuss their problems in a free and uninhibited manner. They get a new perspective and come to realize that the problems that bother them are similar to those faced by their friends.

Discussions and arguments enable the adolescent to present his views to others. Criticism of these views frequently results in their revision, the development of a less dogmatic approach, and a more tolerant attitude toward others whose views are different (1, 68).

Unquestionably one of the chief ways in

which adolescent conversations contribute to socialization is that, through trial and error, the adolescent discovers which topics are interesting and socially acceptable and which forms of presentation are acceptable. He learns, for example, that boasting and destructive critical attacks are not acceptable.

Loafing

Few recreations are as relaxing as "loafing"— time spent in idleness or physical inactivity. Loafing is recreational because the rapid physical growth of early adolescence tends to deplete the adolescent's strength. As growth comes to an end, loafing is less popular.

Whether loafing takes place in the home, at a favorite teen-age meeting place, or on a street corner, it is a pleasurable recreation for the adolescent. It is most pleasurable, however, if it is done with friends. Even though the body is relaxed during loafing, the mind is active. If the adolescent is with friends, he will spend his time talking. If he is alone, he will be daydreaming, reading, watching television, listening to music, or planning what to do next.

Evaluation A reasonable amount of loafing meets certain physical and mental needs. However, when opportunities for more stimulating recreations are lacking, the adolescent will become bored. He may be tempted, as Coleman writes, to "stir up a little excitement" (29). In some instances, this may mean riding around in an automobile or on a motorcycle, or finding a new place to eat and talk; in others, it may mean driving at forbidden speeds, finding a place that will serve liquor and permit drug use and sexual promiscuities. It may mean crashing a party or merely hanging around the house or club where the party is given and watching what is going on (41, 82, 90).

The lonely adolescent who is bored with loafing may watch TV or daydream or ransack the family refrigerator, eating anything he finds available. Many overweight and obese adolescents, Bruch has explained, are lonely loafers (21).

Parties

Parties are a satisfying recreation for three reasons: *First,* they bring boys and girls together socially; *second,* they offer adolescents an opportunity to learn and practice social skills which school and home situations do not offer; and *third,* they are a measure of social status, indicating to others that one is accepted by the peer group.

The status-symbol value of being invited to parties is great. Many adolescents who are not invited deeply resent the snub. Some react aggressively by party-crashing, and some react by dropping out of school or college. Studies reveal that social reasons are a more common cause of dropping out than academic failure. When the economic status of the family makes it impossible for the adolescent to go to school parties or when parents do not want their children to bring guests home because of the expense, confusion, or destruction of home furnishings, the adolescent often feels so out of things that he is motivated to take a job and earn money so that he can attend the parties of his peers.

While youth clubs offer adolescents opportunities for parties, as was pointed out in Chapter 4, many boys and girls, especially those from minority racial and religious groups, do not belong to these clubs. As a result, some of their important social and personal needs go unfulfilled (41, 67, 83).

Throughout adolescence, it is primarily girls who want parties, who make arrangements for them, and who persuade the boys to attend. Girls are more interested in parties than are boys for two reasons: *first,* girls mature earlier, prefer mature social activities earlier, and thus feel more at ease in party situations; *second,* being seen at parties is a far greater status symbol for girls than for boys (47, 66, 86).

Party activities The most popular party activities are *dancing; group singing,* accompanied by a piano or some other instrument played by a member of the group; *games* in which an indefinite number can participate; *listening to the radio; watching television;* and *talking.* *Eating* is an important part of every adolescent party. Simple food has a far greater appeal than adult-approved party food.

While *gambling* is primarily a male activity, girls sometimes shoot crap or play the slot machines when they are with boys. *Smoking* is popular among junior and senior high school students. If the party is to be "fun," many adolescents feel that there must be liquor and drugs. *Drinking* and *drug usage* often begin in early adolescence and are widespread by late adolescence. How these serve as status symbols will be discussed in detail in Chapter 8.

Party activities are greatly influenced by what certain cliques or crowds prefer or can afford and where the parties are held. Some adolescent crowds, for example, are composed mainly of persons who have automobiles and can go a considerable distance from home for their parties; some are limited to school or community parties. At some parties, gambling, drinking, telling off-color jokes, and petting are the favorite activities; at others the entertainment consists mainly of talking, eating, dancing, listening to popular music, or playing games. Parties held away from home, school, or community centers are likely to be "wilder" in the sense that the activities lack parental approval.

Evaluation   If parties are to meet the personal and social needs of the adolescent, they must fulfill three criteria. *First,* the adolescent must be able to relax from the stresses and strains of school and home life. He can do this only when the party is informal. The adolescent does not want to wear formal clothes or behave in an adult-approved fashion. That is why a party that starts out to be formal generally winds up being informal. The young people dance as they like to dance, sit in groups on the floor or porch to talk, and push together the small tables so that they can all be together at one big table when they eat (67, 86).

Second, the adolescent must feel that he does not have to strain to be recognized and accepted as a member of the group. The girl who lacks a dance partner and the boy who

cannot tell an amusing story have little fun because they feel left out of the activities that their peers are enjoying.

Third, the adolescent must feel that being invited to the party is a recognition of his importance and is regarded by others as a symbol of his belonging. The status-symbol value of a party is limited if it is given by a peer who has little status in the larger group and if it is attended only by those whose status is marginal.

Dancing

With sexual maturing comes interest in dancing with members of the opposite sex. During junior high school, dancing is a favorite recreational interest of girls and, to a lesser extent, of boys. At first, dancing is limited mostly to girls while the boys form an interested audience. In high school, dancing is one of the most popular recreations and an important party activity. For the older adolescent, whether in college or in a job, going out to dance is a favorite form of entertainment. Increased interest in dancing throughout the adolescent years can be seen in Figure 7-1. Note the greater interest shown by girls.

Most adolescent parties provide opportunities for dancing and most high school and college athletic programs include classes in different kinds of dancing—ranging from folk to classical and interpretive dancing. Formally organized church and community groups likewise provide opportunities for dancing as well as instruction in social dancing. Only when the adolescent leaves school or college and is too old for the youth groups of the community does he encounter difficulties in finding places where he can dance during his leisure time.

Nondancers   In a culture where high value is placed on the ability to dance, being a nondancer is a serious handicap to social acceptance. The adolescent who cannot dance or will not learn to do so because of religious or moral reasons, because he regards dancing as a waste of time, or because he is afraid of looking foolish is handicapped in all social situations. He acquires the reputation of being a "kid" or a "square." This militates against his ability to form close social relationships with members of his own sex as well as with members of the other sex.

Being a nondancer is more of a problem for girls than for boys, owing to the high value placed on dating and parties by girls. A boy who gains prestige because of his athletic skills can be well accepted and invited to parties even though he does not dance. When there, he can talk to both boys and girls and not be conspicuous. But he is likely to *feel* conspicuous and out of place. This will encourage him to stay away from parties. As a result, he will make poorer social adjustments than he otherwise would have made (18, 29, 114).

Evaluation Since dancing fills certain needs during the adolescent years, the ability to dance affects the kind of personal and social adjustments the adolescent makes. The nondancer is unable to take part in one of the favorite activities of his peer group, and this will make him feel inadequate and inferior.

Among the *personal* needs met by dancing, an opportunity to release the pent-up emotional tensions of school and family life is one of the most important. For many adolescents, the most effective emotional catharsis comes from a style of dancing which, to adults, seems both unconventional and ungraceful.

The need for excitement can also be met by dancing, especially when there is a crowded dance floor, loud music, and a group of peers having a good time together. Many adolescents express their desire to be creative by inventing new dance steps or by changing the conventional dance forms. Many use the dance floor to gratify their desire for peer attention and approval by showing off their dancing skills and, for girls, their figures.

Social needs met by dancing include acceptance by the peer group, self-confidence and self-assurance in social situations, and a feeling of belonging and prestige in peer groups composed of members of both sexes. The adolescent who is rated by peers as a "good dancer" can be assured of a favorable reputa-tion which will open social doors that might otherwise be shut. This is important for boys as well as girls.

Games and sports

During the impressionable freshman and sophomore years in high school, boys discover that the athletes stand out as the heroes of the school. At the same time, girls discover that being an outstanding athlete carries little prestige among peers of either sex. These discoveries influence the attitudes and interests of the young adolescent and affect his recreational activities.

As Coleman has reported, the majority of high school boys would like to be remembered as athletic stars rather than brilliant students, whereas girls would rather be remembered as popular with classmates of both sexes (29, 31). For boys, success in sports is a *visible achievement*. Also, it brings prestige to the school or college, while success in scholarship brings prestige mainly to the student himself. Parents, teachers, and members of the community and the mass media reinforce the prestige of boys' sports and, to a large extent, minimize the prestige of scholastic achievements. Since girls' sports carry little prestige and bring little acclaim, girls' interest is minimal (93, 116).

Boys who lack the body build or skills to become active participants in sports show their interest by talking about sports and by keeping up with sports events reported in newspapers and on radio and television. Since attending school and college games as spectators is a a popular dating activity in middle and late adolescence, girls usually show an interest in boys' athletic activities.

The high prestige associated with certain sports influences the adolescent's participation. While a boy might prefer a less prestigious sport to one with greater prestige, he will participate more in the prestigious one and work harder at being successful in it. The same holds true for girls. Boys claim that their favorite outdoor sports are football, baseball, swimming, and track, while their favorite indoor sports are basketball, swimming, bowling, and ping-pong. For girls, the favorite outdoor sports are swimming, tennis, and ice-skating, while the favorite indoor sports are basketball, roller-skating, and ping-pong (15, 75, 99, 105).

The peak of popularity of active participation in sports comes during the high school years. College students whose skill enables them to play on teams or engage in competitions continue to regard sports as a favorite recreation. Adolescents who go to work after leaving high school often lack opportunities to engage in active sports and, as a result, become spectators (86, 94). In late adolescence, girls show less interest in sports, both as participants or as spectators, than boys. Their lack of interest is due in part at least to cultural attitudes and to social pressures to perform in areas considered more sex appropriate (29, 47).

Games of intellect and gambling As interest in active sports declines, interest in games of intellect, such as puzzles, riddles, guessing games, card games, and games of chance, increases. These games offer the player much of the thrill and excitement formerly derived from sports but without the need to expend physical energy.

Gambling often adds to the excitement and pleasure of games. Gambling is not limited to games of intellect. Few adolescents, for example, find that being a spectator at an athletic contest is as exciting as being a participant. To increase the excitement, they bet on the game whether they watch it on television or on the playing field (85, 95, 99).

Evaluation Games and sports fill many of the same *personal* needs as dancing. They provide a source of emotional catharsis, an opportunity to evaluate oneself in relation to one's peers, a source of excitement, and a means of gratifying the need for peer attention and approval. Because of the low prestige value of sports for girls, their personal needs are less likely to be met by sports than by games, while for boys, the reverse is true.

Games fill fewer *social* needs than sports. Games may offer an opportunity for companionship and acceptance by peers, but they carry far less prestige than sports. A successful card player, for example, is not likely to be chosen as a social leader in adolescence, while a successful athlete often acquires a halo that assures his selection for leadership roles in nonathletic activities. Nor does adolescent success in games usually lead to adult leadership roles. An outstanding athlete in high school or college, however, is likely to be a leader in adult vocational or community life (70, 104, 122).

Sports have greater socialization value than games of intellect because they teach the player to be a cooperative member of a team and to use his energies to further the good of the team. He is not playing for individual glory and prestige as is true in games of intellect. Thus, competition in sports encourages the adolescent to be outer-bound while competition in games of intellect encourages him to be inner-bound (75, 83, 94).

Hobbies

"Hobbies" are activities to which the adolescent devotes some of his leisure time because of the pleasure and satisfaction he derives from them. Since his interest in the activities is strong, often lasting over a period of years, hobbies tend to be persistent.

To an outside observer, an adolescent's hobby might be regarded as a form of work—an activity engaged in to attain some end result. To the adolescent, however, it is a pleasurable relaxation—a recreation. Otherwise, he would not engage in it, because he is neither paid for his efforts nor forced to carry out the activity. The choice of the activity is his alone, and the time and effort given to it are completely voluntary. When his interest in the activity wanes, he feels no compulsion to go on with it, nor does he feel guilty about dropping it.

If a recreational activity is to develop into a hobby, it must be enjoyable to the adolescent and it must satisfy his needs so that he will want to return to it time and time again when he feels a need for recreation and relaxation. Studies of adolescent hobbies reveal that the majority of them fall into two broad categories: constructions and collections.

Constructions Making things just for the fun of doing so is a favorite recreation of many adolescents because they find it relaxing and they have something to show for their efforts. The girl who gets relaxation from knitting or sewing, for example, feels that she is not wasting her time because, eventually, she will have a new article of clothing.

Whether making things will prove to be a pleasurable recreation or a source of stress will depend largely upon the adolescent's skills and experience. A boy who has no mechanical experience or skill may finding tinkering with a cast-off radio quite unrelaxing. Similarly, a girl who has developed no skill in knitting will find making a sweater hard work.

Studies show that boys like to construct or remake cars, bicycles, motorcycles, musical instruments, radios, television sets, boats, or furniture. Girls enjoy making clothing, jewelry, and pottery. They also like to concoct new food combinations, though preparing everyday family meals has little appeal. As girls are expected to assume more responsibility for their clothing and the home than boys, they often regard making things as work. As a result, they generally have fewer such hobbies than boys (1, 4).

Constructive hobbies lose their appeal as the adolescent grows older. He takes a more critical attitude toward his workmanship and thus enjoys it less; he has less leisure time; and, most important, he has a growing interest in crowd life. Relatively few construction activities offer opportunities for being with a group.

One construction activity that retains its popularity throughout adolescence is *drawing*. The adolescent draws just for the fun of drawing, without any thought of displaying his achievements. When his drawing skills are limited, he often turns to doodling, or random scribbling, as a form of relaxation.

This he finds especially pleasurable and relaxing when he is bored in the classroom or while studying. The most common subjects of spontaneous drawing are words printed in a decorative fashion, pictures of men and women, and caricatures. Over 50 percent of the caricatures examined in one study were of men and only 5.6 percent were of women. The caricatures of men emphasized peculiarities of physique, such as a prominent Adam's apple, a receding chin, or a bald head; those of women emphasized badly kept hair or prominent teeth(63). Figure 7-2 shows typical adolescent drawings.

Collections Collecting large quantities of almost anything is a favorite hobby of children. Adolescents, however, collect only those things which are closely related to their school or social interests or which have prestige in the eyes of the peer group (86, 92).

Regardless of current fads, certain items are almost universally collected. Among the most popular items for boys are photographs of friends or of themselves at some memorable event; newspaper clippings about people they know, about people they have crushes on, or about themselves; phonograph records; letters received; badges and awards; old magazines; and programs of athletic events or school plays. Girls collect sweaters, costume jewelry, photographs, letters, articles about their friends or themselves in the newspaper or the school paper, souvenirs of parties, beauty aids—different shades of lipstick and nail polish—and photographs of friends or of themselves in some important dress or costume. The college student, like the high school student, keeps souvenirs of the red-letter days of his college career, often saving these until he reaches middle or old age (73, 92).

Since the job of classifying, labeling, and systematizing a collection is laborious and must be done in solitude, away from the peer group, the adolescent is often unwilling to carry it through. Interest in collecting usually reaches a peak between the ages of 9 and 13 years, the prepuberty and puberty years when the desire for solitude is strong. After the puberty changes have been completed and the young adolescent feels better physically, his interest in peer activities grows and his interest in collecting wanes.

Evaluation Hobbies meet important *personal* needs in the adolescent's life but few of his social needs. Since most hobbies require some activity, they serve as a form of emotional catharsis. As was pointed out earlier, however, this need is successfully met only if the hobby makes use of skills that are so well learned that the adolescent does not have to concentrate on what he is doing. Otherwise the hobby merely adds to the stress that he is trying to get rid of.

Adolescents often derive a strong feeling of personal satisfaction from their construction or collecting achievements. This is especially helpful for adolescents who lack enough social acceptance to gain satisfaction from social achievements. One of the most important needs satisfied by a hobby is the need for autonomy. No matter what a hobby is, it is selected and carried out by the adolescent without pressure or direction from others. The irritation of being told what to do and how to do it is completely absent.

Hobbies that meet important personal needs often become lifelong sources of relaxation and diversion. The man who, as a boy, found relaxation in tinkering around with machinery may find equal satisfaction from working or puttering around in a machine shop in the basement of his home and will use this as a retreat when affairs at the office become stressful. Similarly, the woman who discovered when she was young that experimenting in cooking was pleasurable and relaxing may spend her free time experimenting with new food combinations at the end of a stressful day.

Only when a hobby results in a construction or collection that is admired by the social group and brings prestige to the adolescent does it contribute to his *social* needs. And since social needs become stronger as the adolescent grows older, hobbies begin to lose much of their appeal. Only if they meet per-

Figure 7-2. Typical adolescent drawings.

sonal needs that cannot be met by other recreations are they likely to persist into latter adolescence.

Exploring

Throughout history, it has been recognized that young people grow restless with the accustomed pattern of their lives and want adventure. In the past, many boys and some girls, after completing their schooling, took time out to explore the world before settling down to jobs, homes, and families.

Today this desire to explore is intensified by the boredom that comes with a long period of schooling, often regimented and seemingly irrelevant, and by the possibility of exploring during summer vacations without jeopardizing chances for success in adult life. An equally important development is that the adolescent girl of today can explore almost as freely as the adolescent boy. She is no longer limited to closely supervised summer camps and tightly chaperoned tours.

The adolescent derives little pleasure from exploring his immediate environment. He wants to go afield and explore unfamiliar places. Trips to the country, tramps through the woods, fishing, camping, living in a primitive fashion in the open, and travel to foreign lands are all fun for an adolescent. He likes to do his exploring in unconventional ways. He prefers hitchhiking, riding in busses, or traveling abroad on chartered youth flights or by freighter to the more conventional travel methods enjoyed by adults. Much of the pleasure the adolescent derives from this form of recreation comes from the fact that it is different, exciting, and free from adult supervision (41).

Exploring is popular only when the social interest predominates. Much of the enjoyment comes from being with the crowd or a small group of intimate friends who have much in common. The loner who is rejected by his peers or who voluntarily withdraws from the group rarely engages in this form of recreation.

In the past, interest in exploring waned in middle adolescence when social activities with members of the other sex became prominent. Today, however, with the growth of youth hostels here and abroad and with the relaxing of parental restrictions on the exploratory interests of girls, members of the two sexes can explore the world together in a manner that would once have been considered improper. As a result, interest in exploring remains strong even in late adolescence.

Evaluation Exploring meets some of the most important personal and social needs of the adolescent, and, hence, its popularity as a form of recreation has grown. On the *personal* side, the need for excitement and a wholesome source of emotional catharsis makes exploring especially appealing to adolescents. In addition, it meets their need for autonomy. Getting away from adult supervision and direction gives them a feeling of independence that they can rarely achieve at home or in school. Even the older adolescent who goes to work after completing high school feels this need for autonomy because of the restrictions imposed by his job and by his parents, if he continues to live at home.

Few recreations meet the *social* needs of the adolescent more successfully than exploring. Not only can he be with his peers and engage in activities they prefer without parental supervision, but away from adult pressures, he is less likely to show or experience prejudice and discrimination. He usually becomes more democratic. Thus, exploring helps the adolescent who would suffer from discrimination in his hometown as well as the one who would be pressured to be snobbish.

Daydreaming

Daydreaming is one of the popular recreations of adolescence. With the desire for solitude and withdrawal from the social group at puberty, the adolescent has more time for daydreaming. Furthermore, his greater mental development makes daydreaming a more pleasurable experience than it was in childhood, and to some extent, it replaces the satisfactions formerly derived from active play.

When life becomes too complicated for the young adolescent, he retreats more and more from reality. Throughout high school, daydreaming is a problem for the adolescent himself as well as for his teachers. Though daydreaming decreases as the adolescent grows older, it is common even among college students (24, 27).

Daydreaming is almost universal during the adolescent years, but there are marked variations in the frequency of its occurrence. The well-accepted adolescent, for example, has less time and less need for daydreaming than one who is only marginally accepted or who is neglected or rejected (74, 106, 111).

As shown in Box 7-2, adolescent daydreams can be roughly divided into two major categories (65, 74, 85, 106, 110). Regardless of which category the daydream falls into, it centers around the adolescent's dominant interests *at that time*. The interests are dramatized, and the daydreamer is the central character. Many daydreams are woven around themes popularized by the mass media. As Blazer (13) has explained:

Modern civilization has provided us with "canned fantasies" in the form of movies, radio programs, and television shows. No longer do we have to develop our own daydreams: We can have them brought to us by a flick of the electric switch, or we can view them in technicolor at the neighborhood movie. Through the process of identification we are enabled to incorporate these manufactured dreams into out own repertory, where they serve as models for more dreams of the same type.

Evaluation The pleasant recreation of daydreaming meets some of the adolescent's personal and social needs. It also creates problems. On the positive side, it enables the adolescent to see himself as he would like to be and this is an ego booster at an age when the individual is characteristically unsure of himself and of his worth to society. In addition, daydreaming releases pent-up emotional tension, especially that caused by anxieties and aggressions. In his daydream world, the frustrated adolescent can express his aggressions without fear of social disapproval or punishment; he can run away and hide from anxiety-producing situations without fear of being labeled a "fraidy cat." He can find release for the strong surges of love that accompany sexual maturing. Daydreams also provide a format in which the adolescent can work out a solution to some of his problems. He may, for example, figure out a way to earn the money needed to buy the new car he regards as a must for social acceptance.

On the other hand, daydreaming often leads to poor personal and social adjustments, even though it may meet the adolescent's needs at the time. Blazer points out that "fantasy serves as a substitute for the attainment of goals which would be satisfying, but which are either socially disapproved or are, in the estimation of the individual, beyond his reach." More often, however, it is a form of escape, especially at times of disappointment. Daydreams thus serve as a flight from reality when adolescents cannot successfully meet life's challenges. Under such conditions, as Blazer further explains, many adolescents resort "almost automatically to a favorite fantasy theme whenever they feel bored, insecure, frustrated, or neglected. They use fantasying as a child uses thumb-sucking to comfort and relax themselves" (13). When daydreams lead to no appropriate action, they become harmful. They often waste time which might be more profitably spent on studies or in recreations that have a more socializing influence.

One of the most damaging effects of daydreaming is that it gives the adolescent a distorted concept of himself and his abilities and thus militates against self-acceptance. Day-

BOX 7-2   COMMON CATEGORIES
OF DAYDREAMS

*Daydreams of Superiority
Most daydreams of early and late adolescence fall into this category. The daydreamer sees himself as a conquering hero who is successful in whatever is important to him at the time (sports, romance, or academic work). He is recognized and applauded by his peers, parents, and teachers.

*Daydreams of Inferiority
More daydreams of inferiority occur at puberty than at any other time of life. The daydreamer sees himself as a martyr, misunderstood and mistreated. He gloats over his suffering, but usually, in the end, he turns out to be a hero and gloats over the penitent attitudes of those who made him suffer.

dreams of inferiority, for example, lead to the belief that one's capacities are below those of others. This causes self-dissatisfaction, a tendency to work below capacity, and withdrawal from social contacts. Daydreams of superiority often result in an idealized self-concept which is so remote from reality that it militates against both self-acceptance and social acceptance. The adolescent expects others to treat him in accordance with his idealized self-concept and then becomes angry and resentful when they do not.

Equally damaging, the daydreamer is often so completely satisfied with his imaginary life that he makes little effort to achieve success in real life. He resorts more and more to daydreaming, withdraws from social participation, and is in danger of losing touch with reality. When daydreaming comes from failure or lack of interest in one's environment, it is a retreat from a reality to which the adolescent has little motivation to return.

So long as daydreaming is indulged in with moderation and so long as the adolescent remains in touch with reality, it cannot be totally condemned. As Kuhlen has stressed, "It would be incorrect to assume that all daydreaming or fantasy is fraught with psychological dangers; again it is a matter of the extent to which engaged in'' (73). When the adolescent uses daydreaming as a continual and habitual retreat from reality, however, there is indication of serious underlying maladjustment (62, 65).

Music

Listening to music and producing it can provide recreation for the adolescent. Which activity will be preferred will depend largely upon which offers the most enjoyment and relaxation. The adolescent who, as a child, found piano practice stressful is not as likely to play the piano just for fun as the one who enjoyed piano lessons and did his practicing voluntarily. Even when an adolescent wants to learn to play a currently popular musical instruments—whether it be a guitar, banjo, or ukulele—he will soon lose interest if he finds it hard work or if his skill is so limited that others ridicule his playing. Under such conditions, it will be neither recreational nor pleasurable.

As most adolescents have had some training and practice in singing during their elementary school days, singing can be a pleasurable recreation so long as it is a group activity. Few adolescents sing well enough to want to sing solos, even for a group of peers, and they therefore limit their musical production to group singing.

Listening to music, on the other hand, requires minimum effort and provides maximum pleasure. The favorite music of today's adolescents is that produced by members of the peer group and that heard on radio, television, and records and at pop concerts. Many adolescents prefer radio listening and some carry transistor radios wherever they go. Record music is often more popular because the listener can control what he hears. Even though music produced by members of the peer group is likely to be inferior to that produced commercially, adolescents like to listen to it because it gives them a feeling of belonging to the group.

Musical preferences Studies of musical preferences reveal that adolescents prefer songs to orchestral music because they find it easier to identify with the lyrics or themes of songs. Regardless of whether the music is orchestral or vocal, they like the music that is currently in vogue. As Burke and Grinder have pointed out, their preferences are "oriented toward the peer-group music culture" (22). Some popular music may meet the immediate needs of a particular adolescent best. For example, a social isolate or a fringer usually likes songs that stress loneliness, while one who enjoys greater social acceptance will prefer songs that stress love and independence (23, 64). One who is better adjusted and more stable may prefer music that emphasizes form and quality, such as classical music, while another who is less well adjusted and less stable may prefer highly romantic music that emphasizes feeling (89).

Evaluation Because of its almost universal popularity, music obviously fills important needs during the adolescent years. Among the *personal* needs, the most important is that of emotional catharsis. Few recreations serve this purpose better than music and few are as pleasurable. Almost as important, music offers a source of identification. Many adolescents, when they were younger, derived a feeling of stability from identifying with a parent, teacher, or an older sibling of the same sex. These sources of identification are less satisfactory in adolescence—the reason will be explained in Chapter 13, Transition in Sexuality—and so the adolescent satisfies his need for identification by listening to songs sung by a favorite performer.

The adolescent who can play a musical instrument or sing well gets satisfaction out of being in the limelight and playing the role of leader in peer group song fests.

Because music, especially listening to music, is a group as well as an individual activity, it helps to meet the *social* need of belonging which is so strong in adolescence. Furthermore, discrimination rarely enters into activities that center on music, and so the adolescent whose status in the peer group is insecure can count on a feeling of belonging when the group concentrates its recreation on music, something that is rarely possible in sports, talking, dancing, and many other adolescent recreations (23, 82, 125).

Reading

Whether reading is recreation or work depends not on what is read but on whether reading is voluntary or involuntary. Reading to acquire knowledge, usually regarded as work, can be recreational if the adolescent engages in it voluntarily and if he enjoys it. Recreational reading may involve difficult material presented in a difficult-to-read fashion, as is true of much scientific material which adolescents read just for fun to satisfy their curiosity about scientific matters.

Since needs differ, there are marked variations in what adolescents read for relaxation. Certain topics, however, are almost universally appealing. By the age of 15 years, boys begin to specialize in technical books which relate to their hobbies. Between the tenth and eleven grades, they shift to more mature reading material. After that, the reading interests of boys differ little from those of men. Girls prefer fiction, and unlike boys, they enjoy poetry. Girls become increasingly interested in romance as they grow older, and much of their reading is concentrated on romantic themes (58, 69, 126).

The child limits his reading mainly to books and comics, but the adolescent reads from different media. Box 7-3 describes the adolescent's favorite reading media (16, 20, 44, 120, 126, 128). The adolescent will devote most of his reading time to those media which

---

BOX 7-3   FAVORITE READING MEDIA

*Books
As time available for reading for pleasure decreases, the adolescent reads fewer books. Those he does read are usually by well-known modern authors.

*Magazines
Magazines provide the greatest share of recreational reading. In early adolescence, favorite teen-age magazines emphasize the theme, "How to be attractive in order to be popular in order to have fun." In late adolescence, adult magazines are preferred. Boys enjoy magazines dealing with popular science, humor, and adventure, while girls prefer those which stress romance, beauty, clothes, and glamour.

*Newspapers
The adolescent still enjoys the comic and sports sections, but shows an increasing interest in community, national, and international affairs. Tabloids, with their sensational presentation of news and pictures, appeal to many high school students and older adolescents who go to work. College students prefer regular newspapers.

*Comics
Comic books lose their appeal as adolescence progresses, but comics in newspapers and magazines and satirical magazines in a comics format gain in appeal. Girls prefer comics that concentrate on romance and feminine characters while boys prefer those which emphasize sports, adventure, crime, and violence.

are readily available and which meet his reading needs best. An adolescent from a culturally deprived home, for example, may have access only to comics and tabloids unless he visits the school or neighborhood library where he will find better newspapers, magazines, and books.

Recreational reading is less popular in adolescence than in childhood. Ordinarily, adolescents have less time for recreation than children and, in addition, many adolescents associate reading with school or college work and thus do not regard it as recreation. Instead, they prefer less solitary activities and recreations that are distinctly different from their academic work.

Adolescents read less for pleasure during the summer than during the winter because summer offers more opportunities for outdoor activities. Very bright adolescents read much more for pleasure than do those of average or below average intelligence. The former read with less effort, need less time to prepare their school work, and thus have more time for recreational reading. Girls at every age read more than boys because they have fewer recreational opportunities of other kinds available to them. Adolescents who lack social acceptance often use reading as a major form of recreation (51, 69, 120).

Evaluation Recreational reading meets many of the adolescent's *personal* needs. It offers an opportunity to escape from the real world, which the adolescent often finds dull and boring, into a world of glamour and excitement. Through laughter—from reading humorous stories, jokes, and comics—and through crying—from reading stories with sentimental or tragic themes—the adolescent obtains emotional catharsis. Reading also provides heroes or heroines for the adolescent to identify with; these bolster his ego, increase his feelings of security, and supply models to imitate.

Many of the problems the adolescent faces in real life are mild by comparison with those faced by fictional characters. His problems come to seem less overwhelming, and in reading, he often gains insight into methods of dealing with them. Magazine articles with the "how to" theme likewise help the adolescent solve some of his problems.

Even though reading may temporarily meet some of the important personal needs of the adolescent, undirected reading concentrated on tabloids, magazines, and comics that present life in lurid, exaggerated terms can increase the adolescent's discontent with himself and with the pattern of his life. Even worse, such reading can distort the values he uses to judge people and situations in real life. He may, for example, come to believe that violence offers the easiest way to get what he wants and that respect for the law is characteristic of weaklings.

Reading can meet *social* needs by helping adolescents understand people and social situations and develop socially approved attitudes and better social relationships. It also provides information about social skills and approved behavior which many adolescents find lacking in their home environments. This information helps the adolescent feel more secure in his social relationships and thus improves his social acceptance.

Movies

Though high cost of attending movies and the competition of television have lowered their popularity among adolescents, movies are still a popular recreation. Going to the movies is a favorite dating activity, not only among students but also among adolescents who work. Many go to the movies because they have nowhere else to go on dates, because it helps to pass the time without the necessity of talking, because it gives them a place to pet, and because it is the "thing to do." Those who attend movies when not on dates do so because they are bored with their studies and the recreational activities that are available to them or because members of their cliques want to go (29, 38, 82).

The movies the adolescent sees are not necessarily the ones he *prefers* to see. He sees what is available at the time he is free, what his friends and clique members want to see, and what the movie rating codes permit him to see. Boys prefer movies that deal with adventure, sex, humor, and fighting. Girls prefer those which concentrate on romance with a more subtle treatment of sex. However, since moviegoing is a dating activity, boys often see the movies that girls prefer. When young people of the same sex attend movies, the choices are usually made by the leaders or by the majority of the members of the clique.

Preferences for movies are greatly influenced by the featured stars, with girls having favorite male stars, and boys, favorite female stars. The setting of the movie also influences their choice. Girls, as a group, prefer glamorous settings, the homes of the wealthy or the nobility, while boys prefer foreign settings and outdoor scenes (42, 47, 78).

Influence of movies If a movie comes up to an adolescent's expectations and if it fills some need in his life, he will like it, and this, in turn, will have some influence on his attitudes and behavior. If he is disappointed in the movie, it will have little or no influence on him. Actually, what the adolescent gets from a movie depends upon his background and needs. He takes from the movie what is usable for him or what will function in his life—anything from juvenile delinquency to hair style. How much and what the adolescent remembers from a picture also affects its influence on him. If he identifies with a character whose actions are relevant to his needs or who is similar to him in sex, age, race, and socioeconomic status, the influence is likely to be great (78, 118).

Box 7-4 discusses the most important ways in which adolescents are influenced by movies (41, 78, 120, 121, 125).

Evaluation So many of the adolescent's personal and social needs are met by the movies that moviegoing is a popular recreation even though it is much more expensive than recreations provided by schools, colleges, churches, and other community groups. Movies provide vicarious satisfaction for many desires which are thwarted in real life.

BOX 7-4 HOW MOVIES INFLUENCE ADOLESCENTS

Effects on Behavior
Movies are a major source of information on fashions, makeup, and social behavior. They provide models for the adolescent to imitate.

Effects on Emotions
Movies provide, *first,* a wide range of emotional stimuli which arouse, vicariously, similar emotions in the adolescent, and *second,* models of emotional response which the adolescent assumes are socially approved and which he imitates.

Effects on Values
By vivid presentation of interpersonal behavior in all kinds of relationships, from family life to aggressive attacks, movies help to shape adolescent values and attitudes.

Effects on Social Attitudes
The movies' stereotyped presentation of people of different social, occupational, religious, racial, and national groups and of situations in the home, school, business, community, or national life greatly affect attitudes toward people and situations about which the individual has limited knowledge.

Of the many *personal* needs satisfied by the movies, the need for excitement stands high on the list. If the adolescent is bored with his schooling or the routine of his job, a temporary break brought about by an exciting movie makes him feel better both physically and mentally. Being emotionally stirred up likewise adds excitement, as does the opportunity to vicariously explore new environments and associate with glamorous and nonconventional people. If the adolescent can identify with a character on the screen, personal satisfaction is even greater.

Of longer-term value is the feeling of personal security the adolescent derives from learning how to behave in a socially approved adult way from the models presented on the screen. A girl who is unsure of how to dress and act in different social situations, for instance, loses some of her insecurity when she follows the example of her favorite actress.

For adolescents whose social acceptance in the peer group falls below their desires, many *social* needs are met by the movies. Even when they do not go with a group, just being in the audience with their peers gives them a feeling of belonging. Furthermore, if their poor acceptance is influenced by their lack of social know-how, observing characters on the screen goes a long way toward improving their skills and reducing their self-consciousness.

Movies may meet many of the adolescent's personal and social needs, but they do not always improve his personal and social *adjustments*. Some adolescents, for example, spend too much time on this sedentary recreation. Their physical well-being would be improved if some of this time were spent in more active recreations. Furthermore, too frequent movie attendance may adversely affect the development of self-sufficiency. The adolescent may come to rely upon outside sources of entertainment instead of depending upon his own initiative and efforts.

Equally serious, the values that the adolescent adopts from the movies may lead to poor personal and social adjustments. The boy who develops a romantic and glamorized stereotype of women, for example, may find his own dating and marriage disillusioning. Similarly, a girl who is imbued with the Cinderella happy-ever-after theme of many movies may be bitterly disappointed with her own courtship and marriage.

Excessive moviegoing is a powerful stimulus to fantasy life. If the adolescent is already making poor personal and social adjustments, the problem may be intensified by the movies. But, as Kuhlen has said, if he does not use the movies as a form of escape, he will probably use some other passive activity, such as reading or daydreaming (73).

Radio listening

The popularity of radio listening as an adolescent recreation is demonstrated by the amount of time devoted to this activity. While radio listening does not rate as high as television watching during the junior high school period, its popularity increases as adolescence progresses. During the high school years, adolescents listen to the radio an average of 1 to 3 hours each day. Those who listen to radio programs while studying, who carry transistor sets about, or who have radios in their cars listen even more than the average (5, 11, 29).

Many adolescents turn on the radio as soon as they reach home and keep it going while they study, read, dress, or talk. Listening time varies, however. Adolescents who are well accepted have more interests outside the home than isolates or those who are marginal. Only when radio listening is a popular loafing activity for a clique does the well-accepted adolescent spend as much time on this recreation as the poorly accepted.

Program preferences Adolescents will listen to almost any kind of program that is available when they have time to listen. But, given a choice, their listening preferences parallel their reading interests (73, 77, 121).

Throughout adolescence, programs that present the latest popular music are an increasing source of pleasure. While fads come and go, the adolescent wants to hear the music that his friends are talking about or singing. Classical or semiclassical music appeals to many older adolescents, especially those of the upper socioeconomic groups (10, 20).

In spite of these almost universal preferences, certain variations have been reported. Boys and girls spend approximately the same amount of time listening to the radio, but girls have a broader range of program preferences, with special emphasis on romance and romantic music; boys prefer programs that emphasize adventure and humor. Members of both sexes like quiz and audience-participation programs. Bright adolescents like programs with an intellectual appeal while those of average intelligence prefer programs with an emotional appeal (29, 47, 87).

Evaluation One of the strongest and most universal *personal* needs of adolescents of both sexes is the companionship of others, preferably of their peers. Companionship gives them a feeling not only of security but also of belonging. At times, however, even the most accepted adolescents must of necessity be away from the group. Turning on the radio and hearing someone talk or sing gives them the feeling that they are not alone, and this compensates for the absence of peers. Many adolescents keep their radios turned on while studying, claiming that they can study better that way. It is not the distraction of the radio that helps them to work, but rather the absence of loneliness.

At all ages, music serves as a emotional catharsis, helping the person relax both physically and mentally. Adolescents discover this, often by trial and error, and it accounts to some extent for the growing popularity of musical programs as adolescence progresses.

On the other hand, some adolescents tend to be extremely suggestible and are easily influenced by what they hear on the air. To them, radio speakers are important people and what they say is accepted without question. Such uncritical acceptance is certain to influence the attitudes and values of these adolescents, either favorably or unfavorably, depending upon the kinds of programs they listen to (73, 121).

Television watching

The childhood interest in television carries over into adolescence, though by mid-adolescence, television watching is usually a less popular recreation than radio listening. However, many high school students spend more time on television watching than on their studies or on all other leisure-time activities combined (3, 5, 58).

The decline in television watching as adolescence progresses is due to several factors: Adolescents who are continuing their education or who work have less time for recreations and a greater interest in dating and activities with members of the peer group; they have a more critical attitude toward the programs that are available when they are able to watch; and they cannot watch TV and study or do other things at the same time, as is possible with radio listening. Bright adolescents and well-adjusted adolescents tend to lose interest in television earlier than those who are less bright or less well adjusted (43, 53, 113). The "television addict," the viewer who spends more time on television watching than the average for his age, prefers escapist recreations. As Himmelweit et al. (60) have pointed out:

With escape through television so readily available, the heavy viewer's outside contacts become more restricted still. Such contacts demand much effort and offer little promise of success; they therefore compare unfavorably with the certain, undemanding companionship of television. Within a given intelligence level, social class, and age group, the amount a child views gives an indication of the degree to which his life is satisfactory; heavy viewing is a symptom of unsatisfactory adjustment or of inadequate environmental facilities.

When several television programs are available at the same time, the adolescent will choose the one that appeals to him most. His TV preferences are similar to his radio and reading preferences. Himmelweit et al. write that even the most popular programs were mentioned as favorites by only about one-third of the viewers they questioned: "Within any given age and intelligence group there is . . . a great deal of variation in taste, a fact which seems to be considerably underestimated in popular discussion" (60).

Evaluation Every possible behavior problem, from thumb-sucking to juvenile delinquency, has been ascribed to television watching. Today, however, critics seem to take a more moderate view than formerly. Since children are more avid television watchers than adolescents and are more gullible in their reactions, they are more likely to be influenced, for good or bad, than adolescents.

Most of the research is limited to the effects of television watching on schoolwork and on the various recreations previously enjoyed by adolescents. In one study, for example, 30 percent of the high school students questioned said that television helped them in their schoolwork because it provided educational programs related to their studies. In addition, it opened up new interests, such as science, and encouraged more and better reading to supplement the knowledge gained from educational programs. Seventy percent, however, said that television tempted them to neglect both homework and sports and games (60).

From the relatively small number of studies of the effects of television watching, several influences on attitudes and behavior stand out. Box 7-5 lists the most important effects (8, 40, 43, 53, 103, 113). The effects depend partly on the kind of program the adolescent habitually watches and the amount of time he devotes to watching, but, more importantly, on the kind of person he is and what he brings to his watching—his needs, attitudes, and values.

WHY RECREATIONS SHOULD MEET ADOLESCENT NEEDS

From the detailed description and evaluation of typical adolescent recreations given above, it is apparent that some meet the adolescent's personal and social needs better than others. For two reasons, it is important that recreations meet the adolescent's needs. In the first place, only satisfying recreations contribute to *happiness* and *physical and mental health*. Second, adolescent recreations *set the pattern for recreations in adult life*. With the trend toward shorter work hours and with increased affluence, adults need satisfying recreations if

---

BOX 7-5   SOME EFFECTS OF TELEVISION WATCHING ON ADJUSTMENTS

Family Relationships
The family is closer physically, but social interaction is restricted and there may be friction over which program to watch.

Family Recreational Patterns
Television watching cuts down the number of activities the family engages in as a group. It weakens parental motivation to provide other recreations suited to the ages and needs of different family members.

Adolescent Recreational Activities
Television watching absorbs time that might be devoted to other activities and thus reduces the variety of recreations.

Adolescent Values
Adolescents enjoy programs with excitement and thrills and tend to regard unsocial and destructive behavior as an almost normal occurrence in daily life.

Adolescent Attitudes
Attitudes toward such life experiences as work, family life, romance, and education are colored by dramatic TV presentations of these experiences, and the adolescent is often disillusioned or bored by his own experiences.

Adolescent Physical Well-being
Television watching may disrupt family eating and sleeping routines and thus damage physical well-being.

they are to maintain good physical and mental health.

Whether the adolescent's needs will be met or not depends on what recreational activities are available, what his attitude toward them is, and how well accepted the adolescent is by the peer group that dominates the recreations. Should there be strong social pressures to do well in a particular activity so as to outstrip other members of the peer group, the pleasures and satisfactions that should come from recreation will be replaced by stress and anxiety. When boys are urged to compete with their peers in sports, for example, these sports become work rather than play. Similarly, emphasis on popularity at parties makes party going competitive rather than relaxing (see Fig. 7-3).

While lack of money and lack of recreational facilities in the home, school, and community may limit the adolescent's opportunity to engage in satisfying recreations, they are less formidable and more subject to control than is lack of social acceptance.

The unaccepted adolescent is cut off from the majority of recreations that have prestige value during the adolescent years—parties, movies, dancing, sports, games, and someone to talk to. While he might go to the movies alone or with a family member, he does not want to do so because it would advertise his loneliness and lack of acceptance.

A satisfying recreational program for the adolescent years thus depends upon a reasonably secure status in the peer group. Adolescent recreational problems can be solved satisfactorily only when social-status problems are solved. This is never easy because adolescent social groups are tightly knit and difficult to penetrate and social acceptance previously won can be lost as the interests and values of the peer group change.

HIGHLIGHTS OF CHAPTER 7

1. Recreations—diversions that relax the individual both physically and mentally—fill a need in the adolescent's life just as play fills a need in the child's life.

Figure 7-3. Party going may become a competitive form of work rather than a recreation.

2. Some of the benefits of adolescent recreations are improvement in physical and mental health and in social status, an opportunity for self-evaluation, and opportunities to lay the foundations for adult recreations.

3. To meet the more mature needs of the adolescent, recreational activities must be different from the play activities of childhood. The most important differences between adolescent recreations and childhood play involve the time spent in recreations, the number of recreations engaged in, recreational companions, energy expended in recreations, the degree of formality of recreations, and attitudes toward repetition of recreational activities.

4. Of the many factors that influence the kind of adolescent recreational activities engaged in, the most important are personal interests, opportunities to take part in preferred recreations, physical development, intelligence and sex, environment, family socioeconomic status, peer interests, prestige associated with different recreations, and degree of social acceptance.

5. Some recreations are so popular that they may be regarded as typical of American adolescents today.

6. All the typical adolescent recreations meet

some need in the adolescent's life, though needs vary from one adolescent to another and in the same adolescent from one time to another.

7. Among the most common adolescent recreations are conversations, loafing, parties, dancing, games and sports, hobbies, exploring, daydreaming, music, reading, movies, radio listening, and television watching.

8. While all these recreations meet some need in the adolescent's life at the time, some lead to good personal and social adjustments while others militate against good adjustments.

9. An evaluation of popular adolescent recreations reveals that they come closer to meeting personal needs adequately than social needs. Daydreaming and hobbies, for example, meet personal needs but do little to meet social needs.

10. Many adolescent recreations form the foundation for satisfying adult recreations, for example, conversations, hobbies, reading, radio listening, and television watching.

11. Ideally, recreations should meet the adolescent's needs because satisfying recreations contribute to his happiness and to his physical and mental health, and they set patterns for recreations in adult life.

12. Since many adolescent recreations that are satisfying and prestigious depend on the companionship of peers, lack of social acceptance deprives the adolescent of the benefits of these recreations. The recreational problems of adolescence can, therefore, be solved only when social-status problems are solved.

Chapter 8

Status Symbols

Throughout adolescence, awareness of the importance of social acceptance in achieving a satisfying recreational life spurs the adolescent's desire to improve his acceptance. Increasing awareness also of the role played by one's family's social and economic status in peer acceptance intensifies the adolescent's desire not only to impress his peers but to convince them that his family's status is equal or even superior to theirs.

While still a child, the adolescent discovered that people hold different statuses in the group, that some statuses are more prestigious, and that statuses can be distinguished by certain signs or cues, such as clothes, size and location of homes, and other material possessions. By adolescence, he discovers that his peers and adults as well use these cues to judge other people. Guitar has written, "The most fascinating aspect of our status-conscious society may well be the cool way the younger generation accepts the inevitability of status distinctions" (66).

The adolescent knows from experience that the image others have of him is greatly influenced by these cues. He also knows that a favorable image goes a long way toward ensuring his acceptance by the group. Furthermore, he learns that his image is likely to persist and to form the basis of a reputation which will influence subsequent judgments of him not only by members of the peer group but also by persons who know him only through reputation.

MEANING OF STATUS SYMBOLS

"Status symbols" are the cues or visible signs of something not immediately visible. To an observer, they *suggest* the position, rank, or standing of the individual in the group with which he is identified. To do this, they must be visible. As Guitar (66) has stressed:

Status symbols for the young fall chiefly into the display area. Food and drink labels, family tree, proper address—all so important to their parents— carry little weight with the younger generation. What counts is what you wear, drive, or play.

Symbols come to be associated with status through the process of social learning. Among certain tribes and cultural groups, for example, scarification is a sign of bravery—a trait highly valued by the groups. The same thing is often true of tattooing. It symbolizes bravery, and also symbolizes group membership—belonging to a group that is daring and sometimes delinquent or criminal (152).

The symbols an adolescent values will be those which are highly prized by the group with which he wants to be identified and signify his acceptance by the group. They may include knowing the "right" people, belonging to a prestigious school or community organization, or dating a popular and well-accepted person. See Figure 8-1. As Guitar (66) has explained:

The status symbol is, above all, a means of communication. One guitar player meeting another guitar player needs no verbal contact. The sight of that peerless symbol serves the same purpose today as the aborigine's peace pipe did in times past. It suggests instantly that these two understand one another and can safely become friends. Or, as one boy put it, "Without your blanket, you are nothing. You have to carry your status symbol with you or fade."

The more anxious the adolescent is to be accepted by the peer group or the less secure his status in the group, the more concerned he is about his image. Since status symbols contribute to the quality of the adolescent's personal and social adjustments, their role in his life must be examined.

Evidence of importance of status symbols

There is ample evidence that adolescents are status-symbol-conscious. The most fruitful sources of information are studies of adolescent conversations, writings, and wishes.

In their *conversations* adolescents talk about things that are important to them. What a crowd discusses at a social gathering, what cliques of intimate friends discuss at midnight bull sessions, or what an adolescent and his best friend talk over in confidence—all provide illuminating information about the status symbols they are most concerned with (31, 63, 139).

From adolescents' *writings* in diaries, in letters to friends, in the school "scandal sheets," or in themes or classroom assignments in high school or college, their interest in different status symbols becomes readily apparent. Constant references to clothes, cars, and other material possessions, for example, or to family background and distinguished friends tell what the writers consider important (85, 96, 149).

Perhaps the best method of determining what status symbols adolescents consider most important is to ask what their *wishes* are. Studies reveal that wishes relating to material possessions predominate. Adolescents want things that are prestigious to the group, even though they may not always be valuable (111, 154).

Qualities symbolized

At every age and in every cultural group, the qualities most often symbolized are those which are most valued by the group and whose possession brings individual prestige. Box 8-1 lists a number of the qualities most frequently symbolized and almost universally valued by American adolescents, regardless of sex, socioeconomic status, race, or religion (41, 45, 87, 90, 137).

Which of these qualities an adolescent will be most anxious to proclaim to others through the use of symbols will vary to some extent from one adolescent to another and even in the same adolescent when he is with different groups. Variations occur also in the symbols used to proclaim a quality. Adolescents of all socioeconomic groups want to be considered sex appropriate, for example, but what constitutes sex appropriateness varies. To many of lower socioeconomic groups, masculinity is synonymous with aggressiveness and domination of members of the female sex, while to many of the middle and upper socioeconomic

Figure 8-1. Association with the "right" people is an important status symbol for adolescents.

groups it is more closely related to intellectual strength. This will be discussed in detail in a later chapter.

Because of variations in the value attached to different status symbols, it is impossible to rank them in order of importance. Consequently, in the following sections the most common status symbols used by American adolescents are discussed from the point of view of the qualities they symbolize and the needs they fill in the adolescent's life.

APPEARANCE

The adolescent is well aware that first impressions play a large role in establishing the image others have of him. He also knows that first impressions are greatly influenced by appearance (159). Boys and girls who wear glasses, for example, are regarded as "brains,"

and this image, once formed, tends to persist
(11). In discussing the symbolic value of appearance, Jersild (82) has said:

In everyday speech we note that a person has a
"hang-dog look"; he "looks cranky," "harassed,"
"worried," "gay," "happy," "twinkling," etc. The
relationship between an attitude and appearance
is apparent when a person clearly is trying to falsify
his or her appearance, as happens when a girl's
dyed hair or false eyelashes give her an artificial
look. . . . We see it also when a girl, seemingly unable to accept her own femaleness, selects the styles
that are most likely to cover her from view, such as
high-necked blouses, or loosely cut clothes that
conceal the shapeliness of her body.

According to tradition, girls are far more in-

terested in appearance than boys. In fact, this
difference is often considered a distinguishing
characteristic of the two *sexes*. This distinction
is undoubtedly correct in childhood, but not
in adolescence (60). According to Friedenberg (57), adolescent boys seem to "defy the
male stereotype":

Boys seem to me usually more concerned with their
appearance than girls and also to have more idea of
what they actually look like and how other people
will respond to the way they look. . . . Boys are
often very vain. . . . They bask in physical regard
like alligators on a log.

Qualities symbolized

Appearance symbolizes three qualities in
adolescence. *First*, it tells others that the adolescent conforms to the pattern that is acceptable to the group. The adolescent knows that
group members and their leaders as well are
accepted not only because their abilities are
highly regarded but also because their appearance enables them to represent the group
favorably.

   Equally important, appearance helps to
establish one's social class. A casual appearance, for example, distinguishes adolescents
of the "right" group. Packard (126) emphasizes the symbolic value of a casual appearance in the following illustration:

A sixteen-year-old boy from a limited-success family
was invited to attend a dance for young folks at a
yacht club on the New England coast. His mother
was thrilled and bought him a new blue serge suit
for the occasion. The boy spent a miserable evening. Every boy at the dance except himself was
wearing khakis and an old sports jacket. Among the
yacht-club set this casual uniform was *de rigueur*.

   The *second* quality symbolized by appearance is sex appropriateness. The easiest
way to tell others that one is sex appropriate
in behavior is to look sex appropriate.
   Third, the adolescent uses appearance to
symbolize his maturity. At every age people
are treated according to how old they look
rather than according to their actual ages.
The early maturer, as was pointed out before,

looks older than he is and is given privileges and duties usually associated with older ages.

Every aspect of appearance that plays even the smallest role in affecting the judgments of others is of concern to the adolescent. Some adolescents are willing to withstand great discomfort to correct physical defects or to improve their appearance. Girls often wear uncomfortable shoes to make their feet look smaller, and many go on starvation diets to become slim. Box 8-2 lists those aspects of appearance on which the adolescent concentrates most (108, 115, 138, 143, 167).

Aids to improved appearance

When an adolescent is dissatisfied with his status in the peer group, he tries to improve it. Most often he tries to change the image he *believes* others have of him by trying to change his appearance.

Unlike the pubescent, who shows his concern about his appearance by worrying, the adolescent takes a more constructive approach. He seeks advice and suggestions from others; he follows up magazine, newspaper, or television ads; he reads "beauty aid" columns; and he experiments in a trial-and-error fashion. Of the many aids to an improved appearance, those discussed below are the most widely used.

Diets Adolescence is the age of fad diets. Boys are primarily interested in diets that claim to build muscle tissue and give them a more masculine look. Girls want to look thinner and improve their complexions. When improvement does not occur quickly, adolescents often abandon one diet in favor of another which claims better results (128).

Cosmetics Cosmetics proclaim to others that one is sex appropriate. As Wax has explained, the purpose of cosmetics is to "manipulate one's superficial physical structure so as to make a desired impression" (163):

Cosmetics help to identify a person as a female of our culture and, generally speaking, as a female who views herself and should be treated as socially and sexually mature. The girl who wears cosmetics is insisting on her right to be treated as a woman rather than a child.

To most girls, lipstick is the most important insignia of growing up. Jones (86) has explained the early use of lipstick in this way:

Lipstick symbolizes as well as any one specific item could the sensitization in early adolescence toward a new sex role and toward being grown-up. While its use is confined to girls, opinions about it are not.

Techniques to change body contour Adolescents use many techniques to make their bodies look more attractive and sex appropriate. A boy can have shoulder padding inserted in his coats to create the illusion that he has the sex-approved triangular body. A girl can wear a padded brassiere to give herself the bust shape she wants.

BOX 8-2   FOCAL POINTS OF INTEREST IN APPEARANCE

Body Size and Shape
From the mass media, the adolescent forms an ideal image of the body size and shape for his sex group.

Face
Only when one feature is conspicuously homely or disproportioned is the adolescent concerned about it. Complexion receives more attention than facial features.

Hair
Dissatisfaction with the color of their hair motivates many adolescents to experiment with bleaches and dyes. Their major concern is to find a fashionable hair style that improves their appearance.

Nails
Girls try to color and shape their finger- and toenails according to the prevailing style. Boys merely try to keep their nails clean.

Grooming Tidiness and cleanliness are associated with respectability and belonging to the "right" class of people; good grooming thus helps to create the image of "right" status (126). A deliberately unkempt and sloppy appearance may be the adolescent's way of showing his hostile feelings toward those in authority, mainly parents. If the adolescent makes no attempt to conform to peer standards in his grooming, it suggests that he is at odds with the majority of the peer group as well as with adults. This subject was discussed earlier in Chapter 6.

Clothing One of the greatest aids to improved appearance is clothing. Adolescents use clothes to *enhance* their good physical features and to *camouflage* their poor ones. A slightly overweight girl, for example, finds that dark colors and unadorned garments camouflage her figure (44, 68, 91). Because of the importance of clothing in image creation, this topic is treated at length below.

CLOTHES

The adolescent's interest in clothes stems from the realization that clothes are an important—if not the dominant—determinant of appearance. Appearance, in turn, influences one's status in the social group. As Hoult has explained, clothes are the "symbols by means of which group members judge one another" (77). Interest in clothing varies, however. It depends to a large extent upon whether the adolescent *believes* clothes are important in creating an impression and whether he is dissatisfied with the social status he already has. It cannot be said that *all* adolescents are equally clothes-conscious.

Boys, it has been reported, are as interested in clothes as girls. But girls put slightly more emphasis on clothes as a symbol of social status, while boys use clothes as symbols of individuality and autonomy (57, 138). The socially mobile adolescent who is trying to move up in the world is more aware of the symbolic value of clothes than one who is satisfied to remain in his present economic and social group (10, 157).

Excessive interest in clothes, as compared with the amount normally found among adolescents of a particular age, results from poor personal or social adjustments. Excessive interest is shown in many ways, one of the most common of which is an unreasonable need to find out what others are wearing and where they buy their clothes.

At the opposite end of the continuum of interest is the adolescent who *scorns* clothes, shows no interest in styles, and dresses poorly when he can afford to dress better. Like the individual who is deliberately sloppy and unkempt, such an adolescent is telling the world that he will do as he pleases, regardless of social attitudes. Or he may feel that he has no hope of being accepted by the social group, so why try. Whatever his reason for excessive disinterest in clothes, it suggests poor personal and social adjustments (68, 98).

Qualities symbolized

Adolescents learn, long before childhood is over, that clothes have important symbolic value—that their clothes tell others something about them. Of the many qualities that clothes can symbolize, those discussed below are the most important to the typical American adolescent.

Identification with the peer group When the adolescent looks like the members of his peer group, he feels that he belongs and that others judge him as belonging. During early adolescence especially, belonging to a peer group is regarded as a status symbol. A feeling of belonging helps the adolescent to improve the social acceptance he gains through achievements in activities that are prestigious in the eyes of the group with which he wants to be identified. While many adolescents say they dislike wearing a school uniform because they do not want to be "regimented," they do like the uniform if it helps to identify them with a prestigious school or college (54).

Socioeconomic status Adolescents use clothing in three ways to symbolize their socioeconomic status. The *first* is by wearing clothes made by prestige manufacturers (126, 136). The *second* is by owning a number of garments of each kind. The more evening dresses or sweaters a girl has, for example, the more money she is judged to have for clothing. And *third,* by wearing fashionable clothing—the latest and most extreme styles (17).

Adolescents who are dissatisfied with their family's socioeconomic status and want to improve their lot in life try to create the impression that they belong to a higher socioeconomoc group. In England, for example, many boys of the working class want to "wipe out the old image of the working man—broken fingernails, frayed shirt, and cloth cap." Instead of looking like their fathers, they want to "look smart" like the adolescents of the middle- and upper-class groups (119).

Sex appropriateness The more anxious the adolescent is to show his sex appropriateness, the more emphasis he places on clothes that are symbolic of his own sex. Boys concentrate on sports clothes if they are anxious to proclaim their masculinity. Girls wear ruffles and bows even when plainer clothes would be more becoming.

Individuality While adolescents conform to the prevailing style to show their identity with the group, they want their clothes to symbolize the fact that they are not just like everyone else. To express her own personality, as Bernard has stated, "a girl should dress as the other girls do but with just a touch of individuality" (17).

Maturity Adolescents wear clothes that make them look older as a symbol of their near-adult status. They know, from childhood dramatic play, that dressing up does more than anything else to change one's appearance.

To achieve an older look, adolescents select clothes that are associated with adults and rebel against garments associated with childhood. Because head coverings are worn by children in cold weather, adolescent boys and girls invariably insist on going bareheaded. When a boy goes to work, he wears a tie and jacket to show that he has left behind him the more casual clothes of high school or college.

Independence Since neat clothing is important to adults, sloppiness is an adolescent symbol of rebellion against adult domination. The sloppier the dress, the more others can see that the wearer is in control of his own affairs. Similarly, since adults usually prefer conservative dress, the adolescent symbolizes his autonomy by wearing extreme styles.

Focal points of interest in clothes

While all adolescents are concerned about clothes, they find certain aspects of clothing more interesting than others. They may have discovered that these particular aspects help most to improve their appearance and, hence, their social acceptance, or they may have discovered that these aspects best symbolize the qualities they value and want others to recognize. Box 8-3 contains a description of today's adolescents' focal points of interest in clothes (19, 68, 91, 107, 124, 138).

SPEECH

By adolescence, the individual recognizes the status value of speech and uses it to create in the minds of others the image of himself that he wants them to have. As Lipsett has stated, the verbalizations people make of and about themselves—"self-talk"—are symbols of the way they evaluate themselves (102). The adolescent who verbalizes feelings of inadequacy or inferiority, for example, is telling others that he has a poor opinion of himself. The adolescent who uses tabooed words is telling others that he is independent and not afraid of adult disapproval.

Three aspects of a person's speech can be regarded as symbolic of status: its quality, its content, and its quantity. Either directly or indirectly, each of these tells what the adolescent wants others to know about him.

Quality of speech

How the adolescent speaks—the tonal quality of his voice, his pronunciation, the words he

BOX 8-3 FOCAL POINTS OF INTEREST IN CLOTHES

*Color
The young adolescent likes brightly colored clothes, but with each passing year the preference for more subdued colors grows.

*Ornamentation
Ornaments are most popular in early adolescence. Older adolescents are more conservative, regarding too much ornamentation as poor taste.

*Becomingness
The adolescent is interested in what is most becoming to him, what makes the most of his good features and at the same time covers up his bad features.

*Appropriateness
Knowing that inappropriate clothes create an unfavorable impression, the adolescent is willing to wear whatever is "correct" for the occasion even though he might prefer something different.

*Style
Each year the adolescent becomes more style-conscious, wanting the latest styles and colors whether they are becoming or not.

*Attention Value
The adolescent wants his clothes to attract favorable attention to himself, especially the attention of members of the other sex.

uses, and the correctness of his usage—all this creates an impression on others and tells them things about the speaker. Knowing that others judge him by the quality of his speech, the adolescent becomes speech-conscious.

Tonal quality of voice The child often has a contemptuous attitude toward a "pleasing voice." To a boy, it is a sign of being a sissy (57, 60). In adolescence, however, both boys and girls want to improve their voices. As is characteristic of adolescents, they go to extremes, and the outcome is often an affected, unnatural tone which is a source of amusement to adults and of ridicule to other adolescents (127).

Pronunciation If the adolescent discovers that his pronunciation identifies him with a neighborhood or socioeconomic group that he does not want to be identified with, he will try to change it (18, 36). An adolescent from a *bilingual* family is often more concerned about his foreign accent than about his possible incorrect use of words. His concern is intensified if his accent stems from a language that has little prestige in the eyes of those with whom he wants to be associated. Regardless of prestige, many adolescents, especially boys, prefer not to be different. So long as they have a foreign accent, they feel that they are identified with a minority group (97, 104, 150).

Words Because of the symbolic value of words, many adolescents become "linguistic snobs," trying to impress others by using words that *identify them with the right group* (36).

Studies reveal that certain words identify the speaker with the upper socioeconomic class while other words which convey the same meaning identify the speaker with the middle class. A few samples, given below, illustrate this symbolic use of words (126):

Upper Class	Middle Class
Wash	Launder
Long dress	Formal gown
Rich	Wealthy
Hello	Pleased to meet you
What?	Pardon?
I feel sick	I feel ill
Sweat	Perspiration
Jobs	Positions
Legs	Limbs
Go to work	Go to business

To create the impression that he is *grown-up and sophisticated,* the adolescent adopts a vocabulary of long, technical, and unusual words. Instead of saying that he is "tired," he will say that he is "fatigued"; he will talk about his "paraphernalia" instead of his "equipment." One of the advantages of the courses he takes in high school and college is that he can learn new words to impress others whose education is more limited. The study of psychology, for example, offers unlimited opportunities to acquire new names for well-known patterns of human behavior. These he finds especially impressive if they have a Freudian flavor.

No words serve more effectively as status symbols for adolescents than slang and swear words. By using slang, the adolescent shows that he is an insider; he can communicate with his peers in words that they understand but that outsiders find foreign (17, 127). Since swearing is socially disapproved, the adolescent asserts his independence by using the forbidden words. Furthermore, since swearing is associated with adult males, the adolescent boy shows his sex appropriateness and his near-adult status by swearing. It thus becomes a status symbol. Swearing is considered sex inappropriate for women; therefore, adolescent girls use little swearing (65, 123).

Content of speech

The second aspect of speech which can be regarded as a status symbol is its content. What the adolescent talks about helps to create in the minds of others the image he considers desirable. Box 8-4 lists the various categories of speech content together with a brief description of what each symbolizes (51, 60, 79, 129, 146).

Quantity of speech

The third aspect of a person's speech which is symbolic of status is its quantity. Though less significant than speech quality and content, discussed above, the amount of talking the adolescent does is a cue of his status. Dominating a conversation—determining both the amount of talking he will do and what will be talked about—suggests an *adult status* to the adolescent.

As a child, the adolescent learned that *popular* children do more talking than those who are less well accepted. Consequently, he uses talking as a cue to tell others how popular he is. In addition, he associates amount of talking with *socioeconomic status,* with persons of the upper-class groups talking more than those from "deprived" linguistic environments. Finally, the adolescent associates amount of talking with *sex differences.* He knows that girls talk more than boys and that they tend to dominate the conversation in heterosexual relationships. Girls, as a result, try to show their femininity by talking more than boys; boys attempt to show their masculinity by being strong and silent.

The quiet adolescent may be trying to create an image of being a deep thinker who says little and thinks much. But as adolescents put less value on intellectual than on social and athletic success, such an image carries little peer group prestige.

NAMES AND NICKNAMES

Through the ages, names have been used as symbols to identify people, their family connections, their racial and religious affiliations, their occupations, and their sex. Freud was the first to point out that names are "symbols of self." Freud further stressed the importance of names when he stated that one forgets a person's name when one wants to repress unpleasant associations with the person (56). While this interpretation of forgetting is not wholly accepted, it suggests that, as many people know a person mainly by his name, his name serves as a symbol by which they judge him. As Murphy has pointed out, "One of the most important parts of a person is his name" (114).

Every adolescent has at least two names, a "given" name—his first name—and his "last name," which is his family name or surname. In addition, he may have a middle name or two. He also has one or more "kinship" names and usually at least one "nickname." The kinship names identify his status in the family group—son, brother, grandson, cousin, or nephew. The nickname may be a term of endearment, usually given to him by his parents or some family member—Sonny, Junior, Dear, or Pet—or it may be derogatory—Shorty,

Fatso, or Dumbbell. Other nicknames may be distortions of the individual's given name—Pat or Lizzie—or they may be made up of his initials—Cow or Jaw. With the exception of terms of endearment, most nicknames originate in the peer group.

Many adolescents regard the number of names a person has as symbolic of his status. The more he has, the more important he is. This symbol has come from foreign cultures, notably the British culture, where it is traditional to give children of noble and royal families as many as six or eight names. Being named for someone in the family, especially if it is a prestigious family member, is likewise a status symbol. Boys who add Jr., III, or IV, to their names are regarded as coming from more distinguished families than boys whose names are unrelated to any family member (110, 126).

Despite the symbolic advantage of a number of names, there is a disadvantage that cannot be overlooked—that of confusion of identity. When different "identity symbols" are used, it is difficult for the individual to know which refers to his "real" self. It is equally difficult for others to get a clear image of him if he is referred to by different names. This confusion about one's name has been expressed in the old nursery rhyme (114):

Mother calls me William
Auntie calls me Will
Sister calls me Willie
But Dad calls me Bill

Which of a person's names is used to address him is considered a symbol of his status. If he is called by his given name, for example, it denotes greater familiarity than if he is called by his surname. Being called by a nickname signifies the greatest degree of familiarity.

Qualities symbolized

In every cultural group, physical or psychological characteristics are associated with names. In a study of such associations among American and British people, Sheppard has reported that a person bearing the name of "John" is thought of as trustworthy; "Robin" suggests a young, adventuresome male; "Percy" a sissy; and "Tony" a sociable good guy. "Agnes" suggests a female who is neither young nor good-looking; "Matilda" is associated with a homely girl (144). Figure 8-2 shows some common stereotypes associated with names.

Some names derive their associations from characters in the Bible or in literature; others become associated with characters in the comics, on the screen, or in sports. Still others derive their associations from public figures. Before the Hitler regime in Germany, for example, the name "Adolf" was associated with the nobility. Today the name has such bad connotations that those who bear it are judged unfavorably, not only in Germany but also in many other nations (120).

In addition to the culture-wide associations of names, adolescents create their own associations, based on personal experiences. A girl who has a crush on George, who is the

Figure 8-2. Names are symbols in the minds of others.

| John | Throckmorton | Sue | Abigail |

captain of the football team, will have a far more favorable view of that name than she would if the first George she knew was a pest in her first grade class. Box 8-5 describes the most common qualities symbolized by names (22, 32, 46, 120, 144, 151).

In a democracy, where titles do not exist except when earned by the bearer, the adolescent is still too young to have earned the status-symbol prestige of a title. However, some adolescents are known to their peers and to the adults in their communities as "John Smith, the football captain" or "Mary Smith, the daughter of Judge Smith."

MATERIAL POSSESSIONS

Where high value is placed on wealth, material possessions are important status symbols. As Hechinger and Hechinger have put it, "In a society which judges prestige very largely by outward appearance, what an adolescent owns automatically turns into a yardstick of the entire family's place in the sun" (74). Thus, material possessions may be regarded as objective correlates of status. This is especially true in a mobile society where family background and other status symbols lose, to some extent, their prestige value (41, 42).

To the adolescent, socioeconomic status is measured in terms of the family's home; the make and number of cars, record players, and television sets owned by the family; and the kind of clothing and jewelry family members wear (81, 126). The affluence of the American culture today makes it possible for adolescents to spend money for status symbols which, in past generations, would have been unavailable. As Bernard has stated, our culture can afford a "large leisure class of youngsters who are consumers but not earners" (17). If they do work, they are usually free to spend what they earn on material possessions that are prestigious in the eyes of the peer group.

In Box 8-6 are listed a number of ways in which the adolescent shows how important

---

BOX 8-5 WHAT NAMES SYMBOLIZE

Identification
Common names—John or George or Mary or Anne—give adolescents a feeling of security and belonging. Unusual names with which they cannot identify produce feelings of insecurity and isolation.

Individuality
After the self-conscious stage of early adolescence, adolescents like names that are slightly different from those of their peers. But if they are too different, they are embarrassing.

Sex Appropriateness
A name or nickname that is definitely sex appropriate helps to create an image of a sex-appropriate person. Hybrid names—those used for both sexes (Francis for boys and Frances for girls)—are far more likely to create a sex-inappropriate image.

Degree of Acceptance
Degree of acceptance is symbolized by the name others use in speaking to or about a person. Use of a pet name at home or a favorable nickname in the peer group symbolizes greater acceptance than use of a more formal name. A derogatory nickname symbolizes poor acceptance.

material possessions are to him (6, 21, 66, 153, 156).

Sex differences in interest in material possessions

While all American adolescents recognize that material possessions are status symbols, boys and girls have some different, as well as some overlapping, interests. To both boys and girls, owning records, record players, and transistor radios is important during the adolescent years. Having a large and stylish wardrobe is also important to both (62). In the following paragraphs, the two sexes are discussed separately.

Girls To a girl, clothing and various kinds of ornamentation are important symbols of the socioeconomic status she wants to be identified with because they are readily observable. If she can wear a different dress or sweater to school every day, if she can have a new outfit for every party, and if she has a wide selection of cosmetics and perfume, others will know that her family is well-to-do.

If the home is on the "right" street or in the "right" neighborhood, if it conforms to the prevailing style depicted in magazines or on the screen, and if it has extra rooms—such as a TV room or a recreation room with built-in bar for entertaining—the family's affluence will be immediately recognized. If, in addition, there is a cleaning woman to do the housework and if there are several garages with cars of the "right" make readily available, the symbolism of affluence is greatly increased (66, 126).

Boys Since boys' clothing is more or less standardized and their social activities do not center in the home, their socioeconomic status is largely symbolized by their cars (73). Bernard (17) has stated:

It is taken for granted that every teen-ager will learn to drive and that, if he does not have a car of his own, individually or as a member of a group, he will certainly have access to one. . . . In many cities

---

BOX 8-6 EXPRESSIONS OF INTEREST IN MATERIAL GOODS

*Grumbling about one's own and the family's possessions

*Blaming parents for not providing "sufficient" material possessions

*Envying the material possessions of peers

*Wishing for similar or better possessions than peers

*Dropping out of school and taking a job to buy possessions

*Buying on the installment plan

*Shoplifting or stealing prestigious possessions

*Daydreaming about prestigious possessions

---

it is an accepted pattern that in order to date a girl, a boy must be able to provide a car for transportation; she may not go in a cab or allow herself and her date to be driven by parents. Having acquired a car for transportation, socialization, and dating, a boy becomes so involved in its care and upkeep he has little time or interest left for other activities.

The importance of car ownership to adolescent boys is shown by Figure 8-3, which indicates that ownership increases by 50 percent between the freshman and senior years in high school (37).

"Automania" or an "overobsession with the automobile as a status symbol," as Hechinger and Hechinger describe it, tells the world that the boy is *independent* and can come and go as he pleases, that he is *grown-up* because the law permits him to own and drive a car, and that he is *sex appropriate* because a boy who owns a car is a near man, not "mother's little darling." By driving at speeds beyond the legal limit and by taking chances, the boy further impresses others with his masculinity, indicating that he is not "chicken" or a sissy (73).

If the car is an expensive model, preferably

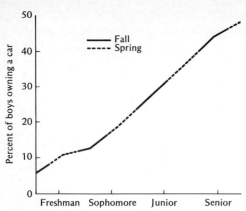

Figure 8-3. Car ownership becomes an increasingly important status symbol for boys as adolescence progresses. (Adapted from J. S. Coleman: *The adolescent society.* New York: Free Press, 1961. Used by permission.)

of foreign make, and a new one rather than a second- or thirdhand jalopy, it implies that the family *socioeconomic status* is superior. When the boy is free to use his car to take members of the crowd for rides, it becomes a "clubhouse on wheels—a medium for holding a party." As adolescent boys explain it, "When you have your own car, you've got it made"—in the sense that the car, as a status symbol, establishes the boy in the eyes of others as the "right kind" (73).

While other material possessions such as radios, television sets, records, sports equipment, and clothes are all-important status symbols, none can compare with a car. Not only is a car readily observable, but the boy can take it wherever he goes. In time, everyone associates it with him.

MONEY

In a culture that places high value on material possessions, money is important for two reasons *First,* money makes it possible to obtain the material possessions that help to establish one's status, and *second,* others tend to attribute favorable qualities to a high-income person and less favorable qualities to one whose income is low or who lives on a hand-to-mouth basis (103).

Even a little child knows that his status in the group is influenced by how much money he has to spend. Later he discovers that teachers and other adults treat children who live in big homes and ride in big cars quite differently from those who live in low-income areas and drive old cars.

The adolescent is well aware that "money counts." But to serve as a status symbol, money must be manifest. This means that it must be spent or available for spending, not held as savings or investments. The typical adolescent will save *voluntarily* only when saving makes it possible for him to buy some larger item than he would be able to buy with his weekly allowance or earnings. A boy is willing to save to buy a car only because of its high prestige value.

American adolescents think of money in terms of *spending,* because spending helps them achieve status. They do not feel guilty about spending for status symbols or about borrowing or buying on the installment plan. Today, unlike in the past, spending more than one has is often regarded as a status symbol (131).

Box 8-7 lists the most important qualities symbolized by money (52, 53, 83, 109, 116, 130).

The amount of money required to satisfy the adolescent's status-symbol needs will vary. If the adolescent is identified with a *group* whose members have more money than he, his allowance will probably be inadequate for his needs. If he has more money than the other members, he may be envied by them.

The adolescent needs more money as he grows *older,* because his status symbols will cost more. His car alone will make a great difference. In addition, he requires more money for entertainment, clothes, and records, as fewer of his needs are supplied by parents, community centers, and schools than when he was younger.

Boys, at all ages, need more money than girls. Boys spend most of their time away from home and must supply their own status symbols instead of relying on the family symbols, as girls do. Also, boys must have money if they are to date.

PRIVILEGES

When the adolescent approaches his mature size and shape, he wants to do the things adults do and to be identified with adults. Once this near-adult image has been created, he expects to be treated as an adult. Since most states permit adolescents to drive cars at some time between the ages of 14 and 18 years and to vote at 18 years, the adolescent discovers the status value of being permitted to engage in adult activities. This whets his appetite for more privileges. Many of today's adolescents look upon the right to vote, drive a car, smoke, and drink as "American puberty rites."

The privileges that mean most to an adolescent are those which are most highly valued by the *group* with which he is identified. Because of the prestige associated with social activities, most of the demands for privileges center on "latchkey problems": the hour one is to come home after a party or other social function, the number of times a week one will be permitted to go out, the people with whom one can associate, and the places one is allowed to go (17, 37, 74).

Boys, as a group, have more privileges than girls; and members of the lower *socioeconomic* groups have more than those of the middle groups. Adolescents of the highest *socioeconomic* groups, like those of the lowest, generally have more privileges than middle-class adolescents. Adolescents who grow up in *large cities* or in *suburban* areas have, as a rule, more privileges than those from small towns or rural districts. And, as would be expected, the adolescent who goes away to college or is working has more privileges than the younger adolescent who is still in high school (45, 126, 132).

Qualities symbolized

Privileges that are readily observable and are related to areas of behavior that are prestig-

---

BOX 8-7 WHAT MONEY SYMBOLIZES

*Socioeconomic Status
Having money readily available at all times, being able to spend money on luxuries and treats for one's friends, and being able to take friends for a ride in one's car—all symbolize high status.

*Identification with the Leading Crowd
Creating the impression of affluence by always having spending money implies that the adolescent belongs to the leading crowd, which normally is relatively well-to-do.

*Sex Appropriateness
Sex appropriateness is shown (1) by how the adolescent gets his spending money and (2) by how he spends it. Earning part of one's spending money at afterschool jobs in stores, factories, or offices is regarded as masculine; relying on an allowance supplemented by baby-sitting jobs is considered feminine. Spending money for sports and dates is regarded as masculine; spending for clothes and beauty aids is regarded as feminine.

*Independence
Whether the adolescent's money comes from an allowance or from earnings, it symbolizes his autonomy. The person who has money is seen as a person who can demand what he wants, can come and go as he pleases, and can buy what he wants without interference.

---

ious in the eyes of the peer group symbolize many of the qualities the adolescent is anxious to have others ascribe to him. Of these, the most important are described in Box 8-8.

Methods of getting privileges

Modern adolescents hold the whip handle when it comes to getting what they want. In an affluent society where parents can provide for their children without their financial help and where young people can earn money while still in school, adolescents have ways of enforcing their demands for privileges that those in a less affluent society or in one where authoritarian child-rearing methods prevail do not have. As Bernard has said, American adolescents of today can demand that adults give them what they want or they will threaten to drop out of school, leave home, and become self-supporting (17).

To enforce their demands for privileges, adolescents who lack social acceptance may play on parental sympathy by blaming their parents for their plight. They may try to look older and more sophisticated than they are and speak with the voice of authority to impress others with their maturity. If all else fails, they may go on an "academic sit-down strike." Knowing that their parents are eager to have them go to college, they are in a favorable bargaining position and generally emerge the winner. If all this does not work, they may drop out of school, take a job, and live away from home where they can do as they please (52).

Difficulties in getting privileges

Adolescents experience different degrees of difficulty in getting the privileges they want and which their peers have. Parents who have used *authoritarian methods of discipline* are rarely willing to relax their control even as their children approach maturity. This is especially true of foreign-born parents. *Firstborn children,* both boys and girls, tend to be more overprotected than their siblings. Even as adolescents, they find obstacles in the way to independence that their younger siblings are not likely to encounter. After a few years of conflict with their first child, parents generally revise their attitudes and grant more privileges. Later children profit by this revision of attitudes and find it easier to get the privileges they demand when they demand them (25, 85).

Girls have more difficulty getting the privileges they want than boys because parents fear that their daughters will acquire an unfavorable reputation. While reluctant to give boys all the privileges they demand, parents sooner or later acquiesce because they do not want their sons to get the reputation of being tied to parental apron strings (45, 90).

The adolescents who have the greatest difficulty gaining privileges are the *late maturers.* By contrast, early maturers are often given

---

BOX 8-8   WHAT PRIVILEGES SYMBOLIZE

Independence
Being allowed to do what age-mates do tells them that the adolescent is no longer tied to parental apron strings. A few more privileges than they have proclaims his greater independence.

Socioeconomic Status
Since too many privileges suggest "wildness," most adolescents who want to create the image of belonging to an upper-class group are willing to accept some limitations on their demands.

Identification with the Right Crowd
If the "nice kids" are restricted in their privileges, the adolescent who is restricted gains the reputation of being a "nice kid."

Sex Appropriateness
In all social classes, masculinity implies the freedom to come and go as one pleases, when one pleases, and with whom one pleases. The image of the sex-appropriate girl is still influenced by the stereotype of the well-protected person with limited privileges.

---

privileges—and responsibilities as well—without having to ask for them (88).

ORGANIZATIONAL AFFILIATION

The adolescent knows that he is judged by the people he associates with. Consequently, he wants to be associated with prestigious organizations, and he wants others to know about his affiliation or membership (145). He is able to symbolize his affiliation in various ways. Many fraternities, sororities, and clubs, for example, have some distinguishing article of *clothing* which only members are permitted to wear. This may be a tie, a cap, a pin, or a ring. In addition, the adolescent can show his affiliation by a *sticker* on his car or luggage or by the use of *writing paper* with the organizational seal on it. Without boasting or bragging, he can casually mention a person or an event related to the organization and thus *talk* about his membership in this indirect fashion.

Most school and college *papers* report the activities of campus organizations. The adolescent who serves as an officer, a committee member, or a committee chairman in an important organization makes sure that reports of his activities are published. The more active he is, the more often his name will appear and the more widely his prestigious affiliation will be known.

The prestige value of one's affiliation with an organization depends on many conditions. Box 8-9 lists the most important sources of prestige (12, 14, 85, 99, 126).

Qualities symbolized

One's organizational affiliation has announcement value. It tells things about the individual, and these are incorporated into the image by which others judge him. Some of the things organizational affiliation tells are discussed below.

Social acceptance The degree of social acceptance an adolescent enjoys is readily manifested by the kind of organization with which

---

BOX 8-9   SOURCES OF PRESTIGE
FROM AFFILIATION

Method of Joining
One may become affiliated with an organization either by being invited or by applying for membership. Greater prestige is associated with being invited to join.

Exclusiveness of the Organization
An organization that carefully screens new members, admits only a few members at a time, and submits them to initiation ceremonies gains the reputation of being exclusive and prestigious.

Activities of the Organization
The major activities of an organization determine how much prestige it will enjoy. Since social and athletic activities are so important to adolescents, social and athletic clubs have greater prestige than academic clubs.

Status in Organization
Being a leader is more prestigious than being a follower. The more prestigious the organization, the greater the prestige of being a leader in it.

---

he is affiliated and the status he occupies in that organization. If he belongs to an organization which admits members only by invitation, this symbolizes his complete acceptance by the other members. Since *everyone*, it is widely assumed, would rather be a leader than a follower, the adolescent who is a follower is regarded as less well accepted than one who holds a leadership role.

Socioeconomic status "Belonging" is a symbol of higher socioeconomic status, not necessarily because only the well-off can afford the financial outlay for membership in an organization, but mainly because they are better accepted.

The higher the adolescent's family on the socioeconomic ladder, the more organizations the adolescent is likely to be identified with. His socioeconomic status, thus, is symbolized by the *number* of his affiliations and the value attributed to them by the social group. It is also symbolized by his *status* in the organizations because adolescent leaders are drawn mainly from those with higher socioeconomic status.

Sex appropriateness Just as women belong to more organizations than men, so do adolescent girls belong to more organizations than boys. In addition, girls take a more active part in organizational affairs than boys; they serve on more committees than boys and do a greater share of the committee work.

The kind of organization one is affiliated with also tells others something about one's sex appropriateness. The boy who belongs to a sports club is regarded as sex appropriate; one who belongs to a social club may be thought of as a sissy. The reverse is true of girls; belonging to a sports club suggests masculinity, while belonging to a social club suggests femininity.

Adult status Belonging to a grown-up kind of organization, playing the role of grown-ups in that organization, and having minimum adult superivsion over the activities—all these suggest to others that the members are near adults.

That organizational affiliation is recognized as a new and important status symbol is well illustrated by the fact that adolescents consciously try to identify themselves with their organizations and let others know of their affiliation. When they speak of their friends, for example, they refer to them as "my fraternity brothers" or "my sorority sisters." This, together with articles of clothing and other similar insignia of membership, leaves no doubt in the minds of others that the adolescent is following an adult pattern in his social life.

TABOOED PLEASURES

Just as Adam and Eve in the Garden of Eden were tempted to eat the only fruit they were forbidden to touch, so the adolescent is tempted to engage in activities that are forbidden. The very fact that they are forbidden gives them a halo of desirability.

Most, though not all, of the activities adolescents are forbidden to engage in are pleasures which adults enjoy. Adults believe that the activities are harmful to adolescents, either phsyically or mentally, or harmful to society. In discussing the use of "pot"—one of the names for marijuana—by high school and college students, *Time* (154) has given the following explanation of why it is forbidden:

How perilous is pot? Medical authorities agree that it is not biochemically addictive, that it does not induce the physiological cravings or withdrawal symptoms of such drugs as heroin or cocaine. It affects the user's judgment, and if used daily, will dull a student's initiative and drive, but on the whole, "marijuana is probably less dangerous than alcohol." . . . What does concern parents, administrators and doctors is the possibility of psychological habituation. . . . "The emotionally susceptible person can get psychologically dependent on anything—caffeine and coffee, nicotine and cigarettes, alcohol or marijuana."

The desirability of many of the tabooed pleasures is constantly called to the attention of the adolescent by the mass media. Ads for alcoholic beverages show adults enjoying these drinks in a gay party setting. The implication is that if you want to have fun at a party, you must drink. Movies, television shows, magazines, newspapers, and radio do their share in glamorizing tabooed pleasures.

In the American culture, certain activities are forbidden to the adolescent until he reaches an age prescribed by law or custom. He may not drive until the *law* of the state in which he lives says he may. He may not buy or be served liquor in a public place until the state in which he lives thinks it safe for him to drink. At no age may he buy narcotics, nor is he allowed to enter houses of prostitution to enjoy the pleasures of sex.

Pleasures that are regarded as less harmful are denied him by *custom* rather than by law. In spite of the supposed linkage between cancer and cigarette smoking, there are no laws saying that a person must wait until a given age to begin smoking or prescribing how much he may smoke. Enforcement of the no-smoking rule is a parental responsibility. In the same way, parents and teachers are expected to chaperon social gatherings to ensure that adolescents do not engage in forbidden sexual activities.

Status values of tabooed pleasures

Frequently a forbidden activity is a far less pleasurable experience than the adolescent had anticipated. It is not uncommon, for example, for the first smoke or drink to make the adolescent slightly nauseated. If engaging in forbidden activities were motivated by plea-surable results alone, many would be abandoned quickly. However, they have great status value, and so the adolescent continues to pursue them. In time, he may develop a liking for them.

As shown in Box 8-10, the status value of forbidden pleasures takes five different forms, each of which tells others important things about the adolescent and influences the image they develop of him (106, 121, 133, 135, 155, 160).

The status value of some forbidden pleasures is so great that adolescents who feel socially insecure and anxious to improve their status in the peer group may engage in them to excess. If drinking hard liquor is regarded as a sign of true masculinity, for example, a boy may regularly overdrink. If group acceptance

---

BOX 8-10   WHAT TABOOES PLEASURES SYMBOLIZE

Independence
To show his autonomy, an adolescent may break rules or laws about smoking, drinking, speeding, and using narcotics. Defying a strict rule or law is more symbolic of autonomy than breaking a lenient rule.

Maturity
Since drinking is almost exclusively associated with adulthood, many junior high school students start drinking to show their near-adult status.

Sex Appropriateness
Many of the tabooed pleasures are most commonly associated with males, and so boys engage in them to show their masculinity; girls refrain in order to show their femininity. Sex appropriateness is symbolized by the manner in which an activity is engaged in. Boys symbolize their masculinity by smoking pipes or unfiltered cigarettes while girls symbolize their femininity by smoking filtered cigarettes.

Identification
Doing what others do implies that one belongs even if this means breaking a rule or law.

Social Class
Among girls, smoking in public is symbolic of middle- and upper-class status. Narcotics are so expensive that they are a status symbol of affluent adolescents. Socially mobile adolescents must give up forbidden pleasures frowned upon by the group with which they hope to be identified and accept new ones which they may enjoy less or even disapprove of.

requires strict adherence to the patterns of behavior approved by the group, excessive drinking may be the price the adolescent must pay to prove to the group that he will be an acceptable member.

Excessive smoking, like excessive drinking, often results from a desire to establish a favorable status in the group. This is true also of the use of narcotics. Smoking marijuana, injecting heroin, or swallowing pills may begin as a thrill promoter when an adolescent is bored or feels inadequate. Not realizing the danger of what he is doing, the adolescent may become an addict.

HIGHLIGHTS OF CHAPTER 8

1. Since the adolescent has learned that the image others have of him is greatly influenced by the cues they use to judge his personal, social, and economic status, he becomes status-symbol-conscious.

2. Status symbols are visible signs of something not immediately visible. Because of their relationship to what can be observed, status symbols suggest certain qualities or properties.

3. The qualities most often symbolized by status symbols are those most highly valued by the group. In adolescence, these qualities are identification with the right group, maturity, autonomy, and sex appropriateness.

4. First impressions are greatly influenced by the individual's appearance; therefore, the adolescent wants to present a pleasing appearance so that the image others have of him will be favorable.

5. Clothes play a very important role in appearance. They are used by adolescents to enhance their good physical characteristics and to camouflage their poor ones. Thus, the adolescent's interest in clothes is focused on color, ornamentation, becomingness, appropriateness, style, and attention value.

6. Three aspects of speech are especially valuable as status symbols because they tell others, either directly or indirectly, what the adolescent wants them to know about him. These three aspects are the quality of speech, its content, and its quantity.

7. In every cultural group, names—surnames, given names, or nicknames—are associated with physical or psychological characteristics. Some of the associations are cultural in origin and some come from personal experiences.

8. In a culture which places high value on wealth, material possessions are status symbols because they are readily visible. The adolescent wants the material possessions that are highly prized by the peer group because he hopes that they will improve his status in the group.

9. Money is a status symbol for adolescents because it enables them to buy the material possessions that raise their status in the group and because it is one measure by which others judge them.

10. The privileges most highly valued by the group are those which are associated with qualities the group expects its members to have. Possession of these privileges is a status symbol which identifies the adolescent's role in the group.

11. Organizational affiliation varies in status-symbol value, depending on the method of joining the organization, the exclusiveness of the organization, its activities, and one's status in it.

12. Tabooed pleasures—activities which the adolescent is forbidden to engage in until he reaches the age prescribed by custom or law—are status symbols which signify the adolescent's independence, maturity, sex appropriateness, identification with the group, and socioeconomic status.

Chapter 9

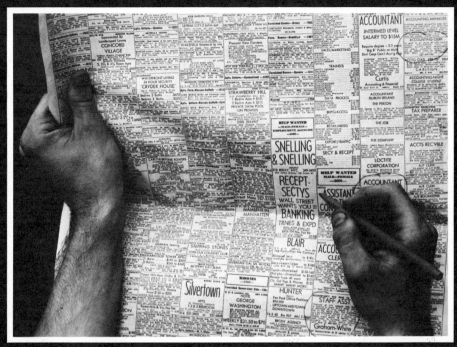

Levels of Aspiration

Photograph by Farrell/Greene
Omikron

Almost everyone would like to rise above his present status. Some may say they are content to stay where they are, but often such a statement is based on a belief that a change is impossible. The only way they can be happy, then, is to convince themselves that they are satisfied. Some may develop a *Pollyanna attitude*—convincing themselves that they are glad things are no worse than they are. Others may adopt a *sour-grapes attitude*—convincing themselves that they do not want more than they have because the things are not worth having.

Traditionally, America is the land of "golden opportunity" where those who are dissatisfied with their lot can better themselves. America has not always been the land of "golden opportunity" that it is today. In early colonial times, *sumptuary laws*—laws restricting the use of material possessions in accordance with the income of the family—made it impossible for citizens to "better themselves." Slavery limited the opportunity for many to follow any life except that prescribed by the slave owners. And low wages meant that a large portion of the population was doomed to the same status as their parents and grandparents.

With the abolition of sumptuary laws and slavery and with the creation of labor unions to demand better wages and working conditions, many barriers to opportunity were removed. As a result, America is more of a land of opportunity *for all* (21).

While people of all ages aspire to better themselves, aspirations are especially strong during adolescence. Typically, adolescence is a time of idealism and romanticism. It is a time of dreaming, high hopes, and confidence. The adolescent has fanciful ideas about the future, about marrying a person with whom he will live happily ever after and having a glamorous job which will provide him with the money he needs for the status symbols he regards as essential to happiness. These status symbols, he believes, will automatically open the doors that have been closed to him.

MEANING OF ASPIRATION

In everyday usage, "ambition" and "aspiration" are synonymous and are used interchangeably. The definition of "ambition," as given in a standard dictionary, means an eagerness for honor, superiority, power, or attainment; it suggests a "personal uplifting." "Aspiration" means a longing for what is above one, with advancement as its end. The subtle distinction lies in the emphasis on "what is above one." Back of all motivation for achievement is the desire for something better—"what is above one"—not just "honor, superiority, power, or attainment." The distinction also explains why achievement, per se, does not always bring satisfaction. An ambitious person will be satisfied with his attainment if it is lauded by others. A person who aspires to better himself will, by contrast, be satisfied only when his achievement comes up to the goal he has set for himself, regardless of how satisfying it may be to others.

"Aspiration" means the goal the individual sets for himself in a task which has intense personal significance for him or in which he is ego-involved. Box 9-1 shows the three important aspects of aspirations (29). Because aspirations are ego-involved, success leads to increased self-esteem, while failure brings embarrassment, remorse, and feelings of personal inadequacy and inferiority.

Kinds of aspirations

Aspirations may be positive or negative, immediate or remote. *Negative* aspirations reflect the desire to avoid failure; *positive* aspirations are oriented toward the goal of achieving success. An example of the first would be the adolescent who is satisfied if he passes an examination; an example of the second would be the adolescent who is satisfied only if he does better than his classmates. Most adolescents aspire positively. Only if they have a history of failure are they likely to set goals centered on the avoidance of failure rather than the achievement of success.

Immediate aspirations are goals the individual sets for himself for the immediate future, such as passing the examination he is scheduled to take tomorrow or winning the tennis tournament he is just entering. *Remote* aspirations are goals set for the future. The more immediate the goal, the more realistic it is likely to be. The adolescent who aspires to win the tournament he is just entering, for example, is more *realistic* in what he hopes to accomplish than the adolescent who aspires to be a doctor when he is still a high school student. The former is able to assess his opponents and to know, within limits, how his athletic skill compares with theirs. Being a doctor is so remote from the experience of the high school student, however, that he has no yardstick by which to measure his potential medical skill.

Strength of aspirations

The strength of aspirations depends not so much on whether they are immediate or remote as on how important they are to the individual. The importance of an aspiration to the individual, in turn, is affected by how hard it is to reach. The more *difficult* it is to reach, the greater its halo, and the more strongly motivated the aspirant is to reach it (110).

Even when a goal is important to an adolescent, the strength of his aspiration to achieve it will be influenced by *realism*. If he questions his ability to achieve the goal, his aspiration to succeed will be weakened. For example, if a student feels that he has little chance of being invited to join an exclusive fraternity because he knows few of its members, his aspiration is likely to be weaker than than if he felt that his chance of being invited to join was greater.

In general, *remote* aspirations are stronger than immediate aspirations. However, if an immediate aspiration is realistic and a remote one is unrealistic, the former will acquire a greater strength.

The strength of an aspiration will determine its effect on the individual's behavior. If an

---

BOX 9-1   ASPECTS OF ASPIRATIONS

*What kind of performance the individual himself considers desirable and important— what he wants to do

*How well he expects to perform

*How important the performance is to him, either as a whole or in its different parts

---

immediate aspiration is stronger than a remote one, the adolescent will satisfy the immediate, even if this interferes with the satisfaction of the remote. If, for example, being popular is more important to a student than a diploma, he will sacrifice his studies in favor of social activities.

Even more important, the strength of an aspiration influences the individual's willingness to do things he has little interest in doing. A boy who dislikes math but is anxious to become a doctor will be willing to work hard to master higher mathematics because it is a requirement for entrance into medical school.

Hierarchy of aspirations

Remote goals may originate as separate and distinct aspirations, but sooner or later, they may fit themselves into the individual's life plan. By adolescence, there is great pressure to formulate remote goals and to combine them into a hierarchy which will provide the adolescent a path to follow to reach the pinnacle of the hierarchy. Even immediate aspirations serve as stepping-stones (24, 83).

If the adolescent aspires to be a doctor, there are many intermediate goals which must be attained before the remote goal is reached. He must graduate from high school and college and satisfy the requirements for admission to medical school. Once he is admitted to medical school, he must concentrate on the areas in which he aspires to specialize and on the more remote goals of internship and residency in hospitals where he can get the special training he needs.

Once a hierarchy of remote goals has been established, the adolescent can direct his energies along a particular path of action. But if his aspirations are unrealistic, the path may lead to failure and disappointment. If the student who aspires to be a doctor is unrealistic about his capacity for this profession, he may upset the entire hierarchy of goals by failing a science course in college. Should his college achievement be only average, he may gain admission to a medical school whose prestige is far below his original aspiration.

MEANING OF LEVEL OF ASPIRATION

"Level of aspiration" is the standard a person expects and hopes to reach in a given performance. It is the *discrepancy between his achieved and his stated goals* (29, 50). It may be realistic in the sense that the person has a good chance of success. Or it may be unrealistic if his chance of reaching his stated goal is in doubt. Realistic levels of aspiration are determined mainly by cognitive factors while unrealistic ones are determined mainly by affective factors (80).

Unrealistic levels of aspiration are usually too high, although they may be too low. As Strang (117) has explained:

Although level of aspiration is an individual matter, people tend to set their levels of aspiration relatively high when they are dissatisfied with their present status, or when they are confident and successful. They tend to set their levels of aspiration relatively low when their motivation is poor, when they fear failure, when they do not face failure frankly, or the situation realistically, when others think poorly of them, and when they feel insecure or have other personality problems.

If an adolescent's chances of reaching unrealistically high goals are fairly good, then his high levels of aspiration should be encouraged and commended. But if his chances of success are nil because of his own inherent limitations or because of environmental obstacles over which there is little or no control,

it is questionable whether such encouragement should be given. Unrealistically high levels of aspiration usually doom the adolescent to failure from the start. Failure, in turn, leads to psychological damage that can adversely affect personal and social adjustments.

Methods of studying levels of aspiration

The psychological damage of unrealistically high or unrealistically low levels of aspiration is great. Only when sufficient scientific knowledge is available will it be possible to guide and encourage the development of levels of aspiration that will lead to a healthy adjustment to life. Scientific interest has centered on discovering what adolescent goals and levels of aspiration are and finding out how levels of aspiration are developed, why they vary, when they develop, and what effects they have on behavior.

One way to find out about an adolescent's aspirations is to ask him. Most adolescents resent this as intrusion into their private lives or they are reticent to disclose their aspirations for fear of being thought presumptuous. Still others do not want to declare themselves and then face the embarrassment that would come should they fall short of their goals (6, 49). Because of the difficulties involved in direct questioning, indirect methods have been used. Of these, the ones given in Box 9-2 have proved to be most fruitful (6, 55, 125, 134, 136, 140).

Social attitudes toward levels of aspiration

In the past, parents and teachers emphasized realistic levels of aspiration in their training of children and adolescents. While young people were not discouraged from being ambitious, they were encouraged to face the facts and to set realistic goals. The aim was to protect the young person from failure, disappointment, and feelings of inadequacy.

With the removal of many obstacles in the path of those who want to get ahead and with the help of scholarships and the expansion of higher education, all this has changed. Children and adolescents are now encouraged to set unrealistic aspirations. (See Fig. 9-2.) They are encouraged to regard what was once unrealistic as realistic. In addition, they are promised any aid their parents can give them to achieve their goals (87, 88).

Adults laud adolescents who aspire to get ahead and confidently predict their success. By contrast, they regard those who are satisfied with things as they are as drifters. Under such conditions, it is not surprising that some adolescents are encouraged to build false hopes.

HOW LEVELS OF ASPIRATION ARE DEVELOPED

Long before the child reaches adolescence, he develops many aspirations for what he will do when he grows up. He also learns to aspire in a way that is characteristically his—realistically or unrealistically. He may develop the habit of allowing himself to be swayed by others in setting his goals; or he may set them with little outside influence, based mainly on an assessment of his abilities acquired from past successes and failures. While environmental pressures and experience will modify the adolescent's pattern of aspiring, it will probably remain relatively the same as in childhood.

Of the many factors that influence adolescent aspiration levels, the following are significant:

Early training

Many adolescents are subjected from babyhood to training which emphasizes high achievement in whatever they do. Their par-

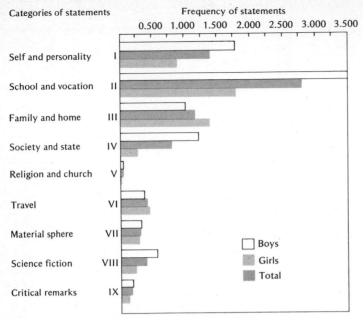

Categories of statements

Frequency of statements

0.500 1.000 1.500 2.000 2.500 3.000 3.500

Self and personality I

School and vocation II

Family and home III

Society and state IV

Religion and church V

Travel VI

Material sphere VII

Science fiction VIII

Critical remarks IX

☐ Boys
▨ Girls
▨ Total

Figure 9-1. Statements made by boys and girls in essays relating to self and future plans give clues to their immediate and remote goals. (Adapted from F. Mönks: Future time perspective in adolescents. *Hum. Develpm.,* 1968, **11,** 107–123. Used by permission.)

ents set the goals they are expected to reach and then show them how to reach them. This training is reinforced by rewards and punishment until the pattern of aspiring becomes internalized and parental guidance is no longer necessary.

Both parents participate in training for achievement, but in a slightly different way. The maternal approach to training is more emotionally involved in the sense that mothers place greater emphasis on warmth and approval for success and disapproval for failure than fathers do (10, 20, 111).

Parental ambitions

Even before a child is born, his parents have a picture of what their dream child will be like and they use this as a model for their aspirations for him throughout his life. Many parents have definite ideas about how much education they want their child to have, what vocation they want him to select, what social and academic achievements they expect of

him, and what sports they want him to excel in.

Many of the ambitions parents set for their children derive from thwarted ambitions of their own and they are determined to see that the obstacles they faced do not handicap their children. High school students, Garrison has reported, say that when they are parents they want their children to have the things they have not had, such as money, cars, friends, dates, and a good education (39). Some parental aspirations come from competition with other parents. Parents want their children to do better than other parents' children, and thus, indirectly, put a feather in their cap. Still other parental ambitions come from personal experiences. Mothers who are career women, for example, expect their children to acquire early the traits that will make them successful.

Schonfeld has referred to parental ambitions as the "great expectation syndrome"—a syndrome composed of aspirations for children to be successful in whatever they undertake, either in extracurricular activities or in academic pursuits. To ensure success, Schonfeld says, parents "cram all kinds of lessons and social experiences down the child's throat," often ignoring his interests and abilities and even his own aspirations (103).

Expectations of significant outsiders

The adolescent's aspirations are greatly influenced by what significant outsiders—especially peers and teachers—expect. If friends expect the adolescent to be a good athlete, for example, his aspirations will center on athletic achievements. The stronger his desire to be accepted by the group, the higher will be his level of aspirations. As Cronbach (29) has explained:

The standard set by one's group affects his goals. A person who thinks of himself as a normal member of a group will strive for the attainments characteristic of that group. . . . He is most influenced by the individual with whom he identifies or the group to which he feels he "belongs." . . . Keeping up with one's group is necessary for self-respect.

The adolescent is influenced to a lesser extent by teachers. If they expect him to achieve academic success, he comes to expect it of himself; if they expect him to fail or squeak through, he lowers his level of aspiration to conform to theirs. How much influence teachers have on student aspirations depends largely upon how prestigious they are and how anxious the adolescent is to conform to their expectations.

Competition with others

Many aspirations are based on a desire to outstrip others. When he was a child, the adolescent competed with older or younger siblings. The older sibling set a pattern which he strove to imitate; the younger set a pattern which he tried to surpass. If, as he grows older, the younger sibling surpasses him, he will aspire to live up to the standard set by the younger sibling.

The habit of competing with others plays an important role in determining what aspirations the adolescent will set for himself. If his friends aspire to be outstanding athletes, he will aspire to be more outstanding than they. When satisfaction from successful competition is great, the adolescent may aspire to perform only in those areas where he can compete successfully, even if it means ignoring his other interests, abilities, and needs.

Cultural traditions

The traditional democratic ideal of equality of opportunity is so widely believed that many children are taught that they can reach the top of the ladder if they will only make the most of what they have. While greater equality probably exists in America than in any other cultural group in the world today, there are still *limitations* to what one can do. Some limitations exist in the individual himself. He may not have the physical or mental capacity or the temperament to achieve what he wants. Other limitations are environmental. The individual may grow up in an environment where there are practically no opportunities to develop his academic abilities or his special

Figure 9-2. Unrealistic levels of aspiration are often fostered by parents. (Adapted from George Clark: "The Neighbors." © 1972 New York News, Inc. World Rights Reserved. Used by permission.)

"Choose your own career, Son. You can be a brain surgeon, banker, diplomat . . ."

skills in the arts. Still other limitations are social. Individuals may be prevented from doing what they are capable of doing because of prejudice. This is especially true of women and of members of minority religious or racial groups.

The adolescent who accepts the belief about equality of opportunity often aspires above his chances of success, even though his level of aspiration may be closely correlated with his abilities. If he fails to consider the obstacles which stand in his way, his level of aspiration will be unrealistically high in spite of his ability and motivation.

Failure to consider personal limitations often accounts for unrealistic levels of aspiration. A student may be unrealistic in aspiring to go to college, for example, if his high grades reflect "effort" more than real academic ability or if his classmates are so poor that he, by comparison, impresses his teachers as being brighter than he is.

Mass media

The traditional American belief about equality of opportunity has been reinforced by books, radio, movies, newspapers, magazines, and television. Even textbooks encourage students to set unrealistic levels of aspiration. Extraordinary achievement in various fields is stressed in many of the books students are expected to read, just as it was in the books read by their parents and grandparents (30).

In childhood as well as in adolescence, the individual identifies with the mass-media character that appeals to him most; that character is generally the hero or the heroine. Furthermore, the adolescent becomes accustomed to happy endings, to having the hero reach his goal even in the face of unbelievable obstacles. And on television, he does it almost instantaneously; within the one-hour time limit, all problems are solved. One cannot be exposed to constant repetition of the theme that all ends well without believing that it holds true in real life also.

Mass media have more influence on remote than on immediate goals. When it comes to the remote future, adolescents can aspire as high as they wish because there is always the possibility that something will happen to enable them to make a fortune or become national heroes.

This is illustrated by the expression of a teen-age girls's vocational aspiration, written after reading a biography of Madam Curie. As reported by Strang (117) the girl wrote:

I should like to be a scientist like Madame Curie. I would like to practice medical science. I want to be a scientist because science is necessary to help our nation grow strong. Our nation must have strong and healthy people free from sickness. There must be scientists to find the necessary things to keep sickness away from our nation . . . to find new discoveries and to improve on the discoveries of others.

Past experiences

Much of the unrealistic aspiring of adolescents can be traced to their limited experience, which makes it impossible for them to assess their capacities realistically. In their vocational aspirations, adolescents with some work experience are more realistic than those with no experience. Lack of experience and the glamorized picture presented in the popular media lead many adolescent girls to regard marriage as a solution to all their problems. Aspirations for large families are likewise based on lack of experience; few adolescent girls realize what it means in terms of work and expense to have a large number of children.

Experience also determines whether the adolescent will aspire to achieve success or to avoid failure. After a failure, he is more likely to hope to avoid another failure than to aspire to achieve success. For example, after failing an exam, his aspiration in taking a makeup examination is usually to pass, not to pass with a brilliant grade.

Interests and values

Adolescent interests influence aspirations in two ways. They determine, *first,* in what areas aspirations will be developed, and *second,* the level of aspirations. An adolescent boy who has discovered the high prestige value of sports will aspire to success in athletics rather than in the area of scholarship where prestige is lower.

Interests and abilities are normally quite closely related. Interest may be stronger than ability, however, if high social prestige is associated with an area of interest. On the other hand, interest may be weaker than ability would justify if environmental conditions have prevented the individual from developing the interest.

When interests are based on abilities, they tend to be stronger and more persistent than when based on group values with little relationship to the individual's own preferences or capacities. When aspirations are developed from interests based on abilities, they are not only stronger but also more realistic than when they are influenced primarily by group values. An adolescent who wishes to become a lawyer because of a sincere interest in law which springs from ability in this area is more realistic in his aspiration than the one who is intrigued by the high social position and income-earning ability associated with the legal profession.

VARIATIONS IN ASPIRATIONS

Among adolescents, goal-setting behavior varies in strength, in degree of realism, and according to degree of remoteness of aspirations. Some adolescents, for example, are "impractical dreamers" in the sense that they aspire above their capacities, while others are "realists" whose levels of aspiration are well within their reach. In commenting on differences in levels of aspiration, Pressey and Kuhlen (92) have remarked:

Some people are not satisfied unless their performance is of top quality, and they may even refuse to participate in an activity in which they cannot do better than most. Others are quite satisfied with a passable performance. Some people have a strong drive for vocational success: some are satisfied with "a living."

Even in the same adolescent, aspirations vary in intensity in different areas of activity. In academic work, aspirations are likely to be higher in subjects which are a stepping-stone to vocational success—such as mathematics and science—than in subjects which are required but seem to have little practical value.

Variations in aspirations and in levels of aspiration come from environmental factors as well as from individual personal characteristics. Some of the factors that affect goal-setting behavior are discussed below.

Cultural ideals

Different cultures have different standards of what they expect of their members. The standards include levels of achievement and attitudes toward achievement. By the time a child reaches adolescence, he is expected to know what his cultural group expects of him and to assume responsibility for guiding his behavior by these standards.

Goal-setting patterns differ among cultures. Studies of the training of Jicarilla Apache Indian boys, for example, reveal a strong emphasis on achievement. Throughout childhood, boys are encouraged by their parents to compete with their age-mates. They are taught the skills needed for successful competition, urged on to higher accomplishments, and ridiculed if they fall below the expected standards. By contrast, the Mountain Arapesh children have few demands for achievement placed on them. They are protected by their parents, are not asked to perform tasks which are exacting or difficult, and are not pressured to acquire skills (23, 79).

Within a cultural group, there are differences in subcultural ideals relating to aspirations. Box 9-3 shows some of the most important subcultural ideals in the American culture (17, 22, 67, 87, 96, 116).

Kind of family

Adolescents from *stable* families tend to concentrate on remote goals and to set higher

BOX 9-3   VARIATIONS IN SUBCULTURAL ASPIRATIONS

Socioeconomic Groups
Middle- and upper-class adolescents are usually trained to set goals for the future and to forgo immediate pleasures that might interfere. Lower-class adolescents are trained to be more present-oriented in their goal setting.

Ethnic Groups
Some groups put little pressure on their children to achieve high vocational and social success while others apply strong pressure. It has been reported that Italians fall in the first category and Greeks in the second.

Religious Groups
Jewish, Protestant, and Catholic parents, in that order, exert varying degrees of pressure on their children to aspire to high achievement.

Environmental Groups
Suburban parents, as a group, put more pressure on their children to aspire high—academically, socially, and vocationally—than do urban and rural parents.

levels of aspiration than those from unstable families. When his family is socially mobile, for example, the adolescent does not know what lies ahead and, consequently, cannot plan for it. If the family is socially stable, he knows what lies ahead and thus has a basis on which to plan (26, 112).

Family size also has an impact on goal setting. Small families are more achievement-oriented than large families. Parents of small families not only pressure their children more but also provide them with more advantages (97, 127).

In a home where the mother is the *dominant parent,* adolescents tend to set higher levels of aspiration. This is because of the emotional tie between mothers and their children, especially their sons (10, 53, 97).

Ordinal position

In middle and upper-class families, parents expect more of the firstborn and give him more advantages, especially if the firstborn is a boy. In lower-class families, by contrast, the youngest child is most likely to be pressured by both parents and older siblings to better

himself. By the time he is ready to go out into the world, his parents are in a better financial position to help him, and his siblings are willing to contribute their share. It is a feather in the cap of every family member to have one of its members move up the educational, vocational, and social ladders (2, 95, 130).

Discipline

Adolescents who have been subjected to strict authoritarian discipline have been reported to aspire, habitually, unrealistically high. By contrast, those whose discipline has been democratic tend to have more realistic aspirations. Since adolescents who have been brought up permissively have acquired the habit of doing much as they please, it is not surprising that they form the habit of aspiring unrealistically low—making little use of their abilities and having little desire to do so (9, 10, 20).

Group status

How much influence the group has on the aspirations of the adolescent varies according to his status in the group and what the group expects of him. If his status is secure and he has no reason to try to impress the group members, his level of aspirations will likely be realistic. The adolescent whose status is marginal, and who sees an opportunity of improving it, may aspire unrealistically high in areas which will increase his prestige in the group. In the case of the social isolate, the group exerts little influence (59, 86, 124).

Use of escape mechanisms

Of the different escape mechanisms, daydreaming has the most pronounced effect on goal-setting behavior. Excessive daydreaming —daydreaming more frequent and more fanciful than is characteristic of the individual's age level—encourages the adolescent to aspire far beyond his capacities. His aspirations are based more on a wishful estimate of his ability than on his real ability. By contrast, the adolescent who uses daydreaming more as a recreation than as a retreat from reality and more as a motivation to action than a retreat from action, will set more realistic goals. Refer to Chapter 7 for a more complete discussion of daydreaming.

The kind of daydream engaged in is also important. When the daydream takes the conquering-hero form, the adolescent develops aspirations for success. The girl who dreams of herself as a concert singer, for example, is likely to set aspirations in that area rather than in homemaking or some other career. (See Fig. 9-3.) If the daydream takes the suffering-hero form, the adolescent may merely aspire to avoid failure. Or he may develop unrealistically high aspirations and then blame his failure to reach his goals on others (19, 105).

Verbalization of aspirations

When the adolescent verbalizes his aspirations to others, he challenges himself to achieve his announced goal and increase his performance level. He knows that others are aware of his hopes and he does not want to be a failure in their eyes.

Aspirations that are verbalized are usually more realistic than those kept private. However, when an adolescent tells his close friends what he hopes to achieve, he is more likely to be unrealistic than when he tells his parents, teachers, or casual acquaintances (33, 58).

Past failures and successes

The adolescent who experiences frequent success tends to develop a *generalized expectation* for future success. In the same way, an adolescent may develop a generalized expectation for failure. These attitudes have a marked effect of the kind of aspiration— whether realistic or unrealistic, high or low— he sets for himself.

Sex

Boys, as a group, feel a need for greater attainment than girls, and their aspirations are concentrated in such areas as athletics, academic work, and sex-appropriate vocations.

Figure 9-3. Conquering-hero daydreams often set the pattern for adolescent aspirations. (Adapted from R. Strang: *The adolescent views himself.* New York: McGraw-Hill, 1957. Used by permission.)

Girls' aspirations, by contrast, relate most often to personal attractiveness and social acceptance—areas that are highly valued among women (11).

A sex difference is also seen in immediate and remote aspirations. Girls tend to have more immediate and fewer remote aspirations than boys. Since most girls regard marriage as their major goal, and since they do not know, during adolescence, when they will marry, whom they will marry, or the socioeconomic status they will have after marriage, it is difficult for them to plan ahead. Even their educational aspirations are often on a month-to-month basis (36, 82, 139).

Both at home and in school, boys are more pressured to achieve than girls. Parents expect more of their sons and so boys are encouraged to aspire unrealistically high in academic work, sports, and vocational choices (113, 127).

Intelligence

When the peer group values high academic performance, many adolescents set unrealistically high levels of aspiration in the hope of winning peer approval. When grades do not matter to the group, however, many bright adolescents set unrealistically low levels of aspiration (18, 46, 53).

Bright adolescents, on the whole, base their aspirations on their interests and capacities rather than on what is prestigious in the peer group. The less bright, by contrast, bow to group values.

Personality

In a number of ways the adolescent's personality affects his goal setting. As a form of compensation, the adolescent who is *self-rejectant* often aspires beyond his capacities. The more dissatisfied he is with himself, the higher and more unrealistic his level of aspiration. Often, excessive ambition is a cover-up for self-dissatisfaction (29, 50).

The *confident,* secure individual sets realistic goals for himself. By contrast, the one who lacks self-confidence is constantly striving to reach goals beyond his capacity; he is never satisfied unless he is "on top" (50, 126).

The adolescent who experiences relatively low *anxiety* tends to set higher goals than the one who is anxious and self-critical. The more anxious the individual, the more he emphasizes his poor past performance and the less optimistic he is about the future. The less anxious adolescent is more influenced by his successes than by his failures. As a result he sets his goals higher, often unrealistically higher, after he has achieved a success in some activity (32, 132).

Emotionally disturbed adolescents, having exaggerated fears or wishes for success, tend to set unrealistically low or high levels of aspiration. Emotionally well-adjusted adolescents are able to maintain a good balance between their hopes and reality and thus aspire more realistically (20, 94, 135).

THE ACHIEVEMENT SYNDROME

Far too many adolescents, accustomed from childhood to having others—mainly parents and teachers—do everything for them, feel that aspiring alone will bring them what they want. While they no longer believe in fairy godmothers and magic wands, they often fail to comprehend what role *they* must play in fulfilling their wishes and how complex their role is. This is not entirely their fault; they have not been given the training needed to achieve their goals, nor have they had to strive to reach their goals unaided.

Instead, they are constantly told how easy things are and are reminded that parents are eager to help. The mass media reinforce this approach. A girl who wants to improve her looks, for example, is told by all the ads for face creams, hair tints, and countless other beauty aids that all she has to do is to buy the foolproof product advertised.

Aspiring is only the first of a whole chain of activities. Whether the adolescent will achieve his aspirations will depend to a large extent on his past experiences and which of these provided him greater satisfaction. He may find satisfaction in daydreams or in identification with some successful person. Or he may be satisfied only if he actively fulfills the aspirations himself.

The complex process leading to achievement has been called the "achievement syndrome," a label which suggests that achievement comes not from one thing alone but from several things that are interrelated. Studies of the achievement syndrome reveal that it is made up of three major elements. Box 9-4 tells what they are and what their role in achievement is (20, 29, 51, 57, 98, 135).

The strength of the achievement syndrome is determined largely by the kind of training the adolescent has received. Parents who have low aspirations for their child give him little training in reaching goals and provide little motivation for him to aspire to success. The adolescent may have sufficient ability but does not learn how to mobilize his energies and use them effectively. As a result, he often gains satisfaction in imaginary successes or blames himself and others for his shortcomings.

Role of motivation

Of the three elements in the achievement syndrome, motivation is the most important. Underlying all aspiration is the fundamental human need for achievement. To fulfill this need, a person is motivated to direct his behavior toward a goal. Many years ago, Adler emphasized the importance of man's innate need for achievement. Everyone, he wrote, has a "life plan"—a purpose or goal which determines his actions. This life plan is developed early in life as a result of certain relationships between the individual and his physical-social environment. The individual develops feelings of inferiority—physical or mental or social in origin—and is motivated to compensate for these feelings by striving to reach a goal and by aspiring to superiority in that goal. Thus, according to Adler, the will to power, which is in everyone, is stimulated by whatever inferiority complex the individual may have developed (1).

Later writers have placed greater emphasis

BOX 9-4   ELEMENTS OF THE
ACHIEVEMENT SYNDROME

Aspiration
In aspiring, the adolescent sets goals which his training at home and in school has taught him are prestigious in the eyes of the group.

Motivation
Motivation provides the drive that the adolescent needs to direct his energies into channels that will lead to the goals he has set. Drive is influenced by rewards and punishment (i.e., social approval and disapproval).

Achievement Value
The adolescent must learn to assess his goals and determine whether they come up to social expectations and are, therefore, worth striving for.

on cultural pressures for achievement and less on a presumed innate need. They have also stressed the role of the social environment in determining aspirations. McClelland has said that the origin of achievement motivation is found in childhood experiences. The strength of the achievement drive will depend on, *first,* the general energy level of the individual, caused by endocrine, metabolic, or other constitutional factors; *second,* cultural influences, especially family values regarding education and success; and *third,* child training to develop independence, self-reliance, self-confidence, and the desire to excel. If child training is too permissive, the achievement motive will be low; if training is strict, the achievement motive will be high (77).

Thus many factors are responsible for the strength of the motive to achieve. Furthermore, social and cultural forces play a more important role than biological factors both in goal-setting behavior and in achievement of the goal that has been set (23, 28).

The achievement drive is usually well established between the ages of 6 and 10 years—the first 5 years of the child's school experience—and changes very little thereafter. As Sontag and Kagan have pointed out, "High levels of achievement behavior at that age (the 'critical age' between 6 and 10 years) are highly correlated with achievement behavior in adulthood" (111). In adolescence, the strength of the individual's drive for achievement is well established. A strong drive is not only easily recognized by the adolescent's peers but is also important in achieving a high level of social acceptance (56).

Outcome of achievement striving

Whether the achievement syndrome will lead to success or failure depends on the adolescent's ability, the use he makes of his ability, and the obstacles in his way. Success and failure are also greatly influenced by personality. If the adolescent feels inadequate, he will have "self-enhancing tendencies"; that is, he will try to make himself seem more adequate and worthy in order to improve his status or gain recognition and approval. His interpretation of his achievement as success or failure will thus be influenced by how well it fulfills his desire for recognition and acceptance (31, 108).

Success and failure can be judged objectively or subjectively. If the adolescent comes up to the expectations others have for him, he will be judged by them as a "success"; if he has done better than they expected, he will be considered a "real success." In spite of this, he may not be satisfied; he may even regard himself as a failure if his achievements do not measure up to his aspirations. Should the expectations of others be unrealistically high in relation to his ability, he will probably accept their expectations as a standard and set his level of aspiration unrealistically high also. As result, he will be both *objectively* and *subjectively* a failure when his achievements fall below both his own and others' expectations for him. Since immediate goals are more likely to be realistic than remote ones, the chances of failure, from a subjective point of view, are greater in the case of remote goals.

SUCCESS

In popular usage, "success" means the favorable termination of a venture; it means doing what you set out to do. As different people have different goals when they set out on a venture, success may have a different meaning for each. As Strang (117) has written:

To a few [success] means having the highest marks in the class. To others it means reaching an individual goal or standard; anything below one's level of aspiration is failure. To many, success means passing in every subject. To some of these, barely "getting by" is enough. . . . To very mature adolescents, success means working up to their optimum capacity, realizing their intellectual potentialities.

Adolescents, like adults, think of success mainly in terms of what is highly valued by the culture in which they live.

Factors contributing to success

Many people attribute success to luck or to influence. They believe that it comes from some outside source and that the successful person contributed little or nothing himself. While some people may *seem* to have "all the luck," the real difference between those who are called lucky and those who are not is that the former take advantage of the opportunities they have and make the most of their potentials; those who are "unlucky" do not. Influence may give a person a start, but unless he does his share, he will not succeed.

Success *must be won.* As stressed earlier, aspirations are not enough, nor is ability. The adolescent must have *training* and *guidance* to know how to use his abilities to the greatest advantage; he must have the *motivation* to use his abilities; he must be willing to *postpone immediate pleasures* for the sake of the larger goal; he must be *flexible* and willing to adjust to new roles and activities if they will contribute to his success, even though they may not be to his liking; he must have opportunities for *experience* to learn how to use his capacities and to assess his strengths and weaknesses; and, above all, he must be *willing to adjust* his levels of aspiration realistically to his abilities (13, 25, 60).

Even when guidance, training, opportunities, and encouragement are given, the adolescent may not reach the level of achievement he should because *they have come too late.* A student who has developed the habit of dawdling over his work may find it difficult or impossible to improve his study habits later when he is shown how to study; the old dawdling habit takes precedence over the new, efficient habit. As Harris has pointed out, "It is possible, indeed likely, that a person who comes late to his training will never realize the full measure of his potential" (45).

Success in one area is often a stepping-stone to success in another, especially when the areas are related. The experience acquired in one situation can be used to advantage in similar situations; in addition, the adolescent discovers what his capacities are and can use this knowledge to adjust his level of aspiration in a new activity. Adolescents whose academic achievements were high, for example, achieve greater occupational status than those whose academic achievements were low. High academic achievements obviously open doors to training opportunities which, in turn, open vocational doors that otherwise would be closed (8, 70).

Obstacles to success

Many adolescents achieve below their potential. In speaking of the relationship between intelligence and academic achievement, Terman has pointed out that "intellect and achievement are far from perfectly correlated" (121). If the adolescent can satisfy his aspirations by *daydreaming* or by *identification* with a hero or heroine in the mass media, his motivation to do what he is capable of doing in real life will be stifled. Or if he is motivated, he may not know how to achieve his goal because of *poor training and guidance.* Also, his motivation may be weakened by an unwillingness to admit or accept his limitations (25, 32, 133).

Even though an adolescent may have guidance, training, and motivation, his success may be blocked by obstacles over which he has little or no control. The obstacles may be *economic;* the adolescent may lack the money needed to do what he wants to do and is capable of doing. They may be *social,* stemming from prejudice based on race, religion, or sex.

Effects of success

While success affects adolescents in various ways, certain effects, as shown in Box 9-5, are almost universal (18, 32, 51, 87, 107, 133).

FAILURE

In the popular conception, "failure" means to fall short; it signifies an unfavorable termination of a venture. Failure may be *objective* or *subjective,* or both. When adults or members of the peer group expect more of the adolescent than he is capable of, they regard his achievement as a failure. If he accepts their level of aspiration for him, he too will judge himself as a failure. Or he may be objectively a success and subjectively a failure because his achievements come up to the expectations of others but fall below his own expectations.

Failures in adolescence are most often subjective. The adolescent is not only unrealistic about what he thinks he can do but he has been so accustomed to having adults help him achieve his goals that he believes his abilities are greater than they actually are.

Failures can also be acknowledged or grandiose. In *acknowledged* failure, the adolescent recognizes that his abilities and the conditions confronting him will prohibit him from reaching the goals he has set for himself or that others expect of him. In *grandiose* failure, the adolescent will not admit his limitations; instead, he convinces himself that he has been blocked in the achievement of his goal by someone or something over which he had no control (32, 38, 51). Figure 9-4 shows the different kinds of failure.

Most of the factors that contribute to failure

BOX 9-5 COMMON EFFECTS OF SUCCESS

Level of Aspiration
If the adolescent is confident that he can repeat or surpass his past successes, he will raise his level of aspiration; if he is not confident, he will play safe, keeping his aspiration level constant or lowering it.

Liking for Activity
The adolescent likes those activities in which he is successful. The greater his success and the more prestigious an activity, the stronger his liking for it.

Motivation
Success strengthens the adolescent's motivation to improve his skills and to put forth effort in subsequent activities—even those unrelated to an activity in which success was earlier achieved.

Desire to Publicize Success
The adolescent wants others to know of his successes because they increase his prestige and raise his status. He publicizes his successes by boasting or by using a more subtle technique, such as wearing athletic insignia.

Satisfaction
Four factors determine how much satisfaction the adolescent will derive from success: the value he attaches to the activity, the prestige associated with the activity, the attitudes of significant people toward his success, and how closely his success fulfills his expectations.

Self-concept
The adolescent who is highly satisfied with his success is proud, confident, and outer-bound—interested in others and generous to them.

Development of Success Complex
Repeated success leads to a generalized expectation of success—the "success complex"—which encourages the adolescent to be so self-confident that he often becomes cocky and arrogant.

are the opposite of those which lead to success. The most important of these are given in Box 9-6.

Effects of failure

Individual reactions to failure are highly varied and difficult to predict. Box 9-7 describes the most frequently reported effects of failure (18, 32, 51, 71, 93, 107).

The difficulty of predicting individual reactions is illustrated in studies of college students who fall below their own and their parents' expectations. One student may pack his bags and leave college with the explanation, "Just say I'm a fish out of water. It's not the school. It's me. I don't fit." Another, "desperately afraid of losing out in the intense competition of college," will "build a psychological buffer for himself by not trying." Others will threaten, attempt, or actually commit suicide rather than face the psychological anguish that comes from their feelings of guilt or shame at letting down those who had pinned their hopes on them. Jackson (52) has reported the following case:

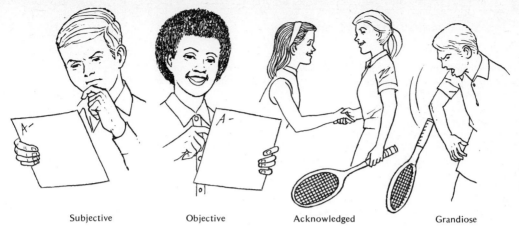

| Subjective | Objective | Acknowledged | Grandiose |

Figure 9-4. There are different kinds of failure.

One freshman was the first from his village to go to Harvard. He was a straight-A student in high school, but went into a psychological tailspin when he got Cs on his first midterm examinations. He wasn't helped when the village band met him at the train station when he came home for Thanksgiving.

Damages of failure

At no other age is failure so damaging and its effects so long-lasting as at adolescence. There are several reasons. *First,* adolescence is the first time that the individual attempts to tackle problems alone. If he fails, he is likely to conclude that he is unable to succeed without the aid of others.

Second, the adolescent is unable to escape from situations that threaten him with failure as he was when he was younger and will be able to do when he is older. As an adult, he can make his own choices, and as a child, he could rely on parental help if he ran into difficulties.

And *third,* this is the time when opinions of others have the most influence on the adolescent's opinion of himself. Furthermore, at no other time is the individual's personal life so open to other people. The closely knit society of the adolescent clique and the freedom with which adolescents talk about their hopes and fears leave the individual little privacy.

Because of the psychological damage that follows frequent and severe failure, it is not fair to encourage the adolescent to set unrealistically high aspirations. Unfortunately, many adults applaud an adolescent's "ambition to get ahead" but do not point out that there may be personal or social limitations to what can be achieved. Since no one can escape the psychological damages of repeated failure, encouraging an adolescent to aspire realistically is the only way to safeguard his mental health.

On the other hand, no adolescent should be encouraged to aspire so low that he will be saved from *all* failure. This, too, is unfair. *First,* if he is always successful, he may develop delusions of grandeur and thus raise his levels of aspiration unrealistically high.

BOX 9-6 FACTORS CONTRIBUTING TO FAILURE

*Limited mental or physical ability

*Lack of recognition of own potential

*Lack of opportunity for training

*Low motivation

*Unrealistically high level of aspiration

BOX 9-7 COMMON EFFECTS OF FAILURE

*Goals
Immediate goals are more likely to be lowered after failure than remote goals. Goals are more likely to be lowered after acknowledged failure than after grandiose failure.

*Dislike for Activity
An occasional failure is ego-deflating enough to condition the adolescent to dislike the activity in which it occurred. Frequent failures may lead to a generalized dislike even for related activities.

*Motivation
Failure may jolt one adolescent out of a state of complacency, but have the opposite effect on another—weakening both his confidence and his motivation.

*Desire to Hide Failure
Pride motivates the adolescent to try to hide his failures from others. The desire to avoid feelings of guilt leads him to project the blame for failure on others or circumstances beyond his control.

*Development of Failure Tolerance
The adolescent who is realistic about his abilities develops failure tolerance—the ability to withstand the effects of failure and to profit by it.

*Use of Escape Mechanisms
Since failure is ego-deflating, the adolescent may use escape mechanisms to avoid failure. He may not set any goal or he may skirt situations where failure seems inevitable.

*Development of Self-realism
Failure can teach the adolescent his strengths and weaknesses, thus helping him to be realistic about his abilities.

*Self-dissatisfaction
How much self-dissatisfaction the adolescent experiences after a failure depends largely on the value he places on the activity, the prestige of the activity, and the attitudes of significant people.

*Group Status
If the adolescent has a secure status in the group, failure will be less devastating to his overall sense of self-worth than if he is a marginal member.

*Self-concept
Failure leads to humiliation, self-derogation, and lack of self-confidence. These cause the adolescent to become self-bound and resentful.

*Development of Failure Complex
If failures come thick and fast, the adolescent is likely to develop a failure complex accompanied by a what's-the-use attitude.

Second, always being successful deprives the adolescent of opportunities to develop failure tolerance, which is essential if he is to cope with the problems of adult life in an adult manner. It is in adulthood that the full impact of the psychological damage will be felt.

HIGHLIGHTS OF CHAPTER 9

1.   An aspiration is a longing for what is above one. Aspirations are always ego-involved and thus have a profound effect on the self-concept.

2.   The strength of aspirations may be negative or positive, depending on how important the aspirations are to the individual; remote aspirations tend to be stronger than immediate ones.

3.   Level of aspiration, which is the discrepancy between the individual's achieved and stated goals, is more often unrealistic than realistic in adolescence. Level of aspiration can best be determined by studying the individual's wishes, ideals, and resolutions and by making laboratory experiments.

4.   Levels of aspiration are developed by family training, parental ambitions, expectations of significant outsiders, competition with siblings and peers, cultural traditions, mass media, past experiences, interests, and values.

5.   Adolescent aspirations vary in strength, degree of realism, and remoteness, depending on such factors as cultural ideals, the kind of family the adolescent grows up in, his ordinal position in the family, the kind of discipline he has been subjected to, his status in the peer group, the type and frequency of use of defense mechanisms, the degree to which he verbalizes his aspirations, the number and severity of his past successes and failures, and his sex, intelligence, and personality.

6.   The complex process leading to achieve-
ment—the "achievement syndrome"—has three important elements: aspiration, motivation, and achievement value.

7.   Whether the achievement syndrome leads to success or failure depends on many conditions, the most important of which are the adolescent's ability, the use he makes of his ability, and the presence or absence of obstacles.

8.   Success—the favorable termination of what one sets out to do—may be objective, in the sense that it is so regarded by others, or subjective, in the sense that it fulfills the individual's aspirations.

9.   Some obstacles to success originate in the adolescent himself, such as limited physical or mental abilities, and some originate in the environment, such as prejudice and discrimination.

10.   Certain effects of success are almost universal; the most important are the effects on level of aspiration, liking for the activity in which success occurs, strengthening of motivation to achieve future success, desire to publicize success, personal satisfaction, favorable effect on the self-concept, and development of a success complex.

11.   Failure, whether subjective or objective, acknowledged or grandiose, may be due to lack of ability (either physical or mental), lack of recognition of one's potential, lack of motivation, lack of opportunity for training, or a level of aspiration unrealistically high for one's abilities.

12.   Failure in adolescence is damaging for three important reasons: Since adolescence is the first time the individual attempts to tackle problems alone, failure may convince him that he lacks the ability to do things without the aid of others; the adolescent is unable to escape from situations that threaten him with failure; and opinions of others have more influence on the self-concept at adolescence that at any other time in the life span.

Chapter 10

Achievements

Photograph by Farrell/Greene
Omikron

To most people, the American dream means vocational success, which allows the individual to rise above his present status. Parents want their children to succeed and to have opportunities for advancement they did not have. They teach their children to set high goals and to develop values which will guide their choices in areas where achievement will make the dream come true. Since World War II, greater opportunities have been opening up for all adolescents, regardless of race, religion, socioeconomic class, and sex, and the American dream of success can now be a reality for many more adolescents than was ever before possible.

The dream of success has long been a part of American ideology, but its attainment has seldom been easy. A study of a high school class of about 50 years ago revealed that few of the class members fell very far below the level of their families in achievement. Similarly, few had climbed to any heights of success, even though they had been told at the time of graduation that, because they live in a "land of equality of opportunity" where "to strive is to succeed," *anyone* can be a "success" (9). Actually, the ones most likely to succeed are those with the greatest ability, though ability alone will not guarantee success (245).

The climb up the socioeconomic ladder is made possible by social mobility, schooling, and vocation. *Social mobility,* or moving up on the social ladder, is largely under the control of parents; whether the adolescent can live in a better community, go to a better school, and come in contact with the "right" people will depend upon the breadwinner of the family. The adolescent's success or failure in *school* and the choice of a lifetime *vocation,* on the other hand, are more nearly under his own control, though not entirely free from parental influences.

Because of his strong desire to improve his status, the adolescent is primarily interested in the kind of success that will help him to get ahead rather than that which will lead to personal satisfaction. The adolescent is more interested in the practical and work-oriented aspects of education, for example, than in the cultural. As Kosa et al. have emphasized, those who want to move up the ladder regard college as "an instrument for social mobility rather than an instrument of scholarship. . . . They accept the middle-class standards, conform to their peers from a higher class and try to ride the trend without much personal effort" (128).

While education is the surest way to success for most adolescents, a few achieve fame and fortune by other means. A great athlete, for example, can attain success even with a limited education. The same is true of movie and television stars, artists, and others who have special talents. But for most, it is schooling which opens the door to prestigious and lucrative vocations; these, in turn, open the door to upward social mobility. The remainder of this chapter will be devoted to a discussion of education, vocational choice, and social mobility; how the adolescent becomes interested in them; and how his interest is expressed.

EDUCATION

Most educators are well aware that the typical American adolescent is not seriously interested in education except as a means to an end. On the surface this statement seems to misinterpret the meaning of overcrowded high schools, increased college enrollments, and the fierce competition for admission to graduate and professional training schools — law, medicine, and engineering especially. But as Hechinger and Hechinger have stated, "There has never been greater concern about getting into college, coupled with so little interest in actual learning" (100). Figure 10-1 shows the spiraling increase in college attendance over the last two decades. Note the great rise in students attending public colleges — not because their academic standards are higher, but because their costs are lower than the private colleges and more within the reach of the majority of students.

Education is actually a means to several ends. Box 10-1 shows what these ends are

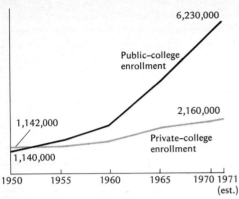

6,230,000

Public–college
enrollment

1,142,000

2,160,000

1,140,000

Private–college
enrollment

1950   1955   1960   1965   1970 1971
(est.)

Figure 10-1. College enrollment has increased dramatically over the last two decades. (Adapted from data from U.S. Dept. of Health, Education and Welfare, 1971.)

and why they are important to adolescents (33, 96, 139, 163, 164, 235).

Areas of major interest

Even before adolescence, the child knows that education and what it symbolizes are highly valued by parents, peers, and teachers. As a result, he too develops a "begrudging respect" for the school system (119), accepting its values and building interests and aspirations around them. While he would like to achieve success in *all* areas which are prestigious, he is realistic enough to know that he must select the areas in which his chances of success are greatest and focus his interests and efforts on them.

The following paragraphs outline the areas of education in which most American adolescents are interested today.

Academic subjects On the whole, students show the greatest interest in subjects they believe will be most valuable to them vocationally and in other areas of adult life. Interest therefore depends to some extent upon sex and upon aspirations for the future. The boy who aspires to a career in business or industry, for example, will be interested in different subjects from a girl whose aspirations center on marriage, homemaking, and child rearing.

Regardless of personal interest or ability, the adolescent's attitude toward school subjects is colored by what is considered *sex appropriate*. Science and mathematics are regarded as "masculine" fields. Even if a girl does well in these subjects, it is believed that they will be of little value as the vocational doors in these areas will be closed to her (12, 64, 200, 212).

Interest and motivation are usually closely correlated, and so the adolescent who has a strong interest in a subject, based on the belief that it will help him achieve his vocational goal, will put great effort into mastering it. As a result, he will do best in the subjects he regards as useful. Success almost always leads to a liking for a subject; liking, in turn, increases motivation, which normally leads to greater success (154, 221).

Grades Adolescents are interested in grades not as an insignia of knowledge but as a means to an end—entrance into college, preferably a "name" college, into a professional training school, or into a good job in a prestigious vocation. Few students are free from worry about their academic work or unconcerned about their grades (148, 209). Why grades are important to an adolescent has been explained thus by Symonds (221):

They indicate success or failure; they determine promotion; they indicate the probability of future success; they influence his parents' attitude toward him. Marks help to determine whether a pupil thinks of himself as successful, smart, or a failure, an outcast, stupid, a nitwit.

Students also worry about how the peer group will react to their grades. They do not want to be resented if they make good grades or regarded as stupid if they make poor ones. Insecure adolescents who are anxious to be socially accepted are most likely to be concerned about peer reaction (51, 222). Figure 10-2 illustrates how one boy solved this problem.

The adolescent who aspires to high grades uses various methods to reach his goal. He may be willing to *sacrifice other interests,* especially sports and social activities, to have enough time to study. He may take *easy courses* even if he is not interested in them. Perhaps the most common method is *cheating* (99, 213), which will be discussed in detail in Chapter 12.

Adolescents whose grades are below their aspirations may try to convince themselves and their friends that good grades are not important. Others are satisfied with what is traditionally called a "gentleman's C," because they spend their time in sports and social activities which they consider more important than grades. Some adolescents blame their teachers for being "against them" and for lowering their grades in revenge. Others claim that lack of privacy, noise, and distractions at home are responsible for their inability to study. To relieve the anxiety that accompanies the drive for high grades, some students lower their levels of aspiration (52, 170, 221).

Academic rewards Most adolescents want a "reward" for the time and effort put into acquiring an education. Some are satisfied with a high school diploma; some with a college degree; and a few, only with a higher degree. These rewards are important to students because they are "salable." When asked why they want a college diploma, many students answer, "Money." As Boroff has pointed out, "It is part of the new folklore of our society that a degree is worth money—lots of money" (33). Packard writes, "Fascination with the diploma as a badge of eligibility apparently is becoming a permanent feature of life at the well-established corporations" (163).

The sales value of an education is increased if the student achieves academic honors in addition to his diploma or degree: the honor roll in high school, the dean's list in college, a scholarship, or cum laude citations. Knowing that honors pay off, some adolescents work hard to achieve them.

Autonomy Most adolescents want autonomy in selecting their courses of study. They object to having to take prescribed courses if they are uninterested in the subject matter,

if they feel they cannot do well in them, or if they can see no practical value to be gained.

In extracurricular matters, protests against regimentation and rules mount. Students want to decide for themselves how much time they will devote to athletics and in what areas they will spend their time; they want to run their clubs and select their speakers; they want to be free to smoke, drink, and pet on the school or college grounds; and they want to be represented on the committees that establish academic and nonacademic policies.

Many adolescents claim that their high schools and colleges are "child-centered" institutions—that they treat the students as if they were still in elementary school. In their demands for autonomy, adolescents sometimes refuse to attend classes unless the rules are changed. Others drop out and get jobs. Chapter 6 contains a more complete discussion of this matter.

Extracurricular activities Sports and social activities make school life tolerable for many students. They are willing to accept the educational aspects to be able to have the extracur-

---

BOX 10-1   IMPORTANT GOALS IN EDUCATION

Social
By being identified with the "right" school or college, the adolescent improves his status in the minds of others. To aid his identification, he makes verbal references to his school and wears its insignia.

Vocational
The more education the adolescent has—the the more diplomas, degrees, and honors— the easier his climb to the top of the vocational pyramid.

Economic
Education is an investment that pays big dividends in increased earning ability. Also, graduation at any level means about twice as much as incompleted training.

FEIFFER'S FABLES

Figure 10-2. The student's attitude toward academic achievement is greatly influenced by peer attitudes. (Adapted from Feifer's Fables. Publishers-Hall Syndicate. *The Philadelphia Evening Bulletin,* Mar. 7, 1965. Used by permission.)

ricular activities that high schools and colleges offer. Even adolescents who find intellectual work interesting and stimulating tend to look upon success in extracurricular activities as more worthwhile (52, 135, 146).

Extracurricular activities are a more important area of education in high school than in college. *First,* the college student finds them a repetition of what he has already had in high school and is somewhat bored with them. *Second,* as the college student approaches the time of getting a job, he realizes the need to make good marks, and so he becomes more serious about his studies (127, 192).

Variations in attitudes toward education

Because of differences in aspirations, backgrounds, and many other factors, adolescents have markedly different attitudes toward education. They enter high school or college with either favorable or unfavorable attitudes and they change very little (127, 146).

Ruthven maintains that there are three kinds of college students, each entering college with a characteristic, long-established attitude. The *first* group he labels "The Noisy Ones"—those who are "determined to be heard. Posing as authorities on almost everything at home and abroad, they insist they should run the university. . . . They usually claim to be liberals and boast of disrespect for authority." The second are "The Playboys and Girls"—those who go to college "only on the insistence of their parents or because it is 'the thing to do' . . . and whose ambition is to get nothing more than to get a 'gentleman's grade' or to get married." The *third* group Ruthven calls "The Dedicated Ones"— those who come to college "with their eyes firmly fixed on at least a general goal. They refuse to be discouraged by adversity or diverted from their course by college sideshows" (184).

Box 10-2 gives the major factors that influence the adolescent's attitudes toward education in general and toward specific aspects, such as teachers and particular subjects (48, 95, 97, 160, 175, 211).

In spite of variations in attitudes, adolescents can be subdivided roughly into those who are satisfied with education and those who are dissatisfied. How satisfaction and dissatisfaction with education in varying degrees affects scholastic achievement and adolescent behavior in the academic milieu are discussed below.

Satisfaction with education

The adolescent who enjoys his studies and feels that his teachers treat him fairly will do good academic work. He may not work up to capacity and his grades may not come up to his aspirations if his major interests and

BOX 10-2 FACTORS AFFECTING ATTITUDES
TOWARD EDUCATION

Cultural Values
While most Americans put a very high value on education, some sub-cultural groups do not, feeling that it will not help them to get ahead.

Social Class Values
In general, attitudes toward education become more favorable as one goes up the socioeconomic ladder.

Parental Attitudes
Middle-class parents, anxious to have their children rise in the world, encourage them to take part in academic and extracurricular activities. Lower-class parents, as a group, show little interest in education and permit their children to drop out of school if they want to go to work.

Ordinal Position
Firstborns, especially in middle- and upper-class families, are likely to receive more encouragement and more educational advantages than later-born siblings.

Peer Group Attitudes
Boys tend to develop more favorable attitudes toward education when they recognize its value to their future. Girls' attitudes become less favorable after the high school sophomore year.

Sex Roles
Boys, as a group, think of education as preparation for their vocation, and girls as a group, for their homemaking and social roles.

Vocational Plans
Adolescents who aspire to go into work that requires higher education have a more favorable attitude toward academic and extracurricular activities than those who aspire to do skilled labor.

Social and Academic Success
Success or failure in extracurricular activities is more important in determining attitudes toward school than success or failure in academic work.

Attitude toward Teachers
Even when an adolescent likes a teacher, his attitude toward school may be unfavorable if he dislikes the subject she teaches, if he does poorly in it, or if he feels it has no practical value for him.

Teaching Techniques
In contrast to the glamour and excitement of movies and television, teaching techniques seem boring and classroom work dull.

Antiwork Attitude
Adolescents who are used to having help from parents and teachers dislike subjects that require work. They may develop a general dislike for school.

values lie in extracurricular areas, but generally he will be satisfied with his grades. The discrepancy between what he hoped to do and what he actually does will be small enough not to disturb him too much. Furthermore, his parents and teachers will be satisfied with his achievements (60).

Many adolescents who are satisfied with school concentrate their efforts on subjects that will help ensure future vocational success even if this deprives them of time for extracurricular activities. They do not feel that good academic work is incompatible with social acceptance in a crowd that is congenial to them.

Satisfaction with education does not mean that the adolescent will not grumble, criticize, or attempt to reform his school or college. He will do all of these but mainly because it is the thing to do. If he criticizes, he generally has a reason, and his suggestions for reform are usually realistic. If a class is poorly taught, he will criticize the teacher for poor instruction, not because he received a poor grade. If he feels that rules are unfair, he will suggest possible changes; he will not simply accuse the school of treating the students like "kids."

On the other hand, he may not vocalize his satisfaction with school. That is not "the thing to do." He does not want the peer group to feel that he is trying to polish the·apple or become teacher's pet.

Variations in satisfaction *Girls,* more often than boys, are satisfied with both academic and extracurricular activities (80). Adolescents from the higher *socioeconomic groups* tend to have more favorable attitudes than those of the lower groups. *Bright* adolescents of all socioeconomic groups are better satisfied than those who are less bright. Being too bright for the group with which they are identified, however, leads to dissatisfaction (74, 78, 251).

Perhaps the greatest variations in satisfaction are related to differences in *personality.* Well-adjusted, mature adolescents tend to be better satisfied with education than those who are poorly adjusted or immature (216).

Furthermore, well-adjusted adolescents develop more efficient study habits than those who suffer from feelings of inadequacy and emotional stress, and thus the well-adjusted do better academic work and have better social relationships in school (73, 158, 253).

Dissatisfaction with education

Unfortunately, the majority of adolescent boys and girls express dissatisfaction with their educational experiences. This may be merely a way of following the crowd. Or it may simply reflect the fact that people of all ages are more vocal about things they dislike than about things they like.

Dissatisfaction varies in intensity from mild to strong. It also varies in a predictable way according to sex, intelligence level, and socioeconomic status. *Boys,* on the whole, are more dissatisfied with their educational experiences than girls and are more vocal about their dissatisfaction. Those who deviate markedly from the mean in *intelligence,* whether below or above, are more dissatisfied than those whose intelligence is close to the mean. Very bright adolescents are especially dissatisfied with their classroom work, with teaching methods, and with their lack of autonomy in extracurricular activities. The less intelligent are dissatisfied with their lack of academic and social success. Adolescents of the lower *socioeconomic* groups are, in general, more dissatisfied than those of the upper groups. Upper-class adolescents are less dissatisfied because schools and colleges often cater to them both academically and socially (60, 78, 80).

Expressions of dissatisfaction Adolescents show their dissatisfaction with school or college in many ways. The following are reported to be the most common.

CRITICISM AND ATTEMPTS TO REFORM As was explained in the chapter on nonconformists, adolescents are often hypercritical of their schools and colleges. They find fault with everything—their studies, their teachers, the extracurricular activities, their classmates, and the administrative policies. Not only do they verbalize their complaints but they offer suggestions, often impractical and unrealistic, about how to improve things.

While dissatisfied students come from all socioeconomic and intelligence levels, the most critical and reform-prone are most likely to come from middle-class backgrounds and to be highly intelligent. The more dissatisfied they are, the more critical and the more avid they are in their attempts at reform. Consciously or unconsciously, they are trying to lower the morale of their classmates and win others to their group.

MISBEHAVIOR It is not uncommon for a dissatisfied student to want to retaliate and cause trouble for those who force him to be in a situation he does not like. He may try to disturb the teacher or other students by cutting up, by interrupting the teacher with irrelevant questions, by disobeying rules, and by showing disrespect for all in authority. If dissatisfaction is very great, an adolescent may express his resentment at having to remain in school by arson, vandalism, and other forms of juvenile delinquency (243, 256). This will be discussed in more detail in Chapter 12.

UNDERACHIEVEMENT In "underachievement" the individual is performing below his tested capacity. The underachiever's performance may not be bad in comparison with that of his classmates, but it is below what he is capable of doing.

Some adolescents are *general* underachievers in the sense that their performance is below their capacities in all or nearly all areas; others are *specific* underachievers, working below their capacities in only certain areas and up to their capacities in others. Underachievement is usually an indication of the adolescent's dissatisfaction.

While underachievement may reach its peak in adolescence, it usually begins during childhood, often as early as the second or third grade. This is the time when the child's attitude toward school often changes from

favorable to less favorable (195). As Shaw and Grubb have pointed out, the underachiever brings the tendency to work below his capacity with him, "at lease in embryo form, when he enters high school" (194).

Studies of underachievement reveal that it has many causes. Furthermore, the underachievement of a particular adolescent is most often the result of a constellation of related causes. In Box 10-3 are given the most common causes of the underachievement syndrome, grouped into large categories (46, 104, 126, 155, 214, 225).

Underachievement is greater among *boys* than among girls. This is usually explained by the fact that girls try to conform more closely to adult expectations and that boys place a lower value on good academic work. *Very bright* adolescents tend to underachieve more than those of average ability; they feel that they must not be distinguished by academic success if they want to gain social acceptance. Among bright adolescents, there is less underachievement among those of the higher *socioeconomic* groups because they know that education is a necessary stepping-stone to success. Adolescents who have learned to *study effectively* tend to underachieve less than those with poor study habits (38, 161).

OVERACHIEVEMENT An "overachiever" performs above his tested ability. By working hard, by impressing his teachers with his conscientiousness, or even by cheating, he does better than his assessed capacity would lead one to expect. Overachievement would seem to suggest satisfaction with education or a high level of intellectual curiosity. More often, however, it is associated with personality factors; it comes from conditions unrelated to the school or college situation, such as feelings of inadequacy.

Studies of overachievers reveal that their dissatisfaction with education comes from two sources. *First,* they are not satisfied with their academic work because their grades have not come up to their expectations or the expectations of their parents, and *second,* they are not satisfied with their social accept-

BOX 10-3   COMMON CAUSES OF UNDERACHIEVEMENT

Home Influences
Parental pressures to achieve academically and socially often make the adolescent resentful. He may try to retaliate by doing what he knows will hurt most—falling below parental expectations. When parents show little interest in the adolescent's academic or extracurricular achievements, his motivation to achieve is weakened.

School Influences
Boring lessons, dull teaching, and unsympathetic or unfair teachers weaken the adolescent's motivation to achieve. Poor study habits and a tendency to be easily distracted and to procrastinate also contribute to underachievement. When the adolescent is constantly unfavorably compared with a sibling who achieves more than he, he becomes resentful and willfully works below his capacity.

Vocational Plans
If the adolescent's vocational plans require only a high school diploma, his motivation to do any more than is necessary to get a diploma will be weak.

Social Rejection
Hostility resulting from peer rejection increases the adolescent's dissatisfaction with school and his tendency to underachieve. Most often, academic success alone gives the adolescent little satisfaction.

Immaturity
Adolescents who are immature for their age tend to underachieve more often than those whose maturity level is average or above.

ance (57, 77, 227). As Coleman has written, academic achievement brings few social rewards, and therefore many potentially good students do not go out for studies, but rather for sports and social activities. As a result, the outstanding students—the "intellectuals" —in many American high schools and colleges are not those with the most intellectual ability. Instead, they are those who hope to improve their social status by achieving distinction in whatever area they can (52).

DROPOUTS   Withdrawing from a situation with which one is dissatisfied is a common reaction. Some people withdraw *mentally* into a daydream world without removing themselves physically. Many more react to dissatisfaction by *physical* withdrawal. They

drop out of school or college before completing the requirements for a diploma or degree (37).

It is possible, often in elementary school, to tell which students are most likely to drop out. Boys and girls who have few friends and belong to no gang show a dislike for school that increases as they grow older. Those who are accepted by peers and teachers have more favorable attitudes toward school and are far less likely to drop out. In colleges, for example, students who join clubs, fraternities, or sororities are less likely to drop out than those who have no such affiliation (14, 252).

Dropping out of school is not ordinarily an overnight decision. Indications of the student's dissatisfaction have probably shown up earlier in school phobias and truancy. A child who develops an abnormal fear of school—a "school phobia"—never completely overcomes his dislike of school. Often he lives for the day when he will no longer have to go. He will play truant or stay away with parental consent if he can persuade his parents that he is not well. Typically, he will drop out before finishing (101, 120).

Most students are motivated to drop out by a constellation of related causes. Furthermore, some drop out voluntarily and some involuntarily. As Box 10-4 shows, the conditions leading to voluntary and involuntary dropout differ (10, 21, 24, 91, 143, 177). Figure 10-3 shows some of the most common reasons for dropping out of high school.

The usual age for boys and girls to drop out of school is 16 years—during the eighth, ninth, and tenth grades. Often they are older than their classmates and feel that they are too old to be with such "kids" (150, 247). College dropouts usually come during the first and second years, often after midyear or final examinations (123, 143). As Boroff has pointed out, "The dropout rate approaches 60 percent, and casualties include the ne'er-do-wells, students whose funds have dried up and those who get bored, restless or married" (33).

Whether dropping out will end or simply interrupt the adolescent's education will depend mainly on when it occurs and why.

Students who drop out of high school are less likely to return to the classroom than those who drop out of college. There are two reasons. First, college dropouts discover that the only kind of job open to them does not come up to their vocational expectations. As Hathaway et al. have written, dropping out of high school or college "is less catastropic for girls than for boys" because most girls expect to marry and leave the labor force (96). Second, college dropouts are more likely to return to the classroom than high school dropouts because they can go to other colleges where, they hope, things will be more to their liking. It is difficult for high school dropouts to transfer to another school. Furthermore, they often find on-the-job training programs in industries which pay good wages and prepare them for a job without a high school diploma.

Whether dropping out will be permanent or temporary also depends on why it occurred. If the adolescent is a voluntary dropout, the chances of his finishing his course of study are slim. One is not strongly motivated to return to a situation with which one is dissatisfied even when the rewards—obtaining a diploma or degree—are high. Later, when the dissatisfaction of being in a dead-end job becomes apparent, family or other responsibilities may make it impossible for the dropout to return to school or college.

The involuntary dropout, by contrast, regards dropping out as an interruption, not as an end to his education. While some involuntary dropouts may never be able to complete their education, they want to and they live in the hope that some day it will be possible. The increase in night high schools for adults

---

BOX 10-4   COMMON CAUSES
                OF ACADEMIC DROPOUT

Involuntary
Involuntary dropouts end their education not because of dissatisfaction with education but because of some necessity, usually economic or familial.

Voluntary
Voluntary dropouts are dissatisfied with education. Conditions that often *predispose* an adolescent to drop out are a feeling of academic or social failure and an inability to see how education will help him to reach his goals for adult life. If these are reinforced by parental and peer attitudes, the adolescent is then motivated to drop out by a desire for money, an academic failure which puts him on probation or requires him to repeat a course, a desire to do what his friends are doing, or parental pressures to end his academic career. Even though an adolescent may be predisposed to drop out of school, he may not drop out unless the motivation to do so is strong. If it is strong, his decision to drop out is likely to be sudden.

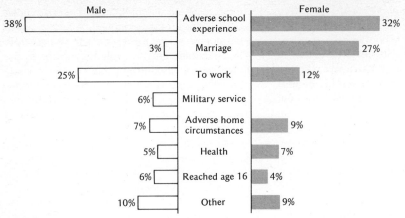

Male		Female
38%	Adverse school experience	32%
3%	Marriage	27%
25%	To work	12%
6%	Military service	
7%	Adverse home circumstances	9%
5%	Health	7%
6%	Reached age 16	4%
10%	Other	9%

Figure 10-3. Common reasons for dropping out of high school. (Adapted from data based on a national survey by U.S. Dept. of Health, Education and Welfare, 1966.)

and in adult education classes on the college campus, correspondence courses for completion of high school or college work, and television courses for college credit—all show how eager some adults are to finish an interrupted education (7, 96, 166, 214).

Damaging effects of dissatisfaction Dissatisfaction with education lowers the student's motivation, and his performance, both quantitatively and qualitatively, will be below his capacity. His performance will also probably be below that of others of equal or inferior ability who are not dissatisfied.

The two most dissatisfied groups are made up of the adolescents at the two ends of the IQ continuum—the brightest and the dullest. Adolescents who are very bright are dissatisfied mainly because they are bored. Those who are dull are dissatisfied because they feel that they are failures—both academically and socially. Students who are dull often drop out of school before completing their courses. Very bright students, as a result of boredom, work below their capacities and often drop out because they, too, find school or college intolerable. Both may become vocational misfits in time.

Adolescents whose dissatisfaction with their education is so great that they decide to drop out of school or college find jobs much harder to get than they had anticipated. Even more damaging, in times of economic depression, the poorly trained are usually the first to be laid off and the last to be rehired when conditions improve.

Idleness and general dissatisfaction lead many adolescents into delinquency. It has been reported, for example, that juvenile delinquency is ten times more frequent among dropouts than among high school graduates. This subject will be discussed in more detail in Chapter 12.

LONG-TERM EFFECTS OF DISSATISFACTION
Added to the immediate effects of dissatisfaction with school are several long-term effects which may far overshadow the consequences just discussed. One of these is the dropout's generalized negative attitude toward book learning. An *antilearning attitude*, which makes many people averse to reading anything except the tabloid newspapers, may prevent the dropout from taking refresher courses to learn new methods in his area of work and from developing new skills. In today's rapidly changing world of work, such an attitude could condemn the individual to a boring and unproductive job for life.

Another long-term consequence of dissatisfaction with education is the effect it has on one's *children*. In discussing dropouts, Schreiber emphasized that "dropout parents breed drop-out sons" (185). This statement can be broadened to read, "Parents who are dissatisfied with education breed children who are dissatisfied with education." As the children of today's adolescents grow up in an age where a lifetime of education is essential to keep pace with the constant changes in business and industry, a negative attitude toward education will unfit them for what life holds in store.

Unless something can be done to make negative attitudes toward education unfashionable in the peer culture, our nation is in for trouble vocationally and psychologically. There will not be enough properly educated workers to do the work that must be done to compete with nations whose adolescents have more positive attitudes toward education. Even worse, there will be many malcontents whose feelings of failure incapacitate them psychologically for doing the only kind of work they are trained to do.

A feeble but important beginning has been made by the "ivy league colleges" to make the scholar as prestigious as the athlete or the fraternity man. However, until high school students can be persuaded that a scholar is not a "square" who causes trouble for them by being a curve raiser, it will not be easy to transfer the halo from the head of the athlete or the "party girl" to the head of the scholar.

VOCATIONS

The American adolescent looks upon his future vocation as a stepping-stone to the better life he craves for himself and his future family. Thus, as in education, the adolescent's attitude toward his vocation is focused more on what it can do for him than on the personal satisfaction he will derive from it. This attitude determines his vocational preference as well as his dedication to his job.

The adolescent's level of vocational aspiration is often unrealistically high. When the time comes to look for a job, the individual often finds that his abilities are not as great as he thought, that his training is incomplete, and that the competition is overwhelming. Consequently, his vocational plans will have to be brought into line with the demands of the marketplace.

Concern about vocational choice

As the child approaches adolescence, his concern about his future vocation grows; he realizes that the time of going to work is just around the corner. The problem of vocational choice that once seemed so remote becomes immediate, personal, and very important.

As Abramovitz has written, "Religion apart, no aspect of human affairs has such pervasive and penetrating consequences as does the way a society makes its living—and how large a living it makes" (1). This is equally true of the individual. The adolescent knows that his whole future will be influenced by the decision he makes now. He further knows that this decision is likely to be for keeps.

In addition, the adolescent is pressured from all sides to make a decision. At home, his *parents* press him to make up his mind about what he "wants to be." At school, his *teachers* press him to decide, in order to know how to prepare him. And, finally, his *friends* are talking and thinking about their future and they want him to do the same.

For many reasons making a vocational choice is of great concern to both boys and girls. Since most girls will eventually marry, their concern is not so great as that of boys. But they are concerned about getting into a field in which they will meet elegible men and to which they may return after their children are old enough not to need constant care. Box 10-5 shows some of the concerns adolescents have about their vocational choices (32, 36, 58, 174, 235, 237).

Age of vocational choice

The age at which adolescents choose their vocations varies greatly. Nor is the choice made rapidly or even finally once it is decided upon.

BOX 10-5 ADOLESCENT CONCERNS ABOUT VOCATIONAL CHOICE

*Specialization and the need for prolonged training make changing vocations, if one is dissatisfied, difficult or impossible.

*Knowing that work will be one of the main activities of his adult life, the adolescent wants to be sure that the vocation he chooses will be to his liking and will fit into his other plans.

*The adolescent does not know if he has the ability or will be able to get the necessary training for one of the limited number of prestige jobs he aspires to.

*Even in times of prosperity, many adolescents are concerned about whether their mediocre academic records will allow them to get and hold a job.

*Because of the rapid change accompanying the spread of automation, the adolescent worries about whether his training will be so out of date in a few years that he will not be fitted for *any* job.

*Limited opportunities to explore a variety of fields and need to acquire specialized training for the jobs he *thinks* he would like to have make the adolescent wonder if it is possible to make a choice that will provide lasting satisfaction.

*As the adolescent becomes aware of the thousands of possible job opportunities in different fields, he is confused about which he might like and be best fitted to do.

As Holden (105) has said, the individual's vocational choice is a

. . . developmental process that spans many years, during which the ultimate decision is determined by a series of actions and occurrences, each one dependent at least in some measure on preceding ones. . . . There comes a time when the general direction followed cannot easily be reversed or changed.

By the time boys and girls reach the seventh or eighth grade, their vocational choices are manifested in a "vocational choice level." They know what level of work they want to go into even though they may not have decided what particular job they want (109, 219, 233).

The age at which vocational choices are made varies according to the kind of work involved. Work that requires specific training over a long period is likely to be decided upon earlier than work that requires little specific training (236).

Even though vocational choices may not be made before adolescence draws to a close, *attitudes* toward different vocations are usually established before adolescence begins. In childhood, the individual may have developed negative attitudes toward certain occupations; he definitely does *not* want to spend the rest of his life in them. At the same time, he often has positive attitudes toward other occupations; they appeal to him and he feels that he could be happy, or at least satisfied, if he selected any one of them as his life work (15, 85, 92).

Once established, these attitudes channel the person's interests into different vocational choice levels. A study of high school seniors, for example, found that interest in teaching was markedly influenced by attitudes formed earlier. Those who were interested in a teaching career liked children and people, wanted to help society, and felt that teaching offered them security and helped them to prepare for marriage. Those whose attitudes toward teaching were unfavorable claimed that children got on their nerves, that they disliked the work connected with teaching, especially the homework and discipline, and that the cost of preparing for a teaching career was too high for the rewards teaching brings (116).

Factors influencing vocational choice

Of the many factors that influence the vocational choices of adolescents, the ones discussed below are the most important.

Family The family's influence on vocational choice may be either positive or negative. *Positive* influence consists mainly of giving advice: direct suggestions about what vocation the adolescent should choose or indirect but sometimes emphatic counsel about certain jobs that the parents consider desirable.

Negative family influence may also be direct or indirect. Parents may tell their children to avoid certain vocations because of poor pay, low prestige, limited opportunities to get ahead, and other disadvantages. Or they may influence their children by incidental remarks. If parents grumble about their own work, for example, adolescents will perceive their parents' jobs unfavorably and develop a negative attitude toward them (83, 151, 168).

Certain variations in family influence on vocational choice are predictable. *Young* adolescents tend to follow parental advice more readily than older adolescents; family influence on vocational choice wanes after the age of 19 years. Of the different *family members,* the father usually exerts the strongest influence, though this varies according to how the adolescent feels about his father (165, 215). Parents exert greater influence over girls' choices than boys' (205). Finally, adolescents from the higher *socioeconomic* groups are, as a whole, subject to greater family influence than those from the lower groups (202, 249).

Sex Since boys and girls often have different attitudes toward vocations, sex differences influence vocational choice. To a boy, the vocation he selects will usually be a lifetime occupation. For that reason he wants to be sure that it will continue to be satisfying as he grows older and he is willing to put a great deal of time and effort into preparing for it (102, 242).

For the average girl, a job is merely a stop-gap between school and marriage. Therefore, she is unwilling to spend much time and effort preparing for a career. Nor is she in a hurry to decide what she wants to do. Furthermore, she is under little pressure to make a once-and-for-all decision (168, 173, 180).

Since more vocations are open to boys, they can afford to be more choosy about what line of work they want to enter. Also, in spite of laws against discrimination, girls know that any job they have is likely to be on a lower level, with less pay and less prestige, than that of boys of similar ability. This militates against the girls' motivation to aspire to jobs that are more closely related to their abilities and interests. Girls often settle for what they know they can get (129, 164).

Long before adolescence, boys and girls recognize that certain vocations are considered masculine, and others, feminine. Boys who wish to go into a "feminine" occupation, such as nursing or elementary school teaching, often discover that unfavorable social attitudes toward their choice mean a lowering of self-esteem and prestige (188).

School The influence of *teachers* in vocational selection is great among adolescents up to 19 years of age. Girls, at all ages, are more influenced by teachers than boys. While *classmates* have some influence, it is less than that of teachers or families in early adolescence. It increases somewhat in late adolescence.

The content of different *school subjects* becomes increasingly important in determining the adolescent's vocational interest in high school and college. *Grades* and academic success likewise influence vocational choice. Students who do well academically aspire to higher-level occupations than those whose intellectual capacity or motivation is limited.

The *extracurricular activities* of the school

also influence vocational aspirations. The adolescent who enjoys sports, for example, is often motivated to go into a line of work in which this interest can find expression. He may become an athletic director in a school or if he is an outstanding athlete, a professional ball player (8, 90, 226).

Degree of realism Lack of realism is shown in both *occupational choice* and *consideration of job opportunities*. Many adolescents of limited ability become interested in occupations in which they cannot possibly succeed. Many want to be in white-collar jobs, but only about 50 percent of the jobs available in the entire country fall in this category; the rest are blue-collar or overall jobs (235, 237).

While lack of realism is most often expressed by aspiring above one's capacities, it may also be expressed in "undershooting" —aspiring too low. Underachievers and adolescents who suffer from feelings of personal inadequacy are most likely to undershoot.

Normally, as adolescence progresses, lack of realism in vocational choice is offset by vocational counseling which acquaints the adolescent with the kinds of jobs available and the abilities needed for different jobs, by a more realistic assessment of abilities, and by opportunities to get some work experience (106, 219). By the end of adolescence, many young people are vocationally mature in the sense that they show increasing wisdom in their vocational preferences and decreasing fantasy (85).

Vocational information Too little vocational information limits the adolescent and often forces him to select an occupation not well suited to his interests and abilities. Too much information may confuse him and delay his vocational choice. Information that stresses the undesirable aspects of an occupation may discourage him from selecting it, even though he has strong preference for such work (134, 174).

Stereotypes Stereotypes of people in various occupations have a profound influence on the adolescent's attitudes toward these occupations. Such stereotypes are myriad: the absentminded professor, the crafty politician, the emotionally unstable artist, and so on (20, 234).

From science fiction and other sources, the adolescent has a composite image of the scientist which is anything but favorable. The scientist is always a man—a brain so engrossed in his work that he does not know what goes on in the world; he has few interests, neglects his family, and is lonely and dedicated (25, 196). The popular stereotype is shown in Figure 10-4.

The stereotype of the teacher is equally as unfavorable as that of the scientist. It is influenced by the mass media, especially books, comics, movies, and television. In literature, for example, the female teacher is usually unattractive, middle-aged, and dowdy. The male teacher is stooped, gaunt, and gray with weariness. In movies, the teacher is often a comic, but occasionally is portrayed as self-sacrificing and weak (81, 186). Inevitably, these images influence vocational selection whether they are valid or not.

Glamour and prestige Long before childhood is over, boys and girls understand the importance of *prestige* to social acceptance. They know which jobs have prestige and which do not, and they are aware of the symbols by which job prestige is judged.

In childhood, the prestige of jobs is judged mainly in terms of the kind of clothing worn by the worker. A job where the worker wears "dress-up clothes"—the white-collar job— is more prestigious than the blue-collar or overall job. Adolescents, by contrast, judge the prestige of jobs in terms of the authority and autonomy of the worker, his salary, and his title. Of these, title is perhaps the most important because it is manifest: *everyone* knows what the worker's title is, but only a few know what his salary is, how much authority he has over his subordinates, and how much independence the job gives him. That is why important-sounding titles have such a strong appeal for adolescents in making their vocational choices (201, 208).

Personality If the adolescent chooses a vocation that fits his personal needs, he will be happy in his work and make good vocational adjustments; if he selects a vocation unsuited to his personality, he will be unhappy in his job, dissatisfied with his achievements, and anxious to change to an occupation that will suit his needs better.

An adolescent who suffers from feelings of inadequacy is not likely to consider an occupation where he would constantly be thrown with other people or where he would be expected to assume responsibility for major policy decisions (13, 23, 179). In a study of chemists, for example, it was found that they preferred work which offered opportunities for solitary achievement and intellectual mastery to that which required close interpersonal relationships (197).

The young adolescent has a limited knowledge of the actual work involved in various vocations. Only after he has had some work experience is he able to determine whether he is in the right kind of work for his individual personality makeup. This is one of the many reasons why vocational choices made early in life are less stable than those made later.

Stability of vocational interests

By the sophomore year of high school, most adolescents begin to express fairly stable vocational interests (168, 207). This does not mean that interests do not change frequently, however. In Box 10-6 are given some of the most common reasons for shifts in interests (36, 58, 67, 85, 174, 207).

Shifts in vocational interests vary according to sex, personality, school influences, intelligence, and guidance. *Sex* differences in favor of the greater stability of girls' choices may be due to one of three causes: the earlier physical maturity of girls, which leads to earlier emotional and social maturity; the more restricted job opportunities for girls; and the less concern girls have about vocations because they tend to regard them as temporary (164, 239).

The *personality* of the adolescent also influences the stability of his vocational in-

Figure 10-4. Popular stereotype of the scientist.

terests. Self-sufficient, secure adolescents tend to have more persistent interests than those who feel insecure and inadequate. The more extroverted the adolescent, the more likely he is to be influenced by the peer group (180, 233).

The more *intelligent* and studious adolescents tend to make more satisfactory, that is, more realistic and appropriate, vocational choices in high school. Vocational interests that develop out of *school* influences survive longer than those derived from outside influences. Finally, adolescents who receive *vocational guidance* in school tend to develop more persistent interests than those who do not (134, 217).

Vocational satisfaction and dissatisfaction

Job dissatisfaction may be due to a number of causes. *First,* the adolescent may have had to take any job he could get, regardless of his interests and preferences.

Second, the adolescent may find the transition from the overprotective atmosphere of the home and school to the impersonal, de-

BOX 10-6 CAUSES OF CHANGE IN VOCATIONAL INTERESTS

Economic Necessity
Parents may be unable to pay for the training needed for the career the adolescent had hoped to have, or he may have to drop out of school to help meet a family financial crisis.

Change in Values
With mental maturity and increased experience, an adolescent develops new values and interests. What seemed like an exciting, glamorous, or interesting career when he was younger may lose its appeal as he grows older.

Vocational Guidance
Guidance gives the adolescent an idea of what different jobs entail and suggests lines of work about which he has little information but which might satisfy his needs and suit his abilities.

Work Experience
Work experience can be an eye-opener to an adolescent whose understanding of different jobs and of working is limited to what he has heard or read or to the cultural stereotypes.

Increased Realism
With vocational guidance and work experience, the adolescent becomes more realistic about job possibilities and his ability for various occupations.

manding atmosphere of the work world hard to adjust to.

Third, the person who has eagerly looked forward to going to work may have a rude awakening when he finds a large discrepancy between what he expected and what actually exists.

Fourth, as the adolescent is forced, through his work experiences, to become more realistic, his dissatisfaction is likely to increase, especially if he has aspired to a job that is beyond his abilities (58, 94, 219).

Expressions of satisfaction and dissatisfaction

The adolescent who likes his job is willing to put more effort into it than is actually required. He is loyal to his employer, and while he may grumble about hours, pay, and countless other things, he generally is only following the pattern set by his coworkers.

Unfortunately, few adolescents have such favorable attitudes toward their work, and ordinarily, attitudes tend to become worse and worse. As shown in Box 10-7, adolescents express their negative attitudes in several common ways (26, 58, 79, 94, 121, 219).

The most dissatisfied adolescents are usually those who are school or college *dropouts.* Furthermore, employers are often more dissatisfied with the work done by the dropout than with that done by other adolescent workers. The very causes that led to dropping out of school—boredom, lack of interest and motivation, unwillingness to work up to capacity —lead to employer dissatisfaction. Furthermore, the adolescent who expects work to be more to his liking than school often finds that it is not (235, 237). By contrast, the more *education* the adolescent has, the more likely he is to be satisfied with his vocational choices. Higher education not only opens up more vocational opportunities and more interesting and prestigious jobs but also great opportunities for rapid advancement (71, 139). Figure 10-5 shows the percentages of adolescents who enter the labor force at various educational levels.

Damaging effects of vocational dissatisfaction

Dissatisfaction is almost universal among adolescents who work part or full time. From friends or parents they acquire an *antiwork attitude* which predisposes them to enter any line of work with the feeling that working is one of the necessary evils of growing up.

Since dissatisfaction lowers motivation to perform well, the adolescent whose attitude toward work is unfavorable will find himself outdistanced in a highly competitive work world by workers who have no greater ability than he. Also, as unfavorable attitudes are sooner or later expressed in *gripes,* the dissatisfied worker will be spotted by his superiors as a troublemaker.

The most damaging aspect of dissatisfaction is that it is so universal that even workers of superior ability often assume a negative attitude, feeling that it is "the thing to do." The result is that those who should supply vocational leadership relinquish this role to persons of lesser ability whose drive for achievement is strong enough to compensate for any dissatisfaction they may have.

Unfavorable attitudes toward work can best be prevented by early vocational guidance, so early in his school career that the child has no opportunity to acquire unrealistic aspirations or negative feelings about any field that he is likely to enter.

SOCIAL MOBILITY

Social mobility enables the individual to improve his status, to climb up the ladder of success. By changing his place of residence, moving from rural to urban areas, from urban to suburban, and from poorer to better neighborhoods, he hopes to become identified with the group he aspires to claim as his friends. No adolescent can change his residence at will; where he lives will depend on where his parents live. However, as most parents are anxious to have their children better themselves, they try to provide them with opportunities to do so.

In addition, parents try to provide their children with the clothes, cars, and other status symbols that will identify them with the preferred social groups. They encourage them to become active in high prestige extracurricular affairs; they join as many of the "right" community organizations as they can gain admission to; and they try to teach their children the approved mores of the group they aspire to be identified with, thus facilitating their acceptance by the group members (36, 163).

Families vary in their desires to alter their social status. In families where both parents are of the same social class, parental interest in having children move up the social ladder is not so great as in families of *divergent* social classes. When the mother comes from a higher social class than the father, ambition to have the children improve their status is usually comparatively strong (28, 67, 124).

> **BOX 10-7 WAYS OF SHOWING JOB DISSATISFACTION**
>
> *Walking off the job, often without giving the customary notice
>
> *Becoming more choosy about accepting a new job, especially one resembling the job held last
>
> *Grumbling, criticizing, and finding fault with everything connected with the job
>
> *Attempting to change working conditions to make them more to one's own liking
>
> *Working below capacity and thus becoming a vocational underachiever
>
> *Compensating for work dissatisfaction by seeking satisfaction in a job-unrelated activity, such as sports
>
> *Glamorizing some aspect of the work, such as its value to others, to compensate for aspects that fail to bring satisfaction

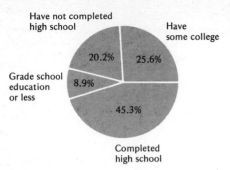

Figure 10-5. Of the 26 million youth entering the labor force between 1960 and 1970, the majority had education below the college level. (Adapted from data from U.S. Dept. of Labor, 1971.)

Desire for social mobility also varies according to the family's *philosophy of life*. When families feel that present pleasures should be sacrificed for greater future rewards, they instill this principle in their children from earliest childhood. As a result, families that are future-oriented are more interested in social mobility than present-oriented families (31, 250).

In addition, the *size of the family* affects its interest in social mobility. In small families, parents are more anxious to have their children rise above them, owing in large part to the fact that parents with few children can provide the assistance needed for upward mobility better than parents of large families. Within a family, *ordinal position* is also important. In middle-class families, first- and second-born children, far more often than their later-born siblings, are given parental assistance in their upward climb. Often, the older children in lower-class families will help the younger ones (4, 5, 210).

Meaning of social mobility

To the layman, "social mobility" means moving upward on the social ladder. To the psychologist and sociologist, it means "changing one's social status." Social and geographic mobility do not necessarily go hand in hand, though geographic mobility facilitates social mobility by burying the past for the individual

and making it possible for him to start over with a clean slate (59, 116).

Social mobility may be either horizontal or vertical. Box 10-8 defines the two terms, gives the names commonly applied to different kinds of mobile people, and explains how much time is usually needed to change positions on the social ladder (59, 63, 67, 110, 250).

Upward social mobility is made possible by such things as vocational success, marriage to a higher-status person, inheritance of wealth, fortunate investment of money earned or inherited, transfer of membership to a higher-status church, purchase of a home in a better district and the use of money to obtain status symbols, and association with people of higher status in community organizations. As Bieri et al. have pointed out, education "provides a primary means by which a person becomes socially mobile in our society" (31).

Downward social mobility is also caused by many factors; the most important are insufficient education to hold a position equivalent to that of one's father; for a woman, marriage to a man whose occupational status is lower than that of her father; incompetence in a chosen occupation; transfer of membership to a lower-status church; immigration from a foreign culture, with loss of status due to acceptance of employment at a lower occupational level; prolonged unemployment; loss of inherited wealth. Divorce or separation may lead to downward mobility by dividing the family income so that the parent who keeps the children will have less to live on than when the family lived together as a unit (31, 163).

Essentials in social mobility

Social mobility does not guarantee social *acceptance*. Because adolescent social groups are so tightly knit, gaining acceptance is more difficult than in a children's gang. If the adolescent tries too hard, he will be regarded as pushy. If he is too passive, he is likely to be overlooked and neglected. Using the *right* amount of aggressiveness may gain him acceptance, but the right amount is difficult to gauge. It varies from group to group and even within a group, depending on the need for new members at a particular time. One thing is certain, however: Gaining acceptance in a new group is a slow process. It often requires more tact and social skill than the average adolescent can be expected to have.

Certain essentials to gaining acceptance are described below.

Desire of the group for a new member Adolescent group members are generally satisfied with one another's company and are not interested in having a stranger join them. Sometimes, however, a closely knit group feels the need for "new blood"—someone who can contribute something new and interesting or prestigious to the group. Under such conditions, a newcomer has a chance of gaining acceptance if he can create the impression that he can fill this need.

Favorable impressions The first and, to a lesser extent, the subsequent impressions the adolescent makes on the members of a group will have a marked influence on how seriously they consider him as a potential member.

Demonstration of valued qualities To gain acceptance in an already-established group, the adolescent must demonstrate to the members his possession of some quality or ability they value highly. Marked ability in a prestigious activity, on the other hand, may be more of a liability than an asset. An outstanding athlete, for example, may be regarded as a threat to the status of the leader of the group. To save his status, the leader may influence other members to reject the newcomer.

Acceptance of similar interests and values The socially mobile adolescent must learn and accept the interests and values of the members of the group with which he wants to be identified if he is to win acceptance. He must dress like the group members and show interest in the recreations they enjoy.

Unless the adolescent has belonged to similar groups or has an opportunity to exchange views with group members, he will have no way of knowing what they value and what their interests are except by watching them or listening to what they say when they are talking among themselves.

Willingness to terminate old associations If the adolescent wishes to gain acceptance in a new group, he must terminate old friendships and his loyalty to members of his old group. He must even try to keep his parents and other relatives in the background if he feels that their appearance and behavior patterns will not be approved by the new group. As Packard (163) has explained:

If we aspire to rise in the world but fail to take on the coloration of the group we aspire to—by failing to discard our old status symbols, friends, club memberships, values, behavior patterns, and acquiring new ones esteemed by the higher group—our chances of success are diminished. Sociologists have found that our home addresses, our friends,

---

BOX 10-8   KINDS OF SOCIAL MOBILITY

Horizontal
The individual moves to a new group similar to the one to which he originally belonged. How long it will take him to be accepted in the group will depend on how closely knit the group is, what he has to offer in the way of sports or social skills, and what is important to the new group.

Vertical
The individual moves from one social stratum to another. One who moves upward is a "climber"; one who moves down on the social ladder is a "decliner" or a "skidder," depending on whether his descent is slow or rapid. It may take years to achieve a secure status in a higher social group. Downward mobility can occur overnight.

Box 10-9 PROBLEMS ARISING
FROM SOCIAL MOBILITY

*Gaps in school or college work due to changes in educational programs and to emotional tension caused by having to adjust to a new environment

*Family friction due to parental pressure to do good academic work and to become identified with the "right" crowd

*Ignorance of the interests and values of the new peer group, which makes identification with its members difficult and leads to anxieties about doing and saying the right thing

*Doubts about how peers in the new social group will react, causing anxiety, overconformity, and a hypercritical attitude toward family members who, the adolescent fears, might "disgrace" him

*A period of being cut off from old peer friendships and from family gatherings, resulting in loneliness and envy of others

our clubs, our values, and even our church affiliations can prove to be "barriers" if we fail to change them with every attempted move up the ladder.

Willingness to wait for acceptance If the adolescent has all the status symbols other adolescents in his class have and if he has learned the approved patterns of behavior for the group, he will assume that lack of acceptance is due to some personal inadequacy. If he becomes resentful or feels inferior, he cannot help revealing his attitudes in his behavior and even in his facial expressions. He will then be less attractive to the group and have even less chance of gaining acceptance.

Satisfactions and dissatisfactions of mobility

An analysis of the satisfactions and dissatisfactions reported in various studies of social

mobility will show how they affect the adolescent's personal and social adjustments.

Satisfactions If the adolescent can achieve social acceptance in the group he wants to be identified with, he will be satisfied; he will feel that he has bettered himself. His satisfaction may, however, be short-lived. Unless his status in the new group is secure, he will experience the dissatisfactions which every fringer experiences. He will live in constant dread of saying or doing something that will weaken the acceptance he has gained.

The downwardly mobile adolescent may, at first, welcome the opportunity to get away from his old group. He may have come to feel like an outsider in it because he was no longer able to afford what group members did. But his insecurity in the new group will be colored by shame and resentment of the conditions which forced him into a lower status.

Satisfactions will be greater if the adolescent is prepared for the problems social mobility creates and if he receives guidance in meeting them. If he knows that *all* socially mobile people meet much the same problems that he is facing, for example, he will not develop feelings of personal inadequacy when he fails to gain immediate acceptance in a new group.

Dissatisfactions Social mobility means uprooting the individual and breaking his ties with the past. Since social relationships are so important to an adolescent, breaking old social ties can be a traumatic experience. The trauma may be mild or intense, depending on the kind of mobility involved. In horizontal mobility, the adolescent can maintain his ties with former friends by visits, telephone calls, or letter writing. In upward mobility, however, he will have to break away from those who could obstruct his climb up the ladder of social success. The downwardly mobile adolescent will be too embarrassed in his new status to try to keep his old friendships alive. For him, the uprooting will be especially traumatic because it will be colored by shame and humiliation.

For two groups of adolescents social mobility is especially difficult. Adolescents from *minority groups* have a marginal status in any situation. Moving to a new group means another struggle to win acceptance and another situation in which they will experience prolonged rejection. Social mobility is more difficult for *girls* than for boys because girls' groups are more tightly knit. Furthermore, lack of social acceptance is apt to be more ego-deflating for girls than for boys (40, 128, 257).

Social mobility creates problems for all adolescents, and is a frequent source of dissatisfaction. Box 10-9 lists the five most common and serious problems (66, 124, 183, 210, 220, 250).

Even if the adolescent is able to gain some acceptance, it does not guarantee satisfaction. His position in the new group is precarious, and he feels too unlike his new associates to be at home with them. He hesitates to confide his problems to them, fearing that he will create an unfavorable impression and jeopardize what acceptance he has achieved. He may feel uncomfortable doing things his old group disapproved of, even though he has the permission or even the urging of his parents to do whatever members of the new group do.

Unquestionably, the most dissatisfied adolescent is the downwardly mobile one. While gaining acceptance may be easier for him than for the upwardly mobile, he does not want acceptance by those whom he regards as his inferiors. If his downward slide has come about through family circumstances over which he has no control, he will develop feelings of martyrdom which will distort his outlook on life and may kill any earlier motivation he had to rise above his present status.

In conclusion, then, it is apparent that many socially mobile adolescents do not immediately find the pot of gold at the end of the rainbow. While many will gain some acceptance in time, they may have a long wait. Even when they achieve acceptance, they may not find it as rewarding as they had anticipated.

HIGHLIGHTS OF CHAPTER 10

1. The American adolescent knows that the climb up the socioeconomic ladder is made possible by education, vocational success, and upward social mobility.

2. The important ends of education for the American adolescent are social, vocational, and economic.

3. For the adolescent, the areas of major interest in education include academic subjects, grades, academic rewards, autonomy, and extracurricular activities.

4. Adolescent attitudes toward education are influenced by such factors as cultural and social class values, parental attitudes, ordinal position in the family, peer group attitudes, sex-role appropriateness, vocational plans, social and academic success, attitudes toward teachers and teaching techniques, and antiwork attitudes.

5. Dissatisfaction with education is expressed in criticism and attempts at reform, misbehavior, under- and overachievement, and dropping out, all of which may have long-term effects on the adolescent's personal and social adjustments.

6. Since adolescents regard their future vocation as an important stepping-stone to success in adult life, they are greatly concerned about selecting a vocation that will help them to fulfill this goal.

7. Many factors influence vocational choice; the most important are the family, the adolescent's sex, his school, degree of realism, vocational information, vocational stereotypes, glamour and prestige of the vocation, and his personality.

8. Vocational interests and choices change often in adolescence, owing to economic necessity, changes in values, vocational guidance, work experience, and increased realism.

9. Vocational dissatisfaction is more common than satisfaction because the adolescent may have to take any job he can get, he may not be prepared for what is expected of him in the work world, and he becomes more realistic about what working means after he has some work experience.

10. Social mobility, which means changing one's social status, may be horizontal (moving to a new, but similar, group) or vertical (moving up or down the social ladder).

11. Gaining acceptance in a new social group

presents many problems for the socially mobile adolescent: the group's desire to have a new member, the need to create a favorable impression on the group, to demonstrate qualities valued by its members and accept its interests and values, and a willingness to terminate old associations and wait for acceptance by members of the new group.

12. The satisfactions the socially mobile adolescent experiences are usually outweighed by the problems social mobility gives rise to: gaps in academic work, friction with family members, ignorance of the interests and values of the members of the new group, uncertainty about how the members of the new group feel about him, and a period of friendlessness between the breaking of old friendships and the establishment of new ones.

Chapter 11

Transition in Religious Beliefs and Observances

Photograph by Farrell/Greene
Omikron

A decline in religious instruction and observances in the home, lack of parental participation in church activities, and absence of religious instruction in the school are the most frequently heard explanations for the minor role religion plays in the lives of modern adolescents. Many people attribute the lack of religious interest to higher education, especially the study of science. Furthermore, it is sometimes contended that concern over pollution, war, financial instability, and discrimination has taken the place of traditional religion.

Much of the instability and irresponsibility of modern youth is said to be the direct result of lack of religion in their lives. The statement is often backed up by the presentation of statistics on the rise in juvenile delinquency; the increase in misdemeanors in the home and school; the increase in drinking, use of narcotics, premarital sexual behavior, illegitimacy, divorce, and venereal disease; and the lack of respect for members of the older generation. These subjects are discussed in other chapters, especially Chapter 12.

ARE ADOLESCENTS IRRELIGIOUS?

It is necessary to know what "religion" means before one can attempt to answer the question, Are adolescents irreligious? Religion consists of two elements: a *faith* which is based on the individual's beliefs and *practices* or religious observances in common with others of the same faith and centered around a place of worship—in the home, school, or community (4, 43, 71). Most people judge an adolescent as religious or irreligious by his practices rather than by his faith.

Equally important, it is essential to know that almost all scientific studies of adolescent religious observances and beliefs have focused on high school and college students. While the high school population is reasonably, though not wholly, representative of all adolescents under 17 years of age, the college population is by no means representative of all older adolescents. Consequently, in studies of the religious attitudes and observances of older adolescents, the results reflect the opinion of only a small percentage of that age group. One cannot therefore, conclude that *all* or even most adolescents would react in a similar manner.

Among adolescents, as was stressed in Chapter 6, it is the thing to do to be antiestablishment. This holds true for the religious "establishment" as well as for other establishments.

With these facts in mind, one notes, with interest, that studies of adolescent religious interests have *not* shown that adolescents are especially irreligious. If they do not attend church or pray regularly, this does not mean that they are irreligious. Nor does questioning certain church doctrines or discarding some of their childhood beliefs mean that they are irreligious. Lack of attendance at chapel services in college, for example, often comes from the kind of service that is held rather than from lack of interest in religion itself (79, 97, 124).

Studies of young adolescents show that their interest in religion is more likely to be revealed by their attitudes than by their participation in religious observances, though most adolescents go to church at least as frequently as their parents (14, 33, 95). They show concern with religion by talking about it with their peers (see Fig. 11-1) and by claiming that they plan to teach their own children about religion and encourage them to believe in God. Interest in religion tends to be greater among girls than boys during high school (48, 63).

Equally favorable attitudes toward religion have been found among older adolescents—those in college as well as those who went to work after high school or are devoting their time to homemaking and parenthood. Older adolescents tend to be moderate in their religion rather than strong believers or nonbelievers (37, 124).

Most older adolescents are trying to find a religion that will meet their needs better than the religion of their childhood. Many change their religious beliefs during late adolescence. No longer do they believe in the fairy-tale aspects of religion that had such strong appeal when they were young. However, *change does not mean discarding religious beliefs.*

It means that the adolescent is trying to find a religion more in keeping with his developing outlook on life (91, 103). In fact, it would be surprising and disturbing if the adolescent did not revise his childhood religious beliefs (as well as his other childish ideas and aspirations) as he becomes more mature.

There is much evidence that adolescents are not only interested in religion but that religion meets a strong need in their lives. They show their interest in religion by discussing it in bull sessions, by taking courses in comparative religion or the philosophy of religion, and by exploring different religions to see if they meet their needs better than the family religion (117, 120). It has been reported, for example, that in recent years a boom in religious studies has occurred at both the graduate and undergraduate levels on college and university campuses (121). There is also a growing interest in religions that deviate from the traditional patterns, such as the "Jesus Movement" (123).

The logical conclusion from the arguments presented above is not that adolescents are irreligious but that some are disenchanted with and alienated from our traditional religious beliefs and observances. Many would probably agree with Rokeach's portrait of the religious-minded churchgoer: one who has a self-centered preoccupation with saving his own soul and an alienated, other-worldly orientation coupled with indifference toward —a tacit endorsement of—a social system that would perpetuate social inequality and injustice (106).

Religious disenchantment among high school dropouts and among many other adolescents who have not continued their education beyond high school is not well documented. As was pointed out earlier, studies of religious interests have through necessity been limited to adolescents who are readily available for study in high school or college.

NEED FOR RELIGION

The adolescent needs *religion*—beliefs that he can accept and observances that are meaningful and helpful to him. He does not neces-

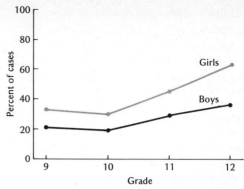

Figure 11-1 Talking about religion increases as adolescence progresses, especially among girls. (Adapted from M. C. Jones: A comparison of the attitudes and interests of ninth-grade students over two generations. *J. educ. Psychol.*, 1960, **51**, 175–186. Used by permission.)

sarily need *theology*—a system of beliefs and observances given to him by some religious establishment.

Adolescence is a period of strain and insecurity, and almost every adolescent needs a religion that can give him faith in life and a feeling of security. *Any* religion that is continuous with life, that is consistent with the workaday world, can give the adolescent a faith to live by and can help him to learn to withstand the conflicts and doubts so characteristic of adolescence. An adolescent needs a religion that is personal and meaningful to him as an individual. As Strang (116) has pointed out:

An adolescent who believes in God as a "very present help" not only in time of trouble but also as a daily source of guidance for his best development, has a certain resource of strength and courage. His concept of himself extends into infinity.

Many adolescents are intolerant of what they regard as "old-fashioned" dogma—in religion as well as in other areas of life. When confronted with dogmatic authority, they try to assert their independence by opposing it. A religion that condemns the pleasures of youth as immoral has little appeal for the adolescent of today.

What the adolescent needs in religion

Few religious beliefs acquired in childhood fulfill adolescent needs. The adolescent wants a religion that can help him, not one that will mystify him or add excitement to his life. Instead of a general religiosity, he now needs specific religious beliefs and attitudes. While he may not be able to define his religious beliefs or state exactly what his religious needs are, that does not mean that he has no need for religion or that he is unaware of his need. Cole and Hall (31) have emphasized three emotional values of religion which help to meet the needs of adolescents:

There is first the catharsis of guilt feelings through prayer, the confessional, or talks with ministers. The resulting feeling of being cleansed of sin, of being given another chance, and of reduced tension is of great value in adjustment. A second value is the increase of security, sometimes relatively superficial and sometimes profound, that may result from religious belief. A trust in God prevents the panic of despair, a belief in personal immortality with its promise of an everlasting perpetuation of the ego prevents the fear of death, the membership in a group gives a sense of belonging, and the chance to work with and help others leads to helpful identifications and attitudes. These values are not all of a religious nature, but they are of assistance in the search for happiness and adjustment. Religion may, therefore, be an important contributing factor to mental health. Finally, religion can become the basis for a sound philosophy of life, even though it does not always do so.

By late adolescence, most individuals feel they have made a satisfactory orientation to religion. When religious adjustment is satisfactory, it gives one a feeling of security and belonging that contributes to his adjustments. It helps him to establish a set of values and goals that are essential to give meaning to his life. Without this, he will have little to live or work for. As Hanawalt (53) has pointed out:

Religious belief is only one of the threads running through the fabric of security feeling and self-esteem. The pattern of the fabric depends upon the nature of the other threads and their interrelationships.

Variations in need for religion No one religion will necessarily meet the needs of all adolescents or even of one adolescent. As Stone and Church (115) have written:

Different religions may appeal to the adolescent in different ways. He may be enthralled by the colorful pageantry of one, by the austere stringency of another, by the militantness of another, or by the castigations of another. In any event, his religion entails a projection of himself beyond mundane reality and into the absolute. His concern with religion is, of course, part and parcel of his concern with the nature of the world into which he is moving; and the nature and existence of God, and the need for and the possibility of faith, are among the topics endlessly debated in adolescent bull sessions.

In Box 11-1 are given some of the factors responsible for variations in the need for religion (14, 25, 41, 50, 72, 83).

Ways of meeting religious needs

While individual needs for religion and religious expression vary, five developmental processes are essential to make any religion fit adolescent needs. These processes, closely correlated with the developmental status of the adolescent, occur in a predictable pattern and at predictable ages. They include religious awakening, doubt or indecision, changes in religious participation, and increased tolerance toward the religious beliefs and practices of others. How these contribute to meeting the adolescent's religious needs will be discussed in the following sections.

RELIGIOUS AWAKENING

"Religious awakening" means an increased interest in religion which leads to a reconstruction of religious beliefs and attitudes. Box 11-2 shows two general kinds of religious awakening, together with their characteristics (10, 42, 43, 113, 114).

Among adolescents of higher intellectual abilities, gradual awakening is far more common than catastrophic awakening. In the lower socioeconomic groups, more emphasis is placed on fervor in religious observances; in

BOX 11-1   CAUSES OF VARIATIONS IN NEED FOR RELIGION

*Home Religious Atmosphere
Adolescents brought up in homes where religion was stressed in childhood feel a greater need for religion than those whose homes ignored religious observances. An authoritarian approach to religion in the home militates against a need to "search" for religion during adolescence.

*Religious Affiliation
Adolescents who have a religious affiliation show greater interest in and need for religion than those who lack an affiliation.

*Peer Attitudes
Adolescents who are identified with a peer group that is active in church affairs and interested in religion will feel a greater need for religion than those whose peers scorn or ignore religion.

*Sex
Girls are usually encouraged to be more active in church affairs than boys, and hence show a greater interest in religion.

*Environment
Religion and church affairs play a more important role in the adolescent's life in rural environments than in urban environments. Church affiliation is a status symbol in the suburbs, and so suburban adolescents are encouraged to take part in church affairs.

*Socioeconomic Status
Adolescents from the lower and middle socioeconomic groups are more dependent on religion than those from the upper socioeconomic groups.

*Religious Denomination
Adolescents whose families belong to the Catholic faith or to small evangelical sects tend, from childhood, to be more interested in religion than those from Protestant or Jewish families.

*Personality
Adolescents with authoritarian personality patterns need religion to give them a feeling of security more than do adolescents with less rigid personality patterns.

the higher socioeconomic groups, more emphasis is placed on formalized religion. As a result, gradual religious awakening is more common in the higher socioeconomic groups, and catastrophic, in the lower. In rural areas, where religious beliefs are less challenged than in urban areas, the catastrophic awakening is very common. The cultural experiences the adolescent has and the practices of the religious denomination with which his family is identified have a marked influence on the kind of religious awakening he will experience. If, for example, the family religion is evangelistic, with a strong appeal to the emotions, the adolescent's religious awakening is likely to be catastrophic (49, 72).

The *temperament* of the adolescent is also
an important factor in determining the course
of his religious awakening. A melancholy or
impetuous temperament predisposes the individual to an unsteady and highly emotion-
alized religious attitude. By contrast, a calm,
even temperament predisposes the individual
to a smooth and peaceful religious awakening. If he is plagued by feelings of guilt, however, he may, to allay these feelings, develop
a strong religious fervor which will excite him
to a sudden catastrophic conversion (35, 85).

Age of religious awakening It is difficult to
tell just when religious awakening begins
unless it takes a catastrophic course. The child
whose mental development has reached a
level of 12 years or more normally shows a
new interest in religion. He begins to expect
logically coherent answers to his questions
about religion, which the less mature child
does not expect (10, 43).

Factors influencing religious awakening

Religious awakening was at one time considered a function of pubescence, a development which grew out of the sexual impulse.
Both, it is true, come at approximately the

same time. But there is no evidence that the
relationship is one of cause and effect.

Traditionally, the individual was converted
to the religion of his parents at about the time
of puberty. His conversion was an important
landmark in his growing up, and much emphasis was placed on a confession of sin and
guilt, on the expression of a desire to lead a
new life, and on the acceptance of an adult
status in the family church. All this contributed
to a heightened interest in religion. Today,
such emotionally toned conversions are relatively infrequent in most religious faiths
(17, 72).

Studies of awakened interest in religion at
adolescence reveal that it is due to a number
of causes. Increased *intelligence* with the
accompanying increased ability to reason
motivates the young adolescent to ponder over
the religious beliefs he accepted unquestioningly during childhood. With increased
knowledge, especially that derived from
scientific studies in school, the adolescent
views his childish beliefs in a new light.
Reasoning has been found to be the most important single cause for changing religious
attitudes and revising childish religious beliefs.
Of less importance is *imitation.* When friends
show a new interest in religion and reevaluate
their faiths, many an adolescent follows the
the crowd in this as in other matters.

Focusing attention on religion, in preparation for joining the church or synagogue as a
full-fledged member with the rights and privileges of the adult members, is certain to
increase the adolescent's thoughts about
religion. As he learns the doctrines and dogmas of his family's faith, and as the ceremonials of the church service are explained to
him, he begins to see the religion of his childhood in a new light and with new meaning.
If joining the family church or synagogue is
an important occasion in his family, and if it
gives him status with his friends who are likewise taking this first step into adult status, the
adolescent may, as Crow and Crow have
pointed out, "experience considerable emotional satisfaction during the period of preparation and the ceremony itself; he may ac-

cept with great seriousness his 'new' church status'' (36). The emotional satisfaction from this experience will lead to an increased interest in religion.

As a child, the individual was accustomed to go to his parents for advice, comfort, and aid. But with the onset of adolescence, boys and girls frequently become alienated from their parents. They then turn to friends and teachers, but they frequently find this an unsatisfactory substitute. As a result they may turn to religion when they find themselves in need of *aid in meeting their personal problems.* Interest in religion is frequently aroused by *experiences of the beautiful,* such as nature and its phenomena, ecclesiastical forms and ceremonies, art, music, and poetry. *Blows of fate,* such as severe illness or death of a loved one, may likewise give rise to a heightened interest in religion. But dramatic incidents and traumatic experiences are less frequently the causes of religious awakening than is reasoning (42, 63, 114).

Effects of religious awakening

Because of the emotional satisfaction the adolescent derives from his new status as a member of the church, he is at first very enthusiastic about religious activities. Not only does he accept his new status with great seriousness, but he is eager to participate in religious conferences with other adolescents. This gives him an opportunity to discuss religious matters with his age-mates and to get their points of view. Many boys and girls, in the early years of adolescence, decide to dedicate their lives to service for their church. They may try to convert their age-mates to their faiths and persuade them to join their churches.

Like most enthusiasms of youth, religious enthusiasm soon begins to wane. As the adolescent analyzes the beliefs he accepted when he joined his church and compares them with the beliefs of his friends, he begins to wonder if he can continue to believe what his church stands for. He even wonders if he would not find some other religion more to his liking. As

doubt and indecision develop, enthusiasm wanes.

There are, however, marked variations in the effect religious awakening has on religious attitudes, interests, and observances. Among adolescents who already have well-established beliefs and pious habits, awakening is merely a more conscious awareness of what he already accepts. On the other hand, a reevaluation of childish beliefs may lead to agnosticism or atheism. Under most circumstances, it will lead to doubts of minor or major severity.

RELIGIOUS DOUBT

Religious doubt is the second common developmental process in the transition from the religion of childhood to that of adulthood. "Doubt" means to waver in opinion, to hesitate in belief, or to be undecided. It may be *active* or *passive.* Active doubt is characteristic of a person who is consciously seeking an answer to a troublesome question. Passive doubt involves little or no effort by the doubter to settle the question one way or the other. It is sometimes referred to as "irrational doubt" because it is accompanied by an attitude of indifference. Active doubt is more heavily weighted with feelings of guilt and fear than is passive doubt. The adolescent who seeks to solve a problem about a religious belief may feel guilty because he is questioning his parents' beliefs; he may even fear the consequences to him either now or in later life if his solution leads him to reject a childhood belief.

The majority of the religious doubts of adolescents fall into three categories: doubts concerned with the Bible; doubts about religious doctrines in general; and doubts concerning doctrines peculiar to a given denomination. Examples of *doubts relating to the Bible* concern the origin of man, the parting of the water, Noah and the ark, and Daniel in the lion's den. The *general religious doctrines* most often doubted may be expressed thus: "The coming of Jesus and the resurrection sound like a fairy tale" and "I don't believe you go to Heaven or Hell when you die. That's the end, there isn't any more." An example of doubting related to *doctrines peculiar to a given denomination* is the question about why it is wrong to dance, go to the movies, play cards, or engage in other worldly pleasures (31, 116)

Box 11-3 lists the most common causes of adolescent doubts about religious beliefs acquired during childhood (41, 49, 54, 55, 74, 93, 101, 117, 127).

Regardless of what gives rise to doubts and in what areas the doubts occur, adolescents vary in the extent, the frequency, and the areas of their doubts. The more *intelligent* the ado-

lescent, the earlier the doubting will begin and the more severe it is likely to be. At all ages, *girls* doubt less than boys and their doubts are less intense. Girls may be more religious than boys or they may simply be more docile in accepting adults' teachings (103).

One of the most important factors influencing variations in doubting is *personality*. Adolescents who are conservative are less likely to doubt (but more likely to be guilt-ridden if they do) than those who are liberal (29, 97).

While doubting begins in childhood, it normally reaches its peak in adolescence. It is

---

BOX 11-3   COMMON CAUSES OF RELIGIOUS DOUBTS

Early Religious Training
Doubting usually starts with the breakdown of the Santa Claus myth, which helps to destroy faith in other early beliefs as knowledge increases

Conflicting Beliefs within the Family
In mixed marriages, the adolescent is confronted with two sets of beliefs and observances. He does not know which to accept or which is correct

Independent Thinking
Adolescents from authoritarian homes are discouraged from thinking independently while those from democratic homes are usually encouraged to do so. By high school age, most begin to take a critical attitude toward what they learn.

Relevance of Religion
If the adolescent cannot see how the religion of his family or church can be applied to the practical problems of life, he questions its teachings and develops a negative attitude toward the value of religion.

Higher Education
With higher education, the adolescent not only learns to question his teaching but also finds contradictions between his childhood faith and the knowledge he acquires from his courses, especially science.

Friends with Different Religious Beliefs
When the adolescent discovers that the beliefs of his friends are different from his own, he wonders which are correct. His doubts are intensified if his religion condemns behavior, such as dancing or card playing; which is permitted in other religions.

Dogmatic Teachings of the Church
Dogmatic teachings give rise to doubt about their relevance to everyday life. Doubt is intensified if the behavior of religious or church leaders fails to conform to the teachings.

usually resolved, in one way or another, by the age of 20. High school seniors, it has been found, are less willing to accept their religion unquestioningly than are freshmen, and college students, less than high school students (31, 55).

Effects of doubting

Doubting in any area leaves its mark on later attitudes and beliefs. This is especially true when emotions are involved. The effects of doubting may be temporary or permanent, mild or severe, depending on how profound the doubting is and on how it is met by parents, teachers, or other adults. Of the many effects of doubting, the following are the most common and the most damaging.

Confusion and uncertainty When religious beliefs established in childhood are challenged by newly acquired knowledge or by conflicts with beliefs of other religious faiths, the adolescent is in a state of uncertainty; he does not know what to believe. As a result, he no longer feels certain about anything related to religion. He then develops a generalized skeptical attitude toward *all* his childhood beliefs and practices.

Acceptance of a creed Doubt makes the adolescent hesitant about accepting a definite creed. If, at the time he joined the church, he was expected to subscribe to certain statements of belief accepted by his church, feelings of guilt will rise if he comes to feel that he can no longer accept them.

Revision of religious beliefs For most adolescents, the period of doubt leads to new or revised religious beliefs which better suit their more mature intellectual status. Which religious beliefs are most subject to revision and how they are revised will be discussed in the next section.

Decrease in religious observances Even though the adolescent accepts the religious faith of his family, he usually shows little interest in religious observances, either in the home or at church. Until doubting leads to a clearer understanding of religion, the adolescent is confused about what to believe; this confusion is intensified by church attendance. As Remmers and Radler (105) have reported, a junior high school girl said:

The reason most kids don't attend church as they used to is because they don't know what to believe. They go to one church and they tell you what is right or wrong and then go to another and hear something entirely different.

Shift to another faith The adolescent whose doubt leads him to be openly critical and cynical often finds his religion no longer useful; he then discards the family religion in favor of another that meets his needs better. This matter will be discussed in more detail later in the chapter.

Value of doubting

Doubting shows that the individual is attempting to make the mental adjustments needed for maturity. Childish religious beliefs, like childish clothes, do not fit when the individual is mature.

A far greater cause for concern occurs when the adolescent makes a snap judgment about religion and decides to reject all religious beliefs because he cannot accept part. Once the adolescent allows his doubts to lead to agnosticism, he is likely to close his mind to the possibility that there might be something of value for him in religion, even though it is not the religion of his parents. Remmers and Radler (105) have written:

In our opinion doubts about religion, rather than causing parental concern, should evoke parental pride. The young man or woman who reaches the doubting stage does so only by *thinking for himself* about the deep and meaningful sphere of religion.

CHANGES IN RELIGIOUS BELIEFS

The third developmental process consists of changes in religious beliefs. Beliefs are based on concepts which broaden and expand with increased knowledge and experience. As

Cole and Hall have said, the child who represents God in a drawing by the back of a man's head because "God's face shone so brightly that one never saw it," cannot, as an adolescent, continue to have such a concept of God; he revises it in keeping with his intellectual capacity and experience (31).

Often, change in religious beliefs is part of the adolescent revolt against *all* authority. The child may question some of his beliefs, but he is not likely to change them; he will cling to them, even though he may doubt their correctness. Not so with the adolescent. Whether he verbalizes his changed concepts and beliefs or keeps them to himself, an adolescent with normal intelligence is bound to make revisions in most of his childhood concepts. The more authoritarian his training, the greater his revolt is likely to be. Some few adolescents are afraid to change their religious beliefs because of threats from parents or fears of supernatural powers or because their personality or limited knowledge and experience prevent their making satisfactory changes. Such adolescents will as adults find themselves in possession of religious beliefs that are more suitable for children than for mature people.

Studies show that specific religious beliefs are most subject to revision, such as the child's concept of God as a person or heaven as a place of eternal happiness and good times after death (1, 92, 107). Young children, Wright and Koppe have reported, think of God as a "big man who watches you all the time." By adolescence, their concepts have become more abstract, as shown by the statement, "God is something we cannot see, something like love, but we know He is here" (132). Box 11–4 lists the beliefs that undergo the most radical change during adolescence (35, 44, 52, 61, 90, 93).

When religious beliefs change

Studies of groups of high school students report that changes in religious beliefs are most pronounced in the early years of high school, when the puberty changes are being completed, and less pronounced as the senior year is approached. This may be explained, in part, by the fact that many religious denominations focus attention on young people at the time of puberty (9, 54, 124).

Many college seniors, when questioned about the changes that had taken place since they entered college, stated that they had entered with half-thought-out religious beliefs which they had accepted from parents, teachers, or religious leaders. The more abstract the beliefs, the less likely they were to change.

While seniors are more tolerant in their religious beliefs than freshmen, the difference is not so great as is generally believed. This suggests that some changes in beliefs took place before the students entered college. Some began in high school, but were not developed until the students came in contact with professors and other students who did not hold the traditional beliefs. Women college students change their religious beliefs less than men students.

The general effect of college training is not to change religious beliefs that are firmly established but rather to lessen the strength of the beliefs. There is a trend toward theological liberalism. The more orthodox the religious faith, however, the more stable the beliefs (35, 57, 107).

Effects of changed beliefs

As the adolescent disassociates himself from his childish religious beliefs and concepts, his attitudes and behavior will inevitably change. What the effects will be and how long they will persist will depend, to a large extent, upon the kind of religious instruction he had in childhood and the reaction of his parents and friends. The longer he has retained his childhood beliefs, the harder it will be for him to change them and the greater his emotional tension.

Changed religious beliefs and attitudes may have any one or any combination of the following four effects.

Decreased interest in religion In late adolescence the individual is likely to have less interest in religion and religious observances.

This changed attitude will make him more tolerant toward people of other religious faiths. These effects will be discussed in later sections of this chapter.

Religious reconstruction Changes in religious beliefs and attitudes generally result in a reconstruction or revision of beliefs that will satisfy the more mature intellectual demands of the adolescent. It is essential, however, that he be able to make the revision without feeling guilty. Frequently the changes are so radical that the reconstruction does not harmonize with any accepted religious faith. It is really a philosophy of life based on religion.

Seashore (109) has described religious reconstruction thus:

The ability to make revisions is one of the finest achievements of a balanced personality. If the educated person does not have that, he will be left holding a discredited doctrine, which he cannot possibly believe, and his religion will fade out or become stagnant.

Acceptance of family faith If the changes in religious belief have been minor, the adoles-

---

BOX 11-4 MOST RADICALLY CHANGED RELIGIOUS BELIEFS

*God
By the late teens, most adolescents have relinquished the Old Testament concept of God as the creator of the world, a powerful ruler who punishes the bad and rewards the good. God is now seen as a friendly, intelligent Being who works in accordance with the laws of nature.

*Heaven and Hell
Few adolescents think of Heaven as eternal happiness and Hell as eternal punishment. Many doubt that there is a Heaven or a Hell or a life after death. See Figure 11-2.

*Death
The childish concept of death as eternal sleep changes to mean the end of life. Most adolescents are skeptical about the belief that only the soul lives after death or that there is any life after death.

*The Bible
Many adolescents doubt that the Bible is the written word of God or that it was even inspired by Him. Many are also skeptical about the Bible's relevance to their lives.

*The Sabbath
Most children regard the Sabbath as a day for religious observance. To adolescents, it is a day free from work, though many feel that some part of it should be spent in religious observance. See Figure 11-3.

*Prayer
No longer does the adolescent believe that prayers must be said daily or used to atone for wrongdoing or to get something he wants. Instead, he regards prayer as a source of help in time of trouble.

*The Church
The child believes that going to church makes you good. The adolescent feels that church is a place where you can *learn* how to be good.

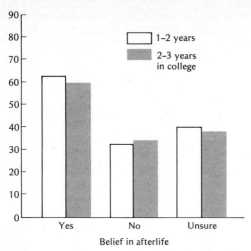

Figure 11-2 Skepticism about life after death increases as adolescents pass through college. (Adapted from S. J. Goldburgh, C. B. Rotman, J. R. Snibbe, and J. W. Ondrack: Attitudes of college students toward personal death. *Adolescence,* 1967, **2,** 211–229. Used by permission.)

cent is likely to retain the faith of his childhood. If they are major, he is likely to adopt another faith, different in most respects from that of his parents.

Among college students, the greatest reshuffling of faiths is reported to occur among Jewish students, and the least among Catholics. The more orthodox the church, the more likely it is to hold its members. When a shift is made, however, it is generally to a more liberal faith. Orthodox religions attract few converts. When parents, especially mothers, are devout, there is less likelihood of adolescents shifting to another faith than when parents are less interested in religion (9, 54, 124).

Agnosticism and atheism When the adolescent revises his religious beliefs, he may accept a religious philosophy of his own, he may accept a different religion, or he may drift into indifference, feeling that religion has little to offer him. He may become an "agnostic"—one who withholds belief because he does not know or is unwilling to accept what evidence is available; or he may become an "atheist"—one who rejects some or all of the essential doctrines of religion and denies the existence of God.

Higher education is often blamed for turning boys and girls into agnostics or atheists. There is little if any evidence, however, to show that college training has much influence at all on religious beliefs (7, 35, 55).

CHANGES IN RELIGIOUS OBSERVANCES

The fourth developmental process necessary to make religion fit adolescent needs involves changes in religious observances. All religious observances show a decline in appeal as adolescence progresses. In the following paragraphs, the most common religious observances will be examined separately to show what decline in participation occurs, when it occurs, and why it occurs.

Church attendance

Studies show a gradual decrease in church and Sunday school attendance as adolescence progresses. Height of attendance occurs in the eleventh grade. In general, boys drop out sooner than girls, and their attendance is less regular. Box 11–5 lists some of the reasons adolescents give for not attending church (37, 64, 73, 79, 87, 117).

Factors that contribute to individual variations in church attendance are discussed below.

CHURCH AFFILIATION Adolescents who are affiliated with a church attend services more regularly than those who are not. The largest percentage of those who do not attend church is found among those with no church affiliation (47, 73).

RELIGIOUS FAITH Attendance is most regular in those faiths which are strict and somewhat authoritarian in their dogmas, such as the Catholic and Lutheran, and in those which have high social prestige value (3, 95).

AGE In high school and in college, freshmen are more church-oriented than seniors. The older adolescent who lives with his family or in the neighborhood in which he grew up attends church more regularly than the college student or the adolescent whose work or military service takes him away from the pressures of family, friends, and neighbors (47, 73).

SEX At every age and in all denominations, girls attend church more regularly than boys (37, 87). The difference in church attendance among adolescent boys and girls is shown in Figure 11-4.

HOME TRAINING Adolescents from homes where authoritarian child-training methods are used, where parents are devout in their beliefs and strict in their religious practices, and where such rituals as grace and evening prayers are part of daily life are usually more conscientious about attending church than those from homes where child-training methods are more democratic and where less emphasis is placed on religious rituals. First-borns in most families are subjected to stronger parental pressures to attend church than their siblings (37, 82).

SCHOOL Adolescents who attended denominational schools and who later attend denominational colleges are more religion-oriented than those who have not had such religious influences in their school lives (47, 68).

PERSONALITY The adolescent who feels insecure and inadequate, who has a tendency toward authoritarianism in his relationships with others, and who has a strong need for religion as a prop in his life will attend church more often and more regularly than one who has greater self-confidence and feelings of security (18, 131).

ENVIRONMENT Churchgoing among adolescents is greater in suburban areas, where it is "the thing to do" to go to church on Sundays and important religious holidays, than in urban centers and, usually, rural areas as well (68, 95).

SOCIOECONOMIC STATUS Church affiliation and church attendance are influenced by the socioeconomic status of the family. Middle- and upper-class adolescents attend church

Figure 11-3 When the child reaches adolescence, his concept of "Sabbath" often changes and with this change comes a changed attitude toward the way to spend the day.

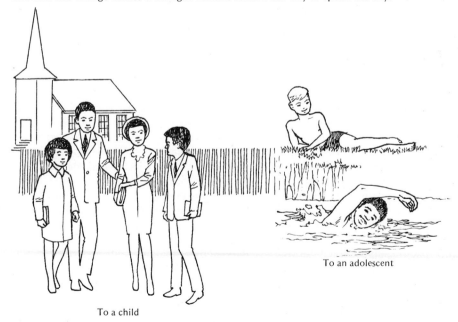

To a child

To an adolescent

more as members of a family group than do those of the lower classes (47, 134).

SOCIAL ACCEPTANCE If the adolescent feels that he is an accepted member of the peer group, he is far more likely to attend church and participate in other church activities (87). Since going to church is the thing to do, many adolescents who are anxious to be identified with the "right" social group continue their churchgoing even after their interest in religion has waned and their beliefs have been shaken by scientific and historical facts.

Church-related activities

Most adolescents are interested in church clubs for social, not religious, reasons. The major determinant of how much time they will devote to church recreations is their degree of social acceptance.

Lack of interest in church recreations today is no doubt due to the many competing school and community organizations which satisfy the recreational and social needs formerly satisfied by the church. Older adolescents, whether in college or at work, often prefer less organized activities or commercial recreations.

Church social clubs appeal to girls more than to boys at all ages, but especially at the high school age. Often, the attitude toward boys who attend such clubs is that they are "a bunch of Christers." Socially mobile adolescents often use church recreational groups as a means of gaining acceptance in the social groups with which they wish to be identified. If they join the "right" group in the "right" church, they hope that this will facilitate their acceptance by the "right" people (69, 95).

Home religious observances

Family religious observances are far less common in America today than in the past. For the most part, observances are limited to holiday celebrations, such as Christmas, Easter, or Passover. They are generally family gatherings of a social nature, with little emphasis on religion (21, 108).

Family rituals are more common in middle- than in upper- and lower-class families and slightly more characteristic of Protestant and Jewish families than of Catholic families; the latter do their worshiping in church (50). In urban and suburban homes, religious rituals are far less common than in rural homes, although rural families have fewer home religious observances today than in the past (21, 37, 95).

Prayer

While adolescents may pray once or twice daily through force of habit, their prayers are likely to be merely a ritual, not a personally rewarding experience. Occasional prayers are said by all except agnostics and atheists. Under unusual circumstances, adolescents will pray at any time or place.

Older adolescents say prayers less frequently than the younger. Like church attendance, however, the frequency of praying is related to religious faith and church affiliation. Those of the Catholic faith pray regularly and regard prayer as part of their daily experience. Protestants pray less regularly than Catholics. Adolescents of the Jewish faith pray least of all and a larger percentage of them say they never pray. Within each faith, boys pray less regularly than girls (8, 43).

The preferred form of prayer is influenced by the adolescent's childhood experience, by his religious affiliation or faith, and by his personality. In Box 11-6 are given some of the common forms of prayer that adolescents use (4, 21, 24, 108, 116).

Reasons for prayer Adolescents have many reasons for praying. In one study, the reasons given by a group of high school students, in order of frequency, as reported by Pixley and Beekman (100) were:

*To ask for personal benefits
*To express thanks
*To talk to God
*To ask for guidance
*To comply with habit
*To seek comfort
*To ask for help for others
*To ask for forgiveness

Ross (108) found that older adolescents who pray fell into four categories:

*Those for whom prayer seems to be a meaningful way of communication with God. Of the group questioned, 17 per cent gave this reason.
*Those for whom prayer approximates a period of self-analysis or meditation—26 per cent.
*Those for whom prayer is a kind of technique—a magical gesture not unlike the proverbial rabbit's foot which is used to bring good luck—which can be used in time of crisis or need. For 42 per cent, prayer served this purpose.
*Those who never pray and have no comment to make about it—15 per cent.

Since the reasons given for prayer suggest that it is used mainly in emergencies, it is not surprising that adolescents pray mostly in un-

usual situations rather than every day. The tenability of this statement is illustrated by the following comments reported by Ross (108):

When I was depressed I often wanted to get drunk, just to lie in the gutter. I didn't care what happened to me, but I always prayed and this helped me. It helped me more than anything else. Prayer helps the self more than anything.

Well, usually before a test I pray to the Lord if He couldn't help me in some way. It gives me courage in myself. I think it helps.

I pray in church on Sundays. I'd pray, too, if I'd get into trouble or if I thought I might die.

Figure 11-4 Sex and degree of social acceptance influence the frequency of adolescent church attendence. (Adapted from E. L. Megargee, G. V. C. Parker, and R. V. Levine: Relationship of familial and social factors to socialization in middle-class college students. *J. abnorm. Psychol.*, 1971, **77**, 76–89. Used by permission.)

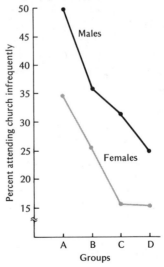

Key

Group A   Poor socialization
Group B   Below average socialization
Group C   Above average socialization
Group D   High socialization

Reasons for not praying For the most part, reasons for not praying are related to doubts about the value of religion. Having been taught as children that prayer was a way of getting God's help or of having God give them something they wanted, young adolescents are often disillusioned when they discover that their prayers are not answered. Pixley and Beekman (100) reported this statement of a high school student:

I don't believe in prayers. When I was ten years old I wanted a bicycle very much, so I prayed in order to get it. I would pray every morning, and at night before I would go to bed; sometimes when I had time during the day I prayed too. I didn't get the bike, so I could never again see any sense in praying. Since that time on I never prayed again.

INCREASE IN RELIGIOUS TOLERANCE

The fifth and perhaps the most significant developmental process in religious change during the adolescent years is increase in religious tolerance. Not only is there a growing tendency to believe that Catholics, Jews, and Protestants are equally good, but there is less tendency to wonder about this question as the adolescent reaches the end of his high school course.

Religious tolerance develops gradually, accompanying the increase in religious doubt. The more the adolescent doubts the religious beliefs he acquired during childhood, the more open-minded he is toward the beliefs of other faiths. As his social horizons broaden and as he comes in contact with persons of other religious faiths in school and in the community, he sees religion in a more mature and more understanding way. Crow and Crow (36) write:

Because of his association with other young people whose respective church affiliations demand that they adhere to specific religious observances that differ from those of his own church, the adolescent considers any such obligations superficial, insignificant, and unrelated to fundamental religious truth. The adolescent's attitude is strengthened by the fact that he admires and respects the other teen-agers.

The more religious the adolescent is, the fewer doubts he has had about his early religious beliefs; and the more dogmatic his religion, the less tolerant will his attitude toward members of other faiths become.

The acceptance of a conventional, externalized religion makes for less tolerance than a personal and internalized religion. Among Catholics, for example, daily communicants are more intolerant of persons of other faiths than occasional communicants. Adolescents who shift from one social group to another have an opportunity to sample the doctrines and teachings of various denominations. As a result, these adolescents are likely to become more tolerant in their attitudes toward other religions than are adolescents who are socially static (18, 98, 111).

Increase in religious tolerance will, inevitably, be expressed in overt behavior. Some such behavior is of only minor significance while some has a profound and long-lasting influence. Of the many effects of an increase in religious tolerance, the following are the most important.

Decrease in prejudice

Increase in tolerance leads to decrease in prejudice against members of minority-group faiths. Decreased prejudice, in turn, breaks down barriers between members of the peer group, with the result that many adolescents form friendships with members of other religious faiths.

Interfaith friendships are often less close than friendships between members of the same faith because of differences in values (111, 131). For example, the social and aspirational values of most Jewish adolescents differ markedly in some respects from those of adolescents of the Protestant and Catholic faiths. To an adolescent Jewish boy, academic achievement is regarded as a very important stepping-stone to vocational and social success. Prot-

estant and Catholic boys, by contrast, put more value on athletic and social achievement. As a result, they regard the Jewish boy as a curve raiser whose interests are quite different from theirs (32, 95).

Change of religious faith

The adolescent whose church has an intolerant attitude toward social activities, whose minister preaches sermons that are primarily doctrinal and authoritarian, and who finds the ritualistic services meaningless and boring is likely to consider joining another church which is more to his liking. His increased tolerance enables him to see the good in other religions. Whether he will change church membership will depend largely on the emotional reactions of his parents; if they put up a great protest, he may abandon the idea. Parents who are devoutly religious do not want their children to change faiths, even when they marry people of another religion (34, 118).

Interfaith dating and marriage

Many parents object to their children dating members of other faiths because they fear that it might lead to an interfaith marriage. This source of friction between parents and adolescent sons and daughters has grown as interfaith dating has become more common.

Interfaith marriages occur most often in the large cities (12, 114). They are frowned upon by the clergy of *all* denominations and regarded as risky in the sense that the divorce rate in interfaith marriages has always been higher than in intrafaith marriages (22, 102). This is illustrated in Figure 11-5. Bossard (20) has explained why interfaith marriages are so risky:

What young people overlook is the real nature of religion and its role in life. Religion is not merely a set of beliefs; it is a way of living and thinking. Roman Catholicism is a culture pattern, as we sociologists put it; so is Judaism, or Methodism or being an Episcopalian.

To minimize the risk in an interfaith marriage, one partner, usually the boy, is often willing to give up his own faith and accept that of the other. To break down the opposition of the girl's family, many a boy is willing to accept her faith, feeling that one religion is as good as another. This usually leads to friction with his own parents and a strained relationship between them, the girl, and her parents (22, 30).

In spite of the hazards involved in interfaith marriages, the chances are that they will become more frequent in the years to come. As more adolescents go to college, where they come in contact with people from many different faiths and where they will not only be encouraged to think independently but will learn facts that contradict their childhood religious concepts, they will become increasingly tolerant toward members of other faiths. Furthermore, interfaith marriages are more common in adolescence than in adulthood, and so long as the trend toward early marriage continues, so will the trend toward more interfaith marriages (104). Box 11-7 gives a number of reasons for the increase in interfaith marriages (12, 15, 22, 62, 95, 102).

College students and adolescents who enter the *armed services* are more likely to marry outside the family faith than are persons who go to work after high school. The democratic atmosphere of the college campus and the

Figure 11-5 The high divorce rate of mixed marriages is one indication of how "risky" such marriages are. (Adapted from G. M. Vernon: Interfaith marriages. *Relig. Educ.*, 1960, **55,** 261–264. Used by permission.)

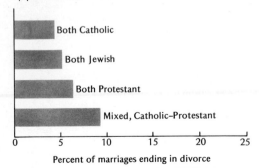

Percent of marriages ending in divorce

armed services leads the adolescent to look for congeniality of interests in the people he meets. Family pressures to select friends of his own religious faith are missing (55, 62).

Adolescents whose families are *socially mobile* are often encouraged by their parents to marry outside their faiths if they come from a minority religious group. Marrying into a family of a more prestigious religious faith, they believe, will aid their climb up the social ladder. By contrast, adolescents from static families are more likely to be encouraged to marry within their faiths, even if this means identification with a minority religious group. Families that are very religious regard education as a better stepping-stone to upward mobility than religion; families that are less religious often consider the "right" religion a necessary stepping-stone in their upward climb (95, 102).

LONG-TERM EFFECTS OF TRANSITIONAL CHANGES

The important changes in religious beliefs, attitudes, and observances discussed in this chapter may have a temporary or a permanent effect on the adolescent's religious interests and activities. For most adolescents, the effects follow a fairly predictable pattern. In this pattern, the late teens are less religious years than the early teens, especially for boys. This relatively low interest in religion extends into the early twenties, which have been called the "least religious period of life" (108).

When the adolescent marries and assumes the responsibilities of parenthood, he often returns to religion. Parents of young children feel that they should teach their children the fundamentals of their own faith and see that they receive proper religious instruction in Sunday school. In addition, they feel that they should set a good example by attending church. They almost always revive the holiday religious practices and rituals that were observed in their own homes (21).

During late adolescence, religious interests and activities are at a low point, and religion lacks the compulsive quality needed to make

BOX 11-7 REASONS FOR INCREASE IN INTERFAITH MARRIAGES

Religious Tolerance
Religious tolerance, which comes from higher education and opportunities for broad social contacts in academic institutions, in the armed services, or at work, makes adolescents less concerned about the religion of those whom they find congenial as dates.

Decreased Interest in Religion
Many adolescents have little interest in religion; they regard other common interests and values as more important in marriage.

Availability of Potential Mates
If persons of their own faith are not available in their communities, adolescents are tempted to marry individuals of other religions. The smaller the number of adolescents of marriageable age in a religious group, the greater the chances that they will marry into another faith.

Opportunity for Social Mobility
If the adolescent is ambitious to move upward on the socioeconomic ladder, he will be motivated to marry outside the family faith if he believes this will facilitate the upward move. Many Jewish-Protestant and Jewish-Catholic marriages are motivated by the desire for upward social mobility.

it a force in the adolescent's life. As Ross has pointed out, religion is then on the "periphery of life" where its influence is indirect (108).

Adolescents who are able to resolve their religious doubts and find a faith that meets their needs gain a feeling of security and add meaning to their lives. The importance of resolving religious doubts becomes clear when one realizes that doubts often become persistent. The adolescent can develop the habit of doubting, of being skeptical, and of feeling that religion is of no value for him. On the other hand, if he can resolve his doubts and embrace some religion, even though it is less conventional than that of his parents, he will be able to receive the help that religion can give (61).

Consequently, to those who claim that young people are irreligious and have no interest in religion, it should be apparent that society must take positive steps to help young people resolve the doubts they experience in adolescence. Even more important, those who lay the child's religious foundations—his parents, grandparents, and Sunday school teachers—must see that these foundations will not lead to troubling doubts and logical disbeliefs as the child grows older. Healthy religious foundations in childhood will go a long way toward producing a healthy attitude toward religion throughout life.

HIGHLIGHTS OF CHAPTER 11

1. Religion consists of two elements: faith and practices. The adolescent is usually judged as religious or irreligious by the latter rather than the former.

2. That modern adolescents are not as irreligious as is popularly believed is shown by their interest in talking about religion, their study of religions in colleges and universities, and their participation in religions that deviate from the traditional patterns.

3. Most adolescents want a religion that meets their needs, though needs vary markedly among adolescents, depending on the religious atmosphere of their homes, religious affiliation, peer attitudes,

sex, environment, socioeconomic status, religious denomination, and personality.

4. Five developmental processes are essential to make a religion fit the needs of adolescents: religious awakening, religious doubt, changes in religious beliefs, changes in religious participation, and increased tolerance toward the beliefs and practices of others.

5. Religious awakening, which means an increased interest in religion leading to a reconstruction of religious beliefs and attitudes, may be gradual or catastrophic. It is due to such factors as increased intelligence and knowledge, focusing attention on religion in preparation for joining the church or synagogue, and acknowledgment of the aid religion can give in meeting personal problems or a blow of fate, such as the death of a loved one.

6. Religious doubt is usually concentrated on the Bible, religious doctrines in general, and doctrines peculiar to a given religious denomination.

7. Religious doubt gives rise to confusion and uncertainty, revision of religious beliefs, a decrease in religious observances, or a shift to another religion.

8. Changes in religious beliefs are most frequent in those beliefs based on specific concepts, such as the childish concepts of God, of prayer, or of Heaven. Such changes have four effects: decreased interest in religion, religious reconstruction, acceptance of the family faith or of a new faith, and agnosticism or atheism.

9. When changed beliefs lead to decreased interest in religion, the adolescent's religious observances are affected in a number of ways: a decline in church attendance, decreased participation in church-related activities, lack of interest in home religious observances, and lowered belief in the value of prayer.

10. Increase in religious tolerance is generally gradual; it accompanies the pattern of religious doubt.

11. Overt expressions of religious tolerance in adolescence include a decrease in prejudice, change of religious faith, and interfaith dating and marriage.

12. The transitional changes in religious beliefs, attitudes, and observances may have temporary or permanent effects on religious attitudes and activities, depending on how the adolescent resolves his religious doubts.

Chapter 12

Transition in Morality

Photograph by Farrell/Greene
Omikron

One of the important developmental tasks of adolescence is to replace childish morality with a morality that will serve as a guide to conduct in adult life. The adolescent is expected to learn that honesty does not merely mean refraining from taking things that belong to others or from telling lies; is means adhering to truth and fair conduct in *all situations*. The adolescent must learn that taking the printed thoughts or words of another and using them without due credit is plagiarism, that copying the work of another with or without his consent is cheating, that saying malicious things about a person behind his back is slander.

In addition to replacing the specific moral concepts of childhood with general moral principles, the adolescent is expected to assume responsibility for the control of his behavior. Morality based on external controls must be replaced by morality based on internal controls. The adolescent is expected to decide what to do in a given situation and stick to his decision without having someone threaten him with punishment if he fails to do so.

MEANING OF MORALITY

"Morality" comes from the Latin word *moralis;* it means "customs, manners, or patterns of behavior that conform to the standards of the group." At every age, the individual is judged by how closely he conforms to the group's standards, and he is labeled "moral" or "immoral" accordingly. What the social group expects is defined in its rules and laws; both are based on the group's prevailing customs.

If the adolescent conforms to society's rules and laws, he is considered a "moral" person. Even if he does not agree with the rules and laws, he often conforms because he realizes that it is the smart thing to do. Wiggam has suggested that moral people "choose the right conduct simply because they see it is the course of action that promises the best consequences" (227).

The "immoral" person is one who fails to conform to group customs, rules, and laws

because he disagrees with group standards or feels little obligation to the group. In most nonconformity, the individual is retaliating against the group for what he considers unfair treatment.

By contrast, an "unmoral" or "nonmoral" person violates social expectations because of ignorance. In adolescence, as in adulthood, there is relatively little unmoral behavior except in situations so unrelated to what has been experienced in the past that the individual has had no opportunity to learn what is expected of him. Thus adolescents who fail to behave as the social group expects usually do so through *intent* rather than through ignorance.

DIFFICULTIES IN MAKING THE TRANSITION TO ADULT MORALITY

The moral values of childhood are no longer adequate to meet all the needs of the adolescent. The individual must now acquire new moral values to meet new needs, especially those arising from relationships with members of the opposite sex and those having to do with alcohol, drugs, and the use of automobiles. One of the major developmental tasks of the adolescent is to learn what the group expects of him and then to conform to the expectations without constant guidance and supervision.

Since the adolescent is anxious to win social approval and avoid disapproval, his motivation to make the transition to a more mature morality is strong. But a number of obstacles stand in the way. Box 12-1 lists the most common ones (1, 102, 124, 206, 213, 223).

Effects of difficulties

In making the transition to adult morality, the adolescent is sometimes confused about what is right and what wrong, what should be done and what should not be. The first effect of this difficulty is to *slow down the learning process* and thus delay the transition. If an adolescent is not sure what code of behavior to accept or if he must learn several contradictory codes, he cannot make the transition quickly and smoothly.

The second effect is to *weaken motivation to conform*. If the adolescent has doubts about the correctness of the socially accepted moral code, his motivation to conform to it will be undermined.

The third effect of the difficulties encountered in making the transition to adult morality stems from a question in the adolescent's mind about the *fairness of adult standards*. When they differ markedly from those of the peer group, the adolescent begins to wonder if they are not irrelevant to his world. In the case of cheating, for example, the adolescent might argue that when his parents were preparing to enter college, competition was not what it is today, nor was a college education so essential to getting a job. Furthermore, he might say, "everyone cheats," and so this gives cheating the stamp of approval. Branding it as dishonest, he concludes, is unfair (22, 81).

The fourth and most adverse consequence of the difficulties faced in making the transition is that the adolescent is caught in a moral dilemma when he must decide between *two or more moral alternatives*. Having to make a decision that could lead to social disapproval as easily as to approval, to punishment as easily as to praise and reward, places the adolescent in a predicament.

Variations in difficulties

Girls, on the whole, have less difficulty making the transition to an adult morality than boys, primarily because their early training has been stricter and they have learned that adhering to cultural values enhances their prestige. Boys, by contrast, know that violating rules and even laws gives them greater prestige, especially in the peer group, than being law-abiding citizens (46, 102).

The *personality pattern* of the adolescent is probably the major factor in determining the ease or difficulty of the transition. Peck and Havighurst (160) have classified moral character according to five "types," varying in the

---

BOX 12-1 OBSTACLES TO DEVELOPING AN ADULT MORALITY

Preparation for Making Moral Decisions
The adolescent brought up in an authoritarian home where decisions were made for him or in a permissive home where there was little motivation to conform to group expectations is less prepared to make moral decisions than one brought up in a democratic home.

Number of Moral Alternatives
The adolescent is faced with learning and obeying more rules, regulations, and laws than the child.

Conflicts in Moral Values
Moral values for different groups sometimes conflict: for the adolescent peer group and the adult group, for the two sexes, for persons of different socio-economic, racial, and religious groups, and for persons from rural and urban environments. Conflicting values make it difficult for the adolescent to decide which to accept.

Pressures from the Peer Group
The more anxious the adolescent is to win social approval among his peers and the less secure his status in the peer group, the more likely he is to ignore adult standards in favor of those of his peers.

difficulty involved in reaching a mature moral status:

1 The *amoral type* lacks internalized principles and has little regard for the consequences of his behavior. This is the most infantile, impulsive, and irresponsible kind of personality.

2 The *expedient type* is one who is primarily self-centered in that he considers other people's welfare only to gain his own ends; he behaves according to the moral standards of the group only so long as it suits his purpose, primarily to get what he wants and to avoid social disapproval.

3 The *conforming type* is one whose main moral principle is to do what others do and what they say *he should do*. This type follows rules and laws specific for each occasion instead of having generalized moral principles.

4 The *rational conscientious type* has his own internal standards of right and wrong by which he judges his acts, but he is rigid in applying his moral principles. To him, an act is "good" or "bad" because he defines it as such, not because of the good or ill effects it may have on others.

5 The *rational altruistic type* represents the highest level of moral maturity. Such a person has a stable set of moral principles by which he guides his behavior. In addition, he tries realistically to appraise the results of a given act and to assess it in terms of whether or not it serves others as well as himself. He is, thus, "rational" in his assessment of his conduct, in the light of his principles and "altruistic" in showing a concern for the welfare of others as well as of himself.

In a follow-up study of a small group of boys and girls from the age of 10 to the age of 17, Peck and Havighurst reported a marked tendency to show the same level of morality at ages 13 and 16 as at 10. "Character type," they concluded, has been established by the age of 10 years, owing to early moral training at home. As a result, in the transition to adult morality, many adolescents are handicapped by personality foundations laid when they were young. The "expedient" adolescent, for example, is in the habit of conforming to social expectations only so long as it suits his purpose; considering the welfare of others would be foreign to his usual pattern of be-

havior. Similarly, the "amoral" adolescent is accustomed to being held back in what he wants to do only by fear or threat of punishment; internalizing a control over his behavior would be a major revision in his usual pattern of behavior (160).

ESSENTIALS IN MAKING THE TRANSITION TO ADULT MORALITY

There is abundant evidence that morality is developed, not inborn. Like all development, it can be controlled and directed so that the individual will acquire the ability to conform to the expectations of his group.

In a successful transition to adult morality, two essentials must be fulfilled: *First,* the adolescent must change the attitudes and values which make up his moral concepts so that they will meet the more mature demands of an adult society, and *second,* he himself must assume control over his behavior.

Changes in moral concepts

From his parents, teachers, and others in authority, the child learns what is regarded as right and what is regarded as wrong. Adults interpret for him the moral codes of the community and punish him when he violates them. The major foundations for the moral codes are laid in the home, although the school and the church also play some role.

In the early days of American education, schools and colleges were church-sponsored and the teachers were often ministers. Gradually, with the growth of secular schools, the teaching of moral values in the schools was deemphasized, except those specifically related to school or college behavior. A study of textbooks used in schools from 1810 to 1950 reveals the change that has taken place (39). While Sunday schools and churches still combine the teaching of morality with the teaching of religion, the decline in interest in religious observances as the child moves into adolescence means that many older children and adolescents do not get the benefit of this instruction.

Regardless of how the child's moral codes are formed, whether at home, in school, in church, or in Sunday school, they are not adequate to meet the more mature needs of the adolescent. They must be revised to conform to the codes that guide the lives of the adult members of the community. This is especially true of moral codes that have a religious foundation. If, for example, the child has learned that God watches him, telling him what to do or what not to do, and then rewards him if he obeys or punishes him if he disobeys, he will no longer accept this concept when he begins to doubt his childish religious beliefs.

Kinds of change Childish moral concepts must be changed in many ways to meet the needs of the adolescent. For one thing, the adolescent is expected to *generalize* his earlier concepts. Generalizing specific moral concepts and incorporating them into a workable code to use in any situation is a gradual process that continues throughout the adolescent years (47).

As the adolescent evaluates different kinds of behavior in terms of moral concepts, he is likely to find some kinds less desirable than others. No longer are "wrong" things wrong to the same degree that they were when he was a child. He now ascribes *degrees of seriousness* to different acts; some of the things that he learned were wrong as a child he now views more tolerantly (168).

In behavior relating to sex, moral values change significantly with age. Attitudes toward masturbation, flirting, petting, and premarital intercourse are often revised in adolescence. Many adolescents regard masturbation as wrong, just as they did in childhood; others may not regard it as wrong, but they usually think of it as socially disapproved. Adolescents likewise show marked variations in their attitudes toward flirting, petting, and premarital intercourse. These changes will be discussed in more detail in Chapter 13. Box 12-2 lists some of the important changes in moral concepts that occur during adolescence (34, 104, 176, 183, 210, 225). Note that some of the changes are in the direction of greater leniency while others are in the direction of greater rigidity.

A final way in which moral concepts must change if they are to meet adolescent needs is that there must be greater concern for the *motives* behind an act. Children tend to condemn an act as right or wrong without considering the reason for the act. If they believe that telling a lie is wrong, they condemn all lying and are unwilling to concede that there *might* be times when a lie is justified. By the age of 12, children gradually begin to liberalize their moral concepts and to understand that certain acts usually labeled wrong may be right under some circumstances. Adolescents must also recognize that punishment may be just and fair under some circumstances and unfair under others (1, 205, 210).

Inner control of behavior

The second essential in making the transition to adult morality is that the adolescent must assume inner control of his own behavior so that external control will no longer be necessary. This change is for the adolescent's own benefit as well as for the good of the social group. As he reaches adulthood, the adolescent will be held responsible for his acts; no longer can he rely on parents and teachers to tell him what to do and what not to do. He must decide for himself and then act in accordance with his decision (167).

The adolescent's conscience is the controlling force that makes external restraints unnecessary. "Conscience" refers to a sense of rightness or wrongness of one's own acts. As Finney has defined it, "Conscience is self-control by inner standards, learned by identification with others' ideals, and maintained by a remorseful or unworthy feeling when one violates it" (55). Eysenck refers to conscience as an "interiorized policeman" or "inner light" (52). Members of the Freudian school of psychologists sometimes refer to it as the "superego" (55). Gesell et al. (61) have explained it in terms of the concept of self:

The self has the strange capacity to commune with itself both as a spectator and as a mentor with a small voice. This most mysterious of all self-phenomena proves to be a profound reality for the growing adolescent. This is his conscience.

Those who believe that a person is born moral or immoral usually hold that conscience is a part of the hereditary endowment. Many people, even today, refer to conscience as the "voice of God" telling the person what to do or what not to do. As Eysenck (52) has explained, they believe that conscience is

. . . some kind of *deus ex machina* implanted in the human being in some mysterious way, which ceaselessly keeps an eye on his activities, and gives him a sharp tweak whenever he deviates from the straight and narrow path of duty.

Just as there is evidence that people are not born moral or immoral but become so through experience, so is there evidence that the individual's conscience is a product of experience. It is often referred to as the "voice of the herd" because the control of the individual's behavior comes from his knowledge of what the cultural group expects of him (26, 124, 195).

Roles of guilt and shame in inner control of behavior Guilt and shame, developed from fear and anxiety, act as deterrents to behavior that falls below social expectations. They are thus internalized controls over behavior. Guilt, as Ausubel (9) states, is a

. . . special kind of negative self-evaluation which occurs when an individual acknowledges that his behavior is at variance with a given moral value to which he feels obligated to conform. . . . It is one of the most important psychological mechanisms through which an individual becomes socialized in the ways of his culture. It is also an important instrument for cultural survival since it constitutes a most efficient watchdog within each individual, serving to keep his behavior compatible with the moral values of the society in which he lives.

If a person felt no guilt, he would have little desire to conform to social expectations. Guilt, therefore, becomes an "internalized watchdog." Before guilt can develop, however, a person must, *first,* accept certain standards of right and wrong or of good and bad as his own; *second,* accept the obligation of regulating his behavior to conform to whatever standards he has adopted and feel accountable for lapses from them; and *third,* possess sufficient self-critical ability to recognize when a discrepancy between behavior and internalized values occurs (9).

"Shame," as Ausubel has explained, differs from guilt in that it is aroused in the individual by an "actual or presumed negative judgment of himself by others resulting in self-depreciation vis-à-vis the group" (9). Shame can be *nonmoral,* as in embarrassment when a person commits a breach of propriety, or it can be *moral,* as when aroused by the negative moral judgments of others. Shame thus relies on external sanctions alone; guilt relies on *both* internal and external sanctions (11, 19). Behavior controlled by shame is "other-directed" while behavior controlled by guilt is "inner-directed" Both are the product of experience (26, 161, 206).

When the adolescent realizes that his behavior is falling below the standards he has set or the expectations of the social group, guilt or shame may lead him to adopt a more lenient attitude toward the behavior. If an adolescent is tempted to cheat, for example, and does so, his attitude toward cheating will become more lenient. If he resists the temptation because of either fear or guilt, his attitude will become more intolerant.

Variations in influence of conscience The degree to which behavior is influenced by conscience varies greatly. Adolescents who are bright or who come from strict backgrounds learn to control their behavior by feelings of guilt sooner than those who are less bright or who come from less strict backgrounds (20, 124). Throughout adolescence, conscience plays a more important role in controlling moral behavior among girls than boys (134, 177). The father's absence from home, especially during the early formative years, has an adverse effect on conscience development in boys (86).

Figure 12-1 When parents condone or encourage cheating, the adolescent's attitudes toward it become lenient. (Adapted from George Clark: "The Neighbors." © 1972 New York News, Inc. World Rights Reserved. Used by permission.)

The Neighbors   *By George Clark*

"I was just telling him some little tricks to help him pass that exam. Like shirt cuff notes and sitting behind the best student and . . ."

Regardless of these variations, every adolescent whose behavior falls short of his own standards has a strong sense of personal inadequacy. Even in the absence of social disapproval, he will have a guilty conscience, which will lead to emotional tension. Unquestionably, some of the unhappiness that every adolescent experiences traces back to a guilty conscience for real or imagined wrongdoing.

ROLE OF DISCIPLINE IN MORAL DEVELOPMENT

"Discipline" comes from the Latin word *disciplina,* which means "teaching" or "instruction." The main purpose of discipline is to teach the individual to conform to social expectations to a reasonable degree. In addition, discipline teaches him that the world responds in an orderly way to his actions, that certain behaviors will always be followed by punishment and others by praise. Also, discipline helps the individual develop self-control and self-direction so that he can make wise decisions.

Adolescents feel a special need for discipline in areas of behavior in which they have no childhood experience to guide them. Because of the complexity of behavior related to members of the opposite sex, adolescents today want guidance in this new area of experience even more than in the past when chaperonage served as a guide (76, 112).

Essentials of discipline

If the adolescent is to learn what society expects of him and be motivated to control his behavior to conform to expectations, discipline must include four essential elements: education in moral concepts, reward for socially approved behavior, punishment for intentional wrongdoing, and consistency in social expectations. Not one of these can be neglected if the adolescent is to achieve the desired goal of self-controlled behavior.

Education in moral concepts Many adults assume that by the time the individual has reached adolescence he has learned what is right or wrong and needs no further moral training. This is far from true. As the social horizons broaden in adolescence, boys and girls must know what the boundaries are in many new situations and what society will tolerate. The function of rules and laws is to teach the individual what the boundaries are, not merely to restrain undesirable behavior.

If the adolescent learns that smoking is not permitted on the school premises, that he is not permitted to stay out after 11 o'clock on school nights, and that the legal limit for driving in the city is 30 miles an hour, he knows what is expected of him. While he may not agree with the rules and laws and may attempt to break them, he still knows that he must face the consequences if he does so. In general, the learning of moral concepts should be completed, or nearly so, when the adolescent reaches legal maturity. After that, he will be held responsible for his own acts (190).

Reward for socially approved behavior Rewards serve two purposes: They are *educational,* informing the adolescent that his behavior has won social approval and is "good" behavior; and they are *ego-bolstering,* stimulating the adolescent to continue to act in that way. Since many adolescents, as a defense against feelings of insecurity, assume a cocky attitude which suggests that they are self-satisfied, many adults feel that rewards encourage adolescents to be conceited. Others argue that threats of punishment, rather than rewards, are a stronger motivation for good behavior.

According to the evidence, rewards do not have bad effects; on the contrary, they provide a strong motivation to conform to society's expectations. As such, they are, as Vincent and Martin have emphasized, a "potent instrument in discipline" (220). To shape behavior, however, rewards must be developmentally appropriate. While a child might respond favorably to such a reward as being allowed to stay up late to watch television if he is "nice to Grandmother," the adolescent would scoff at it.

Material rewards, such as a new article of clothing, new sports equipment, or money, are usually acceptable to an adolescent if they have prestige value in the eyes of the peer group. The greatest reward for most adolescents is praise. Far too often, the comments of parents and teachers are critical; a kind word is a pleasant relief from constant nagging. Not only is praise ego-bolstering but it has great educational value. It tells the adolescent that his act was so acceptable that it was worth commending. To be a "potent instrument in discipline," praise must be used judiciously, not just when a parent or teacher happens to be in a good mood. And the strength of the praise must be regulated according to the acceptability of the act. Indiscriminate use of lavish praise reduces its educational value because the adolescent does not learn to judge the relative acceptability of an act.

Punishment for intentional wrongdoing Like reward, punishment serves two major functions in discipline: It *deters the repetition of socially undesirable acts* and it shows the adolescent *what the social group considers wrong.* If punishment is to encourage the adolescent to avoid behaving in a socially unacceptable way, he must view the punishment as fair and deserved. Otherwise, his resentment will reduce his desire to avoid such acts in the future. Equally as important, punishment must be given only when the "offending" adolescent knew what was expected of him but intentionally violated the expectation. If punishment is to show the adolescent what the social group considers wrong, its severity must be in keeping with the severity of his wrongdoing. He should not be as severely punished for coming into class late as for cheating; nor must he be as severely punished for coming home late at night as for going to forbidden places where liquor is served or where he will be associating with adults of questionable reputation.

Far too often, punishment is imposed by an adult who is angry because of what the adolescent has done. The severity of the punishment then reflects the adult's anger more than the seriousness of the misbehavior. Furthermore, adults judge misbehavior in terms of their own values, not the values of the peer group, and punish accordingly. If adults punish according to adult values, the severity of the punishment may seem out of proportion to the wrongdoing as the adolescent judges it. As a result, the second major function of discipline—to show the adolescent what the group considers wrong—will not be fulfilled. If punishment is to help the adolescent gain self-control, it must have certain characteristics. Box 12-3 lists those which are the most important (12, 65, 155, 190, 199, 220).

Spanking and whipping, so common in childhood, are relatively infrequent forms of punishment for adolescents living in cities and small towns; they are quite frequent for those living in rural areas. By far the most common punishment reported by high school boys and girls is being "talked to" or scolded. Other commonly used punishments are "being made to stay at home," being slapped, and being deprived of pleasures and privileges (12, 65, 199). The kind of punishment used varies according to the size of the family (156). See Figure 12-2, which is based on data from a number of research studies.

Punishment is imposed less frequently as

BOX 12-3   CHARACTERISTICS OF "GOOD" PUNISHMENT

*Should be related in form to the misbehavior

*Must be certain and consistent

*Must seem fair and just to the adolescent

*Must be impersonal

*Should be constructive and conducive to inner control

*Should be withheld until the adolescent's motive is understood

*Should avoid undue arousal of fear

*Should not involve the assignment of extra work that is unrelated to the act for which the punishment is imposed

---

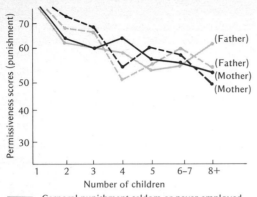

Corporal punishment seldom or never employed

Discussion always or usually—no other punishment

Figure 12-2 The kind of punishment used in the home varies according to family size. (Adapted from F. I. Nye, J. Carlson, and G. Garrett: Family size, interaction, affect, and stress. *J. Marriage & Family,* 1970, **32,** 216–226. Used by permission.)

adolescents approach legal maturity. Whether they do not need punishment as much or whether parents and teachers feel that older adolescents are "too old" to be punished has not been determined. Boys at every age are punished more than girls; boys tend to be more rebellious against rules and laws than girls.

The adolescent views the punishments he receives more critically than the child. The child invariably becomes angry and resentful when punished, no matter how much he may deserve the punishment. When the adolescent feels that the punishment was fair and deserved, he accepts it in a spirit of good sportsmanship. He does not harbor a grudge or interpret the punishment as a sign that his parent does not love him. Nor does he seek revenge by being disobedient.

Adolescents are very critical of certain forms of punishment. They often regard corporal punishment as cruel. Since they are very sensitive to the opinions of their peers, they resent being embarrassed before the group at home or in school. They also resent any punishment that seems unfair, especially when it is a disguised hostility on the part of the parent or teacher.

Consistency in social expectations The importance of consistency in discipline is that it tells the adolescent what his boundaries, limits, and freedoms are. Consistency thus gives the adolescent a feeling of security and eliminates confusion. It teaches him that there is moral orderliness in the world. Even more important, it teaches him that rewards and punishments are predictable, not haphazard.

Inconsistent discipline slows down the learning process. In addition, it causes friction between parents and children. Adolescents consider it unfair to be punished for an act which previously has gone unpunished. In time, inconsistency causes the adolescent to lose respect for his disciplinarians and for their rules.

Parents and teachers are inconsistent in their discipline for many reasons. Those who are inexperienced in their roles are often uncertain about what to do or what to expect of an adolescent. They receive conflicting advice from other adults as well as from adolescents. Inconsistency often stems from an ambivalent attitude toward the adolescent; parents swing from love to resentment, depending on how the adolescent responds to them. More often, however, inconsistency traces its origin to conflicts in parental attitudes. A lenient parent is likely to be less lenient when the stricter parent is present; the strict parent is likely to vacillate when the lenient parent is present. The most lenient and most severe disciplinarians tend to be the most consistent, though they, too, are inconsistent at times (160, 182, 220).

Disciplinary methods

Methods of controlling the behavior of adolescents can be roughly divided into three systems: the authoritarian, the democratic, and the permissive. See Figure 12-3. The systems differ markedly in the way they attempt to control behavior and, as a result, have different effects on the adolescent. Box 12-4 describes the three systems and explains their differences (12, 36, 49, 65, 79, 160).

Which of the three systems of control will be used during adolescence depends largely on which was used when the adolescent was a *child*. If his parents believed that authoritarian control was the best method of bringing up children, or if he went to a school where authoritarian control was used, the chances are that he will be subjected to similar control as an adolescent.

Disciplinary methods vary according to where the family lives, its size, its socioeconomic status, and many other factors (49, 65, 232). As *family size* increases, there is usually less permissiveness for girls but more for boys (156). As the *social status* of the family improves, there is ordinarily a more democratic approach. Middle-class parents, for example, are anxious to train their children to control their own behavior so that they can win social approval. Such parents try to instill self-control in their children by stimulating feelings of guilt and shame and by threats of loss of parental love. Within families, parents tend to be more authoritarian in controlling their *daughters* than their sons—both in adolescence and in childhood (118, 173).

Evaluation of disciplinary methods The success of the method used in disciplining the adolescent must be judged not only in terms

of what effect it has on the adolescent's behavior. It must also be judged in terms of what effect it has on his attitude toward people in authority and on his motivation to try to conform to social expectations.

AUTHORITARIAN DISCIPLINE Under authoritarian discipline, Landis has commented, adolescents "receive their morality ready-made from domineering parents" (120). As a result, they are unprepared to cope with the problems adolescence brings. If they are given more freedom then than they had earlier, it comes too suddenly for them to handle; this makes them unsure of themselves. If, as is more usual, the authoritarian control used in childhood continues, they become either shy and insecure or they compensate by becoming overbold or by rebelling.

Overstrictness, which leads to the feeling that the world is hostile, causes the adolescent to reject authority and to try to assert his independence. As Frank has pointed out, "The stricter the parents, the stronger may be the revolt and the more outrageous the 'hellraising'" (57). Many adolescents, when they find that they cannot get parents or teachers to revise their method of control, leave home

Figure 12-3 Systems of discipline.

Authoritarian   Democratic   Permissive

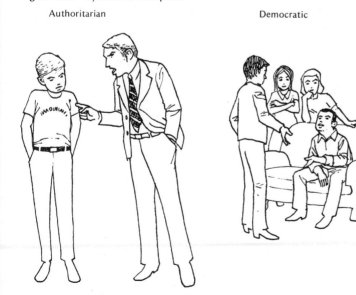

or drop out of school or both. Among girls, one of the reasons for early marriage is to escape parental domination.

PERMISSIVE DISCIPLINE   Unlimited freedom adds to the adolescent's already-present feeling of insecurity. In speaking of the effects permissiveness has on young people, Aldridge (3) has noted:

It is scarcely surprising that the offspring of this way of life, the beneficiaries of all this love and attention and self-sacrifice, should have grown up contemptuous of us or convinced that really we were dead all along and only they were alive. How could people be anything but dead or stupid who had so little regard for themselves? If we gave up our lives for them, it was only reasonable for them to suppose either that we did not value our lives or that they themselves must be terribly important to have provoked us to such fantastic generosity. So we taught them by our example and by our obsequious treatment of them to have no consideration or respect for adults and a grotesquely inflated respect for themselves.

Adolescents who have grown up in permissive homes or whose parents relax discipline when the child reaches adolescence tend to become "spoiled monsters." They are disliked by members of the peer group as well as by adults because of their lack of consideration for others and their uncooperativeness and selfishness.

Perhaps the most damaging effect of permissiveness is that it fails to develop a sense of shame or guilt which would motivate the adolescent to conform to social expectations. When he finds himself in a situation where permissiveness is not accepted, as in college or in the world of business, he will feel mistreated and misunderstood.

DEMOCRATIC DISCIPLINE Adolescent relationships with parents and teachers are far better when discipline is democratic rather than authoritarian or too permissive.

Democratic disciplinarians have greater influence over the adolescent and, in the long run, earn more of his loyalty and respect. As a result, they can guide the adolescent in situations where he feels inadequate and eliminate many of the failures an adolescent who rebels against guidance experiences. Under democratic discipline, the adolescent develops a more cooperative attitude, which is reflected in better relationships with members of the peer group as well as with those in authority.

DISCREPANCIES BETWEEN MORAL KNOWLEDGE AND MORAL BEHAVIOR

Abstract knowledge of right and wrong does not necessarily guarantee behavior consistent with this knowledge. As Crow and Crow (36) have pointed out:

Many adolescents are able to answer correctly all or most of the items on a test designed to discover extent of recognition of generally accepted moral concepts. Yet, in their behavior, at least some of these same young people fail to apply one or more of the conduct standards which, in the form of test items, were answered correctly.

Knowing that it is wrong to cheat will not necessarily keep an adolescent from cheating to improve his own grade or to help a friend. In a study of honesty, a correlation of .25 between moral knowledge and conduct was reported—a marked discrepancy (100). If discrepancies between moral knowledge and behavior are not due to ignorance, then what is responsible for them? Box 12-5 gives the

most common explanations, and they have been backed up by experimental evidence (115, 133, 147, 171, 182, 189).

All people at all ages occasionally engage in behavior which they know is wrong. As Pressey and Kuhlen have put it, "There are no separate groups of saints and sinners. Some people are sometimes honest, sometimes not, sometimes helpful, sometims not—average in virtue as in other traits" (168). Some, however, engage in behavior they know is wrong more frequently than others. Since *girls* conform more and rebel less than boys, there are fewer discrepancies between moral knowledge and behavior among girls (103, 215). However, in both sex groups, *late maturers* are more rebellious against authority than early or average maturers, and there are more discrepancies between moral knowledge and behavior in the former group (99). Normally, discrepancies between knowledge and behavior are greater in early than in late adolescence, not because the *older adolescent* has more moral knowledge but because he is less rebellious (117, 147, 171).

Very strict *authoritarian discipline* encourages discrepancies between moral knowledge and behavior. Studies of honesty in different cultures reveal that children and adolescents from societies where more democratic child-training methods prevail tend to be more honest and law abiding than those from more authoritarian societies (151, 185). But if the adolescent *feels loved*, he is far less likely to do what he knows is wrong, regardless of the system of discipline, than one who feels rejected by his family (12, 65).

Effects of discrepancies

How discrepancies between moral knowledge and behavior will affect the adolescent will depend greatly on whether his misbehavior is *known to others*. If he is caught cheating, he will try to clear himself of blame to avoid having feelings of shame. He may lie, trying to deceive others by proclaiming his innocence. Or he may project the blame on someone else, thus focusing attention on an-

Peer Group Pressures
Since adolescents are anxious to be popular, they are strongly motivated to do what the group thinks is right, even though it may conflict with their own values.

Confusion
Many adolescents are confused when the moral values learned at home differ from those of the peer group or of people who achieve success in the entertainment world.

Immature Control of Strong Urges
When adolescents have a strong urge to engage in self-satisfying but socially disapproved behavior, such as cheating or attention-getting acts, many do not know an acceptable way to attain their goal, so they use any method that will bring the desired result.

Decisions Based on Expediency and Emotional Factors
When a goal is important, adolescents often sacrifice some of their abstract moral beliefs to achieve it.

Striving for Independence
Adolescents who want to be treated as adults may break a rule or law as a form of rebellion against authority.

other person. He may say that the other student looked over his shoulder or copied the answers without his knowledge or consent. If he can convince his accuser of his innocence, he will have no reason to be ashamed.

When misbehavior is *not detected by others,* an adolescent may feel guilty and suffer a lowered self-esteem. To avoid this, he is likely to try to convince himself that the rules or laws are unreasonable, that everyone else does it, or that there are times when violating moral values is justified. He may rationalize a lie by saying that he did not want to tell the truth because another person's feelings would be hurt; therefore, lying was a "kindness" on his part. If he breaks a law, he will argue to himself that "laws are meant to be broken" or that the law is unreasonable and should be changed.

While guilt does act as an internalized policeman to keep the adolescent from repeating an act, rationalization tends to weaken its

restraining value. Only when the adolescent feels that he has narrowly escaped being caught is he likely to be restrained to any marked extent by feelings of guilt. Also rationalization is likely to encourage the adolescent to adopt more lenient moral values and attitudes than he formerly professed (9, 52).

Kinds of discrepancies

Behavior that is not in strict accordance with the standards of the group falls into two general categories: misdemeanors and juvenile delinquencies. When the divergence from the accepted pattern is slight, the misbehavior is generally referred to as a misdemeanor. A misdemeanor is willful badness, mischievousness, or disobedience of a minor sort. More serious divergences are labeled juvenile delinquency. In many instances it is difficult to draw a sharp line of distinction between the two.

The term "misdemeanor" is generally applied to behavior which is in defiance of *rules*—precepts for conduct set by parents, teachers, or other adults in authority. By contrast, "delinquency" is generally applied to misbehavior in defiance of laws—precepts for conduct set by the governing authorities of the community, the state, or the nation.

The important point to note in making this distinction is that misdemeanors are often the forerunners of delinquency. The satisfaction the adolescent derives from misdemeanors will, in time, diminish. Then, more serious misbehavior must be engaged in to provide the satisfaction formerly derived from less serious misbehavior. Studies of juvenile delinquents have stressed, almost universally, that delinquency does not "come out of the blue." Instead, the histories of juvenile delinquents stress that they have misbehaved since earliest childhood, becoming progressively more troublesome with each passing year (109, 231, 233).

MISDEMEANORS

The peak of misdemeanors usually comes between the ages of 13 and 14 years—at puberty. Gradually, during late childhood, the desire to achieve independence from adult control and to win the esteem of members of the peer group increases. This, added to the normal disequilibrium that accompanies the physical changes of puberty, is responsible for the increase in misdemeanors. If the young adolescent is able to achieve greater freedom, his troublesome behavior begins to subside. If adult authority is tightened, however, troublesome behavior will continue (44, 99, 163).

Among older adolescents who are still in college or professional training school, a second peak of misdemeanors often comes just before adulthood. Much of the blowing off of steam in pantie raids, party crashing, and other troublesome behavior during the spring months stems from a flaunting of authority and an attempt to achieve independence while still economically dependent. Older adolescents who achieve independence by entering the work world do not experience this second period of misdemeanors (73, 77).

Misdemeanors are not due to one cause only. Box 12-6 lists the most common causes of misdemeanors in adolescence (29, 61, 115, 117, 133, 171). Note how unimportant ignorance of right and wrong is.

Common forms of misdemeanors

The common misdemeanors of adolescence can be divided into three groups, depending on which rules are broken: home, school, or community.

Home misdemeanors Home misdemeanors include willful disobedience and defiance of parental authority. Many are related to social activities: where adolescents go, what they do, with whom they go, and when they return home. Other home misdemeanors include aggressive verbal attacks on siblings, temper outbursts, breaking and spilling things intentionally, rudeness to family friends and relatives, lying, minor pilfering from parents and siblings, dawdling over routine activities, shirking responsibilities, contradicting parents, and running away from home (82, 108, 189). Figure 12-4 gives the common reasons adolescents have for running away from home.

School misdemeanors Among *high school students,* the most commonly reported misdemeanors are cutting class, being tardy or truant, forging a parent's signature on an excuse note, talking and cutting up in class, cheating, failing to prepare assignments, bullying other students—especially those who are small, members of minority groups, or good students—being rude or insubordinate, smoking, drinking, fighting, throwing things lying, and engaging in illicit sex acts (40, 68, 185). An extensive study of misdemeanors in one high school has shown the relative frequency of misdemeanors in *that school* (234). This is illustrated in Figure 12-5.

College misdemeanors are similar to those in high school. In addition to the ones listed above, the most commonly reported include going to off-limits places, destroying college property, breaking dormitory rules, cutting classes, disrupting classroom work, especially when an inexperienced instructor is in charge, talking in the libraries, taking out books without signing for them, and cutting pages out of library books or writing in them. As in high school, these misdemeanors are more frequent among men than women; they are more frequent during the spring months than at other times of the year (95, 117, 127, 136).

Community misdemeanors   Most community misdemeanors are related to recreational activities and they usually occur when adolescents are not in the home or the school. Unless adolescents have home responsibilities or jobs that keep them busy after school, over weekends, and during vacations, they have plenty of leisure time to get into mischief. In many communities, adolescents complain that there is nothing to do. To stir up some excitement, they often engage in activities that are annoying to others.

Many of the recreations of *younger* adolescents, especially boys, are mischievous, though not actually in conflict with the law. Such activities as playing hooky from school, smoking, drinking, hitching rides, and behaving aggressively toward members of the opposite sex or members of a different clique stem more from the desire for excitement than from an intent to do something wrong (221, 230).

Among *older* adolescents, in junior and senior high school and in college, community misdemeanors are more serious. To stir up some excitement, for example, adolescents may engage in the suicidal game of "chicken" on the highways. Just as reckless driving provides a thrill and brings the admiration of less daring peers, so shoplifting becomes a game where the winner stirs up excitement and at the same time wins the admiration of his peers (188, 221).

Effects of misdemeanors

Even though misdemeanors lead to punishment, the adolescent may feel that the price is worth it if he wins peer attention and esteem. Unfortunately, attention and esteem are often only momentary; the peer group that laughed at his antics in class may regard the adolescent as a pest if he disturbs their study time. Soon he acquires the reputation of being a nuisance or of acting "like a kid"—a reputation that does not bring him the acceptance he was trying to win. Sensing the disapproval of his peers and knowing that he has won the disapproval of adults, the adolescent develops feelings of guilt and shame which, if too strong and too continuous, lead to poor mental health. In time, he may develop a guilt complex.

An even more damaging effect of misdemeanors is that they encourage the adolescent to establish a pattern of adjustment which will not be acceptable as he grows older. Adults, for example, will not find cutting up and bullying others amusing; on the contrary, they will find it childish and a sign of poor sportsmanship and warped values.

Like any stimulant, misdemeanors as ego boosters must be increased in frequency and intensity as time goes on. By mid-adolescence, misbehavior that gives the individual a thrill may be so serious as to be labeled delinquency. However, so long as the individual remains in an environment where his misbehavior is admired or required for acceptance, he will have little desire to learn new adjustive techniques. That is why too close adherence to peer-group morality may prevent the adolescent from learning mature patterns of behavior. Peer morality may be quite different from adult morality. Contact with adults in the home, the school, and the community, either in work or in social life, will go a long way toward showing the adolescent what the adult members of society expect. It will impress upon him the fact that adulthood is just around the corner when he, too, will be judged by the standards of adults and will stand or fall according to their judgments of him.

JUVENILE DELINQUENCY

A delinquent is a minor who has committed an unlawful act for which he would be sent to prison if he were an adult. As Perlman has pointed out, "Legally speaking, a juvenile delinquent is one who commits a delinquent act as defined by law and who is adjudicated as such by an appropriate court" (162). Although state laws vary, most states regard an adolescent as a juvenile if he is under 16 or 18 years of age; adolescents over these ages are usually tried as adults if they commit crimes.

The onset of delinquent behavior, Glueck and Glueck have reported, occurs between 9 and 10 years of age (64). Statistics from different parts of the country show that the largest number of arrests are made of boys and girls between the ages of 17 and 19 years (110, 135, 217). One of the reasons delinquency reaches its peak in middle to late adolescence is that at that time many adolescents are just learning to make social adjustments without the aid of parents or teachers.

New trends in juvenile delinquency

Today, many more *young* adolescents are delinquent than in the past and their delinquent

Figure 12-4 Why adolescents run away from home. (Adapted from J. W. Hildebrand: Why runaways leave home. *J. crim. Law Criminol. police Sci.*, 1963, **54**, 211–216. Used by permission.)

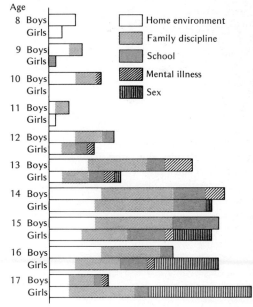

TRANSITION IN MORALITY 261

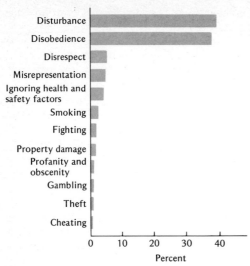

Figure 12-5 Frequency of school misdemeanors in one school. (Adapted from H. Zeitlin: High school discipline. *Calif. J. educ. Res.*, 1962, **13,** 116–125. Used by permission.)

acts are more violent and more destructive of life and property (66, 135, 154).

Under the age of 11 years, delinquent *boys* far outnumber delinquent girls. By middle adolescence, the rapid increase in girl delinquents and the relatively stable rate of increase for boys cuts down the ratio between the two sexes. Young girls are more closely supervised than boys, and so only as girls approach the end of adolescence and have less supervision is their delinquency rate anywhere near that of boys. Furthermore, only in late adolescence do the delinquent acts of girls approximate those of boys in degree of seriousness (114, 153, 154).

Delinquency is found in all *socioeconomic* groups. Even though many cases are not brought to court, the delinquent acts of adolescents of the upper classes today often rival or surpass those of the lower clases in seriousness. The main motive for the rise in affluent delinquency is to "stir up some excitement" (123, 191).

Because *school dropouts* find it difficult to get jobs, there is more delinquency among adolescents who have not finished high school than among those who graduate. The greater the *unemployment* among adolescents, the greater the increase in juvenile delinquency (69, 217).

Causes of juvenile delinquency

From earliest times, attempts have been made to explain why people engage in delinquent acts. Three general explanations have been put forward: The "prescientific mystical" explanation ascribed delinquent behavior to some force outside the individual, such as evil spirits; the early "modern particularistic" explanation attempted to ascribe a specific act to some particular factor, such as heredity, a broken home, endocrine glands, or a physical abnormality; and the "modern quasi-scientific empirical" explanation emphasizes the interrelationship of all the forces or conditions that affect behavior.

The saying, "Like father, like son," illustrates the belief that delinquency is hereditary. Similarly, to say that an adolescent has "bad blood" implies that he has inherited criminal tendencies from a family member. One widely accepted belief is that there is a "delinquent type"—an individual who is predisposed to delinquency. It has also been widely believed that delinquency was found only among "slum kids"—those from the economically and culturally deprived areas of the community—and "dumb kids"—those with low intellectual abilities.

Contradictory scientific evidence Most of the traditional beliefs about the causes of juvenile delinquency have been refuted by scientific studies of delinquents as people and of the conditions that gave rise to their antisocial behavior. There is no evidence that delinquency is hereditary, that it is a product of "bad blood," or that it runs in families. There is, however, some evidence that chromosomal abnormalities (which occur *very* rarely) may be indirectly responsible for delinquency because they lead to physical abnormalities that interfere with the individual's adjustment to the social group (54).

Unlike hereditary traits, which may appear suddenly without any apparent environmental cause, delinquency does not just happen, nor is it an overnight development. Instead, delinquents perform many acts of misconduct, often serious misdemeanors, during their preadolescent years and many show signs of poor personal and social adjustment from their preschool years. Certain "spotting symptoms" can be used to determine whether the individual is making such poor adjustments that he *may* be headed for delinquency. If he has behavior problems not characteristic of his age, such as bed wetting or temper tantrums; if he does unsatisfactory work at school and often engages in truancy; if he makes poor social adjustments not only to the peer group but to adults and older people; and if he has a poor self-concept, characterized by feelings of inadequacy, inferiority, and rejection, he is probably headed for trouble unless remedial steps are taken to correct his patterns of poor adjustment (64, 80, 233).

There is no evidence that delinquency is limited to "slum kids" or that *all* delinquents are "dumb kids." Though there are more mentally defectives among delinquents than among adolescents as a whole, many bright adolescents, even in college, come in conflict with the law while many dull ones do not (27, 60, 219).

Today it is recognized that no such thing as a "delinquent type" exists—an individual with a personality pattern that predisposes him to delinquency. Instead, studies of personality reveal that no one trait is more characteristic of delinquents than of nondelinquents (8, 16, 224). On the other hand, the evidence shows that a delinquent is an ordinary boy or girl who is a product of his environment—his family relationships and his training at home, his neighborhood, school, and associates— and some peculiarity in himself, such as low-grade intelligence or unhappiness. The patterns, attitudes, and practices of the delinquent are transmitted from person to person or from group to group through the influence of the leaders. The adolescent accepts the pattern of delinquent behavior either because of some inadequacy in himself or in his relationship to his environment or because his immedi-ate environment presents predominantly de-viant behavior models (23, 158).

While the causes of juvenile delinquency are many and varied, they may be divided roughly into "predisposing" causes and "mo-tivating" causes. Predisposing causes set the stage or pave the way for delinquent behavior. They heighten the likelihood of delinquency. Motivating causes occur in the lives of *all* adolescents. Depending upon the presence or absence and the relative strength of predis-posing causes, motivating causes drive the adolescent toward delinquent behavior.

Predisposing causes of juvenile delinquency
Some predisposing causes would be adequate alone to set the stage for delinquent behavior; most would not. As Resnick has stated, "Many factors operate to produce an antisocial in-dividual" (178). Of these many factors, the most important are given in Box 12-7 together with a brief explanation of why they predis-pose the adolescent to delinquent behavior (51, 106, 114, 197, 214, 228).

To indicate how many factors may operate to predispose a boy or girl to delinquent be-havior, Kvaraceus has suggested the following "delinquency-producing equation" composed of three complex factors working together, each contributing to the end result—juve-nile delinquency. This equation is: *factors under the skin* (personality makeup) $\times$ *factors in the culture and subculture* $\times$ *factors in com-munity attitude*. When certain conditions and variables are "right," Kvaraceus says, the prob-ability is juvenile delinquency (119).

Some adolescents are more predisposed to delinquency than others. Glueck and Glueck have suggested, for example, that the meso-morphic body build (muscular, strong, and active) is more common among delinquents than the ectomorphic (tall, slender, and rela-tively weak-muscled) or endomorphic (tall, round, and weak-muscled). Mesomorphs are more prone to delinquency, they explain, be-cause they have an excess of energy, a liking for vigorous activity, and a strong response to frustration. Being active, they encounter many frustrations. And being vigorous, they

BOX 12-7 PREDISPOSING CAUSES OF JUVENILE DELINQUENCY

*Low-grade intelligence, which is usually accompanied by lack of foresight and planning, makes it impossible for some adolescents to cope with problems their peers handle successfully.

*Physical defects and deviant sexual maturing lead to feelings of inadequacy which may be compensated for by antisocial behavior.

*Unfavorable attitudes toward school, stemming from academic or social failure, often lead to truancy or dropout and to employment difficulties that give rise to antisocial behavior.

*Confused moral values result from identification with peers whose values differ from those of the home or the larger social group.

*Social acceptance by juvenile gangs, but not by cliques and crowds that have status in the community, means that the adolescent associates too much with the wrong kind of peers. Delinquents may be popular, and even leaders, in their own groups.

*Mass media of communication are indirectly responsible for delinquency only if they reinforce the other unfavorable environmental conditions that often surround potential delinquents.

*Unfavorable home conditions, lack of respect for parents, lack of affectional family relationships, harsh discipline, and markedly deviant patterns of family living make the adolescent feel unloved and predispose him to retaliate in ways that will hurt his parents.

*The personality pattern of potential delinquents is not necessarily maladjusted, though most have unfavorable self-concepts and feelings of inadequacy and inferiority. In situations where they see an opportunity to boost their egos, they may boast or engage in attention-getting behavior. Figure 12-6 shows a comparison of personality traits of delinquents and nondelinquents.

---

react to frustrations in an aggressive manner which often leads to fighting and property damage—behavior which society classes as delinquent (63).

Some of the predisposing causes are more important for girls, and some, for boys. Boys are more group-oriented than girls. Consequently, identity with a delinquent gang and pressures from gang members are more important predispositions to delinquency in boys. Unfavorable home conditions, by contrast, play a more important role in predisposing girls to delinquency (64, 216, 218).

Motivating causes of juvenile delinquency
One or more of the predisposing causes of juvenile delinquency are present in the lives of the majority of adolescents. Motivating

causes, in collaboration with predisposing causes, produce a driving force that is too strong for the individual to resist. The result is behavior that violates the standards of conduct approved by the group to which he belongs.

In the absence of a motivating cause, the predisposing causes would not lead to delinquent behavior even though the adolescent were in a state of readiness to act; the stimulus to release the energy must be applied before the act will be committed. Confused moral values, for example, will not lead to vandalism, reckless driving, or shoplifting unless the adolescent is motivated to engage in these unsocial acts by peers who admire such behavior. If he is accepted by the larger group, behaving in a socially approved way will satisfy him even though he may not fully understand why certain standards are approved and some not.

Delinquent behavior is a response to the thwarting of *some* desire. If only some form of socially disapproved behavior will give the individual personal satisfaction, he will turn to delinquency. If, for example, a girl finds that the only way she can win popularity with boys is to engage in disapproved sex acts, she will become a sex delinquent. Should she be able to satisfy her desire for popularity by more socially approved dating behavior, she will not turn to sex delinquencies.

Studies of the motives of juvenile delinquents reveal that they are the motives of normal but immature young people, rather than of criminals. All normal well-adjusted adolescents want material possessions as status symbols; they want adventure and excitement; and they want to create the impression that they are important members of the peer group. In their desire to satisfy these motives, they may follow behavior patterns which were acceptable when they were younger but are not acceptable as they approach adulthood. The adolescent who discovered when he was younger that he could impress others by exaggeration may become a pathological liar as he grows older. Or he may be motivated to steal prestigious possessions, such as a car or clothing, to satisfy his desire to be a "big shot" in the eyes of the peer group.

Motivating causes in juvenile delinquency may be planned or impulsive. Sometimes the motive is thought out, *planned* in every detail, and carefully executed. Such delinquent acts are "goal-motivated" in the sense that the adolescent carries out the act to achieve a goal which is important to him. Stealing a car may be motivated by a desire to win approval and acceptance by members of a peer group who place high value on material possessions. Most goal-motivated acts of delinquency occur among adolescents who have been exposed to schooling in delinquent techniques, either in the home or as a member of a delinquent gang.

Impulsive motivating causes are based on frustration. The delinquent acts in a fit of anger, jealousy, or envy and bitterly regrets his act after it has been completed. An adolescent may impulsively steal a car he finds unlocked to impress members of a peer group that have rejected him. Impulsive acts are common among delinquents whose lives are full of frustrations. And as most delinquents experience many frustrations, their acts of delinquency are more often impulsive than planned. Whether planned or impulsive, the motivating causes of juvenile delinquency, as shown in Box 12-8, are many and varied (43, 62, 89, 111, 186, 218).

Forms of delinquent behavior

Delinquent acts are usually grouped into four general categories. Box 12-9 lists the categories and gives examples of each (13, 88, 91, 109, 117, 233).

During the last three decades, juvenile crime in all the major categories has increased. Boys of 10 years are now committing the kinds of burglaries and holdups that boys of 15 and

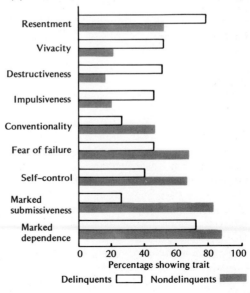

Figure 12-6 Comparison of personality traits of delinquent and nondelinquent boys. Note the more demonstrative traits of the delinquents. (Adapted from L. J. Cronbach: *Educational psychology,* 2d ed. New York: Harcourt, Brace & World, 1963. Used by permission.)

BOX 12-8 MOTIVATING CAUSES OF JUVENILE DELINQUENCY

Desire for Better Things
Dissatisfaction with what he has—often intensified by the mass media—may motivate the adolescent to steal as a quick and easy way to get the status symbols he craves.

Strong Emotions
Strong emotions, especially anger, envy, jealousy, and fear, which the adolescent has not learned to control are often touched off by some minor incident and may lead to fighting, stealing, rioting, and other delinquent behavior.

Boredom
Adolescents with too few responsibilities and too few opportunities for satisfying achievements and wholesome recreations may try to relieve their boredom by breaking laws and stirring up some excitement.

Feelings of Inferiority
The adolescent who feels inferior to his peers—physically, mentally, or socially—is motivated to break laws to prove to others as well as himself that he is not inferior. This motivation is intensified by feelings of sex inappropriateness.

Assertion of Independence
If the adolescent cannot satisfy his desire for independence by breaking home and school rules, he will break laws in the hope of gaining the feeling of independence he craves.

Desire for Social Acceptance
The desire to be accepted, especially by the "right" crowd, motivates the adolescent to follow the crowd even when this means breaking laws.

Desire for Sexual Gratification
Adolescents who feel unloved at home or who have doubts about their sex appropriateness are often motivated to engage in illicit love attachments to compensate for the love they feel they have been denied.

16 used to commit; boys of 15 and 16 are being arrested for the kinds of crimes that used to be committed by young men of 20 or 21. The three most vicious kinds of crime, assault, rape, and criminal homicide, as well as the less vicious, burglary, larceny, and auto theft, have increased greatly (126, 217).

Variations in delinquent behavior Most delinquency among adolescents under the *age of* 13 or 14 years involves offenses against property, such as robbery, burglary, larceny, auto thefts, forgery, fraud, receiving stolen property, and arson. In late adolescence, by contrast, most delinquent acts are offenses against persons—rape, sexual irregularities, intoxication, and attempts at homicide or suicide (110, 229).

Among *boys,* delinquencies consist mainly of stealing, disorderly conduct, burglary, destruction of property, acts of mischief and carelessness, traffic violations, drug use, and injuries to persons. For *girls,* the most common offenses are sexual irregularities, running away, petty stealing, ungovernability, and incorrigibility (29, 176).

Rural offenses are, for the most part, individual acts, such as trespassing on the property of others, threatening to beat up people, hanging around taverns, and being with "bad" associates. *Urban* delinquencies depend mainly on supportive peer group relationships and include such acts as thefts, gambling, truancy, drinking, and using drugs. Delinquent acts in lower *socioeconomic groups* tend to be more serious than those in middle- and upper-class groups. Therefore, the most common kinds of delinquent acts in urban and suburban areas are influenced by the predominant social class in the particular community (59, 123).

Corrective measures

Present trends in dealing with juvenile delinquency emphasize rehabilitation and prevention rather than punishment and vengeance. Prevention, it is believed, offers more hope of controlling the growth of delinquency.

Rehabilitation "Rehabilitation" means curing juvenile delinquency once it has become an established pattern of life for the adolescent. Since juvenile delinquency has no single cause, there can be no one method of cure. It has been recognized for a long time that rehabilitation must be adapted to the conditions that led to delinquency. If delinquency results from personal maladjustment, for example, the adolescent offender may be sent to a clinic for psychiatric treatment. Delinquents who show few signs of personality maladjustment but are from poor social environments may be sent to approved training schools where, it is hoped, environmental conditions will be better than those in which the delinquents have grown up (43, 170).

No matter what method of rehabilitation is used, it will not cure delinquency if the adolescent has no desire to be reformed and if he has found the pattern of his delinquent life satisfying. As Cole and Hall have pointed out, for a delinquent, often there is "*no other life that is so rewarding*" (31).

Prevention If prevention is to be successful, three essentials must be fulfilled: The danger signals indicating potential delinquency must be identified, the important predisposing causes of delinquency must be controlled, and the adolescent must be insulated against delinquency.

IDENTIFICATION OF DANGER SIGNALS Since delinquency is only a step away from nondelinquency and since adolescence is the period when the behavior problems of childhood mature into full-fledged delinquency, the most hopeful preventive measure is to try to identify the potential delinquent and socialize him so that he will fit into the group. Through the use of questionnaires, tests, and observations of behavior, potential delinquents can now be identified and steps can be taken to remedy the conditions that might give rise to later delinquency (64, 160).

Certain patterns of behavior characterize the adolescent who is particularly vulnerable to delinquency. He feels dissatisfied with

---

BOX 12-9 MAJOR CATEGORIES OF DELINQUENT BEHAVIOR

Harm to Self and Others: Assaults on people, muggings, crowd disturbances, attempts at self-destruction by stabbing, shooting, and drowning, etc.

Damage to or Misappropriation of Property: Vandalism, burglaries, larcenies, arson, shoplifting, thefts of all kinds, etc.

Ungovernability: Refusal to obey parental, academic, or legal authority (ranging from defiance to slick surface conformity), truancy, running away from home, driving without a license, buying and drinking liquor, buying and using narcotics, etc.

Acts Leading to Possible Damage to Self or Others: Speeding, use of narcotics, glue sniffing, party crashing, unauthorized use of weapons, sexual misconduct, juvenile prostitution and rape, etc.

school because of poor schoolwork, little scholastic aptitude, or repetition of grades; he plays truant or is a dropout; he belongs to no recognized or supervised peer group; he has low values and ideals; he has an unfavorable home environment; he lives in a high-delinquency neighborhood; he feels rejected in the home, school, or neighborhood; he experiences greater resentments, suspicions, destructiveness, and hostility than other adolescents of the same age; he has poor social insight and shows little sensitivity to conventions and mores; he has difficulties in interpersonal relationships; he solves problems by withdrawal or aggressiveness; he uses more ego defenses than other adolescents of the same age; he has unrealistic levels of aspiration; and he is more emotionally unstable than is usual for his age, as shown in general irritability, low tolerance level, lack of responsibility, and vacillating emotions (62, 66, 91, 208).

Of all the danger signals, the one most indicative of future delinquency is unfavorable home environment. In the investigation of potential delinquency, special emphasis should be placed on the kind of discipline used by the father, the supervision by the mother, the affection of the mother and the father for the child, and the cohesiveness of the family (64, 231).

CONTROL OF PREDISPOSING CAUSES
Most of the factors contributing to delinquency are controllable if they are recognized and dealt with in time. Dealing with one alone is not enough. Certainly it is not enough to blame *parents* for the delinquent behavior of their children. Nor is it fair, as is done in some communities, to punish parents when their children are brought to the juvenile courts. Parents do not *intentionally* train their children to be delinquent. They may not know how to bring up their children so that they will develop more mature attitudes toward their responsibilities to society. Unfavorable home conditions may be beyond the parents' control. Or affluent parents may be mistaken in thinking that it is wise or kind to give their

children a happy, carefree time to enjoy life before they settle down to the problems and responsibilities of adult living.

Schools can do much to prevent juvenile delinquency by controlling the causes that predispose the child to delinquent behavior. They can hire teachers who understand children, study the community and utilize community resources, plan a curriculum that meets the needs of youth and put it into operation, provide child guidance services for the study and treatment of personality disorders, and provide classes for slow learners so that they will not be made to feel inferior (140, 187).

One of the chief ways to control the resentment which often leads to delinquency is to *treat all offenders fairly and equally,* regardless of the socioeconomic status of their parents. Adolescents from slum homes are certain to feel resentful when they are taken to court and punished for acts which adolescents from affluent homes commit with impunity.

INSULATION AGAINST DELINQUENCY   An adolescent who is insulated against delinquency has developed internalized law-abiding norms of behavior and concepts of self which will prevent him from committing delinquencies. Even though he experiences many of the conditions that predispose the adolescent to delinquency and even though the desire to react in a delinquent manner is strong, he will not succumb (184).

By contrast, the adolescent who is not insulated against delinquency may readily succumb to temptations deriving either from his environment or from strong personal drives. As Toby has explained, "Crime arises when the temptation to violate a rule is stronger than the individual's guilt feelings and fear of social disapproval" (211).

No adolescent is born with an insulation against delinquency. What, then, insulates some adolescents against the pressures of delinquency while others succumb? The most obvious answer is fear—fear of social disapproval and rejection or fear of punishment. While unquestionably fear is an insulator against juvenile delinquency, its value is limited. If the adolescent has reason to believe that his misdeed will go undetected, fear will not act as a deterrent.

The best insulation comes from the satisfaction of basic needs in socially acceptable ways. The adolescent is provided with a bulwark against antisocial influences in the peer group and in the neighborhood if he grows up in a family where the emotional ties between the members are strong, where parents teach their children socially acceptable values and patterns of behavior, where they set a good example for the children to imitate, and where they encourage the children to achieve success in school and to avoid social groups whose behavior patterns are socially unacceptable (89, 138, 174).

How long the adolescent will remain insulated against delinquent behavior will depend mainly on his ability to maintain a favorable self-concept. As Scarpitti et al. (184) have pointed out:

Once a favorable self-image has been internalized by pre-adolescents with respect to friends, parents, school and the law, there is every reason to believe that it is as difficult to alter as a delinquent self-image. . . . Thus, internalization of a favorable self-concept is the critical variable in the containment of delinquency.

In conclusion, to cope with juvenile delinquency, the home, school, and community must provide activities in which the adolescent can feel successful and accepted and in which he can find socially approved outlets for his energies. In addition, the adolescent must develop a favorable and realistic self-concept as an insulator against delinquency. If he can see himself as he *really is* and if he is reasonably well satisfied with what he sees, he will not need to try to compensate for self-dissatisfaction by behavior that deviates from the socially approved pattern. As Cole and Hall (31) have emphasized:

The attack upon the problem is indirect and consists essentially in substituting acceptance for rejection by means of activities that are within the established social norms but are *more satisfying to the adolescent than his delinquency*.

HIGHLIGHTS OF CHAPTER 12

1. In making the transition from childish to mature morality, the adolescent must learn what the social group expects of its members and then assume responsibility for his own behavior.

2. The most common obstacles the adolescent faces in making the transition are inadequate preparation for making moral decisions, being confronted with a number of moral alternatives, conflicts in moral values, and pressures from the peer group to conform to peer rather than adult standards.

3. To make a successful transition to adult morality, the adolescent must (1) change the attitudes and values which made up his childish moral concepts so that they will conform to adult standards and (2) assume control of his own behavior.

4. The conscience is the inner controlling force that makes external restraints unnecessary. Guilt and shame act as deterrents to behavior that does not meet social expectations.

5. The role of discipline in moral development is to help the adolescent develop socially approved moral concepts, to reward him for socially approved behavior, to punish him for intentional wrongdoing, and to provide consistent social expectations as an aid in building moral values.

6. Of the three systems of discipline commonly used in controlling adolescent behavior—authoritarian, democratic, and permissive—the democratic produces the best results from the point of view of the adolescent's personal and social development.

7. Discrepancies between moral knowledge and moral behavior in adolescence are due most commonly to peer group pressures, confusion about moral values, immature control of strong urges, decisions based on expediency and emotional factors, and striving for independence.

8. The effects of discrepancies between moral knowledge and behavior depend, to some extent, on whether the adolescent's misbehavior is known to others, how others react to the discrepancies, and how the adolescent himself feels about them.

9. Discrepancies between moral knowledge and behavior may be (1) misdemeanors, or willful misbehavior, resulting from breaking rules established by parents, teachers, and other adults in authority or (2) juvenile delinquency, or willful misbehavior resulting from breaking laws estab-

lished by the governing authorities of the community, state, or nation.

10. Adolescent misdemeanors are most often due to ignorance of right and wrong, frustrations, bids for attention, desire for excitement and thrill, and assertion of independence.

11. Juvenile delinquency is common among adolescents of all socioeconomic levels and both sexes. It results from a combination of predisposing causes and motivating causes. The former include low-grade intelligence, physical defects and deviant sexual maturing, unfavorable attitudes toward school, confused moral values, social acceptance primarily by members of a deviant social group, the influence of mass media, unfavorable home conditions, and an unfavorable personality pattern. Motivating causes include desire for better things, strong but uncontrolled emotions, boredom, feelings of inferiority, assertion of independence, and a desire for social acceptance and sexual gratification.

12. Corrective measures to deal with juvenile delinquency include rehabilitation, or curing juvenile delinquency once it has become an established pattern of life, and prevention. Prevention involves identifying the common danger signals, controlling the predisposing causes, and insulating the adolescent against delinquency.

Chapter 13

Transition in Sexuality

Transition to adult sexuality involves more than the physical changes that occur at puberty, for the adolescent must develop new interests and attitudes and learn new patterns of behavior. In cultures that prepare the child and adolescent for adulthood, the transition is made with relative ease and speed. In the United States and in many other cultural groups where sex education is taboo, limited, or faulty and where the roles of the two sexes are similar, the transition is often difficult and requires the major part of the adolescent years.

To achieve adult sexuality, the adolescent must master several major tasks. He must acquire knowledge about sex and the approved sex roles to motivate him to behave in a socially approved manner, learn the approved patterns of sex behavior, achieve socially approved values as a guide to the selection of a life mate, learn to express "love" for another, and learn to play the approved role for members of his sex. Each of the major tasks will be discussed in detail.

MEANING OF ADULT SEXUALITY

Normally, "adult sexuality" means *heterosexuality* in which sexual interest and affection are focused on members of the opposite sex. In early adolescence, sexual feelings and drives are diffuse and can be fixed on anyone or anything the adolescent has an emotional attachment for. How these feelings and drives will be expressed depends largely on learning and the influence of social pressures. Not until the diffuse sexual feelings and drives are focused on members of the opposite sex and lead to patterns of behavior normally associated with these feelings and drives can the adolescent be considered a heterosexual person or one who has achieved adult sexuality.

Heterosexual interest in childhood is expressed primarily in competition. In adolescence, by contrast, it is accompanied by a strong desire to win the approval of members of the opposite sex.

In early adolescence, this romantic interest is expressed in erotic daydreams, talking about sex and members of the opposite sex, concern about appearance, and crude ways of showing off to attract the attention of members of the opposite sex. As Crow and Crow (40) have explained:

Girls may become shy in the presence of their former boy pals. They may "moon" over the pictures of popular motion-picture actors or television stars. Little cliques of preadolescent girls may display silly, giggling attitudes in the presence of boys, or may seem to evince an attitude of superiority to boys of their own age.

Later this interest shows itself in a desire to dance, to have dates, and to engage in other sociosexual activities.

Conditions contributing to heterosexuality

Heterosexuality is influenced by the *glandular condition* of the individual. Gonadal insufficiency delays the development of sexual responsiveness. Testosterone stimulates sexual responsiveness in both males and females. Pituitary and thyroid deficiencies inhibit sexual responsiveness (96, 140).

Social factors largely determine how heterosexuality will be expressed. Since a strong sex drive is commonly regarded as a sign of masculinity, adolescent boys are motivated to engage in all kinds of heterosexual behavior (96, 174). Girls who look upon marriage as a way of establishing themselves as women are predisposed to date and engage in expressions of love at an earlier age than girls who find other avenues of self-expression rewarding. As Duvall states, "Being in love as a teenager appears, in some cases, to be an escape hatch for those who feel that other doors to the future are closed" (49).

Mass media focus the adolescent's attention on the importance of heterosexual relationships in our culture. Popular songs, movies, television, and literature help the adolescent to identify with the role of lover or loved one and to learn the approved patterns of romantic behavior (78, 166).

Boys respond to more stimuli and are more

easily aroused sexually than girls. While the reasons for these differences have not been fully determined, the following *speculations* are commonly given: Boys have a stronger innate sex drive, the sensory capacity for stimulation is greater in boys, and the sociosexual acculturation of boys is such as to encourage them to respond more openly to sexual feelings and drives. Of the three speculations, the third is most widely accepted (96, 146, 174).

The *age* at which sexual maturing occurs and the *speed* with which it takes place influence the onset and intensity of heterosexual interests. Persons who mature early, for example, not only show an early interest in members of the opposite sex, but they may settle down into a mature relationship of engagement and marriage before they are out of their teens. While delay in sex interest is not apt to have serious permanent consequences, it may mean a relatively unhappy adolescence (86, 140).

Learning to be a heterosexual person will not take place in a vacuum; *opportunities* must be provided for learning, and the adolescent must have the *motivation* necessary to take advantage of the opportunities given. Two environmental conditions are essential to the successful establishment of heterosexual relationships. *First,* there must be a sufficient number of members of the opposite sex of appropriate age, intellectual status, and personality adjustment available to give the adolescent an opportunity to select congenial companions and to have pleasurable social contacts with them. *Second,* there must be an encouraging, sympathetic, and helpful attitude on the part of parents and other adults. If he knows that he has someone to turn to for advice and encouragement, the adolescent is better able to tackle the problems that heterosexual adjustment gives rise to.

An environment in which the sexes are segregated not only increases the adolescent's difficulty in making heterosexual social contacts, but, what is more damaging, it tends to develop in the adolescent a feeling of inadequacy in situations involving members of the opposite sex.

Problems in making the transition

Making the transition from childish to adult sexuality is never easy. In a culture where approved patterns of behavior in heterosexual relationships are changing rapidly, the problems that must be faced are greatly intensified. As Reiss has said, "What was done by a female in 1925 as a rebel and a deviant can be done by a female [today] as a conformist" (147).

Box 13-1 lists the most important transition problems (26, 34, 60, 99, 135, 142). Some of the problems are more troublesome for boys while others are more troublesome for girls. For example, since girls are more harshly judged than boys for deviation from the culturally approved moral-sex standards, problems in this area tend to be more numerous and more serious for girls.

KNOWLEDGE ABOUT SEX AND SEX ROLES

The first important developmental task that must be mastered in the transition to mature sexuality is the acquisition of knowledge about sex and the socially approved roles for members of both sexes. Such knowledge is necessary before the adolescent can make good adjustments to members of the other sex, before he can understand the duties and responsibilities as well as the pleasures and satisfactions of marriage, and before he can play the socially approved sex role. While most boys and girls have considerable information about sex before they reach adolescence, this information is limited and some of it is false.

Typically, the adolescent is preoccupied with sex. He daydreams about it, discusses it with his intimate friends, trades information with his clique mates and other associates, reads everything he can get about sex, and spends much of his time when alone exploring and stimulating different areas of his body to see what sensations he can elicit. Many boys and girls claim that "sex really gets on your mind." Box 13-2 shows some of the major areas of adolescent interest in sex (28, 29, 146, 173, 179, 202).

Sources of information

The usual sources of information about sex are parents, age-mates, books, and siblings. Much information comes from the peer group grapevine and from dirty stories and jokes. Girls get most of their first information about sex from their mothers and girl friends. However, as Figure 13-1 shows, at the time of the menarche many girls have no knowledge about intercourse and many more lack knowledge considered adequate and important for marriage (34, 173).

Friends, dirty stories, and the grapevine are the major sources of first information for boys. When they get their information from parents, mainly fathers, it tends to be concentrated on the origin of babies and the dangers of venereal diseases (29, 167, 202).

Schools are assuming more and more responsibility for sex education. They offer specialized instruction, aided by films and group discussions, or they include the material in science courses. Sometimes the instruction is given by outside doctors and nurses and sometimes by teachers and nurses on the school staff (28, 116).

When young adolescents cannot get adequate information about sex, they may try to satisfy their curiosity by experimentation—manual manipulation, direct observation of persons of the other sex, exhibitionistic sex play, attempts at intercourse, and oral contacts. Boys and girls engage in kissing, manual exploration, and manipulation by the boy of the girl's breasts and genitals. The boy may attempt intercourse, especially if he is dating a younger girl or one who seems receptive. Kissing games are common, as is masturbation. Among older adolescents, petting and attempts at intercourse are common ways of satisfying curiosity. These will be discussed in more detail later in the chapter.

Another way to get information about sex

and love is to write to newspaper and magazine columnists. The peak age for doing so is 18 years. Surprisingly, almost three times as many boys write for advice as girls. The most common problems they seek information about are birth control and approved forms of sexual behavior. Boys are mainly concerned about their own sexual behavior and genital adequacy; girls ask questions mainly about reproduction, their own responsiveness, and their anatomy, such as the size of their breasts (87, 144).

How much and how accurate the adolescent's information is depends largely on its source. In general, the adolescent whose parents are well educated has more information and more accurate information. However, the adolescent's willingness to discuss sexual matters with his parents determines how much information he will receive from them. On the whole, the adolescent with one or both foreign-born parents appears to get more "wholesome" information about sex and to feel more adequately prepared for marriage than the one whose parents are American-born. Adolescents who receive their information from books or from sex education courses in school or church have information that is superior in quality and quantity to that of their peers and they are usually more satisfied with it (28, 48, 92).

Evaluation of sources of information

In any evaluation of the sources of sex information, the adolescent's reactions are the crux of the matter. Adults have marked differences of opinion about who should assume responsibility for sex education. Only when the adolescent's reactions to the information he receives from different sources are taken into consideration can a meaningful evaluation be made.

Parents   Many adolescents feel that their parents should "tell them about sex." Some feel that the school should provide supplementary instruction. Many feel that the information they get from their parents is inadequate or faulty.

Parents are apt to give information about sex in an embarrassed, half-ashamed way that both upsets and embarrasses the adolescent. If the relationship between the adolescent and his parents is at all strained or uneasy, communication will be difficult. Boys, especially, are likely to face this problem.

The quality of home instruction depends not only upon the knowledge the parents have but on their willingness and ability to impart this information. Far too many parents believe they have fulfilled their duty when they tell their children about procreation, when they prepare their daughters for menstruation and their sons for nocturnal emissions, and when they warn them against the dangers of sexual activities. In reality, this leaves large gaps in the knowledge the adolescent would like to have.

BOX 13-2   AREAS OF INTEREST IN SEX

Physiological Changes
The young adolescent is concerned about his physiological changes and those of his age-mates.

Meaning of Love
After puberty, the adolescent becomes interested in the meaning of love—its emotional and social aspects as well as the physical.

Forms of Expression of Love
With interest in members of the opposite sex comes an interest in socially approved expressions of love which will also be satisfying and safe.

Meaning of Marriage and Parenthood
Interest in marriage centers more on the physical aspects than on the economic, in-law, and other problems. Most adolescents are concerned about how to avoid parenthood.

Sex Roles
Interests in socially approved sex roles is more related to dating than to marriage and parenthood.

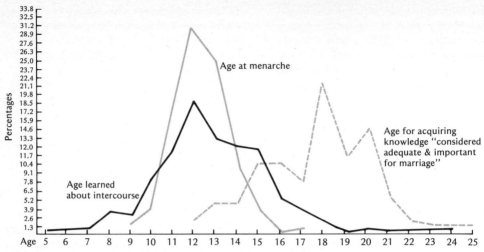

Figure 13-1 Ages at which girls are usually given information about intercourse and marriage. (Adapted from G. Shipman: The psychodynamics of sex education. *Family Coordinator*, 1968, **17**, 3–12. Used by permission.)

Schools Adolescents who feel that their parents cannot give them adequate sex instruction consider the school the most desirable source of information. They claim that the best instruction comes from class discussions, lectures, and suggested readings. As to when the school should initiate instruction, some adolescents feel that it should begin in elementary school; the majority believe it should be given in junior or senior high school, or both.

Most educators feel that sex education should be more than just "reproductive education." It should, they believe, be all-inclusive, covering the psychological and emotional aspects of sex as well as the physical. It should include information about intersex associations, sex roles, pregnancy and its possible complications, childbirth with its potential hazards, the use of contraceptives, the prevention and treatment of venereal disease, the causes and control of deviant sex behavior, especially masturbation and homosexuality, the dangers of abortion, and a host of other related problems. In addition, they believe that more stress should be placed on the development of values in selecting a mate and on preparation for meeting the problems of marriage and parenthood.

Mass media Books, educational films, and magazine articles written by specialists in sex education give both correct and adequate information about sex. However, to romantic, idealistic adolescents, these sources may seem cold and impersonal and the facts too "scientific." Information gleaned from romantic stories, movies, television, or the comics will have more appeal. But the adequacy of this information depends on the adolescent's *interpretation* of what is said or done. The information can readily be distorted—and it often is.

Some of the sex information adolescents get from the peer grapevine is based on facts learned from reliable books and magazine articles; much of it comes from other forms of mass media or from their own experimentation. Not only is such information likely to be distorted by misinterpretations, but, even worse, it is usually colored by the teller's own attitudes toward sex. And since the adolescent who gets personal satisfaction from being in the limelight by virtue of his ability to impart such information may not have his facts straight, much of that information will probably be exaggerated and distorted.

Experimentation Information about sex gained from experimentation is usually correct but it is often badly distorted by the unfavorable attitudes of the experimenter. Knowing that social attitudes toward premarital sex are often very unfavorable may lead the adolescent to feel guilty; if he is caught in his experimentation, he will also feel ashamed. Furthermore, he will be afraid that experimentation will lead to "trouble"—pregnancy for the girl or venereal disease for either girl or boy. In commenting on the dangers of experimentation and the effect on the adolescent's attitudes, Remmers and Radler (150) have written:

Sheer curiosity leads little children to investigate their bodies and those of their playmates. . . . The same experimentation after puberty is another matter. To discourage it completely might prevent teenage boys and girls from ever developing healthy relationships with the other sex. On the other hand, to allow it to go to its logical extreme can cause tragedy, since adolescents are no longer children. Boys can become fathers and girls can become pregnant. The two striking things about sex before marriage are these: (1) it's fun, and (2) it's dangerous. The real solution to the sex problem of the teenage boy or girl is to avoid the dangers but not to miss out on all the fun.

ATTITUDES TOWARD SEX

The second developmental task in the transition to adult sexuality is the development of favorable attitudes. The adolescent's feelings toward sex per se, toward members of the opposite sex, and toward the socially approved roles each sex is expected to play in the culture—all are involved.

Favorable attitudes will lead to good heterosexual adjustments, just as unfavorable attitudes will lead to poor adjustments. Once an attitude has been learned, whether favorable or not, it is likely to remain with the adolescent for life. As Mussen et al. (134) have stated:

No amount of information or reassurance in preadolescence or adolescence will enable the child to adopt a healthy attitude toward sexuality if in the preceding years he has been taught to fear sexual responses. . . . Clinicians have found that when unfavorable sexual attitudes have been built up . . . it is extremely difficult, and sometimes impossible,

to shift them through the use of rational advice given in adolescence. Even extensive psychotherapy may fail to change attitudes which have become too deeply ingrained.

The adolescent's attitudes toward sex are influenced by a number of conditions that trace their origin to his early childhood experiences. Box 13-3 spells out the three most influential conditions (21, 98, 101, 112, 151, 158).

Most boys and girls must change their attitudes radically if they are to achieve a well-adjusted heterosexual adulthood. Since girls reach puberty sooner than boys, their attitudes improve sooner. Girls generally show signs of changed attitudes toward boys during their thirteenth year. However, not until 14 or 15 years of age do they prefer boy friends to girl friends.

Boys begin to show a change in their attitudes a year or two later than girls. The change is from dislike to indifference, however, rather than to accepting and liking. When boys do show a positive attitude toward girls, they are likely to be interested in a *particular* girl, not girls in general.

Throughout adolescence, boys show a progressively better opinion of themselves, of members of the male sex, and of the masculine role; girls, by contrast, have less favorable attitudes toward their own sex, toward the feminine role, and toward themselves as individuals. While girls' attitudes toward their own sex are deteriorating, their attitudes toward the opposite sex are improving. Even though boys' attitudes toward girls and the feminine role improve, there is little evidence that they change radically for the better as adolescence progresses. Boys may *behave* in a socially approved manner when they are with girls but this more often than not is, as McKee and Sherriffs have pointed out, a "veneer of equalitarianism overlying their more firmly established beliefs" (121).

Causes of changed attitudes

While the sex drive, which strengthens with the maturing of the sex organs, is in part re-

BOX 13-3 CONDITIONS AFFECTING ATTITUDES TOWARD SEX

Kind of Sex Information
Adolescents who receive forthright and adequate information from parents or from the school usually have favorable attitudes toward sex. A conspiracy of silence or an overemphasis on "don'ts" leads to unfavorable attitudes. Information based on smutty stories or pornography also encourages unfavorable attitudes.

Attitudes of Significant People
Attitudes developed during the early formative years reflect the parents' attitudes. Even when social contacts broaden, the basic attitudes formed in the home continue to be dominant.

Early Experiences
Adolescents will have unfavorable attitudes toward sex and toward members of the opposite sex if, as children, they experienced parental and teacher favoritism for males, were pressured to avoid members of the opposite sex, or were either the victims or perpetrators of antisocial behavior based on their sex, such as teasing, bullying, and rude or derogatory comments. Boys will develop attitudes of smug superiority in these circumstances, while girls will feel resentful and inadequate.

sponsible for changes in attitudes, social pressures and social expectations are also responsible. Members of the two sexes are subject to quite different social pressures. These tend to accelerate the move toward an improved attitude among girls and to delay it among boys.

Being popular with members of the opposite sex is more prestigious for girls than for boys. As was stressed earlier, for a girl, popularity depends on social success with members of the opposite sex; for a boy, athletic success is the major source of prestige.

Parents, especially mothers, pressure their daughters to date and to marry early. Mothers do not want to "lose" their sons, however, and fathers do not want them to marry early and assume responsibilities that might interfere with their chances of getting ahead in the world.

Members of the peer group pressure the young adolescent boy to avoid girls. Having taken the stand for many years that girls are silly and a waste of time, they find it hard to change their attitudes. Were more prestige associated with dating, these peer influences

might be less severe. And, finally, the boy finds it difficult to change his attitudes because he has verbalized his negative feelings about girls so loudly over the years that it is now ego-deflating to have to admit that he has changed. Parental and peer comments may delay even further the time when he will *show* his changed attitude and get up the courage to appear in public with a girl (101, 112, 135, 166).

Importance of changed attitudes

The importance of changed attitudes in achieving good heterosexual development can best be shown by considering what happens when childhood attitudes are *not* replaced by more mature ones. A *lag* in making the change leads to many social problems. Were the lag limited to the year or slightly more of difference in age of sexual maturing of the two sexes, it would be of less consequence. However, as boys cling to their childhood dislike of girls, they force girls to play a more aggressive role in heterosexual relationships than is approved in our culture. The result is that girls often acquire the reputation of "chasing the boys"—a reputation that dims much of the prestige the girl would otherwise acquire from her social successes.

The neutral attitude boys later develop toward girls leads to *keen* competition among girls to win the attention and interest of boys. As a result, girls form less close and less permanent friendships with members of their own sex than boys do. Even more seriously, they often break friendships with girls who are congenial because they are afraid boys might judge the other girls unfavorably.

Some of the loneliness and maladjustment of adult women may be traced to the keen competitiveness of adolescent girls for masculine attention. Not only does it become a habitual pattern of adjustment for many girls but it leads to the breaking of friendships at a crucial age in friendship formation. If girls carry over into adulthood the attitude of suspicion toward members of their own sex which is an accompaniment of competitiveness, they will form few friendships with other women. This is in direct contrast to the more favorable attitude boys have toward their pals and to the stronger and more stable friendships boys form with one another during the adolescent years.

Unquestionably the most serious effects of the lag in changing attitudes are on the *personalities* of boys and girls in adolescence and on their *life adjustments*. Since boys continue to regard boys more favorably than they regard girls, they treat girls as if they were inferior. Shainess writes, "Men have a self-serving perspective on women. They are a devalued subgroup" (172). This attitude leads to a "female inferiority complex" and a "male superiority complex." As a result, boys tend to overvalue themselves and their abilities and girls tend to undervalue themselves.

These complexes also affect the *relationships* of members of *the two sexes* in social, business, and family life—the three most important areas of life for American adults. Like other minority-group members, women often assume a derogatory attitude toward members of their own group—in this case, other women. Since men regard women as the "inferior

sex," they give women few opportunities to engage in activities with them on an equalitarian basis. Like members of any minority group, women resent this treatment. The resentment, in turn, plays havoc with their loyalty to their employers in the business world and to their happiness in marriage.

PATTERN OF APPROVED HETEROSEXUAL BEHAVIOR

Learning to behave in a socially approved way in heterosexual relationships is the third developmental task in achieving adult sexuality. In mastering this task, adolescents pass through fairly definite and predictable stages. Parents often pressure their children to pass through these stages rapidly and to achieve adult heterosexuality at an earlier age than was regarded as normal in the past. As each stage offers learning opportunities that prepare the adolescent for the next stage, telescoping the stages deprives him of important learning opportunities and leaves him ill-prepared for the problems the next stage gives rise to.

Since the child has little experience in heterosexual relationships, he has much to learn about the approved patterns of behavior when he reaches adolescence. Even with the best possible guidance, the transition is never easy. The pattern of heterosexual relationships and the characteristic behavior at seven stages is illustrated in Figure 13-2. Note the gradual transition to more mature forms of behavior and the fact that, when boys and girls reach adolescence, they must learn altogether new patterns of heterosexual behavior. Box 13-4 describes phases through which adolescents pass in the development of approved heterosexual behavior (5, 47, 62, 120, 122, 161).

Evaluation of phases

Viewed individually, each phase in the developmental pattern leading to adult heterosexuality as expressed in marriage is indicative of sexual immaturity. However, each phase contributes to the adolescent's progress toward maturity.

Infancy–babyhood
Boy and girl interested
only in themselves

Early childhood
Seek companionship
of other children,
regardless of sex

About age 8
Boys prefer to
play with boys,
girls with girls

Ages 10 to 12
Antagonism shown
between sex groups

Ages 13 to 14
Girls become inter-
ested in boys, try to
attract their attention;
boys aloof

Ages 14 to 16
Boy group also shows
interest in girls;
some individuals
begin to pair off

Ages 16 to 17 on
"Going out in couples"
becomes general

Figure 13-2 The seven stages in boy-girl relationships. (Adapted from A. Scheinfeld: *The new you and heredity*. Philadelphia: Lippincott, 1961. Used by permission.)

Many adolescents encounter two difficulties as they pass through these phases. *First,* they may remain too long in one phase before going on to the next. An adolescent who derives so much satisfaction from a crush that he finds age-mates of the opposite sex unattractive may delay his progress to the puppy love phase too long. By the time he loses interest in the older person and wants to shift to a peer relationship, he will seem immature compared with peers who have made normal progress through the puppy love phase and are now dating.

Second, the adolescent may pass through the phases too quickly. This may happen when a late maturer tries to skip a phase and catch up with his age-mates or when parental or peer pressures do not allow the adolescent ade- quate time to complete one phase satisfac- torily before moving on to the next. A late maturer, for example, may just be ready to begin dating when his peers have started to go steady. If he follows their pattern, he will be deprived of some of the learning opportunities that dating offers.

Since each phase contributes to the achievement of adult sexuality, and each has drawbacks if it is lingered in too long, the phases will be evaluated individually.

Crushes Having a crush helps the young adolescent in two of the developmental tasks that every adolescent must master: (1) gaining independence, and (2) deciding what sort of person he is or wants to be, that is, forming his own identity. Too much parental influence may cause the young adolescent to forfeit any individual identity and to model himself as much as possible on the parental pattern. Or it may cause him to "burst out in unhappy rebellion," doing just the opposite of what his parents want. The influence of someone outside the home will prevent either of these from happening. In discussing the value of a crush, Gallagher (62) writes:

Many—perhaps most—adolescent boys and girls,

BOX 13-4 PHASES IN HETEROSEXUAL BEHAVIOR

Crushes and Hero Worship
A strong affectional attachment for an older individual with whom the adolescent has personal contacts is a "crush"; such an attachment for an individual whom the adolescent admires from afar is "hero worship."

Puppy Love
In puppy love—so-called because it is characterized by teasing, roughhousing, and other backhanded ways of showing mutual interest—the adolescent shows affection for someone approximately his own age.

Dating
Unlike "courtship," dating provides pleasant social experiences with no permanent commitment. It begins as a part of clique behavior and in time becomes a single-pair activity, though the members of a pair usually come from the same clique.

Going Steady
After a period of dating different girls, the boy selects one he particularly likes as "his girl." Then both are expected to refrain from dating anyone else.

Pinning
Pinning, a preliminary to engagement, is used by some adolescents to indicate that they are thinking of marriage. It lacks the finality of engagement, and no formal announcement is made. As a token of their understanding, the boy gives the girl a pin with some romantic attachment.

Engagement
If the pinned couple decide to marry, the boy gives the girl an engagement ring. The engagement period is usually shorter than the pinning period.

Marriage
Marriage consists of the union and cohabitation of two people of the opposite sex with a permanent commitment to each other and to their children. If the two people are students or are financially dependent on their parents, the marriage is labeled "early."

though they are perfectly normal and are not being overwhelmed by the changes in their emotions which are part of growing up, would benefit considerably in their emotional development were they to have feelings of admiration and respect for some stable adult outside their family circle. They need such a person because they are uncertain and lack confidence in themselves. At this time the confidence that this person, to whom they have not had close ties, can give will enable them to achieve greater independence more smoothly and gain the knowledge of where they are going that we wish for them.

On the other hand, family friction can result if the adolescent fixes his affection on someone outside the home and talks constantly about that person's good qualities while making hypercritical or derogatory comments about parents or other family members. A boy may belittle his father's business success, for example, but admire and applaud his athletic coach.

Hero worship Hero worship may encourage the adolescent to strive for success; it helps him to formulate values and set goals; it lifts him up when his spirit bogs; it steadies his vacillating conduct and makes for consistency of action. Equally important, in hero worship the adolescent is attempting to develop a concrete picture of the personality he dreams of for himself (161).

If the adolescent's heroes are ill-chosen, if they are not the right ones for him to copy, the effects of hero worship will be harmful. Furthermore, a hero is likely to represent ideals of conduct that, when applied to the adolescent's peers, will make them appear crude and unsophisticated. This may lead the adolescent to take a hypercritical and reforming attitude toward the person he is dating. The result may be a broken romance.

Puppy love Through early experiences with members of the opposite sex, the adolescent learns to appraise them somewhat. He comes to like or dislike certain traits and, as a result, becomes more selective. He learns social skills he had no need for when most of his relationships were with members of his own sex, and he learns what is socially acceptable behavior among members of his own group. Equally important, if all goes well, he builds up self-confidence and security. As this occurs, he develops a more restrained, more polished, and more mature form of behavior.

Since puppy love is very time-, energy-, and attention-consuming, the adolescent may become so engrossed in a romance that he neglects both schoolwork and home responsibilities. This may lead to parental criticism and strained parent-child relationships.

Dating Critics of youthful dating argue that boys and girls who date waste valuable time that might better be spent on their academic work and on preparation for their vocations; that they become so preoccupied with looks and pleasure seeking that they neglect home, community, and other responsibilities; that they—especially girls—tend to develop a competitiveness which militates against good social adjustments; that, with chaperonage a thing of the past, they are too inexperienced to cope with the sexual temptations that dating may give rise to; that they can ill afford the expenses of dating and may drop out of school or college to take a job; and that they spend so little time with their families that family solidarity is impaired (47, 80, 120).

Proponents of adolescent dating point out that, on the whole, its advantages outweigh its disadvantages. Box 13-5 lists the advantages most often reported (80, 120, 143, 147, 176, 205).

Some adolescents, but boys more than girls, date infrequently or not at all. They may be so absorbed in some other activity, such as sports or studies, and gain so much recognition in it that dating seems time-consuming, trivial, and irrelevant. Or, they may be so physically immature that they feel disqualified for the dating game, in which physical readiness for sex is expected. They may lack the clothes and money needed to date. Adolescents who do not date are often slightly maladjusted emotionally and socially reticent. As success in dating depends upon accepting the values of the peer group, adolescents who disapprove of dancing, kissing, or moderate necking are outside the peer culture and probably find few acceptable dating partners.

Nondaters are at a disadvantage in our culture because the social life of adolescence is organized around paired groups. Adolescents who do not date in their high school days do not learn how to behave in social situations with members of the opposite sex. By late adolescence, when they go to college or to work, they feel inadequate and frustrated and turn to more introverted forms of recreation. Self-doubts about their normality and an unfavorable "loner" reputation can play havoc with their personal and social adjustments.

Going steady For both boys and girls, going steady has advantages as well as disadvantages. For girls, the advantages usually predominate, while for boys, the reverse is true. If going steady forces an adolescent into a marriage he does not want *at the time* because he is not emotionally or economically ready for it, the disadvantages are greater than the advantages. Box 13-6 lists some of the pros and cons of going steady during adolescence (22, 56, 65, 106, 154, 158).

Pinning and engagement Because of three very common factors, pinning and engagement are more likely to bring adolescents disillusionment and unhappiness than to prepare them for a successful marriage. These factors are romanticism, role playing, and sexual intimacies.

Romanticism, or the propensity to see the loved one and the marital state in idealized terms, has been heightened in the American culture by the influence of mass media of communication. Girls tend to fall victim to this romantic complex about courtship and marriage more than boys. And because of their greater romanticism, girls are likely to face greater disillusionment and disappointment when they make the transition from engagement to marriage (42, 101, 159). As one young bride said, "It is a big step from the bridal veil to the garbage pail."

Romanticism accounts, in part, for the alarming increase in disillusionment and divorce among those who marry early. Hobart (76) has stated:

Such prevalent disillusionment suggests the existence of important unrealism generating influences in the courtship process. The widespread emphasis on romanticism in the American culture—the so-called romantic cult—which appears to be particularly associated with advanced courtship may in effect be preparing engaged couples for inevitable disillusionment in marriage.

Role playing during the pinning and engagement periods, or an attempt to behave in a manner considered appropriate for one's sex, is the second factor that makes the achievement of adult heterosexuality difficult. Adolescents become familiar with the stereotypes of the "perfect" wife and the "perfect" husband through the mass media. They then expect the person they marry to conform to them (52, 76). To fulfill the stereotype of the

---

BOX 13-5   ADVANTAGES OF DATING

*Tempers highly romantic and unrealistic ideas about love and members of the opposite sex

*Provides experience in adjusting to others in different situations

*Helps to develop poise, self-confidence, and emotional balance

*Reduces emotional excitement on meeting and associating with members of the opposite sex

*Provides opportunities for having a good time

*Enlarges the circle of acquaintances from which a mate may eventually be selected

*Defines the roles of members of the two sexes and the male-female relationship

*Gives the adolescent recognition and prestige in his own group and thus helps to establish his group status

perfect lover, the adolescent boy may write romantic love letters to his girl, bring her gifts, and try to satisfy her every wish. The girl, in turn, plays a role, preparing special foods when her boyfriend comes to her home for a meal and purring over every baby she sees.

Once the engagement has been announced and the date for the wedding set, posing and role playing usually decrease and the characteristic behavior and personalities of the individuals usually emerge. If romantic role playing were permanent, it would not endanger a marriage. But as it is generally only temporary, it is often a source of disillusionment. It can jeopardize a marriage at any age. The danger is greatest in adolescence, however, when romanticism is at its peak. Disillusionment affects both boys and girls, thus increasing the chances that youthful marriages will end in the divorce courts.

Sexual intimacies during the courtship period may be an obstacle to good heterosexual adjustment in marriage. This will be discussed in more detail later in the chapter. However, there is evidence that many adolescent marriages are entered into because of suspected or diagnosed pregnancies. Such marriages—"shotgun marriages," as they were formerly called—are often accompanied by feelings of guilt on the part of the girl and resentment on the part of the boy. This explains to some extent the high divorce rate in teen-age marriages (22, 111, 158).

Early marriage   Short engagements and early marriages are, in part at least, responsible for the rise in the divorce rate and other indications of marital failure: desertions, separations, problem children, juvenile delinquency, and family friction (5, 136, 180). Box 13-7 describes some of the many reasons for the great incidence of failure in early marriages (6, 22, 75, 136, 158).

In spite of the risks involved, some early marriages are never threatened by separation or divorce. While the conditions that contribute to their success vary, five stand out: approval and encouragement from parents; freedom from serious financial difficulties, owing to the ability of the partners to earn money or the willingness of parents to help *without* imposing a state of dependency; a sincere desire to marry early in the belief that growing up with one's children is essential to marital happiness; absence of compulsion to marry because of suspected or diagnosed pregnancy; and an understanding of the realities of marriage and parenthood—a willingness to accept the bad with the good or, as the marriage vow says, "for better or for worse."

ESTABLISHING VALUES IN MATE SELECTION

The adolescent's fourth task in making the transition to adult sexuality is to establish values that will ensure a wise decision in selecting a life mate. The adolescent must learn to judge what is important and what is relatively unimportant not only for the present but for a lifetime.

From *dating* and *going steady*, the adolescent discovers that some of the qualities he valued in a date are not the most important qualities for a potential mate. Some qualities highly valued for dates are illustrated in Figure 13-3. At 14 years of age, for example, girls want boys who are good looking; at 17, they put intelligence ahead of looks. Boys at 14 like "cuties"; at 17, they regard common sense and social skills as of greater importance. When adolescents begin to think seriously of marriage, as Box 13-8 shows, they recognize that emotional maturity, an agreeable personality, financial responsibility, similarity of interests and background, and other qualities are also important (50, 79, 93, 126, 132, 137, 188).

Sex differences in the values by which dates and potential mates are judged are quite marked. Boys want much the same kind of girl for a date as for a future mate, while girls want glamour in a date but practical qualities in a life mate (10, 100, 110, 197).

Even when the adolescent's values conform to a socially approved pattern, certain obstacles may prevent their application when choosing a life mate. These obstacles, as listed in Box 13-9, may result from the adolescent's attitudes or from his environment (79, 93, 132, 149, 165, 188).

The longer the adolescent plays the field and the longer he postpones going steady, pinning, or marrying, the better his chances of developing realistic values. Consequently, the better his chances of finding a life mate who conforms closely to his more mature values. Just as work experience helps an adolescent establish realistic values about a vocation, so does a reasonably long period of dating help him to establish realistic values in heterosexual relationships.

LEARNING TO EXPRESS LOVE

The fifth important task in achieving a mature level of heterosexuality is learning how to ex-

---

BOX 13-7   WHY EARLY MARRIAGES ARE RISKY

Personality Pattern
Persons who marry early are often not ready for marriage psychologically. They may suffer from emotional instability or feelings of personal inadequacy.

Idealism and Romanticism
Many adolescents have such highly romanticized and unrealistic concepts of marriage that disillusionment is almost inevitable.

Financial Problems
Adolescents who cannot afford the pleasures and status symbols they enjoyed before marriage may have to ask their parents for help and thus be forced back into the state of dependency they had hoped to escape.

Social Problems
Married adolescents often find themselves misfits in adolescent social activities, out of touch with their former friends. The more popular the adolescent before marriage, the harder the adjustment to social isolation.

Necessity of Ending Education
If early marriage necessitates dropping out of school or college, adolescents will have to revise their vocational aspirations. This is often a threat to marital happiness.

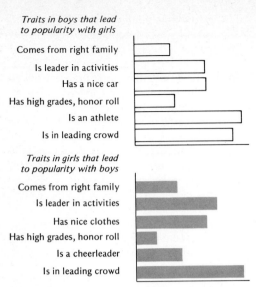

Traits in boys that lead
to popularity with girls

Comes from right family

Is leader in activities

Has a nice car

Has high grades, honor roll

Is an athlete

Is in leading crowd

Traits in girls that lead
to popularity with boys

Comes from right family

Is leader in activities

Has nice clothes

Has high grades, honor roll

Is a cheerleader

Is in leading crowd

Figure 13-3 Some values considered important in selecting dates. (Adapted from J. S. Coleman: *The adolescent society.* New York: Free Press, 1961. Used by permission.)

press the feelings and emotions aroused by the loved one. Children are self-bound; they want to be loved and to have others do things to make them happy. When they are very young, they occasionally show their affection for adults or playmates by hugging or kissing. However, they do not very often demonstrate their affection by doing things to make others happy. When the child reaches school age, he regards *all* demonstration of affection as babyish. True, he may show others that he likes them by slapping them on the back or by saying they are "good guys," but that is his limit. Girls, like boys, are embarrassed by all demonstrations of affection during the closing years of childhood (21, 64).

In making the transition to heterosexuality, the adolescent must learn to be *outer-bound* instead of self-bound, he must learn to show affection as well as receive it, and he must learn to show appreciation for the affectionate demonstrations of others. These are radical changes and they take time. They are more difficult and take longer for boys than girls, because boys, having been taught that show-

ing their tender emotions is unmasculine, have less of a foundation on which to build.

In learning to be outer-bound, the adolescent must master two essentials. *First,* he must learn the socially approved method of showing affection at his age level. Childish ways of showing affection are inappropriate when the individual reaches adolescence. He learns what is appropriate by observing adults and other members of the peer group and the patterns of lovemaking portrayed in the mass media. These he uses as models for his own behavior. *Second,* the adolescent must learn what degree of permissiveness in expressing affection is socially acceptable. Regardless of how much affection he has for another, he must control the overt expression of it, just as he must control his expression of anger, fear, and jealousy. How much permissiveness is acceptable will depend on the mores of the group, the length of time the couple have been dating, and the seriousness of their commitment to each other. Too great permissiveness on early dates will win a girl the reputation of being "loose," and a boy that of being a "wolf." However, as dating progresses, they can be more permissive in their expressions of affection without incurring social disapproval (147).

Girls are almost always more restrained in their expressions of affection than boys because they are more concerned about maintaining a favorable reputation. By contrast, boys who make conquests gain prestige in the eyes of their peers.

With each generation of girls, permissiveness in the expression of affection has increased. This is more true of *college* than of noncollege girls, of the middle and upper *socioeconomic groups* than of the lower, and of the *pinning* and *engagement periods* than of the early, playing-the-field kind of dating.

Permissiveness also varies according to *religious background.* Adolescents with strong religious training in the home, though they may show signs of rebelling, may have a stronger internalized desire to express their affection in socially approved behavior (73). Also adolescents from *rural* areas tend, on the whole, to be less permissive in their sexual behavior than those from urban or suburban areas (69).

Common expressions of love

In the early phases of heterosexual relationships, especially in the crush and hero-worship phase, expressions of affection are mainly nonphysical. Gradually, with the increase in the sex drive after the puberty changes are completed, affection is replaced by love—a strong emotional attachment between individuals of the opposite sex with at least the components of sex desire and tenderness. With this come physical expressions of affection in addition to the nonphysical. In the advanced dating period all the common expressions of affection, both physical and nonphysical, are used to let the loved one know how great the love is. Box 13-10 lists the most common ways of expressing love (8, 45, 59, 91, 114, 118).

Evaluation of expressions of love

All the common expressions of heterosexual love are ego-satisfying, all give the adolescent a feeling of security, and all meet some of his major needs to some extent, especially his sex needs. The simpler expressions, such as the exchange of keepsakes and the desire for constant association, cause no psychological damage. In fact, they are beneficial in helping to change the self-bound adolescent into an outer-bound person and in dissipating the egocentrism that normally accompanies the negative phase of puberty.

The major psychological damage that may come from these simple expressions of affection is that boys may regard them as sex inappropriate. Many boys are trained to believe that *any* expression of affection is sex inappropriate and that inexpressiveness is, as Balswick and Peek have written, "glorified as the epitome of a real man" (3). If, in addition, boys have learned to believe that a "real man" is sexually aggressive, they may want to express their affection in ways which are frightening and distasteful to the girls they love (91).

The psychological damage from the more advanced expressions of love, especially petting and premarital intercourse, is often severe and long-lasting.

Petting One of the arguments commonly raised against petting and to a lesser extent against necking is that they tend to lead to greater sexual liberties, which may result in pregnancy or venereal disease (85, 118, 122). In addition, unpleasant experiences with petting may condition the adolescent unfavorably not only toward a repetition of these experiences but also toward marriage. As may be seen in Figure 13-4, aggressive sexual encounters are especially numerous shortly after girls begin to go steady and before they are experienced enough to handle them successfully (173).

Arguments in favor of petting are given in Box 13-11. These arguments emphasize the value of petting in helping girls make the transition to a mature level of heterosexuality (8, 59, 114, 122, 158). It is quite likely that some, if not all, of the arguments are also applicable to boys.

BOX 13-8 QUALITIES VALUED IN FUTURE MATE

*Physical attractiveness conforming to group standards

*Clothes and grooming in style with group members

*Sex appropriate in appearance and behavior

*Popularity with members of both sexes

*Consideration of and interest in others

*Similar in intelligence and education

*Personality pattern marked by extroversion and maturity

*Desire for normal family life with children

*Similarity of interests and values

*Similarity of family background

*Ability to earn and/or manage money

Whether petting will contribute to marital happiness will depend, to some extent, upon the kind of petting engaged in and the reason for it. Petting "with affection" leads to a more satisfactory relationship before and after marriage than does petting without affection which is motivated more by curiosity or a desire for sexual release. Passive petting, in which the female is the object of the male's sexual advance, has been said to be more predictive of marital happiness than participant petting, in which the female is also active. Regardless of the kind of petting and the motivation for it, too much advanced petting is more likely to be predictive of unhappy than of happy marriages (16, 37, 118).

Premarital intercourse The effects of premarital intercourse on adolescents will depend largely upon their moral values and their belief in its "safety." Girls of all social classes are brought up to believe that premarital intercourse is wrong. Many boys, too, disapprove of it, though they may engage in it if peer pressure is sufficiently strong. Girls, but to a lesser extent, will also give in to peer pressure (14, 123, 175).

When a person does something he believes is wrong, feelings of guilt and shame are inevitable. To ease these feelings, many boys and girls who have premarital affairs rationalize their behavior by saying that they will be married in a few weeks or months. However, if they know their parents disapprove of premarital intercourse, and if they have a close relationship with their parents, even this rationalization is not adequate to reduce their feelings of guilt (45, 108).

In addition to feeling guilty, many adolescents fear being ostracized by the social group if their behavior becomes known; they are also fearful of how their families will react to a premarital pregnancy. While many modern parents react in a positive way—getting the girl married—as compared with the traditional negative way—rejecting and disinheriting her

—many girls do not want a shotgun marriage. They feel that it will interfere with their educational plans and disrupt the educational and vocational aspirations of the boy they love. Many are also afraid that pregnancy would force them to face the social stigma of having an illegitimate child (128, 138, 169).

A marriage entered into out of fear is likely to have more than its share of difficulty. As Dame et al. have said, "Premarital pregnancy imposes additional strains, both emotional and realistic, upon a marriage at a time when the couple has many adjustments to make.

Therefore, it constitutes a severe hazard unless both partners have considerable ego strength" (41).

Some girls are afraid that, by refusing to engage in premarital intercourse with the boy they love, they will lose him. On the other hand, regrets at having started sexual relations before marriage often plague both boys and girls. Once they have started, they find it difficult to stop. This often leads to an earlier marriage than either had planned for. The result is a feeling of being trapped, which is shown in resentments against the marriage partner.

BOX 13-10 COMMON EXPRESSIONS OF LOVE

*Keepsakes
Anything that has belonged to the loved one, especially if selected and used by him, is highly prized because of its symbolic value.

*Constant Association
Even brief separation from the loved one brings unhappiness; every effort is made to be with him and to keep in touch by telephone when parted.

*Confidence
The lover wants to share his joys and sorrows, his hopes and aspirations, and his beliefs and feelings with the loved one.

*Creative Expressions
When parted, the lover composes love letters or poetry, writes in a diary, or, as an outlet for pent-up love, makes something the loved one can use.

*Jealousy
Anyone who shows an interest in or attempts to arouse the affection of the loved one will arouse the lover's jealousy.

*Necking
Physical intimacy characterized by casual kissing and fondling confined to latitudes not lower than the neck is called "necking." It often begins on the first date and increases in frequency and intensity as dating progresses.

*Petting
Physical contact which does not involve union of the genitalia but is used to affect erotic arousal and give sexual release is known as "petting."

*Premarital Intercourse
Most premarital intercourse occurs between the ages of 16 and 20 years. In the advanced period of dating, especially during the pinning and engagement phases, intercourse may occur frequently.

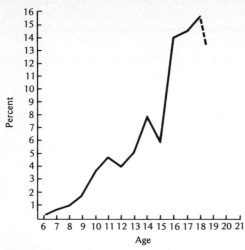

Figure 13-4 Ages at which aggressive sexual encounters are common. (Adapted from G. Shipman: The psychodynamics of sex education. *Family Coordinator,* 1968, **17,** 3-12. Used by permission.)

Boys are far more likely than girls to regret *not* having experienced intercourse before marriage. Few girls have such regrets (73, 129).

LEARNING TO PLAY APPROVED SEX ROLES

Learning to play approved sex roles, the sixth task in achieving mature heterosexuality, is one of the most difficult and most resisted, especially by girls. The *first* difficulty is uncertainty about what are the approved sex roles for members of the two sexes in their social groups. Adolescent concepts about sex roles are often blurred. When children see the mother working outside the home and the father helping with home responsibilities, it is hard for them to realize that their parents' roles are different. In school, all children receive the same training. This suggests to them that they will be playing similar roles when they become adults because the school constantly reminds them that their schooling is a preparation for adult life. Confusion grows when children discover that their peers and the parents of their peers view the approved roles in still different ways.

Because of their blurred concepts, boys and girls approach adolescence without a clear understanding of what society will expect of them. Girls in particular may have to accept roles they have not been prepared for. In addition, they discover that there is a double standard of conduct which permits boys to do things for which girls are often condemned.

Actually, in the American culture, there are two approved standards for the behavior of members of the two sexes: the traditional standard and the egalitarian standard. Box 13-12 describes the characteristics of the traditional and egalitarian roles for men and women (24, 63, 89, 90, 170, 183).

The *second* difficulty which adolescents encounter in learning and accepting approved sex roles derives from social attitudes toward the roles. During childhood, when the father is away from home during the major part of the day and the mother is in control, the child assumes that the mother's role is superior to that of the father. The child interprets this to mean that the role of women is superior to that of men. Before childhood is over, both boys and girls discover that their childhood concepts must be revised. The male role, they learn, both in the home and outside, is more favorable and more prestigious than the female role. As a result, girls become dissatisfied with the female role and resist accepting it, while boys become increasingly satisfied with the role society expects them to play and more willing to accept it.

Effects of sex-role concepts

The concept that the adolescent has of himself as a person will be affected by the sex role— traditional, egalitarian, or a combination—he accepts and whether he accepts it voluntarily or involuntarily. This self-concept will depend partly on the way the adolescent perceives the reactions of others to him and partly on how he feels about the patterns of behavior and the attitudes associated with the role he has accepted.

Traditional roles Acceptance of the concept of the traditional sex roles affects members of the two sexes differently. *Boys* who accept the traditional role experience a feeling of superiority and ego satisfaction from being identified with a role that is prestigious in the eyes of the cultural group. In addition, acceptance of the traditional male role increases the boy's social acceptance with members of both sexes; this leads to better social and personal adjustments and to greater emotional stability.

Feelings of personal superiority—a common accompaniment of identification with the traditional male role—lead to intolerance of any indication of femininity in other boys and to admiration of typically masculine boys. The boy who identifies himself with the traditional masculine role scorns activities considered sex inappropriate. He views any occupations traditionally associated with girls—teaching and nursing, for example—as inferior to those traditionally associated with men—law and medicine, say—and he resents any girl who aspires to enter one of the occupations that "belong to men."

Acceptance of the traditional masculine role leads to the development of personality traits traditionally regarded as characteristic of men. Outstanding among these are self-confidence, egocentrism, authoritarianism, strong drive for achievement, fearlessness, and adventuresomeness. Even boys who find acceptance of the traditional male role difficult derive enough personal and social satisfaction from doing so to justify the sacrifice in personal interests. Consequently, they conform, at least outwardly, to the approved patterns of behavior and attitudes of the traditional male role.

When a *girl* identifies herself with the traditional female role and tries to conform to the socially approved attitudes and behavior patterns of the ideal traditional woman, she will win the approval and acceptance of the social group. These, however, do not guarantee *self-acceptance*—an essential to good adjustment. On the contrary, girls who accept the traditional sex role usually develop unfavorable self-concepts. This is true even when a girl *voluntarily* accepts this role because of earlier training, her own desire to be a wife and mother, parental and peer pressures and

expectations, her religion, or a model of maternal happiness in her own home. Her poor self-concept is due partly to finding that the role she has accepted is boring and frustrating and partly to discovering that the role is even less prestigious than the role she played as a child and far less prestigious than the adult male role.

The greatest damage to good personal and social adjustment comes when a girl *involuntarily* accepts the traditional female role and poses as being happy in it while inwardly rebelling. She may accept the role against her better judgment to please her father or, more often, to please the boy she wants to marry. Many girls start to pose as a traditional female when they discover that this enhances their popularity with members of the opposite sex.

The adolescent girl most likely to pose as being more acceptant of the traditional female role than she actually is is usually intelligent, highly educated, and interested in a career that is traditionally regarded as masculine. Because of the disillusionment and dissatisfaction such a girl sooner or later experiences, the damage to her personal and social adjustment can be severe. As Kiell and Friedman have pointed out, the "rewards of housewifemanship are frustration and lowered self-esteem. Plowed under is the healthy self-concept she

---

BOX 13-11   HOW PETTING HELPS GIRLS ACHIEVE HETEROSEXUALITY

*For most girls, petting provides the first real understanding of a heterosexual experience and, therefore, is a healthy preparation for marriage.

*Petting introduces girls to the physical, psychological, and social problems involved in making emotional adjustments to other individuals. It thus gives them an opportunity to learn how to adjust to various kinds of males.

*Petting prepares the girl for orgasm in marriage.

BOX 13-12   CHARACTERISTICS OF APPROVED SEX ROLES

Traditional

Male Role
In the home, the male is the head of the household, deciding all important matters and determining the pattern of life for every family member. He contributes financially and through his leadership to the welfare of the family. He does not do housework unless it is "too heavy" for a woman. Outside the home, he plays a leadership role in situations which involve women as well as men. At work, he has more power and prestige than the women workers.

Female Role
The adult woman is other-oriented in the sense that she achieves fulfillment by proxy—by serving others in the home, on the job, or in the community. At home or away, she plays a subordinate role, leaving all decision making and other important matters to the male.

Egalitarian

Male Role
The "good" husband and father shares equally with his wife in caring for the home and the children, in making decisions, and in supporting the family economically.

Female Role
The adult female gains self-fulfillment by actualizing her own potentials, rather than solely by helping others achieve theirs. In the home, her role, like her husband's, is to share equally in all matters relating to the support and management of the home and the training and care of the children. Egalitarian roles in adolescence are illustrated in Figure 13-5.

had before marriage" (195). Not only will she become embittered and resentful, but she is likely to verbalize her attitudes to her family, her friends, and her acquaintances. She may develop a deeply disturbed personality and be rejected by the social group because of her unfeminine attitudes.

Egalitarian roles   A *boy* who rejects outright the traditional role for men in favor of the egalitarian role is usually regarded by the social group as effeminate or henpecked. As Koch has written, "It is more serious in our culture for the boy to deviate from the male type than for the girl to deviate from the female type. In other words, a sissy is more frowned upon than a tomboy" (103).

Knowing how the social group feels, the boy who rejects the traditional male role feels that he must use defenses to justify his decision. He may rationalize his interest in "sissy subjects" by explaining that they will be an asset to him in his future vocation. He soon discovers that rationalization is not so effective as a defense mechanism as is compensation. Much of the preoccupation with sex jokes, literature, and movies, aggressive patterns of petting, and authoritarian approach to members of the female sex are blinds which boys use to assert their masculinity and to cover up characteristics that fall short of the traditional virile ideal.

Rejection of the traditional sex role and substitution of the egalitarian role is even more damaging to the personal and social adjustment of *girls* than the outward acceptance but inward rejection of the traditional role. Like boys who accept the egalitarian role, girls are faced with unfavorable social attitudes and poor social acceptance. They know that both boys and girls disapprove of them; they suspect that they are regarded as "freaks"; they sense that they are pitied because they are not popular with boys; and they believe that people accuse them of preferring the egalitarian role because they cannot play the traditional role successfully.

The girl who prefers the egalitarian role knows that society is often highly critical of and punitive toward women who do not know that "woman's place is in the home." If she works after marriage, she realizes that she will be criticized for neglecting her family for selfish reasons. If she expects her children and husband to share some of the home responsibilities, she will be accused of henpecking her husband and spoiling her children's youth. Should her children do poorly in school or get into trouble with the law, she will be accused of putting her own selfish interests ahead of her maternal responsibilities.

To eliminate the damaging effects of social disapproval and rejection on her self-concept, the girl who chooses the egalitarian role will try to erect defenses against her "masculine" behavior. In doing so, she suffers inner conflicts and strains. As a result, many a girl who would prefer the egalitarian role succumbs to the pressures of the social group—against her better judgment—and accepts the traditional feminine role. More often than not, she only increases the psychological damage that was already done by her acceptance of the egalitarian role.

SUCCESS IN MAKING THE TRANSITION TO ADULT SEXUALITY

Few adolescents fail to make the transition into adult heterosexuality. If environmental conditions are unfavorable, however, an adolescent may not progress at the same rate as his contemporaries or may develop a warped attitude toward sex. When an adolescent whose physical development is normal claims to have no interest in members of the other sex, he is left out of most of the social activities of his contemporaries, because these activities are

Figure 13-5 Concepts of egalitarian roles.

planned for mixed groups. He then loses the opportunity to learn social skills. Of equal importance, the awakening sex drives and desires must be satisfied in some way. An adolescent who is isolated or rejected or who for some other reason cannot express his affection or fulfill his needs in the normal ways may develop an unduly heightened interest in sex. In some individuals, the transition may not be completed by the age of legal maturity, owing mainly to the state of dependency that long years of higher education impose. Such delays mean only that progress is being made at a slower-than-normal rate, not that the adolescent is maladjusted in the sense that he *prefers* an immature form of sexuality to a more mature one.

An adolescent who is making satisfactory progress toward heterosexuality will show the characteristics given in Box 13-13 at approximately the same time as his age-mates. How far along the path to adult heterosexuality he will be depends largely upon his age when the judgment is made.

When the adolescent has mastered these learning experiences successfully and has patterned his behavior according to their standards, he will be considered a "psychosexually mature" person. As Brown has stated, "A normal male is one who has identified with, incorporated, and prefers the masculine role: his sexual desire for the female is one aspect of this role" (25). The same characteristics are found in a psychosexually mature female.

HIGHLIGHTS OF CHAPTER 13

1. The transition to adult sexuality, which normally means heterosexuality, is aided by the adolescent's glandular condition, by social factors, and by the mass media. The progress of the transition varies somewhat according to the adolescent's sex, age, motivation, and the attitudes of significant adults toward him.

2. Of the many problems arising from the adolescent's attempts to achieve heterosexuality, the most important are boy-girl relationships, social behavior between members of the two sexes, moral-sex standards, learning to play socially approved sex roles, and abnormal sex behavior.

3. To achieve heterosexuality, the adolescent must acquire adequate and correct knowledge about sex and about the socially approved sex roles for males and females.

4. Among American adolescents, interest in sex centers on the physiological changes that occur during puberty and early adolescence, the meaning of love, the socially approved ways of expressing love, the meaning of marriage and parenthood, and the socially approved sex roles.

5. The major sources of knowledge about sex and sex roles are parents, teachers, mass media, and experimentation.

6. The attitudes of the adolescent toward sex are greatly influenced by childhood experiences, especially those relating to sexual behavior, the kind of sex information he received, and the attitudes of significant people in his life toward sex.

BOX 13-13 CHARACTERISTICS OF SUCCESSFUL TRANSITION TO HETEROSEXUALITY

*The adolescent has learned to manage the sex drive so that its energy can be turned into socially approved patterns of heterosexual behavior. If the drive is too strong and the environmental obstacles too great, the drive will be sublimated in sports or other approved behavior until the obstacles can be removed.

*The individual has abandoned immature forms of sexuality, such as crushes and hero worship, in favor of more mature patterns.

*The adolescent has developed socially approved values for the selection of a mate and understands the practical aspects of the marital role.

*The person has learned to express love in acts that contribute to the happiness and security of the loved one.

*The individual has learned to play the approved role for his sex and to respect the role society expects members of the opposite sex to play.

---

7. As adolescence progresses, improved attitudes toward sex normally contribute to improved personal and social adjustments.

8. Adolescents normally pass through phases of heterosexual behavior which are fairly definite and predictable: crushes and hero worship, puppy love, dating, going steady, pinning, engagement, and marriage. Each phase contributes to the adolescent's heterosexual development.

9. Establishment of values in mate selection is essential in achieving heterosexuality. Values considered important for dates and for future mates are both involved. Establishment of values may be hindered by environmental obstacles or by attitudes resulting from earlier experiences.

10. In making the transition to heterosexuality, the adolescent must learn how to express love for a member of the opposite sex in a socially approved manner and in socially approved degrees of intensity.

11. Learning to play approved sex roles is especially difficult for girls. They are uncertain of what the approved roles for members of the two sexes are and they are frustrated by the negative social attitudes toward the role of girls as compared with that of boys.

12. How successfully the adolescent makes the transition to heterosexuality can be assessed by how well he has learned to manage the sex drive, how willing he is to abandon immature forms of sexuality in favor of more mature ones, his development of socially approved values for the selection of a mate, his learning to express his love for a member of the opposite sex in ways that bring happiness and security to the loved one, and his success in learning to play the role that is socially approved for members of his sex.

Chapter 14

Transition in Family Relationships

The pattern of relationships within any family is highly predictable. Typically, the baby is the center of love and attention. Any disturbing behavior on his part is forgiven on the ground that he is too young to know better. Before he reaches his first birthday, however, his relationships with different family members begin to worsen. This deterioration is shown in a decrease in parental warmth and intellectual stimulation, in greater parental restrictiveness and punitiveness, and in sibling impatience, intolerance, and jealousy.

While family relationships may improve somewhat when the child begins to spend time outside the home, the deterioration continues. As childhood draws to a close, at about the age of 12, friction with *all* members of the family is usual. It reaches a peak between 15 and 17 years. The physical changes at puberty make the child secretive, uncooperative, and quarrelsome, and unless parents recognize the tie-in, they are likely to be overcritical and punitive. The child feels that no one loves him and the gap between parents and child widens.

As the growth spurt of puberty slows down and body homeostasis is gradually restored, the young adolescent begins to feel better. This is reflected in the quality of his behavior, and family relationships gradually improve, beginning between the ages of 15 and 16 years for girls and a year or two later for boys. Improvement depends partly on maturation and partly on environment—how soon family members, especially parents, recognize that the adolescent is no longer a child and revise their habitual way of treating him.

In late adolescence, family relationships are still better. Normally, parents treat their almost-adult sons and daughters more like grown-ups and the adolescents themselves become more mature both socially and emotionally.

EFFECTS OF FAMILY RELATIONSHIPS ON HOME CLIMATE

The home climate—the "psychological atmosphere" of the home—varies markedly from home to home. Some homes have a good climate, some a poor climate, and some a changeable climate. Even within a home, the climate may vary from time to time for any one individual; it is certain to vary for the different children of the family. In general, the home climate is most likely to be poor for the young adolescent because friction with family members is at its peak at this period of his life.

Few adolescents, unfortunately, feel that their home climates favor good interfamily relationships. As a result, most are unhappy, critical, and faultfinding. Other family members, perceiving the adolescents' behavior as unsocial, retaliate by faultfinding and derogatory remarks. When this happens, more and more members of the family are drawn into the deteriorating relationships until everyone is unhappy. See Figure 14-1 for a graphic illustration of the vicious circle of parent-adolescent relationships.

Overt expressions of friction

The effect of frictional relationships on the home climate will depend, to a large extent, upon whether the friction is expressed overtly and what overt expressions are used. In the past, when authoritarian parental control was the norm, only parents and grandparents expressed their annoyance and hostility openly. The emotional climate of the home *appeared* to be calm and peaceful, even though there may have been hidden smoldering resentments.

Under more democratic child training, hostilities between family members—old, young, and in-between—are openly expressed. The young child commonly expresses himself in physical attacks. Gradually, as he discovers that parents, peers, and siblings will not tolerate physical aggressions, he verbalizes his discontents. The more democratic the home, the more outspoken each member is about things that are not to his liking.

Parental nagging, faultfinding, and other expressions of annoyance provide *adolescents* with a model for expressing their own

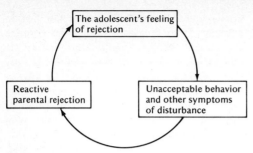

Figure 14-1 The vicious circle of parent-adolescent relationships. (Adapted from D. Hallowitz and B. Stulberg: The vicious cycle of parent-child relationship breakdown. *Soc. Casewk.* 1959, **40,** 268–275. Used by permission.)

grievances. Studies of nagging, for example, reveal that it is rarely limited to one member of the family. As Ellis and Nye (45) have written:

Nagging shows a strong tendency to run in families. If the father nags, one may predict with good accuracy that the mother will nag also. . . . This lends support to the idea that nagging may be a family cultural trait—an approved and expected technique for controlling adolescents.

Adolescents compare their parents unfavorably with the parents of their friends, they nag about being "overprotected" or "deprived," and they find fault with things that are done for them as well as with things that their parents expect them to do for themselves.

Most of the verbal attacks adolescents make on grandparents and other relatives are made behind their backs—in the presence of friends, parents, or siblings. *Grandparents,* on the other hand, have been accustomed to more authoritarian control in the home, and they often openly deplore the democratic give-and-take which they observe in today's families.

Boys do not hesitate to tell their brothers or sisters what they think of them and why; girls then follow suit. As Bossard and Boll have pointed out, sibling relationships are characterized by "stark frankness" in which siblings see each other "with their hair down" (18). That there is plenty of bickering, name calling, faultfinding, and ego-deflating com-

parisons among siblings in most homes is a truism that requires little further emphasis.

Effects of expression of friction

No doubt it is better for the *individual* to be able to express highly charged emotional attitudes openly. But from the point of view of *family relationships,* overt expressions of hostility and annoyance are damaging. The person who is the target of a verbal attack is as emotionally aroused as the attacker himself, but may not have an opportunity to express his resentments adequately to clear his system. This lack of emotional catharsis predisposes him to react unfavorably to other family members.

Unquestionably the overt expression of hostility which produces the most damaging effects on *all* family members is repeated criticism, or nagging. When the adolescent is criticized time and again for neglecting his duties, for wasting time on social activities, or for being rude and impertinent, the cumulative effect makes each verbal attack seem harsher and more difficult to accept. When a mother is constantly criticized for being inefficient and for using "old-fashioned methods" in running the home, each repetition adds to the psychological damage already done to her ego.

No member of the family is spared the damaging effects of overt expressions of hostility. However, as shown in Box 14-1, family members are affected differently (6, 68, 79, 107, 128, 169).

Nonexpression of hostility is damaging not only to family relationships but also to the individual. A controlled hostile emotion predisposes the individual to brood over and exaggerate the cause of the hostility, thus keeping the emotion alive and intensifying it. Sooner or later, it will burst forth in a physical attack or verbal tirade out of all proportion to the situation that gave rise to it. This will nullify all the benefits derived from controlling the hostility, both from the point of view of family relationships and the effect it has on the individual's attitude toward himself.

CONDITIONS AFFECTING THE HOME CLIMATE

While family conflicts are more common in every culture at the time when the children of the family reach adolescence, some evidence suggests that they are most frequent and most severe in the United States. A survey of some of the factors that affect the home climate in America will help to show why conflicts are so common. It will also help us to see which factors are controllable and, thus, how the home climate can be improved.

Of the many conditions and factors that affect the climate of homes in which there are adolescents, the following are the most important:

1. Mutual understanding
2. Conflicts over autonomy
3. Conflict in values
4. Togetherness
5. Parental control
6. Marital relationships
7. Broken homes
8. Family size and composition
9. Invasion by outsiders
10. Socioeconomic status of family
11. Parental occupations
12. Parental aspirations
13. Concepts of family roles
14. Favoritism

Mutual understanding

Just as better social relationships outside the home are achieved when one is able to understand the feelings, thoughts, emotions, and motives of others, so it is in the home. The individual who is capable of *empathy*—of putting himself in the psychological shoes of another and viewing a situation from his frame of reference—makes far better social adjustments than the individual who lacks empathic ability. Refer to Chapters 4 and 5 for a more complete discussion of the role of empathy in social relationships.

There are two aids to understanding: communication and shared experiences. Through *communication,* an individual is able to un-

derstand another's point of view and to present his own point of view so that the other can understand him. Without communication, misunderstanding is common (9, 124, 166). For example, parents who feel that laying down the law to their children is sufficient get poorer cooperation than parents who feel that their children are entitled to know the reasons for restrictions (145).

Understanding is also improved by *sharing experiences* with others, by doing things with them. A teen-age daughter who is critical of her mother's "inefficiency" in preparing meals will get a new perspective on the matter if she helps with meal preparation and has an opportunity to learn how much time and effort are needed to prepare even the simplest meal (141).

BOX 14-1   HOW FRICTION DAMAGES FAMILY MEMBERS

Parents
"Good" parents are deeply hurt by constant criticism from their adolescent children. Mothers are damaged psychologically more than fathers because they come to feel that the years they have devoted to doing things for their children have ended in failure and because they are generally experiencing the physical and emotional crisis of menopause at the time when verbal attacks reach a peak.

Adolescents
The younger the adolescent, the more insecure he is and the more ego-deflating any criticism from *any* source. Expressions of hostility heighten the already-existing feeling of most adolescents that they are misunderstood and unloved.

Elderly Relatives
Elderly relatives are hypersensitive to any suggestion that they are out of step with the times. They are angered by the "impertinence" of young people who say derogatory things to their face. In addition to being hurt, as parents are, they feel indignant.

For parent-child communication to be successful, willingness to communicate must be accompanied by *parental respect* for the child's opinions. Even though there may still be differences of opinion, the home climate will be happier. Adolescents who communicate with their siblings have better relationships with them than those who engage solely in verbal attacks. The siblings with whom they communicate most are the ones with whom they have the best relationships (21, 168).

Adolescents who do things with their families just "for fun" get along with them better than adolescents who spend most of their leisure time with their peers, using the home primarily as a place to eat, sleep, and study. Spending family leisure time together fosters a feeling of mutual understanding. There is thus evidence that understanding and "togetherness" go hand in hand (149). This is illustrated in Figure 14-2.

The breakdown in communication between the adolescent and his parents is more often due to lack of understanding than to lack of shared experiences. Box 14-2 lists the most common causes of the breakdown (54, 124, 128, 138, 145, 166).

Lack of understanding may be due to actual misunderstanding or to a tendency to read extraneous or erroneous meanings into what someone has said. "Misreadings" are very common in adolescent-adult conversations. Hess and Goldblatt (73) have explained:

> One of the central problems of parent–teen-ager relations lies . . . in the fact that each group mistrusts or misunderstands the opinions of the other. Parents and adolescents thus interpret teen-age behavior and problems in different and often contradictory terms.

Conflicts over autonomy

Autonomy is a status symbol for the adolescent. It tells his peers that he is no longer a child but has been granted the status of a near adult. Autonomy is also important personally because the adolescent uses it to measure his adequacy to handle his own affairs.

Even though most parents feel that adolescents must learn to be autonomous, they have many reasons, either conscious or unconscious, for restraining them. Of all the reasons, perhaps the most common is *habit*. In commenting on the failure of parents to adjust to the changed needs of their adolescent children, Bowerman and Kinch (21) have written:

> There would appear to be something like a law of perseveration in human relations, according to which we tend to react to another person in the same manner until there is some force operating, such as a status change imposed on the relationship, which modifies our perception of the other and the way in which we shall react to him. We would expect, for this reason, that parents tend to hold the same demands and expectations of their children until a change in external circumstances forces them to look at their children from a new perspective. These changes are increase in growth and puberty changes and starting high school or junior high school.

If parents deny the adolescent the independence his friends have, he shows his resentment by "parent belittlement." He takes a negative attitude toward his parents and everything they say or do; he turns to outsiders for help, advice, and companionship; he repudiates his parents' plans for his future and tries to do just the opposite. Even more seriously, he experiences a severe blow to the self-

Figure 14-2 Relationship of parental understanding of young people's problems and the frequency with which the adolescent does things for fun with the family. (Adapted from C. L. Stone: Family recreation: A parental dilemma. *Family Life Coordinator,* 1963, **12,** 85–87. Used by permission.)

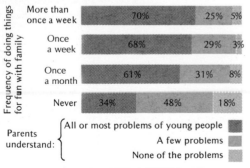

confidence and self-esteem he is trying to build up. When given some independence, but not so much as his friends, he may misuse it in an attempt to convince his peers that he is as independent as they. Parents are then likely to reimpose restraints, and these will increase the adolescent's rebellion.

The adolescent who is given the freedom he demands and then fails to use it successfully blames his parents for babying him too long and not teaching him how to make decisions. Resentment against his parents, combined with the ego-deflating experience of failure, has a devastating effect on his relationships with his parents and upon his attitude toward home and family (79, 128, 163).

Conflict in values

With social and cultural changes come new problems and changes in values. The result is what we have called the cultural generation gap. (See Chap. 6.)

Further complications arise when parents are foreign-born, when they are geographically or socially mobile, and when they are overage, or older than the parents of their children's peers (13, 169). The most serious conflicts in values come in families where parents are overage or are foreign-born. The latter bring with them the values they learned in their own countries—values which are often very different from those of present-day America. Box 14-3 gives some of the reasons for value conflicts between adolescents and overage parents (21, 28, 43, 45, 79, 105).

Conflicts in values are most problematical in those areas in which parents and adolescents have different goals. To parents, for example, thrift, hard work, and a good reputation are goals for which every young person should strive. To adolescents, having fun, being popular, and acquiring status symbols equal or superior to those of their friends are more important.

Whether the adolescent accepts or rejects parental values, there will be friction. If he accepts his parents' values, he will be out of step with his peers and experience some de-

---

BOX 14-2 WHY FAMILY COMMUNICA-
TION BREAKS DOWN

*Because of rapid social and cultural change, the adolescent has experiences which his parents did not have and are unable to understand.

*The adolescent may feel that his parents do not try to understand or sympathize with his problems.

*Generally unsatisfactory relationships with people—by either the adolescent or some of his family members—may create barriers within the family which discourage communication.

*Lack of shared experiences results in few common interests.

---

gree of social rejection. He will then blame his parents for his lack of acceptance. To maintain peace and harmony in the home, many adolescents try to conform, in part at least, to parental standards. They accept parental values but interpret them more liberally than their parents do.

Only when parents revise the values they learned in youth to be more in step with current values can the friction resulting from value clashes be reduced. Sometimes parents' refusal to change their values comes from ignorance of what the new values are. The parent who has limited communication and few shared experiences with his adolescent son or daughter cannot know what the world of youth is like any more than he can know what a foreign land is like if his travels have been limited to his own country.

Togetherness

Togetherness has been extolled as one of the major ideals of American family living. Fathers have been urged to share home duties and child-care responsibilities with their wives; wives have been advised to learn about their husbands' jobs so they can be real helpmates to them; and both parents have been told that if the children share in family decision making, chores, and recreations the home will be a utopia.

While togetherness may produce a good home climate when children are young, this does not necessarily mean that it will when the children become more mature. One of the most important tasks for adolescents—and one which they are most anxious to succeed in—is gaining their autonomy, moving from a status of dependence to one of independence. Furthermore, adolescents are under pressure by parents, teachers, and peers to be socially active in the school and community. They know that social prestige goes with popularity in the peer group, not with clinging to the family (29).

Normally, *young* adolescents spend more time doing things with and for the members of their families than do older adolescents. At every age, *boys* spend more time with their peers and less time with their families than girls. Adolescents from *large families* break away from the togetherness philosophy sooner than those from small families because parents of large families put less pressure on their children to be at home.

The more *popular* the adolescent is with peers of both sexes, the more socially active he will be and the less time he will have to spend with his family. One study shows that adolescents who participate frequently in family recreational activities date less than those who spend less time in family activities (149).

As adolescents become more nonfamily-oriented, outsiders have more influence on their *values* and *decision making* than parents (158). The impact of outsiders depends mainly on how great a gap there is between their values and parental values. This does not mean that adolescents reject *all* parental values and advice. Where they turn for advice will be influenced by the decision to be made. A study of high school girls found that the girls turned to parents for advice in situations which have a long-time consequence, such as the choice of a career, but to their peers in situations where the choice is of immediate consequence, as what dress to wear to a party (25). As the adolescent turns more and more to outsiders, the home has less and less influence on his values.

The breakdown of togetherness also makes the adolescent feel that he no longer *needs his parents* as he did when he was younger. As he comes to realize that he is capable of being independent, economically as well as socially, he often becomes casual in his treatment of his parents, showing them less consideration, respect, and affection than previously.

Parental control

While few adolescents question the need for some parental control or punishment when they willfully violate family rules, they do question the kind of control they are subjected to and the fairness of the punishment meted out. This is what leads to friction. A brief survey of the different kinds of discipline will show how they affect the home climate. Refer to Chapter 12 for a more detailed discussion.

In the *authoritarian* home, the adolescent becomes submissive and is afraid to take the initiative in assuming responsibility. This leads to friction, because his parents expect him to take more responsibility as he grows older. Constantly thwarted in his attempts to achieve independence, the adolescent develops such a strong resentment against his parents that he will not communicate with them or turn to them for advice and help in meeting his problems. This results in a deepening of the parent-adolescent cleavage.

The adolescent whose parents use *democratic* control has more harmonious relationships with his parents. Since they treat him like a near-adult, he likes and respects them and is willing to go to them for advice and help with his problems. He has a less critical

Figure 14-3 Parents who try to appear "young" are often embarrassing to an adolescent because they do not "act their age"; overage parents are embarrassing because they "look like grandparents."

attitude toward them than the adolescent from an authoritarian home, enjoys his home life more, and is more appreciative of what his parents do for him. As a result, the climate of the home is more warm and acceptant.

In a *permissive* home there is no parental control. The adolescent often has little respect for his parents, little appreciation for what they do for him, and little desire to carry his load in the home. Instead, he expects his parents to wait on him while he does little or nothing for them. The adolescent who is permitted to do as he pleases feels resentful and insecure. When things go wrong, he blames his parents for not caring about him and not giving him guidance.

Inconsistency in discipline produces more friction than consistency, regardless of whether parental control is lenient or harsh. When inconsistent discipline leads to unfair punishment, siblings usually side with the adolescent against his parents and defend him as a martyr. This does not help to produce a happy home climate or to foster an affectional bond between the adolescent and his parents.

The greatest source of friction is parental control that differs markedly from that used in the homes of the adolescent's friends. A mother who is much stricter than other mothers, for example, sets the stage for adolescent rebellion. If the father, in a desire to be fair and not harm the children's chances for social acceptance, champions their cause and pleads for greater leniency, the frictional relationship may become overwhelming (19, 114, 134).

Marital relationships

Poor parental relationships is a common cause of family friction. Adolescents who feel that their parents' marriage is happy likewise feel that their homes are happy places in which to live. The reason is clear: The less friction there is between parents, the less there will be between parents and children and between siblings (141).

Marital happiness tends to decline as parents reach middle age. Discontent may be due to unsatisfactory sexual adjustments; dis-

enchantment with marital and parental obligations; personal, social, and economic restrictions; a frictional home climate, which induces feelings of frustration and failure; and changes in interests, causing parents to have less in common as they grow older.

Since deterioration in marital relationships affects the whole family, the home climate may become so emotionally charged that every member is at odds with every other member. It may become so unpleasant for the adolescent that he wants to be out of the house as much as possible.

When parents are preoccupied with their own problems, they give the adolescent the impression that they are disinterested in him. He is hesitant about bringing his friends to his home, not knowing what kind of atmosphere to expect or what sort of reception his friends will get (5).

The most damaging aspect of marital friction is that it is a circular process. That is, once it starts, it is constantly reinforced by the reactions of other family members who are affected by it. The adolescent who is unhappy and disturbed by the emotionally charged atmosphere of his home reacts unfavorably to his parents, his siblings, and his relatives; this establishes a frictional relationship with them. One parent, then, is likely to blame the other for not controlling the adolescent. Marital friction intensifies, and the circle of bad family relationships grows.

Broken homes

When family friction reaches such a peak of intensity that every member is unhappy in his relationship with every other member, a break in the family is likely to occur. If the root of the trouble is marital discontent, it would be logical to assume that family friction would cease as soon as the parents separated. Studies show that, while the home climate does improve after a break, a broken home is far less happy than an unbroken home in which there is no more than the usual amount of family friction. In fact, sometimes a break in the family results in greater friction (27, 76).

Even though an unhappy home climate may improve after a separation or divorce, this does not imply that all sources of unhappiness have been permanently removed. Every home, whether intact or broken by death, separation, or divorce, is susceptible to discord. Box 14-4 explains the most common sources of friction in the "solo" home—a home with only one parent (27, 36, 58, 129, 139, 160).

Which is more damaging to the home climate, a breakup because of parental incompatibility or a half-hearted togetherness marred by parental unhappiness and friction? The question has been answered both ways. One can only answer it in retrospect. A number of variables must be considered. How *unhappy* the home was before the break and how much discord prevailed are important factors. When an unhappy home is broken by a *separation,* usually on a trial basis, every member of the family may have a desire to clear up the problems and end the break. A broken home is more damaging to *adolescents* than to young or grown children. Provisions are usually made for the care of young children, and grown children have their own interests and often their own homes. It is the adolescents who bear the brunt of the break. A break in a *large family* is more damaging than a break in a small family because all problems are intensified. If the parents can meet the socioeconomic and other *needs* of the children, regardless of their ages, the break is less damaging than if it results in privations.

Perhaps the most influential variable is the extent to which the children are *involved* in parental disputes and how much each parent tries to win the loyalty of the children away from the other parent. If the adolescent is used as a go-between in the frictional situation, he will be more emotionally disturbed than if the disputes take place out of his hearing.

A break caused by divorce or separation is more damaging to the home climate than one caused by death. Further, the solo home is less damaging than the reconstructed home. Whether the break is caused by death or divorce, adolescents make better adjustments to their families if the parents do not remarry. Perhaps the most damaging situation is an unhappy home broken by divorce and then reconstructed, so that the adolescent has four rather than two parents (91, 122). More about this in the section on invasion by outsiders.

Family size and composition

The smaller the family, the fewer the interpersonal relationships and the fewer the possibilities for friction. As may be seen in Figure 14-4, the number of interpersonal relationships increases substantially with each additional family member (18).

In *one-child* families, the adolescent may suffer from overprotectiveness and high parental aspirations, both of which are potential sources of family friction. On the other hand, parents with only one child are likely to treat him in a democratic way and to be indulgent about privileges and material possessions. Since the only child is usually the pride of his parents and grandparents, he tends to have a happy, relaxed, nonfrictional home environment. The home is spared the sibling rivalry of families with several children of different ages, both sexes, and different levels of maturity (18, 136).

A family of two or three children—average today, but *small* as compared with past generations—tends to be very frictional. The small family is usually democratically controlled, with every member being encouraged to develop his own individuality and express his thoughts and feelings freely. The result is that there may be many clashes of interests, attitudes, and values. Since a small family is usually economically able to provide the children opportunities to get ahead in life, parental pressure for achievement is strong. Parental resentment and disappointment when children fail to reach the levels of aspiration set for them are a constant source of friction. The small family appears to be particularly vulnerable to parental separation or divorce. Thus the adolescent may have to face the friction-arousing conditions that come with a

BOX 14-4 SOURCES OF FRICTION IN THE SOLO HOME

Economic Condition
If the children live with the mother, as is usual, a shortage of money may force her to accept public assistance, go to work, or live with relatives. Homes broken by the death of a parent lose their main source of earned income or incur the extra expense of paying for a housekeeper.

Downward Mobility
Downward economic or social mobility upsets the status-symbol-conscious adolescent and leads to a frictional attitude toward the parent with whom he lives.

Added Home Responsibilities
As the economic condition of the home deteriorates, the adolescent's social life is curtailed by the necessity of sharing some of the home resonsibilities.

Preoccupation of Remaining Parent
The parent with whom the adolescent lives in a solo home is often so preoccupied with personal problems that the interests and concerns of the adolescent may be ignored.

Overprotectiveness
Even the most preoccupied solo parent sooner or later realizes that he alone is responsible for the care and guidance of the adolescent. His overprotectiveness is resented by the independence-conscious adolescent.

Increased Emotional Tension
When the break in the home is due to death, emotional tension increases after the break; when due to divorce, it increases both before and after. Emotional tension is often reflected in troublesome adolescent behavior—a condition that breeds family friction.

Attachment to One Parent
The absent parent is often glorified by the adolescent. The remaining parent, especially if the break was due to divorce, resents this hero-worshipping attitude.

Being Different
A solo home makes the adolescent different from most of his peers and he interprets this to mean that he is inferior—an attitude that predisposes him to be frictional with the parent with whom he lives.

Stepparent
If broken homes are reconstructed by remarriage, some of the problems may be solved, but often the introduction of new family members brings new problems, as will be explained later in this chapter.

break in the family in *addition* to all the others that are associated with the small family (12, 75).

The *large* family—where there are six or more children—is often less frictional than a small family because the parents tend to use authoritarian methods of control. Otherwise, they feel, a state of anarchy and chaos would prevail (152, 155). While adolescents brought up in a large family are seldom overprotected, they are usually too restricted by economic conditions to use their independence. They have fewer status symbols and educational opportunities than their peers from smaller families. Often, older siblings are deprived of social activities because they must take care of younger siblings. All these limitations lower their opportunities for social acceptance in the peer group with which they would like to be identified.

A family of any size may be either a "nuclear" family—made up of parents and their children—or an "elongated" family—made up of members of three or more generations. Elongated families still exist in the United States, but since the turn of the century nuclear families have become much more common, especially in urban areas (18, 105). As explained in Box 14-5, three major factors influence the home climate of these two kinds of families (15, 72, 80, 82, 147, 159).

Invasion by outsiders

In the nuclear family unit, adolescents become accustomed to a small, closely knit group, flexible enough to meet the needs of all family members. Anything that upsets the homeostasis of family life disturbs the home climate. Invasion by outsiders or by persons whom the adolescent regards as outsiders is always a complicating factor; it is especially so during adolescence when adjustment to parents and siblings is difficult even without

Figure 14-4   To determine the number of interpersonal relationships in the family, use the formula $X = (Y^2 - Y)/2$, in which X represents the number of interpersonal relationships and Y the number of family members.

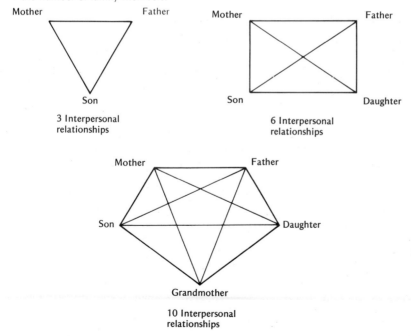

any added complications. Furthermore, when family life is upset, adjustments must be made by *all* family members if homeostasis is to be restored. Some people who come into the home upset the homeostasis of the family more than others.

How much a "paying guest" or *boarder* will upset the family will depend on how much time he spends in the home, whether he takes his meals with the family or shares kitchen privileges, what parts of the house are available for his use, and what his age and sex are. A young teacher "invader," for example, who is in school most of the day and spends his weekends in social activities will be less upsetting to a home than an unemployed middle-aged "invader."

The adolescent who has been accustomed to having his mother do the housework regards part-time domestic workers as intruders. He is critical of their looks, work habits, and speech; he especially resents any authority they may have over him during the mother's absence. Although servants may free the adolescent from household chores, their presence is often a source of friction (121).

Because early adolescence is a self-conscious, hypercritical age, *guests* are likely to be more upsetting to family life at that time than in later adolescence. The young adolescent resents comments about how much he has grown or questions about his interest in members of the opposite sex. He is likely to be critical of the way guests look and behave, of the rigidity of their attitudes, and even of their speech. The older adolescent, who is more tolerant of older people and more poised in social situations, accepts family guests more graciously and may even welcome their presence. At any time during adolescence, the effect of guests on the home climate will depend to some extent upon how typical it is for the family to have guests, how long the guests stay, and how prestigious the guests are in the adolescent's eyes.

A child may enjoy having *relatives* come for a visit, but the adolescent regards them as invaders, especially when living quarters are cramped and they intrude upon his private property, perhaps even taking over his room. Resentment is intensified if they criticize the adolescent, order him around, or have authority over him. If the adolescent and his family have a life style, interests, and values that differ markedly from those of the relatives, friction is likely to persist as long as the relatives remain in the home.

If *grandparents* are financially independent and if they are not expected to play the role of parent surrogate, they may enjoy being with the family. Also, but to a lesser extent, the family may enjoy having them. The presence of grandparents in the home may free adolescent children of many home responsibilities, permitting them to be more active socially with their peers. Under these conditions, the hazards of household invasion are reduced. Grandmothers generally favor their grandsons, and grandfathers, their granddaughters. Thus, there is normally less cross-sex friction than same-sex friction. In any case, grandfathers are a less disturbing influence in the family because they are likely to have more outside interests and to be more remote from the grandchildren (80, 98, 112).

Of all the "invaders," stepparents upset the homeostasis of family life most and for the longest time. A number of factors in the stepparent situation are likely to prove detrimental to a healthy home climate. Box 14-6 lists

---

BOX 14-6 CAUSES OF FRICTION IN THE ADOLESCENT-STEPPARENT RELATIONSHIP

Cultural Stereotypes
Stereotypes of the "wicked" stepmother color the adolescent's attitude toward his own stepmother. There are no common stereotypes of stepfathers.

Attitudes of Peers
If peers regard the adolescent as a "martyr" because he has a stepparent, it may improve his social acceptance but increase his antagonism toward his stepparent.

Attitudes of Stepparent and Stepchild
If the stepparent resents the stepchild, favors his own child, or feels inadequate for the stepparent role, the adolescent will resent the "invader" and his intrusion on the relationship he formerly enjoyed with the solo parent.

Age of Stepchild
In general, very young children and older adolescents who are normally out of the home a great deal can accept a stepparent more easily than a young adolescent.

Sex of Stepchild
As with their own parents, adolescent girls have more clashes with stepmothers than with stepfathers, while adolescent boys have more clashes with stepfathers.

Sex of Stepparent
A stepmother who is too authoritarian or bossy is likely to alienate the adolescent. A stepfather who does not improve the financial status of the family is likely to be resented.

Changes in Home Patterns
The introduction of new methods of discipline, the presence of children belonging to the stepparent, and the arrival of stepsiblings complicate family life and damage the home climate.

Changed Relationships with Own Parent
The adolescent resents his own parent's preoccupation with the stepparent, which is especially marked after remarriage, as well as the influence the stepparent has on his own parent.

---

the most important factors (27, 58, 83, 129, 147).

As Bowerman and Irish have pointed out, in a home where there is a stepparent, there is "more stress, ambivalence, and low cohesiveness" than in normal homes (20). The more disruptive stepparent is likely to be a stepmother. Not only does the stepmother have a more direct and pervasive influence on the children of the family, regardless of their age, but her influence is likely to be more resented. That many more juvenile delinquents come from homes where there are stepmothers than stepfathers would suggest that more often than not the home climate is not improved by the "invasion" of a stepmother (59, 156).

Socioeconomic status of family

The quality of family life and, in turn, the home climate often reflect the family's socioeconomic status. Of the many reasons for the relationship, three are especially important.

First, the kind of home the family has and its location in the community and the clothing, spending money, and other status symbols the adolescent has—all affect his social status in the peer group. When an adolescent feels that his lack of social acceptance is due to lack of money, he may develop strong resentments toward his parents

Second, families that are anxious to improve their socioeconomic status pressure their children to conform to the patterns of behavior and values of the class they aspire to belong to. The demands for conformity may thwart the adolescent's desire for independence and thus create a frictional parent-child relationship.

Third, an insecure or fluctuating socioeconomic status leads to emotional insecurity, which has an adverse effect on the home climate. The adolescent never knows where he stands economically and cannot plan for the future. His insecurity affects his social and personal adjustments and his attitudes toward his family (36, 143, 169).

Parental occupations

Although the social status of a family is largely determined by the occupation of the father, the working mother is often more important in determining what the home climate will be. The effect of her occupation comes mainly from the disruption it causes in the family's accustomed pattern of living. Since the effects of the father's and the mother's occupations on the home climate are very different, they will be discussed separately.

The *father's* occupation affects family relationships in four very important ways. First, the prestige associated with the father's occupation has a direct influence on the adolescent's attitude toward the father. Indirectly, it affects the adolescent's attitude toward himself.

Second, the father's occupation affects the socioeconomic status of the family, which was discussed above.

Third, the father's occupation affects his relationships with his adolescent sons and, to a lesser extent, with his daughters through the influence it has on his aspirations for them and the standards he sets for them. From his experiences in the work world, the father feels that he knows what attitudes, skills, and personal qualities are essential for success. In his attempt to foster them in his sons, he allows the standards of the occupational world to influence the father-son relationship.

Fourth, if the father's job necessitates his absence from home for varying lengths of time, there will be temporary breaks in the family and changes in the home environment. When the father returns, readjustments may be stressful for all family members.

If the adolescent and his mother are satisfied with the father's occupation—with what it does *to* the family as well as *for* the family—it will have a favorable effect on the home climate. A father who is successful, for example, is less resented when he expects his children to do good work at school than a father whose occupation lacks prestige, whose income is low, and who puts pressures on his children to compensate for his own vocational dissatisfaction (117, 143, 144).

A number of conditions related to the *mother's* occupation affect the home climate. Box 14-7 discusses those which have been reported to be most influential (8, 17, 49, 85, 111, 116).

The employment status of the mother affects various family members differently. When the mother works, the *son* has more free time because he may not have to take an afterschool job to earn spending money or to contribute to the family income. The *daughter*, by contrast, is expected to assume more responsi-

---

BOX 14-7   CONDITIONS INFLUENCING EFFECT OF MOTHER'S OCCUPATION ON THE HOME CLIMATE

Age of Children
The adolescent does not need the mother's full-time care, so he is less upset by her going to work than a young child. If he has been accustomed to having the mother at home, however, he, as well as other family members, will have to make adjustments to her being away most of the day.

Reason for Working
If the mother works for personal satisfaction and gain, she may feel guilty because she is not conforming to the cultural stereotype of the good mother. If she works to help support the family, she may gain a new feeling of satisfaction or she may feel resentful.

Husband's Attitude
The father's attitude toward the mother's work will affect their marital relationship and the home climate. If the mother blames the father for not earning enough to provide for the family, he will feel resentful.

Children's Attitudes
Both girls and boys resent having their mothers work if they feel it will make them look different or if working mothers are viewed unfavorably by their peer groups. Girls often resent having to take on household duties which interfere with their social lives.

Attitudes of the Social Group
Adult members of the social group tend to disapprove of working mothers more than adolescents. Awareness of this affects not only the mother's attitude but also that of her husband and children.

Provision for Home Chores
If the mother earns enough to hire outside help to care for the home, her working will not impose additional duties on the other family members or deprive them of shared interests and social activities.

Kind of Work
When a mother's work is prestigious, the pride her family feels in her achievements counteracts some of the unfavorable effects of her being away from home. Part-time work is less damaging to the home climate than full-time work; sporadic work that entails constant readjustments is most damaging.

---

bilities in the home. Furthermore, since the mother contributes more to a girl's socialization than to a boy's, the girl whose mother works often feels that she is handicapped socially.

Maternal employment seems to have little or no effect on the *father-son* relationship. It may strengthen the relationship if both father and son agree that the mother's place is in the home. *Father-daughter* relationships are affected quite differently. As Maccoby (96) has pointed out:

Girls with working mothers [seem] to have more disturbance in their relationships with their fathers than with their mothers. Possibly the mother's working in some way weakens the father's role in the family so that the daughter does not respect him as she might otherwise. An equally possible explanation, however, is that a number of the mothers are working because their husbands are unstable, a quality which might produce negative feelings toward a man on the part of both wife and daughter.

Parental aspirations

Even before a child is born, parental aspirations begin to take shape. By the time he reaches adolescence, parental aspirations are so well set that they encroach on his freedom and may prove damaging to his happiness and to family relationships. When the adolescent comes up to parental expectations, his parents are satisfied and acceptant in their attitudes. This has a favorable influence on the home climate.

Unfortunately, parental expectations are often unrealistically high. When the adolescent cannot fulfill them, his parents remind him of the sacrifices they have made and accuse him of not taking advantage of the opportunities they have provided. This attitude embitters the adolescent and brings about a strained parent-adolescent relationship which is extremely damaging to the home climate and plays havoc with the adolescent's personal adjustments.

The greatest damage comes when the failure of one member to come up to expectations is perceived as a disgrace by the rest of the family. If, for example, an adolescent fails in school—a failure his teachers anticipated on the basis of his ability—his parents may react to it as if it were a disgrace to the entire family.

Subjective disgraces—those based on failure to come up to unrealistically high levels of aspiration—are less damaging than *objective* disgraces—events viewed as disgraceful by the social group. When an adolescent girl has an illegitimate child, the family's reaction will be influenced by the attitudes of the social group with which the family is identified. If the group does not regard illegitimacy as a disgrace, the family's attitude toward the girl will be more tolerant than if the social group rejected her. Whether subjective or objective, disgrace gives rise to family friction and to deep resentments against the offender. While the family, through loyalty, may rally to the support of the disgraced member, this does not mean that the disgrace is forgotten (18, 129, 161).

Concepts of family roles

The "role concepts" held by different family members have a profound effect on expectations and thus on the home climate. Long before the child reaches adolescence, he builds up a concept of his own role in the family as well as concepts of the roles of other family members. Parents and siblings likewise have concepts of the roles various family members should play.

These concepts, like other concepts, are emotionally weighted. The weighting, which may range from strong to weak, determines the degree of liking the individual has for each family member. More important, the emotional weighting determines how easy or difficult it will be to change the concept.

Because of the growth in influence of the mass media, today's adolescents have much more stereotyped concepts of family roles than members of past generations had. Unfortunately, many of the stereotypes are unfavorable. The father is often stereotyped as an overly permissive person or, as Foster has pointed out, the "amiable boob of the situation comedies . . . the ineffectual but lovable bungler" (51). In describing the movie stereotype of the mother, Crowther (34) writes:

Something amazing is happening to the conventional image of Mom (short for American mother) in recent films. It is being severely "dumped on," to use a contemporary phrase. Mother is being presented as a boy's (or a girl's) worst friend. . . . Suddenly [the moviegoer] is confronted by the accumulating idea that mothers are without infallible wisdom and, indeed, can be bad for a kid. And fathers have not come off much better in all the films, though they have usually been subordinate to the mothers and sometimes even victimized by them—all of which makes for further implication of the nefariousness of Mom.

Box 14-8 compares the typical concepts of family roles held by American adolescents and their parents (2, 6, 41, 50, 93, 148).

Unlike the child who thinks of parents as people who do things for him, the independence-conscious adolescent thinks of them as people who guide him and help him to become an adult. With experience, he adds to his concept those qualities which he dislikes in parents, such as overprotectiveness, unfair and inconsistent discipline, interference in his friendships, attempts to influence his decisions without taking his interests or needs into consideration, complaints about his behavior, boastful remarks about him to outsiders, and failure to dress and act their age (2, 92).

BOX 14-8 AMERICAN CONCEPTS OF FAMILY ROLES

Role of Parents
To *adolescents:* Good parents guide and advise the adolescent to help him avoid mistakes. They are interested in his activities and his friends, are readily available when he needs them, and are fair in discipline. They give him a voice in family plans and try to see things from his point of view.

To *parents:* A good parent equips the adolescent for a happy, useful life by either authoritarian or developmental training.

Role of the Adolescent
To *adolescents:* The mass media stereotype of the adolescent's role in the family is widely held. The adolescent is seen as the "boss," the pride, joy, and hope of ambitious, self-sacrificing parents. His parents are his willing servants whose strongest desire is to give him a happy, carefree childhood with few responsibilities except to appear occasionally at family gatherings.

To *parents:* The adolescent is respectful, appreciative of the sacrifices parents have made for him, ambitious and anxious to get ahead, and eager to participate in family activities and make any contribution he can to the running of the home.

Role of Relatives
To *adolescents:* Most relatives are seen as unwelcome guests, intruders, or troublemakers. The most unfavorable concepts relate to female relatives because they are perceived as having greater authority over the adolescents than male relatives.

To *parents:* Because of their age and experience, relatives should be respected and treated with courtesy. Every effort should be made to please them and make them feel welcome in the home.

When one parent does not play the role the other parent thinks appropriate, criticism and friction will follow. If the father thinks he is a good father but his adolescent son does not, friction will develop between them. If the father holds the traditional concept of the good child, he will find it hard to accept the independence and outspokenness of the child brought up by a mother who has strongly developmental concepts of her role.

Thus, it is not the parent-child relationship or the husband-wife relationship, per se, that is important. Rather, it is *how each individual involved in the relationship perceives it*. When parents and their adolescent sons and daughters *both* perceive their relationship as favorable, there will be less friction between them than if either perceived the relationship as unfavorable.

Unrealistic, romanticized role concepts have a highly detrimental effect on the home climate. As Levin (93) has stated, adolescents usually idealize their concept of "father." They want their father

. . . to be ideal, God-like, and when [they] find he is not, [they] are disappointed. Yet circumstances conspire to undermine the ideal. Social change insists that father share his free time with his wife. The widespread disappearance of domestic help propels him into the nursery and kitchen. . . . Suburbia . . . relegates him to ungodlike tasks such as emptying the garbage pail.

Almost as detrimental as romanticized concepts are "imposed" role concepts. These come up in situations in which a member of the family who has strongly developed concepts of the role he should play in the family is forced, through circumstances, to play a role which he feels belongs to another family member. An adolescent daughter, for example, whose concept of a good mother is one who does things for her children, will be resentful when she is expected to assume some of the care of younger siblings.

Favoritism

The final important condition that plays havoc with good family relationships is favoritism. In any human relationship, in the home or outside, it is natural and normal for a person to prefer one individual to another and to feel more comfortable and "at home" with that individual. Certain family members fill the adolescent's needs better than others. This results in a warm, affectionate bond between them and the adolescent—a bond which is recognized or sensed by other family members and often resented.

At every age level, the individual's needs change somewhat as his pattern of life changes. An adolescent, for example, needs someone to whom he can turn for advice and help. If the mother is not only readily available to help him with his problems but is understanding and sympathetic in her attitudes, it is logical that the adolescent would prefer her to his father who is rarely available when he is needed most and, if available, is too tired or preoccupied with his own problems to take time to discuss those of the adolescent.

Preferences are also greatly influenced by the individual's perception of the emotional reactions of others toward him. When an adolescent is aware of the hero-worshiping attitude of a younger sibling, it is logical that he would prefer this sibling to another who goes out of his way to criticize and ridicule everything he does. Because fathers often feel that showing affection is "unmasculine" when directed toward their sons, but "masculine" when directed toward their daughters, boys tend to interpret this to mean that the fathers prefers the girls.

Preferences for certain family members are common in American homes, though they are far from universal. These targets of favoritism are listed in Box 14-9 along with a brief explanation (35, 61, 65, 75, 126, 168).

Two kinds of favoritism are especially damaging to the home climate. The *first* is favoritism that has been shifted from one family member to another. When the adolescent girl begins to prefer her father, the mother is likely to feel hurt and rejected. Sisters who were very close in childhood may develop a frictional relationship when one shifts her affection to an older brother.

The *second* kind of favoritism that is especially damaging to the home climate is that which is concentrated on one family member. If the firstborn son is the favorite of parents and grandparents and the hero of the baby of the family, the other children will resent the attention and affection lavished on him. Similarly, if the children side with the mother against the father, the parental relationship will suffer. Or if the children gang up against a parent whom they perceive as having treated one of them unfairly, the parent-child relationship will suffer.

EFFECTS OF HOME CLIMATE ON THE ADOLESCENT

The psychological atmosphere in which the adolescent grows up has a marked effect on his personal and social adjustments. *Directly,* it influences his characteristic patterns of behavior. If the home climate is happy, he will react to people and things in a happy, positive manner. If it is frictional, he will carry the frictional patterns of behavior learned in the home to situations outside the home and react to them as he habitually reacts to similar situations in the home.

Indirectly, the home climate influences the adolescent by the effect it has on his attitudes. If he learns to resent the authority of his parents because he perceives it as tyrannical and unfair, he will develop attitudes of resentment against *all* in authority. This often leads to radical, nonconforming behavior. A happy home climate, by contrast, will encourage a favorable attitude toward people in authority.

Which of the many conditions within the family has the greatest influence on the ado-

---

BOX 14-9   TARGETS OF FAVORITISM IN THE AMERICAN FAMILY

Children
Parental favoritism usually centers on the firstborn, the youngest in a large family, the one who is bright, ambitious, and a high achiever in academic or extracurricular activities, or the one who is physically or mentally handicapped. Mothers tend to favor sons, and fathers, daughters.

Parents
Both girls and boys favor their mothers in childhood. Girls often shift their preference to their fathers in adolescence because their fathers are less critical and demanding. When boys shift their preference, they tend to like both parents equally.

Siblings
In early adolescence, most girls prefer their sisters; as they grow older, they prefer their brothers. The favorite is usually an older brother who has no anti-girl attitudes. Throughout adolescence, boys tend to prefer their brothers, especially younger ones who hero-worship them. Regardless of the sex of the sibling, both boys and girls favor a sibling who is physically or mentally handicapped or who is "picked on" by one or both parents. The child who is a parent's favorite is rarely a favorite of his siblings.

Relatives
Female relatives—grandmothers and aunts—on the father's side of the family are usually preferred to those on the mother's side. Since male relatives rarely assume positions of authority over the adolescent, the adolescent's preferences are conditioned by the way they treat him and by the prestige of their occupations.

lescent? The answer depends largely on the *kind of person* the adolescent is. A quiet, introspective adolescent will react quite differently to friction between his parents than a more extroverted adolescent whose interests are centered on activities outside the home. As a general rule, the parent-child relationship is the most important single influence in determining the psychological climate of the home and the effect of the home climate on the adolescent. Peck and Havighurst (120) have written:

Each adolescent is just about the kind of person that would be predicted from a knowledge of the way his

Figure 14-5 Relation between early maternal behavior and adolescent behavior of boys. (Adapted from N. Bayley: Research in child development: A longitudinal perspective. *Merrill-Palmer Quart.,* 1965, **11,** 183–208. Used by permission.)

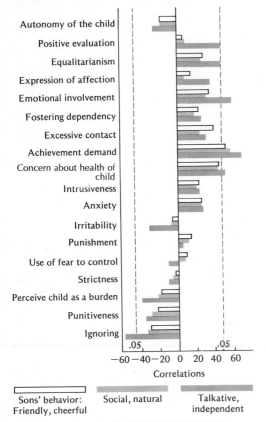

parents treated him. Indeed, it seems reasonable to say that, to an almost startling degree, each child learns to feel and act, psychologically and morally, as just the kind of person his father and mother have been in their relationships with him.

While the home climate affects all areas of the adolescent's life, certain areas are especially influenced by family relationships. The most important of these are discussed below.

Personal adjustment

When the home climate is characterized by affection, respect, cooperation, and tolerance, the adolescent will develop a wholesome self-concept; this will be reflected in good adjustments to life. When the home climate is marked by friction stemming from conflict and destructive competition, it will militate against the development of a wholesome self-concept, especially if the adolescent is directly involved in the conflict.

A study of the effects of parent-child conflicts has shown (see Fig. 14-5) how early maternal behavior affects the behavior of adolescent boys. On the basis of their findings in this study, Schaefer and Bayley (137) concluded:

The data . . . support hypotheses about maternal influence upon the development of the child. An analysis of progressive changes in parent-child correlations suggests that the child's social, emotional, and task-oriented behaviors are, to some extent, a reaction to the parental behaviors he has received throughout the period of childhood.

The mental health of the adolescent is influenced more by the composition and structure of the family and the role the adolescent plays than by the mental health of significant family members (125, 165). This is well illustrated in studies of the effects of ordinal position on the adolescent's adjustments. The firstborn who has been displaced by the arrival of a new sibling will, as Strauss has pointed out, "walk constantly as if with a chip on his shoulder. . . . He has learned from bitter experience that he may be displaced. In line with this, a general attitude of pessimism is common among the first-born." By contrast, according to Strauss, the youngest, who will never be displaced, is likely to be cheerful and happy, to have an optimistic outlook on life, and to make good personal adjustments (151).

The effects of ordinal position on personal admustments do not end with childhood or even with adolescence. Freud wrote many years ago that the child's "position in the sequence of brothers and sisters is of very great significance for the course of his later life" (53). The firstborn is often given greater advantages and encouragement than his siblings, and so is likely to achieve greater success than they. As Schachter (135) has explained:

The repeated findings of a surplus of firstborns among eminent scholars appears to have nothing to do with any direct relationship of birth order to eminence but is simply a reflection of the fact that scholars, eminent or not, derive from a college population in which first-borns are in marked surplus.

Social adjustment

If the home climate is pleasant and the adolescent enjoys doing things with and for the members of the family, he learns to behave in a socially approved way. This makes him popular with his peers as well as with adults. "The home," Warnath says, "thus appears indeed to be a seat of learning for the development of social skills, and perhaps of the desire to participate in activities with other individuals" (164).

The influence of the home climate on the socialization of the adolescent extends to many areas: learning to conform to group mores, to communicate with others, to participate in peer activities, and to express a liking for others. If the adolescent comes from a frictional home, he has doubtless developed the habit of rebelling against home standards—a habit which he will carry into his social relationships outside the home (9, 88).

A poor home climate discourages communication between family members (141). Ability to communicate is essential to popularity and even more so to leadership. Equally important in social acceptance is the ability to express affection for others. The adolescent who comes from a home with a frictional climate finds it difficult to establish affectional relationships with outsiders just as he does with family members (18).

Maturity of behavior

A happy home has been found to be associated with emotional stability and maturity of emotional control (137, 150). Moral maturity, characterized by inner control of behavior, is more characteristic of adolescents from happy homes. Moral immaturity, characterized by intentional misbehavior, misdemeanors, and delinquencies, is more characteristic of adolescents from homes where the psychological climate is poor (102, 128, 163).

Work attitudes

In a happy home, adolescents want to do their share in the running of the home. They develop work attitudes characterized by cooperativeness and a desire to work up to their capacities. These wholesome attitudes are generalized, leading to academic achievement, positive attitudes toward teachers and intellectual interests, good adjustment to the school routine, and a desire to participate in the extracurricular activities (87). As Cottle has remarked, "Good parents produce good students" (32).

The adolescent from a frictional home environment grumbles about the chores assigned to him and does them only under pressure; rarely does he work up to capacity. This unfavorable attitude is responsible for underachievement in school and a critical, faultfinding approach.

Work attitudes developed in the home also affect the individual's vocational adjustment. A little friction in the home may increase achievement motivation and lead to better work and greater success. But this is not likely to happen if friction is persistent or intense (30, 95, 144).

Dating

Adolescents who get along well with their families usually start to date earlier and date more frequently than adolescents from unhappy homes. Since large families tend to have a more frictional home climate than smaller families, adolescents from large families date less than those from smaller families (141, 152). The home climate affects the dating behavior of boys and girls differently. Girls who do not get along well with their mothers are especially eager to date and go steady as a form of compensation for the lack of happiness at home. Boys who get along well with their mothers date less than boys who have a poor mother-son relationship. Also they start to go steady later than girls. This sex difference may be explained by differences in maternal pressures on boys and girls (10, 127). Girls from unhappy homes are far more likely to engage in premarital sex relationships and to have illegitimate babies than girls from happy homes. Refer to Chapter 13 for a more complete discussion of this problem.

Marriage

The happier the parents' marriage and the happier the home climate, the more favorable the adolescent's attitude toward marriage. But, in general, adolescent attitudes toward marriage depend partly on what has caused friction in their homes and partly on their sex. Adolescent boys have a less favorable attitude toward marriage when their parents are divorced than do girls. Girls, by contrast, often feel that they have learned much from their parents' marital failure and that this will enable them to have a happier marriage (94, 140, 144).

Happiness

Primarily, the degree of happiness the adolescent experiences will be determined by the kind of relationship he has with his parents.

When the adolescent receives too little parental affection to meet his needs, he feels unhappy and rejected. While poor relationships with siblings and relatives may lead to unpleasantness, these relationships have less effect on the adolescent's happiness than an overall unhappy home atmosphere that these poor relationships engender (75, 109).

An unhappy home climate during the adolescent years often causes a permanent rift in the family structure. By contrast, a happy home climate generates family loyalty and solidarity. In times of crisis as well as in normal times, the members of a happy family flock together. They enjoy and support one another emotionally even though each may have his own family and his own adult pattern of life.

It is widely acknowledged that the American family is a less stable and less loyal unit than it was a few generations ago. The change is due partly to vocational and social mobility which encourages geographic distance between family members. But a more fundamental cause for the decrease in family cohesiveness is that being together does not necessarily increase happiness. And this is caused mainly by a deterioration in the psychological climate of the American home.

HIGHLIGHTS OF CHAPTER 14

1. The home climate, or the psychological atmosphere of the home, is often marked by friction during the years when the children are going through adolescence. Overt expressions of this friction lead to further deterioration of the home climate.

2. Overt expressions of family friction affect family members—parents, relatives, and the adolescents themselves—differently.

3. The home climate during the adolescent years is greatly improved by mutual understanding, which is largely determined by the ability of family members to communicate and to enjoy shared experiences.

4. When there is a conflict of values between the adolescent and his parents—and this is especially common when parents are foreign-born or overage—the adolescent tends to reject parental

values in favor of peer values. This inevitably leads to family friction with its damaging effects on the home climate.

5. Parental friction or a breakdown in family togetherness disrupts the home and friction tends to persist even when the home is broken by parental separation or divorce.

6. Studies of the effects of various kinds of parental control reveal that democratic control leads to the least friction in the home while both authoritarian and permissive control tend to be friction-instigating.

7. How much family size and composition contribute to a frictional home climate depends more on the quality of family relationships than on the number of relationships. Age, sex, and status in the family largely determine the nature of family relationships.

8. The typical American family is nuclear and adolescents tend to resent the presence of outsiders, be they boarders, part-time domestic helpers, guests, relatives, or stepparents. Thus, homes in which there are outsiders tend to be frictional. Of all outsiders, stepparents are likely to have the most damaging effect on the home climate because adolescents tend to regard them as intruders.

9. The socioeconomic status of the family is determined chiefly by parental occupations. The mother's occupation has a greater effect on the home climate than the father's. If the parent's occupation affects his aspirations for the adolescent, it will affect the parent-child relationship and thus the home climate.

10. When concepts of family roles change, as they do when the child grows older and has wider social contacts, they tend to lead to friction between the adolescent and family members whose appearance, interests, values, and behavior do not coincide with his concepts of what they should be. The more unrealistic the adolescent's concepts of family roles, the more detrimental they will be to a good home climate.

11. The adolescent's preference for one family member usually causes other members to be resentful, just as parental preference for one child arouses the resentment of the other children. Favoritism contributes heavily to family divisiveness.

12. The psychological climate of the home affects the adolescent's personal and social adjustments directly through its influence on his characteristic pattern of behavior, and indirectly, by the effect it has on his attitudes.

Chapter 15

Personality Changes

Just as few adolescents are satisfied with their appearance, so are few satisfied with their personality. The desire to improve both is almost obsessive throughout the adolescent years.

The adolescent has two compelling reasons for wanting to improve his personality. *First,* he knows, from his childhood gang experiences, that personality plays a major role in social acceptance. In discussing the differences between adolescent and adult cultures, Coleman (40) stated:

The importance of having a good personality, or what is a little different, "being friendly" or "being nice to the other kids" . . . is something that adults often fail to realize. Adults often forget how "personality-oriented" children are: they have not yet moved into the world of cold impersonality in which many adults live.

Second, the adolescent is dissatisfied with himself as he is. During the months of withdrawal from the social group, the pubescent becomes self-centered and introverted. He takes stock of himself, of his changing body and feelings, and of his successes and failures and decides that he can stand some improvement. This tends to be more true of boys than girls.

The more aware adolescents are of the value of personality in social relationships the stronger their desire to improve themselves. Dissatisfaction generally reaches its peak between the age of 15 and 16 years. After that both boys and girls become increasingly satisfied with the improvements they have been able to effect.

MEANING OF IMPROVEMENT

"Change" and "improvement" are not synonymous. To "change" means to alter or vary; it does not necessarily mean that the alteration or variation is complete or that the change is for the better. To "improve," on the other hand, means a change for the better. No adolescent merely wants to change; he wants to change for the better.

Changes can be quantitative or qualitative.

In *quantitative* changes, there is a weakening or strengthening of a trait already present. An undesirable trait, such as selfishness, becomes weaker as the child's desire to conform to socially approved standards of behavior becomes stronger. By adolescence or adulthood, the trait may closely approach the mean. In the same way, a socially desirable trait can be strengthened. It may appear that the individual's personality has improved. Actually improvement has come from weakening the socially undesirable trait and strengthening the desirable.

Qualitative changes—or changes in which a socially undesirable trait is completely eliminated and replaced by a desirable one, or vice versa—are unusual, especially in adolescence or adulthood. The adolescent may have a strong desire to get rid of a characteristic he dislikes and replace it with one everybody admires, but it is highly improbable that he will be able to do so.

An observed change in the adolescent's characteristic methods of adjustment may suggest that his personality has improved. However, his changed behavior may be merely a front to win greater social acceptance. The adolescent may be generous with peers whose favor he craves but revert to his usual stingy pattern of behavior with peers he cares little about or with family members. Under such conditions, he has not actually improved his personality even though he may give the impression that he has.

When improvement in personality occurs it is most likely to reflect quantitative changes for the better in *specific traits.* The core of the personality pattern—the concept of self—is least likely to change. With each passing year, it becomes more fixed (89, 141, 198). Box 15-1 lists and explains four conditions that may lead to personality improvement (11, 22, 64, 79, 96, 173).

OBSTACLES TO PERSONALITY IMPROVEMENT

In spite of the adolescent's strong desire to improve his personality, many obstacles stand

Traditional beliefs

There is a widely held traditional belief that
the individual *inherits* his personality from his
parents and other ancestors, just as he does
his eye color or hair texture. Popular justification for the belief is that children resemble
their parents in many of their personality
characteristics, just as their parents resemble
the grandparents. The possibility that the similarity is due to learning rather than heredity
is often overlooked.

It is a well-established scientific fact that
children learn many of their behavior patterns through imitation of those with whom
they are constantly associated. A boy who
hero-worships his father or older brother, for
example, will imitate his hero's aggressiveness or shyness or stinginess, regardless
of whether these are socially approved
traits. They are characteristics of *his hero*
and that is all that is important to him (73,
89, 138).

The belief that personality is inherited is
an obstacle to improvement because it stifles
attempts to change. However dissatisfied the
adolescent may be with himself, he feels that
he was born that way and can do nothing
about it.

Contradictory as it may sound, there is
another widespread belief that the personality
changes, often radically, at the times in life
when the body undergoes radical changes:
at puberty and at the climacteric, or "change
of life" when the reproductive function gradually ends. Unquestionably there are changes
in personality at these times. But all evidence
indicates that the changes are caused by environmental and social factors rather than
heredity and that the direction of the changes
can thus be controlled. The way in which the
pubescent child is treated by parents, teachers,
and peers determines how his personality
will change. This is emphasized by studies
of deviant maturers who are treated in accordance with their physical age rather than
their chronological age. Refer to Chapter 2
for a more complete discussion of deviant
maturing and personality.

It is commonly believed that changes in per-

in the way. Some are of the adolescent's own
making; others are beyond his control. Of the
many obstacles to improvement, those discussed in the following paragraphs are the
most troublesome.

sonality accompanying the physical changes of adolescence will always be in the direction of improvement. This belief is expressed in the saying, "He will *outgrow* that when he is older." If the adolescent accepts this traditional belief, it will weaken his motivation to try to change. Similarly, parents and teachers will fold their hands and do nothing, allowing undesirable personality traits to become reinforced with repetition.

Personality stereotypes

Personality stereotypes are found in every cultural group. Certain desirable or undesirable characteristics are associated with certain racial, religious, and occupational groups, with members of the two sexes, and with certain physical features. When these stereotypes are accepted, there is a tendency to believe that *all* people belonging to a particular group have the same traits (127, 133).

The most widely held stereotypes of personality are those associated with physical features—"physiognomy." For centuries, it has been believed that certain physical features are so universally associated with certain personality characteristics that you can judge a person's personality merely by observing his physical features. However, some physical features are believed to be more revealing than others. The skin texture, height of forehead, fullness of lips, quality of voice, and facial tension, for example, are used more in judging personality than are the width of the face, eyelid visibility, or height of eyebrows (171).

An adolescent who accepts these personality stereotypes comes to think of himself in terms of the stereotype associated with his group or sex or physical features. While not specifically claimed, it is *assumed* that the personality traits associated with a stereotype are hereditary. Consequently, with the acceptance of the stereotypes comes the acceptance of the belief that traits belonging to the stereotyped syndrome cannot be changed. If the adolescent likes the traits associated with a stereotype, no real harm will come from accepting it. But if he dislikes the traits,

he will be dissatisfied with himself and feel that there is nothing he can do about it.

Personality ideal

By *early adolescence,* the crush or hero-worship stage, boys and girls have developed a concept of what they consider the ideal personality. The concept is based on real people, usually adults, who play a prestigious role and have a well-recognized place in society. Today's adolescents draw their ideals mainly from personalities in the entertainment world. Furthermore, they almost always select people from their own culture; American adolescents tend to select Americans for their ideals.

Older adolescents have a more realistic concept of their ideal and they are more influenced by class consciousness. In selecting their ideal, members of both sexes pay particular attention to the qualities that are highly valued in the social group with which they are identified. Their ideal is usually a stereotype composed of traits from different people they have idealized in the past. As they learn that certain traits are more valued than others, their ideal personality stereotype changes (85, 97, 218).

The adolescent uses his ideal for the patterning of his own personality. Should he cling to an unrealistic ideal because of his intense admiration for some glamorized person, he may be in for great disappointment and frustration. If he has not acquired a more realistic concept by the end of high school, he is likely to suffer some degree of maladjustment—to become a distraught idealist.

One other way in which the ideal may become an obstacle to personality improvement is that the adolescent may idealize a person not approved or admired by the social group. In attempting to model his behavior after that of his ideal, the adolescent will develop characteristics that will make him a social misfit.

Complexity of personality pattern

Few adolescents realize what the personality really is or how complex the personality pattern can be. They feel that if they can change some handicapping trait, such as shyness, aggressiveness, or lack of self-confidence, that is all that must be done. Such an approach is too simplistic.

The term "personality" is derived from the Latin word *persona,* meaning a mask worn by an actor while speaking or performing on the stage. The actor revealed the character he was depicting through his speech and actions. Present-day definitions of *personality* stress much the same meaning. While different psychologists define the term differently, all accent the fact that personality is *not* one definite, specific attribute. Instead, it is the quality of the individual's total behavior as revealed by his speech and actions. Psychologists also point out that personality has a physical basis in the individual's neural, glandular, and general bodily states which provide the hereditary foundations for personality and are the driving forces that determine the kind of adjustment the individual makes in his personal and social relationships.

Of all the definitions of personality, that of Allport is probably the most widely accepted and the most often used as a model for definitions by other psychologists. According to Allport, "Personality is the dynamic organization within the individual of those psychophysical systems that determine his characteristic behavior and thought." (7). In this definition are several key terms that need further explanation. The words "dynamic organization" indicate that the characteristics constituting personality are interrelated, that they modify one another. The word "dynamic" tells us that the interrelationships are constantly changing. "Psychophysical systems" means that there are both physical and mental elements in personality. The word "determine" stresses the fact that the psychophysical systems are fundamentally the driving forces or causes of the individual's characteristic patterns of behavior.

The "personality pattern," as suggested above, is highly complex. It is not merely a loose collection of unrelated attributes. Instead, as the term "pattern" suggests, it is an organized unity composed of specific traits or qualities of behavior built up around a "core" or "center of gravity." The core not only serves to integrate and interrelate the different traits but also influences the form they will take. In a healthy, normal personality, the organization of the different parts of the pattern is well integrated and fairly stable over a period of time; in an abnormal personality, the pattern shows some degree of disorganization.

The *core* of the personality pattern is the concept the individual has of himself as a person. As Jersild has explained, it is a "composite of the thoughts and feelings which constitute a person's awareness of his individual existence, his conception of who and what he is" (92). Kinch has described the self-concept as the "organization of qualities that the individual attributes to himself" (103). In Box 15-2 are listed the various elements of the self-concept (28, 66, 85, 97, 172, 218).

The second component of the personality pattern is the specific *traits* or group of related and consistent reactions which characterize the individual's typical manner of personal and social adjustment. They are integrated into the personality pattern and influenced by its core—the self-concept. If the adolescent thinks of himself as superior to others, he will develop a characteristic manner of adjustment which his peers will describe as "having a swelled head." Or if he feels that he is slighted at home because of parental favoritism toward a sibling, he will behave both at home and away from home in a manner that will lead others to say that he "feels sorry for himself" or "suffers from a martyr complex" (7, 187).

Once the personality pattern has been established, it does not change unless steps are taken to produce a change. In young children, the core of the pattern is not well established; it can still be changed without disturbing the total personality balance. By adolescence, however, the personality pattern is less flexible because the self-concept is well formed and the individual's qualities and attitudes are more numerous and more set (7, 204).

As the self-concept becomes more stable,

the traits or qualities of behavior related to it become habitual. The adolescent then assigns himself a role related to his self-concept. As Shane (178) has written:

Children and adults are governed by the concept of self which they develop and make part of themselves. Thus we have boys and girls who assign to themselves the role of clown, good citizen, manager, shrinking violet, little demon, sage, feather-head.

How the concept of self dominates the role the adolescent learns to play is illustrated in Figure 15-1.

The rigidity of the self-concept makes it extremely difficult for others to help the adolescent improve his personality. When the student has come to think of himself as a slow learner, he will, as Walters says, put up a "Gibraltar-like resistance," even when his teachers and counselors can prove that he is as intelligent and as capable of learning quickly as his classmates (208). He is especially likely to reject advice and help if he feels that his self-concept is being threatened.

An equally troublesome obstacle to personality improvement is the adolescent's reputation. One who gains the reputation of being stingy will find it difficult to learn to be more generous if his friends continue to think of him as stingy or if they misinterpret his expressions of generosity as attempts to "buy popularity."

FACTORS INFLUENCING
THE SELF-CONCEPT

The self-concept, as the core of the personality pattern, is largely responsible for the ease or difficulty the adolescent experiences in trying to improve his personality. Of the many factors that influence the development of the self-concept, the following will be discussed here:

1. Physique
2. Physical defects
3. Physical condition
4. Chemique

**BOX 15-2 ELEMENTS OF THE
SELF-CONCEPT**

Physical Self-image: Consists of such qualities as tallness and fatness; sex-appropriate features; blemishes.

Psychological Self-image: Made up of such traits as timidity, honesty, stinginess, and aggressiveness.

Real Self-image: Is a "mirror image" of what the adolescent believes significant people in his life—parents, siblings, teachers, and peers —think of him both physically and psychologically. How they treat him and how they appraise him will determine, to a large extent, how he will appraise himself.

Ideal Self-image: Is a picture of what the adolescent would like to be, physically and psychologically. It serves as an internalized standard made up of his hopes and aspirations based on what he knows members of the social group hold in high esteem.

---

5. Clothes
6. Names and nicknames
7. Intelligence
8. Levels of aspiration
9. Emotions
10. Cultural patterns
11. School and college
12. Social status
13. Family influences

In examining these factors, note that some of them affect the two sexes differently. Note, too, that some of the factors are controllable, and others are not.

Physique

The adolescent knows that his physique— especially his size, sex appropriateness, and personal attractiveness—draws the attention of other people and affects their reaction to him. This, in turn, affects his attitude toward himself. Furthermore, he knows that many

Figure 15-1 The concept of self dominates the role the adolescent learns to play. (Adapted from H. G. Shane: Social experiences and selfhood. *Childhood Educ.*, 1957, **33**, 297–298. Used by permission.)

people accept the cultural stereotypes that relate physical features to personality traits: A wide mouth is believed to indicate friendliness; thick lips, sensuality; and an imposing stature, leadership (128, 171). Figure 15-2 shows how certain "personality types" are popularly associated with body build.

Every cultural group has its own standards of what is "right" in appearance for members of the two sexes. There is a "right" height for boys and for girls; "right" weight for members of each sex; and "right" degree of development of the secondary sex characteristics. Any physical characteristic that deviates from the cultural norm will be regarded as "wrong" and will have an unfavorable effect on the adolescent's self-concept. Being too fat or too thin, too tall or too short, can lead to feelings of inferiority. Being overweight as Bruch has pointed out, can lead to "a disturbance in the maturation of the total personality" (32).

Since few adolescents conform to the norms in every respect, they worry about the features that deviate and are anxious to correct them. Some are concerned about single features, while others are more concerned about the general impression their bodies make on others. A boy, for example, may feel that his small stature and delicate features create the impression that he is a sissy (52, 62, 174). Studies show that juvenile delinquents and adult criminals usually have distorted body images stemming from sex-inappropriate builds. Their antisocial behavior is partially an attempt to compensate for the unfavorable impression that they believe they create on others (44, 69).

Only within limits can the physical factors that have such a profound effect on the adolescent's self-concept be controlled. Dieting may make a fat body more slender or a slender body fatter. However, there is no known way to control height or to help the adolescent who feels that his body is less sex appropriate than he would like. Even though he may, through the use of clothing, acquire an appearance that comes close to his aspirations, the psychological damage caused by earlier resentments and frustrations may never be completely eliminated (109, 112).

Physical defects

Physical defects that were of little consequence during childhood often become the source of embarrassment and feelings of inferiority during adolescence. A slight facial scar or broken tooth, for example, does not disturb a child or attract the attention of his peers. But the self-conscious adolescent feels that any defect is conspicuous; he believes that *everyone* notices it and judges him unfavorably because of it. Thus, it is not the defect per se that affects the adolescent's self-concept but rather the frustrations and resentments he suffers because of his defect.

When a defect is so crippling that the adolescent must be segregated from his peers and put in a special school or home, the effect on the self-concept is especially damaging. The adolescent will lack self-confidence and suffer from generally poor mental health. He will develop negative attitudes not only toward himself but also toward members of the peer group who can have fun and take part in activities from which he is excluded. Deafness and blindness, like crippling, result in social isolation; they lead to poor self-concepts and encourage rigidity because the adolescent is unable to communicate with his peers. By contrast, a defect that does not prevent the adolescent from participating in activities that have high prestige value in the peer group will cause less damage to the self-concept (37, 45, 134).

Minor physical defects can usually be corrected so that they are hardly apparent to others. Major physical defects can often be corrected so that the defective structure can be functionally useful. Poor eyesight, for example, can be corrected by glasses or contact lenses, crooked teeth can be straightened by orthodontic devices, a nose can be reshaped by plastic surgery, and amputations can be overcome by the use of artificial limbs. But the adolescent's attitudes toward these corrective devices may be so negative that the damage to his personality persists (115, 123, 125).

Physical condition

Anything that upsets the homeostasis of the body, whether it be a temporary condition—such as fatigue or hunger—or a more prolonged condition—such as a wasting illness—will have an effect on the self-concept, and this will be reflected in the kind of adjustment the individual makes to life. Upsets in homeostasis are especially common during periods of rapid and uneven growth, as was explained in Chapter 2, but they may occur at any time when health is poor (56).

Should poor health or chronic illness develop in an adolescent whose childhood was healthy, changes in the self-concept are almost inevitable. The adolescent who is suddenly unable to take part in the activities of the group and who has to establish new interests and become self-sufficient finds the adjustment very difficult (37, 62, 161).

As adolescence progresses, most boys and girls come to realize that their health affects not only their looks but also their dispositions. As a result, they become more health-con-

scious and make use of any medical aids they can. With this desire to improve their physical conditions, they improve their self-concepts.

Chemique

The "chemique," or glandular condition produced by hormones from the endocrine system, has a marked influence on personality. A hyperthyroid condition, for example, pre-

Figure 15-2 Many people associate certain "personality types" with body build.

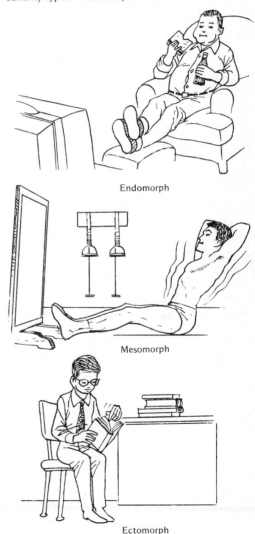

Endomorph

Mesomorph

Ectomorph

disposes the individual to be nervous, irritable, and ready to fly off the handle. Hypothyroidism, by contrast, is primarily responsible for the easygoing, lethargic, indolent personality.

Because of the upset in glandular homeostasis that normally accompanies the menstrual cycle, adolescent girls tend to be depressed and morbid for several days before as well as during the menstrual period. Attempted suicide is reported to be most common during those days (201). Much of the negative-phase behavior of both boys and girls during the early part of puberty can be traced to disturbances in glandular homeostasis. As the glandular condition becomes stabilized, the adolescent usually reverts to his former personality pattern (56).

Indirectly, endocrine glands also affect the personality. The anterior lobe of the pituitary determines whether the individual will be normal in stature or tend toward giantism or dwarfism. Any marked deviation from the average will produce an unfavorable reaction in the social group, and this will affect the adolescent's attitude toward self. The more marked the deviation, the more damaging the effect on the self-concept.

While medical control of the endocrine system is still in an experimental stage, enough is known to be able to control some of the personality disturbances which accompany upsets in endocrine homeostasis. Thyroid treatment, for example, makes the lethargic hypothyroid adolescent more alert, physically and mentally, while estrogen treatment overcomes much of the moodiness and depression the adolescent girl suffers from at the time of her menstrual periods.

Clothes

Clothes are a status symbol for the adolescent and, as such, have a profound effect on his self-concept. For the adolescent whose physique is a source of embarrassment or concern, clothes are especially important because of their camouflage value. Furthermore, since appearance affects one's social acceptance, the adolescent may be able to avoid much of the damage of social rejection if his clothes improve his looks and boost his self-confidence.

Even adolescent boys who, from early childhood, have scorned good clothes as an insignia of a sissy and have delighted in wearing the most slovenly attire, realize that clothes are status symbols that affect social judgments. As they approach the time when they will enter the vocational world, they become increasingly aware of the role clothes play in the impressions others form of them (70, 160). And, like girls, they discover the camouflage value of clothes. For many boys whose physique does not come up to their expectations or to social standards of sex appropriateness, clothes prove to be an important ego booster.

To serve as an aid in improving the self-concept, clothes must add to the adolescent's prestige in the group and enhance his physique. The stores are full of clothing which would serve these two purposes, but there are obstacles which hamper the adolescent's use of it.

First, the adolescent does not know what clothes will best enhance his physique. Sooner or later, through trial and error or comments by others, the adolescent learns to be selective in choosing his clothes and to concentrate on those which improve his looks, even though they may not conform to his preferences.

Second, feelings of insecurity motivate the adolescent to conform to the prevailing styles of the group whether they are becoming to him or not. An overweight girl who is afraid of "being different" may only make herself look more unattractive by wearing dresses with ruffles when that is the prevailing style.

Third, good clothes cost money. Those with prestigious labels often cost more than the adolescent or his family can afford. Nor do all parents, even when they can afford it, feel that such expenditures are justified.

Names and nicknames

How the adolescent feels about his name or nickname will determine its effect on his self-concept. And how he feels about it will be greatly influenced by the attitudes of significant others—or what be *believes* is their attitude. As Abbott and Bruning have stated, "Names may play significant roles in both inter- and intrapersonal behavior" (1). Hartman et al. (81) have spelled out in more detail why this is true:

A child's name, like his somatotype, is generally a settled affair when his first breath is drawn, and his future personality must then grow within its shadow. A powerful mesomorphic boy must experience a different world from his puny counterpart; and, similarly, a boy who answers to a unique, peculiar, or feminine name may well have experiences and feelings in growing up that are quite unknown to John or William. We would expect these childhood experiences to be reflected in the subsequent personality. It is plausible, and confirmed by clinic experience, to assume also that some individuals are seriously affected in their adjustment as a result of a peculiar name.

Should the adolescent like his name and feel that it is approved by the social group with which he is identified, it will give him a feeling of superiority. This will increase his self-confidence. The more dissatisfied he is with his name, the greater psychological hazard it becomes. In commenting on the effect of names and nicknames on the self-concept, Murphy (139) has emphasized that it is not the name, per se, that determines the effect but the attitude of the individual toward his name:

The names of individuals play an important role in the organization of their ego defense patterns and are cathected and utilized from the point of view of ego defenses in a manner similar to an organ or body part. . . . For some, the name may become a part of the core of severe neurosis. . . . The degree of pathological disturbance varies from exaggerated pride or exaggerated shame over one's name, commonly encountered among adolescents, to extremes of psychotic proportions.

Only within limits can the adolescent control the name that becomes a symbol of his self in the eyes of others. If he likes his name or nickname, or some part of it, he can encourage others to use it, though he cannot force them to do so.

Embarrassing family names are not so easy to change. Should the parents be divorced and the mother remarry, for example, the adolescent may be embarrassed to have a name that is different from hers, especially if he is living with her. The only way to avoid this embarrassment is for the stepfather to legally adopt the adolescent—a step that can be taken only with the consent of both parents and the stepfather.

Intelligence

If an adolescent is unable to do the work of the regular high school and is sent to a vocational school, he is likely to develop feelings of inadequacy and inferiority. Because of his inability to comprehend situations as quickly and as well as persons of normal intelligence, the *below-average* adolescent has poor social insight. He says and does many things which arouse his classmates' antagonism. If he recognizes that he is disliked, the unfavorable social attitude will be very damaging to his self-concept. Fortunately, most dull adolescents fail to recognize how unpopular they are, and so social rejection is less damaging to their personality than one might anticipate.

Most adolescents who are *bright* know it and know that others know it. How their peers react to their brightness will depend, to some extent, upon the kind of school they attend. If they are in a school where the majority of the students want to make good grades and go to college, they can be assured of the admiration of their classmates provided they are not cocky or conceited and provided they make some contribution to the school instead of spending all their time studying to make high grades. If they take a superior attitude toward others or if they are self-bound and have difficulty in talking to others and expressing their feelings, they will be disliked and their self-concepts will suffer. In the cultural stereotype, the bright person is "queer" or an "impractical dreamer." Thus the bright adolescent who does not make good social adjustments is likely to regard himself as "different" (10, 76). As a defense against unfavorable social attitudes, he may become an intellectual snob—a person who feels socially inferior but intellectually superior. When this happens, he develops a superiority complex and his belief that he is superior is reflected in his behavior. Thus, brightness, per se, is neither an asset nor a liability to personality; what matters is whether the adolescent makes use of his brightness to win social acceptance.

Average or slightly above average intelligence enables the adolescent to adjust with reasonable success to academic life without being a threat to his classmates. He has enough social insight to size up people and situations and to react to them in an acceptable way. As a result, he feels no need to defend himself against unfavorable peer attitudes. Unlike the very bright or very dull, he runs little risk of developing delusions of grandeur because he feels superior or delusions of persecution because he feels that others misjudge him (3, 130, 150).

At the present time, there is no known way to produce appreciable changes in the intellectual capacity of the individual. However, the *use* the individual makes of his capacity is controllable. An adolescent who is very bright can learn to accept his intellectual superiority as a legacy from his ancestors, not as an indication of personal achievement. He can also learn that his superior intelligence entails a responsibility to make some contribution to society. Instead of spending the major part of his time trying to win academic awards which, though ego satisfying, contribute nothing to the social group, he can participate in activities which are community-oriented and which his less bright peers may not have the time or talent to make worthwhile contributions to. The social attitude toward very bright students is always more favorable if they are well-rounded individuals, participating in the affairs of their institutions and making some contribution to them.

The psychological damage resulting from low-grade intelligence can be greatly minimized by putting adolescents with limited ability together in special classes. Since they will not have to compete with brighter students, the likelihood of their developing feelings of inferiority will be reduced. Furthermore, as friendships are usually established among those who are in the same school classes, the less bright will become identified with a social group where they will have little reason to feel rejected. The major obstacle to this kind of control of the environment is resistance on the part of parents who do not wish to accept the fact that their children are intellectually handicapped.

Levels of aspiration

The adolescent's level of aspiration has a marked influence on his self-concept, determining whether he will see himself as a success or a failure. See Chapter 9 for a complete discussion of levels of aspiration and the importance of objective and subjective success and failure. When the adolescent is successful in reaching the goal he sets for himself, he has a feeling of self-satisfaction and self-confidence. However, if he sets his level of aspiration too low for his abilities and has too many easy successes, he may become cocky and boastful. He may even, on the basis of past successes, raise his goals unrealistically high and then experience a blow to his ego when he fails. While an occasional failure helps the adolescent to keep his feet on the ground and view himself realistically, a series of failures can be devastating.

Failure to reach one's goal undermines self-confidence and leads to feelings of personal inadequacy. It makes the adolescent submissive in his attitudes and apprehensive about the future. To avoid the ego-deflating experience of future failure and to guarantee success, he may set his level of aspiration unrealistically low. Or to ease his feelings of inadequacy, he may project the blame for his failure on others, thus thinking of himself as a martyr. Either path will lead to poor self-concepts, poor adjustment, and unhappiness.

The best way to control the psychological damage resulting from excessive failure or success is to encourage the individual to assess his abilities realistically and to set levels of aspiration which he has a reasonable chance of reaching. Once he has developed the habit of aspiring unrealistically, in either direction, he will resist changing.

A second means of control is to discourage verbalization of levels of aspiration. Many parents and teachers believe that if the adolescent tells his friends what his goal is he will be better motivated to attain it. While it is true that talking about his aspirations may raise his prestige in his own eyes as well as in the eyes of others, the psychological damage from failure is too great to justify this temporary ego satisfaction.

Emotions

Box 15-3 explains four ways in which the emotions affect the self-concept (7, 90, 124, 184, 211). In each case, the effect on the adolescent's self-concept comes from social judgments of his behavior.

Because of the psychological damage emotionality can cause to the self-concept, proper handling of the emotions is essential if the adolescent is to improve his personality. Emotional catharsis, both physical and mental, is the only successful way to handle emotions. See Chapter 3 for a more complete discussion of this matter.

Cultural patterns

Each culture has its own approved pattern for the behavior of its members. Furthermore, every culture and every cultural subgroup establishes behavioral patterns appropriate for

---

BOX 15-3 HOW THE EMOTIONS AFFECT THE SELF-CONCEPT

Upset in Body Homeostasis
Even when overt expressions of the emotions are controlled, an upset in body homeostasis makes the adolescent jittery and ill at ease. Nervous mannerisms such as nail-biting and giggling create the impression that he is silly and immature. Unfavorable social reactions to his behavior lead to feelings of inadequacy and inferiority.

Temperament
The dominant emotions that the adolescent experiences determine his temperament or prevailing mood. If he experiences more anger and resentment than happiness, he will get the reputation of having a disagreeable personality. If he smiles a lot and acts as if he is enjoying life, he will be regarded as happy and good-natured—a reputation that will lead to favorable social judgments and a good self-concept.

Method of Expression
Some adolescents express their emotions on the spot, thus giving the impression that they are impulsive and immature. Some inhibit the expression but release the pent-up energy by directing it at a scapegoat; this is regarded by others as poor sportsmanship. Some inhibit emotional expression and release the pent-up energy later in a socially approved way; this gives the impression that they are mature and well controlled.

Frequency of Expression
Too frequent, too violent, and apparently unjustified emotional outbursts indicate to others that the adolescent is immature. Too much control, on the other hand, will make him moody and disagreeable, creating almost as unfavorable an impression as frequent outbursts.

---

members of the two sexes (21). Within these culturally approved confines, each individual is expected to develop a basic, conforming personality pattern. Even before adolescence, the boy or girl knows that sex-inappropriate behavior must be avoided. In a poem entitled "A Certain Age" (from *Times Three: Selected Verse from Three Decades*. Viking Press, 1960, p. 45), Phyllis McGinley expresses the intensity of the young girl's need to conform:

All of a sudden, bicycles are toys,
Not locomotion. Bicycles are for boys
And seventh-graders, screaming when they talk.
A girl would rather
Take vows, go hungry, put on last year's frock,
Or dance with her own father
Than pedal down the block.

Since personality is a product of cultural influences and is shaped by pressures from the social group, this means, as Stendler has explained, that as "cultures differ, so do the personalities embedded in these cultures" (189). The individual normally comes to think of himself as a member of a particular cultural group, and his conforming behavior becomes habitual.

If necessary and if the motivation is strong enough, the adolescent can break away from his early cultural influences just as he can break any well-learned habit. This he must do if his family is socially mobile. But it is a long, difficult, and often only partially satisfying experience. If he refuses to accept the values of the group, he will become a cultural misfit. The more he rejects the cultural pattern, as in the case of the rugged individualist, the more he will be socially disapproved and the more damage there will be to his self-concept.

School and college

As Solomon has stressed, "The schoolroom must be looked upon as a force secondary in importance to the home in the development of human personality" (183). A number of studies in which adults reported school and college incidents in which they felt embarrassed, inadequate, shy, or insecure indicates how dam-

aging the unpleasant experiences were to their developing self-concepts (33, 88).

The areas of school or college life that have the highest prestige in the eyes of the members of the group with which the adolescent is identified have the greatest influence on his personality development. How he performs in these areas will have a decided influence on his self-concept—on how he rates himself. The areas of campus life that carry the greatest prestige vary from school to school and from time to time, and so no general statements can be made about their relative importance in personality development. However, certain aspects of *every* educational environment affect the adolescent's concept of self. Box 15-4 lists and describes the most important (34, 60, 88, 90, 155, 186).

No one adolescent can change the established pattern of school or college life or the values held by the majority of the students. Therefore, a practical way to control the influence the school or college has on personality is to encourage the adolescent to change and to help him to do so.

Even more important, the adolescent can be helped to assess himself and his abilities more realistically. This will go a long way toward eliminating feelings of academic and social failure. A more realistic attitude toward himself and his abilities will make him more relaxed and may prevent him from dropping out. While dropping out may temporarily remove some of the conditions which are damaging to the self-concept, the dropout inevitably feels that he is a failure.

Social status

Studies of the effects of social status on the self-concept reveal that certain personality characteristics are commonly associated with certain statuses. Adolescents who are *reasonably popular* become extroverted, self-confident, relaxed, and independent in thinking and actions. These personality traits enhance their popularity. Their increased popularity has a favorable effect on their self-concepts. Very *popular* adolescents tend to be somewhat aloof and self-centered because they do not want to offend anyone by playing favorites and because they often have exaggerated opinions of their own importance.

Adolescents who are never selected to play *leadership* roles often develop unfavorable self-concepts along with feelings of failure, resentment, anger, and jealousy. Those who are selected as leaders feel content and self-assured. They may develop self-concepts colored by delusions of grandeur if they are always chosen to lead.

The kind of *unpopularity* the adolescent experiences will determine its effect on his self-concept. The adolescent who is disliked and rejected may develop a chip-on-the-shoulder attitude which causes him to be uncooperative, selfish, and aggressive in his behavior and speech. As Coleman has pointed out, the adolescent will not "sit still while his self-evaluation is being lowered by the social system of the school" (40). He may try to win status by approved acts; more likely, he will try to get even with those who have rejected him.

**BOX 15-4 ASPECTS OF SCHOOL AND COLLEGE LIFE
THAT AFFECT THE SELF-CONCEPT**

Teachers
The teacher's influence comes from the way the adolescent *believes* the teacher judges him, the way the teacher treats him, the method the teacher uses to motivate study, and the personal and social adjustment of the teacher.

Extracurricular Activities
Since athletic achievements are prestigious for boys and social achievements for girls, those who stand out in these areas will develop favorable self-concepts.

Bull Sessions
Intimate conversations with peers give the adolescent new insight into his own problems and help him to realize that he is not unique; they provide an emotional catharsis by giving the adolescent an opportunity to let off pent-up emotional steam; they allow an exchange of views on many subjects and break down any rigidity of thinking; and they enable the adolescent to see himself as others see him and, thus, to change his concept of self.

Prestige of Institution
Being in a school or college that has prestige in the community because of its high academic rating, its athletic successes, or its exclusiveness in student makeup is ego-inflating, while being in one with low ratings in these areas is ego-deflating. See Figure 15-3.

Grades
The adolescent judges himself to a great extent in terms of his grades. The more stress a school or its leading student groups place on grades, the greater their influence on the adolescent's self-concept.

Popularity
The self-concept of the adolescent is more affected by success in extracurricular activities than by grades because students put more value on extracurricular achievements and because their judgments are more important to the adolescent than the judgments of teachers.

Figure 15-3 The prestige of the adolescent's school influences his self-concept.

Adolescents who are overlooked and neglected have many of the same frustrations and resentments as those who are rejected. But, in addition, they come to think of themselves as "different." They feel they have nothing to offer the group, and so become shy and retiring.

In commenting on the damaging effects of unpopularity, Friedenberg (65) writes:

Adolescents lack reserves of self-esteem to sustain them under humiliating conditions. . . . Adolescents are dreadfully concerned about society's appraisal of them and their worth. . . . They cannot easily assimilate an attack on their dignity or worth, for it produces not merely resentment but intense anxiety. The self is threatened while still ill-defined and in its early stages of construction.

While the *voluntary isolate* may be liked by the social group and would be accepted as a member if he wanted to be, he feels that he has little in common with his peers. He as-

sumes an attitude of indifference toward them and shuns their social activities—behavior which leads others to conclude that he is an oddball. This social attitude is then mirrored in his self-concept.

The insecure status of the *fringer* or *climber* leads to anxiety and a strong motivation to do and say whatever the group approves. Most adolescents in this precarious social status become "me-too" personalities (87, 186, 214).

Social status is used by adolescents as a measuring rod of their worth, and an improvement in status would, unquestionably, lead to an improvement in the self-concept. Social status, however, is difficult to control and attempts at improvement are rarely to the adolescent's satisfaction.

One way to improve social status, and perhaps the self-concept, is to change the environment so that the adolescent will have opportunities to associate with people whose interests, abilities, and backgrounds are more similar to his. It is hard, for example, for an adolescent to have a favorable self-concept if his classmates regard him as "different" or "inferior." Changing the environment will not lead to an improved self-concept if the adolescent lacks the qualities needed for acceptance in the group with which he wishes to be identified. He can improve his social acceptance *only* if he develops new interests and skills or is willing to be friends with persons whose abilities and backgrounds are closer to his. Similarly, if he lacks the ability to be a leader, being a cooperative, loyal follower will increase his social acceptance.

Family influences

Parental attitudes and behavior, more than anything else, shape the adolescent's budding personality. Strict, punitive, and demanding parents unwittingly encourage impulsiveness in the adolescent because they do not give him an opportunity to develop internalized controls. Warm, affectionate parents encourage the adolescent to become gregarious and social, while cold and indifferent parents encourage him to be gloomy, seclusive, or socially withdrawn (180). The effects of parent-child relationships on personality development are illustrated in Figure 15-4. Box 15-5 describes the family influences that have the most pronounced effects on the self-concept (18, 19, 100, 106, 122, 176).

Of all the factors that influence the adolescent's self-concept, family influences are, unquestionably, the most difficult to control. The adolescent must be governed by his parents' decisions about where to live and go to school. He cannot do much to change the way his parents treat him and his siblings, nor can he change the training methods they use. Within limits, he can exert some influence over the frictional relationships of the home. But he alone is not responsible for the friction even though he may contribute his share.

Many parents do not recognize the psychological damage that comes from conditions within the home. Unless something disturbs them personally, they often adopt a hands-off policy and allow the children of the family

to cope with unhappy situations as best they can. This is well illustrated in the verbal fighting of siblings. If it annoys parents, they will put a stop to it. But if they feel that it is an inevitable accompaniment of growing up, they will do nothing.

Fortunately, most parents sooner or later realize that treating their adolescent sons and daughters like near adults reduces family friction, improves the dispositions of the children, and encourages them to adopt a more mature pattern of behavior. As the home climate improves, many of the conditions that have been so damaging to the developing self-concept come under better control.

HOW GREAT IS PERSONALITY IMPROVEMENT?

Few adolescents are as successful at improving their personalities as they would like to be. The combined influences of heredity and environment result in the development of rather persistent individual personality patterns.

Because adolescence is characterized by profound and sometimes sudden physical, mental, and emotional changes, it is logical to expect some change in the individual's per-

Figure 15-4 Effects of relationships with parents on personality development. (Adapted from P. E. Slater: Parental behavior and the personality of the child. *J. genet. Psychol.*, 1962, **101**, 52–68. Used by permission.)

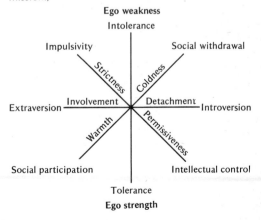

BOX 15-5   HOME INFLUENCES ON THE SELF-CONCEPT

Parental Power
The *amount* of autonomy parents are willing to grant the adolescent greatly influences his self-concept. If parents are confident that the adolescent can handle his affairs successfully, he will be confident also.

Family Friction
Family friction affects the adolescent's personality unfavorably by (1) upsetting his body homeostasis, which leads to anxiety, nervousness, and insecurity, and (2) encouraging aggressive verbal attacks which damage the adolescent's self-esteem.

Family Size
The adolescent from a one-child family generally develops a more wholesome self-concept than one who is subjected to the damaging influence of sibling rivalry and friction.

Status in Family
Firstborn children are under constant pressure to live up to parental expectations, and so they tend to become serious, sensitive, conforming, and dependent; they often suffer from feelings of inadequacy. Later-born children become more peer-oriented, and this makes them more cheerful, friendly, and competitive. They tend to be more popular with their peers than firstborns and this has a favorable effect on their self-concept.

Family Socioeconomic Status
Directly, the effect of socioeconomic status on personality comes from the kind of control parents exercise. Middle-class parents, for example, emphasize the importance of conformity to group standards and this encourages the development of the "conformer" personality pattern. *Indirectly*, the effect comes from the adolescent's comparison of his status with that of his peers. If his status is inferior, the effect on his self-concept will be unfavorable.

sonality at this time. Furthermore, new environmental factors enter the adolescent's life. They, too, leave their mark on his personality. The adolescent years, then, may be regarded as a critical time in the development of personality; during these years it is determined whether the individual will become a mature, resolute, socially conscious individual or one who is frustrated, unsocial, dependent, and immature.

To determine how much improvement takes place in the individual's personality during adolescence, one must examine evidence from studies of persistence in personality to see how much change occurs, what causes it, and what form it takes.

Meaning of persistence

"Persistence" means enduring or constantly recurring. It does not mean that no change occurs; instead, it means that certain traits tend to remain in an unchanged, or relatively unchanged, form. The important thing about personality is, as Allport has pointed out, "its relatively enduring and unique organization" (7).

Persistence of personality is also emphasized by Thompson (199):

Only rarely does there occur a maverick, one whose life experience somehow made him a rebel rather than a conformist. But even then the degree of his deviation is not permitted to be unlimited. Beyond a certain point, society forbids his deviation and few can survive that degree of disapproval.

There are, however, Thompson further explains, two conditions under which the personality pattern will change: First, under circumstances of great stress and temptation, unacceptable patterns of behavior may erupt; and second, when significant people in the individual's life change, he will try to adapt to the new situation.

The fundamental reason for persistence in the personality pattern is to be found in the stability of the self-concept. This is well illustrated in the persistence of feelings of inadequacy, inferiority, and martyrdom that develop as a result of constant exposure to prejudice and discrimination (101).

While the self-concept is the more persistent component of the personality pattern, some traits are markedly persistent also. Those associated with intelligence, physical development, and temperament are the most persistent, while those related to social situations, such as introversion or extroversion, values, and attitudes, are less persistent. Traits that are traditionally sex appropriate for members of the two sexes are also extremely persistent (7, 98, 102). Persistence in different personality traits is illustrated in Figure 15-5 which shows behavior ratings for the same males and females in childhood and in adulthood.

Evidence of persistence

That the personality pattern is persistent has been shown by a number of genetic studies covering a wide age range in the same individuals. "Shirley's babies" showed such consistent personality patterns during the first two years of their lives and 15 years later that they could readily be identified (142). A study of six individuals, rated on 35 personality traits 50 years after judgments about them had been

recorded in their mother's diary, revealed that even after that length of time there was marked persistence in 70 percent of the traits (182). Dependent behavior and striving for achievement and recognition through competence in intellectual or athletic attainments or through improved economic and cultural milieus have likewise been found to be persistent from the early school years into adulthood (98). Personality patterns of early and late maturers, developed as a result of the way they were treated at puberty, have been found to persist into the early thirties (9, 95, 96). Refer to Chapter 2 for a more complete discussion of the effects of deviant sexual maturing on personality.

The best evidence of the difficulties the adolescent faces when he wants to improve his personality comes from studies of the persistence of *maladjustive behavior.* Records of patients in mental hospitals reveal that they have shown poor adjustment since their childhood days. Those who are excitable as adults were excitable as children; those who are schizophrenic as adults were apathetic as children (63, 107). In one study, adults with psychosomatic disorders were found to have made poorer adjustments during childhood

Figure 15-5 Persistence of different personality traits from childhood into early adulthood. (Adapted from J. Kagan and H. A. Moss: *Birth to maturity: A study in psychological development.* New York: Wiley, 1962. Used by permission.)

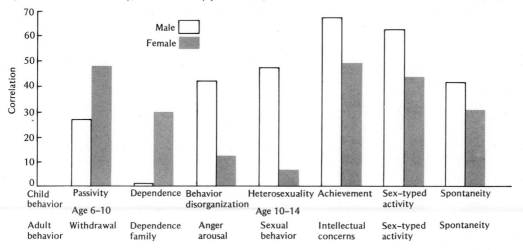

and adolescence than did a symptom-free group used for comparison (190).

Children and adolescents who make good social and personal adjustments tend to make good adjustments in adulthood. They are also far less likely than poorly adjusted youngsters to become involved in delinquent and criminal behavior (14, 162).

Box 15-6 discusses some of the many conditions that contribute to persistence in personality (6, 7, 12, 47, 98, 102, 198).

BOX 15-6 CONDITIONS CONTRIBUTING TO PERSONALITY PERSISTENCE

Heredity
Any trait that is related directly or indirectly to the individual's hereditary endowment will be quite stable over the years. Physical timidity, caused by having a small physique, is not likely to be replaced by physical daring because the individual will not have the physical strength to carry through the change.

Home Training
Because home training tends to be persistent, the self-concept and patterns of behavior related to it become reinforced over the years and develop into well-established habits.

Social Interactions
In the home, the child becomes accustomed to playing the role assigned to him and to thinking of himself as other family members think of him. This pattern developed in the home influences interpersonal relationships outside the home.

Selection of Environment
Once established, the personality pattern determines the kind of environment the individual will select to live and work in and the kind of people he will associate with. He will, for example, select friends whose concept of him causes them to treat him in accordance with his concept of himself.

SELF-ACCEPTANCE AND SELF-REJECTION

Because few adolescents are satisfied with their personalities or with the improvements they are able to make, many find it difficult to like and accept themselves. "Self-acceptance," as Pannes has defined it, is the degree to which an individual, "having considered his personal characteristics, is able and willing to live with them" (149). Jersild (92) has explained in more detail that a person who is self-acceptant

. . . respects himself and lives comfortably with himself; he is able to recognize his own wishes, hopes, fears, and hostilities and to accept his emotional tendencies not in the sense of being smugly self-approving but in the sense of having freedom to be aware of the nature of his feelings; he is freer to make his own decisions and assume responsibility for them.

Because of these self-acceptant attitudes, the person "likes" himself and feels that others also find likable qualities in him. His positive self-regard is stable; it does not fall or rise indiscriminately in relation to criticism or praise.

Many more adolescents are self-rejectant than self-acceptant, especially boys and especially in the early years of adolescence (92, 149). The *self-rejectant* person dislikes himself. He tends to be self-derogatory and to feel that others view him with hostility and disparagement; he does not trust his own feelings and attitudes, and his self-regard vacillates with the attitudes of others toward him; ordinarily he has a grudging attitude toward himself, as shown by an unwillingness to spend money on himself. Self-rejection comes mainly from having a real self-concept that falls short of the ideal self-concept. Even older adolescents tend to have unrealistic objectives and aspirations and to come to college with grandiose expectations. This disparity between what they are and what they would like to be makes it difficult for them to accept themselves (136, 217, 219).

The degree to which the adolescent accepts

himself will determine the kind of life adjustments he makes. No one, at any age, can hope to make good adjustments if he dislikes and rejects himself. On the other hand, a reasonably self-acceptant person will behave in such a way that others will like and accept him. This will increase his self-acceptance. Since self-acceptance and self-rejection become self-perpetuating, maladjustive or adjustive behavior likewise becomes self-perpetuating.

How self-acceptant or self-rejectant the adolescent is will be influenced by his environment. If he is forced to remain in a school year after year where he is constantly subjected to prejudice and discrimination, or if he lives in a home where parents believe that the best way to discipline children is to criticize their weaknesses and ignore their good qualities, the adolescent will find that self-rejection outweighs self-acceptance.

Self-acceptance is easiest when the attitudes of others, especially significant people in the individual's life, are favorable. A baby has no difficulty accepting himself because "everyone loves a baby." The troublesome teen-ager, on the other hand, finds that significant people in his life regard him only as a member of a stereotyped group—the "terrible teens," the "potential juvenile delinquents," or the "smart alecks who know it all."

Effects of self-rejection

When a person rejects himself, he makes poor personal and social adjustments. There are two major kinds of personality maladjustment. The first involves behavior that is personally satisfying but socially unacceptable; the second involves behavior that is socially acceptable but a source of excessive, continuous, and disturbing conflict to the individual. If the adolescent follows the first behavioral pattern, he will gain temporary personal satisfaction by making aggressive physical or verbal attacks on others or by projecting the blame for his socially disapproved behavior on others. This temporary satisfaction will be overshadowed by social disapproval. On the other hand, if he follows the second pattern, he retreats from reality by refusing to come to grips with his problems. His behavior will win social approval, but it will be personally unsatisfying (187, 211).

Maladjustment is far more common in adolescence than is generally realized. Today, it is recognized that juvenile delinquents are maladjusted. It is also recognized that many so-called "normal" adolescents are difficult to live with and have social and personal adjustment problems: Many are underachievers, others do poor work in school and on the job, most have few friends, and almost all are quarrelsome and unhappy at home and in their social relationships outside the home (13, 69, 136).

When maladjustment exists, there are always "danger signals." No one of these alone is necessarily a portent of trouble. When several appear in the same individual, however, and when they seem to fit into a personality pattern—the maladjustive syndrome—they can no longer be ignored. In Box 15-7 are given some of the most common danger signals of personality maladjustment in adolescence (31, 51, 124, 144, 158, 165). Note that many of the danger signals are found in well-adjusted adolescents, but they are found in clusters and in greatly exaggerated form in those who are poorly adjusted.

Whatever form the maladjustive behavior takes, its fundamental purpose is to protect the ego. Washburn has written, "Just as an individual evolves many responses to protect his body, so he does to protect his ego" (211). The smaller the discrepancy between real and ideal self-concepts, the less self-rejectant the adolescent will be and the less need he will have to protect his ego.

Not only must the self-rejectant adolescent protect his ego, but his behavior must compensate for the dissatisfaction that comes with self-rejection. As Lane (105) has stated:

The human personality, as well as the body, is subject to malnutrition. Lacking essential nutrients and rejects critical evaluations of himself and tries to convince others that the evaluations are wrong or unfair or based on false evidence. While this kind of response may alleviate some of his unhappiness, it further increases his maladjustments (83, 88).

Equally damaging is the fact that maladjustive behavior persists and becomes habitual. This has been emphasized by Bennett (20):

Maladjustive behavior shows a tenacious tendency to remain maladjustive. Forms of activity that succeed in doing the individual far more harm than good remain in operation even in the face of the strongest psychotherapeutic efforts. Minor forms of maladjustive behavior become permanent fixtures in the totality of an individual's behavior and often remain throughout his lifetime.

Effects of self-acceptance

The adolescent who sees himself as liked, wanted, and fundamentally worthy; who plays his role and derives satisfaction from it; and who sees himself accurately and realistically will be able to accept himself. His self-acceptance will lead to behavior that is regarded as well-adjusted. Combs (41) has described well-adjusted adolescents thus:

They suffer from no delusions of grandeur or undue humility. They are able to see themselves for what they are and value themselves in accurate and realistic terms. As a consequence, they do not battle ghosts and goblins but are capable of utilizing themselves as effective instruments for the satisfaction of their own needs and others as well.

When adjustment is good, traits or groups of traits are balanced or integrated. As a result, the well-adjusted adolescent enjoys "inner harmony"; he is at peace with himself just as he is at peace with others. Being acceptant of himself and others, he does not need to defend himself. Instead, he is reasonably happy as he is and adjusts himself to life accordingly. This does not mean resignation or defeatism; it means simply *realism* (25, 185).

One of the major reasons an adolescent can accept himself even though he knows he is not perfect is that others accept him. A well-adjusted adolescent makes good *social adjust-*

conditions for growth the personality develops crookedly. The greater number of malnourished personalities become dull. These cause us little trouble, grow up to do work we do not like to do. Others become neurotic. They don't think straight, are undependable and unpredictable but are bothersome principally to their families and immediate neighbors. A smaller portion of the malnourished become aggressive. They strike out, rarely back, in response to deprivation. They are the disorderly ones.

Most adolescents experience unhappiness to some extent. The maladjusted adolescent not only experiences it in a more pronounced form but he also experiences it more often. While the problems he faces are not appreciably different from those of the well-adjusted adolescent, his self-rejecting attitudes make the problems seem insurmountable and this increases his unhappiness.

To counteract some of his unhappiness, the adolescent tries to repress memories that are injurious to his concept of the ideal self; he *ments;* he is able to identify with other people and to have harmonious relationships with them. He is willing to conform to what others value; he is not jealous of others, nor does he try to undermine them; he is not unduly aggressive, unkind, or critical of others; nor does he lose his temper or get easily depressed when things do not go as he wants them to go. In addition, as Barrett-Lennard states, he does not "distort himself to please others, nor does he use them as scapegoats for self-dissatisfaction" (17). Since the well-adjusted adolescent behaves in a manner that makes others like and accept him, his acceptance of self increases and his desire to change himself decreases (50, 71).

The adolescent who does not perceive his social acceptance realistically will behave in a manner that will decrease his social acceptance. One who overaccepts himself believes that he is more popular than he is; he may become intolerant of others and develop an exaggerated notion of his superiority. One who has low self-acceptance depreciates himself; he is self-effacing and denies his own needs and desires in favor of others. Neither the first nor the second would be much fun to have around.

Because of the close relationship between the kind of adjustment the adolescent makes and the degree to which he accepts himself, it is obvious that improvement in adjustment can come only with improvement in self-acceptance. Fundamentally, this resolves itself into bringing the real and ideal self-concepts closer together. Difficult as it is, this gap can be closed. However, it is easier to do in childhood than when the individual reaches the romantic, unrealistic age of adolescence. In attempting to close the gap, the parent, the teacher, or the adolescent himself will find the aids described in Box 15-8 helpful (25, 50, 71, 136, 137, 149).

LEVEL OF ADJUSTMENT AND HAPPINESS

Happiness and good adjustment go hand in hand. Furthermore, since good adjustment depends upon self-acceptance, happiness can be achieved only when a person is reasonably well satisfied with himself. Much of the unhappiness the adolescent experiences could be eliminated if he had a healthier and more realistic concept of self. The adolescent who can see himself as he actually is, not as he would like to be or as his family and friends would like him to be, will make far better adjustments to life than the adolescent whose concept of self has been distorted by wishful thinking. And because he makes better adjustments, he is better satisfied and happier.

While early adolescence is certainly a difficult period, the adolescent who progresses satisfactorily should find his happiness increasing with each passing year. Studies of memories of different ages in the life span indicate that the periods in which the individual was happiest were those in which he felt he

---

BOX 15-8 AIDS TO IMPROVED SELF-ACCEPTANCE

*Convince the adolescent that he will not necessarily outgrow undesirable traits nor will his personality pattern automatically change for the better as his body changes.

*Help the adolescent increase his self-insight so that he has a better understanding of his strengths and weaknesses.

*With better social insight, which can best be achieved by improving self-insight, the adolescent will be able to act in accordance with the way others see him, not as he hopes they see him.

*Because stability of the self-concept is essential to both social and self-acceptance, the adolescent needs help in learning to see himself consistently in one way. Even more important, his stable self-concept must be favorable.

*To improve self-acceptance, the adolescent must be constantly on the alert for minor disturbances and must take immediate steps to correct them before they develop into habits. It may be necessary to change the environment to achieve this goal.

made the best adjustments. The happy adolescent has a philosophy of life that enables him to take the good with the bad, enjoying the good and not being overly disappointed when things are not to his liking (25, 43, 200).

Traditional beliefs about happiness

According to tradition, one can best be happy if one is *carefree*. Childhood is looked upon by people in all cultures, according to Rosenzweig and Rosenzweig, as the "golden days" when the individual can be carefree as will never again be possible (164). Responsibilities are regarded by most people as frustrating and anxiety-provoking. If one can be free from responsibilities, one can be free from frustration and anxiety and, thus, be happy.

Studies of children and adolescents have disproved this belief. Not being given an opportunity to assume responsibility brings unhappiness to both children and adolescents. It means two things to them: first, that significant people in their lives regard them as incapable of handling responsibilities successfully, and second, that they must remain dependent on others. No one who is constantly having to fight for his rights can be happy. Nor can he have a favorable concept of self if significant people in his life think that he is incapable of handling the degree of independence that his age-mates enjoy (43, 200).

An equally common traditional belief is that *material possessions* lead to happiness. This belief has been fostered by different forms of mass media which depict poor people as unhappy and rich people as happy. Furthermore, because of the high status-symbol value of material possessions, many parents and other adults believe that children must have material possessions to be happy. They also believe that more and costlier material possessions make the person more happy.

Material possessions and money to use as he pleases are unquestionably important to the adolescent. They contribute to his social acceptance and, indirectly, to his happiness. On the other hand, material possessions and money will not "buy" social acceptance. Also,

the more the adolescent has, the more likely he is to be envied and regarded as conceited. Studies of socially mobile families have shown that children and adolescents whose families better themselves tend to be less happy than those whose families are more static. Thus, it is apparent that material possessions will not bring happiness *unless they increase the social acceptance* of the individual (121, 148).

A third traditional belief that has been disproved is that a *happy childhood* will guarantee happiness throughout life. Many happy children become unhappy, maladjusted adolescents, adults, or elderly citizens. Many whose childhood was unhappy, by contrast, become happier as life progresses. As was stressed earlier, happiness at any age depends upon the kind of adjustment the individual makes to social expectations at that age. If he conforms to social expectations, he will be happy, whether he is a child, an adolescent, or an adult. The only way that a happy childhood can guarantee future happiness is that it can help train the individual to adjust cheerfully to social expectations. This can be done only if he learns to assess himself and his abilities realistically and to accept and utilize his abilities to their full extent.

Essentials of happiness

Three factors contribute to self-acceptance and thus to good adjustment and happiness. These are acceptance by others, affection, and achievement—the "Three A's" of happiness. A person can be happy only if he feels that others like and accept him. This is especially true in a culture such as our own where high value is placed on *social acceptance*. Just being popular is not enough; to be happy, an adolescent must be accepted by the people he *wants* to be friends with. If his aspirations for friendship and acceptance are unrealistic, he is doomed to be disappointed. This will lead to poor self-concepts and self-rejection.

Social acceptance is accompanied by *affection*—the degree of affection depending on the degree of acceptance the individual enjoys. Affection from others contributes to "ego strength"—the individual's ability to cope with the problems of reality. The adolescent can be happy only if he receives affection from the people who are *important to him*. A girl will be unhappy if she is loved by a boy who means little to her but ignored by one she loves. Similarly, if an adolescent wants affection in the form of romantic love, he will be unhappy if the love he is offered is of the more mature type—companionship love.

The third "A" of happiness is *achievement*. To contribute to happiness, achievement must, first, conform to the adolescent's expectations, and second, be in an area that is prestigious in the eyes of significant people in his life, especially peers. If the adolescent has realistic levels of aspiration, the chances are that he will achieve his goal. This will make him happy. If he does better than he anticipated, he will be happier than he believed possible. How much satisfaction an adolescent derives from his achievements will depend largely upon the prestige associated with them.

In conclusion, to be happy, an adolescent must be realistic about the achievements he is capable of, about the social acceptance he can expect to receive, and about the kind and amount of affection he will receive. Of the three, social acceptance is the most important. A well-accepted adolescent will automatically receive affection from those who accept him and his achievements will win their approval if not their acclaim. Fortunately, happiness is possible for all adolescents provided they are willing to see life and themselves as they are and provided they are willing to accept themselves as they are instead of wanting to be someone else.

HIGHLIGHTS OF CHAPTER 15

1. Personality improvement is aided by a number of conditions, the most important of which are the adolescent's improved physical condition, changes in his environment, social pressures, and self-insight.

2. Most adolescents are anxious to improve their personalities because they recognize the importance of personality in social relationships. They find improvement difficult, however, because of a number of obstacles. These include traditional beliefs about personality, personality stereotypes, personality ideals, and the complexity of the personality pattern.

3. The personality pattern is composed of the self-concept—the core or center of gravity—and specific traits or consistent reactions which are interrelated with and influenced by the self-concept and which are characteristic of the adolescent's typical pattern of adjustment.

4. The self-concept consists of four elements: the physical self-image, the psychological self-image, the real self-image, and the ideal self-image.

5. Of the many factors that influence the development of the self-concept, those which have the greatest effect are physique, physical defects, physical condition, chemique, clothes, names and nicknames, intelligence, levels of aspiration, emotions, cultural patterns, school and college, social status, and a variety of family influences.

6. Studies of the factors that influence the self-concept have revealed that they often affect the two sexes differently.

7. Some of the factors that influence the self-concept are controllable, others can be modified within limits, while still others are beyond control.

8. Studies of persistence in personality reveal that personality improvement is extremely difficult. Conditions that contribute to personality persistence include heredity, home training, social interactions, and environment.

9. Whether the adolescent will be self-acceptant or self-rejectant will depend largely on whether he is satisfied or dissatisfied with his personality and with the improvements he has been able to make in his self-concept and in his characteristic patterns of adjustment.

10. Because self-rejection leads to poor personal and social adjustments, it is important to recognize and correct the common danger signals of maladjustment: excessive irresponsibility, feelings of inadequacy and inferiority, expressions of unsocial behavior, use of defense and retreat mechanisms, hypersensitivity to real or imagined slights, anxiety and worry, perfectionist attitudes, over- or underconcern about appearance, and hostility toward authority.

11. The adolescent who is self-acceptant because he is reasonably satisfied with himself and with the improvements he has been able to achieve in his characteristic patterns of behavior will behave in a way that leads to good personal and social adjustments.

12. Happiness in adolescence goes hand in hand with adjustment and this, in turn, is influenced by the degree to which the adolescent accepts himself.

CHAPTER 1

1. Aarons, Z. A.: Normality and abnormality in adolescence: With a digression on Prince Hal: "The sowing of wild oats." *Psychoanal. Stud. Child.,* 1970, **25,** 309–339.

2. Abel, H., and R. Gingles: Identifying problems of adolescent girls. *J. educ. Res.,* 1965, **58,** 389–392.

3. Adams, J. F.: Adolescents' identification of personal and national problems. *Adolescence,* 1966, **1,** 240–250.

4. Adams, J. F. (ed.): *Understanding adolescence: Current developments in adolescent psychology.* Boston: Allyn and Bacon, 1968.

5. Adelson, J.: What generation gap? *New York Times,* Jan. 18, 1970.

6. Aldridge, J. W.: In the country of the young: Part II. *Harper's Mag.,* November 1969, pp. 93–107.

7. Amatora, Sister M.: Free expression of adolescent's interests. *Genet. Psychol. Monogr.,* 1957, **55,** 173–219.

8. Amos, R. T., and R. M. Washington: A comparison of pupil and teacher perceptions of pupil problems. *J. educ. Psychol.,* 1960, **51,** 255–258.

9. Anderson, J. E.: Behavior and personality. In E. Ginzberg (ed.), *The nation's children.* Vol. 2. *Development and education.* New York: Columbia, 1960, pp. 43–69.

10. Angelino, H.: Developmental tasks and problems of the middle adolescent period. *Education,* 1955, **76,** 226–231.

11. Baer, D. M.: An age-irrelevant concept of development. *Merrill-Palmer Quart.,* 1970, **16,** 238–245.

12. Bailey, J. A., and R. V. Robertson: Students' and teachers' perceptions of student problems. *Personnel Guid. J.,* 1964, **43,** 171–173.

13. Bakan, D.: Adolescence in America: From idea to social fact. *Daedalus,* 1971, **100,** 979–995.

14. Baker, R.: Youth as a tiresome old windbag. *New York Times,* Oct. 17, 1967.

15. Bandura, A.: The stormy decade: Fact or fiction? *Psychology in the Schools,* 1964, **1,** 224–231.

16. Barclay, D.: The battle of the "ages." *New York Times,* Feb. 11, 1962.

17. Barrett-Lennard, G. T.: The mature person. *Ment. Hyg., N.Y.,* 1962, **46,** 98–102.

18. Barter, J. T., D. O. Swabach, and D. Todd: Adolescent suicide attempts. *Arch. gen. Psychiat.,* 1968, **19,** 523–527.

19. Bartlett, C. J., and J. E. Horrocks: A study of the needs status of adolescents from broken homes. *J. genet. Psychol.,* 1958, **93,** 153–159.

20. Bath, J. A., and E. C. Lewis: Attitudes of young female adults toward some areas of parent-adolescent conflict. *J. genet. Psychol.,* 1962, **100,** 241–253.

21. Bealer, R. C., F. K. Willits, and P. R. Maida: The rebellious youth subculture: A myth. *Children,* 1964, **11,** 42–48.

22. Bell, R. R.: Parent-child conflict in sexual values. *J. soc. Issues,* 1966, **22,** no. 2, 34–44.

23. Beller, E. K.: Theories of adolescent development. In J. F. Adams (ed.), *Understanding adolescence: Current developments in adolescent psychology.* Boston: Allyn and Bacon, 1968, pp. 70–100.

24. Benedict, R.: Continuities and discontinuities in cultural conditioning. *Psychiatry,* 1938, **1,** 161–167.

25. Berger, B. M.: Teen-agers are an American invention. *New York Times,* June 13, 1965.

26. Berger, B. M.: The new stage of American man: Almost endless adolescence. *New York Times,* Nov. 2, 1969.

27. Bernard, H. W.: *Human development in western culture,* 3d ed. Boston: Allyn and Bacon, 1970.

28. Bernard, J.: Teen-age culture: An overview. *Ann. Amer. Acad. pol. soc. Sci.,* 1961, **338,** 1–12.

29. Bettelheim, B.: The problem of generations. *Daedalus,* 1962, **91,** 68–96.

30. Bienvenu, M. J.: Measurement of parent-adolescent communication. *Family Coordinator,* 1969, **18,** 117–121.

31. Blos, P.: Prolonged adolescence: The formulation of a syndrome and its therapeutic implications. *Amer. J. Orthopsychiat.,* 1954, **24,** 733–742.

32. Blos, P.: The child analyst looks at the young adolescent. *Daedalus,* 1971, **100,** 961–978.

33. Bonsall, M. R.: Introspections of gifted children. *Calif. J. educ. Res.,* 1960, **11,** 159–166.

34. Brodsky, P.: Problems of adolescence: An Adlerian view. *Adolescence,* 1968, **3,** 9–22.

35. Brown, D.: Helping teen-agers with their family living problems. *Marriage fam. Living,* 1959, **21,** 389–391.

36. Burton, R. V.: Validity of retrospective reports assessed by multitrait-multimethod analysis. *Develpm. Psychol. Monogr.,* 1970, **3,** no. 3.

37. Carroll, J. F. X.: Understanding adolescent needs. *Adolescence,* 1968–1969, **3,** 381–394.

38. Chabassol, D. J., and D. C. Thomas: Age and sex differences in problems and interests of adolescents. *J. exp. Educ.,* 1969, **38,** 16–23.

39. Chapman, A. H.: On managing adolescents. *J. Amer. med. Ass.,* 1960, **174,** 1954–1957.

40. Chilman, C. S., and D. L. Meyer: Single and married undergraduates' measured personality

traits and self-rated happiness. *J. Marriage & Family,* 1966, **28,** 67–76.

41.   Cole, L., and I. N. Hall: *Psychology of adolescence,* 7th ed. New York: Holt, 1970.

42.   Constantinople, A.: Some correlates of average level of happiness among college students. *Develpm. Psychol.,* 1970, **2,** 447.

43.   Crow, L. D., and A. Crow: *Adolescent development and adjustment,* 2d ed. New York: McGraw-Hill, 1965.

44.   Dale, R. R.: The happiness of pupils in co-educational and single sex grammar schools: A comparative assessment. *Brit. J. educ. Psychol.,* 1966, **36,** 39–47.

45.   Dales, R. J.: A method for measuring developmental tasks: Scales for selected tasks at the beginning of adolescence. *Child Develpm.,* 1955, **26,** 111–122.

46.   Dansereau, H. K.: Work and the teenager. *Ann. Amer. Acad. pol. soc. Sci.,* 1961, **338,** 44–52.

47.   Denney, R.: American youth today: A bigger cast, wider screen. *Daedalus,* 1962, **91,** 124–144.

48.   Douvan, E.: Independence and identity in adolescence. *Children,* 1957, **4,** 186–190.

49.   Dubbé, M. C.: What parents are not told may hurt. *Family Life Coordinator,* 1965, **14,** 51–118.

50.   Dunbar, F.: Homeostasis during puberty. *Amer. J. Psychiat.,* 1958, **114,** 673–682.

51.   Duvall, E. M.: Family dilemmas with teenagers. *Family Life Coordinator,* 1965, **14,** 35–38.

52.   Eckerson, L. O.: The teenager problem is the adult. *Personnel Guid. J.,* 1969, **47,** 849–854.

53.   Eisenberg, L.: A developmental approach to adolescence. *Children,* 1965, **12,** 131–135.

54.   Eisenstaudt, S. N.: Archetypal patterns of youth. *Daedalus,* 1962, **91,** 28–46.

55.   Elkind, D.: Egocentrism in adolescence. *Child Develpm.,* 1967, **38,** 1025–1034.

56.   Elkind, D.: *A sympathetic understanding of the child six to sixteen.* Boston: Allyn and Bacon, 1971.

57.   English, H. B.: Chronological divisions of the life span. *J. educ. Psychol.,* 1957, **48,** 437–439.

58.   Epstein, R.: Social class membership and early childhood memories. *Child Develpm.,* 1963, **34,** 503–508.

59.   Feibleman, J. K.: The philosophy of adolescence. *Adolescence,* 1969, **4,** 477–510.

60.   Frank, L. K.: This is the adolescent. *Understanding the Child,* 1949, **18,** 54–69.

61.   Friedenberg, E. Z.: The generation gap. *Ann. Amer. Acad. pol. soc. Sci.,* 1969, **382,** 32–42.

62.   Gaier, E. L.: Adolescence: The current imbroglio. *Adolescence,* 1969, **4,** 89–110.

63.   Garn, S. M.: Growth and development. In E. Ginzberg (ed.), *The nation's children.* Vol. 2. *Development and education.* New York: Columbia, 1960, pp. 24–42.

64.   Garrison, K. C.: Developmental tasks and problems of the late adolescent period. *Education,* 1955, **76,** 232–235.

65.   Garrison, K. C.: A study of the aspirations and concerns of ninth-grade pupils from the public schools of Georgia. *J. soc. Psychol.,* 1966, **69,** 245–252.

66.   Gesell, A., F. L. Ilg, and L. B. Ames: *Youth: The years from ten to sixteen.* New York: Harper & Row, 1956.

67.   Goldman, S.: Profile of an adolescent. *J. Psychol.,* 1962, **54,** 229–240.

68.   Graff. H.: The development of the adolescent. *Penna. Psychiat. Quart.,* 1970, **10,** 27–32.

69.   Grinder, R. E.: The concept of adolescence in the genetic psychology of G. Stanley Hall. *Child Develpm.,* 1969, **40,** 355–369.

70.   Haider, I.: Suicidal attempts in children and adolescents. *Brit. J. Psychiat.,* 1968, **114,** 1133–1134.

71.   Hall, G. S.: *Adolescence.* New York: Appleton-Century-Crofts, 1904.

72.   Harms, E.: Adolescence: Not only a beginning and an end, but a total human experience. *Adolescence,* 1966, **1,** 106–110.

73.   Harris, D. B.: Sex differences in the life problems and interests of adolescents: 1935 and 1957. *Child Develpm.,* 1959, **30,** 453–459.

74.   Harris, D. B.: Work and the adolescent transition to maturity. *Teachers Coll. Rec.,* 1961, **63,** 146–153.

75.   Havighurst, R. J.: *Human development and education.* New York: Longmans, 1953.

76.   Havighurst, R. J.: *Studies of children and society in New Zealand.* Christ Church, N.Z.: Canterbury Univer. Coll. Publications, 1954.

77.   Havighurst, R. J.: Research on the developmental-task concept. *Sch. Rev.,* 1956, **64,** 215–223.

78.   Hays, D. G., and J. W. M. Rothney: Educational decision-making by superior secondary school students and their parents. *Personnel Guid. J.,* 1961, **40,** 26–30.

79.   Hebron, M. E., and W. London: A study of stereotypes in the caretaking of English children. *Brit. J. educ. Psychol.,* 1964, **34,** 125–131.

80.   Hechinger, G., and F. M. Hechinger: *Teenage tyranny.* New York: Morrow, 1963.

81.   Hess, R. D., and I. Greenblatt: The status of adolescents in American society: A problem in social identity. *Child Develpm.,* 1957, **28,** 459–465.

82.   Himber, C.: Inside teenagers. *Adolescence,* 1970, **5,** 285–302.

83.   Hollingworth, L. S.: *The psychology of the adolescent.* New York: Appleton-Century-Crofts, 1928.

84.   Horowitz, E.: Reported embarrassment memories of elementary school, high school, and college students. *J. soc. Psychol.,* 1962, **56,** 317–325.

85. Horrocks, J. E.: *The psychology of adolescence,* 3d ed. Boston: Houghton Mifflin, 1969.

86. Howard, L. P.: Identity conflicts in adolescent girls. *Smith Coll. Stud. soc. Wk,* 1960, **31,** 1–21.

87. Hurlock, E. B.: American adolescents of today: A new species. *Adolescence,* 1966, **1,** 7–21.

88. Jennings, F. G.: Adolescents, aspirations, and the older generation. *Teachers Coll. Rec.,* 1964, **65,** 335–341.

89. Jersild, A. T.: *The psychology of adolescence,* 2d ed. New York: Macmillan, 1963.

90. Jones, M. C.: Psychological correlates of somatic development. *Child Develpm.,* 1965, **36,** 899–911.

91. Jones, W. R.: Affective tolerance and typical problems of married and unmarried college students. *Personnel Guid. J.,* 1958, **37,** 126–128.

92. Joseph, T. P.: Adolescents: From the views of the members of an informal adolescent group. *Genet. Psychol. Monogr.,* 1969, **79,** 3–88.

93. Josselyn, I. M.: Psychological changes in adolescence. *Children,* 1959, **6,** 43–47.

94. Kagan, J.: A conception of early adolescence. *Daedalus,* 1971, **100,** 997–1012.

95. Kagan, J., and H. A. Moss: *Birth to maturity: A study in psychological development.* New York: Wiley, 1962.

96. Kahn, M. D.: The adolescent struggle with identity as a force in psychotherapy. *Adolescence,* 1968–1969, **3,** 395–424.

97. Karlins, M., T. L. Coffman, and G. Walters: On the facting of social stereotypes: Studies in three generations of college students. *J., Pers. soc. Psychol.,* 1969, **13,** 1–16.

98. Kelley, E. C.: Many hold false ideas about youth. In H. F. Clarizio, R. C. Craig, and W. A. Mehrens (eds.), *Contemporary issues in educational psychology.* Boston: Allyn and Bacon, 1970, pp. 155–159.

99. Kelly, H.: Adolescents: A suppressed minority group. *Personnel Guid. J.,* 1969, **47,** 634–640.

100. Keniston, K.: Alienation and the decline of Utopia. *Amer. Scholar,* 1960, **29,** 161–200.

101. Keniston, K.: Social change and youth in America. *Daedalus,* 1962, **91,** 145–171.

102. Keniston, K.: Student activism, moral development, and morality. *Amer. J. Orthopsychiat.,* 1970, **40,** 577–592.

103. Kiell, N.: *The adolescent through fiction.* New York: International Universities Press, 1959.

104. Kreitler, H., and S. Kreitler: Unhappy memories of "the happy past": Studies in cognitive dissonance. *Brit. J. Psychol.,* 1968, **59,** 157–166.

105. Krush, T. P., J. W. Bjord, P. S. Sindell, and J. Nelle: Some thoughts on the formation of personality disorder: Study of an Indian boarding school population. *Amer. J., Psychiat.,* 1966, **122,** 868–876.

106. Kuhlen, R. G.: *The psychology of adolescent development.* New York: Harper & Row, 1952.

107. L'Abate, L.: The status of adolescent psychology. *Develpm. Psychol.,* 1971, **4,** 201–205.

108. Landis, P. H.: The ordering and forbidding technique and teenage adjustment. *Sch. Soc.,* 1954, **80,** 105–106.

109. Lane, H.: The meaning of disorder among youth. *Education,* 1955, **76,** 214–217.

110. Lee, C. B. T.: Campus styles mirror seven decades of change. *New York Times,* Jan. 11, 1971.

111. Lerman, P.: Gangs, networks, and subcultural delinquency. *Amer. J. Sociol.,* 1967, **73,** 63–72.

112. Lester, D.: Suicide as an aggressive act: A replication with a control for neuroticism. *J. gen. Psychol.,* 1968, **79,** 83–86.

113. Levin, P. L.: How to succeed as a teenager. *New York Times,* Apr. 18, 1965.

114. Levy, E.: Toward understanding the adolescent. *Menninger Quart.,* 1969, **23,** 14–21.

115. Lieberman, L. R.: Life satisfaction in the young and the old. *Psychol. Rep.,* 1970, **27,** 75–79.

116. Lief, H. I., and W. C. Thompson: The prediction of behavior from adolescence to adulthood. *Psychiatry,* 1961, **24,** 32–38.

117. Loewenthal, K.: How are "first impressions" formed? *Psychol. Rep.,* 1967, **21,** 834–836.

118. Lucas, C. M., and J. E. Horrocks: An experimental approach to the analysis of adolescent needs. *Child Develpm.,* 1960, **31,** 479–487.

119. Mann, J. W.: Adolescent marginality. *J. genet. Psychol.,* 1965, **106,** 221–235.

120. Martineau, P.: Adulthood in the adolescent perspective. *Adolescence,* 1966, **1,** 272–280.

121. Masterson, J. F., and A. Washburne: The symptomatic adolescent: Psychiatric illness or adolescent turmoil? *Amer. J. Psychiat.,* 1966, **122,** 1240–1248.

122. McCord, J., and W. McCord: Cultural stereotypes and the validity of interviews for research in child development. *Child Develpm.,* 1961, **32,** 171–185.

123. Mead, M.: *Male and female.* New York: Dell, 1968.

124. Meisels, M., and F. M. Canter: A note on the generation gap. *Adolescence,* 1971, 6, 523–530.

125. Meissner, W. W.: Some anxiety indications in the adolescent boy. *J. gen. Psychol.,* 1961, **64,** 251–257.

126. Meissner, W. W.: Parental interaction of the adolescent boy. *J. genet. Psychol.,* 1965, **107,** 225–233.

127. Meltzer, H., and D. Ludwig: Age differences in memory optimism and pessimism of workers. *J. genet. Psychol.,* 1967, **110,** 17–30.

128. Milner, E.: Extreme cultural discontinuity and contemporary American adolescent behavior: A rational analysis. *Int. J. soc. Psychiat.,* 1969, **15,** 314–318.

129. Minuchin, S.: Adolescence: Society's response and responsibility. *Adolescence,* 1969, **4,** 455–476.

130. Morgan, J. C.: Adolescent problems and the Mooney Problem Check List. *Adolescence,* 1969, **4,** 111–126.

131. Murphey, E. B., E. Silber, G. V. Coeho, D. A. Hamburg, and I. Greenberg: Development of autonomy and parent-child interaction in late adolescence. *Amer. J. Orthopsychiat.,* 1963, **33,** 643–652.

132. Musgrove, F.: Intergeneration attitudes. *Brit. J. soc. clin. Psychol.,* 1963, **2,** 209–223.

133. Musgrove, F.: Role-conflict in adolescence. *Brit. J. educ. Psychol.,* 1964, **34,** 34–42.

134. Muus, R. E.: Theories of adolescent development: Their philosophical and historical roots. *Adolescence,* 1966, **1,** 22–44.

135. Nemy, E.: Adolescents today: Are they more disturbed? *New York Times,* Feb. 20, 1970.

136. *New York Times* Report: Loneliness study issue in Britain. Aug. 27, 1964.

137. *Newsweek* Report: The teen-agers. Mar. 21, 1966, pp. 57–75.

138. Nichols, R. C.: Nature and nurture in adolescence. In J. F. Adams (ed.), *Understanding adolescence: Current developments in adolescent psychology.* Boston: Allyn and Bacon, 1968, pp. 101–127.

139. Nixon, R. E.: Psychological normality in adolescence. *Adolescence,* 1966, **1,** 211–223.

140. Norbeck, E., D. E. Walker, and M. Cohen: The interpretation of data: Puberty rites. *Amer. Anthropologist,* 1962, **64,** 463–485.

141. Offer, D.: Studies of normal adolescents. *Adolescence,* 1966, **1,** 305–320.

142. Offer, D.: *The psychological world of the teenager: A study of normal adolescent boys.* New York: Basic Books, 1969.

143. Offer, D., D. Marcus, and J. L. Offer: A longitudinal study of normal adolescent boys. *Amer. J. Psychiat.,* 1970, **126,** 917–924.

144. Parsons, T.: Youth in the context of American society. *Daedalus,* 1962, **91,** 97–123.

145. Porter, B. R.: American teen-agers of the 1960's: Our despair or hope? *J. Marriage & Family,* 1965, **27,** 139–147.

146. Pressey, S. L.: Most important and most neglected topic: Potentials. *J. Gerontologist,* 1963, **3,** 69–70.

147. Price, J. V.: Adolescents/youth. *Amer. J. Orthopsychiat.,* 1971, **41,** 293–306.

148. Quay, H. C., and L. C. Quay: Behavior problems in early adolescence. *Child Develpm.,* 1965, **36,** 215–220.

149. Remmers, H. H.: Cross-cultural studies of teenagers' problems. *J. educ. Psychol.,* 1962, **53,** 254–261.

150. Resnick, H. L. (ed.): *Suicidal behaviors: Diagnosis and management.* Boston: Little, Brown, 1968.

151. Rivenbark, W. H.: Self-disclosure patterns among adolescents. *Psychol. Rep.,* 1971, **28,** 35–42.

152. Robins, J. L.: The problem of the acute identity crisis in adolescence. *Amer. J. Psychoanal.,* 1968, **28,** 37–47.

153. Rosenthal, I.: Reliability of retrospective reports of adolescence. *J. consult. Psychol.,* 1963, **27,** 189–198.

154. Rusk, H. A.: Adolescent problems. *New York Times,* July 13, 1969.

155. Rust, R. E., and J. S. Davie: The personal problems of college students. *Ment. Hyg., N.Y.,* 1961, **45,** 247–257.

156. Schimel, J. L.: Adolescence: On the care and cultivation of weeds. *Adolescence,* 1968–1969, **3,** 339–352.

157. Schonfeld, W. A.: Body-image disturbances in adolescents. *Arch. gen. Psychiat.,* 1966, **15,** 16–21.

158. Schonfeld, W. A.: Socioeconomic affluence as a factor. *N.Y. State J. Med.,* 1967, **67,** 1981–1990.

159. Schrut, A.: Some typical patterns in the behavior and background of adolescent girls who attempt suicide. *Amer. J. Psychiat.,* 1968, **125,** 69–74.

160. Schwartz, R. K.: An interview procedure for studying adolescent perceptions. *Adolescence,* 1970, **5,** 313–322.

161. Sebald, H.: *Adolescence: A sociological analysis.* New York: Appleton-Century-Crofts, 1968.

162. Seidman, J. M. (ed.): *The adolescent: A book of readings,* rev. ed. New York: Holt, 1960.

163. Sieg, A.: Why adolescence occurs. *Adolescence,* 1971, **6,** 337–348.

164. Simpson, R. L., and I. H. Simpson: The school, the peer group, and adolescent development. *J. educ. Sociol.,* 1958, **32,** 37–41.

165. Slocum, W. L., and R. T. Bowles: Attractiveness of occupations to high school students. *Personnel Guid. J.,* 1968, **46,** 754–761.

166. Smith, L. M., and P. F. Kleine: The adolescent and his society. *Rev. educ. Res.,* 1966, **36,** 424–436.

167. Sorenson, R.: Youth's need for challenge and place in society. *Children,* 1962, **9,** 131–138.

168. Spector, S. I.: The "problem" adolescent. *Adolescence,* 1967, **2,** 3–18.

169. Stern, H. H.: A follow-up study of adolescents' views on their personal and vocational future. *Brit. J. educ. Psychol.,* 1961, **31,** 170–182.

170. Stewart, L. H.: Social and emotional adjustment during adolescence as related to the development of psychosomatic illness in adulthood. *Genet. Psychol. Monogr.,* 1962, **65,** 175–215.

171. Stone, L. J., and J. Church: *Childhood and*

adolescence, 2d ed. New York: Random House, 1968.

172. Strang, R.: The transition from childhood to adolescence. In J. P. Adams (ed.), *Understanding adolescence: Current developments in adolescent psychology.* Boston: Allyn and Bacon, 1968, pp. 13–42.

173. Sudia, C., and J. H. Rea: Teenagers discuss age restrictions. *Children, 1971, 18, 232–236.*

174. Sutton-Smith, B.: Developmental laws and the experimentalist's ontology. *Merrill-Palmer Quart., 1970, 16, 253–259.*

175. Teicher, J. D., and J. Jacobs: Adolescents who attempt suicide: Preliminary findings. *Amer. J. Psychiat., 1966, 122, 1248–1257.*

176. Thompson, G. G., and E. F. Gardner: Adolescents' perceptions of happy-successful living. *J. genet. Psychol., 1969, 115, 107–120.*

177. Thompson, O. E.: Student values in transition. *Calif. J. educ. Res., 1968, 19, 77–86.*

178. Thornburg, H.: Adolescence: A re-interpretation. *Adolescence, 1970, 5, 463–484.*

179. Tizard, J.: New trends in developmental psychology. *Brit. J. educ. Psychol., 1970, 40, 1–7.*

180. Tuckman, J.: College students' judgments of the passage of time over the life span. *J. genet. Psychol., 1965, 107, 43–48.*

181. Tuddenham, R. D.: Constancy of personal morale over a fifteen-year interval. *Child Develpm., 1962, 33, 663–673.*

182. Wagner, H.: Adolescent problems resulting from the lengthened educational period. *Adolescence, 1970, 5, 339–346.*

183. Watson, W. C.: Helping adolescents to achieve maturity. *Chicago Sch. J., 1963, 44, 209–216.*

184. Wheeler, D. K.: Expressed wishes of students. *J. genet. Psychol., 1963, 102, 75–81.*

185. Wilkinson, C. B.: The destructiveness of myths. *Amer. J. Psychiat., 1970, 126, 1087–1092.*

186. Wilson, F. M.: The best in life at every age. *Ment. Hyg., N.Y., 1955, 39, 483–488.*

187. Won, G., and D. Yamamura: Expectation of youth in relating to the world of adults. *Family Coordinator, 1970, 19, 219–224.*

188. Yarrow, M. R., J. D. Campbell, and R. V. Burton: Recollections of childhood: A study of the retrospective method. *Monogr. Soc. Res. Child Develpm., 1970, 35, no. 5.*

189. Zaccaria, J. S.: Developmental tasks: Implications for the goals of guidance. *Personnel Guid. J., 1966, 44, 372–375.*

190. Zeligs, R.: Trends in children's New Year's resolutions. *J. exp. Educ., 1957, 26, 133–150.*

CHAPTER 2

1. Acheson, R. M., and C. W. Dupertuis: The relationship between physique and rate of skeletal maturation. *Hum. Biol., 1957, 29, 167–193.*

2. Adams, P. L.: Puberty as a biosocial turning point. *Psychosomatics, 1969, 10, 343–349.*

3. Amatora, Sister M.: Developmental trends in preadolescence and in early adolescence in self-evaluation. *J. genet. Psychol., 1957, 91, 89–97.*

4. Ames, R.: Physical maturing among boys as related to adult social behavior. *Calif. J. educ. Res., 1957, 8, 69–75.*

5. Amundsen, D. W., and C. J. Diers: The age of menarche in classical Greece and Rome. *Hum. Biol., 1969, 41, 125–132.*

6. Andersen, H.: The influence of hormones on human development. In F. Falkner (ed.), *Human development.* Philadelphia: Saunders, 1966, pp. 184–221.

7. Arnhoff, F. N., and E. N. Damianopoulos: Self-body recognition: An empirical approach to the body image. *Merrill-Palmer Quart., 1962, 8, 143–148.*

8. Baldwin, D. C., and N. L. Barnes: Patterns of motivation in families selecting orthodontic treatment. *Int. Ass. dental Res. Abstr., 1966, 44, 142.*

9. Bayley, N.: Consistency of maternal and child behaviors in the Berkeley Growth Study. *Vita Humana, 1964, 7, 73–95.*

10. Bayley, N.: Research in child development: A longitudinal perspective. *Merrill-Palmer Quart., 1965, 11, 183–208.*

11. Blank, L., A. A. Sugerman, and L. Roosa: Body concern, body image and nudity. *Psychol. Rep., 1968, 23, 963–968.*

12. Bojlen, K., and M. W. Bentzon: The influence of climate and nutrition on age at menarche: A historical review and a modern hypothesis. *Hum. Biol., 1968, 46, 69–85.*

13. Brislin, R. W., and S. A. Lewis: Dating and physical attractiveness: Replication. *Psychol. Rep., 1968, 22, 976.*

14. Broderick, C. B.: Sexual behavior among pre-adolescents. *J. soc. Issues, 1966, 22, no. 2, 7–21.*

15. Broverman, D. M., I. K. Broverman, W. Vogel, R. D. Palmer, and E. L. Klaiber: Physique and growth in adolescence. *Child Develpm., 1964, 35, 857–870.*

16. Brŏzek, J. (ed.): Physical growth and body composition. *Monogr. Soc. Res. Child Develpm., 1970, 35, no. 7.*

17. Bruch, H.: Psychological aspects of obesity in adolescence. *Amer. J. publ. Hlth., 1958, 48, 1349–1353.*

18. Bühler, C.: *Das Seelenleben der Jugend-lichen.* Stuttgart: Gustav Fischer Verlag, 1927.

19. Calden, G., R. M. Lundy, and R. J. Schlafer: Sex differences in body concepts. *J. consult. Psychol.,* 1959, **23,** 378.

20. Cauffman, J. G.: Appraisal of the health behavior of junior high school students. *Res. Quart. Amer. Ass. Hlth. Phys. Educ. Recr.,* 1963, **34,** 425–430.

21. Christopherson, V. A.: Role modifications of the disabled male. *Amer. J. Nurs.,* 1968, **68,** 290–293.

22. Clarke, H. H., and D. H. Clarke: Social status and mental health of boys as related to their maturity, structural, and strength characteristics. *Res. Quart. Amer. Ass. Hlth. Phys. Educ. Recr.,* 1961, **32,** 326–334.

23. Clarke, H. H., and E. W. Degutis: Comparison of skeletal age and various physical and motor factors with the pubescent development of 10, 13 and 16 year old boys. *Res. Quart. Amer. Ass. Hlth. Phys. Educ. Recr.,* 1962, **33,** 356–368.

24. Clarke, H. H., and A. L. Olson: Characteristics of 15-year-old boys who demonstrate various accomplishments or difficulties. *Child Develpm.,* 1965, **36,** 559–567.

25. Coleman, J. S.: *The adolescent society.* New York: Free Press, 1961.

26. Compton, N. H.: Body build, clothing and delinquent behavior. *J. Home Econ.,* 1967, **49,** 655–659.

27. Compton, N. H.: Body perception in relation to anxiety among women. *Percept. mot. Skills,* 1969, **28,** 215–218.

28. Corboz, R. J.: Psychological aspects of retarded puberty. *Adolescence,* 1966, **1,** 141–143.

29. Corsini, R. J.: Appearance and criminality. *Amer. J. Sociol.,* 1959, **65,** 39–51.

30. Cortés, J. B., and F. M. Catli: Physique and self-description of temperament. *J. consult. Psychol.,* 1965, **29,** 432–439.

31. Cross, J. F., and J. Cross: Age, sex, race and the perception of facial beauty. *Develpm. Psychol.,* 1971, **5,** 433–439.

32. Cureton, T. K.: Improving the physical fitness of youth. *Monogr. Soc. Res. Child Develpm.,* 1964, **29,** no. 4.

33. Dale, R. J.: A method for measuring developmental tasks: Scales for selected tasks at the beginning of adolescence. *Child Develpm.,* 1955, **26,** 111–122.

34. Damon, A., S. T. Damon, R. B. Reed, and I. Valadian: Age at menarche of mothers and daughters, with a note on accuracy of recall. *Hum. Biol.,* 1969, **41,** 161–175.

35. Dibiase, W. J., and L. A. Hjelle: Body-image stereotypes and body-type preferences among male college students. *Percept. mot. Skills,* 1968, **27,** 1143–1146.

36. Douglas, J. W. B., and J. M. Ross: Age of puberty related to educational ability, attainment, and school leaving age. *J. child Psychol. Psychiat.,* 1964, **5,** 185–196.

37. Dryer, A. S., V. Hulac, and D. Rigler: Differential adjustment to pubescence and cognitive style patterns. *Develpm. Psychol.,* 1971, **4,** 456–462.

38. Dubois, F. S.: Rhythms, cycles, and periods in health and disease. *Amer. J. Psychiat.,* 1959, **116,** 114–119.

39. Duffy, R. J.: Fundamental frequency characteristics of adolescent females. *Lang. Speech,* 1970, **13,** 14–24.

40. Duffy, R. J.: Description and perception of frequency breaks (voice breaks) in adolescent female speakers. *Lang. Speech,* 1970, **13,** 151–161.

41. Dunbar, F.: Homeostasis during puberty. *Amer. J. Psychiat.,* 1958, **114,** 673–682.

42. Dwyer, J., and J. Mayer: Psychological effects of variations in physical appearance during adolescence. *Adolescence,* 1968–1969, **3,** 353–380.

43. Eichorn, D. H.: Biological correlates of behavior. *62d Yearb. nat. Soc. Stud. Educ.,* 1963, pt. 1, 4–61.

44. Eichorn, D. H., and N. Bayley: Growth in head circumference from birth through young adulthood. *Child Develpm.,* 1962, **33,** 257–271.

45. Eichorn, D. H., and J. P. McKee: Physiological stability during adolescence. *Child Develpm.,* 1958, **29,** 255–268.

46. Eisenberg, L.: A developmental approach to adolescence. *Children,* 1965, **12,** 131–135.

47. Faterson, H. F., and H. A. Witkin: Longitudinal study of development of the body concept. *Develpm. Psychol.,* 1970, **2,** 429–438.

48. Fisher, S.: Sex differences in body perception. *Psychol. Monogr.,* 1964, **78,** no. 14.

49. Foll, C. A.: The age at menarche in Assam and Burma. *Arch. Dis. Childh.,* 1961, **36,** 302–304.

50. Frisancho, A. R., S. M. Garn, and C. G. Rohman: Age at menarche: A new method of prediction and retrospective assessment based on hand x-rays. *Hum. Biol.,* 1969, **41,** 42–50.

51. Frisch, R. E., and R. Revelle: Variation in body weights and the age of adolescent growth spurt among Latin American and Asian populations, in relation to caloric supplies. *Hum. Biol.,* 1969, **41,** 185–212.

52. Frisch, R. E., and R. Revelle: The height and weight of adolescent boys and girls at the time of peak velocity of growth in height and weight: Longitudinal data. *Hum. Biol.,* 1969, **41,** 536–559.

53. Frisch, R. E., and R. Revelle: Height and weight at menarche and a hypothesis of critical body weights and adolescent events. *Science,* 1970, **169,** 397–399.

54. Frisk, M., T. Tenhunen, O. Widholm, and H. Hortling: Psychological problems in adolescents

showing advanced or delayed physical maturation. *Adolescence,* 1966, **1,** 126–140.

55. Garn, S. M., and J. A. Haskell: Fat thickness and developmental status in childhood and adolescence. *Amer. J. Dis. Children.* 1960, **99,** 746–751.

56. Garrison, K. C.: Physiological changes in adolescence. In J. F. Adams (ed.), *Understanding adolescence: Current developments in adolescent psychology.* Boston: Allyn and Bacon, 1968, pp. 43–69.

57. Gesell, A., F. L. Ilg, and L. B. Ames: *Youth: The years from ten to sixteen.* New York: Harper & Row, 1956.

58. Gollin, E. S.: An organism oriented concept of development. *Merrill-Palmer Quart.,* 1970, **16,** 246–252.

59. Gording, E. J., and E. Match: Personality changes of certain contact lens patients. *J. Amer. optom. Ass.,* 1968, **39,** 266–269.

60. Hamid, P. N.: Styles of dress as a perceptual cue in impression formation. *Percept. mot. Skills,* 1968, **26,** 904–906.

61. Hampton, M. L., L. R. Shapiro, and R. L. Huenemann: Helping teen-age girls improve their diets. *J. Home Econ.,* 1961, **53,** 835–838.

62. Hanseman, C. F., and M. M. Maresh: A longitudinal study of skeletal maturation. *Amer. J. Dis. Children.* 1961, **101,** 305–321.

63. Harding, V. V.: A method of evaluating osseous development from birth to 14 years. *Child Develpm.,* 1952, **23,** 181–184, 247–271.

64. Harms, E.: Puberty: Physical and mental. *Adolescence,* 1966, **1,** 293–296.

65. Havighurst, R. J.: *Human development and education.* New York: Longmans, 1953.

66. Heald, F. P., M. Daugela, and P. Brunschyber: Physiology of adolescence. *New England J. Med.,* 1963, **268,** 192–198, 243–252, 299–307, 361–366.

67. Henton, C. L.: The effect of socioeconomic and emotional factors on the onset of menarche among Negro and white girls. *J. genet. Psychol.,* 1961, **98,** 255–264.

68. Hurlock, E. B., and S. Sender: The "negative phase" in relation to the behavior of pubescent girls. *Child Develpm.,* 1939, **6,** 325–340.

69. Israel, S. L.: Normal puberty and adolescence. *Ann. N.Y. Acad. Sci.,* 1967, **142,** 773–778.

70. Johnston, F. E.: Individual variation in the rate of skeletal maturation between five and eighteen years. *Child Develpm.,* 1964, **35,** 75–80.

71. Jones, M. C.: The later careers of boys who were early- or late-maturers. *Child Develpm.,* 1957, **28,** 113–128.

72. Jones, M. C.: A study of socialization patterns at the high school level. *J. genet. Psychol.,* 1958, **93,** 87–111.

73. Jones, M. C.: Psychological correlates of somatic development. *Child Develpm.,* 1965, **36,** 899–911.

74. Jones, M. C., and N. Bayley: Physical maturing among boys as related to behavior. *J. educ. Psychol.,* 1950, **41,** 129–148.

75. Jones, M. C., and P. H. Mussen: Self-conceptions, motivations, and interpersonal attitudes of early- and late-maturing girls. *Child Develpm.,* 1958, **29,** 491–501.

76. Joseph, W.: Vocal growth measurements in male adolescents. *J. Res. music Educ.,* 1969, **17,** 423–426.

77. Josselyn, I. M.: Psychological changes in adolescence. *Children,* 1959, **6,** 43–47.

78. Jourard, S. M.: *Personal adjustment,* 2d ed. New York: Macmillan, 1963.

79. Jourard, S. M., and P. F. Secord: Body-cathexis and the ideal female figure. *J. abnorm. soc. Psychol.,* 1955, **50,** 243–246.

80. Kaufman, I., and L. Heims: The body image of the juvenile delinquent. *Amer. J. Orthopsychiat.,* 1958, **28,** 146–159.

81. Klausner, S. Z.: Sacred and profane meanings of blood and alcohol. *J. soc. Psychol.,* 1964, **64,** 27–43.

82. Kleck, R.: Physical stigma and nonverbal cues emitted in face-to-face interaction. *Hum. Relat.,* 1968, **21,** 19–28.

83. Kligman, A. M.: Out damned spots. *Penna. Gazette,* November 1967, p. 35.

84. Koegler, R. R.: Chronic illness and the adolescent. *Ment. Hyg., N.Y.,* 1960, **44,** 111–114.

85. Kralj-Cerek, L.: The influence of food, body build, and social origin on the age at menarche. *Hum. Biol.,* 1956, **28,** 393–406.

86. Krogman, W. M.: Growth of head, face, trunk and limbs in Philadelphia white and Negro children of elementary and high school age. *Monogr. Soc. Res. Child Develpm.,* 1970, **35,** no. 3.

87. Kurtz, R. M.: Sex differences and variations in body attitudes. *J. consult. clin. Psychol.,* 1969, **33,** 625–629.

88. Lane, J. A.: Assessment of physically handicapped adult students in college. *Dissert. Abstr.,* 1968, **28** (9–A), 3511–3512.

89. Larsen, V. L.: Sources of menstrual information: A comparison of age groups. *Family Life Coordinator,* 1961, **10,** 41–43.

90. Lewit, D. W., and K. Virolainen: Conformity and independence in adolescents' motivation for orthodontic treatment. *Child Develpm.,* 1968, **39,** 1189–1200.

91. Linkowski, D. C., M. E. Jaques, and E. L. Gaier: Reactions to disability: A thematic analysis. *J. soc. Psychol.,* 1969, **77,** 201–214.

92. Livson, N., and D. McNeill: The accuracy of recalled age of menarche. *Hum. Biol.,* 1962, **34,** 218–221.

93. Livson, N., and D. McNeill: Physique and maturation rate in male adolescents. *Child Develpm.,* 1962, **33,** 145–152.

94. Livson, N., D. McNeill, and K. Thomas:

Pooled estimates of parent-child correlations in stature from birth to maturity. *Science,* 1962, **138,** 818–819.

95. Lowery, G. H.: Obesity in the adolescent. *Amer. J. publ. Hlth.,* 1958, **48,** 1354–1358.

96. Macfarlane, J., L. Allen, and M. P. Honzik: *A developmental study of the behavior problems of normal children between twenty-one months and fourteen years.* Berkeley: University of California Press, 1954.

97. MacGregor, F. C.: Social and cultural components in the motivations of persons seeking plastic surgery of the nose. *J. Hlth. soc. Behav.,* 1967, **8,** 125–135.

98. Manz, W., and H. E. Lueck: Influence of wearing glasses on personality ratings: Cross cultural validation of an old experiment. *Percept. mot. Skills,* 1968, **27,** 704.

99. Marsden, G., and N. Kalter: Bodily concerns and the WISC Object Assembly subtest. *J. consult. clin. Psychol.,* 1969, **33,** 391–395.

100. Marshall, W. A., and J. M. Tanner: Variations in pattern of pubertal changes in girls. *Arch. Dis. Childh.,* 1969, **44,** 291–303.

101. Marshall, W. A., and J. M. Tanner: Variations in the pattern of pubertal changes in boys. *Arch. Dis. Childh.,* 1970, **45,** 13–23.

102. Martin, P. C., and E. L. Vincent: *Human development.* New York: Ronald, 1960.

103. Masterson, J. G.: True precocious puberty. *Ann. N.Y. Acad. Sci.,* 1967, **142,** 779–782.

104. McCammon, R. W.: Are boys and girls maturing physically at earlier ages? *Amer. J. publ. Hlth.,* 1965, **55,** 103–106.

105. McGuigan, F. J.: *Biological basis for behavior.* Englewood Cliffs, N.J.: Prentice-Hall, 1963.

106. McNeill, D., and N. Livson: Maturation rate and body build in women. *Child Develpm.,* 1963, **34,** 25–32.

107. Meredith, H. V.: A time series analysis of growth of nose height during childhood. *Child Develpm.,* 1958, **29,** 19–34.

108. Meredith, H. V.: Body size of contemporary youth in different parts of the world. *Monogr. Soc. Res. Child Develpm.,* 1969, **34,** no. 7.

109. Meredith, H. V., and J. M. Chadha: A roentgenographic study of changes in head height during childhood and adolescence. *Hum. Biol.,* 1963, **34,** 299–319.

110. Meyer, E., W. E. Jacobson, M. T. Edgerton, and A. Canter: Motivational patterns in patients seeking elective plastic surgery. *Psychosom. Med.,* 1960, **22,** 193–203.

111. Miller, A. G.: Role of physical attractiveness in impression formation. *Psychonomic Sci.,* 1970, **19,** 241–243.

112. Miller, A. R., and R. A. Stewart: Perception of female physiques. *Percept. mot. Skills,* 1968, **27,** 721–722.

113. Montagu, A.: *Human heredity.* New York: Harcourt, Brace & World, 1959.

114. More, D. M.: Developmental concordance and discordance during puberty and early adolescence. *Monogr. Soc. Res. Child Develpm.,* 1953, **18,** 1–128.

115. Morgan, C. T.: *Physiological psychology,* 3d ed. New York: McGraw-Hill, 1965.

116. Mosier, H. D., H. J. Grossman, and H. F. Dingman: Secondary sex development in mentally deficient individuals. *Child Develpm.,* 1962, **33,** 273–286.

117. Muus, R. E.: Puberty rites in primitive and modern societies. *Adolescence,* 1970, **5,** 109–128.

118. Muus, R. E.: Adolescent development and the secular trend. *Adolescence,* 1970, **5,** 267–284.

119. Nash, H.: Assignment of gender to body regions. *J. genet. Psychol.,* 1958, **92,** 113–115.

120. *New York Times* Report: Puberty customs survive in Ghana. Mar. 24, 1966.

121. *New York Times* Report: Teen-agers' habits of eating criticized. Apr. 9, 1966.

122. Newton, M., and M. Issekutz-Wolsky: The effect of parental age on the rate of female maturation. *Gerontologia,* 1969, **15,** 328–331.

123. Nisbet, J. D., R. Illesley, A. E. Sutherland, and M. J. Douse: Puberty and test performance: A further report. *Brit. J. educ. Psychol.,* 1964, **34,** 202–203.

124. Norbeck, E., D. E. Walker, and M. Cohen: The interpretation of data: Puberty rites. *Amer. Anthropologist,* 1962, **64,** 463–485.

125. Owen, G. M., and J. Brŏzek: Influence of age, sex and nutrition on body composition during childhood and adolescence. In F. Falkner (ed.), *Human development.* Philadelphia: Saunders, 1966, pp. 222–238.

126. Parker, E.: *The seven ages of woman.* Baltimore: Johns Hopkins, 1960.

127. Peckos, P. S., and F. F. Heald: Nutrition of adolescents. *Children,* 1964, **11,** 27–30.

128. Poppleton, P. K.: The secular trend in puberty: Has stability been achieved? *Brit. J. educ. Psychol.,* 1966, **36,** 95–100.

129. Prader, A., J. M. Tanner, and G. E. von Harnock: Catch-up growth following illness or starvation. *J. Pediat.,* 1963, **62,** 646–659.

130. Rafferty, F. T., and E. S. Stein: A study of the relationship of early menarche to ego development. *Amer. J. Orthopsychiat.,* 1958, **28,** 170–179.

131. Rakoff, A. E.: Menstrual disorders of the adolescent. *Ann. N.Y. Acad. Sci.,* 1967, **42,** 801–806.

132. Remmers, H. H., and R. H. Radler: *The American teenager.* Indianapolis: Bobbs-Merrill, 1957.

133. Rogers, K. D., and G. Reese: Health studies: Presumably normal high-school students. II. Absence from school. *Amer. J. Dis. Children,* 1965, **109,** 9–27.

134. Ryan, M. S.: *Clothing: A study in human development.* New York: Holt, 1966.

135. Schachter, S.: Obesity and eating. *Science,* 1968, **16,** 751–756.

136. Schauffler, G. C.: Dysmenorrhea in and near puberty. *Ann. N.Y. Acad. Sci.,* 1967, **142,** 794–800.

137. Scheinfeld, A.: *Heredity in humans,* rev. ed. Philadelphia: Lippincott, 1971.

138. Schonfeld, W. A.: Gynecomastia in adolescence. *Arch. gen. Psychiat.,* 1961, **5,** 46–54.

139. Schonfeld, W. A.: Body-image disturbances in adolescents with inappropriate sexual development. *Amer. J. Orthopsychiat.,* 1964, **34,** 493–502.

140. Schonfeld, W. A.: Body-image disturbances in adolescents. *Arch. gen. Psychiat.,* 1966, **15,** 16–21.

141. Schreiber, E. H.: The relationship between personality characteristics and dental disorders in adolescents. *Dissert. Abstr.,* 1967, **28** (4–A), 1313.

142. Shipman, W. G.: Age at menarche and adult personality. *Arch. gen. Psychiat.,* 1964, **10,** 155–159.

143. Shuttleworth, F. K.: The adolescent period: A graphic atlas. *Monogr. Soc. Res. Child Develpm.,* 1949, **14,** no. 1.

144. Sigurjonsdottier, T. J., and A. B. Hayles: Precocious puberty. *Amer. J. Dis. Children,* 1968, **115,** 309–321.

145. Sills, F. D., and P. W. Everett: The relationship of extreme somatotypes to performance in motor and strength tests. *Res. Quart. Amer. Ass. Hlth. Phys. Educ. Recr.,* 1953, **24,** 223–228.

146. Skorepa, C. A., J. E. Horrocks, and G. G. Thompson: A study of friendship fluctuations of college students. *J. genet. Psychol.,* 1963, **102,** 151–157.

147. Smith, S. L., and C. Sander: Food craving, depression and premenstrual problems. *Psychosom. Med.,* 1969, **31,** 281–287.

148. Smith, W. I., E. K. Powell, and S. Ross: Food aversions: Some additional personality correlates. *J. consult. Psychol.,* 1955, **19,** 145–149.

149. Solley, W. H.: Ratio of physical development as a factor in motor coordination of boys ages 10 to 14. *Res. Quart. Amer. Ass. Hlth. Phys. Educ. Recr.,* 1957, **28,** 295–304.

150. Stephens, W. N.: A cross-cultural study of menstrual taboos. *Genet. Psychol. Monogr.,* 1961, **84,** 385–416.

151. Sullivan, W.: Boys and girls are now maturing earlier. *New York Times,* Jan. 24, 1971.

152. Talwar, P. P.: Adolescent sterility in an Indian population. *Hum. Biol.,* 1965, **37,** 256–261.

153. Tanner, J. M.: *Growth at adolescence,* 2d ed. Oxford: Blackwell Scientific Publications, 1962.

154. Tanner, J. M.: The regulation of human growth. *Child Develpm.,* 1963, **34,** 817–847.

155. Tanner, J. M.: Sequence, tempo, and individual variation in the growth and development of boys and girls aged twelve to sixteen. *Daedalus,* 1971, **100,** 907–930.

156. Taylor, C., and G. G. Thompson: Age trends in preferences for certain facial proportions. *Child Develpm.,* 1955, **26,** 97–102.

157. Tejmar, J.: Achievement, body weight and blood pressure in preadolescent girls. *Adolescence,* 1970, **5,** 345–352.

158. Titley, R. W.: Imaginations about the disabled. *Soc. Sci. & Med.,* 1969, **3,** 29–38.

159. Tonks, C. M., P. H. Rack, and M. J. Rose: Attempted suicide and the menstrual cycle. *J. psychosom. Res.,* 1968, **11,** 319–323.

160. Valadian, I., H. C. Stuart, and R. R. Reed: Studies of illnesses of children followed from birth to eighteen years. *Monogr. Soc. Res. Child Develpm.,* 1961, **28,** no. 3.

161. Valsĭk, J. A.: The seasonal rhythm of the menarche: A review. *Hum. Biol.,* 1965, **37,** 75–90.

162. Vamberova, M. P., and J. Tefralova: The effect of puberty on the development of obesity. *Child Develpm. Abstr.,* 1963, **38,** no. 36.

163. Verinis, J. S., and S. Roll: Primary and secondary male characteristics: The hairiness and large penis stereotypes. *Psychol. Rep.,* 1970, **26,** 123–126.

164. Vincent, E. L., and P. C. Martin: *Human psychological development.* New York: Ronald, 1961.

165. Wagonfeld, S., and H. M. Wolowitz: Obesity and the self-help group: A look at TOPS. *Amer. J. Psychiat.,* 1968, **125,** 249–255.

166. Walster, E., V. Aronson, D. Abrahams, and L. Rottmann: Importance of physical attractiveness in dating behavior. *J. Pers. soc. Psychol.,* 1966, **4,** 508–516.

167. Washburn, W. C.: The effects of physique and intrafamily tension on self-concepts in adolescent males. *J. consult. Psychol.,* 1962, **26,** 460–466.

168. Weatherley, D.: Self-perceived rate of physical maturation and personality in late adolescence. *Child Develpm.,* 1964, **35,** 1197–1210.

169. Wickham, M.: The effects of the menstrual cycle on test performance. *Brit. J. Psychol.,* 1958, **49,** 34–41.

170. Wiggins, J. S., N. Wiggins, and J. C. Conger: Correlates of heterosexual somatic preference. *J. Pers. soc. Psychol.,* 1968, **10,** 82–90.

171. Wiggins, N., and J. S. Wiggins: A typological analysis of male preference for female body types. *Multivariate Behav. Res.,* 1969, **4,** 69–109.

172. Young, H. B., A. Zoll, and J. R. Gallagher: Events of puberty in 111 Florentine girls. *Amer. J. Dis. Children,* 1963, **106,** 568–577.

173. Zukowski, W.: The age of menarche in Polish girls. *Hum. Biol.,* 1964, **36,** 233–234.

174. Zwicker, B. L.: Behavior effects of attitudinal change. *Psychol. Rep.,* 1968, **23,** 839–842.

CHAPTER 3

1. Alexander, I. E., and A. M. Adlerstein: Affective responses to the concept of death in a population of children and early adolescents. *J. genet. Psychol.,* 1958, **93,** 167–177.

2. Alpert, R., and R. N. Haber: Anxiety in academic achievement situations. *J. abnorm. soc. Psychol.,* 1960, **61,** 207–215.

3. Amatora, Sister M.: Interests of preadolescent boys and girls. *Genet. Psychol. Monogr.,* 1960, **61,** 77–113.

4. Amatora, Sister M.: Home interests in early adolescence. *Genet. Psychol. Monogr.,* 1962, **65,** 137–174.

5. Ames, L. B., and F. L. Ilg: The developmental point of view with special reference to the principle of reciprocal neuromotor interweaving. *J. genet. Psychol.,* 1964, **105,** 195–209.

6. Angelino, H., J. Dollins, and E. V. Mech: Trends in the "fears and worries" of school children as related to socio-economic status and age. *J. genet. Psychol.,* 1956, **89,** 263–276.

7. Archibald, H. C., D. Bell, C. Miller, and R. D. Tuddenham: Bereavement in childhood and adult psychiatric disturbance. *Psychosom. Med.,* 1962, **24,** 343–351.

8. Averill, J. R.: Grief: Its nature and significance. *Psychol. Bull.,* 1968, **70,** 721–748.

9. Baruch, G. K.: Anne Frank on adolescence. *Adolescence,* 1968–1969, **3,** 425–434.

10. Bateman, M. M., and J. S. Jensen: The effect of religious background on modes of handling anger. *J. soc. Psychol.,* 1958, **47,** 133–141.

11. Bell, E. C.: Nutritional deficiencies and emotional disturbances. *J. Psychol.,* 1958, **45,** 47–74.

12. Berecz, J. M.: Phobias of childhood: Etiology and treatment. *Psychol. Bull.,* 1968, **70,** 694–720.

13. Berger, B. M.: Teen-agers are an American invention. *New York Times,* June 13, 1965.

14. Berger, B. M.: The new stage of American man: Almost endless adolescence. *New York Times,* Nov. 2, 1969.

15. Berkowitz, L.: Aggressive humor as a stimulus to aggressive responses. *J. Pers. soc. Psychol.,* 1970, **16,** 710–717.

16. Berkowitz, L.: Experimental investigations of hostility catharsis. *J. consult. clin. Psychol.,* 1970, **35,** 1–7.

17. Berlyne, D. E.: A theory of human curiosity. *Brit. J. Psychol.,* 1954, **45,** 180–191.

18. Blazer, J. A.: Fantasy and its effects. *J. gen. Psychol.,* 1964, **70,** 163–182.

19. Block, J., and B. Martin: Predicting the behavior of children under frustration. *J. abnorm. soc. Psychol.,* 1955, **51,** 281–285.

20. Bronson, G. W.: The development of fear in man and other animals. *Child Develpm.,* 1968, **39,** 409–431.

21. Bronson, W. C.: Adult derivatives of emotional expressiveness and reactivity control: Developmental continuities from childhood to adulthood. *Child Develpm.,* 1967, **38,** 801–817.

22. Bronzaft, A. L.: Test anxiety, social mobility, and academic achievement. *J. soc. Psychol.,* 1968, **75,** 217–222.

23. Burhenne, D., and H. L. Mirels: Self-disclosure in self-descriptive essays. *J. consult. clin. Psychol.,* 1970, **35,** 409–413.

24. Cason, H.: Common annoyances. *Psychol. Monogr.,* 1930, **48,** no. 2.

25. Chilman, C. S., and D. L. Meyer: Single and married undergraduates' measured personality needs and self-rated happiness. *J. Marriage & Family,* 1966, **28,** 67–76.

26. Chittick, E. V., and P. Himelstein: The manipulation of self-disclosure. *J. Psychol.,* 1967, **65,** 117–121.

27. Cole, L., and I. N. Hall: *Psychology of adolescence,* 7th ed. New York: Holt, 1970.

28. Coser, R. L.: Some social functions of laughter. *Hum. Relat.,* 1959, **12,** 171–182.

29. Croake, J. W.: Adolescent fears. *Adolescence,* 1967, **2,** 459–469.

30. Croake, J. W., and F. H. Knox: A second look at adolescent fears. *Adolescence,* 1971, **6,** 279–284.

31. Crow, L. D., and A. Crow: *Adolescent development and adjustment,* 2d ed. New York: McGraw-Hill, 1965.

32. Davis, J. M.: A reinterpretation of the Barker, Dembo, and Lewin study of frustration and aggression. *Child Develpm.,* 1958, **29,** 503–506.

33. Dimond, R. E., and D. T. Hellkamp: Race, sex, ordinal position of birth, and self-disclosure in high-school students. *Psychol. Rep.,* 1969, **25,** 235–238.

34. Dimond, R. E., and D. C. Munz: Ordinal position of birth and self-disclosure in high-school students. *Psychol. Rep.,* 1967, **21,** 829–833.

35. Doob, A. N.: Catharsis and aggression: The effect of hurting one's enemy. *J. exp. Res. Pers.,* 1970, **4,** 291–296.

36. Dubbé, M. C.: What parents are not told may hurt. *Family Life Coordinator,* 1965, **14,** 51–118.

37. Dunbar, F.: Homeostasis during puberty. *Amer. J. Psychiat.,* 1958, **114,** 673–682.

38. Elkind, D.: Egocentrism in adolescence. *Child Develpm.,* 1967, **38,** 1025–1034.

39. Errera, P.: Some historical aspects of the concept, phobia. *Psychiat. Quart.,* 1962, **36,** 325–336.

40. Feshbach, S.: The drive-reducing function of fantasy behavior. *J. abnorm. soc. Psychol.,* 1955, **50,** 3–11.

41. Frost, B. P.: Anxiety and educational achievement. *Brit. J. educ. Psychol.,* 1968, **38,** 293–301.

42. Gallagher, J. R., and H. I. Harris: *Emotional problems of adolescents,* rev. ed., Fair Lawn, N.J.: Oxford University Press, 1964.

43. Garai, J. E.: Sex differences in mental health. *Genet. Psychol. Monogr.,* 1970, **81,** 123–142.

44. Gesell, A., F. L. Ilg, and L. B. Ames: *Youth: The years from ten to sixteen.* New York: Harper & Row, 1956.

45. Gilley, H. M., and S. Summers: Sex differences in the use of hostile verbs. *Psychol. Rep.,* 1970, **76,** 33–37.

46. Goldstein, J. H., and R. L. Arms: Effects of observing athletic contests on hostility. *Sociometry,* 1971, **34,** 83–90.

47. Goode, W. J.: The theoretical importance of love. *Amer. sociol. Rev.,* 1959, **24,** 38–47.

48. Gotts, E. E.: A note on cross-cultural by age-group comparisons of anxiety scores. *Child Develpm.,* 1968, **39,** 945–947.

49. Greenfeld, N., and E. L. Finkelstein: A comparison of the characteristics of junior high school students. *J. genet. Psychol.,* 1970, **117,** 37–50.

50. Greenwood, E.: The importance of play. *Menninger Quart.,* 1968, **22,** 22–28.

51. Hall, G. S.: *Adolescence.* New York: Appleton-Century-Crofts, 1904.

52. Haring, J.: Freedom of communication between parents and adolescents with problems. *Dissert. Abstr.,* 1967, **27** (11–A), 3956–3957.

53. Harlow, H. F.: The nature of love. *Amer. Psychologist,* 1958, **13,** 673–685.

54. Hartley, R. E.: Some safety valves in play. *Child Study,* 1957, **34,** 12–14.

55. Hartman, B. J.: Survey of college students' problems identified by the Mooney Problem Check List. *Psychol. Rep.,* 1968, **22,** 715–716.

56. Hazard, W. R.: Anxiety and preference for television fantasy. *Journalism Quart.,* 1967, **47,** 461–469.

57. Hechinger, G., and F. M. Hechinger: *Teen-age tyranny.* New York: Morrow, 1963.

58. Hicks, N.: Doctors study link between changes in blood chemistry and depression. *New York Times,* Dec. 8, 1969.

59. Hicks, N.: Drugs to fight depression. *New York Times,* Dec. 14, 1969.

60. Hollon, T. H.: Poor school performance as a symptom of masked depression in children and adolescents. *Amer. J. Psychother.,* 1970, **25,** 258–263.

61. Holt, R. R.: On the interpersonal and intrapersonal consequences of expressing or not expressing anger. *J. consult. clin. Psychol.,* 1970, **35,** 8–12.

62. Hornick, E. J.: Emergencies, anxiety, and adolescence. *N.Y. State J. Med.,* 1967, **67,** 1979–1987.

63. Horowitz, E.: Reported embarrassment memories of elementary school, high school, and college students. *J. soc. Psychol.,* 1962, **56,** 317–325.

64. Horrocks, J. E.: *The psychology of adolescence,* 3d ed. Boston: Houghton Mifflin, 1969.

65. Hountras, P. T., W. E. Grady, and C. W. Vraa: Manifest anxiety and academic achievement of American and Canadian college freshmen. *J. Psychol.,* 1970, **76,** 3–8.

66. Jacobson, E.: Adolescent moods and the remodeling of psychic structures in adolescence. *Psychoanalytic Stud. Child,* 1961, **16,** 164–183.

67. Jennings, F. L.: Religious beliefs and self-disclosure. *Psychol. Rep.,* 1971, **28,** 193–194.

68. Jersild, A. T.: *The psychology of adolescence,* 2d ed. New York: Macmillan, 1963.

69. Jones, M. C.: A study of socialization patterns at the high school level. *J. genet. Psychol.,* 1958, **93,** 87–111.

70. Jones, M. C.: Psychological correlates of somatic development. *Child Develpm.,* 1965, **36,** 899–911.

71. Josselyn, I. M.: Psychological changes in adolescence. *Children,* 1959, **8,** 43–47.

72. Jourard, S. M.: *Personal adjustment.* New York: Macmillan, 1958.

73. Jourard, S. M.: Healthy personality and self-disclosure. *Ment. Hyg., N.Y.,* 1959, **43,** 499–507.

74. Jourard, S. M.: Self-disclosure and other-cathexis. *J. abnorm. soc. Psychol.,* 1959, **59,** 428–443.

75. Jourard, S. M.: Religious denomination and self-disclosure. *Psychol. Rep.,* 1961, **8,** 446.

76. Jourard, S. M., and M. J. Landsman: Cognition, cathexis, and the "Dyadic effect" in men's self-disclosing behavior. *Merrill-Palmer Quart.,* 1960, **6,** 178–186.

77. Jourard, S. M., and J. L. Resnick: Some effects of self-disclosure among college women. *J. humanist Psychol.,* 1970, **10,** 84–93.

78. Jourard, S. M., and P. Richman: Factors in the self-disclosure imputs of college students. *Merrill-Palmer Quart.,* 1963, **9,** 141–148.

79. Kahn, M.: The physiology of catharsis. *J. Pers. soc. Psychol.,* 1966, **3,** 278–286.

80. Kahn, M. H., and K. E. Rudestam: The relationship between liking and perceived self-disclosure in small groups. *J. Psychol.,* 1971, **78,** 81–85.

81. Kates, S. L.: Subjects' evaluations of annoying situations after being described as being well adjusted or poorly adjusted. *J. consult. Psychol.,* 1952, **16,** 429–434.

82. Keislar, E. R.: Experimental development of "like" and "dislike" of others among adolescent girls. *Child Develpm.,* 1961, **32,** 59–69.

83. Khan, S. B.: Dimensions of manifest anxiety and their relationship to college achievement. *J. consult. clin. Psychol.,* 1970, **35,** 223–228.

84. Kreitler, H., and S. Kreitler: Dependence of laughter on cognitive strategies. *Merrill-Palmer Quart.*, 1970, **16**, 163–177.

85. Kuhlen, R. G.: *The psychology of adolescence*, 2d ed. New York: Harper & Row, 1963.

86. L'Abate, L.: Personality correlates of manifest anxiety in children. *J. consult. Psychol.*, 1960, **24**, 342–348.

87. LaGrone, C. W.: Sex and personality differences in relation to fantasy. *J. consult. Psychol.*, 1963, **27**, 270–272.

88. Landy, E., and E. Scanlane: Relationship between school guidance and psychiatry for adolescents. *Amer. J. Orthopsychiat.*, 1962, **32**, 682–690.

89. LaPouse, R., and M. A. Monk: Fears and worries in a representative sample of children. *Amer. J. Orthopsychiat.*, 1959, **29**, 803–818.

90. Lawson, R., and M. H. Marx: Frustration theory and experiment. *Genet. Psychol. Monogr.*, 1958, **57**, 393–464.

91. Lester, D., and E. G. Kam: Effect of a friend dying upon attitudes toward death. *J. soc. Psychol.*, 1971, **83**, 149–150.

92. Levine, J.: Response to humor. *Scient. American*, 1956, **194**, 31–51.

93. Livson, N., and W. C. Bronson: An exploration of patterns of impulse control in early adolescence. *Child Develpm.*, 1961, **32**, 75–88.

94. Lŏvas, O. I.: Effect of exposure to symbolic aggression on aggressive behavior. *Child Develpm.*, 1961, **32**, 37–44.

95. Lowrey, L. G.: Adolescent frustrations and evasions. In P. H. Hoch and J. Zubin (eds.), *Psychopathology of childhood*. New York: Grune & Stratton, 1955, pp. 267–284.

96. Ludwig, L. D.: Intra- and inter-individual relationships between elation-depression and the desire for excitement. *J. Pers.*, 1970, **38**, 167–176.

97. Macfarlane, J., L. Allen, and M. P. Honzik: *A developmental study of the behavior problems of normal children between twenty-one months and fourteen years*. Berkeley: University of California Press, 1954.

98. Mallick, S. K., and B. R. McCandless: A study of catharsis of aggression. *J. Pers. soc. Psychol.*, 1966, **4**, 591–596.

99. Martin, P. C., and E. L. Vincent: *Human development*. New York: Ronald, 1960.

100. Masterman, J. F., and A. Washburne: The symptomatic adolescent: Psychiatric illness or adolescent turmoil? *Amer. J. Psychiat.*, 1966, **122**, 1240–1248.

101. Maw, W. H., and E. W. Maw: Self-concepts of high- and low-curiosity boys. *Child Develpm.*, 1970, **40**, 123–129.

102. Mehrabian, A.: Nonverbal betrayal of feeling. *J. exp. Res. in Pers.*, 1971, **5**, 64–73.

103. Meissner, W. W.: Comparison of anxiety patterns in adolescent boys. *J. genet. Psychol.*, 1961, **99**, 323–329.

104. Meltzer, H., and D. Ludwig: Age differences in memory optimism and pessimism in workers. *J. genet. Psychol.*, 1967, **110**, 17–30.

105. Modigliani, A.: Embarrassment and embarrassability. *Sociometry*, 1968, **31**, 313–326.

106. Moulton, R.: Oral and dental manifestations of anxiety. *Psychiatry*, 1955, **18**, 261–273.

107. Nakamura, C. Y.: The relationship between children's expressions of hostility and methods of discipline exercised by dominant, overprotective parents. *Child Develpm.*, 1959, **30**, 109–117.

108. Nemy, E.: Adolescents today: Are they more disturbed? *New York Times*, Feb. 20, 1970.

109. Neumann, J.: Sex differences in anxiety scores for college freshmen and sophomores. *J. Psychol.*, 1970, **74**, 113–115.

110. O'Connell, W. E.: The adaptive functions of wit and humor. *J. abnorm. soc. Psychol.*, 1960, **61**, 263–270.

111. Packard, V.: *The status seekers*. New York: Pocket Books, 1961.

112. Paivio, A., and W. E. Lambert: Measures and correlates of audience anxiety ("stage fright"). *J. Pers.*, 1959, **27**, 1–17.

113. Palermo, D. S.: Relation between anxiety and the measures of speed in a reaction time test. *Child Develpm.*, 1961, **32**, 401–408.

114. Parker, E.: *The seven ages of woman*. Baltimore: Johns Hopkins, 1960.

115. Peckos, P. S.: Nutrition during growth and development. *Child Develpm.*, 1957, **28**, 273–285.

116. Pedersen, D. M., and V. J. Breglio: Personality correlates of actual self-disclosure. *Psychol. Rep.*, 1968, **22**, 495–501.

117. Pedersen, D. M., and K. L. Higbee: Self-disclosure and relationship to the target person. *Merrill-Palmer Quart.*, 1969, **15**, 213–220.

118. Pflaum, J.: Nature and incidence of manifest anxiety responses among college students. *Psychol. Rep.*, 1964, **15**, 720.

119. Pope, B., T. Blass, A. W. Siegman, and J. Raher: Anxiety and depression in speech. *J. consult. clin. Psychol.*, 1970, **35**, 128–133.

120. Pressey, S. L., and R. G. Kuhlen: *Psychological development through the life span*. New York: Harper & Row, 1957.

121. Rivenbark, W. H.: Self-disclosure patterns among adolescents. *Psychol. Rep.*, 1971, **28**, 35–42.

122. Rosenzweig, S., and S. H. Braun: Adolescent sex differences in reactions to frustration as explored by the Rosenzweig P-F Study. *J. genet. Psychol.*, 1970, **116**, 53–61.

123. Ruebush, B. K.: Interfering and facilitating effects of test anxiety. *J. abnorm. soc. Psychol.*, 1960, **60**, 205–212.

124. Russell, G. W.: Human fears: A factor analytic study of three age levels. *Genet. Psychol. Monogr.*, 1967, **76**, 141–162.

125. Salzinger, K.: A method of analysis of the process of verbal communication between a group of emotionally disturbed adolescents and their friends and relatives. *J. soc. Psychol.*, 1958, **47**, 39–53.

126. Sattler, J. M.: A theoretical, developmental and clinical investigation of embarrassment. *Genet. Psychol. Monogr.*, 1965, **71**, 19–59.

127. Sattler, J. M.: Embarrassment and blushing: A theoretical review. *J. soc. Psychol.*, 1966, **69**, 117–133.

128. Saul, L. J., and E. E. Pulver: The concept of emotional maturity. *Int. J. Psychiat.*, 1966, **2**, 446–460.

129. Schalon, C. L.: Effect of self-esteem upon performance following failure stress. *J. consult. clin. Psychol.*, 1968, **32**, 497.

130. Schrut, A.: Some typical patterns in the behavior and background of adolescent girls who attempt suicide. *Amer. J. Psychiat.*, 1968, **125**, 69–74.

131. Sharma, S.: Manifest anxiety and school achievement of adolescents. *J. consult. clin. Psychol.*, 1970, **34**, 403–407.

132. Singer, J. L.: The importance of daydreaming. *Psychology Today*, pp. 18–27, 1968, no. 1.

133. Smith, S. L., and C. Sander: Food craving, depression and premenstrual problems. *Psychosom. Med.*, 1969, **31**, 281–287.

134. Smith, W., E. K. Powell, and S. Ross: Manifest anxiety and food aversions. *J. abnorm. soc. Psychol.*, 1955, **50**, 101–104.

135. Spiegler, M. D., and R. M. Liebert: Some correlates of self-reported fear. *Psychol. Rep.*, 1970, **26**, 691–695.

136. Sternlicht, M., and Z. W. Wanderer: Catharsis: Tension reduction via relevant cognitive substitution: An experimental demonstration. *J. gen. Psychol.*, 1966, **74**, 173–179.

137. Strickland, J. F.: The effect of motivation arousal on humor preferences. *J. abnorm. soc. Psychol.*, 1959, **59**, 278–281.

138. Sutton-Smith, B., and B. G. Rosenberg: Manifest anxiety and game preferences in children. *Child Develpm.*, 1960, **31**, 307–311.

139. Tanner, J. M.: *Growth at adolescence*, 2d ed. Oxford: Blackwell Scientific Publications, 1962.

140. Thompson, D. F., and L. Meltzer: Communication of emotional intent by facial expression. *J. abnorm. soc. Psychol.*, 1964, **68**, 129–135.

141. Thompson, G. G., and E. F. Gardner: Adolescents' perceptions of happy, successful living. *J. genet. Psychol.*, 1969, **115**, 107–120.

142. Tonks, C. M., P. H. Rack, and M. J. Rose: Attempted suicide and the menstrual cycle. *J. psychosom. Res.*, 1968, **11**, 319–323.

143. Tryon, A. F.: Thumb-sucking and manifest anxiety: A note. *Child Develpm.*, 1968, **39**, 1159–1163.

144. Unger, H. E.: The feeling of happiness. *Psychology*, 1970, **7**, 27–33.

145. Verinis, J. S.: Inhibition of humor enjoyment: Effects of sexual content and introversion-extraversion. *Psychol. Rep.*, 1970, **26**, 167–170.

146. Vincent, E. L., and P. C. Martin: *Human psychological development*. New York: Ronald, 1961.

147. Vondracek, F. W., and M. J. Marshall: Self-disclosure and interpersonal trust: An exploratory study. *Psychol. Rep.*, 1971, **28**, 235–240.

148. Walter, D., L. S. Denzler, and I. G. Sarason: Anxiety and the intellectual performance of high school children. *Child Develpm.*, 1964, **35**, 917–926.

149. Walters, R. H., W. E. Marshall, and J. R. Shooter: Anxiety, isolation, and susceptibility to social influence. *J. Pers.*, 1960, **28**, 518–529.

150. Wart, W. D., and C. R. Day: Manifest anxiety as related to perceived similarity to peers. *Psychol. Rep.*, 1970, **26**, 247–250.

151. Weiner, I. B.: *Psychological disturbances in adolescence*. New York: Wiley, 1970.

152. Weiss, J. H.: Birth order and physiological stress response. *Child Develpm.*, 1970, **41**, 461–470.

153. West, L. W.: Sex differences in the exercise of circumspection in self-disclosure among adolescents. *Psychol. Rep.*, 1970, **26**, 236.

154. Williams, F., and J. Tolch: Communication by facial expression. *J. Commun.*, 1965, **15**, 17–27.

155. Wirt, R. D.: Ideational expression of hostile impulses. *J. consult. Psychol.*, 1956, **20**, 185–189.

156. Worchel, P.: Catharsis and the relief of hostility. *J. abnorm. soc. Psychol.*, 1957, **55**, 238–243.

157. Zander, A.: Group membership and individual security. *Hum. Relat.*, 1958, **11**, 99–111.

158. Zeligs, R.: Children's attitudes toward annoyances. *J. genet. Psychol.*, 1962, **101**, 255–266.

159. Zuk, G. H.: The influence of social context on impulse and control tendencies in preadolescents. *Genet. Psychol. Monogr.*, 1956, **54**, 117–166.

CHAPTER 4

1. Aldridge, J. W.: In the country of the young. Part II. *Harper's Mag.*, November, 1969, pp. 93–107.

2. Allport, G. W.: Prejudice: Is it societal or personal? *Relig. Educ.*, 1964, **59**, 20–29.

3. Amatora, Sister M.: Developmental trends

in pre-adolescence and early adolescence in self-evaluation. *J. genet. Psychol.*, 1957, **91**, 89–97.

4. Arter, R. M.: The effects of prejudice on children. *Children*, 1959, **6**, 185–189.

5. Bach, M. L.: Factors related to student participation in campus social organizations. *J. soc. Psychol.*, 1961, **54**, 337–348.

6. Baker, F., and G. M. O'Brien: Birth order and fraternity affiliation. *J. soc. Psychol.*, 1969, **78**, 41–43.

7. Berger, B. M.: Teen-agers are an American invention. *New York Times*, June 13, 1965.

8. Berger, B. M.: The new stage of American man: Almost endless adolescence. *New York Times*, Nov. 2, 1969.

9. Bernard, J.: Teen-age culture: An overview. *Ann. Amer. Acad. pol. soc. Sci.*, 1961, **338**, 1–12.

10. Blum, B. S., and J. H. Mann: The effect of religious membership on religious prejudice. *J. soc. Psychol.*, 1960, **52**, 97–101.

11. Bogardus, E. S.: Racial distance changes in the United States during the past thirty years. *Sociol. soc. Res.*, 1958, **43**, 127–134.

12. Bowerman, C. E., and J. W. Kinch: Changes in family and peer orientation of children between the fourth and tenth grades. *Soc. Forces*, 1959, **37**, 206–211.

13. Bowlby, J.: Childhood mourning and its implications for psychiatry. *Amer. J. Psychiat.*, 1961, **118**, 481–498.

14. Bretsch, H. S.: Social skills and activities of socially accepted and unaccepted adolescents. *J. educ. Psychol.*, 1952, **43**, 449–458.

15. Brim, O. G., and S. Wheeler: *Socialization after childhood: Two essays.* New York: Wiley, 1966.

16. Bringmann, W., and G. Rieder: Stereotyped attitudes toward the aged in West Germany and the United States. *J. soc. Psychol.*, 1968, **76**, 267–268.

17. Brittain, C. V.: An exploration of the bases of peer-compliance and parent-compliance in adolescence. *Adolescence*, 1967, **2**, 445–458.

18. Brittain, C. V.: A comparison of rural and urban adolescents with respect to peer vs. parent compliance. *Adolescence*, 1969, **4**, 59–68.

19. Burchinal, L. G., and J. D. Cowhig: Rural youth in an urban society. *Children*, 1963, **10**, 167–172.

20. Burlingame, W. V.: An investigation of the correlates of adherence to the adolescent peer culture. *Dissert. Abstr.*, 1967, **28** (5–B), 2118–2119.

21. Caffrey, B., and C. Jones: Racial attitudes of Southern high school seniors: A complex picture. *J. soc. Psychol.*, 1969, **79**, 293–294.

22. Carrier, N. A.: Need correlates of "gullibility." *J. abnorm. soc. Psychol.*, 1963, **66**, 84–86.

23. Cartwright, D. S., and R. J. Robertson: Membership in cliques and achievement. *Amer. J. Sociol.*, 1961, **46**, 441–445.

24. Cashdan, S.: Social participation and sub-cultural influences in the study of adolescent creativity. *Adolescence*, 1971, **6**, 39–52.

25. Chabassol, D.: Prejudice and personality in adolescents. *Alberta J. educ. Res.*, 1970, **16**, 3–12.

26. Chasin, G.: A study of the determinants of friendship choice and of the content of friendship relationships. *Dissert. Abstr.*, 1968, **29**, 681.

27. Child, I. L.: Socialization. In G. Lindzey (ed.), *Handbook of social psychology.* Reading, Mass.: Addison-Wesley, 1954, pp. 655–692.

28. Coleman, J. S.: *The adolescent society.* New York: Free Press, 1961.

29. Coons, F. W.: The resolution of adolescence in college. *Personnel Guid. J.*, 1970, **48**, 533–541.

30. Cooper, J. B.: Emotion in prejudice. *Science*, 1959, **130**, 314–318.

31. Crane, A. R.: The development of moral values in children. IV. Pre-adolescent gangs and the moral development of children. *Brit. J. educ. Psychol.*, 1958, **28**, 201–208.

32. Crow, L. D., and A. Crow: *Adolescent development and adjustment,* 2d ed. New York: McGraw-Hill, 1965.

33. Crowne, D. P., and S. Liverant: Conformity under varying conditions of personal commitment. *J. abnorm. soc. Psychol.*, 1963, **66**, 547–555.

34. Dansereau, H. K.: Work and the teen-ager. *Ann. Amer. Acad. pol. soc. Sci.*, 1961, **338**, 44–52.

35. Dienstbier, R. A.: Positive and negative prejudice interactions of prejudice with race and social desirability. *J. Pers.*, 1970, **38**, 198–215.

36. Dies, R. R.: Need for social approval and blame assignment. *J. consult. clin. Psychol.*, 1970, **35**, 311–316.

37. Doerries, L. E.: Purpose in life and social participation. *J. indiv. Psychol.*, 1970, **26**, 50–53.

38. Douvan, E.: Independence and identity in adolescence. *Children*, 1957, **4**, 186–190.

39. Dreyfus, E. A.: The search for intimacy. *Adolescence*, 1967, **2**, 25–40.

40. Duff, J. C.: Quest for leaders. *J. educ. Sociol.*, 1958, **32**, 90–95.

41. Dunphy, D. C.: The social structure of the urban adolescent peer groups. *Sociometry*, 1963, **26**, 230–246.

42. Ehrlich, H. J., and G. N. vanTubergen: Exploring the structure and salience of stereotypes. *J. soc. Psychol.*, 1971, **83**, 113–127.

43. Elkin, F.: Socialization and the presentation of self. *Marriage fam. Living*, 1958, **20**, 320–325.

44. Elkind, D.: Egocentrism in adolescence. *Child Develpm.*, 1967, **38**, 1025–1034.

45. Fagan, J., and M. O'Neill: A comparison of social-distance scores among college-student samples. *J. soc. Psychol.*, 1965, **66**, 281–290.

46. Farley, F. H., and S. V. Farley: Impulsiveness, sociability, and the preference for varied experience. *Percept. mot. Skills,* 1970, **31,** 47−50.

47. Fletcher, R.: Differences in selected psychological characteristics of participants and nonparticipants in activity. *Percept. mot. Skills,* 1971, **32,** 301−302.

48. Forbes, G. B.: Fraternity or sorority membership and birth order: Sex differences and problems of reliability. *J. soc. Psychol.,* 1970, **82,** 277−278.

49. Friedenberg, E. Z.: *The vanishing adolescent.* Boston: Beacon Press, 1959.

50. Gaier, E. L., and W. F. White: Modes of conformity and career selection of rural and urban high school seniors. *J. soc. Psychol.,* 1965, **67,** 379−391.

51. Gardner, R. C., D. M. Taylor, and H. J. Feenstra: Ethnic stereotypes: Attitudes or beliefs? *Canad. J. Psychol.,* 1970, **24,** 321 334.

52. Gesell, A., F. L. Ilg, and L. B. Ames: *Youth: The years from ten to sixteen.* New York: Harper & Row, 1956.

53. Glad, J. B.: How children may be taught tolerance and cooperation. *Marriage fam. Living,* 1962, **24,** 183−185.

54. Gold, M.: Power in the classroom. *Sociometry,* 1958, **21,** 50−60.

55. Gordon, C.: Social characteristics of early adolescence. *Daedalus,* 1971, **100,** 931−960.

56. Gorlow, L., and B. Barocas: Value preferences and interpersonal behavior. *J. soc. Psychol.,* 1965, **66,** 271−280.

57. Goslin, D. A.: Accuracy of social perception and social acceptance. *Sociometry,* 1962, **25,** 283−296.

58. Hall, R. L., and B. Willerman: The educational influence of dormitory roommates. *Sociometry,* 1963, **26,** 294−318.

59. Hall, W. E., and W. Gaeddert: Social skills and their relationship to scholastic achievement. *J. genet. Psychol.,* 1960, **96,** 269−273.

60. Hardy, K. R., and K. S. Larsen: Personality and selectivity factors as predictors of social conformity among college girls. *J. soc. Psychol.,* 1971, **83,** 147−148.

61. Harmin, M.: General characteristics of participating youth groups. *J. educ. Sociol.,* 1956, **30,** 49−57.

62. Harris, D. B.: Work and the adolescent transition to maturity. *Teachers Coll. Rec.,* 1961, **63,** 146−153.

63. Harris, D. B., and S. C. Tseng: Children's attitudes toward peers and parents as revealed by sentence completions. *Child Develpm.,* 1957, **28,** 401−411.

64. Harris, M.: Caste, class, and minority. *Soc. Forces,* 1959, **37,** 248−254.

65. Harvey, O. J., and J. Rutherford: Status in the informal group: Influence and influencibility at differing age levels. *Child Develpm.,* 1960, **31,** 377−385.

66. Havighurst, R. J.: *Human development and education.* New York: Longmans, 1953.

67. Havighurst, R. J.: The social competence of middle-aged people. *Genet. Psychol. Monogr.,* 1957, **56,** 297−375.

68. Hearn, C. B., and J. Seeman: Personality integration and perception of interpersonal relationships. *J. Pers. soc. Psychol.,* 1971, **18,** 138−143.

69. Hechinger, F. M.: The junior blues. *New York Times,* July 28, 1963.

70. Heilbrun, A. B.: Parental model attributes, nurturant reinforcement, and consistency of behavior in adolescents. *Child Develpm.,* 1964, **35,** 151−167.

71. Heise, D. R., and E. P. M. Roberts: The development of role knowledge. *Genet. Psychol. Monogr.,* 1970, **82,** 83 115.

72. Horrocks, J. E., and M. Benimoff: Stability of adolescents' nominee status, over a one year period, as a friend by their peers. *Adolescence,* 1966, **1,** 224−229.

73. Horrocks, J. E., and M. Benimoff: Isolation from the peer group during adolescence. *Adolescence,* 1967, **2,** 41−52.

74. Izard, C. E.: Personality similarity and friendship: A follow-up study. *J. abnorm. soc. Psychol.,* 1963, **66,** 598−600.

75. Jansen, D. G.: Characteristics of student leaders. *Dissert. Abstr.,* 1968, **28** (9−A), 3768.

76. Jersild, A. T.: *The psychology of adolescence,* 2d ed. New York: Macmillan, 1963.

77. Jones, M. C.: A study of socialization patterns at the high school level. *J. genet. Psychol.,* 1958, **93,** 87−111.

78. Jones, M. C.: A comparison of the attitudes and interests of ninth-grade students over two decades. *J. educ. Psychol.,* 1960, **51,** 175−186.

79. Joseph, T. P.: Adolescents: From the views of the members of an informal adolescent group. *Genet. Psychol. Monogr.,* 1969, **79,** 3−88.

80. Josselyn, I. M.: Psychological changes in adolescence. *Children,* 1959, **6,** 43−47.

81. Julian, J. W., R. M. Ryckman, and E. P. Hollander: Effects of prior group support on conformity. *J. soc. Psychol.,* 1969, **27,** 189−196.

82. Kanous, R. A., L. E. Daugherty, and T. S. Cohn: Relation between heterosexual friendship choices and socioeconomic level. *Child Develpm.,* 1962, **33,** 251−255.

83. Karlins, M., T. L. Coffman, and G. Walters: On the facting of social stereotypes: Studies in three generations of college students. *J. Pers. soc. Psychol.,* 1969, **13,** 1−10.

84. Keislar, E. R.: Experimental development of "like" and "dislike" of others among adolescent girls. *Child Develpm.,* 1961, **32,** 59−66.

85. Kerckhoff, A. C.: Early antecedents of

role-taking and role-playing ability. *Merrill-Palmer Quart.*, 1969, **15,** 229-247.

86. Kievit, M. B.: Social participation and social adjustment. *J. educ. Res.*, 1965, **58,** 303-306.

87. King, M. G.: Sex differences in the perception of friendly and unfriendly interactions. *Brit. J. soc. clin. Psychol.*, 1970, **9,** 212-215.

88. Kipnis, D., and B. Goodstadt: Character structure and friendship relations. *Brit. J. soc. clin. Psychol.*, 1970, **9,** 201-212.

89. Klem, M. W.: Factors related to juvenile gang membership patterns. *Sociol. soc. Res.*, 1966, **51,** 49-62.

90. Klem, M. W.: Impressions of juvenile gang members. *Adolescence*, 1968, **3,** 53-78.

91. Kosa, J., L. D. Rachiele, and C. O. Schommer: The self-image and performance of socially mobile college students. *J. soc. Psychol.*, 1962, **56,** 301-316.

92. Lansbaum, J. B., and E. H. Willis: Conformity in early and late adolescence. *Develpm. Psychol.*, 1971, **4,** 334-337.

93. Lansky, L. M., V. J. Crandall, J. Kagan, and C. T. Baker: Sex differences in aggression and its correlates in middle-class adolescents. *Child Develpm.*, 1961, **32,** 45-58.

94. Laumann, E. O.: Friends of urban man: An assessment of accuracy of reporting their socioeconomic attributes, mutual choice, and attitude agreement. *Sociometry*, 1969, **32,** 54-69.

95. Lerman, P.: Gangs, networks, and subcultural delinquency. *Amer. J. Sociol.*, 1967, **73,** 63-72.

96. Levin, J., and H. Black: Personal appearance as a reflection of social ability: Stereotype or reality? *Psychol. Rep.*, 1970, **27,** 338.

97. Lombardi, D. M.: Peer group influence on attitude. *J. educ. Sociol.*, 1963, **36,** 307-309.

98. Lynch, A. Q.: Perception of peer leadership influence. *J. coll. Stud. Personnel*, 1970, **11,** 203-205.

99. Lynn, R.: Personality characteristics of the mothers of aggressive and nonaggressive children. *J. genet. Psychol.*, 1961, **99,** 159-164.

100. Macdonald, A. P.: Manifestations of differential levels of socialization by birth order. *Develpm. Psychol.*, 1969, **1,** 485-492.

101. Mann, P. A.: Effects of anxiety and defensive style on some aspects of friendship, *J. Pers. soc. Psychol.*, 1971, **18,** 55-61.

102. Martin, J. G., and F. R. Westie: The tolerant personality. *Amer. sociol. Rev.*, 1959, **24,** 521-528.

103. McCord, W., J. McCord, and A. Howard: Early familial experience and bigotry. *Amer. sociol. Rev.*, 1960, **25,** 717-722.

104. Megargee, E. L., G. V. C. Parker, and R. V. Levine: Relationship of familial and social factors to socialization in middle-class college students. *J. abnorm. Psychol.*, 1971, **77,** 76-89.

105. Mehlman, B.: Similarity in friendships. *J. soc. Psychol.*, 1962, **57,** 195-202.

106. Miller, N., D. T. Campbell, H. Twedt, and E. J. O'Connell: Similarity, contrast, and complementarity in friendship choice. *J. Pers. soc. Psychol.*, 1966, **3,** 3-12.

107. Millsom, C. A.: Conformity to peers versus adults in early adolescence. *Dissert. Abstr.*, 1966, **26,** 6892.

108. Mitnick, L. L., and E. McGinnies: Influencing ethnocentrism in small discussion groups through a film communication. *J. abnorm. soc. Psychol.*, 1958, **56,** 82-90.

109. Montagu, A.: Social interest and aggression as potentialities. *J. indiv. Psychol.*, 1970, **26,** 17-31.

110. Moore, J. C., and E. Krupat: Relationships between source status, authoritarianism and conformity in a social influence setting. *Sociometry*, 1971, **34,** 122-134.

111. Morris, D. P., E. Soroker, and G. Burruss: Follow-up studies of shy, withdrawn children. I. Evaluation of later adjustment. *Amer. J. Orthopsychiat.*, 1954, **24,** 743-754.

112. Musgrove, F.: The social needs and satisfactions of some young people. Part 1. At home, in youth clubs, and at work. *Brit. J. educ. Psychol.*, 1966, **36,** 61-71.

113. Myerhoff, B. L., and B. G. Myerhoff: Field observations of "gangs." *Soc. Forces*, 1964, **42,** 328-336.

114. Nelson, P. D.: Similarities and differences among leaders and followers. *J. soc. Psychol.*, 1964, **63,** 161-167.

115. Niab, L. N.: Factors determining group stereotypes. *J. soc. Psychol.*, 1963, **61,** 3-10.

116. Nikelly, A. G.: The dependent adolescent. *Adolescence*, 1971, **6,** 139-144.

117. Noel, D. L.: A theory of the origin of ethnic stratification. *Soc. Probl.*, 1968, **2,** 157-172.

118. Noel, D. L., and A. Pinkney: Correlates of prejudice: Some racial differences and similarities. *Amer. J. Sociol.*, 1964, **29,** 609-622.

119. Nowicki, S., and J. Roundtree: Correlates of locus of control in a secondary school population. *Develpm. Psychol.*, 1971, **4,** 477-478.

120. Packard, V.: *The status seekers.* New York: Pocket Books, 1961.

121. Patterson, F. K.: The youth community participation project. *J. educ. Sociol.*, 1956, **30,** 44-48.

122. Peters, G. R., and C. E. Kennedy: Close friendships in the college community. *J. coll. Stud. Personnel*, 1970, **11,** 449-456.

123. Phelps, H. R., and J. E. Horrocks: Factors influencing informal groups of adolescents. *Child Develpm.*, 1958, **29,** 69-86.

124. Phillips, R. E.: Student activities and self-concept. *J. Negro Educ.*, 1969, **38**, 32–37.

125. Photiadis, J. D.: Education and personality variables related to prejudice. *J. soc. Psychol.*, 1962, **58**, 269–275.

126. Pierce, R. A.: Need similarity and complementarity as determinants of friendship choice. *J. Psychol.*, 1970, **76**, 231–238.

127. Plant, W. T.: Changes in intolerance and authoritarianism for sorority and nonsorority women enrolled in college for two years. *J. soc. Psychol.*, 1966, **68**, 79–83.

128. Pressey, S. L., and R. G. Kuhlen: *Psychological development through the life span.* New York: Harper & Row, 1957.

129. Purnell, R. F.: Socioeconomic status and sex differences in adolescent reference-group orientation. *J. genet. Psychol.*, 1970, **116**, 233–239.

130. Query, J. M. N.: The influence of group pressures on the judgments of children and adolescents: A comparative study. *Adolescence*, 1968, **3**, 153–160.

131. Recreation Survey: Recreational interests and needs of high-school youth: Résumé of study conducted in Schenectady, N. Y. *Recreation*, 1954, **47**, 43–46.

132. Rogers, E. M., and A. E. Havens: Prestige rating and mate selection on a college campus. *Marriage fam. Living*, 1960, **22**, 55–59.

133. Rothaus, P., R. T. Davis, and C. A. Banker: Participation in adolescent autonomous groups. *J. genet. Psychol.*, 1969, **114**, 135–142.

134. Salzinger, K., M. Hammer, S. Portnoy, and S. K. Polgar: Verbal behavior and social distance. *Lang. Speech*, 1970, **13**, 25–37.

135. Schonfield, J.: Differences in smoking, drinking, and social behavior by race and delinquency status in adolescent males. *Adolescence*, 1966, **1**, 367–380.

136. Secord, P. F., and C. W. Backman: Interpersonal congruency, perceived similarity, and friendship. *Sociometry*, 1964, **27**, 115–127.

137. Secord, P. F., and E. Saumer: Identifying Jewish names: Does prejudice increase accuracy? *J. abnorm. soc. Psychol.*, 1960, **61**, 144–145.

138. Serum, C. S., and D. G. Myers: Note on prejudice and personality. *Psychol. Rep.*, 1970, **26**, 65–66.

139. Sheikh, A. A.: Stereotyping in interpersonal perception and intercorrelation between some attitude measures. *J. soc. Psychol.*, 1968, **76**, 175–179.

140. Short, J. F., and F. L. Strodtbeck: Why gangs fight. *Trans-Action*, September-October 1964, pp. 25–29.

141. Sigall, H., and R. Page: Current stereotypes: A little fading, a little faking. *J. Pers. soc. Psychol.*, 1971, **18**, 247–255.

142. Simmons, D. C.: Protest humor: Folkloristic reaction to prejudice. *Amer. J. Psychiat.*, 1963, **120**, 567–570.

143. Sinha, A. K.: Relationship between ethnic stereotypes and social distance. *Psychol. Rep.*, 1971, **28**, 216.

144. Skorepa, C. A., J. E. Horrocks, and G. G. Thompson: A study of friendship fluctuations of college students. *J. genet. Psychol.*, 1963, **102**, 151–157.

145. Smart, R. G.: Social-group membership, leadership, and birth order. *J. soc. Psychol.*, 1965, **67**, 221–225.

146. Smith, K. H.: Conformity as related to masculinity, sex, and other descriptions, suspicion, and artistic preference by sex groups. *J. soc. Psychol.*, 1970, **80**, 79–88.

147. Snyder, E. E.: Socioeconomic variations, values, and social participation among high school students. *J. Marriage & Family*, 1966, **28**, 174–176.

148. Solomon, D.: Influences on the decisions of adolescents. *Hum. Relat.*, 1963, **16**, 45–60.

149. Stone, C. L.: Some family characteristics of socially active and inactive teenagers. *Family Life Coordinator*, 1960, **8**, 53–57.

150. Strang, R.: *The adolescent views himself.* New York: McGraw-Hill, 1957.

151. Stricker, L. J., S. Messick, and D. N. Jackson: Conformity, anticonformity and independence: Their dimensionality and generality. *J. Pers. soc. Psychol.*, 1970, **16**, 494–507.

152. Strickland, B. R., and D. P. Crowne: Conformity under conditions of simulated group pressure as a function of the need for social approval. *J. soc. Psychol.*, 1962, **58**, 171–181.

153. Sugarman, B.: Involvement in youth culture, academic achievement, and conformity in school. *Brit. J. Sociol.*, 1967, **18**, 151–164.

154. Sugarman, B.: Social norms in teenage boys' peer groups. *Hum. Relat.*, 1968, **21**, 41–58.

155. Thornburg, H. D.: Peers: Three distinct groups. *Adolescence*, 1971, **6**, 59–76.

156. Thrasher, F. M.: *The gang.* Chicago: University of Chicago Press, 1963.

157. Triandis, H. C., and V. Vassiliou: Frequency of contact and stereotyping. *J. Pers. soc. Psychol.*, 1967, **7**, 316–328.

158. Van Manen, G. C.: Father roles and adolescent socialization. *Adolescence*, 1968, **3**, 139–152.

159. Vavrik, J., and A. P. Jurich: Self-concept and attitude toward acceptance of females: A note. *Family Coordinator*, 1971, **20**, 151–152.

160. Vraa, C. W.: Influence of need for inclusion on group participation. *Psychol. Rep.*, 1971, **28**, 271–274.

161. Wagner, H.: The increasing importance of the peer group during adolescence. *Adolescence*, 1971, **6**, 53–58.

162. Walster, E., and B. Walster: Effect of expecting to be liked on choice of associates. *J. abnorm. soc. Psychol.*, 1963, **67**, 402–404.

163. Walum, L. R.: Group perception of threat

on non-members. *Sociometry*, 1968, **31**, 278–284.

164. Wedge, B.: Nationality and social perception. *J. Commun.*, 1966, **16**, 273–282.

165. Weller, L.: The relationship of personality and nonpersonality factors to prejudice. *J. soc. Psychol.*, 1964, **63**, 129–137.

166. Werthheimer, R. R.: Consistency of sociometric position in male and female high school students. *J. educ. Psychol.*, 1957, **48**, 385–390.

167. Westley, W. A., and F. Elkin: The protective environment and adolescent socialization. *Soc. Issues*, 1957, **35**, 343–349.

168. Willens, E. P.: Sense of obligation to high school activities as related to school size and marginality of student. *Child Develpm.*, 1967, **38**, 1247–1260.

169. Wilson, W. C.: Development of ethnic attitudes in adolescence. *Child Develpm.*, 1963, **34**, 247–256.

170. Withey, S. B.: The influence of the peer group on the values of youth. *Relig. Educ.*, 1962, **57**, Suppl., 34–44.

171. Witryol, S. L., and J. E. Calkins: Marginal social values of rural school children. *J. genet. Psychol.*, 1958, **92**, 81–93.

172. Zaccaria, J. S.: Developmental tasks: Implications for the goals of guidance. *Personnel Guid. J.*, 1966, **44**, 372–375.

173. Zigler, E.: Social class and the socialization process. *J. educ. Res.*, 1970, **40**, 87–110.

CHAPTER 5

1. Adinolfi, A. A.: Characteristics of highly accepted, highly rejected, and relatively unknown university freshmen. *J. counsel. Psychol.*, 1970, **17**, 456–465.

2. Ahlbrand, W. P., and B. B. Hudgins: Verbal participation and peer status. *Psychology in the Schools*, 1970, **7**, 247–249.

3. Aldridge, J. W.: In the country of the young: Part II. *Harper's Mag.*, November 1969, pp. 93–107.

4. Alexander, C. N.: Ordinal position and sociometric status. *Sociometry*, 1966, **29**, 41–51.

5. Anderson, N. H.: Likeableness ratings of 555 personality-trait words. *J. Pers. soc. Psychol.*, 1968, **9**, 272–279.

6. Ausubel, D. P.: Sociempathy as a function of sociometric status in an adolescent group. *Hum. Relat.*, 1955, **8**, 75–84.

7. Ausubel, D. P., and H. M. Schiff: Some intrapersonal and interpersonal determinants of individual differences in sociempathic ability among adolescents. *J. soc. Psychol.*, 1955, **41**, 39–56.

8. Ausubel, D. P., H. M. Schiff, and E. B. Gasser: A preliminary study of developmental trends in sociempathy: Accuracy of perception of own and others' sociometric status. *Child Develpm.*, 1952, **23**, 111–128.

9. Bach, M. L.: Factors related to student participation in campus social organizations. *J. soc. Psychol.*, 1961, **54**, 337–348.

10. Barclay, D.: Friendship's many faces. *New York Times*, Aug. 13, 1961.

11. Barclay, D.: Leads in developing leadership. *New York Times*, Feb. 4, 1962.

12. Barr, J. A., and K. H. Hoover: Home conditions and influences associated with high school leaders. *Educ. Admin. Supervis.*, 1957, **43**, 271–279.

13. Bernard, J.: Teen-age culture: An overview. *Ann. Amer. Acad. pol. soc. Sci.*, 1961, **338**, 1–12.

14. Bordeau, E., R. Dales, and R. Connor: Relationship of self-concept to 4-H Club leadership. *Rural Sociol.*, 1963, **28**, 413–418.

15. Bossard, J. H. S., and E. S. Boll: *The sociology of child development*, 4th ed. New York: Harper & Row, 1966.

16. Bowerman, C. E., and J. W. Kinch: Changes in family and peer orientation of children between the fourth and tenth grades. *Soc. Forces*, 1959, **37**, 206–211.

17. Brandt, R. M.: The accuracy of self-estimate: A measure of self-concept reality. *Genet. Psychol. Monogr.*, 1958, **58**, 55–99.

18. Bretsch, H. S.: Social skills and activities of socially accepted and unaccepted adolescents. *J. educ. Psychol.*, 1952, **43**, 449–458.

19. Bronson, W. C.: Central orientations: A study of behavior organization from childhood to adolescence. *Child Develpm.*, 1966, **37**, 125–155.

20. Brown, D.: Factors affecting social acceptance of high-school students. *School Review*, 1954, **62**, 151–155.

21. Burke, P. J.: Task and social-emotional leadership role performance. *Sociometry*, 1971, **14**, 22–40.

22. Byles, J. A.: Alienation and social control: A study of adolescents in a suburban community. *Dissert. Abstr.*, 1968, **28** (6–A), 1951–1952.

23. Cannon, K. L.: Stability of sociometric scores of high school students. *J. educ. Res.*, 1958, **52**, 43–48.

24. Cassel, R. N.: A constrict validity study of a leadership and a social insight test for 200 college freshmen students. *J. genet. Psychol.*, 1961, **99**, 165–170.

25. Cassel, R. N., and A. E. Shafer: An experiment in leadership training. *J. Psychol.*, 1961, **51**, 299–305.

26. Chapin, P. S.: Sociometric stars as isolates. *Amer. J. Sociol.*, 1950, **56**, 263–267.

27. Chemers, M. M.: The relationship between

birth order and leadership style. *J. soc. Psychol.,* 1970, **80,** 243–244.

28. Clarke, H. H., and D. H. Clarke: Social status and mental health of boys as related to their maturity, structural and strength characteristics. *Res. Quart. Amer. Ass. Hlth. Phys. Educ. Recr.,* 1961, **32,** 326–334.

29. Clifford, C., and T. S. Cohn: The relationship between leadership and personality attributes perceived by followers. *J. soc. Psychol.,* 1964, **64,** 57–64.

30. Coleman, J. S.: *The adolescent society.* New York: Free Press, 1961.

31. Coleman, J. S.: Teen-agers and their crowd. *PTA Mag.,* 1962, **56,** no. 7, 4–7.

32. Coser, R. L.: Some social functions of laughter. *Hum. Relat.,* 1959, **12,** 171–182.

33. Coster, J. K.: Some characteristics of high-school pupils from three income groups. *J. educ. Psychol.,* 1959, **50,** 55–62.

34. Creson, D. L., and P. M. Blakeney: Social structure in an adolescent milieu program: Implications for treatment. *Adolescence,* 1970, **5,** 407–426.

35. Cruickshank, W. M., and G. O. Johnson: *Education of exceptional children and youth,* 2d ed. Englewood Cliffs, N.J.: Prentice-Hall, 1968.

36. Cunningham, A.: Relation of sense of humor to intelligence. *J. soc. Psychol.,* 1962, **57,** 143–147.

37. Davis, J. M., and A. Farina: Humor appreciation as social communication. *J. Pers. soc. Psychol.,* 1970, **15,** 175–178.

38. DeHaan, R. F.: Social leadership. *57th Yearb. Nat. soc. Stud. Educ.,* 1958, pt. 2, 127–143.

39. DeJung, J. E., and E. F. Gardner: The accuracy of self-role perception: A developmental study. *J. exp. Educ.,* 1962, **31,** 27–41.

40. DeVault, M. V.: Classroom sociometric mutual pairs and residential proximity. *J. educ. Res.,* 1957, **50,** 605–610.

41. Douce, P. D. M.: Selected aspects of personality related to social acceptance and clothing oriented variables. *Dissert. Abstr.,* 1970, **30** (8–B), 3730.

42. Dunphy, D. C.: The social structure of the urban adolescent peer groups. *Sociometry,* 1963, **26,** 230–246.

43. Eagly, A. H.: Leadership style and role differentiation as determinants of group effectiveness. *J. Pers.,* 1970, **38,** 509–524.

44. Elkins, D.: Some factors related to the choice-status of ninety eighth-grade children in a school society. *Genet. Psychol. Monogr.,* 1958, **58,** 207–272.

45. Exline, R. V.: Group interrelations among two dimensions of sociometric status, group congeniality, and accuracy of social perception. *Sociometry,* 1960, **23,** 85–101.

46. Faust, M. S.: Developmental maturity as a determinant in prestige of adolescent girls. *Child Develpm.,* 1960, **31,** 173–184.

47. Feinberg, M. R.: Stability of sociometric status in two adolescent class groups. *J. genet. Psychol.,* 1964, **104,** 83–87.

48. Feinberg, M. R., M. Smith, and R. Schmidt: Analysis of expressions used by adolescents at varying economic levels to describe accepted and rejected peers. *J. genet. Psychol.,* 1958, **93,** 133–148.

49. Feldman, R. A.: Social attributes of the intensely disliked position in children's groups. *Adolescence,* 1969, **4,** 181–198.

50. Feshbach, N., and G. Sones: Sex differences in adolescent reactions toward newcomers. *Develpm. Psychol.,* 1971, **4,** 381–386.

51. Fiedler, F. E.: A note on leadership theory: The effect of social barriers between leaders and followers. *Sociometry,* 1957, **20,** 87–94.

52. Fjeld, S. P.: A longitudinal study of sociometric choice and the communication of values. *J. soc. Psychol.,* 1965, **66,** 297–306.

53. Flanders, N. A., and S. Havumaki: The effect of teacher-pupil contacts involving praise on the sociometric choice of students. *J. educ. Psychol.,* 1960, **51,** 65–68.

54. Frank, F., and L. R. Anderson: Effects of task and group size upon group productivity and member satisfaction. *Sociometry,* 1971, **34,** 135–149.

55. Friedenberg, E. Z.: *The vanishing adolescent.* Boston: Beacon Press, 1959.

56. Friesen, D.: Academic-athletic-popularity syndrome in the Canadian high school society (1967). *Adolescence,* 1968, **3,** 39–52.

57. Fromm-Reichmann, E.: Loneliness. *Psychiatry,* 1959, **22,** 1–15.

58. Frye, R. L.: Relationship between rated leaders and the traits assigned to those leaders. *J. soc. Psychol.,* 1965, **66,** 95–99.

59. Gallagher, J. J.: Social status of children related to intelligence, propinquity, and social perception. *Elem. Sch. J.,* 1958, **58,** 225–231.

60. Gardner, G.: Functional leadership and popularity in small groups. *Hum. Relat.,* 1956, **9,** 491–509.

61. Gesell, A., F. L. Ilg, and L. B. Ames: *Youth: The years from ten to sixteen.* New York: Harper & Row, 1956.

62. Gewirtz, J. L., and D. M. Baer: The effect of brief social deprivation on behaviors for a social reinforcer. *J. abnorm. soc. Psychol.,* 1958, **56,** 49–56.

63. Gilchrist, J. W.: Social psychology and group processes. *Annu. Rev. Psychol.,* 1959, **10,** 233–264.

64. Gold, M.: Power in the classroom. *Sociometry,* 1958, **21,** 50–60.

65. Goodchilds, J. D.: Effects of being witty on position in the social structure of a small group. *Sociometry,* 1959, **22,** 261–272.

66. Goslin, D. A.: Accuracy of self-perception and social acceptance. *Sociometry*, 1962, **25**, 283-296.

67. Gough, H. C.: On making a good impression. *J. educ. Res.*, 1952, **46**, 33-42.

68. Grace, H. A., and N. L. Booth: Is the "gifted" child a social isolate? *Peabody J. Educ.*, 1958, **35**, 195-196.

69. Green, M. E.: Anomie and socioeconomic status among adolescents. *Dissert. Abstr.*, 1968, **29** (6-A), 1964.

70. Grinder, R. E.: Relations of social dating attractions to academic orientation and peer relations. *J. educ. Psychol.*, 1966, **57**, 27-34.

71. Gronlund, N. E., and L. Anderson: Personality characteristics of socially accepted, socially neglected, and socially rejected junior high school pupils. *Educ. Admin. Supervis.*, 1957, **43**, 329-338.

72. Hamilton, J., and J. Warden: The student's role in a high school community and his clothing behavior. *J. Home Econ.*, 1966, **58**, 789-791.

73. Harvey, O. J., and C. Consalvi: Status and conformity to pressure in informal groups. *J. abnorm. soc. Psychol.*, 1960, **60**, 182-187.

74. Havighurst, R. J.: The social competence of middle-aged people. *Genet. Psychol. Monogr.*, 1957, **56**, 297-375.

75. Hendrick, C., and G. Hawkins: Race and belief similarity as determinants of attraction. *Percept. mot. Skills*, 1969, **29**, 710.

76. Horrocks, J. E.: *The psychology of adolescence*, 3d ed. Boston: Houghton Mifflin, 1969.

77. Hutter, M.: Transformation of identity, social mobility, and kinship solidarity. *J. Marriage & Family*, 1970, **32**, 133-137.

78. Jaffee, C. L., and R. L. Lucas: Effects of rates of talking and correctness of decisions on leader choice in small groups. *J. soc. Psychol.*, 1969, **79**, 247-254.

79. Janda, K. F.: Toward the explication of the concept of leadership in terms of the concept of power. *Hum. Relat.*, 1960, **13**, 345-363.

80. Jansen, D. G.: Characteristics of student leaders. *Dissert. Abstr.*, 1968, **28** (9-A), 3768.

81. Johnson, E. E.: Student ratings of popularity and scholastic ability of their peers and actual scholastic performance of those peers. *J. soc. Psychol.*, 1958, **47**, 127-132.

82. Johnson, R. T., and A. N. Frandsen: The California Psychological Inventory profile of student leaders. *Personnel Guid. J.*, 1962, **41**, 343-345.

83. Johnstone, J. W. C., and L. Rosenberg: Sociological observations on the privileged adolescent. In J. F. Adams (ed.), *Understanding adolescence: Current developments in adolescent psychology*. Boston: Allyn and Bacon, 1968, pp. 318-336.

84. Jones, M. C.: A study of socialization patterns at the high school level. *J. genet. Psychol.*, 1958, **93**, 87-111.

85. Jones, M. C.: Psychological correlates of somatic development. *Child Develpm.*, 1965, **36**, 899-911.

86. Jones, R. L., N. W. Gottfried, and A. Owens: The social distance of the exceptional: A study at the high school level. *Except. Children*, 1966, **32**, 551-556.

87. Jones, S. C., and J. S. Shranger: Reputation and self-evaluation as determinants of attractiveness. *Sociometry*, 1970, **33**, 276-286.

88. Kaplan, M. F., and P. V. Olezak: Attraction toward another as a function of similarity and commonality of attitudes. *Psychol. Rep.*, 1971, **28**, 515-521.

89. Karasick, B., T. R. Leidy, and R. Smart: Characteristics differentiating high school leaders from non-leaders. *Purdue Opin. Panel Poll Rep.*, 1968, **27**, 1-18.

90. Keislar, E. R.: The generalization of prestige among adolescent boys. *Calif. J. educ. Res.*, 1959, **10**, 153-156.

91. Keislar, E. R.: Experimental development of "like" and "dislike" of others among adolescent girls. *Child Develpm.*, 1961, **32**, 59-66.

92. Kelly, J. A.: Study of leadership in two contrasting groups. *Sociol. Rev.*, 1963, **11**, 323-335.

93. King, M. G.: Sex differences in the perception of friendly and unfriendly interactions. *Brit. J. soc. clin. Psychol.*, 1970, **9**, 212-215.

94. Kipnis, D., and W. P. Lane: Self-confidence and leadership. *J. appl. Psychol.*, 1962, **46**, 291-295.

95. Kohrs, E. V.: The disadvantaged and lower class adolescent. In J. F. Adams (ed.), *Understanding adolescence: Current developments in adolescent psychology*. Boston: Allyn and Bacon, 1968, pp. 287-317.

96. Krogman, W. M.: Maturation age of 55 boys in the Little League World Series. *Res. Quart. Amer. Ass. Hlth. Phys. Educ. Recr.*, 1959, **30**, 54-56.

97. Krumboltz, J. D.: The relation of extracurricular participation to leadership criteria. *Personnel Guid. J.*, 1957, **35**, 307-314.

98. Kuehne, S. H., and A. M. Creekmore: Relationship among social class, school position and clothing of adolescents. *J. Home Econ.*, 1971, **63**, 555-556.

99. Levine, G. N., and L. A. Sussmann: Social class and sociability in fraternity pledging. *Amer. J. Sociol.*, 1960, **65**, 391-399.

100. Levinson, B. M.: The inner life of the extremely gifted child, as seen from the clinical setting. *J. genet. Psychol.*, 1961, **99**, 83-88.

101. Lott, A. J., B. E. Lott, T. Reed, and T. Crow: Personality-trait descriptions of differentially liked persons. *J. Pers. soc. Psychol.*, 1970, **16**, 284-290.

102. Lott, A. J., B. E. Lott, and M. L. Walsh: Learning of paired associates relevant to differentially liked persons. *J. Pers. soc. Psychol.*, 1970, **16**, 274–283.

103. Lowe, C. A., and J. W. Goldstein: Reciprocal liking and attributes of ability: Mediating effects of perceived intent and personal involvement. *J. Pers. soc. Psychol.*, 1970, **16**, 291–297.

104. Luft, J.: Monetary value and the perception of persons. *J. soc. Psychol.*, 1957, **46**, 245–251.

105. Lynch, A. Q.: Perception of peer leadership influence. *J. coll. Stud. Personnel*, 1970, **11**, 203–205.

106. MacDonald, A. P.: Anxiety, affiliation and social isolation. *Develpm. Psychol.*, 1970, **3**, 242–254.

107. Marak, G. E.: The evolution of leadership structure. *Sociometry*, 1964, **27**, 174–182.

108. Marshall, H. R.: Some factors associated with social acceptance in women's groups. *J. Home Econ.*, 1957, **49**, 173–176.

109. Marshall, H. R.: Prediction of social acceptance in community youth groups. *Child Develpm.*, 1958, **29**, 173–184.

110. Merton, R. K.: The social nature of leadership. *Amer. J. Nurs.*, 1969, **69**, 2614–2618.

111. Miller, A. G.: Role of physical attractiveness in impression formation. *Psychonomic Sci.*, 1970, **19**, 241–243.

112. Mitchell, T. R.: Leadership complexity and leadership style. *J. Pers. soc. Psychol.*, 1970, **16**, 166–174.

113. Mitchell, T. R.: The construct validity of three dimensions of leadership research. *J. soc. Psychol.*, 1970, **80**, 89–94.

114. Moore, N. S.: Status criteria and status variables in an adolescent group. *Dissert. Abstr.*, 1967, **28** (3–A), 1007–1008.

115. Muldoon, J. F.: The concentration of liked and disliked members in groups and the relationship of concentration to group cohesiveness. *Sociometry*, 1955, **18**, 73–81.

116. Muma, J. R.: Peer evaluation and academic performance. *Personnel Guid. J.*, 1965, **44**, 405–409.

117. Naegele, K. N.: Friendship and acquaintances: An exploration of some social distinctions. *Harv. educ. Rev.*, 1958, **28**, 232–252.

118. Nelson, D. O.: Leadership in sports. *Res. Quart. Amer. Ass. Hlth. Phys. Educ. Recr.*, 1966, **37**, 268–275.

119. Nelson, P. D.: Similarities and differences among leaders and followers. *J. soc. Psychol.*, 1964, **63**, 161–167.

120. Newcomb, T. M.: The prediction of interpersonal attraction. *Amer. Psychologist*, 1956, **11**, 575–586.

121. O'Connell, W. E.: The social aspects of wit and humor. *J. soc. Psychol.*, 1969, **79**, 183–193.

122. Orzack, L. H.: Preference and prejudice patterns among rural and urban schoolmates. *Rural Sociol.*, 1956, **21**, 29–33.

123. Ostermeier, A., and J. Eicher: Clothing and appearance as related to social class and social acceptance of adolescent girls. *Quart. Bull. Michigan State Univer. Agricultural Exp. Station*, 1966, **48**, 434–435.

124. Packard, V.: *The status seekers*. New York: Pocket Books, 1961.

125. Pastore, N.: A note on changing toward liked and disliked persons. *J. soc. Psychol.*, 1960, **52**, 173–175.

126. Pauley, B. C.: The effects of transportation and part-time employment upon participation in school activities, school offices held, acceptability for leadership positions, and grade point average among high school seniors. *J. educ. Res.*, 1958, **52**, 3–9.

127. Phelps, H. R., and J. E. Horrocks: Factors influencing informal groups of adolescents. *Child Develpm.*, 1958, **29**, 69–86.

128. Propper, M. M.: Direct and projective assessment of alienation among affluent adolescent males. *J. proj. Tech. pers. Assess.*, 1970, **34**, 41–44.

129. Propper, M. M., V. Kiaune, and J. B. Murray: Alienation syndrome among male adolescents in prestige Catholic and public high schools. *Psychol. Rep.*, 1970, **27**, 311–315.

130. Pryer, M. W., A. W. Flint, and B. M. Bass: Group effectiveness and consistency of leadership. *Sociometry*, 1962, **25**, 391–397.

131. Rose, A. M.: Attitudinal correlates of social participation. *Soc. Forces*, 1959, **37**, 202–206.

132. Ross, A. D.: Control and leadership in women's groups. *Soc. Forces*, 1958, **37**, 124–131.

133. Ryan, M. S.: *Clothing: A study in human behavior*. New York: Holt, 1966.

134. Sarason, S. B., and T. T. Gladwin: Psychological and cultural problems in mental subnormality: A review of research. *Genet. Psychol. Monogr.*, 1958, **57**, 3–284.

135. Scandrette, O. C.: Social distance and the degree of acquaintance. *J. educ. Res.*, 1958, **51**, 367–372.

136. Schachter, S.: Birth order and sociometric choice. *J. abnorm. soc. Psychol.*, 1964, **68**, 453–456.

137. Schneider, B.: Relationship between various criteria of leadership in small groups. *J. soc. Psychol.*, 1970, **82**, 253–261.

138. Sewell, W. H., and A. O. Haller: Factors in the relationship between social status and the personality adjustment of the child. *Amer. sociol. Rev.*, 1959, **24**, 511–520.

139. Simpson, R. L., and I. H. Simpson: The school, the peer group and adolescent development. *J. educ. Sociol.*, 1958, **32**, 37–41.

140. Smart, R. G.: Social-group membership, leadership and birth order. *J. soc. Psychol.*, 1965, **67**, 221–225.

141. Snyder, E. E.: Socioeconomic variables, values, and social participation among high school students. *J. Marriage & Family,* 1966, **28,** 174 – 176.

142. Snyder, E. E.: A longitudinal analysis of social participation in high school and early adulthood voluntary associational participation. *Adolescence,* 1970, **5,** 79 – 88.

143. Stephenson, T. E.: The leader-follower relationship. *Sociol. Rev.,* 1959, **7,** 179 – 195.

144. Stroebe, W., C. A. Insko, V. D. Thompson, and B. D. Layiton: Effects of physical attractiveness, similarity, and sex on various aspects of interpersonal attraction. *J. Pers. soc. Psychol.,* 1971, **18,** 79 – 91.

145. Sutton-Smith, B., and P. Gump: Games and status experience. *Recreation,* 1955, **48,** 172 – 174.

146. Sutton-Smith, B., and B. G. Rosenberg: Peer perceptions of impulsive behavior. *Merrill-Palmer Quart.,* 1961, **7,** 233 – 238.

147. Sutton-Smith, B., and B. G. Rosenberg: Age changes in the effects of ordinal position on sex-role identification. *J. genet. Psychol.,* 1965, **107,** 61 – 73.

148. Taft, R.: The ability to judge people. *Psychol. Bull.,* 1955, **52,** 1 – 23.

149. Terrell, G., and J. Shreffler: A developmental study of leadership. *J. educ. Res.,* 1958, **52,** 69 – 72.

150. Thompson, O. E.: High school students and their values. *Calif. J. educ. Res.,* 1965, **16,** 217 – 227.

151. Treadwell, T. W.: Comparing autocratic and democratic leadership techniques for college women. *Coll. Stud. Survey,* 1970, **4,** 46 – 51.

152. Turner, R. H.: Preoccupation with competitiveness and social acceptance among American and English college students. *Sociometry,* 1960, **23,** 307 – 325.

153. VanKrevelen, A.: Characteristics which "identify" the adolescent to his peers. *J. soc. Psychol.,* 1962, **56,** 285 – 289.

154. Walters, R. H., W. E. Marshall, and J. R. Shooter: Anxiety, isolation, and susceptibility to social influence. *J. Pers.,* 1960, **28,** 518 – 529.

155. Warnath, L. F.: The relation of family cohesiveness and adolescent independence to social effectiveness. *Marriage fam. Living,* 1955, **17,** 346 – 348.

156. Wheeler, D. K.: Popularity among adolescents in Western Australia and in the United States. *School Review,* 1961, **69,** 67 – 81.

157. Williams, M. C., and J. B. Eicher: Teenagers' appearance and social acceptance. *J. Home Econ.,* 1966, **58,** 457 – 461.

158. Yamamoto, K.: Creativity and sociometric choice among adolescents. *J. soc. Psychol.,* 1964, **64,** 249 – 261.

159. Yarnall, C. D.: Relationship of physical fitness to selected measures of personality. *Res. Quart. Amer. Ass. Hlth. Phys. Educ. Recr.,* 1966, **37,** 286 – 288.

160. Ziller, R. C.: Leader acceptance of responsibility for group action under conditions of uncertainty and risk. *J. Psychol.,* 1959, **47,** 57 – 66.

161. Ziller, R. C., and R. D. Behringer: Assimilation of the knowledgeable newcomer under conditions of group success and failure. *J. abnorm. soc. Psychol.,* 1960, **60,** 288 – 291.

162. Ziller, R. C., and R. D. Behringer: A longitudinal study of the assimilation of the new child in the group. *Hum. Relat.,* 1961, **14,** 121 – 133.

163. Ziller, R. C., and R. D. Behringer: Motivational and perceptual effects in orientation toward a newcomer. *J. soc. Psychol.,* 1965, **66,** 79 – 90.

CHAPTER 6

1. Adelson, J.: What generation gap? *New York Times,* Jan. 18, 1970.

2. Adelson, J.: The political imagination of the young adolescent. *Daedalus,* 1971, **100,** 1013 – 1050.

3. Adler, N.: The antinomian personality. *Psychiatry,* 1968, **31,** 325 – 338.

4. Aldridge, J. W.: In the country of the young: Part II. *Harper's Mag.,* November 1969, pp. 93 – 108.

5. Alexander, C. K.: Alcohol and adolescent rebellion. *Soc. Forces,* 1967, **47,** 542 – 550.

6. Alissi, A. S.: Bridging the concept gap in work with youth. *Children,* 1970, **17,** 13 – 18.

7. Altbach, P. C., and P. Peterson: Before Berkeley: Historical perspectives on American student activism. *Ann. Amer. Acad. pol. soc. Sci.,* 1971, **395,** 1 – 14.

8. APA Report: Campus tensions: Analysis and recommendations. *Amer. Psychologist,* 1970, **25,** 694 – 726.

9. Baker, R.: Youth as a tiresome old windbag. *New York Times,* Oct. 17, 1967.

10. Bandura, A.: The stormy decade: Fact or fiction? *Psychology in the Schools,* 1964, **1,** 224 – 231.

11. Barrett, D., and R. Neighbor: Breakdown of family life and permissiveness in the home. *Relig. Educ.,* 1970, **65,** 161 – 162.

12. Bay, C.: Political and apolitical students: Facts in search of theory *J. soc. Issues,* 1967, **23,** no. 3, 76 – 91.

13. Bealer, R. C., F. K. Willits, and P. R. Maida: The rebellious youth subculture: A myth. *Children,* 1964, **11,** 43 – 48.

14. Benedict, R.: Continuities and discontinuities in cultural conditioning. *Psychiatry,* 1938, **1,** 161 – 167.

15. Bernard, J.: Teen-age culture: An overview. *Ann. Amer. Acad. pol. soc. Sci.,* 1961, **338,** 1–12.

16. Bettelheim, B.: The problem of generations. *Daedalus,* 1962, **91,** 68–96.

17. Birenbaum, A.: Sex revolution without the revolution: Sex in contemporary America. *J. sex Res.,* 1970, **6,** 257–267.

18. Blair, G. M., and C. W. Pendleton: Attitudes of youth toward current issues as perceived by teachers and adolescents. *Adolescence,* 1971, **6,** 425–428.

19. Block, J. H., N. Haan, and M. B. Smith: Activism and apathy in contemporary adolescents. In J. F. Adams (ed.), *Understanding adolescence: Current developments in adolescent psychology.* Boston: Allyn and Bacon, 1968, pp. 198–231.

20. Block, J. H., N. Haan, and M. B. Smith: Socialization correlates of student activism. *J. soc. Issues,* 1969, **25,** no. 4, 143–177.

21. Blum, L. H.: The discothèque and the phenomenon of alone-togetherness: A study of the young person's response to the frug and comparable current dances. *Adolescence,* 1966, **1,** 351–366.

22. Bordin, E. S., M. H. Shaevitz, and M. Lacher: Entering college students' preparation for self-regulation. *J. counsel. Psychol.,* 1970, **17,** 291–298.

23. Bossard, J. H. S., and E. S. Boll: *The sociology of child development,* 4th ed. New York: Harper & Row, 1966.

24. Boudon, R.: Sources of student protest in France. *Ann. Amer. Acad. pol. soc. Sci.,* 1971, **395,** 139–149.

25. Brody, J. E.: New laws help minors obtain own health care. *New York Times,* Mar. 5, 1972.

26. Brown, D. R.: Student stress and the institutional environment. *J. soc. Issues,* 1967, **23,** no. 3, 92–107.

27. Brunswick, A. F.: What generation gap? *Soc. Probl.,* 1970, **17,** 358.

28. Burton, W. H.: The preadolescent: Rebel in our society. *Education,* 1955, **76,** 222–225.

29. Cameron, P.: The generation gap: Which generation is believed powerful versus generational members' self-appraisal of power. *Develpm. Psychol.,* 1970, **3,** 403–404.

30. Cantril, H.: A study of aspirations. *Scient. American,* 1963, **208,** no. 2, 41–45.

31. Carroll, J. F. X.: Understanding student rebellion. *Adolescence,* 1969, **4,** 163–180.

32. Conger, J. J.: A world they never knew: The family and social change. *Daedalus,* 1971, **100,** 1105–1138.

33. Count, J.: The conflict factor in adolescent growth. *Adolescence,* 1967, **2,** 167–181.

34. Crow, L. D., and A. Crow: *Adolescent development and adjustment,* 2d ed. New York: McGraw-Hill, 1965.

35. Davis, F., and L. Munoz: Heads and freaks: Patterns and meanings of drug use among Hippies. *J. Hlth. soc. Behav.,* 1968, **9,** 156–164.

36. De Fleur, L. B., and G. R. Garrett: Dimensions of marijuana usage in a land-grant university. *J. counsel. Psychol.,* 1970, **17,** 468–476.

37. Dreger, R. M.: Spontaneous conversations and story-telling of children in a naturalistic setting. *J. Psychol.,* 1970, **40,** 163–180.

38. Dryfoos, S.: Young trustees gain influence. *New York Times,* Jan. 10, 1972.

39. Dunbar, F.: Homeostasis during puberty. *Amer. J. Psychiat.,* 1958, **114,** 673–682.

40. Duvall, E. M.: Teen-agers and the generation gap. *Family Coordinator,* 1969, **18,** 284–286.

41. Eckerson, L. O.: The teenage problem is the adult. *Personnel Guid. J.,* 1969, **47,** 849–854.

42. Eisenberg, L.: Student unrest: Sources and consequences. *Science,* 1970, **167,** 1688–1692.

43. Eisenstaudt, S. N.: Generational conflict and intellectual antinomianism. *Ann. Amer. Acad. pol. soc. Sci.,* 1971, **395,** 68–79.

44. Erikson, E. H.: *Identity: Youth and crises.* New York: Norton, 1968.

45. Erikson, E. H.: Reflections on the dissent of contemporary youth. *Daedalus,* 1970, **99,** 154–176.

46. Flacks, R.: The liberated generation: An exploration of the roots of student protest. *J. soc. Issues,* 1967, **23,** no. 3, 52–75.

47. Flacks, R.: Social and cultural meanings of student revolt: Some informal comparative observations. *Soc. Probl.,* 1970, **17,** 340–357.

48. Flynn, W. R.: The pursuit of purity: A defensive use of drug abuse in adolescence. *Adolescence,* 1970, **5,** 141–150.

49. Friedenberg, E. Z.: *Coming of age in America: Growth and acquiescence.* New York: Random House, 1965.

50. Friedenberg, E. Z.: The generation gap. *Ann. Amer. Acad. pol. soc. Sci.,* 1969, **382,** 32–42.

51. Friedenberg, E. Z.: The high school as a focus of "student unrest." *Ann. Amer. Acad. pol. soc. Sci.,* 1971, **395,** 117–126.

52. Friedman, M.: Youth alienation from and protest against the establishment and middle class culture including church and synagogue: Humanistic values and the generation gap. *Relig. Educ.,* 1970, **65,** 165–170.

53. Gecas, V.: Parental behavior and dimensions of adolescent self-evaluation. *Sociometry,* 1971, **34,** 466–482.

54. Gesell, A., F. L. Ilg, and L. B. Ames: *Youth: The years from ten to sixteen.* New York: Harper & Row, 1956.

55. Gilbert, J. G., and D. N. Lombardi: Personality characteristics of young male narcotic addicts. *J. consult. Psychol.,* 1967, **31,** 536–538.

56. Gilula, M. F., and D. N. Daniels: Violence and man's struggle to adapt. *Science,* 1969, **164,** 396–405.

57. Ginandes, S.: The generation gap widens in America. *Int. J. offender Ther.,* 1969, **13,** 18–20.

58. Gold, M.: Juvenile delinquency as a symp-

tom of alienation. *J. soc. Issues,* 1969, **25,** no. 2, 121–135.

59. Gusfield, J. R.: Student protest and university response. *Ann. Amer. Acad. pol. soc. Sci.,* 1971, **395,** 26–38.

60. Hanna, W. J.: Student protest in independent black Africa. *Ann. Amer. Acad. pol. soc. Sci.,* 1971, **395,** 171–183.

61. Havighurst, R. J.: Conditions productive of superior children. *Teachers Coll. Rec.,* 1961, **62,** 524–531.

62. Herz, S.: Research study on behavioral patterns in sex and drug use on college campus. *Adolescence,* 1970, **5,** 1–16.

63. Herzog, E., and C. E. Sudia: The generation gap in the eyes of youth. *Children,* 1970, **17,** 53–58.

64. Herzog, E., C. E. Sudia, and J. Harwood: Drug use among the young as teenagers see it. *Children,* 1970, **17,** 206–212.

65. Hess, R. D.: Political attitudes in children. *Psychology Today,* 1969, **2,** no. 6, 24–28.

66. Heussenstamm, F. H.: Activism in adolescence: An analysis of the high school underground press. *Adolescence,* 1971, **6,** 317–336.

67. Howard, J. R.: The flowering of the Hippie movement. *Ann. Amer. Acad. pol. soc. Sci.,* 1969, **382,** 43–55.

68. Hurlock, E. B.: American adolescents of today: A new species. *Adolescence,* 1966, **1,** 7–21.

69. Hurlock, E. B.: The adolescent reformer. *Adolescence,* 1968, **3,** 272–306.

70. Jersild, A. T.: *The psychology of adolescence,* 2d ed. New York: Macmillan, 1963.

71. Jersild, A. T.: *Child psychology,* 6th ed. Englewood Cliffs, N.J.: Prentice-Hall, 1969.

72. Johnson, J. J.: The Hippy as a developmental task. *Adolescence,* 1969, **4,** 35–42.

73. Jones, V.: Attitudes of college students and their changes: A 37-year study. *Genet. Psychol. Monogr.,* 1970, **81,** 3–80.

74. Joseph, T. P.: Adolescents: From the views of the members of an informal adolescent group. *Genet. Psychol. Monogr.,* 1969, **79,** 3–88.

75. Karr, S. D., and O. B. Dent: In search of meaning: The generalized rebellion of the hippie. *Adolescence,* 1970, **5,** 187–196.

76. Kelly, H.: Adolescents: A suppressed minority group. *Personnel Guid. J.,* 1969, **47,** 634–640.

77. Keniston, K.: *The uncommitted: Alienated youth in American society.* New York: Dell, 1965.

78. Keniston, K.: The sources of student dissent. *J. soc. Issues,* 1967, **23,** no. 3, 108–137.

79. Keniston, K.: *Young radicals: Notes on committed youths.* New York: Harcourt, Brace & World, 1968.

80. Keniston, K., and M. Lerner: Campus characteristics and campus unrest. *Ann. Amer. Acad. pol. soc. Sci.,* 1971, **395,** 39–53.

81. Keniston, K., and M. Lerner: Selected references on student protest. *Ann. Amer. Acad. pol. soc. Sci.,* 1971, **395,** 184–194.

82. Kerpelman, L. C.: Student political activism and ideology: Comparative characteristics of activists and nonactivists. *J. counsel. Psychol.,* 1969, **16,** 8–13.

83. Kiesler, C. A. (ed.): *The psychology of commitment: Experiments linking behavior to belief.* New York: Academic, 1971.

84. Kirkpatrick, M. E.: The mental hygiene of adolescence in the Anglo-American culture. *Ment. Hyg., N.Y.,* 1952, **36,** 394–403.

85. Kirtley, D., and R. Harkless: Student political activity in relation to personal and social adjustment. *J. Psychol.,* 1970, **75,** 253–256.

86. Klein, A. (ed.): *Natural enemies: Youth and the clash of generations.* Philadelphia: Lippincott, 1969.

87. Kohlberg, L., and C. Gilligan: The adolescent as a philosopher: The discovery of the self in a post-conventional world. *Daedalus,* 1971, **100,** 1051–1086.

88. Kraft, A.: Personality correlates of rebellion-behavior in school. *Adolescence,* 1966, **1,** 251–260.

89. Kuehn, J. L.: The student drug user and his family. *J. coll. Stud. Personnel,* 1970, **11,** 409–413.

90. Laufer, R. S.: Sources of generational consciousness and conflict. *Ann. Amer. Acad. pol. soc. Sci.,* 1971, **395,** 80–94.

91. Lazar, E. A., and C. Klein: What makes parents repulsive? *New York Times,* Feb. 7, 1965.

92. Lee, C. B. T.: Campus styles mirror seven decades of change. *New York Times,* Jan. 11, 1971.

93. Leggett, J.: Metamorphosis of the campus radical. *New York Times,* Jan. 30, 1972.

94. Leo, J.: Studies agree that most campus activists are comparatively intelligent, stable, and unprejudiced. *New York Times,* June 19, 1967.

95. Lerner, R. M., J. Pendoy, and A. Emery: Attitudes of adolescents and adults toward contemporary issues. *Psychol. Rep.,* 1971, **28,** 139–145.

96. Levin, J., and H. Black: Personal appearance as a reflection of social attitudes: Stereotype or reality? *Psychol. Rep.,* 1970, **27,** 338.

97. Liebman, A.: Student activism in Mexico. *Ann. Amer. Acad. pol. soc. Sci.,* 1971, **395,** 159–170.

98. Lipset, S. M.: American student activism in comparative perspective. *Amer. Psychologist,* 1970, **25,** 675–693.

99. Lipset, S. M., and E. C. Ladd: As students age. *New York Times,* Oct. 22, 1971.

100. Lourie, R. S.: The concern of one generation for the next. *Children,* 1970, **17,** 234–235.

101. Macfarlane, J., L. Allen, and M. P. Honzik: *A developmental study of the behavior problems of normal children between twenty-one months and*

fourteen years. Berkeley: University of California Press, 1954.

102. Mankoff, M., and R. Flacks: The changing social base of the American student movement. *Ann. Amer. Acad. pol. soc. Sci.,* 1971, **395,** 54–67.

103. Masters, J. C.: Treatment of "adolescent rebellion" by the reconstrual of stimuli. *J. consult. clin. Psychol.,* 1970, **35,** 213–216.

104. Matza, D.: Subterranean traditions of youth. *Ann. Amer. Acad. pol. soc. Sci.,* 1961, **338,** 102–118.

105. McCleod, J. C.: Youth culture and the generation gap. *Relig. Educ.,* 1970, **65,** 99–108.

106. McCleod, J. C.: Nature and relevance of school and college life and curriculum to the values of youth and the needs of society. *Relig. Educ.,* 1970, **65,** 163–164.

107. McKennell, A. C.: Smoking motivation factors. *Brit. J. soc. clin. Psychol.,* 1970, **9,** 8–22.

108. Mead, M.: *Male and female.* New York: Dell, 1968.

109. Meisels, M., and F. M. Canter: A note on the generation gap. *Adolescence,* 1971, **6,** 523–530.

110. Messer, M.: The predictive value of marijuana use: A note to researchers of student culture. *Sociol. Educ.,* 1969, **42,** 91–97.

111. Middleton, R., and S. Putney: Political expression of adolescent rebellion. *Amer. J. Sociol.,* 1963, **68,** 527–535.

112. Mitchell, K. R., R. J. Kirkby, and D. M. Mitchell: Drug use by university freshmen. *J. coll. Stud. Personnel,* 1970, **11,** 332–336.

113. Mitscherlich, A.: Panel on "protest and revolution." *Int. J. Psychoanal.,* 1970, **51,** 211–218.

114. Mizner, G. L., J. T. Barter, and P. H. Werme: Patterns of drug use among college students: A preliminary report. *Amer. J. Psychiat.,* 1970, **127,** 15–24.

115. Murray, J. B.: The generation gap. *J. genet. Psychol.,* 1971, **118,** 71–80.

116. Myerhoff, B. G.: The revolution as a trip: Symbol and paradox. *Ann. Amer. Acad. pol. soc. Sci.,* 1971, **395,** 105–116.

117. Neal, A. G., and S. Rettig: On the multi-dimensionality of alienation. *Amer. sociol. Rev.,* 1963, **32,** 54–64.

118. *New York Times* Report: Student drug use is laid to tension. Feb. 2, 1969.

119. Nicholi, A. M.: Campus disorders: A problem of adult leadership. *Amer. J. Psychiat.,* 1970, **127,** 424–429.

120. Nikelly, A. G.: Ethical issues in research on student protest. *Amer. Psychologist,* 1971, **26,** 475–478.

121. O'Brien, J. P.: The development of the new left. *Ann. Amer. Acad. pol. soc. Sci.,* 1971, **395,** 15–25.

122. Packard, V.: *The status seekers.* New York: Pocket Books, 1961.

123. Pahnke, W.: Drugs for escape or religious experience. *Relig. Educ.,* 1970, **65,** 176–183.

124. Peterson, R. E.: The student protest movement: Some facts, interpretations, and a plea. In F. F. Korten, S. W. Cook, and J. I. Lacey (eds.), *Psychology and the problems of society.* Washington, D.C.: APA, 1970, 388–394.

125. Pinner, F. A.: Students: A marginal elite in politics. *Ann. Amer. Acad. pol. soc. Sci.,* 1971, **395,** 127–138.

126. Polk, K.: Class, strain and rebellion among adolescents. *Soc. Probl.,* 1969, **17,** 214–224.

127. Pressey, S. L., and R. G. Kuhlen: *Psychological development through the life span.* New York: Harper & Row, 1957.

128. Propper, M. N., V. Kiaune, and J. B. Murray: Alienation syndrome among male adolescents in prestige Catholic and public high schools. *Psychol. Rep.,* 1970, **27,** 311–315.

129. Prugh, D. G.: Youth's challenge and our response: Are we a sick society? *Amer. J. Orthopsychiat.,* 1969, **39,** 548–552.

130. Riester, A. E., and R. A. Zucker: Adolescent social structure and drinking behavior. *Personnel Guid. J.,* 1969, **47,** 304–312.

131. Robins, J. L.: The problem of the acute identity crisis in adolescence. *Amer. J. Psychoanal.,* 1968, **28,** 37–47.

132. Rode, A.: Perceptions of parental behavior among alienated adolescents. *Adolescence,* 1971, **6,** 19–38.

133. Sampson, E. E.: Student activism and the decade of protest. *J. soc. Issues,* 1967, **23,** no. 3, 1–33.

134. Sarbin, F. R.: On the distinction between social roles and social types, with special reference to the Hippie. *Amer. J. Psychiat.,* 1969, **125,** 1024–1031.

135. Schmeck, H. M.: Drugs invade the 3-R scene. *New York Times,* Jan. 10, 1972.

136. Schonfield, J.: Differences in smoking, drinking, and social behavior by race and delinquency status in adolescent males. *Adolescence,* 1966, **1,** 367–380.

137. Scott, J. W., and M. El-Assal: Multiuniversity, university size, university quality and student protest: An impirical study. *Amer. sociol. Rev.,* 1969, **35,** 702–709.

138. Seeley, J. R.: Stances and substances. *Ann. Amer. Acad. pol. soc. Sci.,* 1971, **395,** 95–104.

139. Seeman, M.: On the meaning of alienation. *Amer. sociol. Rev.,* 1959, **24,** 783–791.

140. Sheehan, P. W.: Measurement of a construct of the student-activist personality. *J. consult. clin. Psychol.,* 1971, **36,** 297.

141. Sherif, M.: *Problems of youth: Transition*

to adulthood in a changing world. Chicago: Aldine, 1965.

142. Shimbori, M.: Student radicals in Japan. *Ann. Amer. Acad. pol. soc. Sci.,* 1971, **395,** 150–158.

143. Shore, M. F., and J. L. Massimo: The alienated adolescent: A challenge to the mental health profession. *Adolescence,* 1969, **4,** 19–34.

144. Smith, D. E., and J. Sternfield: The hippie communal movement effects on child birth and development. *Amer. J. Orthopsychiat.,* 1970, **40,** 527–530.

145. Spiegel, J. P.: Campus disorders: A transactional approach. *Psychoanal. Rev.,* 1970, **57,** 472–504.

146. Stevens, W. K.: Reform drive now key issue in education. *New York Times,* Jan. 11, 1971.

147. Stewart, L., and N. Livson: Smoking and rebelliousness: A longitudinal study from childhood to maturity. *J. consult. Psychol.,* 1966, **30,** 225–229.

148. Stinchcombe, A. L.: *Rebellion in a high school.* Chicago: Quadrangle, 1964.

149. Strean, H. S.: Youth as advisers to adults and vice versa. *Children,* 1970, **17,** 59–62.

150. Sudia, C., and J. H. Rea: Teenagers discuss age restrictions. *Children,* 1971, **18,** 232–236.

151. Sullivan, R. J.: Reluctant rebels. *Parents' Mag.,* April 1971, pp. 56–57, 92–93.

152. Tennyson, A.: *The poetical works of Alfred Lord Tennyson.* New York: Macmillan, 1894.

153. Thomas, L. E.: Family correlates of student political activism. *Develpm. Psychol.,* 1971, **4,** 206–214.

154. Thompson, O. E.: Student values in transition. *Calif. J. educ. Res.,* 1968, **19,** 77–86.

155. *Time* Report: The new commandment: Thou shalt not—maybe. Dec. 13, 1971, pp. 73–74.

156. Trent, J. W., and J. L. Craise: Commitment and conformity in the American college. *J. soc. Issues,* 1967, **23,** no. 3, 34–51.

157. *U.S. News & World Report:* End of the youth revolt? Survey of changing mood. Aug. 9, 1971, pp. 26–31.

158. *U.S. News & World Report:* What schools are doing to train young voters. Oct. 18, 1971, pp. 92–95.

159. *U.S. News & World Report:* Turn from campus violence. Oct. 25, 1971, pp. 40–43.

160. *U.S. News & World Report:* Newest campus crusade: Equal rights for women. Dec. 13, 1971, pp. 79–81.

161. Watts, W. A., S. Lynch, and D. Whittaker: Alienation and activism in today's college-age youth: Socialization patterns and current family relationships. *J. counsel. Psychol.,* 1969, **16,** 1–7.

162. Weiner, I. B.: The generation gap: Fact and fancy. *Adolescence,* 1971, **6,** 155–166.

163. Westby, D. L., and R. G. Baumgart: Class and politics in the family backgrounds of student political activists. *Amer. sociol. Rev.,* 1966, **31,** 690–692.

164. Whittaker, D.: The psychological adjustment of intellectual nonconformists. *Adolescence,* 1971, **6,** 415–424.

165. Whittaker, D., and W. A. Watts: Personality characteristics associated with activism and disaffiliation in today's college-age youth. *J. counsel. Psychol.,* 1971, **18,** 200–206.

166. Wittenberg, R. M.: *The troubled generation.* New York: Association Press, 1967.

167. Wolfenden, J.: Students' strains and stresses. *Brit. J. Psychiat.,* 1970, **116,** 577–585.

168. Wyatt, F.: Motives of rebellion: Psychological comments on the crisis of authority among students. *Humanitas,* 1969, **4,** 355–373.

CHAPTER 7

1. Adelson, J., and P. P. O'Neil: Growth of political ideas in adolescence. *J. Pers. soc. Psychol.,* 1966, **4,** 295–306.

2. Albert, R. S., and H. G. Meline: The influence of social status on the uses of television. *Publ. Opin. Quart.,* 1958, **22,** 145–151.

3. Allport, G. W.: Values and our youth. *Teachers Coll. Rec.,* 1961, **63,** 211–219.

4. Amatora, Sister M: Analyses of certain recreational interests and activities and other variables in the large family. *J. soc. Psychol.,* 1959, **50,** 225–231.

5. Amatora, Sister M.: Home interests in early adolescence. *Genet. Psychol. Monogr.,* 1962, **65,** 137–174.

6. Anast, P.: Personality determinants of mass media preferences. *Journalism Quart.,* 1966, **43,** 729–732.

7. Anast, P.: Differential movie appeals as correlates of attendance. *Journalism Quart.,* 1967, **44,** 86–90.

8. Appell, C. T.: Television's impact upon middle-class family life. *Teachers Coll. Rec.,* 1960, **61,** 265–274.

9. Baranowski, M. D.: Television and the adolescent. *Adolescence,* 1971, **6,** 369–396.

10. Baumann, V. H.: Teen-age music preferences. *J. Res. mus. Educ.,* 1960, **8,** 75–84.

11. Bernard, J.: Teen-age culture: An overview. *Ann. Amer. Acad. pol. soc. Sci.,* 1961, **338,** 1–12.

12. Bishop, D. W., and P. A. Witt: Sources of behavioral variance during leisure time. *J. Pers. soc. Psychol.,* 1970, **16,** 352–360.

13. Blazer, J. A.: Fantasy and its effects. *J. gen. Psychol.,* 1964, **70,** 163–182.

14. Blum, L. H.: The discothèque and the phenomenon of alone-togetherness: A study of the young person's response to the frug and comparable current dances. *Adolescence,* 1966, **1,** 351–366.

15. Blumenfeld, W. S., and H. H. Remmers: Research note on high school spectator sports preferences of high school students. *Percept. mot. Skills,* 1965, **20,** 166.

16. Bowen, E.: Comeback for Goldilocks et al. *New York Times,* Aug. 26, 1962.

17. Boyers, R.: Attitudes toward sex in American "high culture." *Ann. Amer. Acad. pol. soc. Sci.,* 1968, **376,** 36–52.

18. Bretsch, H. S.: Social skills and activities of socially accepted and unaccepted adolescents. *J. educ. Psychol.,* 1952, **43,** 449–458.

19. Brough, J. R., and M. L. Reeves: Activities of suburban and inner-city youth. *Personnel Guid. J.,* 1968, **47,** 209–212.

20. Brown, C. H.: Self-portrait: The teen-age magazine. *Ann. Amer. Acad. pol. soc. Sci.,* 1961, **338,** 13–21.

21. Bruch, H.: Psychological aspects of obesity in adolescence. *Amer. J. publ. Hlth.,* 1958, **48,** 1349–1353.

22. Burke, R. S., and R. E. Grinder: Personality-oriented themes and listening patterns in teenage music and their relation to certain academic and peer variables. *School Review,* 1966, **74,** 196–211.

23. Bush, P. A., and R. G. Pease: Pop records and connotation saliation: Test of Jakobovits theory. *Psychol. Rep.,* 1968, **23,** 871–875.

24. Cameron, P.: The words college students use and what they talk about. *J. commun. Disord.,* 1970, **3,** 36–46.

25. Cannon, K. L.: The relationship of social acceptance to socio-economic status and residence of high-school students. *Rural Sociol.,* 1957, **22,** 142–148.

26. Carlett, H. A.: A study of the fantasy behavior of children at three age levels. *Dissert. Abstr.,* 1965, **26,** 1167–1168.

27. Clarke, A. C.: The use of leisure and its relation to levels of occupational prestige. *Amer. sociol. Rev.,* 1956, **21,** 301–307.

28. Coffin, T. E.: Television's impact on society. *Amer. Psychologist,* 1955, **10,** 630–641.

29. Coleman, J. S.: *The adolescent society.* New York: Free Press, 1961.

30. Coleman, J. S.: Athletics in high school *Ann. Amer. Acad. pol. soc. Sci.,* 1961, **338,** 33–42.

31. Coleman, J. S.: The competition for adolescent energies. In H. F. Clarizio, R. C. Craig, and W. A. Mehrens (eds.), *Contemporary issues in educational psychology.* Boston: Allyn and Bacon, 1970, pp. 574–586.

32. Collier, M. J., and E. L. Gaier: The hero of the preferred childhood stories of college men. *Amer. Imago,* 1959, **16,** 177–194.

33. Coser, R. L.: Laughter among colleagues. *Psychiatry,* 1960, **23,** 81–95.

34. Crow, L. D., and A. Crow: *Adolescent development and adjustment,* 2d ed. New York: McGraw-Hill, 1965.

35. De Fleur, M. L.: Mass communication and social change. *Soc. Forces,* 1966, **44,** 314–326.

36. Donald, M. N., and R. J. Havighurst: The meaning of leisure. *Soc. Forces,* 1959, **37,** 355–360.

37. Dunkelberger, C. J., and L. E. Tyler: Interest stability and personality traits. *J. counsel. Psychol.,* 1961, **8,** 70–74.

38. Dunphy, D. C.: The social structure of the urban adolescent peer groups. *Sociometry,* 1963, **26,** 230–246.

39. Ellis, D. S.: Speech and social status in America. *Soc. Forces,* 1967, **45,** 431–437.

40. Ellison, J.: Television: Stimulant to violence. *Nation,* 1963, **197,** 433–436.

41. Farley, F. H., and O. Cox: Stimulus-seeking motivation in adolescents as a function of age and sex. *Adolescence,* 1971, **6,** 207–218.

42. Farley, F. H., and S. V. Farley: Impulsiveness, sociability, and the preference for varied experience. *Percept. mot. Skills,* 1970, **31,** 47–50.

43. Faust, M.: Televiewing habits of retarded and gifted pupils. *Education,* 1961, **81,** 300–302.

44. Felker, D. W., and D. M. Hunter: Sex and age differences in response to cartoons depicting subjects of different ages and sex. *J. Psychol.,* 1970, **76,** 19–21.

45. Fingarette, H.: All work and no play. *Humanitas,* 1969, **5,** 5–19.

46. Fitzsimmons, S. J., and H. C. Osburn: The impact of social issues and public affairs television documentaries. *Publ. Opin. Quart.,* 1968, **32,** 380–397.

47. Garai, J. E., and A. Scheinfeld: Sex differences in mental and behavioral traits. *Genet. Psychol. Monogr.,* 1968, **77,** 169–299.

48. Gesell, A., F. L. Ilg, and L. B. Ames: *Youth: The years from ten to sixteen.* New York: Harper & Row, 1956.

49. Glucksberg, S., and R. M. Krauss: What do people say after they have learned to talk? Studies of the development of referential communication. *Merrill-Palmer Quart.,* 1967, **13,** 309–316.

50. Goodchilds, J. D.: Effects of being witty on position in the social structure of a small group. *Sociometry,* 1959, **22,** 261–272.

51. Gottsdanker, J. S.: Intellectual interest patterns of gifted college students. *Educ. psychol. Measmt.,* 1968, **28,** 361–366.

52. Gould, J.: TV violence held unharmful to youth. *New York Times,* Jan. 11, 1972.

53. Hamilton, R. V., R. H. Lawless, and R. W. Marshall: Television within the social matrix. II. Trends after 18 months of ownership. *J. soc. Psychol.,* 1960, **52,** 77–86.

54. Harris, D. B.: Sex differences in the life problems and interests of adolescents: 1935 and 1957. *Child Develpm.*, 1959, **30,** 453–459.

55. Hechinger, G., and F. M. Hechinger: *Teen-age tyranny.* New York: Morrow, 1963.

56. Hein, H.: Play as an aesthetic concept. *Humanitas,* 1969, **5,** 21–28.

57. Heller, M. S., and S. Polsky: Television violence: Guidelines for evaluation. *Arch. gen. Psychiat.,* 1971, **24,** 279–285.

58. Hemmerling, R. L., and H. Hurst: The effects of leisure time activities on scholastic achievement. *Calif. J. educ. Res.,* 1961, **12,** 86–90.

59. Herron, R. E., and B. Sutton-Smith (eds): *Child's play.* New York: Wiley, 1971.

60. Himmelweit, H. T., A. N. Oppenheim, and P. Vince: *Television and the child.* London: Oxford University Press, 1958.

61. Holton, S. M.: The pursuit of happiness. *High Sch. J.,* 1954, **37,** 165–168.

62. Horrocks, J. E.: *The psychology of adolescence,* 3d ed. Boston: Houghton Mifflin, 1969.

63. Hurlock, E. B.: The spontaneous drawings of adolescents. *J. genet. Psychol.,* 1943, **63,** 141–156.

64. Jakobovits, L. A.: Studies of fads. I. The "Hit Parade." *Psychol. Rep.,* 1966, **18,** 443–450.

65. Jersild, A. T.: *The psychology of adolescence,* 2d ed. New York: Macmillan, 1963.

66. Jones, M. C.: A study of socialization patterns at the high school level. *J. genet. Psychol.,* 1958, **93,** 87–111.

67. Jones, M. C.: A comparison of the attitudes and interests of ninth-grade students over two decades. *J. educ. Psychol.,* 1960, **51,** 175–186.

68. Jones, V.: Attitudes of college students and their changes: A 37-year study. *Genet. Psychol. Monogr.,* 1970, **81,** 3–80.

69. Jungeblut, A., and J. H. Coleman: Reading content that interests seventh, eighth, and ninth grade students. *J. educ. Res.,* 1965, **58,** 393–401.

70. Kelley, H. H., and A. J. Stahelski: Social interaction basis of cooperators' and competitors' beliefs about others. *J. Pers. soc. Psychol.,* 1970, **16,** 66–91.

71. Kelly, H. S.: The meaning of current dance forms to adolescent girls: An exploratory study. *Nurs. Res.,* 1969, **17,** 573–579.

72. Krumboltz, J. D., R. E. Christal, and J. H. Ward: Predicting leadership ratings from high school activities. *J. educ. Psychol.,* 1959, **50,** 105–110.

73. Kuhlen, R. G.: *The psychology of adolescent development,* 2d ed. New York: Harper & Row, 1963.

74. La Grone, C. W.: Sex and personality differences in relation to fantasy. *J. consult. Psychol.,* 1963, **27,** 270–272.

75. Lamphear, S. C.: Personality and recreation: A study of participant behavior in selected outdoor recreation activities. *Dissert. Abstr.,* 1970, **30** (12–B), 5314.

76. Levinson, B. M.: The inner life of the extremely gifted child, as seen from the clinical setting. *J. genet. Psychol.,* 1961, **99,** 83–88.

77. Lyness, P. I.: Patterns in mass communications tastes of the young audience. *J. educ. Psychol.,* 1951, **42,** 449–467.

78. Maccoby, E. E., W. C. Wilson, and R. V. Burton: Differential movie-viewing behavior of male and female viewers. *J. Pers.,* 1958, **26,** 259–267.

79. Margolin, E.: Work and play: Are they really opposites? *Elem. Sch. J.,* 1967, **67,** 343–353.

80. McKellar, F., and R. Harris: Radio preferences of adolescents and children. *Brit. J. educ. Psychol.,* 1952, **22,** 101–113.

81. Mehrabian, A., and S. G. Diamond: Seating arrangement and conversation. *Sociometry,* 1971, **34,** 281–289.

82. *Newsweek* Report: The teen-agers. Mar. 21, 1966, pp. 57–75.

83. Noe, F. P.: An instrumental conception of leisure for the adolescent. *Adolescence,* 1969, **4,** 385–400.

84. Noe, F. P.: A pre-industrial examination of adolescent leisure in a cross-cultural setting. *Adolescence,* 1971, **6,** 349–368.

85. Norbeck, E.: Human play and its cultural expression. *Humanitas,* 1969, **5,** 43–55.

86. Packard, V.: *The status seekers.* New York: Pocket Books, 1961.

87. Pate, J. L., and E. Broughton: Game-playing behavior as a function of incentive. *Psychol. Rep.,* 1970, **27,** 36.

88. Pauley, G. G.: The effects of transportation and part-time employment upon participation in school activities, school offices held, acceptability for leadership positions, and grade point average among high school seniors. *J. educ. Res.,* 1958, **52,** 3–9.

89. Payne, E.: Musical taste and personality. *Brit. J. Psychol.,* 1967, **58,** 133–138.

90. Phelps, H. R., and J. E. Horrocks: Factors influencing informal groups of adolescents. *Child Develpm.,* 1958, **29,** 69–86.

91. Pressey, S. L., and R. G. Kuhlen: *Psychological development through the life span.* New York: Harper & Row, 1957.

92. Recreation Survey: Recreational interests and needs of high-school youth: Résumé of study conducted in Schenectady, N. Y. *Recreation,* 1954, **47,** 43–46.

93. Rehberg, R. A.: Behavior and attitudinal consequences of high interscholastic sports: A speculative consideration. *Adolescence,* 1969, **4,** 69–88.

94. Richardson, C. E.: Thurstone Scale for Measuring Attitudes of college students toward physical fitness and exercise. *Res. Quart. Amer. Ass. Hlth. Phys. Educ. Recr.,* 1960, **31,** 638–643.

95. Roberts, J. M., M. J. Arth, and R. R. Bush:

Games in culture. *Amer. Anthropologist*, 1959, **61**, 597–605.

96. Robinson, J. P.: Television and leisure time: Yesterday, today, and (maybe) tomorrow. *Publ. Opin. Quart.*, 1969, **33**, 210–222.

97. Robinson, J. P., and P. Hirsch: It's the sound that does it. *Psychology Today*, 1969, **3**, October, pp. 42–45.

98. Rogers, V. R.: Children's musical preferences as related to grade level and other factors. *Elem. Sch. J.*, 1957, **57**, 433–435.

99. Rosenblatt, P. C.: Functions of games: An examination of individual difference hypotheses derived from a cross-cultural study. *J. soc. Psychol.*, 1962, **58**, 17–22.

100. Sadler, W. A.: Creative existence: Play as a pathway to personal freedom and community. *Humanitas*, 1969, **5**, 57–97.

101. Salzinger, K., M. Hammer, S. Portnoy, and S. K. Polgar: Verbal behavior and social distance. *Lang. Speech*, 1970, **13**, 25–37.

102. Schramm, W.: Patterns in children's reading of newspapers. *Journalism Quart.*, 1960, **37**, 35–40.

103. Schramm, W.: *The effects of television on children and adolescents*. New York: UNESCO Bull., 1965.

104. Sermat, V.: Is game behavior related to behavior in other interpersonal situations? *J. Pers. soc. Psychol.*, 1970, **16**, 92–109.

105. Sessoms, H. D.: An analysis of selected variables affecting outdoor recreation patterns. *Sociol. Rev.*, 1963, **42**, 112–115.

106. Shaffer, L. F., and E. J. Shoben: *The psychology of adjustment*, 2d ed. Boston: Houghton Mifflin, 1956.

107. Simpson, R. L., and I. H. Simpson: The school, the peer group, and adolescent development. *J. educ. Sociol.*, 1968, **32**, 37–41.

108. Singer, J. L.: The importance of daydreaming. *Psychology Today*, 1968, **1**, 18–27.

109. Singer, J. L., and V. G. McCraven: Some characteristics of adult daydreaming. *J. Psychol.*, 1961, **51**, 151–164.

110. Singer, J. L., and R. Rowe: An experimental study of some relationships between daydreaming and anxiety. *J. consult. Psychol.*, 1962, **26**, 446–454.

111. Singer, J. L., and R. A. Schonbar: Correlates of daydreaming: A dimension of self-awareness. *J. consult. Psychol.*, 1961, **25**, 1–6.

112. Smedley, D. A.: Language and social class among grammar school children. *Brit. J. educ. Psychol.*, 1969, **39**, 95–96.

113. Steiner, B. A.: *The people look at television: A study of audience attitudes*. New York: Knopf, 1963.

114. Strang, R.: *The adolescent views himself*. New York: McGraw-Hill, 1957.

115. Sutton-Smith, B.: Play preference and play behavior: A validity study. *Psychol. Rep.*, 1965, **16**, 65–66.

116. Sutton-Smith, B., and P. Gump: Games and status experiences. *Recreation*, 1955, **48**, 172–174.

117. Vincent, E. L., and P. C. Martin: *Human psychological development*. New York: Ronald, 1961.

118. Wall, W. D., and W. A. Simson: The responses of adolescent groups to certain films. *Brit. J. educ. Psychol.*, 1951, **21**, 81–88.

119. Webster's *Third new international dictionary*. Springfield, Mass.: Merriam, 1967.

120. Wertham, F.: The scientific study of mass media effects. *Amer. J. Psychiat.*, 1962, **119**, 306–311.

121. Whitehead, P. C.: Sex, violence, and crime in the mass media. *Canad. ment. Hlth.*, 1970, **18**, 20–23.

122. Wichman, H.: Effects of isolation and communication on cooperation in a two-person game. *J. Pers. soc. Psychol.*, 1970, **16**, 114–120.

123. Winick, C.: Teenagers, satire and *Mad. Merrill-Palmer Quart.*, 1962, **8**, 183–203.

124. Witty, P. A.: Studies of children's interests: A brief summary. *Elem. Eng.*, 1960, **37**, 469–475.

125. Witty, P. A.: A study of pupils' interests: Grades 9, 10, 11, 12. *Education*, 1961, **82**, 39–45, 100–110, 169–174.

126. Witty, P. A.: Studies of the mass media: 1949–1965. *Science Educ.*, 1966, **50**, 119–126.

127. Witty, P. A., P. Kinsella, and A. Coomer: A summary of yearly studies of televiewing: 1949–1963. *Elem. Eng.*, 1963, **40**, 590–597.

128. Young, R., and M. Frye: Some are laughing: Some are not—why? *Psychol. Rep.*, 1966, **18**, 747–754.

129. Zuckerman, M.: Dimensions of sensation seeking. *J. consult. clin. Psychol.*, 1971, **36**, 45–52.

CHAPTER 8

1. Aaronson, B. S.: Drugs: Personality: Drugs. *Psychol. Rep.*, 1970, **26**, 811–818.

2. Adelson, D.: Attitudes toward first names: An investigation of the relationship between self-acceptance, self-identity, and group and individual attitudes toward first names. *Dissert. Abstr.*, 1957, **16**, 1831.

3. Aiken, L. R.: The relationship of dress to selected measures of personality in undergraduate women. *J. soc. Psychol.*, 1963, **59**, 119–128.

4. Albott, W. L., and J. L. Bruning: Given names: A neglected social variable. *Psychol. Rec.,* 1970, **20,** 527–533.

5. Allport, G. W.: Values and our youth. *Teachers Coll. Rec.,* 1961, **63,** 211–219.

6. Amatora, Sister M.: Free expression of adolescent interests. *Genet. Psychol. Monogr.,* 1957, **56,** 173–219.

7. Amatora, Sister M.: Home interests in early adolescence. *Genet. Psychol. Monogr.,* 1962, **65,** 137–174.

8. Amo, M. F., and J. R. Bittner: College student attitudes toward marijuana. *Coll. Stud. Survey,* 1970, **4,** 52–54.

9. Angelino, H., L. A. Barnes, and C. L. Shedd: Attitudes of mothers and adolescent daughters concerning clothing and grooming. *J. Home Econ.,* 1956, **48,** 779–782.

10. Anspach, K.: Clothing selection and the mobility concept. *J. Home Econ.,* 1961, **53,** 428–430.

11. Argyle, M., and R. McHenry: Do spectacles really affect judgments of intelligence? *Brit. J. soc. clin. Psychol.,* 1971, **10,** 27–29.

12. Aronson, E., and J. Mills: The effect of severity of imitation on liking for a group. *J. abnorm. soc. Psychol.,* 1959, **59,** 177–181.

13. Babchuk, N., R. Marsey, and C. W. Gordon: Men and women in community organizations: A note on power and prestige. *Amer. sociol. Rev.,* 1960, **25,** 399–403.

14. Bach, M. L.: Factors related to student participation in campus social organizations. *J. soc. Psychol.,* 1961, **54,** 337–348.

15. Baer, D. J., and J. M. Katkin: Limitation of smoking by sons and daughters who smoke and smoking behavior of parents. *J. genet. Psychol.,* 1971, **118,** 293–296.

16. Barker, G. H., and W. T. Adams: Glue sniffers. *Sociol. soc. Res.,* 1963, **47,** 298–310.

17. Bernard, J.: Teen-age culture: An overview. *Ann. Amer. Acad. pol. soc. Sci.,* 1961, **338,** 1–12.

18. Bernstein, B.: Language and social class. *Brit. J. Sociol.,* 1960, **11,** 271–276.

19. Bjerstedt, A.: Warm-cold color preferences as potential personality indicators: Preliminary note. *Percept. mot. Skills,* 1960, **10,** 31–34.

20. Blain, M. J., and M. Ramirez: Increasing sociometric rank, meaningfulness, and discriminability of children's names through reinforcement and interaction. *Child Develpm.,* 1968, **39,** 949–955.

21. Blazer, J. A.: Fantasy and its effects. *J. gen. Psychol.,* 1964, **70,** 163–182.

22. Boshier, R.: Attitudes toward self and one's proper names. *J. indiv. Psychol.,* 1968, **24,** 63–66.

23. Boshier, R.: Self-esteem and first names in children. *Psychol. Rep.,* 1968, **22,** 762.

24. Bossard, J. H. S., and E. S. Boll: *The sociology of child development,* 4th ed. New York: Harper & Row, 1966.

25. Bowerman, C. E., and J. W. Kinch: Changes in family and peer orientation of children between fourth and tenth grades. *Soc. Forces,* 1959, **37,** 206–211.

26. Brotman, K., I. Silverman, and F. Suffet: Some social correlates of student drug use. *Crime & Delinqu.,* 1970, **16,** 67–74.

27. Brown, C. H.: Self-portrait: The teen-age magazine. *Ann. Amer. Acad. pol. soc. Sci.,* 1961, **338,** 13–21.

28. Brown, R., and M. Ford: Address in American English. *J. abnorm. soc. Psychol.,* 1961, **62,** 375–385.

29. Bush, G., and P. London: On the disappearance of knickers: Hypotheses for the functional analysis of the psychology of clothing. *J. soc. Psychol.,* 1960, **51,** 359–366.

30. Cabe, P. A.: Name length as a factor in mate selection: Age controlled. *Psychol. Rep.,* 1968, **22,** 794.

31. Cameron, P.: The words college students use and what they talk about. *J. commun. Disord.,* 1970, **3,** 36–46.

32. Catton, W. R.: What's in a name? A study of role inertia. *J. Marriage & Family,* 1969, **31,** 15–18.

33. Cavan, R. S.: *Juvenile delinquency.* Philadelphia: Lippincott, 1962.

34. Chamberlin, C.: Youth and drugs. *Menninger Quart.,* 1969, **23,** 12–21.

35. Christiansen, K., and A. Kernaleguen: Orthodoxy and conservatism: Modesty in clothing selection. *J. Home Econ.,* 1971, **63,** 251–255.

36. Cohn, W.: On the language of lower-class children. *School Review,* 1959, **67,** 435–440.

37. Coleman, J. S.: *The adolescent society.* New York: Free Press, 1961.

38. Curtis, R. F.: Occupational mobility and membership in formal voluntary associations: A note on research. *Amer. sociol. Rev.,* 1959, **24,** 846–848.

39. Cwalina, G. E.: Drug use on high school and college campuses. *J. sch. Hlth.,* 1968, **38,** 638–646.

40. Danziger, K.: The child's understanding of kinship terms: A study in the development of rational concepts. *J. genet. Psychol.,* 1957, **91,** 213–232.

41. Davis, J. A.: Status symbols and the measurement of status perception. *Sociometry,* 1956, **19,** 154–165.

42. Dodson, D. W.: Reassessing values in the present age. *J. educ. Sociol.,* 1958, **32,** 49–61.

43. Donald, M. N., and R. J. Havighurst: The meaning of leisure. *Soc. Forces,* 1959, **37,** 355–360.

44. Douce, P. D. M.: Selected aspects of personality related to social acceptance and clothing

oriented variables. *Dissert. Abstr.,* 1970, **30** (8–B), 3730.

45. Douvan, E.: Independence and identity in adolescence. *Children,* 1957, **4,** 186–190.

46. Drake, D.: On pet names. *Amer. Imago,* 1957, **14,** 41–43.

47. Dunphy, D. C.: The social structure of the urban adolescent peer groups. *Sociometry,* 1963, **26,** 230–246.

48. Dunsing, M.: Spending money of adolescents. *J. Home Econ.,* 1956, **48,** 405–408.

49. Duvall, E. M.: Teenagers and the automobile. *Marriage fam. Living,* 1961, **23,** 190–191.

50. Eldridge, W. B.: *Narcotics and the law: A critique of the American experiment in narcotic drug control.* New York: New York University Press, 1962.

51. Ellis, D. S.: Speech and social status in America. *Soc. Forces,* 1967, **45,** 431–437.

52. Engel, M., G. Marsden, and S. Woodaman: Orientation to work in children. *Amer. J. Orthopsychiat.,* 1968, **38,** 137–143.

53. Feldman, F. M.: Money: An index to personal problems in adolescents. *Marriage fam. Living,* 1963, **25,** 364–376.

54. Fellows, L.: Schoolboy dress scored in Britain. *New York Times,* Aug. 11, 1963.

55. Forbes, G. B.: Smoking behavior and birth order. *Psychol. Rep.,* 1970, **26,** 766.

56. Freud, S.: *The standard edition of the complete psychological works of Sigmund Freud.* London: Hogarth, 1953–1962.

57. Friedenberg, E. Z.: *The vanishing adolescent.* New York: Dell, 1962.

58. Garrison, K. C.: *Psychology of adolescence,* 6th ed. Englewood Cliffs, N.J.: Prentice-Hall, 1964.

59. Gellert, E., J. S. Girgus, and J. Cohen: Children's awareness of their bodily appearance: A developmental study of factors associated with body percept. *Genet. Psychol. Monogr.,* 1971, **84,** 69–174.

60. Gesell, A., F. L. Ilg, and L. B. Ames: *Youth: The years from ten to sixteen.* New York: Harper & Row, 1956.

61. Glenn, N. D.: Negro prestige criteria: A case study in the bases of prestige. *Amer. J. Sociol.,* 1963, **68,** 645–657.

62. Glickman, A. S.: Clothing leadership among boys. *Dissert. Abstr.,* 1958, **18,** 682–684.

63. Glucksberg, S., and R. M. Krauss: What do people say after they have learned to talk? Studies of the development of referential communication. *Merrill-Palmer Quart.,* 1967, **13,** 309–316.

64. Goodman, N.: Adolescent norms and behavior: Organization and conformity. *Merrill-Palmer Quart.,* 1969, **15,** 199–211.

65. Grosser, G. S., and W. J. Laczek: Prior parochial vs. secular education and utterance latencies to taboo words. *J. Psychol.,* 1963, **55,** 263–277.

66. Guitar, M. A.: Status seekers, junior grade. *New York Times,* Aug. 16, 1964.

67. Hager, D. L., A. M. Vener, and C. S. Stewart: Patterns of adolescent drug use in Middle America. *J. counsel. Psychol.,* 1971, **18,** 292–297.

68. Hamid, P. N.: Style of dress as a perceptual cue in impression formation. *Percept. mot. Skills,* 1968, **26,** 904–906.

69. Hartman, A. A.: Name style in relation to personality. *J. gen. Psychol.,* 1958, **59,** 289–294.

70. Hartman, A. A., R. C. Nicolay, and J. Hurley: Unique personal names as a social adjustment factor. *J. soc. Psychol.,* 1968, **75,** 107–110.

71. Havighurst, R. J., and K. Feigenbaum: Leisure and life style. *Amer. J. Sociol.,* 1959, **64,** 396–404.

72. Hechinger, F. M.: Drug issue. *New York Times,* Feb. 28, 1965.

73. Hechinger, G., and F. M. Hechinger: Serious epidemic of "automania." *New York Times,* Aug. 11, 1963.

74. Hechinger, G., and F. M. Hechinger: *Teenage tyranny.* New York: Morrow, 1963.

75. Hodgkins, B. J.: Preadolescent awareness of clothing and appearance as related to age and sex. *Dissert. Abstr.,* 1970, **31** (1–A), 494.

76. Hogan, R., D. Mankin, J. Conway, and S. Fox: Personality correlates of undergraduate marijuana use. *J. consult. clin. Psychol.,* 1970, **35,** 58–63.

77. Hoult, T. F.: Experimental measurement of clothing as a factor in some social ratings of selected American men. *Amer. sociol. Rev.,* 1954, **19,** 324–328.

78. Hunt, L. A.: A developmental study of factors related to children's clothing preferences. *Monogr. Soc. Res. Child Develpm.,* 1959, **24,** no. 1.

79. Hunt, R. G., and T. K. Lin: Accuracy of judgments of personal attributes from speech. *J. Pers. soc. Psychol.,* 1967, **6,** 450–453.

80. Hurlock, E. B.: Motivation in fashion. *Arch. Psychol., N.Y.,* 1929, no. 111.

81. Jahoda, G.: Development of the perception of social differences in children from 6 to 10. *Brit. J. Psychol.,* 1959, **50,** 159–175.

82. Jersild, A. T.: *The psychology of adolescence,* 2d ed. New York: Macmillan, 1963.

83. Johannis, T. B.: Participation by fathers, mothers, and teenage sons and daughters in selected family economic activity. *Family Life Coordinator,* 1957, **6,** 15–16.

84. Johnson, P. A., and J. R. Staffieri: Stereotypic affective properties of personal names and somatotypes in children. *Develpm. Psychol.,* 1971, **5,** 176.

85. Jones, M. C.: A study of socialization patterns at the high school level. *J. genet. Psychol.,* 1958, **93,** 87–111.

86. Jones, M. C.: Lipstick charts maturity. *New York Times,* Mar. 21, 1959.

87. Jones, M. C.: A comparison of attitudes and interests of ninth-grade students over two decades. *J. educ. Psychol.*, 1960, **51**, 175–186.

88. Jones, M. C.: Psychological correlates of somatic development. *Child Develpm.*, 1965, **36**, 899–911.

89. Jones, M. C.: Personality antecedents and correlates of drinking patterns in women. *J. consult. clin. Psychol.*, 1971, **36**, 61–69.

90. Josselyn, I. M.: Psychological changes in adolescence. *Children*, 1959, **6**, 43–47.

91. Kernaleguen, A. P., and N. H. Compton: Body-field perceptual differentiation related to peer perception of attitudes toward clothing. *Percept. mot. Skills*, 1968, **27**, 195–198.

92. Kilborn, S. K.: Perception and creativity in clothing. *Percept. mot. Skills*, 1971, **32**, 24–26.

93. King, F. W.: Marijuana and LSD usage among college students: Prevalence rate, frequency, and self-estimates of future use. *Psychiatry*, 1969, **32**, 265–276.

94. Kolansky, H., and W. T. Moore: Effects of marijuana on adolescents and young adults. *J. Amer. med. Ass.*, 1971, **216**, 486–492.

95. Kuehne, S. H., and A. M. Creekmore: Relationship among social class, school position and clothing of adolescents. *J. Home Econ.*, 1971, **63**, 555–556.

96. Kuhlen, R. G.: *The psychology of adolescent development*, 2d ed. New York: Harper & Row, 1963.

97. Lambert, W. E., H. Frankel, and G. R. Tucker: Judging personality through speech: A French-Canadian example. *J. Commun.*, 1966, **16**, 305–321.

98. Levin, J., and H. Black: Personal appearance as a reflection of social attitudes: Stereotype or reality? *Psychol. Rep.*, 1970, **27**, 338.

99. Levine, G. N., and L. A. Sussmann: Social class and sociability in fraternity pledging. *Amer. J. Sociol.*, 1960, **65**, 391–399.

100. Levitt, E. E., and J. A. Edwards: A multivariate study of correlative factors in youthful cigarette smoking. *Develpm. Psychol.*, 1970, **2**, 5–11.

101. Levy, N. J.: The use of drugs by teenagers for sanctuary and illusion. *Amer. J. Psychoanal.*, 1968, **28**, 48–58.

102. Lipsett, L. P.: A self-concept scale for children and its relationship to the children's form of the Manifest Anxiety Scale. *Child Develpm.*, 1958, **29**, 463–472.

103. Luft, J.: Monetary value and the perception of persons. *J. soc. Psychol.*, 1957, **46**, 245–251.

104. Markel, N. N., R. M. Eisler, and H. W. Reese: Judging personality from dialect. *J. verb. Learning verb. Behav.*, 1967, **6**, 33–35.

105. Martin, W. A.: Word fluency: Intellect or personality? *J. genet. Psychol.*, 1971, **118**, 17–24.

106. McGlothlin, W. H., and L. J. West: The marijuana problem: An overview. *Amer. J. Psychiat.*, 1968, **125**, 370–378.

107. McInnes, J. H., and J. K. Shearer: Relationship between color choice and selected preferences of the individual. *J. Home Econ.*, 1964, **56**, 181–187.

108. Mead, M.: *Male and female*. New York: Dell, 1968.

109. Mehlman, B., and R. G. Warehime: Social class and social desirability. *J. soc. Psychol.*, 1962, **58**, 167–170.

110. Middleton, D.: In Britain, names denote status and the more the better. *New York Times*, July 5, 1960.

111. Milgram, N. A., and W. W. Riedel: Developmental and experiential factors in making wishes. *Child Develpm.*, 1969, **40**, 763–771.

112. Miller, A. G.: Role of physical attractiveness in impression formation. *Psychonomic Sci.*, 1970, **19**, 241–243.

113. Mitchell, K. R., R. J. Kirkby, and D. M. Mitchell: Note on sex differences in student drug use. *Psychol. Rep.*, 1970, **27**, 116.

114. Murphy, W. F.: A note on the significance of names. *Psychoanal. Quart.*, 1957, **26**, 91–106.

115. Nash, H.: Recognition of body surface regions. *Genet. Psychol. Monogr.*, 1969, **79**, 297–340.

116. Neisser, E. G.: Emotional and social values attached to money. *Marriage fam. Living*, 1960, **22**, 132–139.

117. *New York Times* Report: Trend is to Anthony in naming babies. July 15, 1962.

118. *New York Times* Report: Narcotics a growing problem of affluent youth. Jan. 4, 1965.

119. *New York Times* Report: Britain's best-dressed: The youthful mods. Feb. 24, 1965.

120. *New York Times* Report: Once-proud name of Adolf shunned by West Germans. Jan. 19, 1969.

121. *New York Times* Report: Student drug use is laid to tension. Feb. 2, 1969.

122. *New York Times* Report: College students these days don't throw money around. Mar. 27, 1972.

123. *Newsweek* Report: The teen-agers. Mar. 21, 1966, pp. 57–75.

124. Ostermeier, A. L.: Adolescent behavior as manifested in clothing. *Bull. State Univer. College, Buffalo*, 1967, **3**, 1–9.

125. Ostermeier, A. L., and J. Eicher: Clothing and appearance as related to social class and social acceptance of adolescent girls. *Quart. Bull. Michigan State Univer. Agricultural Exp. Station*, 1966, **48**, 434–435.

126. Packard, V.: *The status seekers*. New York: Pocket Books, 1961.

127. Pear, T. H.: *Personality, appearance and speech*. London: G. Allen, 1957.

128. Peckos, P. S., and R. F. Heald: Nutrition in adolescents. *Children*, 1964, **11**, 27–30.

129. Penny, R.: Age and sex differences in motivational orientation to the communicative act. *Child Develpm.*, 1958, **29**, 163–171.

130. Powell, K. S., and D. A. Gover: The adolescent as a consumer: Facts and implications. *Marriage fam. Living*, 1963, **25**, 359–364.

131. Pressey, S. L., and A. W. Jones: 1923–1953 and 20–60 age changes in moral codes, anxieties, and interests, as shown by the "X-O Tests." *J. Psychol.*, 1955, **39**, 485–502.

132. Psathas, G.: Ethnicity, social class and adolescent independence from parental control. *Amer. sociol. Rev.*, 1957, **22**, 415–423.

133. Reiter, H. H.: Note on some personality differences between heavy and light drinkers. *Percept. mot. Skills*, 1970, **30**, 762.

134. Richards, E. A., and R. E. Hawthorne: Values, body cathexis, and clothing of male university students. *J. Home Econ.*, 1971, **63**, 190–194.

135. Riester, A. E., and R. A. Zucker: Adolescent social structure and drinking behavior. *Personnel Guid. J.*, 1968, **47**, 304–312.

136. Roach, M. E.: The influence of social class on clothing practices and orientation at early adolescence: A study of clothing-related behavior in seventh grade girls. *Dissert. Abstr.*, 1962, **22**, 2897–2898.

137. Roucek, J. S.: Age as a prestige factor. *Sociol. soc. Res.*, 1958, **42**, 349–352.

138. Ryan, M. S.: *Clothing: A study in human behavior*. New York: Holt, 1966.

139. Salzinger, K., M. Hammer, S. Portnoy, and S. K. Polgar: Verbal behavior and social distance. *Lang. Speech*, 1970, **13**, 25–37.

140. Schmeck, H. M.: Drugs invade the 3-R scene. *New York Times*, Jan. 10, 1972.

141. Schneider, D. M., and G. C. Homans: Kinship terminology and the American kinship system. *Amer. Anthropologist*, 1955, **57**, 1194–1208.

142. Schneider, N. G., and J. P. Houston: Smoking and anxiety. *Psychol. Rep.*, 1970, **26**, 941–942.

143. Schonfeld, W. A.: Body-image disturbances in adolescents. *Arch. gen. Psychiat.*, 1966, **15**, 16–21.

144. Sheppard, D.: Characteristics associated with Christian names. *Brit. J. Psychol.*, 1963, **54**, 167–174.

145. Silverman, D.: An evaluation of the relationship between attitudes toward self and attitudes toward a vocational high school. *J. educ. Sociol.*, 1963, **36**, 410–418.

146. Smedley, D. A.: Language and social class among grammar school children. *Brit. J. educ. Psychol.*, 1969, **39**, 95–96.

147. Smith, G. M.: Relations between personality and smoking behavior in preadult subjects. *J. consult. clin. Psychol.*, 1969, **33**, 710–715.

148. Stout, D. R., and A. Latzke: Values college women consider in clothing selection. *J. Home Econ.*, 1958, **50**, 43–44.

149. Strang, R.: *The adolescent views himself.* New York: McGraw-Hill, 1957.

150. Strongman, K. T., and J. Woosley: Stereotyped reactions to regional accents. *Brit. J. soc. clin. Psychol.*, 1967, **6**, 164–167.

151. Strunk, O.: Attitudes toward one's name and one's self. *J. Indiv. Psychol.*, 1958, **14**, 64–67.

152. Taylor, A. J. W.: Tattooing among male and female offenders of different ages in different types of institutions. *Genet. Psychol. Monogr.*, 1970, **81**, 81–119.

153. *Time* Report: Students: "On the fringe of a golden era." Jan. 29, 1965, pp. 56–59.

154. *Time* Report: The pot problem. Mar. 12, 1965, p. 49.

155. *Time* Report: Pop drugs: The high is a way of life. Sept. 26, 1969, pp. 68–78.

156. *U.S. News & World Report:* Will teenagers make the sixties soar? Oct. 26, 1964, pp. 102–104.

157. Vener, A. M.: Clothes tell a story. *New York Times*, Apr. 28, 1959.

158. Vener, A. M., and C. R. Hoffer: Adolescent orientation to clothing. In M. E. Roach and J. B. Eicher (eds.), *Dress, ornamentation and the social order*. New York: Wiley, 1965, pp. 76–81.

159. Vielhaber, D. P., and E. Gottheil: First impressions and subsequent ratings of performance. *Psychol. Rep.*, 1965, **17**, 916.

160. Walker, R. E., R. C. Nicolay, R. Kluceny, and R. E. Riedel: Psychological correlates of smoking. *J. clin. Psychol.*, 1969, **25**, 42–44.

161. Warburton, F. E.: The lab coat as a status symbol. *Science*, 1960, **131**, 895.

162. Wass, B., and J. Eicher: Clothing as related to role behavior in teenage girls. *Quart. Bull. Michigan State Univer. Agricultural Exp. Station*, 1964, **47**, 206–208, 211–213.

163. Wax, M.: Themes in cosmetics and grooming. *Amer. J. Sociol.*, 1957, **62**, 588–593.

164. Wheeler, D. K.: Expressed wishes of students. *J. genet. Psychol.*, 1963, **102**, 75–81.

165. Williams, J. E., J. K. Morland, and W. L. Underwood: Connotations of color names in the United States, Europe, and Asia. *J. soc. Psychol.*, 1970, **82**, 3–14.

166. Winick, C.: Taboo and disapproved colors and symbols in varying foreign countries. *J. soc. Psychol.*, 1963, **59**, 361–368.

167. Winick, C.: The Beige Epoch: Depolarization of sex roles in America. *Ann. Amer. Acad. pol. soc. Sci.*, 1968, **376**, 18–24.

CHAPTER 9

1. Adler, A.: *Individual psychology.* New York: Harcourt, Brace & World, 1924.

2. Alexander, C. D.: Ordinal position and social mobility. *Sociometry,* 1968, **31,** 285–293.

3. Alexander, C. N., and E. Q. Campbell: Peer influences on adolescent educational aspirations and attainments. *Amer. sociol. Rev.,* 1964, **29,** 568–575.

4. Allport, G. W.: Values and our youth. *Teachers Coll. Rec.,* 1961, **63,** 211–219.

5. Altus, W. D.: Birth order and its sequelae. *Science,* 1966, **151,** 44–49.

6. Amatora, Sister M.: Free expressions of adolescents' interests. *Genet. Psychol. Monogr.,* 1957, **55,** 173–219.

7. Baird, L. L., and J. L. Holland: The flow of high school students to schools, colleges, and jobs. *ACT Res. Rep.,* 1968, no. 26.

8. Beilin, H.: The mobility and achievement of a 1926 class of high school graduates. *J. counsel. Psychol.,* 1954, **1,** 144–148.

9. Beilin, H.: The pattern of postponability and its relation to social class mobility. *J. soc. Psychol.,* 1956, **44,** 33–48.

10. Bell, G. D.: Processes in the formation of adolescents' aspirations. *Soc. Forces,* 1963, **42,** 179–186.

11. Bennett, E. M., and L. R. Cohen: Men and women: Personality patterns and contrasts. *Genet. Psychol. Monogr.,* 1959, **59,** 101–155.

12. Bennett, W. S., and N. P. Gist: Class and family influence on student aspirations. *Soc. Forces,* 1964, **43,** 167–173.

13. Berger, E. M.: Willingness to accept limitations and college achievement: A replication. *J. counsel. Psychol.,* 1963, **10,** 176–178.

14. Bernstein, E.: Fear of failure, achievement motivation, and aspiring to prestigeful occupations. *J. abnorm. soc. Psychol.,* 1963, **67,** 189–193.

15. Blackman, L. S., and H. Kahn: Success and failure as determinants of aspirational shifts in retardates and normals. *Amer. J. ment. Defic.,* 1963, **67,** 751–755.

16. Bossard, J. H. S., and E. S. Boll: *The sociology of child development,* 4th ed. New York: Harper & Row, 1966.

17. Boyle, R. P.: The effect of the high school on students' aspirations. *Amer. J. Sociol.,* 1966, **71,** 628–639.

18. Byers, J. L.: A study of the level of aspiration of academically successful and unsuccessful high school students. *Calif. J. educ. Res.,* 1962, **13,** 209–216.

19. Calogeras, R. C.: Some relationships between fantasy and self-report behavior. *Genet. Psychol. Monogr.,* 1958, **59,** 273–325.

20. Campanello, T.: Maturational development of adolescents. *Education,* 1965, **85,** 310–313.

21. Cantril, H.: A study of aspirations. *Scient. American,* 1963, **208,** no. 2, 41–45.

22. Caro, F. G., and C. T. Pihlbad: Aspirations and expectations: A reexamination of the bases for social class differences in the occupational orientations of male high school students. *Sociol. soc. Res.,* 1965, **49,** 465–475.

23. Child, I. L., and M. K. Bacon: Cultural pressures and achievement motivation. In P. H. Hoch and J. Zubin (eds.), *Psychopathology of childhood.* New York: Grune & Stratton, 1955, pp. 166–176.

24. Christensen, H. T.: Lifetime family and occupational role projections of high school students. *Marriage fam. Living,* 1961, **23,** 181–183.

25. Clark, R. D., and E. P. Willems: Risk preferences as related to judged consequences of failure. *Psychol. Rep.,* 1969, **25,** 827–830.

26. Cohen, E. G.: Parental factors in educational mobility. *Sociol. Educ.,* 1965, **38,** 404–425.

27. Collier, M. J.: The psychological appeal of the Cinderella theme. *Amer. Imago,* 1961, **18,** 399–411.

28. Crandall, V. C., S. Good, and V. J. Crandall: Reinforcement effect of adult reactions and nonreactions to children's achievement expectations: A replication study. *Child Develpm.,* 1964, **35,** 485–497.

29. Cronbach, L. J.: *Educational psychology,* 2d ed. New York: Harcourt, Brace & World, 1963.

30. De Charms, R., and G. H. Moeller: Values expressed in children's readers: 1800–1950. *J. abnorm. soc. Psychol.,* 1962, **64,** 136–142.

31. D'Heurle, A., J. C. Mellinger, and E. A. Haggard: Personality, intellectual, and achievement patterns in gifted children. *Psychol. Monogr.,* 1959, **73,** no. 13.

32. Distefano, M. K., M. W. Pryer, and D. P. Rice: Changes in success-failure attitudes during adolescence. *J. genet. Psychol.,* 1970, **116,** 11–13.

33. Dubbé, M. C.: What parents are not told may hurt. *Fam. Life Coordinator,* 1965, **14,** 51–118.

34. Elder, G. H.: Achievement motivation and intelligence in occupational mobility: A longitudinal analysis. *Sociometry,* 1968, **31,** 327–354.

35. Elliott, J. L., and D. H. Elliott: Effects of birth order and age gap on aspiration level. *Proc. Annu. Convent. APA,* 1970, **5,** pt. 1, 369–370.

36. Farley, J.: Graduate women: Career aspirations and desired family size. *Amer. Psychologist,* 1970, **25,** 1099–1100.

37. Fischer, E. H., C. F. Wells, and S. L. Cohen: Birth order and expressed interest in becoming a college professor. *J. counsel. Psychol.,* 1968, **15,** 111–116.

38. Ford, L. H.: Reaction to failure as a function of expectancy for success. *J. abnorm. soc. Psychol.,* 1963, **67,** 340–348.

39. Garrison, K. C.: The attitudes and concerns about marriage and the family of ninth-grade pupils from the public schools of Georgia. *Adolescence*, 1966, **1**, 54–59.

40. Gist, N. P., and W. S. Bennett: Aspirations of Negro and white students. *Soc. Forces*, 1963, **42**, 40–58.

41. Gottlieb, D.: Goal aspirations and goal fulfillment: Differences between deprived and affluent American adolescents. *Amer. J. Orthopsychiat.*, 1964, **34**, 934–941.

42. Greene, R. L., and J. R. Clark: Birth order and college attendance in a cross-cultural setting. *J. soc. Psychol.*, 1968, **75**, 289–290.

43. Greenfeld, N., and E. L. Finkelstein: A comparison of the characteristics of junior high school students. *J. genet. Psychol.*, 1970, **117**, 37–50.

44. Haller, A. O., and W. H. Sewell: Farm residence and level of educational and occupational aspiration. *Amer. J. Sociol.*, 1957, **62**, 407–411.

45. Harris, D. B.: The development of potentiality. *Teachers Coll. Rec.*, 1960, **61**, 423–428.

46. Harrison, F.: Aspirations as related to school performance and sociometric status. *Sociometry*, 1969, **32**, 70–79.

47. Hartman, B. J.: Motives for college attendance. *Psychol. Rep.*, 1968, **22**, 783–784.

48. Hecht, R. M., J. E. Aron, and S. Lirtzman: Let's stop worrying about aptitudes and look at attitudes. *Personnel Guid. J.*, 1965, **44**, 616–619.

49. Hermans, H. J. M.: A questionnaire measure of achievement motivation. *J. appl. Psychol.*, 1970, **50**, 353–363.

50. Hilgard, E. R.: *Introduction to psychology*, 5th ed. New York: Harcourt, Brace & World, 1971.

51. Isen, A. M.: Success, failure, attention and reaction to others. *J. Pers. soc. Psychol.*, 1970, **13**, 294–301.

52. Jackson, D.: Crack-ups on campus. *Life Mag.*, Jan. 8, 1965, pp. 72–73.

53. Jacobson, R. B.: An explanation of parental encouragement as an intervening variable in occupational and educational learning of children. *J. Marriage & Family*, 1971, **33**, 174–182.

54. Jencks, C.: Social stratification and higher education. *Harv. educ. Rev.*, 1968, **38**, 277–316.

55. Jennings, F. G.: Adolescents, aspirations and the older generation. *Teachers Coll. Rec.*, 1964, **65**, 335–341.

56. Jones, M. C.: A study of socialization patterns at the high school level. *J. genet. Psychol.*, 1958, **93**, 87–111.

57. Jones, V.: Attitudes of college students and their changes: A 37-year study. *Genet. Psychol. Monogr.*, 1970, **81**, 3–80.

58. Jourard, S. M., and P. Richman: Factors in the self-disclosure inputs of college students. *Merrill-Palmer Quart.*, 1963, **9**, 141–148.

59. Kandel, D. B., and G. S. Lesser: Parental and peer influences on educational plans of adolescents. *Amer. sociol. Rev.*, 1969, **34**, 212–223.

60. Katz, F. M.: The meaning of success: Some differences in value systems of social classes. *J. soc. Psychol.*, 1964, **62**, 141–148.

61. Kausler, D. H.: Aspiration level as a determinant of performance. *J. Pers.*, 1959, **27**, 346–351.

62. Kinnane, J. F., and Sister M. M. Bannon: Perceived parental influence and work-value orientation. *Personnel Guid. J.*, 1964, **43**, 273–279.

63. Kinnane, J. F., and M. W. Pable: Family background and work-value orientation. *J. counsel. Psychol.*, 1962, **9**, 320–325.

64. Koch, H. L.: The relation of certain formal attributes of siblings to attitudes held toward each other and toward their parents. *Monogr. Soc. Res. Child Develpm.*, 1960, **25**, no. 4.

65. Kolb, D. A., and R. E. Boyatzis: Goal-setting and self-directed behavior change. *Hum. Relat.*, 1970, **23**, 439–457.

66. Kosa, J., L. D. Rachiele, and C. O. Schommer: The self-image and performance of socially mobile college students. *J. soc. Psychol.*, 1962, **56**, 301–316.

67. Krauss, I.: Sources of educational aspirations among working-class youth. *Amer. sociol. Rev.*, 1964, **29**, 867–879.

68. Krippner, S.: The educational plans and preferences of upper-middle-class junior high school pupils. *Vocat. Guid. Quart.*, 1965, **13**, 257–260.

69. Kuhweide, K., H. E. Lueck, and E. Timaeus: Occupational prestige: A cross-cultural comparison. *Percept. mot. Skills*, 1968, **27**, 154.

70. Lehman, H. C.: *Age and achievement*. Princeton, N.J.: Princeton University Press, 1953.

71. Levin, H., and A. L. Baldwin: The choice to exhibit. *Child Develpm.*, 1958, **29**, 373–380.

72. Lewin, K., T. Dembo, L. Festinger, and P. S. Sears: Level of aspiration. In J. McV. Hunt (ed.), *Personality and the behavior disorders*. New York: Ronald, 1944, pp. 333–378.

73. Lockwood, W. V.: Realism of vocational preference. *Personnel Guid. J.*, 1958, **37**, 98–106.

74. Maccoby, E. E., W. C. Wilson, and R. V. Burton: Differential movie-viewing behavior of male and female viewers. *J. Pers.*, 1958, **26**, 259–267.

75. Matthews, E., and D. V. Tiedman: Attitudes toward career and marriage and the development of life style in young women. *J. counsel. Psychol.*, 1964, **11**, 375–384.

76. McCann, D. J., and J. W. Reich: Social and numerical anchoring effects on the level of aspiration. *Psychol. Rec.*, 1969, **19**, 617–622.

77. McClelland, D. C.: *The achievement motive*. New York: Appleton-Century-Crofts, 1953.

78. McDill, E. L., and J. Coleman: Family and peer influences in college plans for high school students. *Sociol. Educ.*, 1964, **38**, 112–126.

79. Mead, M.: *Male and female*. New York: Dell, 1968.

80. Meade, R. D.: Realism of aspiration level in Indian and American college students. *J. soc. Psychol.,* 1968, **75,** 169–173.

81. Mitchell, J. V.: Goal-setting behavior as a function of self-acceptance, over- and under-achievement, and related personality variables. *J. educ. Psychol.,* 1959, **50,** 93–104.

82. Moerk, E., and P. Becker: Attitudes of high school students toward future marriage and college education. *Family Coordinator,* 1971, **20,** 67–73.

83. Mönks, F.: Future time perspective in adolescents. *Hum. Develpm.,* 1968, **11,** 107–123.

84. Mulvey, M. C.: Psychological and social factors in prediction of career patterns of women. *Genet. Psychol. Monogr.,* 1963, **68,** 309–386.

85. Ninane, P., and F. E. Fiedler: Member reactions to success and failure of group tasks. *Hum. Relat.,* 1970, **23,** 3–13.

86. O'Shea, A. J.: Peer relationships and male academic achievement: A review of suggested clarifications. *Personnel Guid. J.,* 1969, **47,** 417–423.

87. Packard, V.: *The status seekers.* New York: Pocket Books, 1961.

88. Packard, V.: *The pyramid climbers.* New York: McGraw-Hill, 1962.

89. Parker, A. W.: Career and marriage orientation in the vocational development of college women. *J. appl. Psychol.,* 1966, **50,** 232–235.

90. Parsons, O. A.: Status needs and performance under failure. *J. Pers.,* 1958, **26,** 123–138.

91. Pavalko, R. M., and M. H. Walizer: Parental educational differences and the college plans of youth. *Sociol. soc. Res.,* 1969, **54,** 80–89.

92. Pressey, S. L., and R. G. Kuhlen: *Psychological development through the life span.* New York: Harper & Row, 1957.

93. Rao, K. U., and R. W. Russell: Effects of stress on goal setting behavior. *J. abnorm. soc. Psychol.,* 1960, **61,** 380–388.

94. Raynor, J. O.: Relationships between achievement-related motives, future-orientation, and academic performance. *J. Pers. soc. Psychol.,* 1970, **15,** 28–33.

95. Rhine, W. R.: Birth order differences in conformity and level of achievement arousal. *Child Develpm.,* 1968, **39,** 987–996.

96. Rosen, B. C.: Race, ethnicity and achievement syndrome. *Amer. sociol. Rev.,* 1959, **24,** 47–60.

97. Rosen, B. C.: Family structure and achievement motivation. *Amer. sociol. Rev.,* 1961, **26,** 574–585.

98. Rosen, B. C., and R. D'Andrade: The psychological origins of achievement motivation. *Sociometry,* 1959, **22,** 185–218.

99. Rosenfeld, H., and A. Zander: The influence of teachers on aspirations of students. *J. educ. Psychol.,* 1961, **52,** 1–11.

100. Rushing, W. A.: Adolescent-parent relationship and mobility aspirations. *Soc. Forces,* 1964, **43,** 157–166.

101. Sandeen, C. A.: Aspirations for college. *Personnel Guid. J.,* 1968, **46,** 462–465.

102. Schachter, S.: Birth order, eminence, and higher education. *Amer. sociol. Rev.,* 1963, **28,** 757–768.

103. Schonfeld, W. A.: Socioeconomic affluence as a factor. *N.Y. State J. Med.,* 1967, **67,** 1981–1990.

104. Sewell, W. H., and V. P. Shah: Parents' education and children's educational aspirations and achievements. *Amer. sociol. Rev.,* 1968, **33,** 191–200.

105. Shaffer, L. F., and E. J. Shoben: *The psychology of adjustment,* 2d ed. Boston: Houghton Mifflin, 1956.

106. Sherif, M., and C. W. Sherif: Adolescent attitudes and behavior in their reference groups within differing sociocultural settings. In J. P. Hill (ed.), *Minnesota symposia on child psychology.* Minneapolis: University of Minnesota Press, 1969, vol. 3, pp. 97–130.

107. Shrauger, J. S., and S. E. Rosenberg: Self-esteem and the effects of success and failure feedback on performance. *J. Pers.,* 1970, **38,** 404–417.

108. Silverman, I.: Self-esteem and differential responsiveness to success and failure. *J. abnorm. soc. Psychol.,* 1964, **69,** 115–119.

109. Simpson, R. L.: Parental influence, anticipatory socialization, and social mobility. *Amer. sociol. Rev.,* 1962, **27,** 517–522.

110. Smith, D. C., and L. Wing: Developmental changes in preference for goals difficult to attain. *Child Develpm.,* 1961, **32,** 29–36.

111. Sontag, L. W., and J. Kagan: The emergence of intellectual achievement motives. *Amer. J. Orthopsychiat.,* 1963, **33,** 532–534.

112. Spady, W. G.: Educational mobility and access: Growth and paradoxes. *Amer. J. Sociol.,* 1967, **73,** 273–286.

113. Stein, A. H.: The effects of sex-role standards for achievement and sex-role preference on three determinants of achievement motivation. *Develpm. Psychol.,* 1971, **4,** 219–231.

114. Stotland, E., S. Thornley, E. Thomas, and A. R. Cohen: The effects of group expectations and self-esteem upon self-evaluation. *J. abnorm. soc. Psychol.,* 1957, **54,** 55–63.

115. Stotland, E., and A. Zander: Effects of public and private failure on self-evaluation. *J. abnorm. soc. Psychol.,* 1958, **56,** 223–229.

116. Stout, R. T.: Social class and occupational aspirations: A Weberian analysis. *Personnel Guid. J.,* 1969, **47,** 650–654.

117. Strang, R.: *The adolescent views himself.* New York: McGraw-Hill, 1957.

118. Strodtbeck, F. L., M. R. McDonald, and B. C. Rosen: Evaluation of occupations: A reflection

of Jewish and Italian mobility differences. *Amer. sociol. Rev.*, 1957, **22,** 546–553.

119. Symonds, P. M.: What education has to learn from psychology. VI. Emotion and learning. *Teachers Coll. Rec.*, 1958, **60,** 9–22.

120. Taylor, R. Q., and G. R. Hanson: Interest and persistence. *J. counsel. Psychol.*, 1970, **17,** 506–509.

121. Terman, L. M.: The discovery and encouragement of exceptional talent. *Amer. Psychologist*, 1954, **9,** 221–230.

122. Thistlewaite, D. L., and N. Wheeler: Effects of teacher and peer subcultures upon student aspirations. *J. educ. Psychol.*, 1966, **57,** 35–47.

123. Thompson, O. E.: Student values in transition. *Calif. J. educ. Res.*, 1968, **19,** 77–86.

124. Tomeh, A. K.: The impact of reference groups on the educational and occupational aspirations of women college students. *J. Marriage & Family*, 1968, **30,** 102–110.

125. Torrance, E. P., and D. C. Dauw: Aspirations and dreams of three groups of creatively gifted high school seniors and a comparable unselected group. *Gifted Child Quart.*, 1965, **9,** 177–183.

126. Tseng, M. S., and A. R. Carter: Achievement motivation and fear of failure as determinants of vocational choice, vocational aspirations, and perception of vocational prestige. *J. counsel. Psychol.*, 1970, **17,** 150–156.

127. Turner, R. H.: Some family determinants of ambition. *Sociol. soc. Res.*, 1962, **46,** 397–411.

128. Turner, R. H.: Some aspects of women's ambition. *Amer. J. Sociol.*, 1964, **70,** 271–285.

129. Urell, C.: What do they want out of life? *Teachers Coll. Rec.*, 1960, **61,** 318–330.

130. Very, P. S., and R. W. Prull: Birth order, personality development, and the choice of law as a profession. *J. genet. Psychol.*, 1970, **116,** 219–221.

131. Wallace, J. L., and T. H. Leonard: Factors affecting vocational and educational decision making of high school girls. *J. Home Econ.*, 1971, **63,** 241–245.

132. Watson, D. L.: Anxiety and the structure of motivation. *Gawein*, 1969, **17,** 122–133.

133. Weiner, B., and A. Kukla: An attitudinal analysis of achievement motivation. *J. Pers. soc. Psychol.*, 1970, **15,** 1–20.

134. Wheeler, D. K.: Expressed wishes of students. *J. genet. Psychol.*, 1963, **102,** 75–81.

135. Wilburn, W. V.: Testing Talcott Parsons' theory of motivation. *J. soc. Psychol.*, 1970, **80,** 239–240.

136. Witty, P. A.: A study of pupils' interests: Grades 9, 10, 11, 12. *Education*, 1961, **82,** 39–45, 100–110.

137. Won, G., and D. Yamamura: Expectation of youth in relating to the world of adults. *Family Coordinator*, 1970, **19,** 219–224.

138. Zaccaria, J. S.: Developmental tasks: Implications for the goals of guidance. *Personnel Guid. J.*, 1966, **44,** 372–375.

139. Zelen, S. L., and G. J. Zelen: Life-span expectations and achievement expectations of underprivileged and middle-class adolescents. *J. soc. Psychol.*, 1970, **80,** 111–112.

140. Zeligs, R.: Trends in children's New Year's resolutions. *J. exp. Educ.*, 1957, **26,** 133–150.

CHAPTER 10

1. Abramovitz, M.: Growing up in an affluent society. In E. Ginzberg (ed.), *The nation's children*. Vol. 1. *The family and social change*. New York: Columbia, 1960, pp. 158–169.

2. Adams, B. N., and M. T. Meidam: Economics, family structure, and college attendance. *Amer. J. Sociol.*, 1968, **74,** 230–239.

3. Alden, V. R.: Just how much is a degree worth? *New York Times,* Jan. 10, 1972.

4. Alexander, C. N.: Ordinal position and social mobility. *Sociometry*, 1968, **31,** 285–293.

5. Altus, W. D.: Birth order and its sequelae. *Science*, 1966, **151,** 44–49.

6. Amatora, Sister M.: School interests of early adolescents. *J. genet. Psychol.*, 1961, **98,** 133–145.

7. Ames, L. B., and R. N. Walker: A note on school dropouts: A longitudinal research with late adolescents. *J. genet. Psychol.*, 1965, **107,** 277–279.

8. Andersen, D. G., and R. A. Heimann: Vocational maturity of junior high school girls. *Vocat. Guid. Quart.*, 1967, **15,** 191–195.

9. Anderson, D.: What a high school class did with fifty years of life. *Personnel Guid. J.*, 1966, **45,** 116–123.

10. Anderson, J. A., and J. C. Follman: Attitudes of dropouts toward school. *Psychol. Rep.*, 1968, **23,** 1142.

11. Anspach, J.: Clothing selection and the mobility concept. *J. Home Econ.*, 1961, **54,** 428–430.

12. Anttonen, R. G.: A longitudinal study of mathematics attitude. *J. educ. Res.*, 1969, **62,** 467–471.

13. Appleton, G. M., and J. C. Hansen: Parent-child relations, need-nurturance, and vocational orientation. *Personnel Guid. J.*, 1969, **47,** 794–799.

14. Astin, A. W.: Personal and environmental factors associated with college dropouts among high aptitude students. *J. educ. Psychol.*, 1964, **55,** 219–227.

15. Astin, H. S.: Stability and change in the career plans of ninth grade girls. *Personnel Guid. J.,* 1968, **46,** 961–966.

16. Bachelis, W. D., and J. Pierce-Jones: Adolescents' social mobility orientation in relation to F-scale behavior. *Psychol. Rep.,* 1964, **14,** 75–79.

17. Bachtold, L. M.: Personality differences among high ability underachievers. *J. educ. Res.,* 1969, **63,** 16–18.

18. Baird, L. L.: The effects of college residence groups on students' self-concepts, goals and achievement. *Personnel Guid. J.,* 1969, **47,** 1015–1021.

19. Baker, R. W., and T. O. Madell: Susceptibility to distraction in academically underachieving and achieving male college students. *J. consult. Psychol.,* 1965, **29,** 173–177.

20. Banducci, R.: Accuracy of occupational stereotypes of grade-twelve boys. *J. counsel. Psychol.,* 1970, **17,** 534–539.

21. Barclay, A., and L. F. Cervantes: The Thematic Apperception Test as an index of personality attributes characterizing the adolescent academic dropout. *Adolescence,* 1969, **4,** 525–540.

22. Barnett, R.: Personality correlates of vocational planning. *Genet. Psychol. Monogr.,* 1971, **83,** 309–356.

23. Barry, W. A., and E. S. Bordin: Personality development and the vocational choice of the ministry. *J. counsel. Psychol.,* 1967, **14,** 395–403.

24. Bayer, A. E.: The college dropout: Factors affecting senior college completion. *Sociol. Educ.,* 1968, **41,** 305–316.

25. Beardslee, D. G., and D. D. O'Dowd: The college student's image of the scientist. *Science,* 1961, **133,** 997–1001.

26. Berdie, R. F., and A. B. Hood: Personal values and attitudes as determinants of post-high school plans. *Personnel Guid. J.,* 1964, **42,** 754–759.

27. Bergland, B. W., and J. D. Krumboltz: An optimal grade level for career exploration. *Vocat. Guid. Quart.,* 1969, **18,** 29–33.

28. Berkowitz, L., and J. R. Macaulay: Some effects of differences in status level and status stability. *Hum. Relat.,* 1961, **14,** 135–148.

29. Berman, G., and M. Eisenberg: Psychosocial aspects of academic achievement. *Amer. J. Orthopsychiat.,* 1971, **41,** 406–415.

30. Betz, R. L., K. B. Engle, and G. G. Mallinson: Perceptions of non-college-bound vocationally oriented high school graduates. *Personnel Guid. J.,* 1969, **47,** 988–994.

31. Bieri, J., R. Lobeck, and H. Plotnick: Psychological factors in differential social mobility. *J. soc. Psychol.,* 1962, **58,** 183–200.

32. Blum, S. H.: The desire for security: An element in the vocational choice of college men. *J. educ. Psychol.,* 1961, **52,** 317–321.

33. Boroff, D.: American fetish: The college degree. *New York Times,* Feb. 14, 1960.

34. Borow, H.: The adolescent in a world of work. In J. F. Adams (ed.), *Understanding adolescence: Current developments in adolescent psychology.* Boston: Allyn and Bacon, 1968, pp. 337–360.

35. Breed, W.: Occupational mobility and suicide among white males. *Amer. sociol. Rev.,* 1963, **28,** 179–188.

36. Brenton, N.: 21,741 choices for a career. *New York Times,* Oct. 25, 1970.

37. Brown, F. C.: Identifying college dropouts with the Minnesota Counseling Inventory. *Personnel Guid. J.,* 1961, **39,** 280–282.

38. Brown, F. G.: Study habits and attitudes, college experience, and college success. *Personnel Guid. J.,* 1964, **42,** 287–292.

39. Buck, C. W.: Crystallization of vocational interests as a function of vocational exploration in college. *J. counsel. Psychol.,* 1970, **17,** 347–351.

40. Burchinal, L. G., and J. D. Cowhig: Rural youth in an urban society. *Children,* 1963, **10,** 167–172.

41. Burnstein, E.: Fear of failure, achievement motivation, and aspiring to prestigeful occupations. *J. abnorm. soc. Psychol.,* 1963, **67,** 189–192.

42. Cameron, H. K.: Nonintellectual correlates of academic achievement. *J. Negro Educ.,* 1968, **37,** 252–257.

43. Capp, L. A.: A repertoire of perceptions on the professor's role. *Dissert. Abstr.,* 1968, **28** (9–A), 3474.

44. Child, D.: Some aspects of study habits in higher education. *Educ. Sci.,* 1970, **4,** 11–20.

45. Choppin, B.: Social class and educational achievement. *Educ. Res.,* 1968, **10,** 213–217.

46. Chopra, S. L.: Cultural deprivation and academic achievement. *J. educ. Res.,* 1969, **62,** 435–438.

47. Chown, S. M.: Personality factors in the formation of occupational choice. *Brit. J. educ. Psychol.,* 1959, **29,** 23–33.

48. Clarke, J. H.: The image of the teacher. *Brit. J. educ. Psychol.,* 1968, **38,** 280–285.

49. Cohen, D.: Differentiating motivation underlying vocational choice. *J. educ. Res.,* 1971, **64,** 229–234.

50. Cole, L., and I. N. Hall: *Psychology of adolescence,* 7th ed. New York: Holt, 1970.

51. Coleman, J. S.: Academic achievement and the structure of competition. *Harv. educ. Rev.,* 1959, **29,** 330–351.

52. Coleman, J. S.: *The adolescent society.* New York: Free Press, 1961.

53. Constantinople, A.: Perceived instrumentality of the college as a measure of attitudes toward college. *J. Pers. soc. Psychol.,* 1967, **5,** 196–201.

54. Crandall, V. C., and E. S. Battle: The ante-

cedents and adult correlates of academic and intellectual achievement effort. In J. P. Hill (ed.), *Minnesota symposia on child psychology.* Minneapolis: University of Minnesota Press, 1970, vol. 4, pp. 36–93.

55. Dale, R. R.: Pupil-teacher relationships in co-educational and single-sex grammar schools. *Brit. J. educ. Psychol.,* 1966, **36,** 267–271.

56. Damos, G. D.: Attitudes of Mexican-American and Anglo-American groups toward education. *J. soc. Psychol.,* 1962, **57,** 249–256.

57. Danesino, A., and W. A. Layman: Contrasting personality patterns of high and low achievers among college students of Italian and Irish descent. *J. Psychol.,* 1969, **72,** 71–83.

58. Dansereau, H. K.: Work and the teenager. *Ann. Amer. Acad. pol. soc. Sci.,* 1961, **338,** 44–52.

59. Davis, A.: Personality and social mobility. *School Review,* 1957, **65,** 134–143.

60. Diedrich, R. C., and P. W. Jackson: Satisfied and dissatisfied students. *Personnel Guid. J.,* 1969, **47,** 641–649.

61. Dienstfrey, H.: Doctors, lawyers, and other TV heroes. *Commentary,* 1963, **35,** 519–524.

62. Dooley, B. J., and W. F. White: Motivational patterns of a select group of adult evening college students. *J. educ. Res.,* 1968, **62,** 65–66.

63. Duncan, O. D.: The trend of occupational mobility in the United States. *Amer. sociol. Rev.,* 1965, **30,** 491–498.

64. Dutton, W. H.: Another look at attitudes of junior high school pupils toward arithmetic. *Elem. Sch. J.,* 1968, **68,** 265–268.

65. Eckland, B. K.: Social class and college graduation: Some misconceptions corrected. *Amer. J. Sociol.,* 1964, **70,** 36–50.

66. Elder, G. H.: Achievement motivation and intelligence in occupational mobility: A longitudinal analysis. *Sociometry,* 1968, **31,** 327–354.

67. Ellis, R. A., and W. C. Lane: Social mobility and career orientation. *Sociol. soc. Res.,* 1966, **50,** 280–296.

68. Emans, R.: Teacher attitudes as a function of values. *J. educ. Res.,* 1969, **62,** 459–463.

69. Empey, L. T.: Social class and occupational aspirations: A comparison of absolute and relative measurement. *Amer. sociol. Rev.,* 1956, **21,** 703–709.

70. Engel, M., G. Marsden, and S. Woodaman: Orientation to work in children. *Amer. J. Orthopsychiat.,* 1968, **38,** 137–143.

71. Falk, L. L.: Occupational satisfaction of female college graduates. *J. Marriage & Family,* 1966, **28,** 177–185.

72. Field, T. W., and M. E. Poole: Intellectual style and achievement of arts and science undergraduates. *Brit. J. educ. Psychol.,* 1970, **40,** 338–341.

73. Fink, M. B.: Self-concept as it relates to academic underachievement. *Calif. J. educ. Res.,* 1962, **13,** 57–62.

74. Finlayson, D. S.: A follow-up study of school achievement in relation to personality. *Brit. J. educ. Psychol.,* 1970, **40,** 344–348.

75. Fischer, E. H., C. F. Wells, and S. L. Cohen: Birth order and expressed interest in becoming a college professor. *J. counsel. Psychol.,* 1968, **15,** 111–116.

76. Fitzsimmons, S. J., J. Cheever, E. Leonard, and D. Macunovich: School failures: Now and tomorrow. *Develpm. Psychol.,* 1969, **1,** 134–146.

77. Flaherty, Sister M. R., and E. Reutzel: Personality traits of high and low achievers in college. *J. educ. Res.,* 1965, **58,** 409–411.

78. Frandsen, A., and M. Sorenson: Interests as motives in academic achievement. *J. sch. Psychol.,* 1968–69, **7,** no. 1, 52–56.

79. Friedlander, F.: Underlying sources of job satisfaction. *J. appl. Psychol.,* 1963, **47,** 246–250.

80. Garai, J. E., and A. Scheinfeld: Sex differences in mental and behavioral traits. *Genet. Psychol. Monogr.,* 1968, **77,** 169–229.

81. Gerbner, G.: Images across cultures: Teachers in mass media fiction and drama, *School Review,* 1966, **74,** 212–230.

82. Goldberg, J. B.: Influence of pupils' attitudes on perception of teachers' behavior and on consequent school work. *J. educ. Psychol.,* 1968, **59,** 1–5.

83. Green, L. B., and H. J. Parker: Parental influence on adolescents' occupational choice: A test of an aspect of Roe's theory. *J. counsel. Psychol.,* 1965, **12,** 379–393.

84. Greenfeld, N., and E. L. Finkelstein: A comparison of the characteristics of junior high school students. *J. genet. Psychol.,* 1970, **117,** 37–50.

85. Gribbons, W. D., and P. R. Lohnes: Eighth-grade vocational maturity in relation to nine-year career patterns. *J. counsel. Psychol.,* 1969, **16,** 557–562.

86. Gurman, A. S.: The role of the family in underachievement. *J. sch. Psychol.,* 1970, **8,** 48–53.

87. Hackman, R. B.: Vocational counseling with adolescents. In J. F. Adams (ed.), *Understanding adolescence: Current developments in adolescent psychology.* Boston: Allyn and Bacon, 1968, pp. 361–386.

88. Halbertsam, M. J.: An MD reviews Dr. Welby on TV. *New York Times,* Jan. 16, 1972.

89. Hall, R. L., and B. Willerman: The educational influence of dormitory roommates. *Sociometry,* 1963, **26,** 294–318.

90. Haller, A. G., and C. E. Butterworth: Peer influences on levels of occupational and educational aspiration. *Soc. Forces,* 1960, **38,** 289–295.

91. Hanson, G. R., and R. G. Taylor: Interac-

tion of ability and personality: Another look at the drop-out problem in an institute of technology. *J. counsel. Psychol.,* 1970, **17,** 540–545.

92. Hanson, J. T.: Ninth-grade girls' vocational choices and their parents' occupational level. *Vocat. Guid. Quart.,* 1965, **13,** 261–264.

93. Harris, C. M.: Scholastic self-concept in early and middle adolescence. *Adolescence,* 1971, **6,** 269–278.

94. Harris, D. B.: Work and the adolescent: Transition to maturity. *Teachers Coll. Rec.,* 1961, **63,** 146–153.

95. Harrison, F. I.: Relationship between home background, school success, and adolescent attitudes. *Merrill-Palmer Quart.,* 1968, **14,** 331–344.

96. Hathaway, S. R., P. C. Reynolds, and E. D. Monachesi: Follow-up of 812 girls 10 years after high school dropout. *J. consult. clin. Psychol.,* 1969, **33,** 383–390.

97. Havighurst, R. J.: Social-class influences on American education. *60th Yearb. Nat. Soc. Stud. Educ.,* 1961, pt. 2, 120–143.

98. Hawley, W.: What women think men think: Does it affect their career choice? *J. counsel. Psychol.,* 1971, **18,** 193–199.

99. Hechinger, F. M.: On cheating. *New York Times,* Jan. 31, 1965.

100. Hechinger, G., and F. M. Hechinger: *Teenage tyranny.* New York: Morrow, 1963.

101. Hersov, L. A.: Persistent non-attendance at school. *J. child Psychol. Psychiat.,* 1960, **1,** 130–136.

102. Hill, G. B.: Choice of career by grammar school boys. *Occup. Psychol.,* 1965, **39,** 279–287.

103. Hill, J. P.: Similarity and accordance between parents and sons in attitudes toward mathematics. *Child Develpm.,* 1967, **38,** 777–791.

104. Hilliard, T., and R. M. Roth: Maternal attitudes and the non-achievement syndrome. *Personnel Guid. J.,* 1969, **47,** 424–428.

105. Holden, G. S.: Scholastic aptitude and the relative persistence of vocational choice. *Personnel Guid. J.,* 1961, **40,** 36–41.

106. Hollander, J. W.: Development of vocational decisions during adolescence. *J. counsel. Psychol.,* 1971, **18,** 244–248.

107. Hollander, M. A., and H. J. Parker: Occupational stereotypes and needs: Their relationship to vocational choice. *Vocat. Guid. Quart.,* 1969, **18,** 91–98.

108. Hulin, C. L.: Effects of change in job satisfaction levels on employee turnover. *J. appl. Psychol.,* 1968, **52,** 122–126.

109. Hulson, P. W.: Vocational choices: 1930 and 1961. *Vocat. Guid. Quart.,* 1962, **10,** 218–222.

110. Jackson, E. F., and H. J. Crockett: Occupational mobility in the United States: A point estimate and trend comparison. *Amer. sociol. Rev.,* 1964, **29,** 5–15.

111. Jackson, E. F., W. S. Fox, and H. J. Crockett: Religion and occupational achievement. *Amer. sociol. Rev.,* 1970, **35,** 48–63.

112. Jackson, R. M.: In support of the concept of underachievement. *Personnel Guid. J.,* 1968, **47,** 56–62.

113. Jacobsen, R. B.: An exploration of parental encouragement as an intervening variable in occupational-educational learning in children. *J. Marriage & Family,* 1971, **33,** 174–182.

114. Jennings, F. G.: Adolescents, aspirations, and the older generation. *Teachers Coll. Rec.,* 1964, **65,** 335–341.

115. Jersild, A. T.: *The psychology of adolescence,* 2d ed. New York: Macmillan, 1963.

116. Johnson, A. H.: The responses of high school seniors to a set of structured situations concerning teaching as a career. *J. exp. Educ.,* 1958, **26,** 263–314.

117. Joiner, L. M., E. L. Erickson, and W. B. Brookover: Socioeconomic status and perceived expectations as measures of family influence. *Personnel Guid. J.,* 1969, **47,** 655–659.

118. Jones, V.: Attitudes of college students and their changes: A 37-year study. *Genet. Psychol. Monogr.,* 1970, **81,** 3–80.

119. Joseph, T. P.: Adolescents: From the views of members of an informal adolescent group. *Genet. Psychol. Monogr.,* 1969, **79,** 3–88.

120. Kahn, J. H., and G. P. Nursten: School refusal: A comprehensive view of school phobia and other failures of school attendance. *Amer. J. Orthopsychiat.,* 1962, **32,** 707–718.

121. Katz, F. M.: The meaning of success: Some differences in value systems of social class. *J. soc. Psychol.,* 1964, **62,** 141–148.

122. Kauffman, J. M., S. J. Weaver, and A. Weaver: Age and intelligence as correlates of perceived family relationships of underachievers. *Psychol. Rep.,* 1971, **28,** 522.

123. Kellogg, R. L.: A direct approach to sex-role identification of school-related objects. *Psychol. Rep.,* 1969, **24,** 839–841.

124. Kinloch, G. C., and R. Perrucci: Social origins, academic achievement, and mobility channels: Sponsored and contest mobility among college graduates. *Soc. Forces,* 1969, **48,** 36–45.

125. Kinnane, J. P., and M. W. Pable: Family background and work value orientation. *J. counsel. Psychol.,* 1962, **9,** 320–329.

126. Kipnis, D., and J. H. Resnick: Experimental prevention of underachievement among intelligent, impulsive college students. *J. consult. clin. Psychol.,* 1971, **36,** 53–60.

127. Kniveton, B. H.: An investigation of the attitudes of adolescents to aspects of their schooling. *Brit. J. educ. Psychol.,* 1969, **39,** 78–81.

128. Kosa, J., L. D. Rachiele, and C. O. Schommer: The self-image and performance of socially mobile college students. *J. soc. Psychol.,* 1962, **56,** 301–316.

129. Krippner, S.: Science as a vocational preference among junior high school pupils. *Vocat. Guid. Quart.,* 1963, **11,** 129–134.

130. Krippner, S.: The educational plans and preferences of upper-middle-class junior high school pupils. *Vocat. Guid. Quart.,* 1965, **13,** 257–260.

131. Kuhweide, K., H. E. Lueck, and E. Timaeus: Occupational prestige: A cross-cultural comparison. *Percept. mot. Skills,* 1968, **27,** 154.

132. Kurtzman, K. A.: A study of school attitudes, peer acceptance and personality of creative adolescents. *Except. Children,* 1967, **34,** 157–162.

133. Kuvlesky, W. P., and R. C. Bealer: The relevance of adolescents' occupational aspirations for subsequent job attainments. *Rural Sociol.,* 1967, **32,** 290–301.

134. Leonard, R. S.: Vocational guidance in junior high: One school's answer. *Vocat. Guid. Quart.,* 1969, **17,** 221–222.

135. Lewis, G. M.: Interpersonal relations and school achievement. *Children,* 1964, **11,** 235–236.

136. Lipset, S. M.: Constant values in American society. *Children,* 1959, **6,** 219–224.

137. Lockwood, W. V.: Realism of vocational preference. *Personnel Guid. J.,* 1958, **37,** 98–106.

138. Macomber, F. G.: The role of educational institutions in adolescent development. In J. F. Adams (ed.), *Understanding adolescence: Current developments in adolescent psychology.* Boston: Allyn and Bacon, 1968, pp. 232–247.

139. Maeroff, G. L.: Study finds college is means to more satisfying life. *New York Times,* Oct. 6, 1971.

140. Maeroff, G. L.: Home life linked to school success. *New York Times,* Jan. 30, 1972.

141. Maeroff, G. L.: Reasons for college dropouts studied. *New York Times,* Feb. 14, 1972.

142. Marr, E.: Vocational maturity and specification of a preference. *Vocat. Guid. Quart.,* 1969, **18,** 45–48.

143. Marsh, L. M.: College dropouts: A review. *Personnel Guid. J.,* 1966, **44,** 475–481.

144. Marso, R. N.: The influence of test difficulty upon study efforts and achievement. *Amer. educ. Res. J.,* 1969, **6,** 621–632.

145. Martin, E. C.: Reflections on the early adolescent in school. *Daedalus,* 1971, **100,** 1087–1103.

146. McDill, E. L., and J. Coleman: Family and peer influences in college plans for junior high school students. *Sociol. Educ.,* 1965, **38,** 112–126.

147. McIntire, W. G., and D. C. Payne: The relationship of family functioning to school achievement. *Family Coordinator,* 1971, **20,** 265–268.

148. Meissner, W. W.: Some indications of sources of anxiety in adolescent boys. *J. genet. Psychol.,* 1961, **99,** 65–73.

149. Miller, G. W.: Factors in school achievement and social class. *J. educ. Psychol.,* 1970, **61,** 260–269.

150. Moller, A., and W. Asher: Comment on "A comparison of dropouts and nondropouts on participation in school activities." *Psychol. Rep.,* 1968, **22,** 1243–1244.

151. Mowsesian, R., B. R. G. Heath, and J. W. M. Rothney: Superior students' occupational preferences and their fathers' occupations. *Personnel Guid. J.,* 1967, **45,** 238–242.

152. Mueller, R. H., P. J. Roach, and J. A. Malone: College students' views of the characteristics of an "ideal" professor. *Psychology in the Schools,* 1971, **8,** 161–167.

153. Muma, J. R.: Peer evaluation and academic performance. *Personnel Guid. J.,* 1966, **44,** 405–409.

154. Neale, D. C., N. Gill, and W. Tismer: Relationship between attitudes toward school subjects and school achievement. *J. educ. Res.,* 1970, **63,** 232–237.

155. Nelson, D. D.: A study of school achievement among adolescent children with working and nonworking mothers. *J. educ. Res.,* 1969, **62,** 456–458.

156. *New York Times* Report: 50% of working men in blue collar jobs. July 26, 1963.

157. *New York Times* Report: Truancy: Any number can play, and do. Jan. 30, 1972.

158. Oakland, J. A.: Measurement of personality correlates of academic achievement in high school students. *J. counsel. Psychol.,* 1969, **16,** 452–453.

159. Oberlander, M., N. Jenkin, K. Houlihan, and J. Jackson: Family size and birth order as determinants of scholastic attitude and achievement in a sample of eighth graders. *J. consult. clin. Psychol.,* 1970, **34,** 19–21.

160. O'Shea, A. J.: Peer relationships and male academic achievement: A review and suggested clarification. *Personnel Guid. J.,* 1969, **47,** 417–423.

161. O'Shea, A. J.: Low achievement syndrome among bright junior high school boys. *J. educ. Res.,* 1970, **63,** 257–262.

162. Osipow, S. H.: Perceptions of occupation as a function of titles and descriptions. *J. counsel. Psychol.,* 1962, **9,** 106–109.

163. Packard, V.: *The status seekers.* New York: Pocket Books, 1961.

164. Packard, V.: *The pyramid climbers.* New York: McGraw-Hill, 1962.

165. Pallone, N. J., F. S. Rickard, and R. B. Hurley: Key influences of occupational preference among black youth. *J. counsel. Psychol.,* 1970, **17,** 498–501.

166. Pang, H.: Undistinguished school experiences of distinguished persons. *Adolescence,* 1968, **3,** 319–329.

167. Parker, A. W.: Career and marriage ori-

entation in the vocational development of college women. *J. appl. Psychol.*, 1966, **50,** 232–235.

168. Perrone, P. A.: Stability of values of junior high school pupils and their parents over two years. *Personnel Guid. J.*, 1967, **46,** 268–274.

169. Pervin, L. A., and D. B. Rubin: Student dissatisfaction with college and the college dropout: A transactional approach. *J. soc. Psychol.*, 1967, **72,** 285–295.

170. Pickup, A. J., and W. S. Anthony: Teachers' marks and pupils' expectations: The short-term effects of discrepancies upon classroom performance in secondary school. *Brit. J. educ. Psychol.*, 1968, **38,** 302–309.

171. Powell, M., and V. Bloom: Development of and reasons for vocational choices of adolescents through the high school years. *J. educ. Res.*, 1962, **56,** 126–133.

172. Propper, M. M., and E. T. Clark: Alienation: Another dimension of underachievement. *J. Psychol.*, 1970, **75,** 13–18.

173. Psathas, G.: Toward a theory of vocational choice for women. *Sociol. soc. Res.*, 1968, **52,** 253–268.

174. Rauner, T. M.: Occupational information and occupational choice. *Personnel Guid. J.*, 1962, **41,** 311–317.

175. Raynor, J. O.: Relationships between achievement-related motives, future orientation, and academic performance. *J. Pers. soc. Psychol.*, 1970, **15,** 28–33.

176. Rehberg, R. A., W. E. Schafer, and J. Sinclair: Toward a temporal sequence of adolescent achievement variables. *Amer. sociol. Rev.*, 1970, **35,** 34–48.

177. Reinhold, R.: Harvard study calls emotional illness major cause of dropouts. *New York Times*, Oct. 25, 1970.

178. Rensberger, D.: Study finds school dropouts do not appear to suffer. *New York Times*, Nov. 6, 1971.

179. Resnick, H., M. L. Fauble, and S. H. Osipow: Vocational crystallization and self-esteem in college students. *J. counsel. Psychol.*, 1970, **17,** 465–467.

180. Rezler, A. G.: Characteristics of high school girls choosing traditional or pioneer vocations. *Personnel Guid. J.*, 1967, **45,** 659–665.

181. Rolcik, J. W.: Scholastic achievement of teenagers and parental attitudes toward and interest in schoolwork. *Family Coordinator*, 1965, **14,** 158–160.

182. Rosen, B. C.: Race, ethnicity, and the achievement syndrome. *Amer. sociol. Rev.*, 1959, **24,** 47–60.

183. Rushing, W. A.: Adolescent-parent relationship and mobility aspirations. *Soc. Forces*, 1964, **43,** 157–166.

184. Ruthven, A. G.: *Naturalist in two worlds.* Ann Arbor: University of Michigan Press, 1963.

185. Schreiber, D.: The dropout and the delinquent. *Phi Delta Kappan,* 1963, **44,** 215–221.

186. Schwartz, J.: The portrayal of educators in motion pictures: 1950–1958. *J. educ. Sociol.*, 1960, **34,** 82–90.

187. Seeman, M.: On the personal consequences of alienation in work. *Amer. sociol. Rev.*, 1967, **32,** 273–285.

188. Segal, B. E.: Male nurses: A case study in status contradiction and prestige loss. *Soc. Forces*, 1962, **41,** 31–38.

189. Seidel, H. E.: Attitudes, goals, achievements and educational needs of adolescents from two Appalachian communities. *J. educ. Res.*, 1970, **63,** 424–429.

190. Sewell, W. H., and V. P. Shah: Social class, parental encouragement and educational aspirations. *Amer. J. Sociol.*, 1968, **73,** 559–572.

191. Sharp, R.: Relative importance of interest and ability in vocational decision making. *J. counsel. Psychol.*, 1970, **17,** 258–267.

192. Sharples, D.: Children's attitudes toward junior school activities. *Brit. J. educ. Psychol.*, 1969, **39,** 72–77.

193. Shaw, M. C.: Note on parent attitudes toward independence training and the academic achievement of their children. *J. educ. Psychol.*, 1964, **55,** 371–374.

194. Shaw, M. C., and J. Grubb: Hostility and able high school underachievers. *J. counsel. Psychol.*, 1958, **5,** 263–266.

195. Shaw, M. C., and J. T. McCuen: The onset of academic underachievement in bright children. *J. educ. Psychol.*, 1960, **51,** 103–108.

196. Shenker, I.: Caricatures put scientists on pedestal. *New York Times,* Dec. 12, 1969.

197. Siegelman, M., and R. F. Peck: Personality patterns related to occupational roles. *Genet. Psychol. Monogr.*, 1960, **61,** 291–349.

198. Silverman, D.: An evaluation of the relationship between attitudes toward self and attitudes toward a vocational high school. *J. educ. Sociol.*, 1963, **36,** 410–418.

199. Silverman, M.: Developmental trends in the vocational interests of special education and normal students. *J. genet. Psychol.*, 1971, **118,** 157–172.

200. Slee, F. W.: The feminine image factor in girls' attitudes toward school subjects. *Brit. J. educ. Psychol.*, 1968, **38,** 212–214.

201. Slocum, W. L., and R. T. Bowles: Attractiveness of occupations to high school students. *Personnel Guid J*, 1968, **46,** 754–761.

202. Smelser, W. T.: Adolescent and adult occupational choice as a function of family socioeconomic history. *Sociometry*, 1963, **26,** 393–409.

203. Smelser, W. T., and L. H. Stewart: Where are the siblings? A re-evaluation of the relationship

between birth order and college attendance. *Sociometry,* 1968, **31,** 294–303.

204. Smith, L.: A 5-year follow-up study of high ability achieving and nonachieving college freshmen. *J. educ. Res.,* 1971, **64,** 220–222.

205. Smith, R. J., C. E. Ramsey, and C. Castello: Parental authority and job choice: Sex differences in three cultures. *Amer. J. Sociol.,* 1963, **69,** 143–149.

206. Soucar, E.: Students' perceptions of liked and disliked teachers. *Percept. mot. Skills,* 1970, **31,** 19–24.

207. Southworth, J. A., and M. E. Morningstar: Persistence of occupational choice and personality congruence. *J. counsel. Psychol.,* 1970, **17,** 409–412.

208. Spaeth, J. L.: Occupational prestige expectations among male college graduates. *Amer. J. Sociol.,* 1968, **73,** 548–558.

209. Spiegelberger, C. D., and W. G. Kalzenmeyer: Manifest anxiety, intelligence and college grades. *J. consult. Psychol.,* 1959, **23,** 78.

210. Stacey, B.: Some psychological consequences of intergeneration mobility. *Hum. Relat.,* 1967, **20,** 3–12.

211. Stein, A. H.: The effects of sex-role standards for achievement and sex-role preferences on three determinants of academic motivation. *Develpm. Psychol.,* 1971, **4,** 219–231.

212. Stein, A. H., and J. Smithells: Age and sex differences in children's sex-role standards about achievement. *Develpm. Psychol.,* 1969, **1,** 252–259.

213. Steininger, M., R. E. Johnson, and D. K. Kirts: Cheating on college examinations as a function of situationally aroused anxiety and hostility. *J. educ. Psychol.,* 1964, **55,** 317–324.

214. Stennett, R. G., and H. J. Feenstra: Late bloomers: Fact or fancy? *J. educ. Res.,* 1970, **63,** 344–346.

215. Stewart, L. H.: Mother-son identification and vocational interest. *Genet. Psychol. Monogr.,* 1959, **60,** 31–63.

216. Stout, R. T.: Social class and educational aspirations: A Weberian analysis. *Personnel Guid. J.,* 1969, **47,** 650–654.

217. Strong, E. K.: Satisfaction and interests. *Amer. Psychologist,* 1958, **13,** 449–456.

218. Sturtz, S. A.: Sex differences in college student satisfaction. *J. coll. Stud. Personnel,* 1971, **12,** 220–222.

219. Super, D. E., and P. L. Overstreet: *The vocational maturity of ninth grade boys.* New York: Teachers College, Columbia, 1960.

220. Switzer, R. E., J. C. Hirschberg, L. Myers, E. Gray, N. H. Evers, and R. Forman: The effect of family moves on children. *Ment. Hyg., N.Y.,* 1961, **45,** 528–536.

221. Symonds, P. M.: What education has to learn from psychology. VI. Emotions and learning. *Teachers Coll. Rec.,* 1959, **60,** 9–22.

222. Tannenbaum, A. J.: *Adolescent attitudes toward academic brilliance.* New York: Teachers College, Columbia, 1962.

223. Taylor, R. Q., and G. R. Hanson: Interest and persistence. *J. counsel. Psychol.,* 1970, **17,** 506–509.

224. Terman, L. M.: Are scientists different? *Scient. American,* 1955, **192,** no. 1, 25–29.

225. Thelen, M. H., and C. S. Hartis: Personality of college underachievers who improve with group psychotherapy. *Personnel Guid. J.,* 1968, **46,** 561–566.

226. Thompson, O. E.: Occupational values of high school students. *Personnel Guid. J.,* 1966, **44,** 850–853.

227. Thorndike, R. L.: *The concepts of over- and underachievement.* New York: Teachers College, Columbia, 1963.

228. Tomeh, A. K.: The impact of reference groups on the educational and occupational aspirations of women college students. *J. Marriage & Family,* 1968, **30,** 102–110.

229. Torrance, E. P., and D. C. Dauw: Aspirations and dreams of three groups of creatively gifted high school seniors and a comparable unselected group. *Gifted Child Quart.,* 1965, **9,** 177–182.

230. Trickett, E. J., and R. H. Moos: Generality and specificity of student reactions in high school classrooms. *Adolescence,* 1970, **5,** 373–390.

231. Tseng, M. S., and A. R. Carter: Achievement motivation and fear of failure as determinants of vocational choice, vocational aspiration and perception of vocational prestige. *J. counsel. Psychol.,* 1970, **17,** 150–156.

232. Turner, R. H.: Some aspects of women's ambition. *Amer. J. Sociol.,* 1964, **70,** 271–284.

233. Tyler, L. E.: The antecedents of two varieties of vocational interests. *Genet. Psychol. Monogr.,* 1964, **70,** 177–227.

234. Ulrich, G., H. Hecklik, and E. C. Roeber: Occupational stereotypes of high school students. *Voc. Guid. Quart.,* 1966, **14,** 169–174.

235. *U.S. News & World Report:* Jobs for all: Anytime soon? Aug. 2, 1971, pp. 30–32.

236. *U.S. News & World Report:* Is hard work going out of style? Aug. 23, 1971, pp. 52–56.

237. *U.S. News & World Report:* Where the jobs will be in the '70s. Sept. 6, 1971, pp. 68–71.

238. *U.S. News & World Report:* Record year on American campuses. Sept. 20, 1971, p. 38.

239. *U.S. News & World Report:* Bias in jobs: Tighter rules in sight. Sept. 27, 1971, pp. 91–92.

240. Vaz, D.: High school senior boys' attitudes toward nursing as a career. *Nurs. Res.,* 1969, **17,** 533–538.

241. Very, P. S.: Real and ideal characteristics of the teacher-student relationship. *Percept. mot. Skills,* 1968, **27,** 880–882.

242. Wagman, M.: Sex and age differences in

occupational values. *Personnel Guid. J.,* 1965, **44,** 258–262.

243. Walz, G., and J. Miller: School climates and student behavior: Implications for counselor role. *Personnel Guid. J.,* 1969, **47,** 859–867.

244. Waterman, A. S., and C. K. Waterman: The relationship between ego identity status and satisfaction with college. *J. educ. Res.,* 1970, **64,** 165–168.

245. Watley, D. J.: Career progress of merit scholars. *Nat. Merit Scholarship Corp. Res. Rep.,* 1968, **4,** no. 1.

246. Watley, D. J., and R. C. Nichols: Career decisions of talented youth: Trends over the past decade. *Nat. Merit Scholarship Corp. Res. Rep.,* 1969, **5,** 1–14.

247. Weber, G. H., and A. B. Motz: School as perceived by the dropout. *J. Negro Educ.,* 1968, **37,** 127–134.

248. Weiss, R. L., S. M. Sales, and S. Bode: Student authoritarianism and teacher authoritarianism as factors in the determination of student performance and attitudes. *J. exp. Educ.,* 1970, **38,** 83–87.

249. Werts, C. E.: Paternal influence on career choice. *J. counsel. Psychol.,* 1968, **15,** 48–52.

250. Westoff, C. F., M. Bressler, and P. C. Sagi: The concept of social mobility: An empirical inquiry. *Amer. sociol. Rev.,* 1960, **25,** 375–385.

251. Williams, R. L.: Personality, ability and achievement correlates of scholastic attitudes. *J. educ. Res.,* 1970, **63,** 401–403.

252. Willingham, W. W.: College performance of fraternity members and independent students. *Personnel Guid. J.,* 1962, **41,** 29–31.

253. Wilson, R. C., and W. R. Morrow: School and career adjustment of bright high-achieving and under-achieving high school boys. *J. genet. Psychol.,* 1962, **101,** 91–103.

254. Yamamoto, K., E. C. Thomas, and E. A. Karns: School-related attitudes of middle-school age students. *Amer. educ. Res. J.,* 1969, **6,** 191–206.

255. Yee, A. H., and P. J. Runkel: Simplicial structures of middle-class and lower-class pupils' attitudes toward teachers. *Develpm. Psychol.,* 1969, **1,** 646–652.

256. Zeitlin, H.: High school discipline. *Calif. J. educ. Res.,* 1962, **13,** 116–125.

257. Ziller, R. C., and R. D. Behringer: A longitudinal study of the assimilation of the new child in the group. *Hum. Relat.,* 1961, **14,** 121–133.

258. Ziniles, H., B. Biber, W. Rabinowitz, and L. Hay: Personality aspects of teaching: A predictive study. *Genet. Psychol. Monogr.,* 1964, **69,** 101–149.

259. Zytowski, D. G.: Toward a theory of career development for women. *Personnel Guid. J.,* 1969, **47,** 660–664.

CHAPTER 11

1. Adinarayan, S. P., and M. Rajamanickam: A study of student attitudes toward religion and the spiritual and the supernatural. *J. soc. Psychol.,* 1962, **57,** 105–111.

2. Ahlstrom, S. E.: The radical turn in theology and ethics: Why it occurred in the 1960s. *Ann. Amer. Acad. pol. soc. Sci.,* 1970, **387,** 1–13.

3. Allen, E. E., and R. W. Hites: Factors in religious attitudes of older adolescents. *J. soc. Psychol.,* 1961, **55,** 265–273.

4. Allport, G. W.: *The individual and his religion.* New York: Macmillan, 1950.

5. Amatora, Sister M.: Needed research on religious development during adolescence. *Catholic psych. Rec.,* 1963, **1,** 1–9.

6. Anderson, G. C.: Maturing religion. *Pastoral Psychol.,* 1971, **22,** 17–20.

7. Ansbacher, H. L.: Religion and individual psychology: Introduction. *J. indiv. Psychol.,* 1971, **27,** 3–9.

8. Ash, R. T.: Jewish adolescents' attitudes toward religion and ethnicity. *Adolescence,* 1969, **4,** 245–282.

9. Babin, P.: The faith of adolescents toward the end of school. *Relig. Educ.,* 1962, **57,** 128–131.

10. Bagwell, H. R.: The abrupt religious conversion experience. *J. Relig. & Hlth.,* 1969, **8,** 163–178.

11. Bailey, F. E.: Youth's response to the Bible. *Relig. Educ.,* 1964, **59,** 241–249.

12. Barnett, L. D.: Research into interreligious dating and marriage. *Marriage fam. Living,* 1962, **24,** 191–194.

13. Barnett, L. D.: Religious differentials in fertility planning and fertility in the United States. *Family Life Coordinator,* 1965, **14,** 161–170.

14. Bealer, R. C., and F. C. Willits: The religious interests of American high school youth: A survey of recent research. *Relig. Educ.,* 1967, **62,** 435–444.

15. Bealer, R. C., F. K. Willits, and G. W. Bender: Religious exogamy: A study of social distance. *Sociol. soc. Res.,* 1963, **48,** 69–79.

16. Beit-Hallahmi, B.: The rise and fall of the psychology of religion movement. *Proc. Annu. Convent. APA,* 1971, **6,** pt. 2, 727–728.

17. Bellah, R. N.: Religious evolution. *Amer. sociol. Rev.,* 1964, **29,** 358–374.

18. Blum, B. S., and J. H. Mann: The effect of religious membership on religious prejudice. *J. soc. Psychol.,* 1960, **52,** 97–101.

19. Blumenfeld, W. S., R. D. Franklin, and

H. H. Remmers: Teenagers' attitudes toward study habits, vocational plans, religious beliefs, and luck. *Purdue Opin. Panel Poll Rep.,* 1962, **22,** no. 67.

20. Bossard, J. H. S.: Eight reasons why marriages go wrong. *New York Times,* June 24, 1956.

21. Bossard, J. H. S., and E. S. Boll: *Ritual in family living.* Philadelphia: University of Pennsylvania Press, 1950.

22. Bossard, J. H. S., and E. S. Boll: *One marriage, two faiths.* New York: Ronald, 1957.

23. Brown, C. M., and L. W. Ferguson: Self-concept and religious belief. *Psychol. Rep.,* 1968, **22,** 266.

24. Brown, L. B.: Egocentric thought in petitionary prayer: A cross-cultural study. *J. soc. Psychol.,* 1966, **68,** 197–210.

25. Brown, L. B., and D. J. Pallant: Religious belief and social pressure. *Psychol. Rep.,* 1962, **10,** 813–814.

26. Burchinal, L. G.: Membership groups and attitudes toward cross-religious dating and marriage. *Marriage fam. Living,* 1960, **22,** 248–253.

27. Burchinal, L. G.: Farm-nonfarm differences in religious beliefs and practices. *Rural Sociol.,* 1961, **26,** 414–418.

28. Christensen, H. T., and K. E. Barber: Interfaith versus intrafaith marriage in Indiana. *J. Marriage & Family,* 1967, **29,** 461–469.

29. Clarke, W. H.: Religion as a response to the search for meaning: Its relation to skepticism and creativity. *J. soc. Psychol.,* 1963, **60,** 127–137.

30. Cogley, J.: Many converts called nominal. *New York Times,* July 19, 1965.

31. Cole, L., and I. N. Hall: *Psychology of adolescence,* 7th ed. New York: Holt, 1970.

32. Coleman, J. S.: *The adolescent society.* New York: Free Press, 1961.

33. Connley, W. H.: Do adolescents have faith? *Catholic soc. J.,* 1969, **69,** 4–8, 10.

34. Cooke, T. F.: Interpersonal correlates of religious beliefs. *Dissert. Abstr.,* 1962, **23,** 1103.

35. Cottle, R. E.: Religion in the university: "Messiah" or "Antichrist"? *Relig. Educ.,* 1971, **66,** 254–256.

36. Crow, L. D., and A. Crow: *Adolescent development and adjustment,* 2d ed. New York: McGraw-Hill, 1965.

37. De Bord, L. W.: Adolescent religious participation: An examination of sib-structure and church attendance. *Adolescence,* 1969, **4,** 557–570.

38. Dickstein, L. S., and S. J. Blatt: Death concern, futurity and anticipation. *J. consult. Psychol.,* 1966, **30,** 11–17.

39. Diggory, J. C., and D. Z. Rothman: Values destroyed by death. *J. abnorm. soc. Psychol.,* 1961, **63,** 205–210.

40. Di Guiseppe, R. A.: Dogmatism correlation with strength of religious conviction. *Psychol. Rep.,* 1971, **28,** 64.

41. Dillingham, H. C.: Protestant religion and social status. *Amer. J. Sociol.,* 1965, **70,** 416–422.

42. Drapela, V. J.: Personality adjustment and religious growth. *J. Relig. & Hlth.,* 1969, **8,** 87–97.

43. Elkind, D., and S. Elkind: Varieties of religious experiences in young adolescents. In R. E. Grinder (ed.), *Studies in adolescence.* New York: Macmillan, 1963, pp. 247–261.

44. Feifel, H. (ed.): *The meaning of death.* New York: McGraw-Hill, 1959.

45. Fiske, E. B.: Evangelicalism: The strong current of spiritual revival. *New York Times,* Mar. 5, 1972.

46. Ford, T. R.: Status, residence, and fundamentalist religious beliefs in the Southern Appalachians. *Soc. Forces,* 1960, **38,** 41–49.

47. Garrison, K. C.: The relationship of certain variables to church-sect typology among college students. *J. soc. Psychol.,* 1962, **56,** 29–32.

48. Garrison, K. C.: The attitudes and concerns about marriage and the family of ninth-grade pupils from the public schools of Georgia. *Adolescence,* 1966, **1,** 54–59.

49. Glandstone, R., and G. C. Gupta: A cross cultural study of the behavioral aspects of the concept of religion. *J. soc. Psychol.,* 1963, **60,** 203–211.

50. Glasner, Rabbi S.: Family religion as a matrix of personal growth. *Marriage fam. Living,* 1961, **23,** 291–293.

51. Glass, K. D.: A study of religious belief and practice as related to anxiety and dogmatism in college women. *Dissert. Abstr. Int.,* 1971, **31** (7–A), 3637.

52. Golburgh, S. J., C. B. Rotman, J. R. Snibbe, and J. W. Ondrack: Attitudes of college students toward personal death. *Adolescence,* 1967, **2,** 211–229.

53. Hanawalt, N. G.: Feelings of security and the self-esteem in relation to religious belief. *J. soc. Psychol.,* 1963, **59,** 347–353.

54. Havens, J.: A study of religious conflict in college students. *J. soc. Psychol.,* 1964, **64,** 77–87.

55. Havens, J.: The course of college religious conflict. *Relig. Educ.,* 1970, **65,** 257–264.

56. Heiss, J. S.: Interfaith marriage and marital outcome. *Marriage fam. Living,* 1961, **23,** 228–233.

57. Hites, R. W.: Changes in religious attitudes during four years of college. *J. soc. Psychol.,* 1965, **66,** 51–63.

58. Hogan, R. A.: Adolescent views of death. *Adolescence,* 1970, **5,** 55–66.

59. Hollingshead, A. DeB.: *Elmtown's youth.* New York: Wiley, 1949.

60. Hollingworth, L. S.: *Children above 180 IQ: Origin and development.* New York: Harcourt, Brace & World, 1950.

61. Hyde, K. E.: The religious concepts of adolescents. *Relig. Educ.,* 1961, **56,** 329–334.

62. Jacks, I.: Attitudes of college freshmen and sophomores toward interfaith marriage. *Adolescence,* 1967, **2,** 183 – 209.

63. Jones, M. C.: A comparison of the attitudes and interests of ninth-grade students over two generations. *J. educ. Psychol.,* 1960, **51,** 175 – 186.

64. Jones, V.: Attitudes of college students and their changes: A 37-year study. *Genet. Psychol. Monogr.,* 1970, **81,** 3 – 88.

65. Kalish, R. A.: Some variables in death attitudes. *J. soc. Psychol.,* 1963, **59,** 137 – 145.

66. Kennedy, W. A.: A multi-dimensional study of mathematically gifted adolescents. *Child Develpm.,* 1960, **31,** 655 – 666.

67. Kneeland, D. E.: The Jesus movement spreading on campus. *New York Times,* Dec. 26, 1971.

68. Kosa, J., and C. O. Schommer: Religious participation, religious knowledge, and scholastic aptitude: An empirical study. *J. scient. Stud. Relig.,* 1961, **1,** 88 – 97.

69. Kosa, J., and C. O. Schommer: Sex differences in the religious attitudes of Catholic college students. *Psychol. Rep.,* 1962, **10,** 285 – 286.

70. Kuhlen, R. G.: *The psychology of adolescent development,* 2d ed. New York: Harper & Row, 1963.

71. Landis, B. Y.: Religion and youth. In E. Ginzberg (ed.), *The nation's children.* Vol. 2. *Development and education.* New York: Columbia, 1960, pp. 186 – 206.

72. Landis, J. T.: Religiousness, family relationships, and family values in Protestant, Catholic and Jewish families. *Marriage fam. Living,* 1960, **22,** 341 – 347.

73. Lazerwitz, B.: Variations in church attendance. *Soc. Forces,* 1963, **39,** 301 – 309.

74. Lazerwitz, B., and L. Rowitz: The three-generation hypotheses. *Amer. J. Sociol.,* 1964, **69,** 529 – 538.

75. Lehmann, I. J., K. B. Sinha, and R. T. Hartnett: Changes in attitudes and values associated with college attendance. *J. educ. Psychol.,* 1966, **57,** 89 – 98.

76. Lester, D.: Relation of fear of death in subjects to fear of death in their parents. *Psychol. Rec.,* 1970, **20,** 540 – 543.

77. Lester, D.: Sex differences in attitudes toward death: A replication. *Psychol. Rep.,* 1971, **28,** 754.

78. Lester, D., and E. G. Kam: Effect of a friend dying upon attitudes toward death. *J. soc. Psychol.,* 1971, **83,** 149 – 150.

79. Lieberman, J. N.: The relationship of religious observance to faith: An attempt at a developmental interpretation. *Relig. Educ.,* 1964, **59,** 253 – 257.

80. London, P., R. E. Schulman, and M. S. Black: Religion, guilt, and ethical standards. *J. soc. Psychol.,* 1964, **63,** 145 – 159.

81. Long, D., D. Elkind, and B. Spilka: The child's conception of prayer. *J. scient. Stud. Relig.,* 1967, **6,** 101 – 109.

82. MacDonald, A. P.: Birth order and religious affiliation. *Develpm. Psychol.,* 1969, **1,** 628.

83. Martin, C., and R. C. Nichols: Personality and religious belief. *J. soc. Psychol.,* 1962, **56,** 3 – 8.

84. Martin, D., and L. S. Wrightsman: Religion and fears about death: A critical review of research. *Relig. Educ.,* 1964, **57,** 174 – 176.

85. Maurer, A.: Adolescent attitudes toward death. *J. genet. Psychol.,* 1964, **105,** 75 – 90.

86. McKenna, Sister H. V.: Religious attitudes and personality traits. *J. soc. Psychol.,* 1961, **54,** 379 – 388.

87. Megargee, E. L., G. V. C. Parker, and R. V. Levine: Relationship of familial and social factors to socialization in middle-class college students. *J. abnorm. Psychol.,* 1971, **77,** 76 – 89.

88. Meissner, W. W.: Parental interaction of the adolescent boy. *J. genet. Psychol.,* 1965, **107,** 225 – 233.

89. Middleton, R., and S. Putney: Religion, normative standards and behavior. *Sociometry,* 1962, **25,** 141 – 152.

90. Neidhart, W.: What the Bible means to children and adolescents. *Relig. Educ.,* 1968, **63,** 112 – 119.

91. Nelson, C. E.: Can Protestantism make it with the "new generation"? *Relig. Educ.,* 1969, **64,** 374 – 383.

92. Nelson, M. O.: The concept of God and feelings toward parents. *J. indiv. Psychol.,* 1971, **27,** 46 – 49.

93. Nordberg, R. B.: Developing the idea of God in children. *Relig. Educ.,* 1971, **66,** 376 – 379.

94. Ostow, M.: The nature of religious controls. *Amer. Psychologist,* 1958, **13,** 571 – 574.

95. Packard, V.: *The status seekers.* New York: Pocket Books, 1961.

96. Pahnke, W.: Drugs for escape or religious experience. *Relig. Educ.,* 1970, **65,** 176 – 183.

97. Parsons, H. L.: Religious beliefs of students at six colleges and universities. *Relig. Educ.,* 1963, **58,** 538 – 544.

98. Photiadis, J. D., and J. Biggar: Religiosity, education and ethnic distance. *Amer. J. Sociol.,* 1962, **67,** 666 – 672.

99. Pilkington, G. W., P. K. Poppleton, and G. Robertshaw: Changes in religious attitudes and practices among students during university degree courses. *Brit. J. educ. Psychol.,* 1965, **35,** 150 – 157.

100. Pixley, E., and E. Beekman: The faith of youth as shown by a survey in public schools in Los Angeles. *Relig. Educ.,* 1949, **44,** 336 – 342.

101. Poppleton, P. K., and G. W. Pilkington: The measurement of religious attitudes in a university population. *Brit. J. soc. clin. Psychol.,* 1963, **2,** 20 – 36.

102. Prince, A. J.: A study of 194 cross-religious marriages. *Family Life Coordinator,* 1962, **11,** 3–7.

103. Putney, S., and R. Middleton: Rebellion, conformity, and parental religious ideology. *Sociometry,* 1961, **24,** 125–135.

104. Reiss, P. J.: The trend in interfaith marriages. *J. scient. Stud. Relig.,* 1965, **5,** 64–67.

105. Remmers, H. H., and D. H. Radler: *The American teenager.* Indianapolis: Bobbs-Merrill, 1957.

106. Rokeach, M.: Faith, hope, and bigotry. *Psychology Today,* 1970, **3,** no. 11, 33–37, 58.

107. Roscoe, J. T.: Religious beliefs of American college students. *Coll. Stud. Surv.,* 1968, **2,** 49–55.

108. Ross, M. C.: *Religious beliefs of youth.* New York: Association Press, 1950.

109. Seashore, C. E.: The religion of the educated person. *J. higher Educ.,* 1947, **18,** 71–76.

110. Selfors, S. A., R. K. Leik, and E. King: Values in mate selection: Education versus religion. *Marriage fam. Living,* 1962, **24,** 399–401.

111. Siegman, A. W.: A cross-cultural investigation of the relationship between religiosity, ethnic prejudice, and authoritarianism. *Psychol. Rep.,* 1962, **11,** 419–424.

112. Somerville, R. M.: Death education as part of family life education: Using imaginative literature for insights into family crises. *Family Coordinator,* 1971, **20,** 209–224.

113. Spellman, C. M., G. D. Baskett, and D. Byrne: Manifest anxiety as a contributing factor in religious conversion. *J. consult. clin. Psychol.,* 1971, **36,** 245–247.

114. Stanley, G.: Personality and attitude correlates of religious conversion. *J. scient. Stud. Relig.,* 1964, **4,** 60–63.

115. Stone, L. J., and J. Church: *Childhood and adolescence,* 2d ed. New York: Random House, 1968.

116. Strang, R.: *The adolescent views himself.* New York: McGraw-Hill, 1957.

117. Strommen, M. P.: Alienation, gratification and disenchantment. *Relig. Educ.,* 1969, **64,** 362–368.

118. Tamney, J. B.: An exploratory study of religious conversion. *Dissert. Abstr.,* 1962, **23,** 2237.

119. Thompson, O. E.: High school students and their values. *Calif. J. educ. Res.,* 1965, **16,** 217–227.

120. *Time* Report: Fellow traveling with Jesus. Sept. 6, 1971, pp. 54–55.

121. *Time* Report: The boom in religious studies. Oct. 18, 1971, pp. 83–84.

122. *Time* Report: The new commandment: Thou shalt not—maybe. Dec. 13, 1971, pp. 73–74.

123. *Time* Report: Whose children? Jan. 24, 1972, pp. 51–52.

124. Van Dyke, P., and J. Pierce-Jones: The psychology of religion of middle and late adolescence: A review of empirical research: 1950–1960. *Relig. Educ.,* 1963, **58,** 529–537.

125. Vernon, G. M.: Interfaith marriages. *Relig. Educ.,* 1960, **55,** 261–264.

126. Weigert, A. J., and D. L. Thomas: Socialization and religiosity: A cross-national analysis of Catholic adolescents. *Sociometry,* 1970, **33,** 305–326.

127. Wells, H. K.: Religious attitudes at a small denominational college as compared with Harvard and Radcliffe. *J. Psychol.,* 1962, **53,** 349–382.

128. Weltha, D. A.: Some relationships between religious attitudes and the self-concept. *Dissert. Abstr.,* 1969, **30** (6 –B), 2782.

129. Williams, R.: A theory of God-concept readiness: From the Piagetian theories of child artificialism and the origin of religious feeling in children. *Relig. Educ.,* 1971, **66,** 62–66.

130. Willits, F. C., R. C. Bealer, and G. W. Bender: Interreligious marriage among Pennsylvania rural youth. *Marriage fam. Living,* 1963, **25,** 433–438.

131. Wilson, W. C.: Extrinsic religious values and prejudice. *J. abnorm. soc. Psychol.,* 1960, **60,** 286–288.

132. Wright, H. D., and W. A. Koppe: Children's potential religious concepts. *Charact. Potential,* 1964, **2,** 83–87.

133. Young, R. K., D. S. Dustin, and W. H. Holtzman: Changes in attitude toward religion in a Southern university. *Psychol. Rep.,* 1966, **18,** 39–46.

134. Zimmer B. G., and A. H. Hawley: Suburbanization and church participation. *Soc. Forces,* 1959, **37,** 348–354.

CHAPTER 12

1. Adelson, J., B. Green, and R. O'Neil: Growth of the idea of law in adolescence. *Develpm. Psychol.,* 1969, **1,** 327–332.

2. Aldrich, C. K.: Thief: Expect a boy to steal and he won't disappoint you. *Psychology Today,* 1971, **4,** no. 3, 66–69.

3. Aldridge, J. W.: In the country of the young. *Harper's Mag.,* October 1969, pp. 49–64.

4. Allen, V. L.: Effect of knowledge of deception on conformity. *J. soc. Psychol.,* 1966, **69,** 101–106.

5. Allinsmith, W.: Conscience and conflict: The moral force in personality. *Child Develpm.,* 1957, **28,** 460–476.

6. Anderson, H. H., G. L. Anderson, L. R. Cohen, and F. D. Nutt: Image of the teacher by

adolescent children in four countries: Germany, England, Mexico, and the United States. *J. soc. Psychol.,* 1959, **50,** 47–55.

7. Anderson, R. E.: Where's Dad? Paternal deprivation and delinquency. *Arch. gen. Psychiat.,* 1968, **18,** 641–649.

8. Asuni, T.: Maladjustment and delinquency: A comparison of two samples. *J. child Psychol. Psychiat.,* 1963, **4,** 219–228.

9. Ausubel, D. P.: Relationships between shame and guilt in the socialization process. *Psychol. Rev.,* 1955, **62,** 378–390.

10. Barclay, D.: "Law course" for the young. *New York Times,* Apr. 16, 1961.

11. Bartemeier, L. H.: Character formation. *Bull. Menninger Clinic,* 1969, **33,** 346–351.

12. Baumrind, D.: Authoritarian vs. authoritative parental control. *Adolescence,* 1968, **3,** 255–272.

13. Beattie, R. H., and J. P. Kenney: Aggressive crimes. *Ann. Amer. Acad. pol. soc. Sci.,* 1966, **364,** 73–85.

14. Becker, L. J.: The changing moral values of students. *J. Home Econ.,* 1963, **55,** 646–648.

15. Berninghausen, D. K., and R. W. Faunce: An exploratory study of juvenile delinquency and the reading of sensational books. *J. exp. Educ.,* 1964, **33,** 161–168.

16. Berry, G. W.: Personality patterns and delinquency. *Brit. J. educ. Psychol.,* 1971, **41,** 221–222.

17. Bettelheim, B.: Violence: Neglected mode of behavior. *Ann. Amer. Acad. pol. soc. Sci.,* 1966, **364,** 50–59.

18. Bittner, J. R.: Student value profiles of state and church-related colleges. *Coll. Stud. Survey,* 1968, **2,** 1–4.

19. Black, M. S., and P. London: The dimensions of guilt, religion and personal ethics. *J. soc. Psychol.,* 1966, **69,** 39–54.

20. Boehm, L., and M. C. Nass: Social class differences in conscience development. *Child Develpm.,* 1962, **33,** 565–574.

21. Bonjean, C. M., and E. McGee: Scholastic dishonesty among undergraduates in differing systems of social control. *Sociol. Educ.,* 1965, **38,** 127–137.

22. Borup, J., and W. F. Elliott: College students' attitudes toward laws, courts and enforcers. *Coll. Stud. Survey,* 1970, **4,** 24–27.

23. Briggs, P. F., R. D. Wirt, and R. Johnson: An application of prediction tables to the study of delinquency. *J. consult. Psychol.,* 1961, **25,** 46–50.

24. Brontenbrenner, U.: The role of age, sex, class, and culture in studies of moral development. *Relig. Educ.,* 1962, **57,** S-3–S-17.

25. Bruno, R., and W. H. Tedford: Rule learning by adolescents. *Psychol. Rep.,* 1969, **25,** 800–802.

26. Campbell, E. Q.: The internalization of moral norms. *Sociometry,* 1964, **27,** 391–412.

27. Caplan, N. S., and L. A. Siebart: Distribution of juvenile delinquent intelligence scores over a thirty-four year period. *J. clin. Psychol.,* 1964, **20,** 242–247.

28. Centra, J. A.: College freshmen attitudes toward cheating. *Personnel Guid. J.,* 1970, **48,** 366–373.

29. Clark, J. P., and E. W. Haurek: Age and sex roles of adolescents and their involvement in misconduct: A reappraisal. *Sociol. soc. Res.,* 1966, **50,** 495–508.

30. Clark, J. P., and E. P. Wenninger: The attitude of juveniles toward the legal institution. *J. crim. Law Criminol. police Sci.,* 1964, **55,** 482–489.

31. Cole, L., and I. N. Hall: *Psychology of adolescence,* 7th ed. New York: Holt, 1970.

32. Cole, M., F. M. Fletcher, and S. L. Pressey: Forty-year changes in college student attitudes. *J. counsel. Psychol.,* 1963, **10,** 53–55.

33. Conant, J. B.: Social dynamite in our large cities. *Crime & Delinqu.,* 1962, **18,** 102–115.

34. Corry, J.: Drugs: A growing campus problem. *New York Times,* Mar. 21, 1966.

35. Crane, A. R.: The development of moral values in children. IV. Preadolescent gangs and the moral development of children. *Brit. J. educ. Psychol.,* 1958, **28,** 201–208.

36. Crow, L. D., and A. Crow: *Adolescent development and adjustment,* 2d ed. New York: McGraw-Hill, 1965.

37. Cummins, E. J.: Are disciplinary students different? *Personnel Guid. J.,* 1966, **44,** 624–627.

38. Davis, D. B.: Violence in American literature. *Ann. Amer. Acad. pol. soc. Sci.,* 1966, **364,** 28–36.

39. de Charms, R., and G. H. Moeller: Values expressed in children's readers: 1900–1950. *J. abnorm. soc. Psychol.,* 1962, **64,** 136–142.

40. Demsch, B., and J. Garth: A multi-disciplinary approach to truancy. *Psychology in the Schools,* 1970, **7,** 194–197.

41. Dentler, R. A., and L. J. Monroe: *Problem behavior in junior high school youth in Kansas.* Bureau of Child Research, University of Kansas Child Res. Series no. 8, 1961.

42. Devereux, E. C.: The role of peer-group experience in moral development. In J. P. Hill (ed.), *Minnesota symposia on child psychology.* Minneapolis: University of Minnesota Press, 1970, vol. 4, pp. 94–140.

43. Didato, S. V.: Delinquents in group therapy: Some new techniques. *Adolescence,* 1970, **5,** 207–222.

44. Dunbar, F.: Homeostasis during puberty. *Amer. J. Psychiat.,* 1958, **114,** 673–682.

45. Duncan, D. F.: Stigma and delinquency. *Cornell J. soc. Relat.,* 1969, **4,** 41–48.

46. Durkheim, E. (ed.): *Moral education*. New York: Free Press, 1961.

47. Durkin, D.: The specificity of children's moral judgments. *J. genet. Psychol.*, 1961, **98,** 3–13.

48. Eisenman, R.: Values and attitudes in adolescence. In J. F. Adams (ed.), *Understanding adolescence: Current developments in adolescent psychology*. Boston: Allyn and Bacon, 1968, pp. 183–197.

49. Elder, G. H.: Parental power legitimation and its effect on the adolescent. *Sociometry,* 1963, **26,** 50–65.

50. Epstein, E. M.: The self-concept of the delinquent female. *Smith Coll. Stud. soc. Wk.,* 1962, **32,** 220–234.

51. Erickson, M. C., and L. T. Empey: Class position, peers and delinquency. *Sociol. soc. Res.,* 1965, **49,** 268–282.

52. Eysenck, H. J.: The development of moral values in children. VII. The contribution of learning theory. *Brit. J. educ. Psychol.,* 1960, **30,** 11–21.

53. Farnsworth, D. L.: Sexual morality and the dilemma of the college. *Amer. J. Orthopsychiat.,* 1965, **35,** 676–681.

54. Ferdon, N. K.: Chromosomal characteristics and antisocial behavior. *J. genet. Psychol.,* 1971, **118,** 281–292.

55. Finney, J. C.: Some maternal influences on children's personality and character. *Genet. Psychol. Monogr.,* 1961, **63,** 199–278.

56. Fodor, E. M.: Moral judgment in Negro and white adolescents. *J. soc. Psychol.,* 1969, **79,** 289–291.

57. Frank, L. K.: This is the adolescent. *Understanding the Child,* 1949, **18,** 65–69.

58. Gallatin, J. E.: The development of the concept of rights in adolescence. *Dissert. Abstr.,* 1968, **28** (12–B), 5204.

59. Gallenkamp, C. R., and J. F. Rychlak: Parental attitudes of sanction in middle-class adolescent male delinquency. *J. soc. Psychol.,* 1968, **75,** 255–260.

60. Gath, D., G. Tennent, and R. Pidduck: Educational characteristics of bright delinquents. *Brit. J. educ. Psychol.,* 1970, **40,** 216–219.

61. Gesell, A., F. L. Ilg, and L. B. Ames: *Youth: The years from ten to sixteen.* New York: Harper & Row, 1956.

62. Giannell, A. S.: Psychological needs characteristic of four criminal-offender groups. *J. soc. Psychol.,* 1966, **69,** 55–72.

63. Glueck, S., and E. T. Glueck: *Physique and delinquency.* New York: Harper & Row, 1956.

64. Glueck, S., and E. T. Glueck: *Family environment and delinquency.* Boston: Houghton Mifflin, 1962.

65. Gnagey, T.: Let's individualize discipline. *Adolescence,* 1970, **5,** 101–108.

66. Goshen, C. E.: The characterology of ado-

lescent offenders and the management of prisons. *Adolescence,* 1971, **6,** 167–186.

67. Gottlieb, D., and C. Ramsey: *The American adolescent.* Homewood, Ill.: Dorsey, 1964.

68. Greene, J. E.: Alleged "misdemeanors" among senior high school students. *J. soc. Psychol.,* 1962, **58,** 371–382.

69. Gregory, I.: Anterospective data following childhood loss of a parent: Delinquency and high school dropout. *Arch. gen. Psychiat.,* 1965, **13,** 99–109.

70. Hampden-Turner, C., and P. Whitten: Morals left and right, *Psychology Today,* Apr. 4, 1971, pp. 39–43, 74–76.

71. Harp, J., and T. Taietz: Academic integrity and social structure: A study of cheating among college students. *Soc. Probl.,* 1966, **13,** 365–373.

72. Harris, H.: Development of moral values in white and Negro boys. *Develpm. Psychol.,* 1970, **2,** 376–383.

73. Harrison, E.: Youth and spring equal explosion. *New York Times,* May 3, 1964.

74. Havighurst, R. J.: Moral character and religious education. *Relig. Educ.,* 1956, **51,** 163–169.

75. Hechinger, F. M.: Adults vs. teenagers. *New York Times,* Dec. 12, 1964.

76. Hechinger, G., and F. M. Hechinger: *Teen-age tyranny.* New York: Morrow, 1963.

77. Hechinger, G., and F. M. Hechinger: College morals mirror our society. *New York Times,* Apr. 14, 1963.

78. Heilbrun, A. B.: Social values: Social behavior consistency, parental identification, and aggression in late adolescence. *J. genet. Psychol.,* 1964, **104,** 135–146.

79. Henry, J.: Permissiveness and morality: *Ment. Hyg., N.Y.,* 1961, **45,** 282–287.

80. Herzog, E.: *Identifying potential delinquents.* U.S. Dept. of Health, Education and Welfare, 1960.

81. Hetherington, E. M., and S. E. Feldman: College cheating as a function of subject and situational variables. *J. educ. Psychol.,* 1964, **55,** 212–218.

82. Hildebrand, J. W.: Why runaways leave home. *J. crim. Law Criminol. police Sci.,* 1963, **54,** 211–216.

83. Hill, J. P., and R. A. Kochendorfer: Knowledge of peer success and risk of detection as determinants of cheating. *Develpm. Psychol.,* 1969, **1,** 231–238.

84. Hindelang, M. J.: The commitment of delinquents to their misdeeds: Do delinquents drift? *Soc. Probl.,* 1970, **17,** 502–509.

85. Hirsch, T., and R. Stark: Hell fire and delinquency. *Soc. Probl.,* 1969, **17,** 202–213.

86. Hoffman, M. L.: Father absence and conscience development. *Develpm. Psychol.,* 1971, **4,** 400–406.

87. Hogan, R.: A dimension of moral judgment.

J. consult clin. Psychol., 1970, **35,** 205–212.

88. Hooke, J. F.: Rating delinquent behavior. *Psychol. Rep.,* 1970, **27,** 155–158.

89. Horrocks, J. E., and N. W. Gottfried: Psychological needs and verbally expressed aggression of adolescent delinquent boys. *J. Psychol.,* 1966, **62,** 179–194.

90. Huntley, C. W.: Changes in values during the four years of college. *Coll. Stud. Survey,* 1967, **1,** 43–48.

91. Hurwitz, J. I.: Three delinquent types: A multivariate analysis. *J. crim. Law Criminol. police Sci.,* 1965, **56,** 328–334.

92. Jacobson, L. J., E. Berger, and J. Millham: Individual differences in cheating during a temptation period when confronting failure. *J. Pers. soc. Psychol.,* 1970, **15,** 48–56.

93. Jaffe, N.: Shame found key to delinquency. *New York Times,* Apr. 17, 1966.

94. Jersild, A. T.: *The psychology of adolescence,* 2d ed. New York: Macmillan, 1963.

95. Johnson, C. D., and J. Gormly: Achievement, sociability and task importance in relation to academic cheating. *Psychol. Rep.,* 1971, **28,** 302.

96. Johnson, R. E., and M. S. Klores: Attitudes toward cheating as a function of classroom dissatisfaction and peer norms. *J. educ. Res.,* 1968, **62,** 60–64.

97. Johnston, N.: *The sociology of punishment and correction.* New York: Wiley, 1962.

98. Jones, M. C.: A comparison of the attitudes and interests of ninth grade students over two decades. *J. educ. Psychol.,* 1960, **51,** 175–186.

99. Jones, M. C.: Psychological correlates of somatic development. *Child Develpm.,* 1965, **36,** 899–911.

100. Jones, V.: Character development in children: An objective approach. In L. Carmichael (ed.), *Manual of child psychology,* 2d ed. New York: Wiley, 1954, pp. 781–832.

101. Joseph, T. P.: Adolescents: From the views of the members of an informal adolescent group. *Genet. Psychol. Monogr.,* 1969, **79,** 3–88.

102. Kay, A. W.: *Moral development: A psychological study of moral growth from childhood to adolescence.* New York: Schocken Books, 1969.

103. Keasey, C. B.: Sex differences in yielding to temptation: A function of the situation. *J. genet. Psychol.,* 1971, **118,** 25–28.

104. Kellmir-Pringle, M. L., and J. B. Edwards: Some moral concepts and judgments of junior school children. *Brit. J. soc. clin. Psychol.,* 1964, **3,** 196–215.

105. Kelly, F. J., and D. J. Baer: Age of male delinquents when father left home and recidivism. *Psychol. Rep.,* 1969, **25,** 1010.

106. Kelly, F. J., and D. J. Veldman: Delinquency and school dropout behavior as a function of impulsivity and nondominant values. *J. abnorm. soc. Psychol.,* 1964, **69,** 190–194.

107. Keniston, K.: Student activism, moral development, and morality. *Amer. J. Orthopsychiat.,* 1970, **40,** 577–592.

108. Kessler, C. C., and J. Wieland: Experimental study of risk-taking behavior in runaway girls. *Psychol. Rep.,* 1970, **26,** 810.

109. Kimsey, L. R.: Some observations on the psychodynamics of juvenile delinquents. *Adolescence,* 1970, **5,** 197–206.

110. King, W.: Children's crime rising across U.S. *New York Times,* Oct. 5, 1971.

111. Klein, M. W.: Impressions of juvenile gang members. *Adolescence,* 1968, **3,** 53–78.

112. Klemer, R. H.: Student attitudes toward guidance in sexual morality. *Marriage fam. Living,* 1962, **24,** 260–264.

113. Klinger, E., A. Albaum, and M. Hethering: Factors influencing the severity of moral judgments. *J. soc. Psychol.,* 1964, **63,** 319–326.

114. Konopka, G.: Adolescent delinquent girls. *Children,* 1964, **11,** 21–26.

115. Kudirka, N. Z.: Defiance of authority under peer influence. *Dissert. Abstr.,* 1965, **26,** 4103.

116. Kulik, J. A., T. R. Sarbin, and K. B. Stein: Language, socialization and delinquency. *Develpm. Psychol.,* 1971, **4,** 434–439.

117. Kulik, J. A., K. B. Stein, and T. R. Sarbin: Dimensions and patterns of adolescent antisocial behavior. *J. consult. clin. Psychol.,* 1968, **32,** 375–382.

118. Kunz, P. R.: Religious influences on parental discipline and achievement demands. *Marriage fam. Living,* 1963, **25,** 224–225.

119. Kvaraceus, W. C.: The delinquent. *J. educ. Res.,* 1959, **29,** 545–552.

120. Landis, P. H.: The ordering and forbidding technique and teen-age adjustment. *Sch. Soc.,* 1954, **80,** 105–106.

121. Laney, J. T.: The new morality and the religious communities. *Ann. Amer. Acad. pol. soc. Sci.,* 1970, **387,** 14–21.

122. Larsen, O. N.: Controversies about the mass communication of violence. *Ann. Amer. Acad. pol. soc. Sci.,* 1966, **364,** 37–49.

123. Larson, J. D., B. J. Fitzgerald, and R. Martin: Social class, reported parental behavior and delinquency status. *Psychol. Rep.,* 1971, **28,** 323–328.

124. Lee, L. C.: The concomitant development of cognitive and moral modes of thought: A test of selected deductions from Piaget's theory. *Genet. Psychol. Monogr.,* 1971, **83,** 93–146.

125. Lehmann, I. J., B. K. Sinha, and R. T. Hartnett: Changes in attitudes and values associated with college attendance. *J. educ. Psychol.,* 1966, **57,** 89–98.

126. Lelyveld, J.: The paradoxical case of the

affluent delinquent. *New York Times,* Oct. 4, 1964.

127. Le May, M. L.: Birth order and college misconduct. *J. indiv. Psychol.,* 1968, **24,** 167–169.

128. Lerman, P.: Gangs, networks and subcultural delinquency. *Amer. J. Sociol.,* 1967, **73,** 63–72.

129. Lerman, P.: Individual values, peer values and subcultural delinquency. *Amer. sociol. Rev.,* 1968, **33,** 219–235.

130. Leveque, K. L., and R. E. Walker: Correlates of high school cheating behavior. *Psychology in the Schools,* 1970, **7,** 159–163.

131. Levinson, B., and H. Mezei: Self-concepts and ideal-self concepts of run-away youths: Counseling implications. *Psychol. Rep.,* 1970, **26,** 871–874.

132. Light, H. K.: Attitudes of rural and urban adolescent girls toward selected concepts. *Family Coordinator,* 1970, **19,** 225–227.

133. London, E. S.: An inquiry into boredom and thrill seeking. *Dissert. Abstr.,* 1966, **26,** 4853.

134. London, P., R. E. Schulman, and M. S. Black: Religion, guilt, and ethical standards. *J. soc. Psychol.,* 1964, **63,** 145–149.

135. Lubasch, A. H.: Crimes by children reported increasing at an alarming rate. *New York Times,* Oct. 24, 1971.

136. Luchins, A. S., and E. H. Luchins: Strengthening motivational factors to tell the truth. *J. soc. Psychol.,* 1970, **81,** 55–62.

137. Macfarlane, J., L. Allen, and M. P. Honzik: *A developmental study of the behavior problems of normal children between twenty-one months and fourteen years.* Berkeley: University of California Press, 1954.

138. MacIver, R. M.: Juvenile delinquency. In E. Ginzberg (ed.), *The nation's children.* III. *Problems and Prospects.* New York: Columbia, 1960, pp. 103–123.

139. Marshall, T. F., and A. Mason: A framework for the analysis of juvenile delinquency causation. *Brit. J. Sociol.,* 1968, **19,** 130–142.

140. Martin, L. M.: Three approaches to delinquency prevention. *Crime & Delinqu.,* 1961, **7,** 16–24.

141. Medinnus, G. R.: Delinquents' perceptions of their parents. *J. consult. Psychol.,* 1965, **29,** 592–593.

142. Menninger, W.: Youth and violence. *Menninger Quart.,* 1969, **23,** 22–30.

143. Milgrim, S. A.: A comparison of the effects of classics and contemporary literary works on high-school students' declared attitudes toward certain moral values. *Dissert. Abstr.,* 1968, **28** (10–A), 3899.

144. Miller, W. B.: Violent crimes in city gangs. *Ann. Amer. Acad. pol. soc. Sci.,* 1966, **364,** 96–112.

145. Morris, J. F.: The development of adolescent value-judgments. *Brit. J. educ. Psychol.,* 1958, **28,** 1–14.

146. Mosher, D. L., and J. B. Mosher: Relationships between authoritarian attitudes in delinquent girls and the authoritarian attitudes and authoritarian rearing practices of their mothers. *Psychol. Rep.,* 1965, **16,** 23–30.

147. Mussen, P. H., E. Rutherford, S. Harris, and C. B. Keasey: Honesty and altruism among preadolescents. *Develpm. Psychol.,* 1970, **3,** 169–194.

148. Naess, S.: Mother-separation and delinquency. *Brit. J. Criminol.,* 1962, **2,** 361–374.

149. Needham, M. A., and E. M. Schur: Student punitiveness toward sexual deviation. *Marriage fam. Living,* 1963, **25,** 227–229.

150. Nelson, E. A., R. E. Grinder, and M. C. Mutterer: Sources of variance in behavioral measures of honesty in temptation situations: Methodological analysis. *Develpm. Psychol.,* 1969, **1,** 265–279.

151. *New York Times* Report: U.S. children top list for honesty. Sept. 4, 1961.

152. *New York Times* Report: Young offenders studied by U.N. Nov. 15, 1965.

153. *New York Times* Report: Delinquent girls outpaced boys in '65. Dec. 23, 1966.

154. *New York Times* Report: Crime figures show something new. Sept. 1, 1968.

155. *Newsweek* Report: The teen-agers. Mar. 21, 1966, pp. 57–75.

156. Nye, F. I., J. Carlson, and G. Garrett: Family size, interaction, affect and stress. *J. Marriage & Family,* 1970, **32,** 216–226.

157. Palmai, G., P. B. Storey, and O. Briscoe: Social class and the young offender. *Brit. J. Psychiat.,* 1967, **113,** 1073–1082.

158. Palmore, E. B., and P. E. Hammond: Interacting factors in juvenile delinquency. *Amer. sociol. Rev.,* 1964, **29,** 848–854.

159. Patterson, C. H.: Are ethics different in different settings? *Personnel Guid. J.,* 1971, **50,** 254–259.

160. Peck, R. F., and R. J. Havighurst: *The psychology of character development.* New York: Wiley, 1962.

161. Peretti, P. O.: Guilt in moral development. A comparative study. *Psychol. Rep.,* 1969, **25,** 739–745.

162. Perlman, I. R.: Delinquency prevention: The size of the problem. *Ann. Amer. Acad. pol. soc. Sci.,* 1959, **322,** 1–9.

163. Peterson, D. R.: Behavior problems of middle childhood. *J. consult. Psychol.,* 1961, **25,** 205–209.

164. Pierson, G. R., W. W. Langille, and D. E. Swenson: A factor analysis of the playground behavior of delinquent boys. *J. genet. Psychol.,* 1965, **106,** 287–291.

165. Piliavin, I., and S. Briar: Police encounters

with juveniles. *Amer. J. Sociol.,* 1964, **70,** 206–214.

166.   Pine, G. J.: Occupational and educational aspirations and delinquent behavior. *Vocat. Guid. Quart.,* 1965, **13,** 107–111.

167.   Poffenberger, T.: The control of adolescent premarital coitus. *Marriage fam. Living,* 1962, **24,** 254–260.

168.   Pressey, S. L., and R. G. Kuhlen: *Psychological development through the life span.* New York: Harper & Row, 1957.

169.   Putney, S., and R. Middleton: Effect of husband-wife interaction on the strictness of attitudes toward child rearing. *Marriage fam. Living,* 1960, **22,** 171–173.

170.   Quarter, J. J., and R. M. Laxer: A structured program of teaching and counseling for conduct problem students in the junior high school. *J. educ. Res.,* 1970, **63,** 229–231.

171.   Quay, H. C., and L. C. Quay: Behavior problems in early adolescence. *Child Develpm.,* 1965, **36,** 215–220.

172.   Query, J. M. N.: The influence of group pressures on the judgments of children and adolescents: A comparative study. *Adolescence,* 1968, **3,** 153–160.

173.   Rapp, D. W.: Child rearing attitudes of mothers in Germany and the United States. *Child Develpm.,* 1961, **32,** 669–678.

174.   Reckless, W. C., and S. Dinitz: Pioneering with self-concept as a vulnerability factor in delinquency. *J. crim. Law Criminol. police Sci.,* 1967, **58,** 515–523.

175.   Reiss, A. J., and A. L. Rhodes: The distribution of juvenile delinquency in the social class structure. *Amer. sociol. Rev.,* 1961, **26,** 720–732.

176.   Reiss, I. L.: The sexual renaissance: A summary and analysis. *J. soc. Issues,* 1966, **22,** no. 2, 123–137.

177.   Rempel, H., and E. I. Signori: Sex differences in self-ratings of conscience as a determinant of behavior. *Psychol. Rep.,* 1964, **15,** 277–278.

178.   Resnick, J.: The juvenile delinquent: An explanation. *Educ. Admin. Supervis.,* 1955, **41,** 218–223.

179.   Rettig, S., and B. Pasamanick: Differential judgment of ethical risk by cheaters and noncheaters. *J. abnorm. soc. Psychol.,* 1964, **69,** 109–113.

180.   Robey, A., R. J. Rosenwald, J. E. Snell, and R. E. Lee: The runaway girl: A reaction to family stress. *Amer. J. Orthopsychiat.,* 1964, **34,** 762–767.

181.   Rosenfeld, H. M,: Delinquent acting-out in adolescent males and the task of sexual identification. *Smith Coll. Stud. soc. Wk.,* 1969, **40,** 1–29.

182.   Rosenthal, M. J.: The syndrome of the inconsistent mother. *Amer. J. Orthopsychiat.,* 1962, **32,** 637–644.

183.   Roskens, R. W., and H. F. Dizney: A study of unethical academic behavior in high school and college. *J. educ. Res.,* 1966, **59,** 231–234.

184.   Scarpitti, F. R., E. Murray, S. Dinitz, and W. C. Reckless: The "good" boy in a high delinquency area: Four years later. *Amer. sociol. Rev.,* 1960, **25,** 555–558.

185.   Schab, F.: Honor and dishonor in the secondary schools in three cultures. *Adolescence,* 1971, **6,** 145–154.

186.   Scharr, J. H.: Violence in juvenile gangs: Some notes and a few analogies. *Amer. J. Orthopsychiat.,* 1963, **33,** 29–37.

187.   Schmid, A. C.: Susceptibility to social influence and retention of opinion change in two types of delinquents. *J. abnorm. Psychol.,* 1970, **76,** 123–129.

188.   Schreiber, D.: Dropout and the delinquent: Promising practices gleaned from a year of study. *Phi Delta Kappan,* 1963, **44,** 215–221.

189.   Sebald, H.: *Adolescence: A sociological analysis.* New York: Appleton-Century-Crofts, 1968.

190.   Settlage, C. F.: The values of limits in child rearing. *Children,* 1958, **5,** 175–178.

191.   Shanley, F. J.: Middle-class delinquency as a social problem. *Sociol. soc. Res.,* 1967, **51,** 185–198.

192.   Shellow, R., J. R. Schamp, E. Liebow, and E. Unger: Suburban runaways of the 1960's. *Monogr. Soc. Res. Child Develpm.,* 1967, **32,** no. 3.

193.   Shelton, J., and J. P. Hill: Effects on cheating of achievement anxiety and knowledge of peer performance. *Develpm. Psychol.,* 1969, **1,** 449–455.

194.   Short, J. F., R. Rivera, and R. A. Tennyson: Perceived opportunities, gang membership and delinquency. *Amer. sociol. Rev.,* 1965, **30,** 56–67.

195.   Shybut, J.: Internal vs. external control, time perspective and delay of gratification of high and low ego strength groups. *J. clin. Psychol.,* 1970, **26,** 430–431.

196.   Simpson, J. E., T. G. Eynon, and W. C. Reckless: Institutionalization as perceived by the juvenile offender. *Sociol. soc. Res.,* 1963, **48,** 13–23.

197.   Slocum, W. L., and C. L. Stone: Family culture patterns and delinquent-type behavior. *Marriage fam. Living,* 1963, **25,** 202–208.

198.   Smith, H.: Soviet troubled by teen-age crime. *New York Times,* Feb. 13, 1972.

199.   Solomon, R. L.: Punishment. *Amer. Psychologist,* 1964, **19,** 239–253.

200.   Sowles, R. C., and J. H. Gill: Institutional and community adjustment of delinquents following counseling. *J. consult. clin. Psychol.,* 1970, **34,** 398–407.

201.   Steininger, M.: Attitudes toward cheating:

General and specific. *Psychol. Rep.,* 1968, **22,** 1101–1107.

202. Steininger, M., R. E. Johnson, and D. K. Kirts: Cheating on college examinations as a function of situationally aroused anxiety and hostility. *J. educ. Psychol.,* 1964, **55,** 317–324.

203. Stewart, L., and N. Livson: Smoking and rebelliousness: A longitudinal study from childhood to maturity. *J. consult. Psychol.,* 1966, **30,** 225–229.

204. Stokes, W. R.: Our changing sex ethics. *Marriage fam. Living,* 1962, **24,** 269–272.

205. Sugarman, P.: Social norms in teenage boys' peer groups. *Hum. Relat.,* 1968, **21,** 41–58.

206. Sullivan, E. V., G. McCullough, and M. Stager: A developmental study of the relationship between conceptual, ego and moral development. *Child Develpm.,* 1970, **41,** 399–411.

207. Sutton-Smith, B., and B. G. Rosenberg: Peer perceptions of impulsive behavior. *Merrill-Palmer Quart.,* 1961, **7,** 233–238.

208. Taylor, A. J. W.: Tattooing among male and female offenders of different ages in different types of institutions. *Genet. Psychol. Monogr.,* 1970, **81,** 81–119.

209. Tennent, T. G.: Truancy and stealing. *Brit. J. Psychiat.,* 1970, **116,** 587–592.

210. Thompson, O. E.: High school students and their values. *Calif. J. educ. Res.,* 1965, **16,** 217–227.

211. Toby, J.: The differential effect of family disorganization. *Amer. sociol. Rev.,* 1957, **22,** 505–512.

212. Toby, J.: Violence and the masculine ideal: Some qualitative data. *Ann. Amer. Acad. pol. soc. Sci.,* 1966, **364,** 19–27.

213. Troll, L. E., B. L. Neugarten, and R. J. Kraines: Similarity in values and other personality characteristics in college students and their parents. *Merrill-Palmer Quart.,* 1969, **15,** 323–336.

214. Tsubouchi, K., and R. L. Jenkins: Three types of delinquents: Their performance on MMPI and PCR. *J. clin. Psychol.,* 1969, **25,** 353–358.

215. Tuma, E., and N. Livson: Family socioeconomic status and adolescent attitudes toward authority. *Child Develpm.,* 1960, **31,** 387–399.

216. *U.S. News & World Report:* Why young people "go bad." Apr. 26, 1965, pp. 56–62.

217. *U.S. News & World Report:* Crisis in juvenile courts. Mar. 24, 1969, pp. 62–64.

218. *U.S. News & World Report:* We're reaping a harvest of permissiveness. Sept. 27, 1971, p. 22.

219. *U.S. News & World Report:* Runaway children. Apr. 24, 1972, pp. 38–42.

220. Vincent, E. L., and P. C. Martin: *Human psychological development.* New York: Ronald, 1961.

221. Wallace, R.: Where's the party—let's crash it! *Life Mag.,* July 5, 1963, pp. 63–67.

222. Watson, G.: Some personality differences in children related to strict or permissive parental discipline. *J. Psychol.,* 1957, **44,** 227–249.

223. Weisbroth, S. P.: Moral judgment, sex, and parental identification in adults. *Develpm. Psychol.,* 1970, **2,** 396–402.

224. Wert, R. D., and P. F. Briggs: Personality and environmental factors in the development of delinquency. *Psychol. Monogr.,* 1959, **73,** no. 13.

225. White, W. F., and N. J. Minden: Risky-shift phenomenon in moral attitudes of high school boys and girls. *Psychol. Rep.,* 1969, **25,** 515–518.

226. White, W. F., and T. L. Porter: Multivariate analysis of attitudes and personality characteristics among youthful offenders. *Psychol. Rep.,* 1970, **26,** 487–491.

227. Wiggam, R. A.: Do brains and character go together? *Sch. Soc.,* 1941, **54,** 261–265.

228. Willie, C. V.: The relative contribution of family status and economic status to juvenile delinquency. *Soc. Probl.,* 1967, **14,** 326–335.

229. Withers, S.: Putting the label on stealing. *New York Times,* July 21, 1963.

230. Witryol, S. L., and J. E. Calkins: Marginal social values of rural school children. *J. genet. Psychol.,* 1958, **92,** 81–93.

231. Wolman, R. N.: Early recollections and the perception of others: A study of delinquent adolescents. *J. genet. Psychol.,* 1970, **116,** 157–163.

232. Woods, P. J., K. B. Glavin, and C. M. Kettle: A mother-daughter comparison on selected aspects of child rearing in a higher socioeconomic group. *Child Develpm.,* 1960, **31,** 121–128.

233. Yablonsky, L. *The violent gang.* New York: Macmillan, 1962.

234. Zeitlin, H.: High school discipline. *Calif. J. educ. Res.,* 1962, **13,** 116–125.

CHAPTER 13

1. Altus, W. D.: Sex role dissatisfaction, birth order and parental favoritism. *Proc. Annu. Convent. APA,* 1971, **6,** pt. 1, 161–162.

2. Angrist, S. S.: Role constellation as a variable in women's leisure activities. *Soc. Forces,* 1967, **45,** 423–431.

3. Balswick, J. O., and C. W. Peek: The inexpressive male: A tragedy of American society. *Family Coordinator,* 1971, **20,** 363–368.

4. Barglow, P., M. Bornstein, D. B. Exum, M. K Wright, and H. M. Visotsky: Some psychiatric aspects of illegitimate pregnancy in early adolescence. *Amer. J. Orthopsychiat.,* 1968, **38,** 672–687.

5. Bayer, A. E.: Early dating and early marriage. *J. Marriage & Family,* 1968, **30,** 628–632.

6. Beigel, H. G.: Romantic love. *Amer. sociol. Rev.,* 1951, **16,** 326–334.

7. Bell, R. R.: The marital expectations of adolescents. In J. F. Adams (ed.), *Understanding adolescence: Current developments in adolescent psychology.* Boston: Allyn and Bacon, 1968, pp. 272–286.

8. Bell, R. R., and J. B. Chaskes: Premarital sexual experience among coeds: 1958 and 1968. *J. Marriage & Family,* 1970, **32,** 81–84.

9. Bernard, J.: Marital stability and patterns of status variables. *J. Marriage & Family,* 1966, **28,** 421–448.

10. Berscheid, E., and K. Dion: Physical attractiveness and dating choice: A test of the matching hypothesis. *J. exp. soc. Psychol.,* 1971, **7,** 173–189.

11. Biller, H. B., and R. M. Bahn: Father absence, perceived maternal behavior and masculinity of self-concept among high school boys. *Develpm. Psychol.,* 1971, **4,** 178–181.

12. Biller, H. B., and D. A. Liebman: Body build, sex-role preference and sex-role adoption in junior high school boys. *J. genet. Psychol.,* 1971, **118,** 81–86.

13. Biller, H. B., and S. D. Weiss: The father-daughter relationship and the personality development of the female. *J. genet. Psychol.,* 1970, **116,** 79–93.

14. Birdwhistell, M.: Adolescents and the pill culture. *Family Coordinator,* 1968, **17,** 27–32.

15. Birenbaum, A.: Revolution without the revolution: Sex in contemporary America. *J. sex Res.,* 1970, **6,** 257–267.

16. Blaine, G. B.: Sex and the adolescent. *N.Y. State J. Med.,* 1967, **67,** 1967–1975.

17. Boyers, R.: Attitudes toward sex in American "high culture." *Ann. Amer. Acad. pol. soc. Sci.,* 1968, **376,** 36–52.

18. Braaten, L. J., and C. D. Darling: Overt and covert homosexual problems among male college students. *Genet. Psychol. Monogr.,* 1965, **71,** 269–310.

19. Braen, B. B.: The evaluation of a therapeutic group approach to school-age pregnant girls. *Adolescence,* 1970, **5,** 171–186.

20. Brislin, R. W., and S. A. Lewis: Dating and physical attractiveness: Replication. *Psychol. Rep.,* 1968, **22,** 976.

21. Broderick, C. B., and S. E. Fowler: New patterns in relationships between the sexes among preadolescents. *Marriage fam. Living,* 1961, **23,** 27–30.

22. Broderick, C. B., and G. Rowe: A scale of preadolescent heterosexual development. *J. Marriage & Family,* 1968, **30,** 97–101.

23. Brody, J.: Homosexuality: Parents aren't always to blame. *New York Times,* Jan. 10, 1971.

24. Brotman, J., and R. J. Sentes: Attitudes toward feminism in different national student groups. *J. soc. Psychol.,* 1968, **76,** 137–138.

25. Brown, D. G.: Sex-role development in a changing culture. *Psychol. Bull.,* 1958, **55,** 232–242.

26. Brown, D. G., and D. B. Lynn: Human sexual development: An outline of components and concepts. *J. Marriage & Family,* 1966, **28,** 155–162.

27. Burchinal, L. G.: Sources and adequacy of sex knowledge among Iowa high school girls. *Marriage fam. Living,* 1960, **22,** 268–269.

28. Calderone, M. S.: Sex education and the roles of school and church. *Ann. Amer. Acad. pol. soc. Sci.,* 1968, **376,** 53–60.

29. Calderwood, D.: Adolescents' views on sex education. *J. Marriage & Family,* 1965, **27,** 291–298.

30. Cameron, P.: Note on time spent thinking about sex. *Psychol. Rep.,* 1967, **20,** 741–742.

31. Cameron, P.: The generation gap: Beliefs about sexuality and self-reported sexuality. *Develpm. Psychol.,* 1970, **3,** 272.

32. Cannon, K. L., and R. Long: Premarital sexual behavior in the sixties. *J. Marriage & Family,* 1971, **33,** 36–49.

33. Christensen, H. T., and R. E. Barber: Interfaith versus intrafaith marriage in Indiana. *J. Marriage & Family,* 1967, **29,** 461–469.

34. Cole, L., and I. N. Hall: *Psychology of adolescence,* 7th ed. New York: Holt, 1970.

35. Coleman, J. S.: *The adolescent society.* New York: Free Press, 1961.

36. Connell, D. M., and J. E. Johnson: Relation between sex-role identification and self-esteem in early adolescents. *Develpm. Psychol.,* 1970, **3,** 268.

37. Coombs, R. H.: Value consensus and partner satisfaction among dating couples. *J. Marriage & Family,* 1966, **28,** 166–173.

38. Cooper, A. J.: "Neurosis" and disorders of sexual potency in the male. *J. psychosom. Res.,* 1968, **12,** 141–144.

39. Couch, G. B.: Youth looks at sex. *Adolescence,* 1967, **2,** 258–266.

40. Crow, L. D., and A. Crow: *Adolescent development and adjustment,* 2d ed. New York: McGraw-Hill, 1965.

41. Dame, N. G., G. H. Finck, R. G. Mayos, B. S. Reiner, and B. O. Smith: Conflict in marriage following premarital pregnancy. *Amer. J. Orthopsychiat.,* 1966, **36,** 468–475.

42. Dean, D. G.: Romanticism and emotional maturity: A further exploration. *Soc. Forces,* 1964, **42,** 299–303.

43. de Jung, J. E., and E. F. Gardner: The accuracy of self-role perception: A developmental study. *J. exp. Educ.,* 1962, **31,** 27–41.

44. De Lora, J.: Social systems of dating on a

college campus. *Marriage fam. Living,* 1963, **25,** 81–84.

45. Diamant, L.: Premarital sexual behavior, attitudes, and emotional adjustment. *J. soc. Psychol.,* 1970, **82,** 75–80.

46. Dickinson, G. E.: Dating patterns of black and white adolescents in a Southern community. *Adolescence,* 1971, **6,** 285–298.

47. Douvan, E., and J. Adelson: American dating patterns. In D. Rogers (ed.), *Issues in adolescent psychology.* New York: Appleton-Century-Crofts, 1969, pp. 386–395.

48. Dubbé, M. C.: What parents are not told may hurt. *Family Life Coordinator,* 1965, **14,** 51–118.

49. Duvall, E. M.: Adolescent love as a reflection of teen-agers' search for identity. *J. Marriage & Family,* 1964, **26,** 226–229.

50. Elder, G. H.: Appearance and education in marriage mobility. *Amer. sociol. Rev.,* 1969, **34,** 519–533.

51. Ellis, A.: Sexual manifestations of emotionally disturbed behavior. *Ann. Amer. Acad. pol. soc. Sci.,* 1968, **376,** 96–105.

52. England, R. W.: Images of love and courtship in family-magazine fiction. *Marriage fam. Living,* 1960, **22,** 162–165.

53. Evans, R. B.: Childhood parental relationships of homosexual men. *J. consult. clin. Psychol.,* 1969, **33,** 129–135.

54. Farley, J.: Graduate women: Career aspirations and desired family size. *Amer. Psychologist,* 1970, **25,** 1099–1100.

55. Farnsworth, D. L.: Sexual morality and the dilemma of the colleges. *Amer. J. Orthopsychiat.,* 1965, **35,** 676–681.

56. Ferdinand, T. N.: Sex behavior and the American class structure: A mosaic. *Ann. Amer. Acad. pol. soc. Sci.,* 1968, **376,** 76–85.

57. Fine, B.: Battle of the sexes begins at start of grammar school. *New York Times,* May 27, 1962.

58. Fleck, S.: Pregnancy as a symptom of adolescent maladjustment. *Int. J. soc. Psychiat.,* 1956, **2,** 118–131.

59. Freedman, M. B.: The sexual behavior of American college women: An empirical study and an historical survey. *Merrill-Palmer Quart.,* 1965, **11,** 33–48.

60. Gagnon, J. H., and W. Simon: Sexual deviance in contemporary America. *Ann. Amer. Acad. pol. soc. Sci.,* 1968, **376,** 106–122.

61. Gagnon, J. H., and W. Simon: They're going to learn in the street anyway. *Psychology Today,* July 1969, pp. 46–47, 71.

62. Gallagher, J. R.: That favorite teacher: A parent's enemy or ally? *Marriage fam. Living,* 1961, **23,** 400–402.

63. Geiken, K. F.: Expectations concerning husband-wife responsibilities in the home. *J. Marriage & Family,* 1964, **26,** 349–352.

64. Gesell, A., F. L. Ilg, and L. B. Ames: *Youth: The years from ten to sixteen.* New York: Harper & Row, 1956.

65. Grinder, R. E.: Relations of social dating attractions to academic orientation and peer relations. *J. educ. Psychol.,* 1966, **57,** 27–34.

66. Halleck, S. L.: Mental health on the campus. *J. Amer. med. Ass.,* 1967, **200,** 684–690.

67. Harlow, H. F.: The nature of love. *Amer. Psychologist,* 1958, **13,** 673–685.

68. Harris, D. B., and S. C. Tseng: Children's attitudes toward peers and parents as revealed by sentence completions. *Child Develpm.,* 1957, **28,** 401–411.

69. Harrison, D. E., W. H. Bennett, and G. Globetti: Attitudes of rural youth toward premarital sexual permissiveness. *J. Marriage & Family,* 1969, **31,** 783–787.

70. Hechinger, G.: Slowing down the social pace. *New York Times,* Apr. 14, 1963.

71. Heilbrun, A. B.: Sex-role identity in adolescent females: A theoretical paradox. *Adolescence,* 1968, **3,** 79–88.

72. Heise, D. R., and E. P. M. Roberts: The development of role knowledge. *Genet. Psychol. Monogr.,* 1970, **82,** 83–115.

73. Heltsley, M. E., and C. B. Broderick: Religiosity and premarital permissiveness: Reexamination of Reiss's traditionalism proposition. *J. Marriage & Family,* 1969, **31,** 441–443.

74. Henton, J. M.: The effects of married high-school students on their unmarried classmates. *J. Marriage & Family,* 1964, **26,** 87–88.

75. Hermann, R. O.: Expectations and attitudes as a source of financial problems in teenage marriages. *J. Marriage & Family,* 1965, **27,** 89–91.

76. Hobart, C. W.: Disillusionment in marriage and romanticism. *Marriage fam. Living,* 1958, **20,** 156–162.

77. Holmes, M., C. Nicol, and R. Stubbs: Sex attitudes of young people. *Educ. Res.,* 1968, **11,** 38–42.

78. Horton, D.: The dialogue of courtship in popular songs. *Amer. J. Sociol.,* 1957, **62,** 562–578.

79. Hudson, J. W., and L. F. Henze: Campus values in mate selection: A replication. *J. Marriage & Family,* 1969, **31,** 772–775.

80. Husbands, C. T.: Some social and psychological consequences of the American dating system. *Adolescence,* 1970, **5,** 451–462.

81. Inselberg, R. M.: Social and psychological factors associated with high school marriages. *J. Home Econ.,* 1961, **53,** 766–772.

82. Jacks, I.: Attitudes of college freshmen and sophomores toward interfaith marriage. *Adolescence,* 1967, **2,** 183–209.

83. Jenkin, N., and K. Vroegh: Contemporary

concepts of masculinity and femininity. *Psychol. Rep.,* 1969, **25,** 679–697.

84. Johnson, M. M.: Sex-role learning in the nuclear family. *Child Develpm.,* 1963, **34,** 319–333.

85. Johnson, R. E.: Some correlates of extramarital coitus. *J. Marriage & Family,* 1970, **32,** 449–456.

86. Jones, M. C.: Psychological correlates of somatic development. *Child Develpm.,* 1965, **36,** 899–911.

87. Juhasz, A. M.: Background factors, extent of sex knowledge and source of information. *J. Sch. Hlth.,* 1969, **39,** 32–39.

88. Kaats, G. R., and K. E. Davis: The dynamics of sexual behavior of college students. *J. Marriage & Family,* 1970, **32,** 390–399.

89. Kalish, R. A., M. Maloney, and A. Arkoff: Cross-cultural comparisons of college student marital-role preferences. *J. soc. Psychol.,* 1966, **68,** 41–47.

90. Kammeyer, K.: The feminine role: An analysis of attitude consistency. *J. Marriage & Family,* 1964, **26,** 295–305.

91. Kanin, E. J.: Sexually aggressive college males. *J. coll. Stud. Personnel,* 1971, **12,** 107–110.

92. Kariel, P. E.: Social class, age, and educational group differences in childbirth information. *Marriage fam. Living,* 1963, **25,** 353–355.

93. Karp, E. S., J. H. Jackson, and D. Lester: Ideal-self fulfillment in mate selection: A corollary to the complementary need theory of mate selection. *J. Marriage & Family,* 1970, **32,** 269–272.

94. Kerckhoff, A. C.: Early antecedents of role-taking and role-playing ability. *Merrill-Palmer Quart.,* 1969, **15,** 229–247.

95. Kiell, N., and B. Friedman: Culture lag and housewifemanship: The role of the married female college student. *J. educ. Sociol.,* 1957, **31,** 87–95.

96. Kirkendall, L. A.: Toward a clarification of the concept of male sex drive. *Marriage fam. Living,* 1958, **20,** 367–372.

97. Kirkendall, L. A.: Circumstances associated with teenage boys' use of prostitution. *Marriage fam. Living,* 1960, **22,** 145–149.

98. Kirkendall, L. A., and D. S. Brody: The arousal of fear: Does it have a place in sex education? *Family Life Coordinator,* 1964, **13,** 14–16.

99. Kirkendall, L. A., and R. W. Libby: Interpersonal relationships: Crux of the sexual renaissance. *J. soc. Issues,* 1966, **22,** no. 2, 45–59.

100. Klemer, R. H.: Self-esteem and college dating experience as factors in mate selection and marital happiness. A longitudinal study. *J. Marriage & Family,* 1971, **33,** 183–187.

101. Knox, D. H.: Conceptions of love at three developmental levels. *Family Coordinator,* 1970, **19,** 151–157.

102. Knox, D. H., and M. J. Sporakowski: Attitudes of college students toward love. *J. Marriage & Family,* 1968, **30,** 638–642.

103. Koch, H. L.: The relation of certain formal attributes of siblings to attitudes held toward each other and toward their parents. *Monogr. Soc. Res. Child Develpm.,* 1960, **25,** no. 4.

104. Kogan, W. S., E. E. Boe, and E. F. Gocka: Personality changes in unwed mothers following parturition. *J. clin. Psychol.,* 1968, **24,** 3–11.

105. Kuhlen, R. G., and N. B. Houlihan: Adolescent heterosexual interest in 1942 and 1963. *Child Develpm.,* 1965, **36,** 1049–1052.

106. Kunz, P. R.: Romantic love and reciprocity. *Family Coordinator,* 1969, **18,** 111–116.

107. Landis, J. T.: Dating maturation of children from happy and unhappy marriages. *Marriage fam. Living,* 1963, **25,** 351–353.

108. Lester, D.: Adolescent suicide and premarital sexual behavior. *J. soc. Psychol.,* 1970, **82,** 131–132.

109. Leventhal, G. S.: Influence of brothers and sisters on sex-role behavior. *J. Pers. soc. Psychol.,* 1970, **16,** 452–465.

110. Levinger, G.: Note on need complementarity in marriage. *Psychol. Bull.,* 1964, **61,** 153–157.

111. Lowrie, S. H.: Early marriage: Premarital pregnancy and associated factors. *J. Marriage & Family,* 1965, **27,** 48–56.

112. Luckey, E. B., and G. D. Nass: A comparison of sexual attitudes and behavior in an international sample. *J. Marriage & Family,* 1969, **31,** 364–379.

113. MacNamara, D. E. J.: Sex offenses and sex offenders. *Ann. Amer. Acad. pol. soc. Sci.,* 1968, **376,** 148–155.

114. Maranell, G. M., D. A. Dodder, and D. F. Mitchell: Social class and sexual permissiveness: A subsequent test. *J. Marriage & Family,* 1970, **32,** 85–88.

11⁻. Martelle, D. L.: Interracial marriage attitudes among high school students. *Psychol. Rep.,* 1970, **27,** 1007–1010.

116. Martin, P. C.: Objectives in teaching high school youth about pregnancy and child bearing. *Marriage fam. Living,* 1962, **24,** 403–406.

117. Martinson, F. M.: Ego deficiency as a factor in marriage: A male sample. *Marriage fam. Living,* 1959, **21,** 48–52.

118. Masters, W. H., and V. E. Johnson: *Human sexual response.* Boston: Little, Brown, 1965.

119. Matthews, E., and D. V. Tiedman: Attitudes toward career and marriage and the development of life style in young women. *J. counsel. Psychol.,* 1964, **11,** 375–384.

120. McDaniel, C. O.: Dating roles and reasons for dating. *J. Marriage & Family,* 1969, **31,** 97–107.

121. McKee, J. P., and A. C. Sherriffs: The differential evaluation of males and females. *J. Pers.,* 1957, **25,** 356–371.

122. Mead, M.: *Male and female*. New York: Dell, 1968.

123. Middendor, P., C. P. Brinkman, and W. Koomen: Determinants of premarital sexual permissiveness: A secondary analysis. *J. Marriage & Family*, 1970, **32**, 369–379.

124. Miller, A. R., and R. A. Stewart: Perception of female physique. *Percept. mot. Skills*, 1968, **27**, 721–722.

125. Miller, H., and W. Wilson: Relation of sexual behaviors, values and conflict to avowed happiness and personal adjustment. *Psychol. Rep.*, 1968, **23**, 1075–1086.

126. Miller, H. L., and W. H. Rivenbark: Sexual differences in physical attractiveness as a determinant of heterosexual liking. *Psychol. Rep.*, 1970, **27**, 701–702.

127. Mirande, A. M.: Reference group theory and adolescent sexual behavior. *J. Marriage & Family*, 1968, **30**, 572–577.

128. Mosher, D. L., and H. J. Cross: Sex guilt and premarital sexual experiences of college students. *J. consult. clin. Psychol.*, 1971, **36**, 27–32.

129. Moss, J. J., F. Apolonio, and M. Jensen: The premarital dyad during the sixties. *J. Marriage & Family*, 1971, **33**, 50–69.

130. Moss, J. J., and R. Gingles: The relationship of personality to the incidence of early marriage. *Marriage fam. Living*, 1959, **21**, 373–377.

131. Murdock, P. H.: Birth order and age at marriage. *Brit. J. soc. clin. Psychol.*, 1966, **5**, 24–29.

132. Murstein, B. L.: Stimulus-value-role: A theory of marital choice. *J. Marriage & Family*, 1970, **32**, 465–481.

133. Mussen, P. H.: Long-term consequents of masculinity of interests in adolescence. *J. consult. Psychol.*, 1962, **26**, 435–440.

134. Mussen, P. H., J. J. Conger, and J. Kagan: *Child development and personality*, 3d ed. New York: Harper & Row, 1969.

135. *New York Times* Report: Youth views seen shifting on sex. June 22, 1969.

136. *New York Times* Report: Divorce rise tied to "20-year-slump." Dec. 9, 1970.

137. Noerk, E., and P. Becker: Attitudes of high school students toward future marriage and college education. *Family Coordinator*, 1971, **20**, 67–73.

138. Osofsky, H. J.: *The pregnant teen-ager*. Springfield, Ill.: Charles C Thomas, 1968.

139. Paris, B. L., and E. B. Luckey: A longitudinal study in marital satisfaction. *Sociol. soc. Res.*, 1966, **50**, 212–222.

140. Parker, E.: *The seven ages of woman*. Baltimore: Johns Hopkins. 1960.

141. Pavalko, R. M., and N. Nager: Contingencies of marriage to high-status men. *Soc. Forces*, 1968, **46**, 523–531.

142. Poffenberger, T.: Three papers on going steady. *Family Life Coordinator*, 1964, **13**, 7–13.

143. Pollis, C. A.: Dating involvement and patterns of idealization: A test of Waller's hypothesis. *J. Marriage & Family*, 1969, **31**, 765–771.

144. Pomeroy, W. B.: An analysis of questions on sex. *Psychol. Rec.*, 1960, **10**, 191–201.

145. Rappaport, A. F., D. Payne, and A. Steinmann: Perceptual differences between married and single college women for the concepts of self, ideal women and man's ideal women. *J. Marriage & Family*, 1970, **32**, 441–442.

146. Reevy, W. R.: Adolescent sexuality. In A. Ellis and A. Abarbanel (eds.), *The encyclopedia of sexual behavior*. Englewood Cliffs, N.J.: Hawthorn, 1961, pp. 52–67.

147. Reiss, I. L.: The sexual renaissance: A summary and analysis. *J. soc. Issues*, 1966, **22**, no. 2, 123–137.

148. Reiss, I. L.: Premarital sex as deviant behavior: An application of current approaches to deviance. *Amer. sociol. Rev.*, 1970, **35**, 78–87.

149. Reiss, P. J.: The trend in interfaith marriages. *J. sci. Stud. Relig.*, 1965, **5**, 64–67.

150. Remmers, H. H., and D. A. Radler: *The American teen-ager*. Indianapolis: Bobbs-Merrill, 1957.

151. Robinson, I. E., K. King, C. J. Dudley, and F. J. Cline: Change in sexual behavior and attitudes of college students. *Family Coordinator*, 1968, **17**, 119–123.

152. Rodgers, D. A., and F. J. Ziegler: Changes in sexual behavior consequent to use of noncoital procedures of contraception. *Psychosomat. Med.*, 1968, **30**, 495–505.

153. Roessler, R. T.: Sexuality and identity: Masculine differentiation and feminine constancy. *Adolescence*, 1971, **6**, 187–196.

154. Rosenberg, B., and J. Bensman: Sexual patterns in three ethnic subcultures of an American underclass. *Ann. Amer. Acad. pol. soc. Sci.*, 1968, **376**, 61–75.

155. Rosenberg, B. G., and B. Sutton-Smith: Sex-role identity and sibling composition. *J. genet. Psychol.*, 1971, **118**, 29–32.

156. Rosenkrantz, P., S. Vogel, H. Bee, I. Broverman, and D. M. Broverman: Sex-role stereotypes and self-concepts in college students. *J. consult. clin. Psychol.*, 1968, **32**, 287–295.

157. Rosenthal, J.: Divorce found twice as likely among those marrying young. *New York Times*, Oct. 11, 1971.

158. Rubin, I., and L. A. Kirkendall: *Sex in the adolescent years*. New York: Association Press, 1968.

159. Rubin, Z.: Measurement of romantic love. *J. Pers. soc. Psychol.*, 1970, **16**, 265–273.

160. Rudy, A. J.: Sex-role perceptions in early adolescence. *Adolescence*, 1968, **3**, 453–470.

161. Ryback, W.: Notes on crushes and hero-

worship of adolescents. *Psychiat. Quart. Suppl.,* 1969, **39,** 48-53.

162. Ryder, R. G., J. S. Kafka, and D. H. Olson: Separating and joining influences in courtship and early marriage. *Amer. J. Orthopsychiat.,* 1971, **41,** 450-464.

163. Sacks, S. R.: Widening the perspective on adolescent sex problems. *Adolescence,* 1966, **1,** 79-90.

164. Saucier, J. F.: Psychodynamics of interethnic marriage. *Canad. Psychol. Ass. J.,* 1970, **15,** 129-134.

165. Schab, F.: Some attitudes of the male undergraduate concerning the female undergraduate. *J. Home Econ.,* 1966, **58,** 204-205.

166. Schmidt, G., and V. Sigusch: Sex differences in response to psychosexual stimulation by films and slides. *J. sex Res.,* 1970, **6,** 268-283.

167. Schwartz, M. S.: A report on sex information knowledge of 87 lower class ninth grade boys. *Family Coordinator,* 1969, **18,** 361-371.

168. Scott, J. F.: The American college sorority: Its role in class and ethnic endogamy. *Amer. sociol. Rev.,* 1965, **30,** 514-527.

169. Semmens, J. P., and W. M. Lamers: *Teenage pregnancy.* Springfield, Ill.: Charles C Thomas, 1968.

170. Seward, G. H., and W. R. Larson: Adolescent concepts of social sex roles in the United States and the two Germanies. *Hum. Develpm.,* 1968, **11,** 217-248.

171. Sexton, P.: How the American boy is feminized. *Psychology Today,* 1970, **3,** Jan., pp. 23-29, 66-67.

172. Shainess, N.: Images of women: Past and present, overt and obscured. *Amer. J. Psychother.,* 1969, **23,** 77-97.

173. Shipman, G.: The psychodynamics of sex education. *Family Coordinator,* 1968, **17,** 3-12.

174. Shuttleworth, F. K.: A biosocial and developmental theory of male and female sexuality. *Marriage fam. Living,* 1959, **21,** 163-170.

175. Signell, K. A.: Prevention of teenage illegitimate pregnancy: A consultation approach to sex education. *Family Coordinator,* 1969, **18,** 222-225.

176. Skipper, J. K., and G. Nass: Dating behavior: A framework for analysis and an illustration. *J. Marriage & Family,* 1966, **28,** 412-420.

177. Smigel, E. O., and R. Seiden: The decline and fall of the double standard. *Ann. Amer. Acad. pol. soc. Sci.,* 1968, **376,** 6-17.

178. Snyder, E. C.: Attitudes: A study of homogamy and marital selectivity. *J. Marriage & Family,* 1964, **26,** 332-336.

179. Somerville, R. M.: Family life and sex education in the turbulent sixties. *J. Marriage & Family,* 1971, **33,** 11-35.

180. Sporakowski, M. J.: Marital preparedness, prediction and adjustment. *Family Coordinator,* 1968, **17,** 155-161.

181. Staton, T. F.: Sex education for adolescents. In J. F. Adams (ed.), *Understanding adolescence: Current developments in adolescent psychology.* Boston: Allyn and Bacon, 1968, pp. 248-271.

182. Stein, A. H., and J. Smithells: Age and sex differences in children's sex-role standards about achievement. *Develpm. Psychol.,* 1969, **1,** 252-259.

183. Steinmann, A., and D. J. Fox: Malefemale perceptions of the female role in the United States. *J. Psychol.,* 1966, **64,** 265-276.

184. Sterrett, J. E., and S. R. Bollman: Factors related to adolescents' expectations of marital roles. *Family Coordinator,* 1970, **19,** 353-356.

185. Stinnett, N.: An investigation of selected attitudes of college students toward marriage. *J. Home Econ.,* 1971, **63,** 33-37.

186. Stone, C. L.: Family recreation: A parental dilemma. *Family Life Coordinator,* 1963, **12,** 85-87.

187. Theodorson, G. A.: Romanticism and motivation to marry in the United States, Singapore, Burma, and India. *Soc. Forces,* 1965, **44,** 17-27.

188. Udry, J. R.: The influence of the ideal mate image on mate selection and mate perception. *J. Marriage & Family,* 1965, **27,** 477-482.

189. *U.S. News & World Report:* Woman's changing role in America. Sept. 8, 1969, pp. 44-46.

190. Vavrik, J., and A. P. Jurich: Self-concept and attitude toward acceptance of females: A note. *Family Coordinator,* 1971, **20,** 151-152.

191. Verinis, J. S.: Inhibition of humor enjoyment: Effects of sexual content and introversion-extraversion. *Psychol. Rep.,* 1970, **26,** 167-170.

192. Vincent, C. E.: Teen-age unwed mothers in American society. *J. soc. Issues,* 1966, **22,** no. 2, 22-33.

193. Vogel, S. R., I. K. Broverman, D. M. Broverman, F. E. Clarkson, and P. S. Rosenkrantz: Maternal employment and perception of sex-roles among college students. *Develpm. Psychol.,* 1970, **3,** 384-391.

194. Vroegh, K.: Masculinity and femininity in the elementary and junior high school years. *Develpm. Psychol.,* 1971, **4,** 254-261.

195. Vroegh, K.: The relationship of birth order and sex of siblings to gender role identity. *Develpm. Psychol.,* 1971, **4,** 407-411.

196. Wagman, M.: Interests and values of career and homemaking oriented women. *Personnel Guid. J.,* 1966, **44,** 794-801.

197. Walster, E., V. Aronson, D. Abrahams, and L. Rottmann: Importance of physical attractiveness in dating behavior. *J. Pers. soc. Psychol.,* 1966, **4,** 508-516.

198. Walters, P. A.: Promiscuity in adolescence. *Amer. J. Orthopsychiat.,* 1965, **35,** 670-675.

199. Ward, W. D.: Process of sex-role devel-

opment. *Develpm. Psychol.,* 1969, **1,** 163–168.

200. Webb, A. P.: Sex-role preferences and adjustment in early adolescents. *Child Develpm.,* 1963, **34,** 609–618.

201. Whalen, R. E.: Sexual motivation. *Psychol. Rev.,* 1966, **73,** 151–163.

202. Wiechmann, G. H., and A. L. Ellis: A study of the effects of "sex education" on premarital petting and coital behavior. *Family Coordinator,* 1969, **18,** 231–234.

203. Wiggins, J. S., N. Wiggins, and J. C. Conger: Correlates of heterosexual somatic preference. *J. Pers. soc. Psychol.,* 1968, **10,** 82–90.

204. Winick, C.: The Beige Epoch: Depolarization of sex roles in America. *Ann. Amer. Acad. pol. soc. Sci.,* 1968, **376,** 18–24.

205. Wittman, J. S.: Dating patterns of rural and urban Kentucky teenagers. *Family Coordinator,* 1971, **20,** 63–66.

206. Zucker, R. A.: Sex-role identity patterns and drinking behavior in adolescents. *Quart. J. Stud. Alcohol,* 1968, **29,** 868–884.

207. Zuk, G. H.: Sex-appropriate behavior in adolescence. *J. genet. Psychol.,* 1958, **93,** 15–32.

CHAPTER 14

1. Albrecht, R.: Intergeneration parent patterns. *J. Home Econ.,* 1954, **46,** 29–32.

2. Aldous, J.: A study of parental role functions. *Family Life Coordinator,* 1961, **10,** 43–44.

3. Alexander, C. N.: Ordinal position and social mobility. *Sociometry,* 1968, **31,** 285–293.

4. Altus, W. D.: Birth order and academic primogeniture. *J. Pers. soc. Psychol.,* 1965, **2,** 872–876.

5. Arasteh, J. D.: Parenthood: Some antecedents and consequences: A preliminary survey of the mental health literature. *J. genet. Psychol.,* 1971, **118,** 179–202.

6. Arnhoff, F. N., H. V. Leon, and I. Lorge: Cross-cultural acceptance of stereotypes toward aging. *J. soc. Psychol.,* 1964, **63,** 41–58.

7. Baer, D. J., and J. M. Katkin: Limitation of smoking by sons and daughters who smoke and smoking behavior of parents. *J. genet. Psychol.,* 1971, **118,** 293–296.

8. Bailyn, L.: Career and family orientations of husbands and wives in relation to marital happiness. *Hum. Relat.,* 1970, **23,** 97–113.

9. Baker, F., and G. M. St. L. O'Brien: Birth order and fraternity affiliation. *J. soc. Psychol.,* 1969, **78,** 41–43.

10. Baker, L. G.: The personal and social adjustments of the never-married woman. *J. Marriage & Family,* 1968, **30,** 473–479.

11. Barclay, A., and D. R. Cusumano: Father absence, cross-sex identity, and field-dependent behavior in male adolescents. *Child Develpm.,* 1967, **38,** 243–250.

12. Bath, J. A., and E. C. Lewis: Attitudes of young females toward some areas of parent-adolescent conflict. *J. genet. Psychol.,* 1962, **100,** 241–253.

13. Bealer, R. C., F. K. Willits, and P. R. Maida: The rebellious youth subculture. *Children,* 1964, **11,** 43–48.

14. Berger, B. M.: Teen-agers are an American invention. *New York Times,* June 13, 1965.

15. Berger, B. M.: The new stage of American man: Almost endless adolescence. *New York Times,* Nov. 2, 1969.

16. Bienvenu, M. L.: Measurement of parent-adolescent communication. *Family Coordinator,* 1969, **18,** 117–121.

17. Blood, R. O.: Long-range causes and consequences of the employment of married women. *J. Marriage & Family,* 1965, **27,** 43–47.

18. Bossard, J. H. S., and E. S. Boll: *The sociology of child development,* 4th ed. New York: Harper & Row, 1966.

19. Bowerman, C. E., and G. H. Elder: Variations in adolescent perception of family power structure. *Amer. sociol. Rev.,* 1964, **29,** 551–567.

20. Bowerman, C. E., and D. P. Irish: Some relationships of stepchildren to their parents. *Marriage fam. Living,* 1962, **24,** 113–121.

21. Bowerman, C. E., and J. W. Kinch: Changes in family and peer orientation of children between the fourth and tenth grades. *Soc. Forces,* 1959, **37,** 206–211.

22. Bradley, R. W., and M. P. Sanborn: Ordinal position of high school students identified by their teachers as superior. *J. educ. Psychol.,* 1969, **60,** 41–45.

23. Bragg, W. E.: Academic primogeniture and sex-role contrast of the second born. *J. indiv. Psychol.,* 1970, **28,** 196–199.

24. Breznitz, S., and S. Kugelmass: The perception of parents by adolescents. *Hum. Relat.,* 1965, **18,** 103–113.

25. Brittain, C. V.: An exploration of the bases of peer-compliance and parent-compliance in adolescence. *Adolescence,* 1967, **2,** 445–458.

26. Bronson, W. C., E. S. Katten, and N. Livson: Patterns of authority and affection in two generations. *J. abnorm. soc. Psychol.,* 1959, **58,** 143–152.

27. Burchinal, L. G.: Characteristics of adolescents from unbroken, broken, and reconstituted families. *J. Marriage & Family,* 1964, **26,** 44–51.

28. Chorost, S. B.: Parental child-rearing atti-

tudes and their correlates in adolescent hostility. *Genet. Psychol. Monogr.,* 1962, **66,** 49–90.

29. Coleman, J. S.: *The adolescent society.* New York: Free Press, 1961.

30. Cooper, J. B., and H. H. Lewis: Parent evaluation as related to social ideology and academic achievement. *J. genet. Psychol.,* 1962, **101,** 135–143.

31. Costin, F.: Effects of child psychology on students' perceptions of their parents' attitudes toward parent-child relationships. *Child Develpm.,* 1963, **34,** 227–236.

32. Cottle, T. J.: Family perceptions, sex role identify and the prediction of school performance. *Educ. psychol. Measmt.,* 1968, **28,** 861–886.

33. Crosby, J. F.: The effect of family life education on the values and attitudes of adolescents. *Family Coordinator,* 1971, **20,** 137–140.

34. Crowther, B.: Poor Mom. *New York Times,* Apr. 22, 1962.

35. Cummings, E., and D. M. Schneider: Sibling solidarity: A property of American kinship. *Amer. Anthropologist,* 1961, **63,** 498–505.

36. Cutright, P.: Income and family events: Marital stability. *J. Marriage & Family,* 1971, **33,** 291–306.

37. Dahlem, N. W.: Young Americans' reported perceptions of their parents. *J. Psychol.,* 1970, **74,** 187–194.

38. deLint, J. E. E.: A note on Smart's study of birth rank and affiliation in male university students. *J. Psychol.,* 1966, **62,** 177–178.

39. Despert, J. L.: *Children of divorce.* Garden City, N.Y.: Doubleday, 1953.

40. Dreger, R. M., and A. Sweetland: Traits of fatherhood as revealed by the factor-analysis of a parent attitude scale. *J. genet. Psychol.,* 1960, **96,** 115–122.

41. Droppleman, L. F., and E. S. Schaefer: Boys' and girls' reports of maternal and paternal behavior. *J. abnorm. soc. Psychol.,* 1963, **67,** 648–654.

42. Duncan, L. W., and P. W. Fitzgerald: Increasing the parent-child communication through counselor-parent conferences. *Personnel Guid. J.,* 1969, **47,** 514–517.

43. Duvall, E. M.: Teen-agers and the generation gap. *Family Coordinator,* 1969, **18,** 284–286.

44. Elder, G. H.: Structural variations in the child rearing relationship. *Sociometry,* 1962, **25,** 241–262.

45. Ellis, D., and F. I. Nye: The nagging parent. *Family Life Coordinator,* 1959, **8,** 8–10.

46. Esty, J. F.: Early and current parent-child relationships perceived by college student leaders and non-leaders. *Dissert. Abstr.,* 1968, **29** (3–B), 1169–1170.

47. Farber, B., and W. C. Jenné: Interaction with retarded siblings and life goals of children. *Marriage fam. Living,* 1963, **25,** 96–98.

48. Farley, F. H., R. Hatch, P. Murphy, and K. Miller: Sibling structure and masculinity-femininity in male adolescents. *Adolescence,* 1971, **6,** 441–450.

49. Farley, J.: Maternal employment and child behavior. *Cornell J. soc. Behav.,* 1968, **3,** 58–71.

50. Fitzgerald, M. P.: Sex differences in the perception of the parental role for middle and working class adolescents. *J. clin. Psychol.,* 1966, **22,** 15–16.

51. Foster, J. E.: Father images: Television and ideal. *J. Marriage & Family,* 1964, **26,** 353–355.

52. Frankel, E.: Characteristics of working and non-working mothers among intellectually gifted high and low achievers. *Personnel Guid. J.,* 1964, **42,** 776–780.

53. Freud, S.: *The standard edition of the complete psychological works of Sigmund Freud.* London: Hogarth, 1953–1962.

54. Friedenberg, E. Z.: The generation gap. *Ann. Amer. Acad. pol. soc. Sci.,* 1969, **382,** 32–42.

55. Fromm, E.: Mother. *Psychology Today,* 1971, **4,** March, pp. 74–77.

56. George, E. L., and M. Thomas: A comparative study of children of employed mothers and unemployed mothers. *Psychol. Studies,* 1967, **12,** 32–38.

57. Gilbert, E.: Allowance, chores, cars, dates are rated high on conflict list. *New York Times,* Mar. 1, 1963.

58. Glick, P. C., and A. J. Norton: Frequency, duration, and probability of marriage and divorce. *J. Marriage & Family,* 1971, **33,** 307–317.

59. Glueck, S., and E. T. Glueck: *Family environment and delinquency.* Boston: Houghton Mifflin, 1962.

60. Goode, W. J.: *After divorce.* New York: Free Press, 1956.

61. Greene, R. L., and J. R. Clark: Adler's theory of birth order. *Psychol. Rep.,* 1970, **26,** 387–390.

62. Grinder, R. E., and J. C. Spector: Sex differences in adolescents' perception of parental resource control. *J. genet. Psychol.,* 1965, **106,** 337–344.

63. Gustav, A.: Ritual in families of dissident and non-dissident students. *Psychol. Rep.,* 1971, **28,** 563–567.

64. Hallowitz, D., and B. Stulberg: The vicious cycle of parent-child relationship breakdown. *Soc. Casewk.,* 1959, **40,** 268–275.

65. Hammer, M.: Preference for a male child: Cultural factor. *J. indiv. Psychol.,* 1970, **28,** 54–56.

66. Hearn, J. L., D. C. Charles, and L. Wolins: Life history antecedents of measured personality variables. *J. genet. Psychol.,* 1965, **107,** 99–110.

67. Heer, D. M.: Husband and wife perceptions of family power structure. *Marriage fam. Living,* 1962, **24,** 65–67.

68. Heilbrun, A. B.: Social value–social behavior inconsistency and early signs of psychopathology in adolescence. *Child Develpm.*, 1963, **34**, 187–194.

69. Heilbrun, A. B.: Perceived maternal child rearing practices and subsequent deviance in adolescence. *Adolescence, 1966,* **1**, 152–179.

70. Heilbrun, A. B.: Parental identification and the patterning of vocational interests in college males and females. *J. counsel. Psychol.*, 1969, **16**, 342–347.

71. Heilbrun, A. B., and D. K. Fromme: Parental identification of late adolescents and level of adjustment: The importance of parent-model attributes, ordinal position and sex of the child. *J. genet. Psychol.*, 1965, **107**, 49–59.

72. Heise, D. R., and E. P. M. Roberts: The development of role knowledge. *Genet. Psychol. Monogr.*, 1970, **82**, 83–115.

73. Hess, R. D., and I. Goldblatt: The status of adolescents in American society: A problem in social identity. *Child Develpm.*, 1957, **28**, 459–468.

74. Ianni, F. A. J.: The Italo-American teenagers. *Ann. Amer. Acad. pol. soc. Sci.*, 1961, **338**, 70–78.

75. Irish, D. P.: Sibling interaction: A neglected aspect in family life research. *Soc. Forces*, 1964, **42**, 279–288.

76. Jackson, J. K., and H. S. Ripley: Broken homes and attempted and completed suicide. *Arch. gen. Psychiat.*, 1965, **12**, 213–216.

77. Jacobs, J., and J. D. Teicher: Broken homes and social isolation in attempted suicide of adolescents. *Int. J. soc. Psychiat.*, 1967, **13**, 139–149.

78. Johannis, T. B., and J. M. Rollins: Teenagers' perception of family decision making about social activity. *Family Life Coordinator*, 1960, **8**, 59–60.

79. Joseph, T. P.: Adolescents: From the views of an informal adolescent group. *Genet. Psychol. Monogr.*, 1969, **79**, 3–88.

80. Kahana, B., and E. Kahana: Grandparenthood from the perspective of the developing grandchild. *Develpm. Psychol.*, 1970, **3**, 98–105.

81. Kandel, D., and G. S. Lesser: Parent-adolescent relationships and adolescent independence in the United States and Denmark. *J. Marriage & Family*, 1969, **31**, 348–358.

82. Katz, H. A., and J. B. Rotter: Interpersonal trust scores of college students and their parents. *Child Develpm.*, 1969, **40**, 657–661.

83. Kavanaugh, G.: The influence of a stepmother's motivation in marriage upon her stepchild's symptom formation. *Smith Coll. Stud. soc. Wk.*, 1961, **32**, 65–66.

84. Kennedy, C. E.: Patterns of parent-student communication. *J. Home Econ.*, 1971, **63**, 513–520.

85. King, K., J. McIntyre, and L. J. Axelson: Adolescents' views of maternal employment as a threat to the marital relationship. *J. Marriage & Family*, 1968, **30**, 633–637.

86. Kohn, M. L., and E. E. Carroll: Social class and allocation of parental responsibilities. *Sociometry*, 1960, **23**, 372–392.

87. Kopf, K. E.: Family variables and school adjustment of eighth-grade father-absent boys. *Family Coordinator*, 1970, **19**, 145–150.

88. Landers, D. M.: Sibling-sex status and ordinal position effects of females' sport participation and interests. *J. soc. Psychol.*, 1970, **80**, 247–248.

89. Landis, J. T.: A comparison of children from divorced and non-divorced unhappy marriages. *Family Life Coordinator*, 1962, **11**, 61–65.

90. Landis, J. T.: A re-examination of the role of the father as an index of family integration. *Marriage fam. Living*, 1962, **24**, 122–128.

91. Landis, J. T.: Social correlates of divorce and nondivorce among the unhappy married. *Marriage fam. Living*, 1963, **25**, 178–180.

92. Lazar, E. A., and C. Klein: What makes parents repulsive. *New York Times*, Feb. 7, 1965.

93. Levin, P. L.: Putting down father. *New York Times*, Mar. 21, 1965.

94. Lewis, J. M.: Family homeostasis: A view from an adolescent service. *Adolescence*, 1968–1969, **3**, 447–452.

95. Longstreth, L. E., and R. E. Rice: Perceptions of parental behavior and identification with parents by three groups of boys differing in school adjustment. *J. educ. Psychol.*, 1964, **55**, 144–151.

96. Maccoby, E. E.: Children and working mothers. *Children*, 1958, **5**, 83–89.

97. Mandelbaum, A.: Youth and family. *Menninger Quart.*, 1969, **23**, 4–11.

98. Marcus, I. M.: Family interaction in adolescents with learning difficulties. *Adolescence*, 1966, **1**, 261–271.

99. Martineau, P.: Adulthood in the adolescent perspective. *Adolescence*, 1966, **1**, 272–280.

100. Masters, W. H., and V. E. Johnson: *Human sexual response*. Boston: Little, Brown, 1966.

101. Maxwell, P. H., R. Connor, and J. Walters: Family member perception of parent role performance. *Merrill-Palmer Quart.*, 1961, **7**, 31–37.

102. McArthur, A.: Developmental tasks and parent-adolescent conflict. *Marriage fam. Living*, 1962, **24**, 189–191.

103. McGahey, C., and M. J. Sporakowski: Intergenerational attitudes toward child bearing and child rearing. *J. Home Econ.*, 1972, **64**, 27–37.

104. McIntire, W. G., and D. C. Payne: The relationship of family functioning to school achievement. *Family Coordinator*, 1971, **20**, 265–268.

105. Mead, M.: The changing American family. *Children*, 1963, **10**, 173–174.

106. Medinnus, G. R.: Adolescents' self-accept-

ance and perceptions of their parents. *J. consult. Psychol.*, 1965, **29**, 150–154.

107. Meissner, W. W.: Parental interaction of the adolescent boy. *J. genet. Psychol.*, 1965, **107**, 225–233.

108. Murphy, E. B., E. Silber, C. V. Coelho, D. A. Hamburg, and I. Greenberg: Development of autonomy and parent-child interaction in late adolescence. *Amer. J. Orthopsychiat.*, 1963, **33**, 643–652.

109. Mussen, P. H., H. B. Young, R. Gaddini, and L. Morante: The influence of father-son relationships on adolescent personality and attitudes. *J. child Psychol. Psychiat.*, 1963, **4**, 3–16.

110. Nelson, D. D.: A study of personality adjustment among adolescent children with working and nonworking mothers. *J. educ. Res.*, 1971, **64**, 328–330.

111. Nelson, H. Y., and P. R. Goldman: Attitudes of high school students and young adults toward the gainful employment of married women. *Family Coordinator*, 1969, **18**, 251–255.

112. Neugarten, B. L., and K. K. Weinstein: The changing American grandparent. *J. Marriage & Family*, 1964, **26**, 199–204.

113. *New York Times* Report: Few teen-age marriages turn out well, survey shows. Apr. 14, 1965.

114. Nikally, A. G.: Maternal indulgence and neglect and maladjustment in adolescence. *J. clin. Psychol.*, 1967, **23**, 148–150.

115. Nye, F. I., J. Carlson, and G. Garrett: Family size, interaction, affect and stress. *J. Marriage & Family*, 1970, **32**, 216–226.

116. Orden, S. R., and N. M. Bradburn: Working wives and marriage happiness. *Amer. J. Sociol.*, 1969, **74**, 392–407.

117. Packard, V.: *The status seekers*. New York: Pocket Books, 1961.

118. Parker, E.: *The seven ages of woman*. Baltimore: Johns Hopkins, 1960.

119. Peck, R. F.: Family patterns correlated with adolescent personality structure. *J. abnorm. soc. Psychol.*, 1958, **57**, 347–350.

120. Peck, R. F., and R. J. Havighurst: *The psychology of character development*. New York: Wiley, 1962.

121. Perry, J. B.: The mother substitute of employed mothers: An exploratory inquiry. *Marriage fam. Living*, 1961, **23**, 361–367.

122. Perry, J. B., and E. H. Pfuhl: Adjustment of children in "solo" and "remarriage" homes. *Marriage fam. Living*, 1963, **25**, 221–223.

123. Pollock, O.: Some challenges to the American family. *Children*, 1964, **11**, 19–20.

124. Rallings, E. M.: Problems of communication in family living. *Family Coordinator*, 1969, **18**, 289–291.

125. Reddy, N. Y.: A study of the relationship between ordinal position of adolescents and their adjustment. *Psychol. Stud.*, 1967, **12**, 91–100.

126. Reiss, P. J.: The extended kinship system: Correlates of and attitudes on frequency of interaction. *Marriage fam. Living*, 1962, **24**, 333–339.

127. Robey, A., R. J. Rosenwald, J. E. Snell, and R. E. Lee: The runaway girl: A reaction to family stress. *Amer. J. Orthopsychiat.*, 1964, **34**, 262–267.

128. Rode, A.: Perceptions of parental behavior among alienated adolescents. *Adolescence*, 1971, **6**, 19–38.

129. Rodman, H., F. R. Nichols, and P. Voydanoff: Lower-class attitudes toward "deviant" family patterns: A cross-cultural study. *J. Marriage & Family*, 1969, **31**, 315–321.

130. Rosenberg, B. G., and B. Sutton-Smith: Family interaction effects on masculinity-femininity. *J. Pers. soc. Psychol.*, 1968, **8**, 117–120.

131. Rossmann, J. E., and D. P. Campbell: Why college-trained mothers work. *Personnel Guid. J.*, 1965, **43**, 986–992.

132. Ryan, M. S.: *Clothing: A study in human behavior*. New York: Holt, 1966.

133. Sampson, E. E.: Birth order, need achievement and conformity. *J. abnorm. soc. Psychol.*, 1962, **64**, 155–159.

134. Schab, F.: Adolescent attitudes about parental control. *J. Home Econ.*, 1970, **62**, 54–56.

135. Schachter, S.: Birth order, eminence and higher education. *Amer. sociol. Rev.*, 1963, **28**, 757–768.

136. Schachter, S.: Birth order and sociometric choice. *J. abnorm. soc. Psychol.*, 1964, **68**, 453–456.

137. Schaefer, E. S., and N. Bayley: Consistency of maternal behavior from infancy to preadolescence. *J. abnorm. soc. Psychol.*, 1960, **61**, 1–6.

138. Schaimberg, L.: Some sociocultural factors in adolescent-parent conflict: A cross-cultural comparison of selected cultures. *Adolescence*, 1969, **4**, 333–360.

139. Sennett, R.: Break up the family. *New York Times*, July 19, 1971.

140. Skipper, J. K., J. K. Hadden, and G. D. Tucker: Three dimensions of parental kinship terminology: Situation, subgroup identity, and sentiment. *J. Marriage & Family*, 1968, **30**, 592–596.

141. Slocum, W. L.: Some factors associated with happiness in unbroken homes. *Family Life Coordinator*, 1958, **6**, 35–39.

142. Smelser, W. T., and L. H. Stewart: Where are the siblings? A reevaluation of the relationship between birth order and college attendance. *Sociometry*, 1968, **31**, 294–303.

143. Smith, T. E.: Social class and attitudes toward fathers. *Sociol. soc. Res.*, 1969, **53**, 217–226.

144. Smith, T. E.: Some bases for parental influence upon late adolescents: An application of a social power model. *Adolescence*, 1970, **5**, 323–338.

145. Steiner, G. J.: Parent-teen education: An

exercise in communication. *Family Coordinator,* 1970, **19,** 213–218.

146. Stinnett, N.: An investigation of selected attitudes of college students toward marriage. *J. Home Econ.,* 1971, **63,** 33–37.

147. Stinnett, N., and J. E. Montgomery: Youth's perceptions of marriages of older persons. *J. Marriage & Family,* 1968, **30,** 392–396.

148. Stone, C. L.: Three-generation influences on teen-agers' conceptions of family culture patterns and parent-child relationships. *Marriage fam. Living,* 1962, **24,** 287–288.

149. Stone, C. L.: Family recreation: A parental dilemma. *Family Life Coordinator,* 1963, **12,** 85–87.

150. Straus, M. A.: Conjugal power structure and adolescent personality. *Marriage fam. Living,* 1962, **24,** 17–25.

151. Strauss, B. V.: The dynamics of ordinal position effects. *Quart. J. child Behav.,* 1951, **3,** 133–145.

152. Templeton, J. A.: The influence of family size on some aspects of teen-agers' attitudes, behavior, and perceptions of home life. *Family Life Coordinator,* 1962, **11,** 51–57.

153. *Time* Report: The command generation. July 29, 1966, pp. 50–54.

154. Tomeh, A. K.: Birth order and friendship associations. *J. Marriage & Family,* 1970, **32,** 360–369.

155. Troll, L. E.: The family in later life: A decade review, *J. Marriage & Family,* 1971, **33,** 263–290.

156. *U.S. News & World Report:* Why young people "go bad." Apr. 26, 1965, pp. 56–62.

157. *U.S. News & World Report:* How women's role in U.S. is changing. May 30, 1966, pp. 58–60.

158. Utech, D. A., and K. L. Hoving: Parents and peers as competing influences in the decisions of children of different ages. *J. soc. Psychol.,* 1969, **78,** 267–274.

159. Vander Veen, F., and H. W. Haberland: Family satisfaction and congruence of family concepts among adolescents and their parents. *Proc. Annu. Convent. APA.,* 1971, **6,** pt. 1, 147–148.

160. VanManen, G. C.: Father roles and adolescent socialization. *Adolescence,* 1969, **3,** 139–152.

161. Vogel, W., and C. G. Lauterbach: Relationships between normal and disturbed sons' percepts of their parents' behavior and personality attributes of the parents and sons. *J. clin. Psychol.,* 1963, **19,** 52–56.

162. Wakefield, W. M.: Awareness, affection and perceived similarity in the parent-child relationship. *J. genet. Psychol.,* 1970, **117,** 91–97.

163. Walters, J., and N. Stinnett: Parent-child relationships: A decade review of research. *J. Marriage & Family,* 1971, **33,** 70–111.

164. Warnath, C. F.: The relation of family cohesiveness and adolescent independence to social effectiveness. *Marriage fam. Living,* 1955, **17,** 346–348.

165. Westley, W. A., and N. B. Epstein: Family structure and emotional health: A case study approach. *Marriage fam. Living,* 1960, **22,** 25–27.

166. Won, G. Y. M., D. S. Yamamura, and K. Ikeda: The relation of communication with parents and peers to deviant behavior of youth. *J. Marriage & Family,* 1969, **31,** 43–47.

167. Wyatt, F.: A clinical view of parenthood. *Bull. Menninger Clin.,* 1971, **35,** 167–181.

168. Yourglich, A.: Explorations in sociological study of sibling systems. *Family Life Coordinator,* 1964, **13,** 91–94.

169. Zunich, M.: Attitudes of lower-class families. *J. soc. Psychol.,* 1964, **63,** 367–371.

CHAPTER 15

1. Abbott, W. L., and J. L. Bruning: Given names: A neglected social variable. *Psychol. Rec.,* 1970, **20,** 527–533.

2. Abu-Laban, B.: Self-conception and appraisal by others: A study of community leaders. *Sociol. soc. Res.,* 1963, **48,** 32–37.

3. Adams, H. L., E. P. Mason, and D. F. Blood: Personality characteristics of American and English, bright and average college freshmen. *Psychol. Rep.,* 1970, **26,** 831–834.

4. Aiken, L. R.: The relationships of dress to selected measures of personality in undergraduate women. *J. soc. Psychol.,* 1963, **59,** 119–128.

5. Aldridge, J. W.: In the country of the young: Part II. *Harper's Mag.,* November 1969, pp. 93–107.

6. Allen, M. G.: Psychoanalytic theory of infant gratification and adult personality. *J. genet. Psychol.,* 1964, **104,** 265–274.

7. Allport, G. W.: *Pattern and growth in personality.* New York: Holt, 1961.

8. Amatora, Sister M.: Developmental trends in pre-adolescence and in early adolescence in self evaluation. *J. genet. Psychol.,* 1959, **91,** 89–97.

9. Ames, L. B.: Longitudinal survey of child Rorschach responses: Older subjects aged 10 to 16 years. *Genet. Psychol. Monogr.,* 1960, **62,** 185–229.

10. Argyle, M., and R. McHenry: Do spectacles really affect judgments of intelligence? *Brit. J. soc. clin. Psychol.,* 1971, **10,** 27–29.

11. Arsenian, S.: Change in evaluative attitudes during twenty-five years. *J. appl. Psychol.,* 1970, **54,** 302–304.

12. Backman, C. W., P. F. Secord, and J. R.

Pierce: Resistance to change in the self-concept as a function of consensus among significant others. *Sociometry*, 1963, **26**, 102–111.

13. Bailey, R. C.: Self-concept differences in low and high achieving students. *J. clin. Psychol.*, 1971, **27**, 188–191.

14. Baker, J. W., and A. Holzworth: Social histories of successful and unsuccessful children. *Child Develpm.*, 1961, **32**, 135–149.

15. Baldwin, D. C., and M. L. Barnes: Patterns of motivation in families seeking orthodontic treatment. *Int. Ass. dental Res. Abstr.*, 1966, **44**, 142.

16. Baron, R. M., A. R. Bass, and P. M. Vietze: Type and frequency of praise as determinants of favorability of self-image: An experiment in a field setting. *J. Pers.*, 1971, **39**, 493–511.

17. Barrett-Lennard, G. T.: The mature person. *Ment. Hyg., N.Y.*, 1962, **46**, 98–102.

18. Becker, G.: Situational discrimination in repressor-type and sensitized-type approval seekers and the birth order by subject sex interaction. *J. soc. Psychol.*, 1970, **82**, 81–97.

19. Bell, A. P.: Role modelship and interaction in adolescence and young adulthood. *Develpm. Psychol.*, 1970, **2**, 123–128.

20. Bennett, E. M.: A socio-cultural interpretation of maladjustive behavior. *J. soc. Psychol.*, 1953, **37**, 19–26.

21. Bennett, E. M., and L. R. Cohen: Men and women: Personality patterns and contrasts. *Genet. Psychol. Monogr.*, 1959, **59**, 101–155.

22. Berdie, R. F.: Personality changes from high school entrance to college matriculation. *J. counsel. Psychol.*, 1968, **15**, 376–380.

23. Blain, M. J., and M. Ramirez: Increasing sociometric rank, meaningfulness and discriminability of children's names through reinforcement and interaction. *Child Develpm.*, 1968, **39**, 949–955.

24. Blank, L., A. A. Sugerman, and L. Roosa: Body concern, body image and nudity. *Psychol. Rep.*, 1968, **23**, 963–968.

25. Bloom, R.: Dimensions of mental health in adolescent boys. *J. clin. Psychol.*, 1970, **26**, 35–38.

26. Boshier, R.: Attitudes toward self and one's proper names. *J. indiv. Psychol.*, 1968, **24**, 63–66.

27. Boshier, R.: Self-esteem and first names in children. *Psychol. Rep.*, 1968, **22**, 762.

28. Boshier, R.: Self-regarding attitudes: A bibliography. *Psychol. Rep.*, 1970, **26**, 218.

29. Bossard, J. H. S., and E. S. Boll: *The sociology of child development*, 4th ed. New York: Harper & Row, 1966.

30. Brehm, M. L., and K. W. Back: Self-image and attitudes toward drugs. *J. Pers.*, 1968, **36**, 299–314.

31. Brill, N. Q., E. Crumpton, and H. N. Grayson: Personality factors in marihuana use. *Arch. gen. Psychiat.*, 1971, **24**, 163–165.

32. Bruch, H.: Developmental obesity and schizophrenia. *Psychiatry*, 1958, **21**, 65–70.

33. Bühler, C.: School as a phase of human life. *Education*, 1952, **73**, 219–222.

34. Cartwright, R. D.: Self-conception patterns of college students and adjustment to college life. *J. counsel. Psychol.*, 1963, **10**, 47–52.

35. Catton, W. R.: What's in a name? A study of role inertia. *J. Marriage & Family*, 1969, **31**, 15–18.

36. Cavior, N., and P. R. Dokecki: Physical attractiveness and self-concept: A test of Mead's hypothesis. *Proc. Annu. Convent. APA*, 1971, **6**, pt. 1, 319–320.

37. Christopherson, V. A.: Role modifications of the disabled male. *Amer. J. Nurs.*, 1968, **68**, 290–293.

38. Cobliner, W. G.: Social factors in mental disorders: A contribution to the etiology of mental illness. *Genet. Psychol. Monogr.*, 1963, **67**, 151–215.

39. Cohen, H. A., and R. Miller: Mobility as a factor in adolescent identity problems. *Psychol. Rep.*, 1969, **25**, 775–778.

40. Coleman, J. S.: *The adolescent society*. New York: Free Press, 1961.

41. Combs, A. W.: New horizons in field research: The self concept. *Educ. Leadership*, 1958, **15**, 315–319, 328.

42. Constantinople, A.: An Eriksonian measure of personality development in college students. *Develpm. Psychol.*, 1969, **1**, 357–372.

43. Constantinople, A.: Some correlates of average level of happiness among college students. *Develpm. Psychol.*, 1970, **2**, 447.

44. Corsini, R. J.: Appearance and criminality. *Amer. J. Sociol.*, 1959, **65**, 49–51.

45. Cruickshank, W. M., and G. O. Johnson: *Education of exceptional children and youth*, 2d ed. Englewood Cliffs, N.J.: Prentice-Hall, 1967.

46. Dale, R. R.: The happiness of pupils in co-educational and single-sex grammar schools: A comparative assessment. *Brit. J. educ. Psychol.*, 1966, **36**, 39–47.

47. Davis, R. E., and R. A. Ruiz: Infant feeding method and adolescent personality. *Amer. J. Psychiat.*, 1965, **122**, 673–678.

48. Dean, D. G.: Romanticism and emotional maturity. *Marriage fam. Living*, 1961, **23**, 44–45.

49. DeJung, J. E., and E. F. Gardner: The accuracy of self-role perception: A developmental study. *J. exp. Educ.*, 1962, **31**, 27–41.

50. DeLeon, P. H., J. H. DeLeon, and P. J. Swihart: Relation of accuracy of self-perception and peer ratings. *Percept. mot. Skills*, 1969, **29**, 966.

51. Deo, P., and S. Sharma: Self-ideal discrepancy and school achievement. *Adolescence*, 1970, **5**, 353–359.

52. Dibiase, W. J., and L. A. Hjelle: Body-image stereotypes and body-type preferences among

male college students. *Percept. mot. Skills,* 1968, **27,** 1143–1146.

53. Dien, D. S., and E. W. Vinacke: Self-concept and parental identification of young adults with mixed Caucasian-Japanese parentage. *J. abnorm. soc. Psychol.,* 1964, **69,** 463–466.

54. Douce, P. D. M.: Selected aspects of personality related to social acceptance and clothing oriented variables. *Dissert. Abstr.,* 1970, **30** (8–B), 3730.

55. Douvan, E.: Independence and identity in adolescence. *Children,* 1957, **4,** 186–190.

56. Dunbar, F.: Homeostasis during puberty. *Amer. J. Psychiat.,* 1958, **114,** 673–682.

57. Eismann, E. P.: Ego ideal maturation in late adolescence. *Dissert. Abstr.,* 1968, **28** (10–B), 4294.

58. Elkind, D.: Egocentrism in adolescence. *Child Develpm.,* 1967, **38,** 1025–1034.

59. Elton, C. F., and H. A. Rose: The face of change. *J. counsel. Psychol.,* 1968, **15,** 372–375.

60. Engel, M., G. Marsden, and S. Woodaman: Orientation to work in children. *Amer. J. Orthopsychiat.,* 1968, **38,** 137–143.

61. Eysenck, H. J.: Relation between intelligence and personality. *Percept. mot. Skills,* 1971, **32,** 637–638.

62. Fletcher, R., and L. Dowell: Selected personality characteristics of high school athletes and nonathletes. *J. Psychol.,* 1971, **77,** 39–41.

63. Freedman, A. M., and L. Bender: When the childhood schizophrenic grows up. *Ment. Hyg., N.Y.,* 1957, **27,** 553–565.

64. Freedman, M. B., and C. Bereiter: A longitudinal study of personality development in college alumnae. *Merrill-Palmer Quart.,* 1963, **9,** 295–302.

65. Friedenberg, E. Z.: *The vanishing adolescent.* Boston: Beacon Press, 1959.

66. Gergen, K. J.: *The concept of self.* New York: Holt, 1971.

67. Gerjuoy, H., and B. S. Aaronson: Multidimensional scaling of terms used to describe personality. *Psychol. Rep.,* 1970, **26,** 3–8.

68. Glöckel, H.: A comparative study of the self-ideal in youth. *Child Develpm. Abstr.,* 1960, **34,** no. 649.

69. Glueck, S., and E. T. Glueck: *Physique and delinquency.* New York: Harper & Row, 1956.

70. Good, E. H., and E. A. Kelley: Teenage boys' perceptions of the role clothing plays in the occupational world. *J. Home Econ.,* 1971, **63,** 332–336.

71. Goodman, N.: Adolescent norms and behavior: Organization and conformity. *Merrill-Palmer Quart.,* 1969, **15,** 199–211.

72. Gording, E. J., and E. Match: Personality changes of certain contact lens patients. *J. Amer. optomet. Ass.,* 1968, **39,** 266–269.

73. Gottesman, I. L.: Heritability of personality. *Psychol. Monogr.,* 1963, **77,** no. 9.

74. Guerney, B., and J. L. Burton: Relationships among anxiety and self, typical peer, and ideal percepts of college women. *J. soc. Psychol.,* 1963, **61,** 335–344.

75. Haller, A. O., and S. Thomas: Personality correlates of the socioeconomic status of adolescent males. *Sociometry,* 1962, **25,** 398–404.

76. Hamid, P. N.: Style of dress as a perceptual cue in impression formation. *Percept. mot. Skills,* 1968, **26,** 904–906.

77. Hamilton, J., and J. Warden: The student's role in a high school community and his clothing behavior. *J. Home Econ.,* 1966, **58,** 789–791.

78. Hammer, E. F.: Personality patterns in young creative artists. *Adolescence,* 1966, **1,** 327–350.

79. Harrow, M., D. A. Fox, K. L. Markhus, R. Stillman, and C. B. Hallowell: Changes in adolescents' self-concepts and their parents' perceptions during psychiatric hospitalization. *J. ment. nerv. Dis.,* 1968, **147,** 252–259.

80. Hartman, A. A.: Name styles in relation to personality. *J. gen. Psychol.,* 1958, **59,** 289–294.

81. Hartman, A. A., R. C. Nicolay, and J. Hurley: Unique personal names as a social adjustment factor. *J. soc. Psychol.,* 1968, **75,** 107–110.

82. Hartnagel, T. F.: Father absence and self-conception among lower class white and Negro boys. *Soc. Probl.,* 1970, **18,** 162–163.

83. Harvey, O. J., H. H. Kelley, and M. M. Shapiro: Reactions to unfavorable evaluations of the self made by other persons. *J. Pers.,* 1957, **25,** 393–411.

84. Helson, R.: Personality characteristics and developmental history of creative college women. *Genet. Psychol. Monogr.,* 1967, **76,** 205–256.

85. Hess, A. L., and H. L. Bradshaw: Positiveness of self-concept and ideal self-concept as a function of age. *J. genet. Psychol.,* 1970, **117,** 57–67.

86. Hicks, J. M.: The influence of group flattery upon self evaluation. *J. soc. Psychol.,* 1962, **58,** 147–151.

87. Hodson, N. G.: Growth promoting in adolescence through interpersonal relations. *Adolescence,* 1966, **1,** 230–239.

88. Horowitz, E.: Reported embarrassment memories in elementary school, high school, and college students. *J. soc. Psychol.,* 1962, **56,** 317–325.

89. Horrocks, J. E., and S. A. Weinberg: Psychological needs and their development during adolescence. *J. Psychol.,* 1970, **74,** 51–69.

90. Houston, K.: Sources, effects and individual vulnerability of psychological problems for college students. *J. counsel. Psychol.,* 1971, **18,** 157–165.

91. Humphrey, C., M. Klaasen, and A. M. Creekmore: Clothing and self-concept of adolescents. *J. Home Econ.,* 1971, **63,** 246–250.

92. Jersild, A. T.: *The psychology of adolescence,* 2d ed. New York: Macmillan, 1963.

93. Joesting, J., and R. Joesting: Future problems of gifted girls. *Gifted Child Quart.,* 1970, **14,** 82–86.

94. Johnson, P. A., and J. R. Staffieri: Stereotypic affective properties of personal names and somatotypes in children. *Develpm. Psychol.,* 1971, **5,** 176.

95. Jones, M. C.: Psychological correlates of somatic development. *Child Develpm.,* 1965, **36,** 899–911.

96. Jones, M. C.: A report on three growth studies at the University of California. *Gerontologist,* 1967, **7,** 49–54.

97. Jorgensen, E. C., and R. H. Howell: Changes in self, ideal-self correlations from ages 8 through 18. *J. soc. Psychol.,* 1969, **79,** 63–67.

98. Kagan, J., and H. A. Moss: *Birth to maturity: A study in psychological development.* New York: Wiley, 1962.

99. Kaplan, M. F.: Forming impressions of personality: The effect of the initial impression. *Psychonomic Sci.,* 1970, **18,** 255–256.

100. Karabenick, S. A.: On the relation between personality and birth order. *Psychol. Rep.,* 1971, **28,** 258.

101. Katz, I.; Review of evidence relating to effects of segregation on the intellectual performance of Negroes. *Amer. Psychologist,* 1964, **19,** 381–399.

102. Kelly, E. L.: Constancy of the adult personality. *Amer. Psychologist,* 1955, **10,** 659–681.

103. Kinch, J. W.: A formalized theory of the self-concept. *Amer. J. Sociol.,* 1963, **68,** 481–486.

104. Klineberg, O.: Black and white in international perspective. *Amer. Psychologist,* 1971, **26,** 119–128.

105. Lane, H.: The meaning of disorder among youth. *Education,* 1955, **76,** 214–217.

106. Langsley, D. G., R. H. Fairbairn, and C. D. DeYoung: Adolescence and family crises. *Canad. psychiat. Ass. J.,* 1968, **13,** 125–133.

107. Lantz, H. R.: Number of childhood friends as reported in the life histories of a psychiatrically diagnosed group of 1,000. *Marriage fam. Living,* 1956, **18,** 107–109.

108. Lawson, L. D.: Hair color, personality, and the observer. *Psychol. Rep.,* 1971, **28,** 311–322.

109. Lerner, R. M.: The development of stereotyped expectancies of body build–behavior relations. *Child Develpm.,* 1969, **40,** 137–141.

110. Lester, D.: Factors affecting choice of method of suicide. *J. clin. Psychol.,* 1970, **26,** 437.

111. Levenson, M., and C. Neuringer: Intropunitiveness in suicidal adolescents. *J. proj. Tech. pers. Assess.,* 1970, **34,** 409–411.

112. Levin, J., and H. Black: Personal appearance as a reflection of social attitudes: Stereotype or reality. *Psychol. Rep.,* 1970, **27,** 338.

113. Levin, P. L.: How to succeed as a teenager. *New York Times,* Apr. 18, 1965.

114. Levy, N. J.: The use of drugs by teenagers for sanctuary and illusion. *Amer. J. Psychoanal.,* 1968, **28,** 48–58.

115. Lewit, D. W., and K. Virolainen: Conformity and independence in adolescents' motivation for orthodontic treatment. *Child Develpm.,* 1968, **39,** 1189–1200.

116. Lief, H. I., and W. C. Thompson: The prediction of behavior from adolescence to adulthood. *Psychiatry,* 1961, **24,** 32–38.

117. Lipscomb, I. F.: The effects of counseling, both group and individual, on changes in self-concept of high school sophomore girls of low socioeconomic background. *Dissert. Abstr.,* 1968, **28** (9–A), 3466–3467.

118. Loewenthal, K.: How are "first impressions" formed? *Psychol. Rep.,* 1967, **21,** 834–836.

119. Long, B. H., R. C. Ziller, and E. H. Henderson: Developmental changes in the self-concept during adolescence. *School Review,* 1968, **76,** 210–230.

120. Looft, W. R.: Egocentrism and social interaction in adolescence. *Adolescence,* 1971, **6,** 485–494.

121. Luft, J.: Monetary value of the perception of persons. *J. soc. Psychol.,* 1957, **46,** 245–251.

122. MacDonald, A. P.: Birth order and personality. *J. consult. clin. Psychol.,* 1971, **36,** 171–176.

123. MacGregor, F. C.: Social and cultural components in the motivations of persons seeking plastic surgery of the nose. *J. Hlth. soc. Behav.,* 1967, **8,** 125–135.

124. Mann, C. W.: Pro-rationalization: A defense mechanism. *Psychol. Rep.,* 1970, **36,** 636–638.

125. Manz, W., and H. E. Lueck: Influence of wearing glasses on personality ratings: Cross cultural validation of an old experiment. *Percept. mot. Skills,* 1968, **27,** 704.

126. Marcia, J. E., and M. L. Friedman: Ego identity status in college women. *J. Pers.,* 1970, **38,** 249–263.

127. Markel, N. N., M. Meisels, and J. E. Houck: Judging personality from voice quality. *J. abnorm. soc. Psychol.,* 1964, **68,** 458–463.

128. Martin, J. C.: Racial ethnocentrism and judgment of beauty. *J. soc. Psychol.,* 1964, **63,** 59–63.

129. Mason, E. P.: Cross-validation study of personality characteristics of junior high students from American, Indian, Mexican and Caucasian ethnic backgrounds. *J. soc. Psychol.,* 1969, **77,** 15–24.

130. Mason, E. P., H. L. Adams, and D. F. Blood: Further study of personality characteristics of bright college freshmen. *Psychol. Rep.,* 1968, **23,** 395–400.

131. Masterson, J. F., and A. Washburne: The symptomatic adolescent: Psychiatric illness or ado-

lescent turmoil? *Amer. J. Psychiat.*, 1966, **122,** 1240–1248.

132. McCullers, J. C., and W. T. Plant: Personal and social development: Cultural influences. *Rev. educ. Res.*, 1964, **34,** 599–610.

133. McDonald, R. L.: Effects of sex, race and class on self, ideal-self, and parental ratings in Southern adolescents. *Percept. mot. Skills*, 1968, **27,** 15–25.

134. Merriman, J. B.: Relationship of personality traits to motor ability. *Res. Quart. Amer. Ass. Hlth. Phys. Educ. Recr.*, 1960, **31,** 163–173.

135. Meyer, E., W. E. Jacobson, M. T. Edgerton, and A. Canter: Motivational patterns in patients seeking elective plastic surgery. *Psychosom. Med.*, 1960, **22,** 193–203.

136. Moore, C. H., and J. C. Ascough: Self-acceptance and adjustment revisited: A replication. *Psychol. Rep.*, 1970, **26,** 855–858.

137. Moore, R.: Helping adolescents achieve psychological growth. *Adolescence*, 1970, **5,** 37–54.

138. Morse, S., and K. J. Gergen: Social comparison, self-consistency and the concept of self. *J. Pers. soc. Psychol.*, 1970, **16,** 148–156.

139. Murphy, W. F.: A note on the significance of names. *Psychoanal. Quart.*, 1957, **26,** 91–106.

140. Mussen, P. H., H. B. Young, R. Gaddini, and L. Morante: The influence of father-son relationships on adolescent personality and attitudes. *J. child Psychol. Psychiat.*, 1963, **4,** 3–16.

141. Nawas, M. M.: Change in efficiency of ego functioning and complexity from adolescence to young adulthood. *Develpm. Psychol.*, 1971, **4,** 412–415.

142. Neilon, P.: Shirley's babies after 15 years: A personality study. *J. genet. Psychol.*, 1948, **73,** 175–186.

143. *New York Times* Report: What's in a name? Nov. 10, 1964.

144. Nikelly, A. G.: The dependent adolescent. *Adolescence*, 1971, **6,** 139–144.

145. Norton, D. L.: The rites of passage from dependency to autonomy. *School Review,* 1970, **79,** 19–41.

146. Oberlander, M. L., K. L. Frauenfelder, and H. Heath: Ordinal position, sex of sibling, sex and personal preferences in a group of eighteen-year-olds. *J. consult. clin. Psychol.*, 1970, **35,** 122–125.

147. Ostermeier, A. L.: Adolescent behavior as manifested in clothing. *Child Study Center Bull., State Univer. Coll., Buffalo,* 1967, **3,** 1–9.

148. Packard, V.: *The status seekers*. New York: Pocket Books, 1961.

149. Pannes, E. D.: The relationship between self-acceptance and dogmatism in junior-senior high school students. *J. educ. Sociol.*, 1963, **36,** 419–426.

150. Parloff, M. B., M. Kleman, and J. H. Handlon: Personality characteristics which differentiate creative male adolescents and adults. *J. Pers.*, 1968, **36,** 528–552.

151. Peck, R. F.: Family patterns correlated with adolescent personality structure. *J. abnorm. soc. Psychol.*, 1958, **57,** 347–350.

152. Peck, R. F., and R. J. Havighurst: *The psychology of character development*. New York: Wiley, 1962.

153. Peck, R. F., and R. G. Richek: Personality and social development: Family influences. *Rev. educ. Res.*, 1964, **34,** 574–587.

154. Peterson, D. R.: Behavior problems of middle childhood. *J. consult. Psychol.*, 1961, **25,** 205–209.

155. Phillips, R. E.: Student activities and self-concept. *J. Negro Educ.*, 1969, **38,** 32–37.

156. Plant, W. T.: Changes in intolerance and authoritarianism for sorority and nonsorority women enrolled in college for two years. *J. soc. Psychol.*, 1966, **68,** 79–83.

157. Platt, J. J., and R. Eisenman: Homesickness incidence and stability. *Psychology*, 1970, **7,** 42–45.

158. Reiter, H. H.: Note on some personality differences between heavy and light drinkers. *Percept. mot. Skills*, 1970, **30,** 762.

159. Resnick, H. L. (ed.): *Suicidal behaviors: Diagnosis and management*. Boston: Little, Brown, 1968.

160. Richards, E. A., and R. E. Hawthorn: Values, body cathexis, and clothing of male university students. *J. Home Econ.*, 1971, **63,** 190–194.

161. Robbins, P. R.: Personality and psychosomatic illness: A selected review of research. *Genet. Psychol. Monogr.*, 1969, **80,** 51–90.

162. Robins, L. N., and P. O'Neal: The adult prognosis of runaway children. *Amer. J. Orthopsychiat.*, 1959, **29,** 752–761.

163. Rosenberg, M.: Parental interest and children's self-conceptions. *Sociometry*, 1963, **26,** 35–49.

164. Rosenzweig, S., and L. Rosenzweig: Aggression in problem children and normals as evaluated by the Rosenzweig Picture Frustration Study. *J. abnorm. soc. Psychol.*, 1952, **47,** 683–688.

165. Rudestam, K. E.: Stockholm and Los Angeles: A cross-cultural study of the communication of suicidal intent. *J. consult. clin. Psychol.*, 1971, **36,** 82–90.

166. Rusk, H. A.: Adolescent problems. *New York Times,* July 13, 1969.

167. Ryan, M. S.: *Clothing: A study in human behavior*. New York: Holt, 1966.

168. Sappenfield, B. R.: Perceived similarity to self as related to the stereotypically perceived "ideal personality." *J. exp. Res. in Pers.*, 1970, **4,** 297–302.

169. Schaefer, C. E.: Imaginary companions and

creative adolescents. *Develpm. Psychol.*, 1969, **1**, 747–749.

170. Schaefer, C. E.: A psychological study of 10 exceptionally creative girls. *Except. Children*, 1970, **36**, 431–441.

171. Scheinfeld, A.: *Heredity in humans*, rev. ed. Philadelphia: Lippincott, 1971.

172. Schludermann, S., and E. Schludermann: Personality correlates of adolescent self-concepts and security-insecurity. *J. Pers.*, 1970, **74**, 85–90.

173. Schmidt, M. R.: Personality change in college women. *J. coll. Stud. Personnel*, 1970, **11**, 414–418.

174. Schonfeld, W. A.: Body-image disturbances in adolescents with inappropriate sexual development. *Amer. J. Orthopsychiat.*, 1964, **34**, 493–502.

175. Schreiber, E. H.: The relationship between personality characteristics and dental disorders in adolescents. *Dissert. Abstr.*, 1967, **28** (4–A), 1313.

176. Schulhofer, E.: The handling of adolescent crises as a preventive measure for family functioning. *Psychother. & Psychosom.*, 1967, **15**, 60.

177. Schwendman, G., K. S. Larsen, and F. Dunn: Social position, social desirability, and self-esteem. *Psychol. Rep.*, 1970, **27**, 117–118.

178. Shane, H. G.: Social experiences and selfhood. *Childhood Educ.*, 1957, **33**, 297–298.

179. Silverman, D.: An evaluation of the relationship between attitudes toward self and attitudes toward a vocational high school. *J. educ. Sociol.*, 1963, **36**, 410–418.

180. Slater, P. E.: Parental behavior and the personality of the child. *J. genet. Psychol.*, 1962, **101**, 52–68.

181. Smith, G. M.: Relations between personality and smoking behavior in preadult subjects. *J. consult. clin. Psychol.*, 1969, **33**, 710–715.

182. Smith, M. E.: A comparison of certain personality traits rated in the same individuals in childhood and fifty years later. *Child Develpm.*, 1952, **23**, 159–180.

183. Solomon, J. C.: Neuroses of school teachers. *Ment. Hyg., N.Y.*, 1960, **44**, 79–90.

184. Sontag, L. W., C. T. Baker, and V. L. Nelson: Mental growth and personality development: A longitudinal study. *Monogr. Soc. Res. Child Develpm.*, 1958, **23**, no. 2.

185. Spaights, E.: Accuracy of self-estimation of junior high school students. *J. educ. Res.*, 1965, **58**, 416–419.

186. Spaulding, R. L.: Personality and social development: Peer and school influences. *Rev. educ. Res.*, 1964, **34**, 588–598.

187. Stagner, R.: *Psychology of personality*, 3d ed. New York: McGraw-Hill, 1961.

188. Stanley, E. J., and J. T. Barter: Adolescent suicidal behavior. *Amer. J. Orthopsychiat.*, 1970, **40**, 87–96.

189. Stendler, C. B.: The learning of certain secondary drives by Parisian and American children. *Marriage fam. Living*, 1954, **16**, 195–200.

190. Stewart, L. H.: Social and emotional adjustment during adolescence as related to the development of psychosomatic illness in adulthood. *Genet. Psychol. Monogr.*, 1962, **65**, 175–215.

191. Sticht, T. G., and W. Fox: Geographical mobility and dogmatism, anxiety, and age. *J. soc. Psychol.*, 1966, **68**, 171–174.

192. Stiller, A., H. A. Schwartz, and E. L. Cowen: The social desirability of trait-descriptive terms among high-school students. *Child Develpm.*, 1965, **36**, 981–1002.

193. Stone, G. P.: Appearance and self. In M. E. Roach and J. B. Eicher (eds.), *Dress, adornment, and the social order*. New York: Wiley, 1965, pp. 216–245.

194. Stott, L. H.: The persistency effects of early family experiences upon personality development. *Merrill-Palmer Quart.*, 1957, **3**, 145–159.

195. Strang, R.: *The adolescent views himself.* New York: McGraw-Hill, 1957.

196. Suinn, R. M.: The relationship between self-acceptance and acceptance of others: A learning theory analysis. *J. abnorm. soc. Psychol.*, 1961, **63**, 37–42.

197. Symonds, P. M.: Pupil evaluation and self evaluation. *Teachers Coll. Rec.*, 1952, **54**, 138–149.

198. Thomas, A., S. Chess, and H. G. Birch: The origin of personality. *Scient. American*, 1970, **223**, no. 7, pp. 102–109.

199. Thompson, C.: Concepts of the self in interpersonal theory. *Amer. J. Psychother.*, 1958, **12**, 5–17.

200. Thompson, G. G., and E. F. Gardner: Adolescent perceptions of happy, successful living. *J. genet. Psychol.*, 1969, **115**, 107–120.

201. Tonks, C. M., P. H. Rack, and M. J. Rose: Attempted suicide and the menstrual cycle. *J. psychosom. Res.*, 1968, **11**, 319–323.

202. Torda, C.: Some observations on the creative process. *Percept. mot. Skills*, 1970, **31**, 107–126.

203. Torrance, E. P., and J. Khatena: "What kind of person are you?" A brief screening device for identifying creatively gifted adolescents and adults. *Gifted Child Quart.*, 1970, **14**, 71–75.

204. Tuddenham, R. D.: The constancy of the personality ratings over two decades. *Genet. Psychol. Monogr.*, 1959, **60**, 3–29.

205. Van den Daele, L.: A developmental study of the ego-ideal. *Genet. Psychol. Monogr.*, 1968, **78**, 191–256.

206. Vener, A. M., and C. R. Hoffer: Adolescent orientation to clothing. In M. E. Roach and J. B. Eicher (eds.), *Dress, adornment, and the social order*. New York: Wiley, 1965, pp. 76–81.

207. Walker, R. E., R. C. Nicolay, R. Kluceny,

and R. E. Riedel: Psychological correlates of smoking. *J. clin. Psychol.,* 1969, **25,** 42–44.

208.   Walters, Sister A.: The role of the school in personality development. *Education,* 1957, **77,** 214–219.

209.   Warren, J. A., and P. A. Heist: Personality attributes of gifted college students. *Science,* 1960, **132,** 330–337.

210.   Washburn, W. C.: The effects of physique and intrafamily tension on self-concepts in adolescent males. *J. consult. Psychol.,* 1962, **26,** 460–466.

211.   Washburn, W. C.: Patterns of protective attitudes in relation to differences in self-evaluation and anxiety level among high school students. *Calif. J. educ. Res.,* 1962, **13,** 84–94.

212.   Wass, B., and J. B. Eicher: Clothing as related to role behavior of teenage girls. *Quart. Bull. Michigan State Univer. Agriculture Exp. Station,* 1964, **47,** 206–208, 211–213.

213.   Waterman, A. S., and C. K. Waterman: A longitudinal study of changes in ego identity status during the freshman year at college. *Develpm. Psychol.,* 1971, **5,** 167–173.

214.   Weiner, I. B.: *Psychological disturbances in adolescence.* New York: Wiley, 1970.

215.   Werner, E., and E. Gallistel: Prediction of outstanding performance, delinquency, and mental disturbance from childhood evaluations. *Child Develpm.,* 1961, **32,** 255–260.

216.   Wertheimer, M.: The defense mechanisms that students report in their own behavior. *J. genet. Psychol.,* 1958, **92,** 111–112.

217.   Wilcox, A. H., and B. R. Fritz: Actual-ideal discrepancy and adjustment. *J. counsel. Psychol.,* 1971, **18,** 166–169.

218.   Winick, C.: Trends in the conceptions of celebrities: A study of news magazine profiles and television interviews. *J. soc. Psychol.,* 1963, **60,** 301–310.

219.   Winkler, R. C., and R. A. Myers: Some concomitants of self-ideal discrepancy measures and self-acceptance. *J. counsel. Psychol.,* 1963, **10,** 83–86.

220.   Yarrow, M. R., J. D. Campbell, and R. V. Burton: Recollections of childhood: A study of the retrospective method. *Monogr. Soc. Res. Child Develpm.,* 1970, **35,** no. 5.

Index